Tilting at
DON QUIXOTE

Other books by Nicholas Wollaston

TRAVEL

Handles of Chance
China in the Morning
Red Rumba
Winter in England

FICTION

Jupiter Laughs
Pharaoh's Chicken
The Tale Bearer
Eclipse
Mr Thistlewood
The Stones of Bau
Café de Paris

BIOGRAPHY

The Man on the Ice Cap

Tilting at
DON QUIXOTE

NICHOLAS
WOLLASTON

ANDRE DEUTSCH

First published 1990 by
André Deutsch Limited
105 Great Russell Street
London WC1B 3LJ

British Library Cataloguing in Publication Data

Wollaston, Nicholas, *1926–*
  Tilting at Don Quixote.
  1. Fiction in English, 1945 — Biographies
  I. Title
  823'.914'09

ISBN 0 233 98551 4

Phototypeset by Input Typesetting Ltd, London
Printed and bound by
WSOY Finland

'We will never remember anything by sitting in one place waiting for the memories to come back to us of their own accord. Memories are scattered all over the world. We must travel if we want to find them and flush them from their hiding places.'

Milan Kundera: *The Book of Laughter and Forgetting*

ONE

May 14, Manzanares. At midday, getting off the train from Madrid, I can't discover when there is a bus to Argamasilla de Alba, forty kilometres from here. The man in the ticket office is no help: trains are his business, not buses, and if there was ever a line to Argamasilla it has been closed.

I don't mind, I'm in no hurry – I have given myself a month. It's a fine spring day, touched with anticipation. I sense an emptiness ahead, stimulating and alarming and all my own. Somehow, like my notebook, I must fill it.

Cervantes knew the feeling. In his prologue to *Don Quixote* he described the suspense before the words came: 'Many times I took up my pen to write and many times I put it down, not knowing what to say.' It's a familiar state: 'Hesitating, the paper in front of me, elbow on the desk, fingers on my cheek, thinking . . .'

The station plaza is deserted. A taxi-driver dozes in his car, a dog lies in the sun by the wall. I walk over to a bench under the new-leafed planes and sit down with my rucksack. After ten minutes a bus comes into the plaza, from Albacete to Ciudad Real – no use to me. I must get to Argamasilla, my proper starting place. It was Don Quixote's home, though in the first sentence of his novel Cervantes was careful not to identify it: 'In a village of La Mancha, whose name I don't wish to remember, there lived not long ago a gentleman . . .'

Don Quixote was verging on fifty, younger than me, but I'm the same shape – tall and thin and bony – and I can guess his pleasure as he started on his journey across the plain, slipping away from home one morning unobserved, telling nobody of his intentions. He was happy to find how easy it was to begin.

At London airport yesterday the papers shouted, 'They're off!' The 1987 general election was also starting, with a month to go: a month to show up the low point of British cynicism, selfishness, greed. I'm glad to escape the stampede for power, beyond reach of the TV pundits, out of earshot of the lies and arrogance. But I shall be home on election day, to vote for something that promises more humility and compassion, even a little imagination: something nearer Don Quixote's idealism, his foolish dream of justice, checked by Sancho Panza's practicality.

A telephone rings in a box on one of the trees, waking the taxi-driver. He gets out to answer it, trying to hurry, and speaks for a while, too quietly for me to overhear; then hangs up. The dog stirs, stands up uneasily, yawns and hops over to the man to be stroked – it has only three legs. When the man returns to his taxi the dog comes to me and rubs its mange on my trousers. To get rid of it I go over and ask the taxi-driver, before he is asleep again, where the Argamasilla bus departs from. But he doesn't know – taxis are his business.

In the train from Madrid there were two Englishmen on their way to the Costa del Sol. One of them asked the ticket collector, '*Quelle heure – arriver?*' They were his few words of a foreign language and he didn't care that it was the wrong one, but tapped his watch and added in English, 'Malaga, I mean?' In silence, politely, the Spaniard wrote the answer on a piece of paper.

I will do better, I hope.

A grey-haired man in a tricycle chair, winding himself along with hand pedals, comes at speed down a street into the plaza. He has no legs at all, he is unluckier than the dog. He could have been wounded as a boy soldier in the Civil War fifty years ago. He circles the plaza once, heeling over on his three wheels; circles it again and disappears up another street.

In the bar on the train I had a hunk of bread with dark raw ham, *jamón serrano*, and a beer, and now I feel sleepy and indecisive. I will see what happens, if I can keep awake. I should be alert for details and reactions, ready to scribble them down. But though I have a compulsion to follow Don Quixote through La Mancha and write a book, I can't yet tell its shape, I can only watch. It has its own existence and will emerge with the least nudging from me. Don Quixote spoke of a painter, busy with brush and canvas, who was asked what he was painting and replied, 'Whatever it turns out to be.'

I feel the same. Sometimes I have written a synopsis to be fleshed out later but this time the bones, ungainly, disjointed, like Don Quixote's, will fall together in a random way, assembled from my disordered thoughts.

I'm aware of two women approaching my bench under the trees, coming from the station. In wide black skirts they look like gypsies, one fat and one thin, their hair drawn back from their foreheads. They are handsome, confident, humorous, but not beautiful.

'*Buenas tardes*,' they say and sit down with me, arranging their bundles. 'Where are you from?'

'From Madrid.' But I know they mean what country.

'He's American,' the fat one tells the thin one.

'No, he's French,' the thin one says.

I ask them about the bus to Argamasilla, and the fat woman lifts her eyes to the bright Manchegan sky: 'The Lord, *el Señor*, knows.' But the thin one says that the bus to Tomelloso passes through Argamasilla. They are going on it themselves tomorrow morning – there is a fiesta in Tomelloso.

When I ask if they are local people they laugh. They come from Mallorca, they go to all the fiestas in Spain, and they launch into a stream of incomprehensible language, laughing more – at me, I think. The fat one shuffles her big black-skirted bottom closer on the bench and asks for the price of a coffee for them both in the station bar. How much? Twenty *duros* will do – a hundred pesetas – and she drops my coin into one of her bundles.

A man walks from the station across the plaza to a block of flats. The fat woman calls to him and he waves back but, seeing me with them, he doesn't stop.

'My friend's lover,' the thin woman explains and makes a sign of copulation with her fingers.

The fat woman laughs: 'Yes, but he doesn't pay much.'

It was two laughing whores at the door of an inn who set Don Quixote off on his first adventure. He rode up on his equally skinny horse, Rocinante, a grotesque figure in armour with a spear, and in his deluded vision – or his limitless imagination – they were beautiful maidens at a castle gate. At that moment a swineherd blew a horn to collect his pigs, which for Don Quixote was a trumpet call from the battlements to herald his approach. Reality wasn't good enough for such a man, and after their first fright at this curious visitor the two women got the idea. Amused by his madness, flattered by his gallantry, they would be princesses for him, not whores. It was a new way to please a man.

Travelling through La Mancha in Don Quixote's company, it will be hard not to catch his twisted vision of things or be infected with his fantasy. Through La Mancha: through life itself. I take Cervantes's book, the first modern novel, to be a parable of life – everyone's, but especially a writer's. So fact may slide into fiction sometimes, and the truth be stretched.

The two women of Manzanares extract what fun they can from me, as well as my hundred pesetas, then go back into the station for their coffee. A man standing in an empty cart pulled by a mule comes into the plaza, shouting something unintelligible. I get up and walk into the town, where I learn that the bus to Argamasilla tomorrow leaves not from the station but from the hospital.

On the top floor of the Mesón Sancho, commemorating Don Quixote's earthy, ever-realistic squire Sancho Panza, I find a room with a window among the roof tiles, and late in the evening have supper in a bar owned by a toothless old man whom I can't understand. My Spanish is bad, but at least I have teeth for it.

From the TV in the corner I discover that there are elections in Spain too – I didn't escape after all. Then it switches to the celebrations in Madrid today for the king's and queen's twenty-fifth wedding anniversary. It was mine and Deirdre's also, in Spain last summer. We didn't drive through the streets in a coach like these two, but drank Spanish champagne with one of our sons and a few friends on the terrace of a rented house, with olive trees stacked on the Andalusian hills and the sea in the distance.

I still marvel that we have been married nearly half my life and much more than half Deirdre's. Though I have never dedicated a book to anyone, and she won't like this any more than the others, it is for her. It's the least I can do – a gesture of what I used to call my love, in memory of hers.

After a *copa* of brandy with the toothless man I sit for half an hour in the main plaza. This is the time of the *paseo*, the nightly social stroll, and half Manzanares is on parade. V. S. Pritchett said that the Spanish treat the street as their place of entertainment, like a drawing-room. A pram is parked close to the floodlit fountain for the baby to be kept happy by the illuminated jets, the incandescent froth. What bemused ideas do they convey? Astonishingly, in this small town in the middle of Spain, a black woman in a purple dress shaped by her African body goes tripping smartly across the square.

Opposite stands the church, bathed in electric light. Nothing is symmetrical or architected in that glowing holy edifice, yet it rules the plaza with its age, dignity, haphazard disproportions. The people driving past in new cars, the couples kissing on the benches, the baby's gossiping family, all know it. They are nothing to that accumulation of human love. Swifts scream across the darkening sky, and pigeons flop in and out of their nesting niches on the church, impatient for the floodlights to be switched off, and the black woman comes tripping back, and the baby is pushed home, the fountain still splashing in its eyes, and I have another *copa* in a bar on my way back to the Mesón Sancho.

And one more. And then a final one.

I'm still not clear what my purpose is, beyond catching tomorrow's bus to Argamasilla de Alba. The vagabond life on the roads of La Mancha gave Cervantes a formula for his book. And Don Quixote himself, stepping out of the pages of the second volume to criticize the first, which had already been published, said the author must have written it down gropingly, without method, letting it turn out anyhow.

The future will be conjured from the present and the past with, I hope, an extra essence to transform it. To Don Quixote – the Knight of the Sad Countenance, as Sancho called him – that essence was life itself: the untruth that enhances truth.

TWO

My father was fifty-five and I was nearly four when he was shot dead in his room at King's College, Cambridge. He was the Tutor, though he never taught anyone and was far from academic. 'A plain man among scholars,' someone called him. His job was to interview new students, advise and help them in their time at university, and generally be their friend.

He was an explorer, whose name was given to a mountain in central Africa, a giant African lobelia, a primula in the Himalayas and a kind of Tibetan rabbit. But if he had had to choose the place to die it might have been King's. 'I have loved the college and chapel more than any other spot in the world,' he told the woman he married. Lying with fever in the Congo or cutting through the New Guinea jungle he never failed to toast the feast-day of the college patron, St Nicholas, after whom he named his only son.

He qualified as a doctor but wrote, 'I made a horrible mistake when I went in for a profession which I loathe.' Two days after starting his first hospital job he heard of an expedition to the Ruwenzori mountains in need of a doctor, and resigned. Once, for a month between expeditions, he was public health inspector at Guildford. And on the day the First World War broke out, though he was near the age limit and wouldn't have been called up, he joined the navy and served as a doctor for five years.

He met my mother before the war in London, at a concert in the Queen's Hall. An old King's friend was there with his wife, who said to her husband afterwards, 'I liked that man.' So he was invited to their house and introduced to one of the wife's many sisters – my mother.

She was fourteen years younger. While he was exploring in New

Guinea she had travelled alone in the Caucasus, Armenia, Kurdistan. Preparing another expedition, my father summoned his courage to invite her out. He was thirty-seven, but hadn't entertained a woman before: 'I know so little of people, apart from men, that I never dreamt it was even possible to ask you to come to tea.' She didn't come, and he went back to New Guinea for another year.

Over the years they seldom met, or even wrote. In the war my mother joined the Land Army and drove a team of carthorses on a farm. Afterwards she did relief work in Poland with the Quakers. In 1921 my father went as doctor and naturalist on the first Everest expedition, probably the most enjoyable of them all. Nobody before had been near the mountain and nobody this time seriously tried to climb it. But there were unknown valleys and glaciers and lesser peaks to explore: 'My chief delight,' he wrote to my mother from Tibet, 'has lain more in the indescribable beauty of the flowers and the sight of these mountains than in the conquest of Everest itself.'

He was asked to go again the following year, but declined. He wanted to take a third expedition to New Guinea and was trying to collect funds. Also, he had discovered something else. Recently he had been shattered by the death from pneumonia of a favourite godson: 'He made a manful struggle but was beaten last Tuesday, three days after his sixth birthday. He was the most lovable child and we trusted each other uncommonly. It is a bitter blow and a proper punishment to me for keeping the love and trust of a child and taking none of the responsibilities. I have been so wrapped up in my own affairs that it only just begins to occur to me that I have made a mess of things and have missed the best in life. I am still a bit bewildered.'

In 1923 he asked my mother to marry him. She refused, and in the opinion of one of my father's few woman friends she lost the chance of her life. He was less certain: 'She would find me a mighty difficult problem. All the same, I have not yet given up this quest and do not intend to, until I have been knocked down flat again. She came with me to a theatre on Tuesday, so I am not entirely excommunicated.' A fortnight later they dined at a restaurant. 'She likes me very very much,' he told the friend, 'but says she could never get to care for anybody in that sort of way, so it seems there is no more to be said. Unfortunately I care a good deal more than I thought. It is a bitter business, like one of those dreams where you suddenly fall through space with a sickening bump. But I suppose there is a purpose in all these things. I wish I could believe that, or could know what the purpose is.'

Nobody had money for a long expedition to New Guinea, and when my father was told of a mountain range in Colombia which had never been explored and would be cheaper he changed plans. He and my mother spent a day together in the country: 'She loves to be with me, but she does not love me, so we have said goodbye until she finds she wants me, which I am afraid will never be. It is a rotten business and makes me very wretched.' One of her sisters told her she was a little fool. One of his oldest friends, father of four children, killed himself, which increased the gloom. But soon he would be lost in the mountains, doing what he was best at.

At a restaurant a fortnight before he was due to sail he talked of Colombia. My mother wished she could go with him. Only as his wife, he said. She decided she did love him: 'She doesn't yet know how much or why or in what way. If I were half a man I would pick her up and carry her off to the nearest parson or registry office, but I think all will be well. It might conceivably happen that she will sail with me. Wouldn't that be great!'

A week later it was fixed: 'The whole face of the world is changed. I was going to be a crusty old bear, and now I am never going to be anything of the kind. Isn't it too glorious!' To another friend, the poet Henry Newbolt, he wrote, 'Don't think it was a sudden inspiration. But you wouldn't, if you knew her. I am beside myself with happiness. Think of me, at forty-eight! The whole world is turned upside down. "Poor old boy," you will say.' They were married in King's chapel in time to catch the boat. Within seven years his ashes were buried in the crypt.

For a honeymoon Colombia was a good testing-ground. They endured a stormy voyage along the coast in a small schooner, living in two dog kennels on deck, prostrated by seasickness. They were cheated over the price of mules, floundered through swamps in tropical heat, were thrown into rivers thick with crocodiles, exchanged the mules for oxen which bolted and smashed their baggage, were pestered by sandflies and horseflies and mosquitoes, spent every evening pulling ticks out of each other, were deserted by their porters who refused to go up into the mountains, got ill with hunger, gave up exploring and tried to get up-river to Bogotá, but the water fell and they had to camp for a week on a mud bank before retreating to the coast in a rowing-boat. The natives – puny, unfriendly, thieving and drugged on coca or drunk on sugar wine – were a disappointment. Worse, for my father, was the lack of wildlife: few birds or butterflies and only three flowers worth noting.

8

But my mother seemed happy, getting out her penny whistle when the natives played their reed pipes.

On their return they bought a house, Bencombe, on a steep Cotswold hillside and I believe – I must believe – they were extraordinarily happy for the four years they lived there. Though he was fifty and she was thirty-six, they walked hand in hand through the garden like young lovers at the beginning of the world. All his life my father had been, as he put it, 'simply dogged by good fortune' and the luck held till the very end.

I was born at Bencombe in 1926, the middle of three children with a sister on either side. My chronology is vague. I ran down the field through the waist-high summer grass, and battled in the snow, laughing then crying for the cold. I stood in the kitchen with my eyes at table level, I sat by my mother while she read a story, I lay in my parents' bed where I could see my father's shadow through the door, shaving in his dressing-gown. He, or his shadow again, played with us on the terrace while my mother with her 'pocket folding' Kodak stepped out the distance, heel to toe, then turned to shade the viewfinder with her hand and squeezed the rubber bulb. I rode up the stairs to bed on someone's back – my father's, I suppose. An adder lay coiled and basking, a goldfinch nested in the quince tree, a sparrowhawk took a fantail pigeon from the dovecote, foxes killed our chickens; and people came to stay, mostly aunts.

There were stone balls along the garden wall, and an oil engine in the stables to make electricity, driving a belt that cracked like a whip, and a brass telephone in the hall with a winding handle for calling the exchange. (Twenty-five years later I had one like that in my house in Kenya.) I can smell the stale air and mothballs behind the empty clothes in the cupboard on the landing. I can hear the doorbell in the village shop and the whine of our car going up the hill in low gear.

I know that black Austin Twelve better than any later car, even its number; and the big door handles, the mock leather panels on the outside, the bees stuck in the honeycomb of the radiator, the thermometer for a mascot on the front of the bonnet, the silver St Christopher on the dashboard, the knobbly steering-wheel with throttle and ignition levers, the pockets full of Bartholomew's half-inch maps. There was room to walk about and open the little skylight in the roof and pull the cord above the driver's head for the back window blind. I can hear the clunk of the gate-change on the gears, the dying hum of the flywheel, the bark of the electric horn, used only for lorries, and the sad bellow of the air horn – I could just blow it with two hands.

Our nurserymaid was Alice Moon, granddaughter of a toothless old road-mender with a beard and pickaxe. Four of his sons had been killed in the war. I had no grandfather, so Grampy would do. Pushing the pram or driving the pony trap, Alice took the road where she knew he was filling holes, trimming the verge. A grass snake wriggled across the road and Grampy killed it with his shovel. We left it half squashed, half still thrashing, and whipped up the pony to get home for tea.

The cook was Mabel, the gardener was Davis. When I was born Davis said I was the spit of my father, a story I liked to hear. After my father's death my mother sent Davis his old suits. I was holding one of Davis's wooden labels, for marking seed beds and young plants, when I ran down the drive and fell over. It stuck into my nose and I screamed; and screamed in the Austin all the way to the doctor's, where my father held me while I was stitched; and screamed till he bought me a clock-work steam-roller and stuffed a cloud of toilet paper in the funnel, for smoke. I keep a small scar at the corner of my nostril, a link with one of the few visions I have of him.

When he was elected Tutor of King's College he wrote, 'This comes straight from heaven,' and began work at Cambridge while looking for a house. 'I like the young men,' he told my mother, whom he saw only at odd weekends and in the vacation, 'and I really believe they like me.' The secret may lie in a remark by another King's don, Maynard Keynes, who described him as 'a man to whom it was unusually easy to speak the truth, who could unlock hearts with a word and a look, and break down everyone's reserve except his own'.

I came to rely on quotations and the memory of people who knew him for a picture of my father. Apart from three or four incidents I had only a sense of his presence – a person my mother talked to, less substantial than his clothes and pipe and tobacco tins. For years, greedy for whatever I could be told, I would treat anyone who added to the portrait as a messenger from him, bringing fresh news. 'I can only remember him,' somebody once wrote, 'as a quiet reserved man with an amused smile at the general scene,' and I got another glimpse.

Nearly fifty years after my father's death, at a party in the London zoo to celebrate someone's second marriage (an even worse disaster than the first, though mercifully briefer), I met Professor I. A. Richards, poet and literary pundit, author of a book with the stunning title, *The Meaning of Meaning*. When we were introduced, and through the party noise – through the cries from monkey cage and lion house – the old professor heard my name, he asked if I was the son of the explorer. It was a chance to pick the memory of one of my father's friends and he told me something I hadn't heard before, something new and precious which he had got from my father and which gave a glimpse of him in a strange light.

It concerned an expedition to the mountains of New Guinea, which my father hoped to be the first to climb. The only other white man in the party was a Dutchman, the rest were native porters. For weeks they cut into the interior from the coast, through the jungle towards the foothills. It was exploring in the classic style, with naked savages and poisoned arrows and a whiff of cannibalism. The Dutchman died of fever, the porters mutinied or ran away, and in one of the infested rivers my father's dugout capsized with the loss of scientific instruments, medicines, diaries, guns – everything. He never reached the mountains, never got more than an agonizing view of distant snows, and had to turn back.

I knew all that, because it was in the book my father wrote, but to the account of the retreat to the coast – over endless ridges of the foothills, along tortuous jungle tracks, down unhealthy streams that backed and turned for ever – Professor Richards supplied a fresh twist. The party was struck by fatigue and sickness and the terrible climate, and my father, himself weak with malaria, struggled to bring them out alive. But through the tropical mists and heat haze and rainstorms he was led on by another white man in the distance ahead, the back view of a stranger travelling in the same direction, towards the coast. Each time my father topped another ridge the man was going over the farther one, and each time my father turned another bend of a path or river the man was disappearing round the next.

Yet was he really a stranger? He looked maddeningly familiar and even in his feverish state my father thought he recognized him from long ago, but he could never catch up to make sure. When he got close enough to shout, the man wouldn't stop or turn round to show his face. All my father knew was that another explorer, pressing on in front, kept him going and rescued the expedition.

At last they reached the coast where the stranger gave him the slip once more and disappeared for good. Though my father tried to settle

11

the mystery, making inquiries about other travellers in the country, he discovered nothing. He paid off his porters and on the long voyage home forgot about it, till a year or two later when he went to a London tailor to be measured for a suit. In the fitting-room he tried on the jacket and watched the tailor in the mirror, marking the front, snipping and pinning, then turning him round to show him the back. There in the glass was the elusive figure that my father had followed in the jungle, who had saved his life.

I liked the story for the new, literary angle it gave to my father's image. It was told by a man for whom a sensitivity to poetry was the best testimony to an imaginative life; and if poetry creates something truer than the facts Don Quixote might have liked it too. Ambiguities, uncertainties, conundrums beset him. Nothing had a fixed identity except his quest for the most absolute, unbending justice.

At Cambridge my father found a house in West Road, three minutes' walk from King's College, to rent at eighty pounds a year. My mother went to see it, and back at Bencombe she drew a picture for us. It had a hole in the garden, big enough to get lost in, and I imagined a shaft like a mine.

Bencombe was sold, but West Road wasn't ready. My sisters and I were taken to a hotel on Minchinhampton Common, where we had a winter picnic in a quarry pit. As if the cold wasn't enough I was given an orange with a sugar lump in it, and got juice over my wrists and inside my sleeves – sticky fingers still trouble me. Then my mother took a flat near Notting Hill Gate, convenient for her friends and family and for Kensington Gardens. It was the time of Christopher Robin and *When We Were Very Young*. We went to the Round Pond and the statue of Peter Pan, and at breakfast, swallowing burnt porridge, we watched a service lift rising past the window with coal for the flats above.

At Cambridge station, in the early summer of 1930, my father met us in the Austin and drove us to West Road. Beside him in the front seat I put out my hand to turn into the gate, recognizing the house from my mother's picture. It had a fire bell on the chimney and green shutters and traces of a Regency veranda, now removed except the porch. The gardener was turfing over the fussy rose beds in the lawn but the hole, instead of a mine shaft, was a wide grass bowl that might

12

once have been a fish pond. We rolled into it and later, every year, had our Guy Fawkes bonfire there.

I have one more blurred, oblique vision of my father at West Road during the next two weeks – the last two of his life. At tea he lifted me on to his knee and helped himself to more quince jam, spooning it from a blue pot to his bread and butter. It was his favourite jam.

THREE

May 15, Argamasilla de Alba. Don Quixote rode a horse and Sancho Panza a donkey, but I'm no good with animals. I considered a bicycle before settling for local buses and *la coche de San Francisco*, St Francis's carriage – my own legs.

The bus from Manzanares took an erratic route here, cutting a line across the Manchegan plain from one village to the next, turning sharply and heading for another. 'Forbidden to eat pips' was written above the driver's head.

Cervantes deliberately chose this country, flat and blank, without features except the long straight roads for his two characters to ride along. The land waits for something to happen on it, like the empty page in the typewriter each morning, waiting for words to appear, for people to emerge and act. Sometimes there is a solitary man at work in the landscape, chopping at the soil with a mattock, a story in himself. Or a man standing motionless with a fishing-rod like a heron by a ditch, more weed and mud than water: unbelievable that he will ever catch anything.

I wonder about a man alone in the world, without colleagues: the essential human condition. There was an Arab I once saw riding a camel across the Sinai desert, going somewhere else, and a Polynesian far out in the Pacific Ocean, paddling his canoe from one horizon to another. Don Quixote's quest too was a lonely one, merely shadowed by Sancho riding behind him: the ideal tailed by the real, the virtue of madness dogged by the sterility of common sense.

The stones have been cleared off the land into huge heaps or long banks, and the fields watered. Strips of green barley are laid between the vines, daubed with scarlet poppies – weedkillers are not much used.

The vines, stuck like cloves into the ground, are sprouting bright leaves. Their precisely measured rows, at right angles to the road, change into other rows as the bus passes, at thirty degrees or forty-five or sixty, all a little different in character. Nothing is the same from another angle – seen, as it were, by another person. The wind stirs the barley, a hoopoe flops through the sunlit morning.

In Argamasilla the figure on a plinth in the middle of the town is not Don Quixote, not even one of the caricatures of him, all knobbly knees and goofy travesty, but another cartoon clown – Mickey Mouse, laughing at the traffic. Don Quixote and Sancho stand under the trees in a small park behind the church. The church is locked, also the Quixote House. I don't mind, I'm not here for culture, I haven't even brought a guidebook. But there is nowhere to stay and I have six hours before the bus to Tomelloso.

Lorries thunder past on their way to Valencia, Madrid, Cadiz, even Holland, rolling dust into the bar where I sit. A dwarf perches on the chair next to me and says proudly, 'This is Argamasilla de Alba, the home of Don Quixote.' We share a plate of green beans – *judias verdes*, green Jewesses, they are called, but the dwarf can't tell me why.

It strikes me that I haven't seen a priest in Spain yet, and hardly a nun. In the afternoon two boys' bands appear in the town, one in blue serge, the other in crimson satin, with bugles and drums to drown the traffic. Their teacher's whistle, trying to control them, only adds to the noise. Then a girls' band joins them, in pink and white with ribbons in their hair and silver wands flicking in their fingers, as fragile as butterflies. I have a sudden vision of one of the lorries swerving off the road, ploughing through them. Don Quixote would ride out into the traffic to fight it, and get knocked down.

FOUR

My father's murderer was called Potts. I know his other name, but simply Potts is enough to define him in my mind. Brief and abrupt, it suits his stunted life. He was nineteen in the summer of 1930 when he shot my father and a policeman. For me it has become a short story, melodramatic but plausible, with near-fictitious characters I have invented.

Potts might still be alive, in his late seventies, if he hadn't turned the stolen pistol on himself and pulled the trigger once more. But I can't perceive the old age of someone who was always young; who never reached twenty and, if not reprieved for insanity, would have died anyway, hanged for the double murder. He was over eighteen, the legal age for hanging.

I was three, nearly four. All I knew was that my father was dead and my mother was in tears, though I didn't see the connection. 'Why are you crying?' I asked when she came down to breakfast. I knew nothing of Potts or the shooting for years. My mother kept it from me till she thought I was old enough to stand the shock.

I was ten when she told me the story one autumn evening in our Cambridge house, suddenly getting up from the sofa to stand at the mantelpiece with a handkerchief. She turned to kick the coals so that I shouldn't see her face, and I felt a kind of privilege, watching her in tears again. I could cry too, it was something we had in common: not so much that she was crying like a child, but that I could cry like a grown-up. I also felt a twinge of superiority, because she was telling me what I knew already.

At school another boy had let it out: 'Your father was shot by an undergraduate, wasn't he?'

'No, he wasn't.' I denied it, because for me it wasn't true. My father had died, that was all. Not that he was any less real for being dead – he was just different from other boys' fathers. His presence, made of facts and figments, was what I loved above all. I knew him dead better than I had known him alive, so that he lived now as he never had before. But the manner of his death was no part of the myth, and to discover it might kill my most precious treasure.

The boy at school had the tact not to argue, though without saying more he showed that he knew better. And from the way his words began to work like grubs in my imagination I came to know that they were true.

So when my mother judged that it was time to tell me she found her secret had been kept to no purpose. It was a lesson I should have learnt: never to save something for a better moment without being sure that nobody will get there first. But often, like missed chances, there have been things I have put off, to find when the time came that it was too late. 'In delay,' Don Quixote said more than once, 'there is usually danger.'

After my mother died too, when I was sixteen, I found an envelope of my father's obituaries which she had cut out. One in the *Church Times* ended with sympathy for the bereaved and a hope that my father and the policeman might rest in peace – also the young murderer 'who most needs our prayers'. It drove me wild. Let the villain roast. Nothing was too terrible for the man who had left me without a father, who had destroyed or broken so many lives one afternoon when all he need have done was take his own. But in time my feelings changed from rage to indifference, then to curiosity. I grew to recognize an uncanny, tenuous connection with my father's killer, as I do with my characters in a novel.

Potts was in his first year, having gone to Cambridge with a scholarship and a reputation for being unusual. I can see him clearly: tall, slim, debonair, his hair smoothed back in the style of 1930. He played the drums in a jazz band, hired a piano for his room, ran up debts. His friends were in other colleges, and at King's he was elusive though conspicuous. You didn't forget him, they said, once you noticed him. He wore polo-necked sweaters and plus-fours with check stockings like the Prince of Wales, and brown and white golf shoes. Dressing-up was part of the act, with exaggeration and boasting, verging on the theatrical. The words that were used afterwards – nervous, excitable, highly strung – sound harmless. But Potts overdid it, and sometimes wore a false moustache or took a more flamboyant name.

At home in the Easter vacation he talked seriously about his future, which must have pleased his father, a businessman who had settled several unpaid Cambridge bills. But after he went back for the summer term his family heard nothing for a month, till a letter came from my father, the college Tutor. Potts was absent without permission, nobody knew where. The Cambridge police were told, then the county police, finally the London police.

The police, though they were unaware, had been given a clue when another undergraduate reported a stolen pistol. He had bought an automatic with a box of ammunition for use in South America where he was going after Cambridge, but early in May it was missing.

Potts had taken it. He showed it to Newman, who played the trumpet in the same band and shared some of his fantasies, and suggested a career of crime together. Newman bought a revolver and on an old motorbike they toured the Cambridgeshire villages, telling stories in pubs, spending money, borrowing more and perhaps earning a little on the piano and trumpet. To anyone who would listen Potts claimed to have royal blood, to own fifty suits, to have his life insured for twenty thousands pounds, to be heir to the principality of Alsace-Lorraine and entitled to be called Prince Lorraine. At least one girl fell for it and thought she was engaged to him. It was the good life, far from lectures and college rules. Sooner or later the two would be expelled from Cambridge, but they couldn't stick it anyway. They applied for passports, they would go abroad, they would get jobs.

Then Potts got a demand for five pounds which he had borrowed. He telegraphed half the money and Bolton, a friend in Newman's college, gave them another loan. The motorbike would have to be sold, but first they would ride it to London. In the last week of May they quit Cambridge, swearing that nothing would drag them back.

In London they got twenty pounds for the bike but it was Saturday, the banks were shut, they couldn't cash the cheque till Monday. They drifted through the West End and slept on the steps of St Martin's-in-the-Fields. They were young and fit, and masters of their fate. When the motorbike money was gone there would be something else to sell or someone to borrow from.

But five days down-and-out were enough. They wanted excitement, glamour, company, to match their dreams. On Thursday night, when it began to rain, one of them remembered an old address passed on by someone at Cambridge – a flat in Shaftesbury Avenue where Madge

Miller lived. In the early hours of Friday, wet and tired and dirty, they rang her bell.

Madge was twenty-five, auburn and petite, living with her maid. She worked at a night-club, calling herself a dance instructress, and wasn't surprised to be knocked up by strange young men-about-town with money to spend – though these two were broke. But Madge, a figure from fiction with a heart of gold, put them in her spare room. It was the start of a very lost weekend – the platitudes, like the clouds, were closing in.

In the morning the maid brought tea and French bread, probably the regular breakfast at Madge's. Potts spoke of a man at the Savoy Hotel who might lend them money, and he and Newman went off in search, but had no luck. Potts pawned his onyx cufflinks, bought a pair of horn-rimmed glasses and false whiskers, and had his hair waved and dyed a shade of ginger. That evening he and Newman took Madge to the movies, then to a restaurant, finishing with a show at the Holborn Empire. After Potts's money ran out Madge borrowed from a friend. It was raining again, and they went back to her flat to play poker for matches.

When Madge discovered the guns Potts resorted to bravado: 'If the cops come to get us we've got these to show!' Madge told him not to be a fool. Over the weekend she learnt a little of what was going on in his mind. If he went back to Cambridge he might be arrested for fraud, and he spoke of a loan from a friend, the heir to the Russian throne. Madge wasn't impressed, she knew about romantic young men: 'Take my advice – go back and face the music.' But the music might be too painful, and Potts boasted of another warrant concerning a smashed car. Nobody could tell the truth of his stories or predict his mood – he veered from defiance to despair. 'If anyone comes through that door,' he cried, waving his pistol, 'I'll shoot myself.' Newman caught the spirit and threatened the same. Madge said, 'Not in my flat, you won't.'

On Saturday they pawned Newman's watch. Potts wrote to Bolton, the Cambridge friend who had lent them money, enclosing the pawn ticket: Bolton could keep the watch or sell it to get his money back. Potts asked him to send his dress clothes from Cambridge – to sell or to wear, nobody could tell – addressed to the post office, Charing Cross.

That night, after Potts had pawned a platinum watch chain and Madge had borrowed more money, they went to the movies again. On Sunday, leading them through the empty streets, Potts showed them his father's office in High Holborn – he had never seen it before. On Monday, her butter finished and her patience running out, Madge gave them bread and dripping for breakfast. Potts wanted to watch the king at the Trooping of the Colour next day and go to the Derby the day after, but Madge wouldn't pay for any more. Potts and Newman said goodbye and left.

Again they drifted all day and most of the night. Trying to sleep on the Embankment – the place for tramps, the plot was wearing thin – Potts pulled out his pistol and brandished it into the dark. He seemed to enjoy his desperation, revelling in the hunt, though he swore the police would never get him, Cambridge wouldn't see his face again, he would never be handed over to King's College or his parents.

On Tuesday morning they went to Charing Cross to collect the parcel from Bolton. But Bolton was there himself, waiting in the post office – he had been asked to bring them back to Cambridge in his car.

After ten days on the run Newman was soon persuaded. But Potts was in a fright. This wasn't part of his fantasy. He had lost control of the action, he didn't know his lines, he was running out of ideas. In the end he agreed to go with them. On the way he said, 'I feel I'm putting my head in a hornet's nest.' Bolton, who didn't know about the guns, said, 'Cheer up – it won't be as bad as you think.'

It was the third of June, 1930. That morning my mother went by train in the opposite direction, on a cheap day ticket to London. She would do some shopping for the new house and see one of her sisters, or go to a gallery. She loved a day in London.

At Cambridge Bolton and Newman drove to their college, leaving Potts to walk to King's alone. His feelings – resentment, ignominy, pride – would remain his secret. What he didn't know, though he must have guessed the police were on his track, was that he had been seen by a detective who followed him through the town. Then by chance, outside his college, he met the very man who was the proper one to go and see: a man of whom another undergraduate at King's wrote a few days later, 'It was possible to go and tell him things and to ask for his advice as if he were a father.' He was mine.

The meeting was fatal to both men and to the third who was watching them. The players were moving into place for the last scene – one turning murderer, the others becoming victims. What Potts and the Tutor, prodigal and explorer, said was never known. Together they walked through the gate into the college. My father, an uneasy agent of

20

discipline, must have dreaded the interview. 'Men *took* exeats in my day,' he would tell undergraduates who came to ask for permission to leave Cambridge.

His rooms were on the ground floor in Gibb's building, the large classical block across the front court next to the chapel. They consisted, behind tall windows, of a big outer room facing the court and two smaller rooms, a bedroom and study, overlooking the great lawn down to the river and the Backs. Somewhere over there, across the bridge and beyond the trees, was the house in West Road where his three children were finishing lunch and where, that evening, he would expect to hear about my mother's day in London. 'You might justly say that we have all that we deserve,' he had written to a friend recently, hoping for a visit. 'We are fortunate people and the most unlikely things happen to us.' Now, at half-past one on a summer afternoon, fortune was taking the unlikeliest turn of all.

Shortly after he and Potts had gone in, Detective Sergeant Willis called at the porter's lodge with a warrant for Potts's arrest and was directed to the Tutor's rooms. My father, talking to Potts in the study, came into the outer room to meet Willis. 'You'd better go in and see him,' he said, and they went back into the study. Unaware of danger my father stood by the empty fireplace while Willis arraigned Potts. The three were close to each other in the small room. It was all over in a minute.

Willis cautioned Potts, told him he would have to come to the police station and began reading out the warrant. Potts didn't let him get far – the first bullet hit Willis's shoulder. Willis struggled to get at Potts and push my father aside to save him, but fell over a chair. Potts fired twice at my father, then again at Willis. Finally, for which everyone later must have been thankful, he fired at his own head.

Mortally wounded, Willis lay trying to remember how many shots he had heard. He kept still, afraid that Potts might have another bullet. In time he looked up and saw Potts lying with his head in a pool of blood, with my father beside him near the fireplace. Willis somehow got to his feet, staggered through the outer room and reached the door above the front steps. 'Help!' he called, sinking to the ground. 'He shot me – I shall be dead in ten minutes.' But he lived sixteen hours, long enough to tell the story.

The quiet of a Cambridge college was broken. A man who had explored unknown lands and reached the top of unclimbed mountains died with a policeman and a student in a crazy shoot-up like something from the Wild West. And I lost a father and gained a myth.

The news rocked the college and raced through the town. Before the end of the afternoon it reached the London papers. My mother, coming out of the Leicester Galleries, saw a terrifying headline across the *Evening Standard*: UNDERGRADUATE SHOOTS TUTOR DEAD: AMAZING DRAMA AT CAMBRIDGE. Blindly she fumbled for a penny and gave it to the man. 'Read all about it,' he said, and she did.

FIVE

May 15, Tomelloso. A cheap hotel room is either up among the tiles and TV aerials, with swifts and swallows hurling themselves across the pale sky, or it looks darkly into an inner well, with the smell of yesterday's cooking coming from below and no sky visible through the drying laundry. Last night in Tomelloso I had a gloomy cell in the middle of a building, and the fiesta promised by the two women at Manzanares was a lie.

I'm learning the difficulty of getting supper in Spain. There may be a dining-room at the back of a bar or upstairs, but nobody wants to use it. '*Comer* – eat?' the barman asks in surprise, and puts his fingers to his mouth, munching the air to make sure of my meaning. 'Later – nine o'clock, nine-thirty, *más o menos*, more or less . . .' He rocks his hand as though it's a toss-up, a matter of luck whether they will open it at all tonight and cook a meal for anyone. The chance is small if there is a bullfight or football on TV.

At last, towards ten o'clock, the barman's assistant reluctantly takes charge of the dining-room and lets me in. He turns on the lights and TV and pulls a bow tie from a drawer in the dresser, clipping it to his shirt, preening in front of a mirror. I see his annoyance at being dragged from the bar and I half share it. There are twenty tables laid with glasses and cutlery, and a big refrigerator humming with pork and fish and water melons and old apples, and racks of bottles ready for a party. Sometimes it must happen, but not tonight.

Though supper alone is improved by the delay and my hunger, I can hear the liveliness from the bar and wish I had stayed there, getting drunk on dark Manchegan wine with a piece of hard white Manchegan cheese tasting of sheep. Somewhere on the road today I saw a flock of them crammed into a forty-ton lorry, their tails hanging out, roaring through a village.

SIX

'When the strength for fiction fails the writer,' Salman Rushdie wrote of a book by V. S. Naipaul, 'what remains is autobiography.'

So I write about myself when I can't think of anything better: scraping the barrel, or coming clean at last, or not dishing myself up as someone else. The danger, it seems, is of squandering myself; of giving away too much, spending all I have. Will there be anything left to live on – to write about – afterwards? There is a primitive fear that to tell your name to someone is to give him power over you. You are no longer a free agent, master of yourself, having surrendered more than your name but your identity too, even your soul. To disclose yourself, expose yourself, in a whole book is asking for trouble. Self-revelation is a kind of suicide.

But it works the other way too. Tapping my life out on a typewriter generally used for more original work, I can't drop the old habits. It's what the imagination is for – to ferment the raw stuff and inject it with Saul Bellow's 'transforming additive, the gift of poetry'. A woman in a novel of mine, watching a waiter pour champagne into her glass, decides that more fizz is what the world needs. Her life would have been flat enough if she hadn't blown some bubbles into it.

Somewhere this will turn almost into a novel, advancing into fiction, retreating into biography, straddling the frontier in the haze where fact meets fantasy, before advancing again. It will have to happen, if only because I have lived it once and can't go through it all a second time, or not exactly as before. Fiction, Kipling wrote, is truth's elder sister.

Deirdre has hardly appeared yet. She will be on the watershed, one foot in experience and one in invention, a no-woman for a no-man's land. Bits of her may have occurred in novels here and there, but never the entire Deirdre. She won't recognize herself because only part of her is the truth. Which part? – she and I would disagree. The rest is a patchwork of people, real and imaginary, known or dreamed of. No doubt it contains aspects of myself, like any character made of my words, whether in fiction or not. When I wrote the biography of a polar explorer I couldn't feel the man, the nearest to becoming him, without breaking into fiction. The alternative was to follow him and spend a winter, as he had done, alone under the arctic ice.

I was never much good at a sustained relationship before meeting Deirdre. Probably she would say I haven't improved. Now she is the woman in my life; the only one I might be able to live with if I had to live with anyone; the one I haven't met.

The woman in my life – or nearly half of it. But I can detect her in the early part too, though for most of my childhood she wasn't yet born. (She once felt the same, and wrote in a letter before we were married, 'Did I half love you before I ever met you?') If she is a figment, a character in a book who lives in words, there is no reason why she shouldn't inhabit words about her that belong to a time before her birth. The future was in the past, just as the past will be in the pages I haven't written yet.

SEVEN

May 16, Tomelloso. The bus leaves before dawn. A hare crosses the road in the headlights. Slowly, like a stage after the curtain goes up, the land grows visible. The plain begins to fold and wrinkle, turning into low hills with lagoons lying in the slits between.

At Ruidera, where the bus drops me as daylight breaks, I have a coffee in a bar. Two men drinking *aguardiente* for breakfast silently eye the thin, bald foreigner. I leave my rucksack in the bar and walk through the village; walk for hours along the line of lagoons, the way Don Quixote came, in the cool, grey, clouded morning.

A big fish jumps – the pike of Ruidera are famous. Waterbirds splash and quack in the reeds, cuckoos call over the lagoons. And such nightingales! I stand under the poplars while they drench me with song. This is a Spain I haven't heard of. Nobody comes along the road – I have the morning, the lagoons, the nightingales to myself.

By midday I'm walking up into the hills, through clumps of rosemary to the Cave of Montesinos: a rustic picnic bench, a litter bin, a notice for tourists pointing to the cave – a crack slanting down into the hillside, perhaps the shaft of an old copper mine.

Don Quixote found the mouth choked with thorns, wild figs, brambles. When he slashed at them with his sword a flock of crows and jackdaws flew out, knocking him over. A lesser man would have taken it as a bad omen but Don Quixote tied on a rope, prayed for God's help and the protection of his mistress, the lovely, matchless Dulcinea, to whose love he dedicated this dangerous adventure, and began the descent. He only wished he had brought a bell so that Sancho Panza, paying out the rope and making a thousand signs of the cross, would

27

know he was alive. 'God be your guide,' Sancho called as his master vanished into the dark, 'and bring you back safely to the light of the world.'

Don Quixote climbed down, shouting for more rope till there was none left. After waiting a while Sancho pulled the rope up. Don Quixote returned to the surface, his eyes shut, and had to be shaken and slapped before he stretched his limbs, as if waking from deep sleep. What had he seen in that hell down there?

'Hell you call it!' he cried. 'You have snatched me from the sweetest life, the loveliest vision that man has ever had. Now I know that the pleasures of this life are a dream – they pass like a shadow, they wither like flowers in the field.' He had found himself in a meadow – a madman's fantasy, Sancho thought – where a wonderful castle was revealed, with battlements of crystal, the scene for unimaginable episodes of romance and chivalry. He believed he had spent three days in that enchanted land, and had had a glimpse of Dulcinea.

Sancho knew that Dulcinea was an uncouth village girl, far from lovely, and told his master he was talking nonsense.

'Sancho,' Don Quixote said, 'I know you too well – it's because you love me that you speak like that. You have no experience of world affairs, so anything you don't understand seems impossible. But the time will come when you will believe what I saw down there. The truth allows no argument.' And Don Quixote, though mad, was incapable of a lie.

This afternoon I go a short way down into the cave and shout, 'Don Quixote!' hoping for an echo or perhaps a frightened bat – even a sight of Dulcinea – but nothing happens. It isn't a pleasant place, I don't stay long, but I don't doubt the reality of Don Quixote's vision. Reality, for him, was the illusion that led him into action.

On the long walk back the nightingales are silent. Instead, blue dragonflies slide through the bushes by the lagoons. At Ruidera the bar is shut, with my rucksack locked inside. I rattle the door and a girl comes out with it from the next house. The early morning quiet is forgotten as a motorbike rally tears through the village. On their huge machines the drivers and their pillion girls, hair streaming, wear their crash helmets strapped to their arms.

EIGHT

Oscar Wilde wrote, 'Where there is sorrow there is holy ground,' and after my father's murder a sort of sanctity fell on the rest of my mother's life, though nothing could soften the utter pain. ('I think of your mother losing your father,' Deirdre said in a letter when she was expecting our first baby, 'and do not understand how she could bear such sadness.') Despite his many friends my father probably wasn't easy to know and still more difficult to love, which made the loss more devastating. But my mother shielded her children from the events and for me it was a time of dissolving darkness, emerging consciousness.

Birthdays stand as beacons and the first I remember was my fourth, twenty days after my father died, with a chocolate cake and the garden through the window. On my fifth birthday my mother cut my hair short and kept a golden lock of it tied with blue silk in a piece of tissue paper. More than fifty years later, with indefinable horror, I put it in the fire.

Among the shadows are the servants, allies of a child in a land colonized by grown-ups, though they lived in dark attics where we weren't allowed. A housemaid might get forty pounds a year, a parlour-maid sixty, a cook eighty, with keep and uniform, half a day off each week and a fortnight in the summer.

Ivy was housemaid, superseded by Peggy from Scotland in a flurry of bedmaking and brooms, carrying coal scuttles and water cans, laying fires, emptying slops, pushing the carpet sweeper, helping my mother with the Monday laundry. Edith was parlourmaid, stern in black and white with starched cuffs, who polished the silver in the pantry, turned the knife grinder, rolled the butter pats with wooden paddles, served in

29

the dining-room and didn't upset her tray of glasses when I dropped a toy bomb behind her from the top of the stairs. She laughed once, when I was made to apologize for ringing the front door bell and hiding behind the Wellingtonia. When she gave notice her place was taken by her sister Winnie, jollier but less reliable.

The cook was Nellie, tiny and shiny and pink like a shrimp boiled in one of her saucepans. After breakfast my mother went into the kitchen to order the meals, writing on a slate. Copper jelly moulds were ranged on the shelf and a smell of soup hung among the flypapers. We had roast meat or a chicken and steamed pudding on Sunday, shepherd's pie or rissoles on Monday, fish on Friday, sausages for Sunday breakfast, porridge in the winter. My mother liked plain cooking – Irish stew, boiled halibut with egg sauce, apple charlotte and custard, plenty of milk puddings and junket. I learnt to eat anything except artichoke soup and tapioca. Garlic wasn't heard of, except the wild kind in the shrubbery that I can still smell at the thought of hide-and-seek. Seed cake, flavoured with caraways, was considered dangerously spicy and exotic. Olive oil was for ear ache.

Doggett, the first gardener at West Road, was useless and had to be replaced by Fishpool, who had some skill with vegetables though none with flowers, and was best with the mowing-machine or backing the old Austin into the yard to wash it: he thought we ought to have a modern streamlined car. He came on a tall bicycle with an acetylene lamp and his dinner tied to the carrier, and ate it cross-legged on the potting-shed bench – bread and cheese cut with a broken dining-room knife in his earthy fingers and cold tea in a bottle. He earned less than two pounds a week.

The butcher Joey – or was that his horse? – trotted up the drive, riding on a sort of meat-safe on wheels. The milk float, with measures to dip into the churns, had a pale dairy-cream horse. The grocer's and greengrocer's boys had bicycles, the baker brought stone-ground bread in a basket on his arm. In the winter the muffin man, with a tray on his head, walked up the road ringing his bell. If an onion man from Brittany came to the kitchen door my mother was sent for, to speak French.

At Cambridge as an undergraduate in 1947 I could still see – though they had vanished – the lamplighter whistling on his bicycle, coming up West Road at dusk to turn on the gaslamps with a pole, and the coal wagon pulled by carthorses leaving a trail of dung, and the funerals that were always connected with my father: no wonder people stopped in the street as the hearse passed and men took off their hats, and my sisters' riding-master stood up in his stirrups.

Nannies, who sank into the oblivion they deserved, were replaced by Vera who was closer to my own age, seven, than to my mother's forty-four. She came bicycling and punting on the river, helped with photography, played rummy and for four years occupied a special inside-outside place, a valve for family pressure. When I became asthmatic she looked after me, not as a nurse but a friend, knowing what she could do that my mother and a doctor couldn't. And, as she probably intended, she was the first woman I saw naked. We were on holiday at Bamburgh – picnics on the sand, trips to the Farne Islands and Lindisfarne – staying above the bakery, going on the bread round in a van with the baker's son, who later fought in the Spanish Civil War. When I was drying myself after a bath Vera decided to have one too, undressing and stepping in, then standing in front of me to soap her breasts and the triangle of ginger hair below. The secrets I had guessed at looked so simple – I was grateful to her for showing me.

Encouraged by Vera I wrote a letter and put it, with an envelope addressed to myself, in a ginger beer bottle. We sealed it with red sealing-wax and threw it in the sea from a boat among the Farne Islands. A year later the envelope came back from Norway, where a man had picked it up on the shore a hundred miles north of Bergen.

Vera read the *Daily Mail* and after tea she watched from the window for Ron, a student in a college scarf who came on his racing bike to court her. On her half-day they went to a cinema or ate waffles in a café. I was sure that Ron never saw what I had seen in the bathroom. He went to India as a teacher, and letters came from Cawnpore with the king in purple on the stamp, the price in annas. But Ron counted for less in Vera's heart than Africa. After four years with us my mother found her a job in Rhodesia and gave her a necklace of green peridots. When we took her to the station, to our delight and with almost no hesitation my mother kissed her.

Education began for my elder sister and me one morning after breakfast when my mother started *Reading Without Tears* and gave us copybooks for tracing a florid script with a steel nib dipped in an inkpot, all loops and ligatures and blots. She also made us write gothic letters in Indian ink, perhaps because she remembered it from her own childhood with a vague emotion, pleasant or not, which she wanted to pass on.

She made us learn 'Piping down the valleys wild' and 'When Dick the shepherd blows his nail' and 'For men may come and men may go', and the Lord's Prayer and Psalm 23 though she had no religion, not even any convinced atheism. (When she was dying she took the sacraments for the first time, from a retired missionary bishop who brought friendship and comfort.) Soon she began arithmetic, but was herself defeated by the simplest sum. Lessons had a quality of adventure – much of it was new to her too. She produced a globe, and an atlas with the phases of the moon, and a history book, *Our Island Story*, with Alfred burning the cakes, Canute and the waves, the princes in the tower, Raleigh laying his cloak in the mud, Drake and his bowls.

One day she introduced a horror called Mademoiselle, all fluttering lace and French gush, scented enough to make us sick, who put us through the present tense of *donner*. 'You'll have to do it when you go to school,' my mother said. We told her we never would go to school, not with much hope: the limit of her teaching would soon be reached.

I was seven and my sister eight when we walked with Vera across the meadows to Mrs Smith's, next to the Greene King brewery. Mrs Smith was spiky with a pale face and lifeless black hair, in a dark mannish suit, satin blouse, tie and tiepin. She put me in the bottom class and my sister in the second, but I bellowed all morning – we had always done lessons together, I was as good as her – and in a few hours I won. But next day Mademoiselle turned up, still teaching *donner*, with extra perfume against the smell of fermenting beer from next door.

All his life my father kept a diary – I was given one when I was seven. It had pages of facts and at once I was a grown-up with everything a man-about-town should need: the weight of a truss of straw, the value of a Polish zloty, the gallons in a pipe of port. I looked up the cost of a letter to Egypt, the high tide at London Bridge, Princess Elizabeth's birthday, the beginning of Michaelmas law sittings. As a Jew I checked the Day of Atonement, a Muslim the first of Ramadan, a Christian the conversion of St Paul. I knew when the Royal Academy opened, pheasant shooting ended, fire policies expired and the moon entered the penumbra of an eclipse. There were spaces for my Cash Summary and for Things Lent, for my telegraphic address, number of my car and bank book and season ticket, times of my trains To Town and From Town, details of insurance for my servants whose wages I could calculate in pounds or guineas. For a dishonest moment I was a barrister or city gent.

But I had to record something on the blank pages. On January 1st (circumcision, bank holiday in Scotland, holiday at Stock Exchange) my mother started me off: 'Saw first snipe.'

I got the idea and was soon seeing a chiffchaff, linnet, stonechat, redwing, great titmouse. But it was all lies, I couldn't identify any of them. I was on safer ground with the weather: 'Lovely sun, great gale, hard frost, began to rain.' And food: 'Had duck's eggs for tea, had first new potatoes, had raspberry ice, bought doughnuts.' For pages I was simply 'in bed', till one day 'got up for breakfast' and at last 'went back to school'. Usually it was a list of going somewhere: 'Went to get straw for guinea pigs, went to the doctor, went in the car and went through a ford, went to a birthday party, went to the cobbler's, went on bicycles, went to the midsummer fair, went bathing and went out of my depth, went to have hair cut, went to buy winter clothes.' Occasionally I changed the verb: 'Tried to catch some newts but failed, skated on the Grantchester meadows, began algebra at school.'

The diary was for events, not ideas. I entered birthdays – my father's too – and the visits of relations. Every Sunday my mother's undergraduate nephews and nieces and their friends came to lunch, a bright spot for her in an alien town and a treat for us. 'John and Patrick played sardines with us, Sylvia climbed a tree, Victor hosed us with no clothes on, Teresa stayed for tea.'

One of the cousins, my mother's favourite in that pre-war Cambridge of fervent socialism, joined the Jarrow marchers ('How nice of him,' the cook said) and was pelted with tomatoes by Mosley's fascists. Probably my mother would have liked to join him. Her politics were instinctively left-wing but haunted by my father's conservatism, and we grew up with no strong principles, religious or political, to confess or deny. Sometimes I have wished for roots in a living faith, even if I was to cut them later, just as I have envied anyone devoted to the lives of others, knowing how far I am from real charity or the dedication of a believer – the selflessness of Don Quixote.

We roller-skated on the empty roads, and played penny whistles, and invited an old professor of astronomy to tea, to see him come in his carriage with two chestnut horses and a coachman; and entertained him with musical boxes and a puppet show. In the garden, when I pushed

33

the swing all one summer afternoon for a girl called June while the others were being Indians in a wigwam, my sisters teased me for being in love, till I thought I was. Forty years later I met June again and she politely said she remembered too, but I knew she was lying.

NINE

May 16, Tomelloso. There should be an afternoon bus to Alcázar de San Juan, capital of La Mancha. For an hour I wait in the bus station before a man tells me that the timetable is wrong: there are no more buses today, Saturday, and nothing to anywhere on Sunday. Unwilling to wait till Monday I walk out of town and stand at the beginning of the Alcázar road. I haven't hitch-hiked since I was a young man in Australia, writing my first book, and am glad to be doing it again.

The first are local cars, signalling that they are turning off shortly. One of them stops and the man offers to take me three kilometres. I say I will try for something better: Alcázar is only thirty kilometres or so, there will soon be a car going there. Twenty minutes later he comes back down the other side of the road and blows his horn: I am still here, in the bitter Manchegan wind – a wind, they boast, that can kill a man but can't blow out a candle.

Big new cars, all with empty seats, accelerate on seeing me, the drivers' eyes fixed on the road ahead. Crowded families stare out at me as they pass, and turn to stare again through the back window. For a time it rains. A tractor with a girl beside the driver looks like stopping, but changes its mind. I give myself till seven o'clock, then I will go back to Tomelloso for the weekend. A disabled man, perhaps legless, stops and points to the crutches propped on the seat beside him and the boxes of lettuces that fill the back, and says he is sorry. I stand by the road for an hour and a half. La Mancha, I have read, is a land of nine months' winter, three months' hell. I wish the hell would come.

At last Benito comes, in a small Renault van. He isn't going to Alcázar, but to Campo de Criptana where he keeps a bar: 'You know – where Don Quixote tilted at the windmills.'

That suits me better.

Benito wears a shiny black shirt, shiny black trousers, shiny black hair in the Elvis Presley style. He is surprised I had to wait so long for a lift and apologizes for Spain, making room for me between crates of beer, Coca Cola, fizzy fruit drinks. '*Mi sueño* – my dream,' he says, 'is to go to America.'

'*La Vida es Sueño*, Life is a Dream,' is a play by Calderón written thirty years after Cervantes published the first volume of *Don Quixote*. Three centuries later the philosopher Unamuno wrote, 'If life is a dream, why should we so obstinately deny that dreams are life? And all that is life is truth.'

On the straight flat road to Campo de Criptana, rattling among Benito's bottles, it's easy to see why Don Quixote, born on this empty plain and free of worldly attachments, lived in dreams; easy to understand the vision of the great madman when there was so little else to focus on. It's a country of hallucinations.

TEN

Our windows shook when foundations for a new university library were driven into the clay on the other side of West Road. King George V and Queen Mary came in a Daimler to open it, and we sat on the garden fence to cheer – they had come for us. We saw them again at Hyde Park Corner in the Silver Jubilee procession, and then one morning the postman told us the king was dead. I was glad – I had the same birthday as the Prince of Wales and now I would share it with the king. But after one birthday together Edward VIII let me down by abdicating.

Childhood faded into a pattern of details brightened by incidents unfixed to any date: driving in the Austin to the Gog Magog hills for a picnic – 'saw a silver-washed fritillary', I put in my diary, frightened of being caught out by my father's ghost; skating on the frozen fens – 'bought roast chestnuts'; seeing the airship R101 drifting over Ely, soon to crash on its way to India – 'had jam puffs for tea'; punting up the river to Byron's Pool where Rupert Brooke bathed naked with Virginia Woolf – 'swam five strokes without touching the bottom'.

Many of the details belonged in the bathroom: the smell of Wright's coal tar soap, the twice-daily Pepsodent toothpaste and weekly Palmolive shampoo, my mother's enormous loofah, the scales she weighed us on and measurements of our height pencilled on the door. In a red cupboard was the bottle of iodine that stung on a cut, with the horrors of milk of magnesia, liquid paraffin, syrup of figs, to put colour back in our tongues or settle our 'motions'.

Though my mother allowed new medicines like Radio Malt and glucose, she preferred the ones of her own childhood: Parrish's Food, a tonic that shot a stream of black lava from one's bowels, to be inspected before being flushed away; *Pomade Divine*, a precious ointment in a jar with a glass stopper, scented with mysterious goodness but so stiff it had to be softened in hot water; 'gold beater's skin', a brown transparent membrane, reluctantly given up when Elastoplast was invented; scalding poultices of fuller's earth, blackcurrant lozenges, Elliman's embrocation (originally for horses), calamine lotion, camphorated oil, witch hazel, Brand's Essence and Benger's Food – a store of remedies, welcome or disagreeable, smelling indefinably of tears and relief.

Clothes were a feature as large as food and medicine: socks knitted by my mother and kept up with elastic garters, viyella shirts, chilprufe vests, aertex sleeping suits, combinations in the winter, leggings for the snow, fingerless cotton gloves tied round my wrists to stop me scratching my eczema. I wanted a sailor suit but never got it, and was sent to parties in an Eton jacket with waistcoat and striped trousers, broad starched collar, patent leather pumps – enough to set off an attack of asthma. I hated party games, I wouldn't dance, I clamoured to go home.

Every Christmas ('lovely big turkey and plum pudding', and I listed my presents) the dons of King's College gave a children's party. Jolliest, funniest, fattest of them was Beves, who had become Tutor on my father's death. In a paper hat and silk handkerchief over his eyes for blind man's buff, or breaking the rules of general post, or leading the party in 'Here we go gathering nuts in May', he was our favourite. At the climax, in a flourish of streamers and cheers, a chef brought in a huge pie baked in the college kitchens. Beves cut the pastry and pulled out a surprise for each of us.

Fifteen years later, as an undergraduate, I took my weekly essay to Beves's elegant room overlooking the river. He offered cigarettes from a silver box and sherry in a goblet from his collection of old glass. I was a dull student, lucky to get a degree, but not beyond his kindness and persuasion. He would introduce me to French novelists, a fat man moving nimbly among his friends, or turn in his chair, eyebrows raised, to steer one of my banalities into a question worth discussing.

Long after his death he smiled again from the front page of *The Times*. Fabulous party-giver, fastidious collector, connoisseur of food and wine who spent the summer touring France in his Rolls-Royce, author of a thesis on the Holy Grail, translator of Rabelais, the portly figure in a surplice reading the lesson in King's chapel, the life and soul of Cambridge dramatics who played a hilarious gravedigger in my first *Hamlet* – Beves was found to have been a more talented actor than anyone suspected. He was unmasked as the man who, at the time of those children's parties, was secretly enlisting undergraduates as Russian spies; whose three famous recruits were Burgess, Maclean and Philby. Beves was the missing fourth man. He had pulled his biggest surprise out of the Christmas pie.

It came as a shock, as *The Times* said, but it was also a delight. A man was revealed as not what he was seen to be – not so simple or obvious as he appeared. He was all the things that made him conspicuous and loved, and far more: the keeper of a private life hidden under a colossal public deception, a last laugh at our gullibility. His career as Cambridge don was a masquerade, a performance surpassed by his versatility, making fools look foolish. The fantasy was ours, not his. The man we knew was a character from fiction – the reality was espionage.

Being naturally subversive I marvelled how the hero of those party games and patient teacher of an indifferent student could be this villain in the news, accused of 'distasteful activities' as an enemy agent. I could admire his duplicity and envy his inner certainty, the faith of a Don Quixote through the looking-glass, impelling him for years without reward but with great danger. I saw his life, not as a record of treason leading to hundreds of deaths and an international scandal, but as one man's secret journey. And it was nice to know that, after bequeathing his books and glass collection and a lot of money to King's, he died of a heart attack in his college room, not in exile among his bleak Moscow masters; and not shot, like his predecessor, by one of his students with a stolen pistol.

In fact *The Times* got it wrong. They had been tipped off that the fourth man was a Cambridge don and given a crossword clue – five letters beginning with B. They picked on Beves of King's, but really it was Blunt of Trinity.

Before my ninth birthday, with purple-topped stockings and a fleur-de-lis on my cap, I went to the King's Choir School in West Road, three minutes from home. The headmaster, a man like a monkey called Fidd, had private ideas about teaching and wrote his own textbooks. He used to hitch a big roller to his car, fix the throttle and steering-wheel and set it to run in circles over the cricket field while he went indoors to teach; occasionally he looked out to see if it was on course. In the summer, before going home, boys had to pull the roller over the pitch with masters sitting on top to give weight.

Some masters were undergraduates earning money to pay for university. One was Wickers, with a crimson pig face and a voice developed for coaching rowing crews. In Latin, if a boy got a word wrong, Wickers made him stand up. At a second mistake he had to stand on the seat of his desk. At a third Wickers smacked the back of his bare legs with a ruler till the boy got it right or began to cry. Tears were probably Wickers's preference, though with his bright and noisy ways he was more popular than other masters – unless we only laughed with him like frightened rabbits, waiting for the ruler. He stayed on, becoming headmaster after Fidd, but resigned over a case of 'intimacy' with one of his boys.

Fear was part of school. The worst terror was one of Fidd's beatings, which were more a matter of luck than justice. Often it came as a surprise – a trivial crime, a misunderstanding, a sharp summons to the study – and would be ferociously delivered. I never got one and was terrified of the danger, though I envied the glory that went with it and even ached for the unknown sting of a cane.

I wasn't a goody-goody nor quite a sneak, and wished I had the courage to be naughty. The worst I did was report that I had a cold, which wasn't true, to get out of games, which I hated. Instead I would go for a bicycle ride alone. I felt safe, confident that I could lie my way out of trouble.

In the 1935 school photograph I am cross-legged on the ground between a boy called Luard who became a member of parliament and one called James who became a bishop. Eighty boys are locked into the mid-thirties, as motionless as the summer chestnut trees above us, never to give conkers, never to fall. I know them by their surnames only, even the ones I called my friends.

Among them is Smart, smaller than myself, who told me the secret my mother was keeping from me, and Holden who said I looked like a parrot, and Forsyth who acted *Alice* in the school play – each year the same play with the same girlish freckled boy. Farrant, the placid somnolent son of a judge; Pickthorn, the quick-tempered son of a politician who became a baronet; and Hankey, the erratic, desperate footballing son of a clergyman, later a vicar himself. Westmacott, who went away in the middle of term and died, but has survived no less truly than the others who were stopped by the photographer, cut short on a summer day. Spens, too pretty in the photo to be a bully, who forced me and other small boys to hold hands in a ring while he sent an electric current through us, which tingled and twisted like a liquid corkscrew and caused, I was sure, the diarrhoea I got next day. Carter-Jonas, an estate agent's son whose name was on all the House For Sale boards in town. Lennard-Jones, a professor's son who guarded the changing-room door and wouldn't let me through without the password, whose name I once saw among the doctors in a hospital for diseases of the rectum. Waddams, whom I found again in a Covent Garden pub in the interval of a Wagner opera.

All of them are evoked in the photo by the grinning, scowling, dismal, happy faces of Cambridge boys with famous Cambridge names – Ryle, Adrian, Hoskyns, Burnaby, Loewe, Keynes – in grey shorts and cricket shirts, fixed by the camera, unlikely ever to grow up. Near me at the front is the boy who emptied his bowels during a history lesson but sat on in the mess and stink, not daring to move. Afterwards we teased him and pulled up his shorts to see, though he still denied that anything had happened. Later he joined the Foreign Office.

In a striped blazer between Fidd and Wickers is the choirmaster, with an understandable big smile: he was acquitted of indecency with the choirboys – sodomy was rife in Cambridge. Next to Mrs Fidd is a master who told us that he once left his sailing-boat tied to the quay, to find when he came back that the tide had dropped and the boat was hanging in the air. He spent hundreds of hours teaching Latin pronouns or French declensions or algebra equations, but only the memory of his dangling boat survives.

Beyond the chestnut trees, through a gothic door, was the concrete floor where you could strike sparks with your football boots. And rows of lockers where private things were safe – in mine I had a lump of pitch that spread into a soft black pool over my Bible. And the lavatory, the Bog, where you could have your arm seized from behind and twisted nearly off. And the immense communal bath, a tank lined with white tiles, full of steam and muddy footballers, where I learnt about circumcision.

I learnt some of the things I was taught, but wondered what they had to do with me. Past participles and Pythagoras and the Plantagenets might be right for other boys, like sport, though not for me. I would do what was expected, so long as nobody got the idea that it was relevant.

ELEVEN

May 16, Campo de Criptana. In the evening there is a wedding, the bride and bridegroom posing endlessly outside the church for the cameras – a photographer is more important than a priest. After the flashbulbs someone lets off bangers in the crowd and rice bags are thrown like bombs over the couple. Struggling to a car with ribbons on the aerial, bumpers, door handles, they fall into a bed of white flowers and drive away in a burst of satin and petals.

After dark I walk up to see the windmills on a hill above the town where they catch the relentless Manchegan wind, ten white towers capped with grey, their sails ready to turn.

'What luck, friend Sancho!' Don Quixote cried as they rode across the plain. 'Look at those monster giants – more than forty of them! I'm going into battle, I'll kill them all.'

'What giants?' Sancho asked.

'Over there, with long arms.'

'Watch out, sir! – those are windmills.'

'You know nothing about it,' Don Quixote retorted. 'They're giants, and if you're frightened keep away and say your prayers while I attack.' He dug his spurs into Rocinante, ignoring Sancho's shouts and the breeze that stirred the windmill sails: 'Don't flee, you cowards! – it's only one man fighting you.' Commending himself with all his heart to Dulcinea, putting up his shield, urging Rocinante into a gallop, he charged the first windmill and drove his spear into its sail. But the wind caught it, smashed the spear, dragged horse and rider with it and threw them to the ground.

'My God, didn't I tell you?' Sancho said, helping Don Quixote to his feet. 'Nobody could mistake them, unless he had windmills on the brain.'

'Be quiet, Sancho,' his master replied. 'The giants were turned by magic into windmills, to cheat me of the glory of conquering them.'

They rode on towards the Pass of Lápice and though it was soon dinner time Don Quixote, battered by his fall, had no appetite. Sancho ate as they went, helping himself from his saddle-bags and drinking heavily from his wine bottle, deciding that these mad adventures were quite fun after all; and when they stopped at night under the trees he fell asleep. But Don Quixote tore off a branch for a makeshift spear and stayed awake all night, thinking of his impossible, unattainable, non-existent but totally believable Dulcinea: dreams that weren't so different from other men's, though his were excused by lunacy.

In tonight's breeze, when I climb the hill above Campo de Criptana after supper, the windmills are motionless and silent as they have been for years, no longer grinding flour for bread but truly giants with a monstrous inhuman look. No wonder Sancho was frightened or that Don Quixote attacked. And Sancho was right: his master had windmills on the brain, grinding reality into his peculiar idea of truth.

TWELVE

My mother had a talent for holidays. Bright glimpses survive and the earliest, for their quickness and isolation, are the most intense. At Caister-on-Sea I splashed up and down the shallows with a bamboo spear, patrolling my sisters' sandcastle, while herring drifters edged along the grey horizon. At Rustington I got sand in my teeth from damp jam sandwiches. At Thorpeness an aunt fell into the lake. On the beach we wore waterproof pants with elastic round the thighs and pinch-tight rubber sandshoes, and were given gingernuts and bitter chocolate after bathing. On the Isle of Wight a vanilla ice burst through its cone over my shorts and the new *Queen Mary*, coming home from America, was a swindle – it had fewer funnels than the old *Aquitania*.

At Bembridge, across the road from The Limes, a black-haired Jewish boy was staying in another boarding-house. He had come from Germany where he wasn't wanted, and shouted his latest English sentence from the window: 'I am your friend, Niklaus.' Up the road in a bungalow called The Nest an old sea captain showed me model ships, a tropical bird's nest, nautical instruments, weapons, a shrunken head and masks. But they were unbearable – the images of someone else's future, not mine. I wanted to play on the beach.

My mother's old nurse, an enveloping person with a bristly chin and a smell I didn't like, perhaps of the cowslip wine she brewed, won a thousand pounds in the Irish sweepstake and gave my mother fifty. It took us, after typhoid injections in the bathroom, to Tangier for six days, tourist class in a P. and O. liner: mahogany and brass and crimson plush and potted plants – said to be the Prince of Wales's favourite ship after an Empire tour. Through our porthole we saw Tilbury docks slip into the night. Next morning Dover Castle floated in the December

44

sky, lifted on a bank of mist. Soon all the family except me were seasick in our cabin, and stewards were fetching basins down the corridor.

I went up on the lurching spray-blown promenade and for the first time felt the sea all round me, the biggest desert in the world. A tall man with a moustache told me that eight times round the deck was a mile, and marched away – he was on his way to India. I was busy with a loose tooth, probing at sharp roots with my tongue and tasting blood. I threw it into the Bay of Biscay on New Year's Day, 1934. This year I would be eight.

Porpoises rolled in the waves and a few passengers came out, pale like spring flowers, to watch the coast of Portugal: army families going back to the North-West Frontier, civil servants bound for another tour in Bengal or the Sudan, elderly globetrotters avoiding the English winter. They knew it well, they often passed this way on the Empire shuttle.

After Suez it would start heating up, the tall man with a moustache told me. He wanted to make friends, which flattered me at first. He said it was a pity I was getting off at Tangier, it gave us so little time. And I would miss the best part of the voyage. In the Red Sea there was usually a death from heat-stroke among the stokers in the boiler-room: the officers kept quiet but he could always tell – the engines stopped in the night while the body was put overboard.

He asked my name and about my family. Why was my mother alone with three small children? That made me, he said, the only man in the family. I became defensive, afraid he was going to call me 'son' and give me half-a-crown. At Tangier he waved from the rail as we climbed down into a tender to be ferried ashore, on to the edge of Africa.

Mosquito nets, tents of cobweb, hung over our hotel beds. A smell of narcissus filled the dining-room. We rode mules, picked tangerines, bought leather purses, collected shells. Wrapped in a huge Buick tourer we started for the Gates of Hercules, but got bogged in mud and picnicked on a hillside. White egrets pecked the fields, threadbare old men filled their goatskin water-bags and loped off into the desert, a ragged shepherd boy played his flute: it was all done for us, it seemed, and perhaps it was.

We toiled round a Moorish palace and saw a pair of storks and ate *oeufs au plat*, and too soon were sailing home in another liner, a new white one with a nursery and three yellow funnels. I caught whooping-cough from another child on board and in bed at home, in paints or chalks, I endlessly drew Tangier bay with a three-funnelled liner at anchor.

Twenty years later I was a passenger in that same liner from Australia to India. Two of the funnels had been taken off – they were dummies, put there for the thirties' fashion (so what else was false in childhood?). My own style was also reduced and with no sweepstake winnings I was alone in a six-berth emigrant cabin below the waterline, close to the screws.

But I slipped up through the first class barrier to watch the ship break away from the Adelaide dockside. A tangle of paper streamers snapped as the gap widened. Gathering way, heading for the open sea, turning into the sunset – it was something out of a bad movie. Australians hung over the side and sang about jolly swagmen, tucker bags, coolibah trees, the ritual memories of a land they never knew, before drifting below, settling down for the first night at sea.

In the dusk a girl and I were left at the rail, she with a long streamer in her fingers, I trying to reach the other end as it blew my way. I caught it, pulled gently, felt a tug in answer. It was all the clichés I could think of. Fingering towards each other along yards of coloured paper, meeting in the middle, touching – it was worse than any movie.

She was travelling first class. Going to England. Never been out of Australia before. Seeing Europe – Venice, the Alhambra, Madame Tussauds – the way girls did. The Parthenon, the Prado, the planetarium, all those places. Especially Scotland. A city girl, a wool broker's daughter – a broken engagement back there, somewhere in the dark astern. Sharing a first class cabin with another girl. Dad paid for the ticket – first class Dad. And lovely first class breasts.

We went into the bar, but the steward wouldn't let me buy drinks – I was the wrong class, I belonged down at the bottom of the ship. The girl laughed, apologizing for her Dad. Next day I tracked her to her cabin. The friend was sick – love or something, not the sea – but we could go up on deck. I was her guest if anyone asked. So that was the Great Australian Bight, she said greedily, and stretched her arms along the horizon, her shirt front brushing the lucky rail. And how did I like Australia? What was I doing in Adelaide anyway? – it was a dump, a real wowser, the only cemetery with lights on.

Well, I hadn't meant to go there at all, to be honest. I was on the loose. Writing my first book. A writer? – well, not yet, but give me time. I was still knocking around. I landed in Sydney by chance. Someone gave me an address in South Australia, a sheep station, and said if I turned up I'd be put to work and paid. So I hitch-hiked – ten days from Sydney to Adelaide.

Typical Englishman, the girl on the liner said. Just what she'd expect. Pity I couldn't join her in the first class pool. But I must have seen more of Australia than she ever had. I could tell her about it. Up through the Blue Mountains, across the Riverina, down the Murray. Pommies were popular, more than the Poles, Balts, Serbs, Greeks, that lot. I was recognized at once, standing by the road with a thumb out. Picked up and fed and offered jobs. Taken home to meet the family: 'Why Pommie, we fight the same wars!'

Beer was popular too. Too popular, the girl agreed – Australian men were awful. The game was to swallow the maximum between leaving work at five o'clock and closing-time at six. Men crowded the pubs with an eye on the clock, lining up beers and knocking them back. It was a fight to get through to the bar, till someone heard my accent: 'Two schooners for the Pommie! Make it four!' I came from the second best country in the world.

On the station there were twenty thousand sheep. That was nothing to some places, the girl said. But this was out in the 'trace element' country where they were still clearing the bush, ploughing it up, scattering chemicals and grass seed. The girl's Dad had money in one of those companies – otherwise it would go in taxes. He was lucky to have only one daughter to send to Europe.

They made me a jackaroo. Mutton chops and eggs and potatoes at four in the morning, with ketchup sloshed over everything. Sometimes it was steak instead of chops. Then all day out in the paddocks. Not like an English paddock, I told her, with an apple tree and a patch of nettles and an old tin bath for the pony. But she wouldn't know about that. Wait till she got to England and saw for herself. These were thousand-acre blocks of desert. From the middle the boundary fence was out of sight, or just a mirage on the horizon with a billabong upside down in the haze. Sheets of water vanished when you reached them. Amazing how those farmers found their way without a sextant. Sextant? – the thing the captain had up on the bridge, to tell him where we were.

Sheep and kangaroos and emus floated in the distance like ships at sea. To me they looked the same from far away. Someone would point at a sickly ewe or a stray lamb when there was nothing there. Had to chase it into a corner, inspect its wool and feet, prod its ribs. But she was a wool broker's daughter, I didn't have to tell her.

I was sent out alone to bury the dead – all an English jackaroo was fit for, the girl supposed. Given a jeep with a spade and crowbar in the back, and let loose in the paddocks. Driving for ever, looking for a corpse before it went rotten – too late, too often. They died of disease, old age, whatever. Dig a grave, tip it in, cover it up, look for another. A dozen burials in a good day. But what about a sheep that was still dying? Finish it off with the crowbar? I never could, but drove away, hoping I could find it again. One evening I raced a kangaroo along the boundary fence back to the station.

Tea at six – mutton chops and eggs and potatoes again, with a fresh bottle of ketchup. Push the plate aside and empty the bottle on to slabs of bread and butter – lashings of it, never enough. And beer, for ever. Sometimes we went into town to tank up, and came back for ketchup on whatever was left.

All day mending fences, straining wire. All day in the shearing-shed, sweeping up. Or baling wool and weighing it. Or wading into the pens, grabbing sheep and holding them ready for the shearers – they were paid piecework, they wouldn't be kept waiting. When the shearing was over I was sent out to pick mushrooms – we had them for tea, sunk in ketchup.

Once we drove a mob of cattle to the railway, two days away. I was offered a horse like a proper jackaroo, but said I'd walk and they laughed. So did the girl on the liner, and said she'd smuggle me into the first class cinema. Bullocks got lost in the bush and a cow calved on the way, the first birth I'd ever seen. We made billy tea on a camp fire and baked a damper in the ashes: 'Real Australia for you, Pommie.'

The girl had never had a damper. I could tell her about England too. Piccadilly, Paris, Scotland, anywhere. She'd be sharing a flat in Earl's Court like them all. But I was getting off at Bombay. I'd wander off into India. Through Persia and Turkey perhaps, collecting material. Back in London next year or so. She'd be home in Australia by then.

We didn't have much time. After Bombay she could find another man, a first class one. She had a nice cabin up there – pity about the friend, though. We could go down and have a look at mine. About twenty decks lower. Down all these stairs. Right at the stern, under the sea. Down under – how far could you sink? But it was the best I could do. My Dad was never a wool broker.

I was treating her like a little tart, she said. Standing back to slap, I thought. But she grabbed me lower down. That was a lovely pair she had, and we fished one out. Six nights to Bombay, six bunks to ourselves. No porthole, only a stream of tropical air from the ventilator – what they used to call a punkah. She could turn the jet anywhere she fancied. Better not on the bare stomach, though, or she'd have a chill by morning. People at home had laughed and said she'd be in bed with an Englishman before she knew she'd got there. Truer than they thought – hardly out of Australian waters. Soon we'd be across the equator. First time in the northern hemisphere for her, first time under the sea for us both. The throbbing went on and on – the screws twisting, shaking, so you thought they must fall off. Pushing us through the water, me to Bombay, her to Earl's Court.

She was an old ship now, vibrating all day, all night. If the engines stopped it meant that a stoker had died of heat in the boiler-room and they were dropping him overboard. How did I know? I'd sailed in her once before, as a little boy.

The summer after Tangier we went to Norway, to an island in the Oslo fiord. At three shillings and sixpence a day all in, and two shillings and sixpence for children, it was cheaper than England. But we missed the boat train from King's Cross to Newcastle and caught the next. My mother stood in the corridor, watching the stations go by, counting the minutes to sailing time – we would never make it. The train drew into Newcastle, already late, and we were at the door, ready to leap. A river, a castle, a cathedral – it was only Durham. Another half-hour at least. We were lost, the boat would never wait.

But it did. Children and luggage were heaped into a taxi, we raced to the docks. Officers at the gangway, the captain on the bridge, sailors at the ropes – five minutes more and they would have sailed without us or missed the tide. We piled aboard and were away down river. Other passengers made sure we knew that they had arrived on time and been kept waiting.

On the island we lived in a wooden bungalow with an earth closet at the back; caught mackerel, climbed rocks, took trips to see the whaling fleet, ate bowls of sour milk and bilberries, cut slices of brown cheese with a special razor. Eight was a good age, moving from infancy to proper boyhood. But I sneezed when we rode in a hay wagon and was expected to make notes of meadow pipits or swallowtail butterflies, like my father.

Next year it was Wimereux, up the coast from Boulogne. We stayed at the Hôtel des Bains, with tram bells in the street and memories of Mademoiselle stirred by the manageress, blue-spectacled and strict. There was a lighthouse, a fish market, a yellow kite like an eagle on the beach, and pinewoods perfumed in the heat as though flushed with disinfectant. We drank sickly grenadine, while my mother read *Paris Soir* and made friends with a fragile but happy Englishwoman in a deckchair, younger than herself. She was Winifred Holtby, correcting proofs of her new novel – soon to be published posthumously; eking out the last few months of cancer. For a child of nine it was like shaking hands with an angel, somebody who had stepped halfway into death and might have seen my father there.

She died later that year and long afterwards I read her *Letter to a Goddaughter*: 'Ask yourself sometimes: If I knew I had only six more months to live, how would I choose to spend those six months? Then do it. Take no heed of conventions and gestures and personal influences which beckon you aside. Find your métier, equip yourself to follow it; then follow it.' It was advice that Don Quixote would approve of: 'Find something that you care about more than yourself, and serve it.' She shared another of his beliefs: 'Get rid of the passion for Possession – never mind how. In a life where one is liable to lose one's money, one's health and one's loves all too easily, the appetite for possession is fatal to happiness.' At Wimereux she was with a friend who had two children, one of them a little girl on top of a sandcastle – perhaps the goddaughter – later known as Shirley Williams.

After eating Wimereux mussels I had my first asthma attack. Something gripped my chest, tightening like a belt, fighting for mastery. I struggled, gasped, whooped for breath, fighting back. Yet my lungs were full, not of air but of another force inside, expanding outwards, which I couldn't expel. I was locked, unable to breathe in or out. Sweat formed on my face, though my hands and feet were ice cold. The noises – whistles, squeaks, a tuneless moan like an old harmonium – alarmed my mother, squeezing my hand to comfort us both. The hotel manageress, her eyes starting behind the blue lenses, called a doctor who gave me ephedrine pills to be sucked slowly under the tongue: tasting of something dead, beetles perhaps, inducing shivers and a dry, bitter mouth. I dreaded the next pill more than another attack, and came home from Wimereux an asthmatic.

THIRTEEN

May 17, Campo de Criptana. Even in daylight, this Sunday morning, the silence of the windmills is eerie and menacing. But I would like to test the danger – I want them to advance towards me over the hilltop, their arms wheeling. I'm on the point of believing that with some faith unknown to me, though almost within reach, they might creakingly begin to move. The truth is subjective: windmills are giants because, to Don Quixote once, that is what they were.

Below the hill, beyond the white town, La Mancha goes on forever with sheets of water, or perhaps plastic, catching the light. Far across the plain, on another hill near Alcázar de San Juan, four more white windmills gleam in a patch of sunshine before a rainstorm douses them. It falls on fifty little girls too, emerging from church in Campo de Criptana after their first communion. Miniatures of yesterday's bride, no bigger than dolls, they hoist their fairy-white skirts and run through the downpour, or get swept up and carried home.

After the rain, with the sun coaxing fumes from the road, I start walking ten kilometres to Alcázar between limitless vines. The tiny grapes are like broccoli flowers under the new leaves. Two National Guardsmen drive past on big Honda bikes and I half hope they will stop to question me. Dead dogs have been squashed flat on the highway by multiple lorry tyres, one as big as a wolf, now as thin as cardboard, rolled into the tarmac – it would happen to me if I was run over. On a piece of stony ground two more dogs, rather less dead, with a goatherd carrying a hefty stick, watch his goats nibbling among the thistles.

It was to some goatherds, munching cheese and acorns and helping themselves from a wineskin hanging in a tree to cool while a pot of goat meat stewed over a fire, that Don Quixote delivered a harangue on the golden age of history: a time, he told them, when anyone could stretch out and pick the fruits of nature, when the words 'mine' and 'yours' were unknown because all things belonged to everyone, when shepherdesses danced over the hills with no more clothes than modesty required, when truth wasn't tainted with malice or justice assailed by prejudice and self-interest, when all was peace and amity and concord. But in this hateful modern age, he said, it was his duty to defy the wickedness. Spurred by a mythical past to win an unattainable future he must search the corners of the world, penetrate the most intricate labyrinth, attempt the impossible.

The goatherds only gaped in amazement, saying nothing till he had stopped. Then one of them, sitting on a log to tune his fiddle, sang a song for this garrulous but harmless knight who talked such nonsense about love and hope, and would have sung another but Sancho Panza, after many visits to the wineskin, opted for sleep rather than more music.

Along the road the ten windmills on their hill at Campo de Criptana watch me from behind, and the four at Alcázar from ahead, as I walk through the chequered day between patches of sun and rain.

FOURTEEN

Too much was expected. I was supposed to like birds, as my father had done. He could walk into a garden, I was often told, and listen for a moment, then say there was a chaffinch in the copper beech, a willow warbler in the hedge, a pair of flycatchers somewhere else. He knew what rare nest he was likely to find and the place to look for it, and I was meant to be the same. When a woodpecker settled on the lawn I was sent to fetch his binoculars, but I wished it would fly away.

I was taught carpentry so that I could make a bird-table and learn which birds came to our garden. I was given an egg-blowing outfit and a notebook with bird names in English and Latin for me to mark the ones I had seen, male and female and juvenile, and add my observations. I hated it, not only because I was no good. When my mother said, 'But you're not very interested, are you?' I felt wounded and the tears began. I too expected more from myself than I knew was possible.

The same with butterflies and moths. My father's collection had gone to museums, but we still had a mahogany cabinet with the ones he had kept for himself. A smaller version was found for me, and a net, killing-bottle, setting-boards, pins. Hardly protesting, I started my own collection. A famous Cambridge zoologist took me to his laboratory and gave me a Parnassus and a Red Underwing. But instead of the treasure he intended, they were a mockery to boost my shame.

I wanted to be like my father, knowing how hopeless it was. The father I had never had was the man I would never be. My failure could be measured by his fame. His study, a shrine for my hopelessness, was kept as he left it, the fire laid for lighting. Once a year my mother moved into it from the drawing-room for a few weeks, to sit among his things: the explorer's trophies on the walls, the Papuan stone axes and

African elephant's tail, the photos of mountains and forests, the great bookcase and a jar of spills and feathers on the mantelpiece for lighting and cleaning his pipe. Sometimes my mother smoked a pipe too and struck Swan Vesta matches between the fireplace tiles, the way he had.

When she talked about him a smile came into her brown eyes, a catch into her voice. She said she didn't know how she could have survived without her children, though we were no substitute – the love for a man couldn't be turned to a child. She loved us, I think, without often showing it. I was proud when she told me that my hand in hers felt like my father's, with the same shape of palm, but I knew I could never win his place. Once I asked if she loved me more than she had loved her own mother, knowing I was breaking the rules. Though I got the answer I wanted, I felt guilty for having demanded it and doubted if it was true. If I could cheat, so could she.

I told myself that I loved my father – it was the least I could do, to show I was worthy of him. But what would he have been really like? It never struck me that I might be lucky he had died. He could have been far sterner than I imagined, a worse tyrant in life than he was in death. Not knowing him, I couldn't tell what I had escaped.

He dwelt everywhere. My bedroom carpet was his favourite blue, his macintosh hung in the downstairs lavatory, his hammer and nails and pliers lived in the tool box. Exploring down in the cellar I held up a bottle of his whisky to the light, showing off to my sisters, and dropped it on the brick floor. It was a crime against my father, a blasphemy, and we fled.

For years he hovered on the edge of life, standing in dark corners, watching at the end of my bed, sitting in an empty chair. I wasn't sure that the crocodile living in the mat at the foot of the stairs, ready to catch me if I didn't jump over him and fly up to bed, wasn't my father in disguise. The stuffed albino mole in a glass case on my mantelpiece – useless to cuddle, secretly hated – was a relic of my father's childhood and therefore sacred: though blind, it could still see into my thoughts after the light was turned out, and report them to my father.

My terror was that he hadn't died at all but was coming back to live with us one day, and unless I could escape or hide he would see what I was like. Even as a man, alone in a room and aware of his presence quite close, I would sometimes challenge him aloud to make himself visible and speak.

It was a long time before I realized that I needn't feel unworthy of him – that in fact he might even have approved of me. 'Don't try to be

54

like me,' I could hear him saying. 'Be yourself. Be all the things I never was. Do what I would have liked to do, but didn't dare.' It was an immense relief.

Don Quixote was a *hidalgo*, a gentleman. But the word is a contraction of *hijo de algo*, son of something – a somebody, not a nobody. Was I too a son of something? Of what?

Possibly, I thought, the truth was being kept from me, like the story of my father's death. I wasn't really myself, but someone else – an heir of some kind, born for a destiny to be revealed one day. If I could get through childhood I would succeed to the 'something' that was my right – a comforting belief, but also frightening: whatever was due to me, at the end I would fail to deserve it, which was why they never let me into the secret. I didn't learn for years that the future was only a vital aspiration of the present and nothing would come to me except by my own efforts.

Still, if not a *hijo de algo*, I was the son of my father before anything, responsible for the family continuity. Heredity was important. Some of the Wollaston ancestors hung on the walls like an abiding conscience. The aunts, when they came to stay, smiled at them as old friends and talked of them intimately. I tried not to look them in the eye in case they caught me in some lapse. The feeling, and the portraits, still live with me and I shall not be free till I have sold them. I know the scorn they will throw at me as they are taken away to be auctioned – I have been putting it off for years.

The Wollastons have been traced to Norman times and once were yeoman farmers. Later they had pretensions to gentility and occasional prosperity, but if they made money they lost it. At times they lived in big houses in London or the country, then moved somewhere humbler. In a debtors' prison they could count on being bailed out by their relations. A family chronicler calls them reserved, self-contained men, tending to be reclusive or puritanical, and says little about the women.

Among them is a draper, a haberdasher, an upholsterer, a keeper of Newgate prison, a philosopher, a gambler, an accountant for the Gas Company, even a lord mayor of London and two members of parliament. There are few soldiers and no artists, though Hogarth and Gainsborough painted them. I feel special affection for one who was a country squire in Leicestershire during the Civil War. In a mild way he probably favoured the royalists, though he was too old or too timid to take part in the fighting. And he was so frightened of giving offence to the winning side that when the two armies met in 1644 on Bosworth Field, where he could have watched the battle from his house, he left home and hid in London till the war passed to a safer distance.

Several went to America, Australia, South Africa, India, Burma and France, where the name lingers. Some were drawn to religion, but questioned its orthodoxy and found comfort in their huge families or in the stars. One of them, a country vicar in the eighteenth century and father of seventeen children, wrote a book called *The Secret History of a Private Man*. Others were scientists, including the most illustrious, my great great great uncle, famous for his discoveries and his modesty. I sit in his chair and tell the time by his clock.

My grandfather, who died before I was born, was a master at Clifton College, a brilliant but stern lecturer of the things that a cultivated boy should know. My grandmother was a Richmond – daughter, niece, cousin and granddaughter of painters, but great granddaughter of the groom at the Coach and Horses pub in Kew. I knew her as an old granny in a black straw hat sitting in the garden at West Road, annoyed that I wasn't called William, the proper name for a Wollaston.

The austere, intolerant mood in that schoolmaster's house may have helped drive my father on his travels. He hardly mentioned his family to my mother and it was years before she learnt that he had a brother and six sisters. After they were married he took her to meet his parents for the first time, but a short day's visit was all he could bear.

My father's only brother escaped to a fruit farm in British Columbia and sent us a box of apples every Christmas, large and mushy, not as good as our own. He came once or twice to stay, wearing spats and taking the number of a Haydn record which he liked; and died an old bachelor in the Vancouver Club. 'We *think* he had no children,' one of the sisters said, rather touched by the number of letters from Canadian women at his death.

None of the six sisters – proud and intimidating and clever – had any children either. Aunt Thea, the eldest, told me that marriage was a possibility she had declined. She was eighty at the time, tall with blue eyes, hair that had once been golden, a bosom that fell to her skirt, a sonorous contralto voice and a small beard; a lifelong schoolmistress who couldn't resist reminding me that I was the last male between our branch of the family and extinction. I wondered about her chances of ever marrying – her suitors would have been young schoolmasters, probably clergymen, easily frightened – and also about that ancient virginity. 'Let's have lunch in a pub – how I would love that!' she cried, game for something mannish and perhaps remembering the groom at the Coach and Horses. We had beer and sausages in the Volunteer at the top of Baker Street, feeling guilty that we hadn't earned it with a hearty walk. Aged nearly ninety she was found alone, long after her death, in her filthy little flat in Maida Vale.

Next was Aunt Katty, dressed in eternal grey, a lady's companion in Somerset. The best thing about her was her dead husband, a coal merchant who had been posted missing in the First World War. I went to stay with her, the first time I had been away from home alone, comforted by my toy leopard cub in bed with me. The unknown uncle's picture was everywhere, a dim khaki figure in Sam Browne belt and puttees. 'Missing' was a terrifying fate, and I was haunted by the thought of him still wandering among the empty trenches or tangled for the last twenty years in barbed wire. I dreaded, yet half hoped, that he would choose this week to come home. In the evenings Aunt Katty dictated my diary – 'your father never missed a day' – though she omitted the chicken she had run over in her little grey car and left dying in the road behind us, a flapping mess of feathers in the back window. She was going for a holiday abroad and begged to take my leopard with her. For months she didn't send it back, so I wrote to her and at last a leopard came, but it wasn't mine. She had lost it and bought another, thinking I wouldn't notice – perhaps the missing uncle was wise to stay away. Among the half-dozen people at her cremation the only other aunt chided me for wearing a black tie – a double snub, for me and for the woman in the coffin.

Aunt Charlotte, a schools inspector, married late in life and soon her husband was wishing she had put it off for ever. He was a gentle, melancholy painter whose joy was to play his viola – no match for her. She was considered amusing and was admired for the speed and sharpness of her wit, though few people felt its full sting. To me she found it best to be rude, rebuking me when I left Cambridge without a degree and got a job in Africa, rebuking me again when I gave up the job and went back to Cambridge to finish my degree. She mocked my writing, knowing the way to hurt me, though after the painter died she was happy to let me take her to concerts and weed her garden. In her will she left me some books, then thought better of it and crossed me off – luckily she had already given me the books. I kept quiet when I got married, afraid of her tongue, but she found out and told me that in two years I would abandon my wife whose name, Deirdre, she wouldn't utter but spoke of as 'that girl'.

Aunt Agnes, after failing as a freelance typist, took to coaching girls in French and ended up in a Sussex convent where the nuns kept her supplied with brandy.

Aunt Connie, the youngest, lived mostly abroad and was said to be some kind of teacher too, though nobody would explain the mystery about her. 'Spoilt and impossible' was all I was told, suggesting a scandal, but probably she just preferred to avoid her relations. I saw her only once, when I was an undergraduate at Cambridge and a don invited us both to lunch. I liked her and thought she liked me, though she didn't take much notice, concentrating on the don. She talked and laughed, then vanished again – perhaps she felt that one glimpse was enough for a lifetime. 'Connie went her own rather erratic way and died first of all of us,' Aunt Christy, the last survivor, said, illuminating nothing.

Aunt Christy was the best of my father's sisters, his own favourite. I put her, or parts of someone like her, into a novel, and now it's hard to separate the two. I loved them both, and one of them is still alive.

'I've got an aunt,' the narrator in the novel tells his girl friend untruthfully to give himself an alibi, and invents a story. He is a writer (but not me) and enjoys the fiction. 'She was a delicate girl of eighteen just like any other. Dying of consumption. The doctors said she had six months to live.' I think it's what happened to Aunt Christy, who was sent to Switzerland as her only hope and lived till she was ninety-three. 'When it was obvious she wasn't going to die she married a Swiss lawyer,' the fictitious writer says, half in love with his doubly fictitious aunt. His girl friend accuses him of making it all up but he denies it: 'Not a word, it's the truth.' Real or imaginary, fact or fiction – both are true.

Aunt Christy's husband was an advocate in Lausanne. They lived at the top of an old house overlooking the Lake of Geneva, with a wine press in the cellar and vineyards rising in the hills behind. But after fifty-two years of marriage her husband let her down by dying first, which was her only complaint. She went to live alone in a tiny chalet in the mountains, her 'home *de bois*' where she once gave me supper of a baked potato, Gruyère cheese and a bottle of local white wine, as the aunt in the novel does for her nephew. 'She's my favourite woman,' he tells his girl friend, who isn't pleased.

All her life Aunt Christy was beautiful. In old age the soft English girl, with six months to live if she was lucky, was still visible – the wrinkles a document, an engraving of those rescued years. And the great grey eyes, bleached and almost blind, held something of a young girl's pain but more of a long life's gratitude. At eighty-eight she was no nearer death than at eighteen, and could ignore the terror she had already faced all that time ago. Preserved in the old but youthful woman was the young but dying girl.

Towards the end she could hardly see the mountains but knew at any hour exactly what they looked like, just as she could sit in silence and hear Mozart or Schubert. When she was the last of the aunts alive she came to stay with me and Deirdre and our three children in our home in Islington.

'She'll die on you,' one of my sisters warned. But Deirdre, with more imagination, said it would be a wonderful thing, a compliment to us, and Aunt Christy agreed: 'I think you would take it the way I want you to.'

Her adult life had been spent as a foreigner abroad, but now she belonged among English people, in England where her childhood was – 'a very dithery, tottery, *hors-de-la-réalité* Anglo-Swiss aunt,' she called herself. If it was awkward and painful to fit into our haphazard modern ways she didn't show it, and once she had fallen in love with our baby son, whom she watched for hours as he slept – joined by the decades that separated them – everything was happiness. Hampstead Heath, Epping Forest, Kew Gardens, a concert, a street market, the National Gallery in a wheelchair, all the little non-adventures of domestic life in London – '*je nage dans le bonheur* of having been with you,' she wrote, back in her chalet and homesick for our house. 'You can't know what you are to me, but I believe Deirdre guesses.'

She came again when she was ninety, and again at ninety-one. As if liberated by the death of everyone of her age she was the liveliest, most alert person in the house. 'She has more friends and more letters every day than I do,' the fictional writer says. 'She cuts across the generations.' When his girl friend asks why he doesn't write a novel about her he replies, 'I've never done it as blatantly as that. I love her, I'd rather not tamper with her and I should have to disguise her so much, there'd be nothing left.'

Perhaps she saw in me something of my father, and I felt I had passed a test at last – I was fit to be his son. I wanted her to talk about him, but either she couldn't trust herself or she thought that stories were unnecessary and I must already know anything she could tell me. She

59

read my first novel, but didn't like the characters and was sorry for me, for knowing such people. When she met my friends she was reassured.

'More than half my life is seeing everything in the light of all that has been good and lovely and rose-coloured bespectacled,' she said. Though the anguish growling under our semblance of family contentment – my fragile but just glimmering belief in myself as a writer, Deirdre's tenderness and exhaustion from the strain of small children, my exasperation with seemingly hollow domestic rituals, Deirdre's perplexity when my self-discontent broke out in irritability towards her or obsessive fussiness about the house, my reticence and fear of quarrels, Deirdre's need to show anger if she felt it and her relief and cheerfulness after an explosion which would leave me confused and miserable for days, the false expectations, the times in any relationship between a man and woman that reach such a dead end, as Solzhenitsyn said, when everything that could be said has been said and all arguments have been exhausted and there is nothing to do but sit down and howl, all this shadowing two people who could appear such a happy loving couple – though the anguish of modern marriage can't have escaped Aunt Christy she chose to remember the delights. 'What wonderful days I had with you – I rather live in them, and would like them to be in my mind when I slip off.'

For too long she hadn't seen the sea. She wanted to stand at the edge of England as she had as a child and watch the infinite horizon. So we took her to Hastings and left her alone on a bench on the seafront. Though a tiresome old pensioner, twenty years younger, came and spoilt Aunt Christy's solitude with chatter, and though the grey English Channel wasn't the blue Atlantic of her memory, the endless breakers rolled in her ears again and in her dim eyes the rim of the world stretched for ever.

One year she didn't come. She had become a Catholic on condition that she could still use the English prayer book. Now she was lying in a little room, being looked after by nuns, with a few of her own things and a small piece of mountain visible through the window.

The last time I saw her she was in a pretty dress again, as if for supper in our Islington kitchen, a thin black rosary twisted in her waxen fingers, her head on a new pillow. A nun patted her forehead as one would a sleeping child, but I couldn't bring myself to kiss her though I wanted to. I was nearly fifty and had never seen the corpse of someone I loved. We took her up to a little cemetery in her proud high mountains – where on a visit to her once, leaving her and our children in the village for a long walk alone above the forest, Deirdre and I had made love among summer herbs and whistling marmots; where now, on a December day in 1974, the snow fell softly into her Alpine grave before they filled it in.

When I went home and told my children that I had seen Aunt Christy the youngest looked at me in horror. It was impossible – she was dead, she didn't exist. Then his face changed to admiration: I had come back from heaven.

FIFTEEN

May 18, Alcázar de San Juan. I'm old enough to stop a pretty girl in the street, less than half my age. She is tall with loose black hair to her shoulders and her long legs have a better sprung, less solid tread than a Spanish woman's. We may be the only foreigners in the town and clearly she is alone like me, which is all we have in common. I cross the street and walk beside her, wishing I had been so bold many years ago. 'You can't be Spanish,' I tell her in English, forgiving myself the banality.

'Nor are you,' she says in return.

'Japanese?' I suggest, aware that other people are watching us.

'Of course. And you are Engrish?' She has trouble with L and R which are uncertain, often interchangeable.

'Of course.' We walk down the street and I steer her towards the plaza where I know there are statues of Don Quixote and Sancho Panza.

'You are travelling?' she asks. The word is a muddle of consonants, something like 'tlaverring'. But there is no doubt about the statues which are awful – Don Quixote an elongated stick-man, Sancho a spherical dolt, pantomime comics on a horse and donkey that belong in Disneyland. 'Oh, I rike!' the Japanese girl cries, and claps her hands.

She is hungry, or hungly, and rooking for a lestaurant. I lead her to a bar and order her a hamburger and orange juice, a beer for myself. She is twenty-five and tells me her birthday, and writes her name in my notebook: a secletaly, from a town near Fujiyama. I draw a picture of the famous mountain beside her name, not very skilful but not very difficult, and she laughs delightfully. I have never talked to a Japanese before and nobody has ever applauded my drawing.

She left Yokohama a month ago, travelled by ship to Russia, then by train across Siberia to Moscow, Vienna, Paris, Madrid. Budapest is her favourite so far, because of the Brue Danube.

'Why come to Alcázar?' I ask.

'For the windmiaws – there are no windmiaws in Japan.' Today she is going by bus to Campo de Criptana to see them.

So we have something else in common, and I draw windmills on the slopes of my Fujiyama. She laughs and claps her hands, and eats her hamburger to the last crumb.

From here she will go to Granada, Seville, Lisbon, London, Chester where she will attend a language school for a month, then Edinburgh, Dublin, Venice, Florence, Athens – they become strange new places, the way she pronounces them – and back to Japan after eight months, to tell her mother all about it: 'I want to talk to my mother so much, but it is too expensive – inte'lational caw.' She telephoned from Paris and will again from Chester.

We have another orange juice and beer, and talk about films. She loved *Out of Africa* and anything by Tarkovsky. I tell her that *Crocodile Dundee* is on in Alcázar, and she claps: 'Oh, I rike to see!'

'Let's go then,' I say. It would be fun – *Clocodi'e Dundee* in Spanish with a Japanese girl.

But she must catch her bus to the windmills, and we go out into the street. 'Can I take your picture?' she asks, opening her camera.

I would prefer not, with people staring at us: 'Save it for the windmills.' We shake hands twice and she bows deeply several times, almost to my knees with a little hiss, before slipping away on those well-sprung legs.

I go back to the bar for one more beer, and wonder at the improbability: two strangers brought here from Suffolk and Japan by Don Quixote. I ask myself if it really happened – not even my picture of windmills on Fujiyama is enough to prove it. Anything in my notebook, the moment I put it there, is already distanced from me, existing independently.

At another table a young man in uniform, a gun at his belt, has an arm round a girl in denims – another uniform. One of her hands, crimson-nailed and dextrous, is twined with his, while the other runs through her own hair. Suddenly he gets up to push a coin into the fruit machine, pull a lever, watch the lights – this illusion of glory, like Don Quixote's; then shrugs and returns to the comfort of the crimson-tipped fingers.

We hope, and put out fingertips for contact with someone else, who does the same. But it's only fingertips – the rest is apart, ourselves.

SIXTEEN

For three years, more often than not, I was ill with asthma. Hay fever and eczema were something extra. At the sight of a horse I was led away before an attack began. Animals, feathers and dust, games under the beds or in the cupboards, cushions and rugs and lofts would set me off. Perhaps there were psychogenic causes too, linked to unconscious conflicts in me. Sometimes I lay curled on the sofa like a dog – 'liverish' was the word – before starting to wheeze and being put to bed. A kettle with a long fishtail spout bubbled on a gas ring, wafting friar's balsam into the room, or I sat under a towel inhaling vapour from a china urn. Medicines stood on the mantelpiece but only ephedrine, a drug know to the Chinese for four thousand years and also to the Romans, brought relief.

I was kept in bed for weeks, living on beef tea and boiled fish, playing halma and ludo; reading the *Just So Stories* or Harrods' annual catalogue, or the *Illustrated London News* with pictures of Mussolini's soldiers goose-stepping into Abyssinia and Hitler's pocket battleships, or old Christmas magazines, *Holly Leaves* with reproductions of 'The Blue Boy' and 'The Age of Innocence' and 'When did you last see your father?' (When did I last see mine?) In time I was allowed up to sit by the gas fire or play trains, and at last taken to London by my mother to see another specialist, once even a homœopath.

The London trips were an excuse for a treat taken on my mother's impulse, for her pleasure too. 'Went in a hansom cab,' I put in my diary. It was the last hansom in London and we drove round Hyde Park, my mother shouting about old times to the driver through the little hatch above us, till the horse made me wheeze. 'Saw some cheetahs racing,' I wrote. Hearing that they had been brought to England by an eccentric Kenya settler to compete with greyhounds, my mother took me to watch them being trained to chase an electric hare. Later we heard that they were sent back to Africa in disgrace: on the racetrack they had turned from the hare and pounced on the dogs.

'Had an ice at Gunter's' was more fun than 'went to the Natural History Museum', which wasn't the treat it was meant to be. I was bored by those stuffed mammals, except the whales swimming above me; and the birds and butterflies, jogging my guilt, made me impatient for *Tiger Tim's Weekly* which my mother would buy for the train home.

Long afterwards, working in the museum library, I was led into the fossil room by an archivist. She watched me, totally a woman of the moment, careful not to release her own love for those trapped old animals: the tracery of fin and claw, the fragment of a filigree bone, the vivid shaking of a wing a million years ago or just this instant. A track of enormous footprints paced across the floor where a prehistoric creature had walked through the museum that morning – soon he would be back; and suddenly the archivist laughed at my pleasure in that quiet hall. She had once been a dancer, and moved about the library as if about to break into flight. Locked alone together in the Rare Books Room we seemed at moments to be on the brink of some ecstatic *pas de deux*, but were stopped by shyness and perhaps the suspicion of a limitless affinity that frightened us. 'I love your gentleness,' she said, surprising me with something I didn't know about myself, 'but wish you were more gentle with yourself.'

I felt a sort of privilege in asthma. This was *my* disease, a unique possession that nobody could take away. Later I was to become ashamed to the point of denying it, but as a child it was a talent of my own, something even my father hadn't had: my private enemy to be conquered, almost my friend to console me. It was useful too – I could be let off games at school.

One bad winter my mother took me to Hastings for a few days, away from the Cambridge damp and cold and from the family. At the station a taxi-driver suggested the Albany Hotel on the seafront – out-of-season and half-inhabited by old residents shuffling through the public rooms, sheltering like us from the climate. A page boy – silver buttons from throat to navel and cheeky tight trousers that I eyed with mystifying envy, close to lust – pulled the rope in the lift and swung us up to our bedroom. The English Channel lay beyond our balcony, a chambermaid brought tea and macaroons. In the evening, before taking her Times Book Club book to the lounge, my mother slipped me into the billiard room where, among talk of breaks and pots and cannons, I heard men use words I didn't know, spoken quietly between shots with a glance at the boy watching from the half-dark. I was sure my mother didn't know them either.

We were friends for a while, though we never said so. We listened to the hotel radio and my mother said she must buy one when we got home; and walked along the winter beach to the fishermen's tall black sheds; and went to Bodiam castle, Pevensey castle, Battle abbey, mostly in silence but enjoying each other. She was soothing and calm, and I was happy till the old inadequacy returned.

'What will you be when you grow up?'

An explorer like my father. Or a sailor – an admiral, no less. Or governor of a colony, Sir Nicholas in a plumed hat ruling my own West Indian island. Or briefly, for no pious reason, only for the robes and glitter, I wanted to be a bishop. But none of them were believable. I would never even drive a tram, a secret dream. The disappointment was my mother's too, I knew, all the worse for being unspoken. I wouldn't be anything, I would never grow up – it was unthinkable to be a man.

On the pier we pushed pennies into slot machines. One of them was a prison scene, a little group standing on an execution platform. My penny fell, the wheels whirred, the priest flapped his Bible up and down, the governor raised his hand, the hangman pulled a lever, the murderer dropped into the pit. It would have happened to Potts.

At last my mother heard of a doctor from a clinic at Mont Dore in the Auvergne, *providence des asthmatiques*, who was in London. At first he refused to see us but relented, though he scarcely looked at me, only scribbled out a diet and wouldn't accept a fee. No cream or eggs, no oranges or sugar, no fat, nothing rich, absolutely no wine or spirits – it wasn't drastic. But my asthma improved and after I was sent away to a boarding-school near the sea, aged eleven, it hardly bothered me till I was twenty-five. The ephedrine pills that I carried but seldom used were a furtive link with childhood, to keep quiet about.

The novelist Patrick White has called asthma 'that curse of half my life'. And the novelist John Updike, for whom an asthma attack feels like two walls being drawn closer and closer till they are pressed together, has said the same about his first marriage, comparing it to 'a household whose walls seemed to be shrinking around me, squeezing my chest'. When he left home and was divorced his asthma got better.

For Proust, the most articulate victim, asthma was nearly an obsession. Unconsciously he needed the disease – 'a dread master, a faithful servant,' his biographer called it – preferring the way of life it demanded and using it as a sanctuary in which he could write his fiction. He went to Mont Dore for treatment and in his masterpiece *A la Recherche du Temps Perdu* he describes a doctor like the one in my childhood, briskly ordering a diet for an asthmatic boy with the same success it had on me. Later he writes of illness enhancing the pleasures of memory, his famous theme. At the end of the huge work – *de si longue haleine*, so long a breath, a true asthmatic's cry – the narrator records his ambivalence to a disease which, by compelling him to retire from the world, enables him to write yet destroys his strength to do so.

My mother's family, called Meinertzhagen, was quite unlike the Wollastons. Her grandfather came to London from Bremen in the eighteen-twenties, got a job with a German banker who had a Spanish wife, married the banker's daughter and became a partner. My mother's father, who liked fishing and shooting more than banking, was three quarters German and one quarter Spanish. She was ninth of his ten children.

My mother's mother was as English as possible, one of nine sisters, granddaughters of 'Radical Dick' Potter, a Yorkshire draper's son who went to Manchester and became a liberal MP and founder of the *Guardian*. Another of the sisters was my great-aunt Bo – Beatrice Webb, wife of Sidney. But the family fame, such as it was, dwindled with its fortune, leaving a huge number of cousins to share some silver spoons and a legacy of radical enterprise that was soon squandered. When the Webbs' ashes were buried in Westminster Abbey we looked a motley lot standing with our cousin Stafford Cripps, who was chancellor of the exchequer, and the prime minister, Attlee, and Bernard Shaw.

A generation later one of the cousins gave a party for several hundred descendants of those nine sisters, most of us strangers to each other. We wore coloured badges to show which sister was our grandmother and searched among the faces for common ground, or even a friend. There were a few rich bankers and brokers, some civil servants and academics, doctors and architects, farmers, a casino manager, a psycho-analyst, a baronet, a handful of pretty women and many plain ones. As individuals we might signify something, even achieve something. As a family, a committee of relations, we didn't matter.

But blood connections can be stirred in curious ways. Harmlessly eating my chicken salad I was stalked by a woman who hailed me from several yards away: 'I've been admiring your *nose!*' I was speechless and only afterwards thought what I should have replied – her own nose was negligible. She came close, searching the branches of the family tree for the genetic strain: 'I wonder where you got it?'

Missing from the party, having died on a train in Italy, was my favourite cousin Andreas, an asthmatic and thus as ally, always aloof though his family feeling was stronger than mine. He kept track of the remotest members and wrote to me after reading my first novel, 'How cruelly well you describe us, the ineffectual grandsons who think they are special and almost get away with it.' It wasn't at all what I had meant and was perhaps a review of the book Andreas himself would have liked to write.

Recently at family occasions – a funeral, a golden wedding, a far-fetched gathering for some ancient self-preserving purpose – I have eyed my stockbroking life-broken cousins, bankrupt millionaires, and rejoiced to feel no strong affinity; no envy either.

Though my grandfather died sixteen years before I was born I have familiar, vivid glimpses of him. He had a bathtub under his bed, filled with hot water in the morning by his valet who then shaved him. He toasted his breakfast sausages on a fork at the dining-room fire. At the bank, if a telegram came to say there was a hatch of mayfly and the trout were rising, he caught the next train home. Family cares were tiresome and he behaved to his children rather as a benevolent uncle, turning up sometimes to give them a treat. In the carriage on the way to christen one of the babies he asked what name was to be given. 'Cunegunde,' my grandmother told him – she had been reading Voltaire. 'Nonsense,' he said, 'we'll call her Beatrice', which became Bobo.

My grandmother read the *Guardian*, faithful to her forebears, and wrote letters to *Country Life* about the chaffinch that tapped on her window every morning, impatient for its breakfast. She wasn't interested in her husband's city life or his sporting friends. 'I never feel quite sure that you are not better pleased to be free to go your own way without me,' she wrote to him, and complained that often she cried her eyes out alone at home. No doubt there were other women to console him. Beatrice Webb (who described marriage as a form of suicide, but called her own childless one *Our Partnership*) wrote of her sister, 'It was her misfortune to marry a man of narrow sympathies, of many conventions and more prejudices, and with no sense of humour.'

My mother was born at Mottisfont, an old abbey by a Hampshire river where a crazy but magic feudal life survived into this century. Her childhood in that haunted paradise, enhanced by stories and photos, became a dream for us too, which we could share with her and her brothers and sisters but never find for ourselves. They exchanged and polished their memories, creating a mythology of happiness, till I felt a longing for a life I had never known and only later, after learning of my grandparents' miserable marriage, began to suspect. When I took my own children to Mottisfont, now a National Trust property with ices and souvenirs and guided tours, we found it closed. For a moment I was insulted, turned away from my mother's birthplace, then relieved that another generation was spared my secondhand nostalgia.

Her eldest brother, Uncle Dan, kept an aviary of rare eagles and owls at Mottisfont. Charming, gifted, a legend among the others, he died of appendicitis as a young man and was quickly canonized. Aunt Bardie, a tiny aristocratic bird, was a dedicated Fabian socialist, champion of the campaign for milk in schools, but happy to receive profits from one of her nephews, a stockbroker, who looked after her investments. Aunt Margy, a violinist and rather sensual kind of saint, had six children of her own and then, when my mother died, took on my two sisters and me.

Uncle Dick was a soldier, brilliant intelligence officer, traveller, ornithologist, collector of birds and expert on their parasites, self-styled spy and fervent Zionist; a proud, restless, unorthodox, opinionated, intolerant man whose early life in Africa was marked by the slaughter of wild animals and his fellow men. Revelations by a biographer that he was a liar and a thief were no surprise to his relations.

In the First World War he rode out in front of the Turkish lines till the enemy gave chase, then galloped away, dropping a dispatch bag with his lunch, maps, English money, a dummy love letter written by my mother and some false but convincing plans for the British tactics – thus helping to win the battle of Gaza. Another trick was to fly over the enemy and drop cigarettes laced with opium. In the thirties, never short of confidence (his telegraphic address was simply 'Montezuma London'), he had an interview with Hitler who saluted him: 'Heil Hitler!' Uncle Dick saluted back: 'Heil Meinertzhagen!' Aged seventy, finding himself in Haifa during the British departure from Palestine, he borrowed a uniform and rifle and had what he called a glorious day shooting Arabs, which he celebrated with champagne.

Finding that his first wife, on their wedding night, wasn't a virgin he had no more to do with her. He was posted to India and chose to go to the frontier where wives couldn't follow – she was left to enjoy society back in the cantonment. As a gentleman he let her divorce him, and when asked where the writ could be served on him replied, 'It's a monkey business – I'll be in the monkey house at the zoo.' His second wife, a Scottish heiress, was shot through the head when they were alone together on a moor, practising pistol shooting – enough to feed another legend.

His elder son, my cousin Dan, was killed in the Second World War, darkening Uncle Dick's last years. But he was always kind to me though too honest to hide his impatience with any of us, which meant most of us, who didn't bring honour to the family. I met him in Kenya after I had crossed the Sahara in a lorry and he questioned me about the birds I had seen – for him no corner of the desert was empty. I had a business job, not the kind of thing he liked any more than I did, but it was a fine country for a young man, he said, fixing me in the eye and wishing me luck.

I saw him off at Nairobi station on the Mombasa train, on his way to visit a friend in Arabia, St John Philby, father of the traitor Kim, and met him next on a London bus. 'Where are you off to?' he asked, as though it should be the Upper Nile or Lhasa. He himself, as he might once have travelled through Baluchistan in search of a rare partridge, was off to buy a lettuce in the Army and Navy Stores, the best place for them.

When my first travel book was published he told another nephew, who passed it on, 'It's about absolutely nothing.' But he put me on his list for dinner parties, which were mostly champagne in huge goblets, oxtail stew and chestnut pudding. Every year he hired a London bus for the Derby, filled the bottom deck with lunch and more champagne, the top deck with his friends, and drove off to Epsom. But the races didn't interest him – he looked the other way.

Towards the end, like an old lion, he began to lose his battles. A quarrel about a neighbour's dog ended in Uncle Dick being knocked down and fighting an unsuccessful lawsuit. He bought a harpsichord, hoping it might bring him peace, but it was often out of tune and his fingers wouldn't work. He sat in his dressing-gown, a white-bearded predator among a hundred bound volumes of his diary, cases full of bird skins, captured German flags, a big pair of the original orange glass Belisha beacons and memories of a fantastic life, true or fabricated, till within a few months of his ninetieth birthday.

Aunt Lawrencina, who introduced my father to my mother, was the prettiest and most untamed. Strangers would be gladdened to see her take off her shoes and stockings, hitch up her skirt and dance across the lawn.

Aunt Bobo, playwright and novelist and mystic, was known to recite her poems in Trafalgar Square. Once when I was in naval officer's uniform I saw her in a subway at Euston station, a thin silver-haired woman in glasses weaving towards me and calling, 'Which is the platform for Nottingham?' She was more pleased at her mistake than at meeting me (what was the use of a nephew at Euston if not to direct her?) and hurried away to catch a train to visit a relation in a mental hospital. Years later she said, 'I'm told your wife is beautiful,' and I tried to see beyond the fragile figure in a chair, out of her dingy room to the flat where Deirdre was expecting our first baby. 'That's why I married her,' I said too hastily, and Aunt Bobo said, 'I hope that isn't true.'

Uncle Fritz, another asthmatic, studied medicine for a time, then disappeared for years in South Africa. Later he had an antique shop near Oxford Circus and wrote a scholarly book on Japanese netsukes. Some of the finest in his collection were said to be his own work. Once at West Road he took out of his pocket a marvellous little tortoise that he had carved from a piece of amber. His letters were full of delicately coloured, often lewd, illustrations and one of my cousins has an exquisite study of an erect penis – presumably Uncle Fritz's own. After his marriage to an actress broke down he went to live at Bow, in the East End, with a waitress whom he adored. He was near to being a communist without joining the party and was believed to have been a hero in the blitz, which he never denied. Unlike Uncle Dick he wrote to say he had enjoyed my first book, and I could hear the chuckle of a man who had arranged his life better than most people. But when the waitress died of cancer he found he couldn't live without her. A fortnight later a cousin received an ominous letter from Bow and rang the police urgently to investigate. They were too late – Uncle Fritz had killed himself.

Uncle Louis, the gentlest of the brothers, followed my grandfather into the bank and watched it decline. Perhaps he was too fond of his garden, his collection of French stamps, his beautiful wife, to care about the City; or perhaps he wasn't fond enough of any of them. Early in the Second World War, after being mugged in the London black-out, he died of shock and sadness.

Aunt Betty, youngest of the ten, was an actress but too impetuous to be successful. As one of Macbeth's witches at the Old Vic she got bored with the 'bubble, bubble, toil and trouble' routine and switched to 'thirty days hath September, April, June and November', which had the same rhythm, but it didn't please the director. 'D'you think I should have a baby,' she asked Aunt Margy, 'to look after me when I'm old?' Briefly she had a husband but no baby, and never grew old. She smoked cigars, had an operation to alter her nose, a fine hook, which made it grotesque, and died of drink.

As a big family they had a mutual sufficiency, an unworldiness that sometimes put them out of touch with real things. Any dottiness, a favourite word, they believed was due to a gypsy strain somewhere in the blood. Such myths were passed on to us – my mother's childhood permeated my own. I could see her nursery and schoolroom, the bedroom haunted by a monk from the demolished abbey, the entertainments put on by my grandmother in the village hall. I knew all about Uncle Dick's horses, Aunt Betty's donkeys, Uncle Fritz's tempers and the time Uncle Dan, after hearing Sousa's band, played the music again on the Mottisfont piano, stamping the floor and hitting notes with his fists and elbows to get the right noise.

Though my grandparents were incompatible and unhappy in marriage, they were carried by the momentum of the world they made at Mottisfont. Its aura outlived their ten children and touched their twenty-four grandchildren, including me.

SEVENTEEN

May 18, Alcázar de San Juan. I take a train to Albacete – *Al Basit* in Arabic, meaning the plain, and there is hardly a bend in the line for two hours. The girl in the opposite seat crosses herself before we start, and settles down to read in a magazine about the marriage difficulties of the Prince and Princess of Wales.

La Mancha is a desperate land, flattened by monotony and stagnation. Time passes slowly, the human spirit sleeps. It's a place fit for eccentrics – individualists, mystics, madmen – though it has been transformed since Don Quixote's time. I try to imagine ploughing it with oxen, and to see pack mules on the roads, treading for ever across the flatness, shrivelled by wind, blinded by the dust they kick up. But machinery and irrigation – water above all – have turned dust into good earth.

Somewhere over there, stopping at an inn, Don Quixote and Sancho Panza were entertained with a puppet show, a story of a lady rescued by her lover from the Moors. But the drama was too much for Don Quixote, champion of the wronged, and when the Moors gave chase he leapt on the stage with his sword and hacked them to pieces. Besides, he was no respecter of make-believe: the falsity of puppets was intolerable. Like any cardboard figures manipulated by some showman – or by hypocrisy, pomposity, the hollow gestures of convention – they deserved to be broken up.

La Mancha imparts an indefinable anxiety, a sense of travelling without firm contact with the earth. I feel a vague longing to be elsewhere. Sometimes mountains appear on the horizon like distant islands, solid land at the edge of this unwaving sea. They make me restless. If they aren't imaginary, or put there like brush-strokes to define the plain, they must be a reminder of real country somewhere. One day I shall get back there.

EIGHTEEN

'It's a trap to spend time writing about your childhood,' Norman Mailer wrote. 'Self-pity comes into the voice.' But I feel no self-pity, only surprise that it happened as I remember. Perhaps it didn't.

Long trousers flapped round my ankles and tears blurred my eyes to mark my banishment from home. In 1937, after George VI's coronation, my mother put me on the school train at Waterloo and watched me slip away. Last night I had cried in her bed, wondering why this should be done by someone who was supposed to love me. If she felt miserable too, packing me off to Dorset, it was no comfort.

In charge of the train was Miss Cartwright, young but ample, all yellow hair and face powder and trembling bust under her turquoise cardigan. She was cloying, I was inconsolable. Most boys, racing up and down the corridor, looked happy that the holidays were over. 'I've got a wizard cricket bat, I'll get my second eleven colours this term, it'll be hard cheese if I don't.' They must have awful homes or no mother or sisters worse than mine.

'Say your prayers!' the captain of my dormitory, Jonathan, shouted that night. Clever, musical, friendly, he wrote letters to me later from his public school; then was killed in the war and had a book of poems published after his death.

My mother didn't believe in prayers, she hadn't shown me what to do. I copied the other boys and knelt by my bed, watching through my fingers. I would pray to be at home if it wasn't too tender to think of – I had to force it from my mind. The dormitory windows had no curtains, the bed was hard and narrow with a thin red blanket and my father's old rug, that he had had at school – he had pursued me here.

Next morning a bell rang, the boys jumped out of bed, stripped and ran naked down the passage. I followed in alarm, hoping it was only for another kind of prayer. But it was worse: three baths of cold water with showers pouring in and fifty boys lining up for a dip, while a rabbitty little woman saw that nobody shirked. The captains had big genitals in a nest of pubic hair, something I hadn't seen before. My own tiny spout shrank to nothing in the cold water – everyone else's was bigger. We grabbed a towel and ran back to our dormitories, slipping on the linoleum.

At breakfast I got two little brown things on a plate, one like a thin bit of bark, the other a piece of broken tile – bacon and fried bread. When I cut them they scattered across the table. Other boys knew the trick: swallow them whole. They came back to me years later in Goa where I was shown St Francis Xavier's toe, a fragment of shrivelled protein bitten off his pickled corpse by a pilgrim who had been made to spit it out. At the end of each table a master sat eating a proper breakfast, eggs and sausages with toast and butter and marmalade instead of our half-slice of bread and margarine. On the dining-room wall hung the shields of public schools where boys had won scholarships and, like a shrine with last year's poppies, photos of five pale heroes killed in the First World War, including one with the Victoria Cross.

The school was owned by the Crow, now elderly and crusty. His rule had slipped into benign laxity, broken by sudden hot-headed attacks with the cane. The place was in decline, economies were obvious. Fees at fifty pounds a term couldn't be raised, but parents were asked to donate prizes and sports cups, and any boy with a birthday was expected to get a cake sent from home, big enough to feed us all. 'Three cheers for Nick Wollaston!' the captain of the school shouted at tea and for five minutes I was popular though my cake, like my penis, was smaller than most. A pair of twin brothers from Somerset who were sent regular quantities of clotted cream, saving the school jam, were favourites of the Crow. Long afterwards I met one of them on a mountain path in Wales: he had become a wine merchant and his twin was master of the Exmoor staghounds.

After breakfast, before lessons, we played a game of escape and capture on the gravel outside, with rules invented over generations, a torment for new boys who couldn't run fast. But nobody cheated: punishment by other boys was the worst kind. Then the Crow put us through exercises – press ups, touch your toes, arms bend, running on the spot; and drilled us like a platoon – quick march, right wheel, about turn, form fours, though the army had changed to threes long ago. My asthma was left behind, at home.

In class the Crow lined us up round his desk for a daily Latin grammar test. He liked to pull the short hairs above one's ear with a circular motion, to twist the right answer out. The pain was matched by his pleasure, repeating the question through his teeth. My mother spoke of the twinkle in his eye, but she never saw the way it flashed when he had one's hair in his fingers.

Humiliation went with economy. It was dished up in food that only hungry boys would eat: scrambled eggs with lumps of un-reconstituted powder, tubs of swilling mince, dark slabs of bubble-and-squeak believed to be seaweed, interchangeable gravy and custard that oozed like cooling lava over the plate, mummified suet puddings, white or pink or brown blancmange with a skin of rubber, mugs of watery grey milk. At night on our way to bed, with a film of cocoa grit in our teeth, we saw the Crow and his wife with the masters and matron in evening dress, sitting down to dine by candlelight.

The ticking of an alarm clock still takes me to a dormitory. I had it muffled under my pillow, set for three in the morning. Lisping to make less noise, we felt our way down to the kitchen with a torch masked in a sock and stood barefoot on the cold floor, stuffing ourselves with sultanas, shivering with fear. At the end of the Christmas term we broke out after dark and went carol-singing to collect money for sweets. Though we put on Dorset accents a women at the first house challenged us: we weren't real village boys, we ought to be ashamed, she would report us. We sprinted back to school to get alibis.

Homesickness took the place of asthma. My mother's visit at half-term made it worse – an agony of precious, vanishing hours. Her letters, in bundles in a locker over my bed, were unbearable. I kept them for twenty years and read them, then threw them away, before I got married; knowing, perhaps, that I was shutting Deirdre out of my childhood. Too poignant and distressing for my mood, I had to hold them at a distance, refusing to be affected.

Other boys didn't suffer or hid it better. Anyway their parents, fixed in studio portraits on their lockers – dead-eyed men with jowls and moustaches, hard women with perms and pearls – were different. When they came for sports day they still looked artificial, only less imposing than in their photos. My mother alone was real, but somehow failed to show it. How could anyone else see that she was the best – a mother and father in one? She was older than most, with greying hair. She hated lipstick, her clothes weren't smart. Embarrassed, dreading explanations, I would steer her away and have her to myself.

The Crow's wife, fragile with a smile of chronic disappointment, attempted a chilling motherliness of her own. Sunday was her day. Before morning church she censored our letters home, which had to be left unsealed. Later she opened the library and checked our reading. There wasn't much choice: shelves of Baroness Orczy, John Buchan, Jeffrey Farnol, Edgar Wallace, Dornford Yates, in the same flat-backed red covers, with cricketers' memoirs and stories of the First World War. On Sunday evening in her drawing-room she read aloud *Beau Geste* or *The Man in the Iron Mask* or *With Kitchener to Khartoum*.

I don't like schools, I still feel uneasy when I pass one and didn't enjoy going into my own children's. But the Crow's was probably less unpleasant than most of its kind. Rose-beds and lawns led to the playing fields, creepers clung to the old stone buildings, flowers ramped over the walls. From the dormitory windows we saw destroyers heliographing to each other in Swanage Bay and at night the Needles lighthouse flashed at us from the Isle of Wight, twenty miles away. The Dorset hills rolled into the distance, the Purbeck cliffs fell into the sea.

On summer mornings, packing up lessons, we ran over the hills to Dancing Ledge, a miraculous shelf of rock between the cliffs and the sea. A rough pool had been blasted out of the rock, washed by the tide, but boys who could swim jumped naked off the edge into the sea, sixty feet deep. After this the thought of lunch – pease pudding or toad-in-the-hole – and a wasted afternoon on the cricket field, with more lessons before tea, became less bleak.

On Saturdays, if there was no cricket match, we went to other coves along the coast, with a picnic hamper on the back of the Crow's car and a tin of lemonade powder to be diluted under his wife's eye. We walked through stone-walled fields of hay and clover; and found a quarry still working – a shaft slanting under ground and trucks being pulled up by winch and a man chiselling London kerbstones; and sat at the wheel of a derelict lorry, a rusty carcass with solid rubber tyres and a sump of green oil in the back axle; and swapped dirty stories and swear words, the way we swapped stamps or cigarette cards. Down on the shore we fished for bass and sailed our boats and knocked limpets off the rocks. The first time I touched a woman's moist and gentle secret, as her lover, I remembered the feel of sea anemones in those Dorset pools.

Hitler was arming, Chamberlain was appeasing, and one summer day we were taken to the cliffs above Weymouth Bay to watch the fleet return from exercises: squadrons of battleships and cruisers steaming over the horizon with their destroyer escort, then anchoring with a flurry of signals in front of us – a vast spectacle of power across the sea. For about a week the navy would be my life. I longed, with an erotic longing, to command one of those destroyers.

Sometimes in the winter instead of football, in boiler suits with knives and axes, we ran down through the woods to a narrow valley where we built houses of sticks and bracken, hacking the foundations out of the hillside; and had great battles with mud pellets flipped from the tip of a hazel rod. A shot of mud the size of a golf ball, slung by a boy who hated you, could sting through denim and leave a bruise like a purple plum.

The masters were underpaid young men in baggy grey flannels and striped ties, with leather patches on their elbows. Keats, severe but popular because of his cricket, was believed to own a secret wife though nobody had seen her. In arithmetic he taught us how to calculate compound interest on the stocks and shares which eventually all of us were sure to hold. During an exam someone put a stink bomb under his desk and bad eggs filled the room, with chokes and giggles. He sat on in silence, refusing to open the window, showing nothing till the end, then asked who had done it. Andrew, with the worst temper in the school, often baited for the fun of his rages and one day to become a frequent letter-writer to *The Times*, slowly stood up. Keats took him to the masters' common room and gave him the most vicious beating we had heard of. After that his cricket was admired still more. Later I found him running a fishing pub in Kenya, no more pleased to be reminded of that time than I was.

Other masters were noted for their cars. Wrench, in tight oily curls and a cloud of whisky, had a two-seater with a dicky and solid wheels. Pike, wide-mouthed, huge-footed, drove a sporty MG usually smoth-ered with boys. Chadwick, in a pale blue jacket, tried to drive his Standard Eight forwards on the gravel while the wheels spun backwards, like in films. In his English class we read *Journey's End*, taking the parts of young officers in the trenches twenty years ago. He also wrote his own plays for us and collected rare books and told us to write the first page of a novel. I turned in a pastoral scene with lowing cattle and church bells ringing across the valley, knowing it was good. He gave it back with top marks and a photo clipped to it – a country landscape, 'This England', cut out of a Worthington beer advert. In my last term he let me read Robert Graves's *Goodbye to All That*, a view of the war to upset my prejudices and teach me some new bad words.

Years afterwards in Mallorca a woman and I, on a rock by a deserted beach, saw a lone swimmer enter the bay, heading straight for us, a sun-brown god coming out of the sea. He landed at our feet – 'you must be English,' he said, 'you couldn't be anything else' – and introduced himself: Robert Graves, large and broken-nosed, a myth of his own. He came to sit on our rocks and I told him what his book had once done for a boy of twelve. 'Put it down in words,' he advised me, watching the two of us. He led us up through the olive trees and took the hand of his small son who was standing on the path; and told a story from the Odyssey as we climbed to his house where he poured out tumblers of wine – he might have been Homer himself.

The matron's room was a sanctuary, the nearest thing to home. After spoons of malt and doses of Mist Scillae, a general cure she poured from huge bottles, we stayed to read her *Daily Mirror* and listen to 'Monday Night at Eight' or 'Band Wagon' on her radio. In the sickroom, for anyone not ill enough to be sent to the sanatorium, a tin bungalow beyond the playing fields, she kept a set of the Wonder Books – a remedy for most diseases. Having flu there, with a sense of privilege in the whiff of antiseptic, I could almost be in West Road. Even the Crow's wife's smile, on her daily visit, cracked less sharply.

Epidemics tore through the school, not just mumps and chickenpox but a craze for model aeroplanes, the Saint books, county cricket, black strips of liquorice. Though I was nearly immune, except for a bout of roller-skating, nobody could avoid the latest bug. The school was sucking aniseed balls one week, gobstoppers the next. Photography was the rage, then French cricket, hawk moth caterpillars, Jew's harps, mouth organs. Potato pistols gave way to water pistols, which fell to catapults. Enthusiasm was catching, but never lasted. Hours were spent folding paper into bullets for a wet afternoon, when desks were piled into fortresses with rubber bands stretched between them and battles fought across the room. War still meant a slinging match from trench to trench, and the five dead heroes on the dining-room wall would have recognized the scene. But on the next rainy day we were playing whist.

Most of the boys, briefly my friends or enemies in that time of flickering peace – the Munich crisis, the invasion of Austria and Czechoslovakia – vanished from my life. Sometimes I have imagined them in the army or the foreign office or the church, inheriting family businesses or farms, becoming masters at schools like the Crow's. Any glimpses I have caught were based on almost nothing. Sebastian, a strange fair little boy with glasses who had an epileptic fit in the changing-room, walked from Cape Horn to Panama and wrote a book, a tale of courage and romance that was sent to me for review. Nicholas, a wicket-keeper who yelled 'Howzat!' aggressively enough to sway the umpire, was the personnel officer in a cloud of pipe smoke who interviewed me for a job at the BBC. In Broadcasting House I saw him, as dormitory captain, whacking smaller boys with a slipper and rubbing his feet with eau-de-cologne, a shilling a bottle, before going to bed. He offered me the job, but I didn't take it.

Dacre, a long-legged red-haired short-sighted boy, though useless at work and games, was popular because at home his father, an admiral, beat him with the back of a long-handled clothes brush when the term report came, with an extra beating for any he had had at school and another for being fond of wild flowers. I saw him again, loping unmistakably through the tropical sun in the naval base at Trincomalee in Sri Lanka. But I was an officer and he was a rating on the lower deck – a disgrace for the admiral, who with luck had been sewn into his hammock with the clothes brush and buried at sea – and because he should salute me I avoided him. Then the disgrace was mine.

Others have survived on trivial points, like the ones at the Cambridge choir school but with Christian names. Tim, who could tell an Avro Anson bomber by the sound of its engines without looking up. John, who picked the Crow's tobacco plants and smoked them in a Woolworth's pipe. Another John, a famous belcher who taught me the word 'bugger' but not its meaning, and his friend Derek who told me I was effeminate, which hurt for years. Peter, who belonged to a bible-reading fellowship and kept a silver threepenny bit under his foreskin. Robin, a future ambassador to Yugoslavia, who asked me to go camping in Herefordshire where we poured petrol into a lake and lit it, then watched the birds skittering over the water to escape the flames – enough to raise my father's ghost.

Odd details catch in the memory, flashes of recognition like those destroyers signalling in the bay, leaving the rest of a character blank. Pat had foul breath and sherbet powder down his jersey, Rex had brown scum on his teeth, Simon had been born with a cleft palate and Christopher with no thumbs, Anthony's bed was chocked up at the foot to control his bladder at night, Brian collected us round him after he had been beaten, to show off his stripes. Klaus, a Jewish refugee, arrived from Germany and we were told to be kind to him, so he was treated as if he wasn't there. There was no telling, at the time, what would be memorable about any of them – or, for them, about me.

I went back to the school in 1963, hoping to find that it wasn't there, afraid that it might be. But even after the Crow's successor had shown me round I wasn't convinced. It was a return, not to the place but to that queer summer of 1939, to childhood, to thoughts and hopes and dreads that had escaped me. Much came flooding back, that had ebbed into the dark where I would have liked to keep it. And suddenly I was glad to be middle-aged, not a small boy with those twenty-four years ahead of me, still to be gone through.

NINETEEN

May 19, Albacete. For a time in the Civil War this was headquarters of the International Brigade. Now old stone buildings round the cathedral, even ornate imperial offices in the commercial part, are being torn down in favour of angular blocks with no grace or humour, monuments to the peseta. It's all illusion and Don Quixote's style was less greedy, more humane.

The road south-west from Albacete runs dead straight for thirty kilometres, not a flicker of the bus driver's fingers on the wheel, to the first hills. It's like coming ashore at last, climbing up among poplars and small fields; no longer the far horizon and the infinite eye-strain.

We follow an abandoned railway: embankments and cuttings and tunnels that engineers of the last century sweated over, now holding their rusty rails like bloodless arteries; and derelict country stations, still tiled and whitewashed, once the pride of some local functionary, his whistle silenced like the hiss of steam and clank of buffers. The road takes over, ripping through the sierra, being widened and straightened and flattened, doing more damage than the railway ever did.

Spain often wears a wrinkled, unchanging face. But often too there is a new factory, a cement works, a mill. It was the noise of local industry, one dark night when they were lost, that Don Quixote and Sancho Panza heard. Riding near a stream, they were struck by sounds of thudding iron and rattling chains. Don Quixote brandished his spear, ready to charge and even die for the sake of Dulcinea, but his squire persuaded him to wait till dawn, though he had to tie up Rocinante's legs to stop him. Sancho was petrified, trembling all night till his bowels burst, then forgetting his terror in the morning and mocking Don

Quixote when they found that the noise was only the machinery of a cloth mill.

'It's no joke,' Don Quixote said, hitting Sancho with his spear. To him, the evidence of cold reality meant nothing. In the dark his courage had made no distinction between a factory and a dragon, and in the light of day his idealism was above ridicule.

Mercifully the giant billboards in the landscape of Franco's time – *Todo por la Patria!* – have gone. Even the sinister green-uniformed tricorn-hatted Civil Guards, in pairs to emphasize their menace, are rare now. Yet under a lingering whiff of violence there remains an element of surrender in the people's character. They give in, to the rich men's gain and the baffled disadvantage of the rest. The national *fate*, the agony, the submission, are still there. Sometimes Spain seems too terrible to live with. It has no benevolence or bounty, but only the hard bleached sierras, the dried rivers, the unremitting sun. No wonder men conquered America from here: it was impossible to stay at home.

No wonder also that Cervantes's two travellers are still relevant. Things are not what they appear, in Spain as elsewhere. Unlike Sancho, who saw only what was visible, Don Quixote elevated it into a dream. He was the greatest conquistador of all, fixed on some inner vision – of the human soul, no less – blind to the facts of life around him. His story, though a picaresque adventure, is spiritual and universal – the revelation of oneself. Sometimes the facts may have proved him wrong but nobody, not even Sancho, was any better for the facts.

In the bus the copper-skinned gypsy and her daughter, having slept till now across the Machegan plain, wake up as we wind through the first olive groves of Andalusia and begin cracking melon seeds in their teeth.

TWENTY

'By the by,' my mother said, casually but ominously, the day I started school at Winchester in 1939, a fortnight after war broke out.

It was the way she would announce anything momentous: 'By the by,' she had once said, 'I'm having my hair cut off,' and she came back without the thick long hair that, from the dimmest time, I had watched her curl with tongs heated over a small burner on her dressing-table – solid white fuel and a blue flame – and pin up, with a sour whiff of singeing, into a bun. Or, 'By the by, I've got to start wearing spectacles,' which meant that now she was old. Or, less darkly, 'By the by, I've got tickets for the circus next week.'

'By the by,' she had said in 1938, 'there's a German girl coming to stay for the summer, to learn English.' One evening, encouraged by my mother, the girl talked about the Nazi terror at home, the shortages and suspicions and fear. Next morning, troubled by her recklessness, she begged my mother to keep quiet about it: even Cambridge wasn't beyond reach of the Gestapo. 'By the by,' my mother said before long, 'Irene told me terrible things about Germany . . .' It all came out, and I passed it on to my friends.

'By the by,' she had said a fortnight earlier, in September 1939, when my sisters and I came home from the town swimming-pool for Sunday lunch, having missed Chamberlain's broadcast, and she met us at the door: 'We're at war with Germany.'

Now she said it again, warning me of something dire and dreadful: 'By the by, I expect you'll get quite a shock from some of the things you see – you know, among the bigger boys.'

My present worry was to get my shirt collar straight – I couldn't see how it worked. Nothing fitted, nothing in my father's stud box was any use – nor was my mother. In the end, with collar and tie twisted round my neck, we went to an outfitter's in the town where a salesman gave me a lesson.

At tea with the housemaster among other new boys I got the sort of shock I thought my mother meant. The tall man with a moustache who ignored us but joked with our parents – another master, I thought – turned out to be the senior prefect, only five years older than me. So before I left this place I would become a man. In fact I was one already – a 'new man', despite my smooth cheeks and child's voice.

The first thing to learn was the language. A new man's pitch-up, his family relations, disappeared after tea and wouldn't be seen again till there was a hatch thoke, a holiday. Some men got a quill from brocking – a pleasure from bullying. To jockey a man's baker or his benjamin when he was continent was tug non licet – to steal a boy's cushion or ruler when he was ill was absolutely forbidden. 'On a toll last half-remedy I saw a cud girl' meant that I saw a pretty one on a run last half-holiday. There was a printed dictionary and I had to be fluent in a fortnight.

I also had to know six Latin verses of the school song, *Dulce Domum*, the long inscription round the war memorial cloister, all the house-masters and senior prefects and house colours, captains of games, competitions and prizes, names and nicknames of countless people and places, the answers to a catechism of absurd questions, with a rigmarole of Greek and Latin tags and obscure but hallowed jokes. After two weeks I would be tested by the prefects, whose punishment for failure was too frightening to risk. They ruled the house, and in the tub-room I saw the purple bruises they could make.

I never stopped to think that this extraordinary stuff was silly. It had been forced on the prefects when they first came and one day, unbelievably, I would be in their place. On top of St Catherine's Hill overlooking the school I ran round a maze cut in the turf with a pebble in each hand, then laid them on a cross in the middle and knelt to kiss it in front of dozens of other boys. For nearly half my thirteen years I had been preparing for Winchester, and this was it, and I didn't yet know how many years afterwards I would spend trying to live it down. To my sorrow I can still recite the house colours and some of the jargon memorized in that awful fortnight.

Fagging–sweating, it was called – was an extra anxiety in the timetable of work and sport. I polished a prefect's shoes, filled his tub to the depth and temperature he liked, pressed and laid out his clothes, remembering which shirt and tie and socks went with the blue pin-stripe, the grey flannel, the brown check. On Wednesday his Corps uniform had to be brushed, his puttees ironed and rolled, his belt and pouch and bayonet frog sandpapered, then spat on and boned with a toothbrush handle before polishing. The torment of button-sticks and toecaps left no time for the maths I hadn't done, the history I hadn't read. On Saturday I had to report the games I had played that week, including a three-mile run that nearly brought back my asthma. On Sunday I made sandwiches for the prefects' tea, and at any time a bell might ring for an errand or some idiotic ritual.

Life was absorbed by demands and the need to keep up. I learnt to be alert and remember who was dangerous, when to be in chapel – nine times a week – and how many buttons on my jacket I could leave undone. Fear was rife and warnings were welcome, though sometimes too cautious. When I lined up with other new boys to be tested for the choral society I was advised to sing the wrong notes – it would take up an evening a week and carry no prestige, anyway till my voice had broken. But I couldn't sing out of tune, though I tried. I joined the trebles and sang Bach my first term, thankful to have passed.

Centuries of dogma and tradition, collected like weed on a ship's bottom, slowed the place down but never stopped it. Momentum was kept going by a covenant with the past, guarded by old boys who came back to see that we were carrying on properly and by the historic ones who watched us from their niches. Most of us conformed without question and slowly rose from 'junior' to 'inferior', shedding slavery, acquiring privileges, waiting for eventual power. Anyone who rebelled, if he wasn't beaten into orthodoxy, was rolled downstairs from his 'gallery', dormitory, to 'conduit', the changing room, in a laundry basket and abandoned under a cold shower. Only a few brave characters managed to steer independently alongside the rest of us, admired for their imagination but considered rather treacherous for their disdain. I belonged to the majority, neither happily nor unhappily, but only shamefully long afterwards.

My house was known as a bad one, a joke in the school with the fewest boys in the top form and none in the football or cricket teams; with too many pansies in suede shoes and a new suit every term, who oiled their hair with bay rum or smoked Russian cigarettes. We didn't mind losing house matches and wore the gaudiest ribbon on our straw hats to show our decadence, our 'low moral tone'. Cynical about house pride, ambitious only to get by with the least pain – it suited me. And though the prefects could be as tyrannical as in other houses I was glad not to have one of the strenuous games-mad housemasters, driving everyone to success.

My housemaster was a burly, gentle, faded man with a sad moustache who let out a small moan before speaking. Whatever kept him from interfering – shyness or indifference or deep unhappiness – was something to be grateful for. At times some dim passion glimmered through his melancholy, but he was too aloof to stimulate the forty adolescents in his house; too unnoticeable to be liked or disliked. A maths teacher, he ran up the long stairs to his classroom with a stopwatch, and calculated from his weight and the staircase height the horsepower he had generated; but somehow he made it boring. He coached rowing, like a hunched old heron bicycling along the towpath, and on a fine night would set up a telescope on the lawn and show the moons of Venus to anyone interested – few of us were. Perhaps he was wasted on us. His wife followed him like a small dog, straight from the pet parlour after a shampoo and trim.

One winter evening he called me to his study (school reminiscences always have this scene) and in a roundabout way, with the black-out curtains drawn, he struggled with his duty. Probably I had a thing I called my cock, he said with effort, and near it were my balls, and one night I would have a wet dream if I hadn't already, but it was normal and not important, really nothing at all, I needn't worry when it came. He was apologizing for nature as well as for his confusion, for the little sighs and grunts as his sad eyes swam round the room, never settling on mine. He couldn't cope with our crude puberty. A year or two later he became ill and one day while we were having lunch he died. We got another housemaster, keen to win matches, who set about 'pulling the house together' and 'raising the tone'.

Beating went in phases, like the fashion for paisley ties or double-breasted waistcoats. There would be a year of terror as a generation of sadists became prefects, and then it died down. We had one senior prefect, a handsome boy of eighteen with a strong moustache, who beat the juniors mercilessly, perhaps because he failed to reach the top of the school or become captain of any games. Soon after he left school his name appeared on the roll of honour outside the chapel door, killed in action, and there was rejoicing in the house.

A character in a novel (again, not me) remembers waiting in pyjamas for the summons downstairs, overcome with fear; being told to take off his dressing-gown and show there was no handkerchief inside his trousers; bending over a table with a cushion on his head in case of ricochets; then the relief of the cane burning into him and the feel, in bed afterwards, of the hot corrugations on his skin and the uncontrollable erection.

It was roughly like that, with allowances for fiction; and so fraught with pain, resentment, shame, that I don't forgive those boys who beat me. One of them emerged years later from behind a pillar in Salisbury cathedral and I couldn't avoid him, or remind him of that old indignity. Another came into the Kensington public library where I was writing a book and I kept my head down, with no cushion on it this time, till he had gone out. For a moment he brought back the last thing I remembered seeing before the first stroke of his cane: the wooden propeller of a German aeroplane shot down in the First World War by a member of the house, hanging on the wall. I did become a prefect, but never beat anyone.

More than anything, more than the famous teaching or character-building, the war marked my five years at Winchester, a ground bass rumbling under the trivialities. It was always out there beyond the school, out of reach of masters and prefects, the future itself and almost a friend – it couldn't be worse than this. One day I would escape to it and be lost, though I knew my name would never go up on the chapel door.

France fell one hot day of my first summer term. The Germans would be here next week and briefly the fear of defeat overlaid the dread of cricket to be played, Horace to be translated, a prefect's Sunday clothes to be sponged. But more pressing anxieties returned. Lying in the sun by the river, in the fenced-off section where we bathed naked, I was less concerned by the flight of Spitfires thundering overhead than by the livid marks of a cane on another boy's buttocks or the sudden need to jump into the water and subdue the first twitchings of love, unwanted and too visible.

We had our week's butter and margarine rations, two ounces each, on saucers down the table with our names; ludicrously, to mock austerity, a boy with a glass eye rolled it towards me, a winking marble between the saucers. For the war effort we kept pigs and geese and grew potatoes. The cricket pavilion was filled with tear gas and we stood inside to test our gas masks; then some of us took them off for bravado, and came out with eyes streaming. In the summer holidays we went to harvest or forestry camps, stooking corn, working on the first combine harvesters, picking up potatoes or stones, hoeing cabbages, felling trees for pit props: three weeks in tents, neither school nor home but an uneasy alliance with masters and the wives who cooked for us, a time of beer in tin mugs from a barrel and promenade concerts on someone's radio and the shooting stars of August – freedom of a sort.

A few boys were sent to America and came back after the invasion scare had passed, with accents and zoot suits. When the air raid siren sounded we trooped down to the concrete shelter under the drive and waited for the all clear. If the raid lasted long enough we were let off morning lessons before breakfast. Later, bunks were built and we spent the night down there, listening to the bombs on Southampton. But though one or two fell on Winchester and we watched a dog fight one afternoon, the war meant dreariness more than excitement.

Many of the younger, brighter masters were called up. Two took holy orders – to avoid conscription, we assumed – and retired men were dragged back. In a German lesson a veteran of the First World War, still limping on a wounded leg, described his night lying in a shell crater where he had heard another man's death rattle, the exact guttural sound that he was trying to teach us, from the next crater.

Art almost disappeared and drama totally. Only music struggled on. I was taught the flute by someone who couldn't play it – he was the teatime violinist at a café in the town. The head of music, an inspiring man with an incomparable stammer and illicit lusts, drove us through oratorios and symphonies but was never more appreciated than on Home Guard exercises, his battledress awry, helplessly tangled with his rifle. He took me as a piano pupil after my teacher joined a bomber crew, though I was no good, and there is a slow movement of a Beethoven sonata I can't hear without feeling him behind me, unbuttoning my shirt and running his fingers down my chest.

Long afterwards my eye was caught by an obituary: died suddenly aged fifty, ex-captain of the Coldstream Guards, a baronet and justice of the peace, beloved husband of Anastasia and father of three daughters. I could see him, a tall sergeant-major in the Corps, stamping and shouting louder than anyone, the future guardsman on parade. I could also see him playing César Franck on his violin, a cool stylish performance which Anastasia and the girls never heard. But he left them more than a million pounds.

There were ways of escape and a boy in my house, Tony, older than me, took me walking in Wales in the Easter holidays: in yellow cycle capes and stiff new boots, butting through rain and cloud, blistered, hungry, cold and soaked, sore from rucksack straps, lost but drunk with exhilaration. Drunk with beer too, among wet clothes and saucepans of tinned soup in the youth hostels at night.

Tony read modern poetry to me, and plied me with more beer and Gold Flake cigarettes which I hated, but wasn't child enough or man enough to refuse. I hadn't begun to shave, I lied about my age to get into the hostels as an adult, not a junior. Other hostellers bellowed their raucous songs, the socks steamed, the soup boiled over, the room tilted and revolved, my eyes swam round my head with the *Love Song of J. Alfred Prufrock*, I lurched to a bunk and into my sleeping-bag, lowered my reeling head to the pillow but was tipped on to the floor and rushed out in time to vomit into the night, where tomorrow's mountains were wrapped in the hush of wind and water.

Back at school, after T. S. Eliot and Louis MacNeice and the infinite mountains, everything had diminished a little.

TWENTY-ONE

May 20, Ubeda. I feel guilty in this town on the fringe of Andalusia. It isn't Don Quixote's country – he needed the empty scenery of La Mancha. This is the South, another land, facing the Mediterranean, Africa, the Moors. The churches are built on old mosques, the music in the bars has another rhythm. The spirit is personified by a bullfighter, not by a madman on a horse. The poet Antonio Machado called Ubeda '*reina y gitana*', queen and gypsy. The days are warmer, the voices softer, the prices higher.

But I had to come here. It was a painter from Ubeda, an uncertain fumbling character mentioned by Don Quixote, who couldn't tell what he was painting till it was finished. He painted a cock, but so unlike one that he had to write under it, 'This is a cock,' in case it was mistaken for a fox.

I make a tourist's gesture and for half an hour in the morning enjoy the opulence, passion, arrogance, voluptuous joy of baroque architecture. A team of young men and girls in dungarees and straw hats is clipping the hedges in the plaza, ready for the summer season. The first coaches feel their way among the constricted streets and park against the old buildings, too big and bright to be inoffensive. Two Englishwomen poised outside the Parador, cameras slung and guidebooks handy for a couple of churches before lunch, congratulate themselves on such lucky weather. Later in the day the souvenir shop, if only for postcards home, will be a sanctuary in their punishing timetable of sightseeing.

I'm uneasy, a feeble tourist, more renegade than rubberneck. I'm not meant to be among these renaissance façades and aristocratic palaces. I have no place here, I belong on the road, on the plain and in the mountains, the open country where incidents occur or can be invented

93

– a better scene for a writer. I must go back to the blank La Mancha. To escape I buy *El País* and take it to a bench under the trees. From an inside page I'm given a cold grin by Mrs Thatcher. Thank God not to be in England now.

Restlessly I walk through the town: flowerpots in the windows, canary cages, glassed-in balconies; a glimpse into the cool of a courtyard with some watered greenery and a woman in black with a broom, sweeping round her son's motorbike. A few sun-bleached palm leaves remain tied to the balconies, from Palm Sunday a month ago. A helicopter comes rattling overhead, circling low, a man leaning out with a camera.

The Spanish elections are the day before the British and there are posters everywhere, for a multitude of parties. On a wall is written, 'There will be no peace in the world till Gaddafi is dead,' but Gaddafi has been crossed out and Reagan put in, with another sentence: 'Vote No to the Yanqui bases in Spain.'

At the edge of town, where a rubbish tip drops abruptly into olive groves that stretch into the sierras, a guineafowl screeches from a roof-top. 'That's a partridge,' a little girl tells her younger sister. I tell her she is wrong and for a moment they stare at me in amazement – this gangling stranger, hook-nosed under a sun hat – then grab each other's hands and flee.

The afternoon surrenders to a torpid quiet. Even the children and the caged songbirds are silenced in the streets. A dog wakes up long enough to scratch. Sometimes a motorbike cracks the numbness like a jab coming through the dentist's anaesthetic.

Slowly towards evening the pace quickens. A van with loudspeakers drives past, shouting politics. Shops open up again. A doctor in a big Renault with a stunningly pretty woman parks in a narrow street and they get out. Without a word or glance or smile she walks away, while he locks the car and unlocks the shiny door of an old house. A metal plate on it says that he is a specialist in the digestive apparatus. Starting to write a story about them in my mind, I go into a bar.

A man in a smaller Renault drives from bar to bar with a box and a bunch of keys, emptying the fruit machines of money. They have English names, Lucky Player or Wolf Man or Lemon Baby, and their jingle tunes are a dominant sound of Spain, chiming more frequently than church bells. But the TV screen is paramount for veneration, with faces at the bar turned, as they might once have been towards the host at the altar, to the bullfight or football or a dubbed soap opera. When an election programme comes on, the faces turn away.

I find a less aggressive slogan on a wall: '*La Paz es verde* – peace is green,' echoing the Andalusian poet Lorca, '*Verde, que te quiero verde. Verde viento. Verdes ramas.* Green, how I love you green. Green wind. Green branches.' There is a Green Party in Spain, working for Green Peace. It doesn't fit the national image of armoured conquistadors fighting to win an empire and red blood on the bullring sand.

In a shop for surgical goods an elderly man in a white coat awaits customers for his orthopædic callipers, hernia trusses, corn pads, even a wheelchair or a glass eye. The white coat, with his grey hair and strong tanned face, gives him authority: you would trust him with your deformity – he looks like a scientist or anyway a TV actor. He doesn't have to wait long for someone to enter the shop, a woman limping on a blocked-up boot. In Spain – where young men, otherwise still youthful, soon develop an unhealthy bulging stomach – there seem to be more people with club feet or crutches than in other countries. Only the very oldest men, with one leg or half an arm, can be victims of the Civil War.

In the evening, in the falling dusk, the wheeling swifts and swallows vacate the sky for bats, flying lower among the plaza trees, and I choose a restaurant for supper. Here too, among the wrought iron and darkened woodwork and bottle racks and antique crockery, the room's focus is a TV set. I order *tortilla de la casa* and it comes with mushrooms, asparagus, onions, potatoes, infinite herbs. I would have preferred a plain omelette – simple food, one taste at a time.

Across the room is a couple at another table. He, obviously an Englishman with a sports sweater knotted loosely over his shoulders, is trying to be relaxed and confident with a girl I can't place, possibly Spanish, totally silent and uninterested. He is having trouble with her, but won't admit it. He will boast about her when he gets back to his London office or his pub – 'I was with this smashing bird in Spain' – praising his own success.

She hardly looks at him or opens her mouth, unless to put a piece of lettuce in it, while he talks continuously. I'm too far away to hear his words, except occasionally, 'I say . . .' She isn't quite rude to him, and only her big sorrowful eyes show how bored she is. I try to catch them and for an instant, across the tables, I'm fixed by a profound, helpless sadness before they move away.

She toys with an *agua mineral* but he, having drunk half a bottle of wine, orders another and jokes with the waiter, practising his Spanish. Later he refuses a dessert and has a coffee, watching the girl dab at a slice of water melon. He presses her to a glass of sweet white wine and she accepts, a concession to ritual, putting her lips in it but swallowing nothing. Her eyes stray to the TV, his to her breasts – they look good to me.

I'm a little envious, of course, and try to draw those sad eyes to me again, but they refuse to come. Instead the man stares at me, still talking, recognizing another Englishman. I wonder what the rest of their story is, looking in on a brief moment of it, inventing even that moment. And I wonder how the night will end. Perhaps they do too. The girl eats less than half her water melon: that is what they are grown for – to be left mutilated on the plate.

After a *copa* of brandy with my coffee I leave, passing their table. The man is saying, 'I say . . .' but not to me, and the girl's eyes turn to him for the first time, avoiding me deliberately.

The woman behind the bar down the street puts her hands on her hips as if about to break into an Andalusian dance, waiting for the click of castanets, and I say, '*Una copa.*'

Another brandy? You've had enough, you fool.

TWENTY-TWO

My mother died in the Easter holidays, 1943, when I was sixteen. At the beginning of the war she had made room at home for three other children and, after they went to America, for an elderly couple in flight from the air raids. In the first winter she volunteered as an ambulance driver, practising at night with masked headlights; and tried to tune in to Hitler on the radio but got Lord Haw-Haw, the English traitor in Berlin, instead. Next winter, after the blitz began, she was prosecuted for breaking the black-out – a chink of light through the curtains – and fined a pound.

The war brought an extra darkness to widowhood and perhaps she knew she wouldn't see the end of it. She sent my sisters and me for holidays alone, to a boarding-house near Windermere with our bicycles and to a family in Dorset who kept a cow and ferrets. (In a novel two boys release a ferret and a rabbit together in a stable to watch the slow killing, starting with the rabbit's eyes.) After the worst of the blitz she gave us tickets for London matinées – Gielgud as Macbeth and Shylock, *Dear Brutus, Watch on the Rhine, Arsenic and Old Lace* – with money for ices in the interval. Probably she already knew what was killing her.

'By the by, I've got to have an operation.' She didn't speak of it as a disease like my asthma, even when she had to have more surgery: 'I've got this silly ulcer.' When I went to see her in hospital she showed me the tube in her stomach, fixed with plaster and a safety-pin, for feeding her. I saw it again when I had a drainpipe in me, with peritonitis after a burst appendix at about her age.

I wasn't frightened – there was no threat. But for some time she had seemed to keep me at a distance, as if the end of childhood was the limit of her concern. I had no suspicion that she was abandoning me, I only knew that I was growing up and leaving her. We looked at each other sideways across the gap, recognizing that now there were things we wouldn't share. She might guess at mine, but never hinted at her own. It wasn't a denial of love so much as a retreat from its blinding agony. Neither of us could trust ourselves to face the truth.

In bed at home, mystifying my sisters and me, she discussed our uncles, aunts, cousins, friends, with their virtues and failings. Which of them did we like best, for ourselves? – but we refused to see what she was preparing us for. And in her loneliness the sight of her children round her must have multiplied the pain. We belonged to next summer, to the peace after the war, to the future she wouldn't be in. She spoke of the hazards and traps we should look out for, and went back to hospital for radium treatment.

In time, growing weaker in the ward, she was convinced by her doctor's gloom. Hardly able to hold a pen she wrote to a sister and brother-in-law, Aunt Margy and Uncle George: 'It has taken me a very long time to bring myself to write this letter, for I even now cannot see that I will not for certain be here . . .' She asked them, now in their mid-sixties after bringing up six children of their own, to be guardians of hers. 'I am really unfit to write or think. Do please say yes.' Next day, exhausted and weeping, she waited for their answer. When it came she was overwhelmed: 'You can't think what a blessing it is . . . I feel a little stronger today and have less pain.'

A will was drawn up and the solicitor raged at the hospital nurses for refusing to witness it: 'Bring me a doctor! Bring me anyone – I can't believe in this huge establishment there is nobody who will witness a signature.' The nurses flew through the wards and came back with a young man who obliged. The end of 'this tiresome business', as my mother called it, was a relief and despite the bitter finality she managed to brighten her doctor's face – 'but it takes some doing'. At the end of the winter he allowed her home with a nurse.

For a few days in early spring, from a chair in the window, she watched the days grow longer. The sun shone through the glass, her daffodils came up, she would soon be strong enough to go out. But one day she stayed in bed and never left it.

'What are you doing in the holidays?' a boy at school asked.

I had no idea: 'It depends what happens to my mother.' I hardly knew what I meant. My consciousness had a mechanism for self-protection, switching off at the threat of danger. Perhaps I should have guessed, or been told, that my mother was dying. But all I dared accept was that something was happening, too big to be talked about, and I was close to the centre of it.

At home Aunt Margy and Uncle George moved in. On the radio after supper we listened to Yehudi Menuhin, who had braved the Atlantic U-boats to entertain American troops in England, play Brahms' violin concerto. Aunt Margy, a violinist, sat flushed with the power of music, which affected me as never before. Somehow it belonged to the essence of things, to the wonder of life and the futility of hope, the ache of adolescence and the awe of whatever was happening up in my mother's bedroom.

Long afterwards a publisher asked me to write Menuhin's autobiography – it would be anonymous, but well paid. 'A ghost?' I suggested, and he looked pained. This wasn't hack stuff but would mean re-living Menuhin's career, attending his concerts and master classes, absorbing his philosophy, even moving into his household. It would help if I learnt to play the violin. But at the time, trying hard to be myself, I couldn't also be turned into someone else. (The last surviving aunt was disappointed – she had hoped for fame in the family and would have liked Menuhin for a nephew.) When the book came out it was praised by *The Times* critic, though he suspected the tactful hand of an editor in it and for a moment I was sorry it wasn't me. Shelving my life for six months to become Menuhin might have given scope for fiction too, and I would have tried to show thanks for what he once did for a boy.

I asked the nurse if I could practise my flute in the room next to my mother's, without disturbing her. I hated that chilly starched woman, an intruder in our house with her drugs and towels, her false charity and knowing looks. Sniffing back her arrogance she said that my mother was probably too sedated to notice, implying that I wasn't worth hearing anyway. But didn't the nurse know? – it was my mother's birthday. Fifty-four today. I played my flute for all I was worth, hoping to fill her room and reach the abyss where her mind had sunk. She was *alive*, and I could still be her son.

But I too was half-drugged. Later I wished that I had been more conscious during those precious days. I was numbed by people's kindness, aware only of the need for continuity and survival. Everything was unreal, or too real to bear. The day-to-day uncertainty was kept suspended and any stab of grief was soothed.

On a table I found a letter lying open, and my own name caught my eye. It was to Aunt Margy from one of the other aunts, saying how sorry she felt for us three children but especially for me, 'the most sensitive'. I was outraged. *Sensitive*! It was an extra wound added to whatever else they had in store. These aunts had got it wrong. I was tough, almost a man, and could take anything that was coming. ('What sort of school is Winchester, for God's sake,' Deirdre wondered when I told her, 'that it makes a boy ashamed of being sensitive?')

The last time I saw my mother has become an ambiguous occasion, poised between my actual visit to her bedroom and the account of it by Paul, the character in a novel. Both our memories are valid, though mine has been overlaid by Paul's sharper one. The fact is only in my mind, an invention of my own, grey and shadowy. But the fiction is in hard words told by another man – a more reliable one – printed in a book, black and white. The truth belongs equally to the novel's reality and the event's illusion. Or perhaps unequally, balanced in favour of fiction.

I sat alone beside her bed – the huge bed where she had slept with my father for six and a half years and with nobody for twice as long, where I had been conceived and born, where I had lain crying before going back to school – and watched her breathing, deep among the bedclothes. Her shrunken head sank like an old stone into the pillows, her neck had withered to a stem, her body hardly raised the sheets. Only her hair and eyebrows were still my mother's. Slowly she pulled a hand out, bent and fleshless, and touched my chin, cheeks, lips, innocent except for the first hopeful traces of a moustache. But I didn't take her hand or kiss her. (Twenty years later Uncle George showed me a cheque with her last feeble signature – the bank had refused to honour it.) On her wrist was the silver bangle given to her as a girl by her father which, as her hand grew too big to slip it off, she had kept on for life – and now for death. She murmured something I didn't hear – 'by the by', perhaps – and opened her eyes, blinked without seeing me and closed them. I hardly knew whether I loved her any more. Her diminishment, from my mother into this, had come too fast.

The nurse came in and said that that was enough. Ever since, I have wished for those five minutes again. That night in my bedroom I was overcome with desolation and gave way, sobbing into my pillow: 'Don't die! Don't die! Oh God, don't let her die, you fool.' But it wasn't any good, I knew.

Shopping in the town with Aunt Margy I heard her say, 'We thought she would die last night,' and wait for my response.

It was the first admission – nobody had been so blunt before – and I was speechless.

100

'Her heart keeps going, it's amazing.'

But I wasn't amazed – I knew my mother.

'It's a terrible disease isn't it?'

What was?

'Cancer.'

So that was it. They had kept it from me and now it was too late. It was a plot cooked up by that hard-lipped nurse and the faceless doctor who came every day. They had given my mother cancer, something that went with flag days and appeals, not a disease for our family. We had tuberculosis or went mad or committed suicide, or died of strokes or heart attacks or drink. But nobody got cancer – it was obscene, it was sabotage.

She lived longer than they thought possible, lying in a false drug-death, the real one denied by a heart that refused to do what was expected. But a funeral was arranged, a grave chosen, her children's future planned. Then one early morning I heard Aunt Margy's steps coming to my bedroom door and knew what she had to say: 'Your mother died,' and she kissed me.

Next day some of the aunts and uncles collected and sat with us, trying awkwardly to smile and fill the silence. Uncle Dick said, 'Your voice has broken.' The nurse had left. We could hear men carrying something downstairs and out of the house – it was time to go. We walked quickly through the April chill, but my mother had got there first. I didn't trust myself to look at her. Though she was in a box on a table at the altar steps, I might see inside. I must try not to imagine the unimaginable. Whatever she was now, for sixteen years she had been my mother. Fear and bewilderment assaulted me with the priest's ominous voice, the sorrow of my relations, the stark bright blankness of tomorrow. We mumbled some prayers and shuffled out. Childhood was finished.

Suddenly I was angry as well as frightened, and ashamed too. They've got it wrong, they've made a gigantic blunder. Why are they being so stupid? My mother always said she would be cremated like my father, and have Psalm 23 and 'As pants the hart for cooling streams'. They should have asked me. Or I should have told them. Why don't I stand up for her? I've let her down. Oh God, make her alive again so that we can do it the way she wanted.

Black cars took us to the drizzle-blown cemetery, my mother leading the way, by roads that we had often bicycled along. Standing by the grave the priest read the dreadful words while the wind grabbed the pages of his prayer book and his surplice tore loose like a wet sail, flapping round his legs. Four men – four crows in fake mourning for a stranger – lifted the box on ropes and dropped it out of sight. My heart almost cracked, the stopped-up tears burst at last. The priest shut his book, hauled in his surplice and said kind things. One of my sisters stepped forward and tossed a bunch of spring flowers into the hole. Down there, on the lid, a shiny metal plate was engraved with my mother's name and the dates of her birth and death – her whole life scratched on a piece of brass.

My father hadn't died as finally as this. For me his death was the beginning of my invention of him, which could never leave me. But my mother's death, because I had known her, was the end – as real as her life had been.

To disturb me, as my sisters grew older, I sometimes caught visions of my mother in them. And once by luck, to the surprise of us both, I met her again, or at least I saw her large brown eyes looking at me, long afterwards in India.

I had been asked by Amnesty International to try and visit a woman political prisoner, a veteran socialist who had fought against the government for the independence of Kashmir. For two years she had been under house arrest in Ahmedabad, where no journalist was allowed to see her. But Amnesty had made contact and given me the address of an office in Bombay, an exporter of cotton piece goods. People there seemed uneasy at my inquiry and sent me to the Gymkhana Club. I had tea on the veranda overlooking the cricket field with a lawyer, a furtive man who mentioned names and wrote a letter for me to take to Ahmedabad, but didn't sign it.

My picture of house arrest was revised when I got there and took a motor rickshaw to the address. Audacity was the key, I saw, and my driver rattled past the sentries into a garden of great trees and shaded lawns, an oasis of luxury at the edge of a hot, impoverished, teeming city. The prisoner's father was a multi-millionaire, a prince of capitalism whose home, full of children and grandchildren, was the centre of one of the world's great textile empires. A swimming pool lay among the beautiful pavilions. Fountains splashed in courtyards. Idols danced over limpid pools, servants padded across the speckless marble, gardeners sprinkled the gaudy lilies, peacocks did what peacocks do.

Trying to reach the prisoner, locked somewhere in this fantasy, was like the fragments of a dream. My letter was taken by a man who vanished. Another man came and questioned me; led me to a different part of paradise and left me there. A third man moved me on again. I tried the names I had been given in Bombay, but nobody owned or recognized them. I asked about my motor rickshaw which I had left in the garden, and was told it had been paid off and sent away. I might, I felt, be kept for ever in this wonderland. Did Amnesty, with its emblem of a candle encircled by barbed wire and its index of victims, appreciate their true condition?

After two hours of Indian deviousness, with my impatience soothed by such unreality and the scent of jasmine, I was abandoned near a four-armed goddess in the twilight. Perhaps she herself, in that unlikely prison, was the woman I had come to see. But there was a muffled gasp and from behind a pillar the prisoner emerged, barefoot on the marble. She wore cropped hair and rumpled white pyjamas, and had my mother's eyes.

On behalf of Amnesty I presented her with a sticky box of chocolates, and in return she pressed on me two red roses. She led me to the corner of a cloister where we talked in the falling night while somewhere close, I was aware, a sentry waited to escort me to the gate.

Next day I went back and she gave me lunch, rice and lentils in our fingers, a prison diet in a tycoon's palace. It was like meeting an old socialist of an earlier, gentler and more aristocratic kind, a Fabian in a golden cage, and when I got to know her better I told her that she reminded me of my great aunt Beatrice Webb. But it was my mother's eyes, with a wild elusive light in them, that smiled at me. I had come twenty-four years and half across the world to find them in this extraordinary Indian woman, who was about my mother's age when she died.

I was flying back to England and she gave me a basket of mangoes to take with me, for my children. In London they tasted strangely of another world.

TWENTY-THREE

May 21, Ubeda. I take an early bus back towards La Mancha, the arid heartland of Spain, before I'm caught – I can see the danger. Two days after putting my foot in the treacherous, seductive South I'm withdrawing, mindful of the caged birds that don't sing in the afternoon, impatient for something more exacting.

The road leads north over the marvellous olive hills to Arquillos, Vilches, La Carolina. An olive 'grove' is no word – too intimate and biblical – for these huge plantations spreading up and down the landscape: endless patterns of trees on the terracotta soil, an unbelievable sea of future olive oil, now with a pale dusting of blossom. Beehives are massed on the slopes below the hilltops for the wild flowers.

I leave the bus at Santa Elena on *el general*, the highway from Córdoba and Granada to Madrid, and have a second breakfast of coffee and toast – for a thousand pesetas I can have a roast partridge if I want. From here *el general* runs in a double route through the mountains, north and south traffic sometimes several kilometres apart. I find a path between the two, among pinewoods full of birds and flowers, with another nightingale and the smell of pine needles. Later, nearing the Desfiladero de Despeñaperros, the Gorge of the Overthrown Dogs, I'm forced back on *el general*.

At a road junction a man in a car stops to offer a lift up into the sierras, not the way I'm going. 'Are you sure?' he asks when I say I will continue on foot through the Desfiladero. Obstinately I plod on, wishing I had gone with him. *Carpe diem*, seize the day, is the motto of a man in a novel I wrote, a fantasy I have never kept. The sweat off my back is soaking into my rucksack.

Don Quixote, knowing what adventures could lie in such country, rejoiced as he and Sancho Panza rode into these mountains. But Sancho, without his master's trust or vision, was uneasy.

They had just met a gang of men chained together, marching under guard: convicts, Sancho explained, on their way to slavery in the royal galleys. Hearing that they were going by force, not willingly, and believing that human liberty was sacred, Don Quixote asked the sergeant to set the men free. To him, justice was something beyond mere guilt and punishment, which were matters for God, not the king.

The sergeant only laughed: 'Funny joke!' At which Don Quixote, compassionate, brave, dedicated protector of the oppressed and hater of cold authority, attacked with spear and shield, and broke the chains. Before they scattered he ordered the freed men to go to El Toboso, home of Dulcinea, and present her with an account of his latest feat. But their gratitude turned to mockery and they began stoning this crazy liberator, knocking him off his horse and robbing him.

'I've always heard,' the Knight of the Sad Countenance said, hobbling on with Sancho, 'that to do good for villains is to pour water into the sea. But now it's done – patience! And it'll be a lesson for the future.'

Sancho knew better: 'You'll never learn, or I'm a Turk.' That night they slept under the cork trees where one of the freed convicts, still not satisfied, stole Sancho's donkey. Though they recovered it later, Sancho's grief and his terror as they travelled deeper into the mountains were only soothed by Don Quixote's mad, infectious faith. The squire saw his master's lunacy, but despite himself he needed it. Sancho was on the way to being quixotized.

This morning I'm buffeted by the suction of passing lorries and nearly jump off the verge at the sudden hiss of air brakes or the blast of a horn, blown either to salute or scare me. Often I can follow a path or the old road or a dried river bed. Sometimes I walk in the shade under a concrete flyover, with lorries thundering overhead. Once I have to trudge through a long tunnel where slimy puddles lie underfoot and the roar of diesels is intensified. The light at the end seems an unreachable joy.

At Venta de Cárdenas I drink two bottles of orange juice, regretting the partridge I didn't eat this morning, and walk another kilometre to the next café where I drink two more.

Somewhere among these mountains, where a stream came through the trees into a meadow of grass and flowers, Don Quixote announced that he would do penance for Dulcinea:'Oh day of my night, glory of my grief, pole-star of my travels, light of my fortune . . . !' She deserved to be mistress of the universe, he told Sancho.

'I know her well,' Sancho said. 'She's a fine wench, every inch of her. The muscles on her! And her voice! Once she went up the church tower to call the men in from her father's field a couple of miles away and they heard her as if they were in the churchyard. She keeps nothing back, she'll have fun with anyone. I tell you, you're quite right – though it's a long time since I've seen her and she must have changed. All day out in the sun and wind – it ruins a woman's looks. But I thought you were in love with a princess or someone, to deserve the things you've done for her. And probably she's winnowing or threshing . . .'

'Sancho, you talk a lot of gibberish.' For Don Quixote's purpose, as he dimly recognized, Dulcinea was as good as the finest princess on earth: 'In my imagination everything I say is true, neither more nor less, and so I draw her as I want her.'

'You're always right,' Sancho said, 'and I'm an ass.'

His master was less certain: 'Really Sancho, as far as I can tell, you're no saner than me.' He stripped off his trousers and, in only his shirt, kicked twice in the air and turned two somersaults, revealing things which moved Sancho to cover Rocinante's eyes. Then he tore a piece off his shirt-tail, knotted it into a rosary and recited a million Ave Marias; and spent three days wandering about, fasting and sighing for his Dulcinea, scratching poems of love and sorrow on the ground or carving them on trees. In penance for nothing, acting the raving lover of nobody, he turned logic upside down and with self-mockery ridiculed the curse of common sense – a virtue dear to Sancho Panza but unknown to Don Quixote's peculiar reality.

Several times this afternoon I dodge off the road and crawl under a tree for half an hour, and wonder at what a fool I am. This might be a penance for having left La Mancha, a price for my two days in Andalusia, but really it is madness. I feel no pity for myself, only scorn. Butterflies zigzag among the poppies, lizards rattle the stones. Once a long green snake slithers over the road in front.

I meet a shepherd with a flock of lean shorn sheep and a few goats standing on their hind legs to reach the bush tops. 'Are they yours?' I ask, knowing it's unlikely.

He shakes his head, saying nothing.

'How many kilometres to Almuradiel?'

He holds up four fingers.

'Is that it, at the top of the road?' I can see white buildings in the distance.

He nods – perhaps he is dumb.

'*Adíos.*'

Another hour at least, I reckon. But I'm glad to be off *el general* and the afternoon is cooling down. I pass two more shepherds with their flocks, who are almost as untalkative. 'Twenty minutes to Almuradiel?' I ask. It's difficult to judge the distance, I have been deceived so often. 'Thirty? Forty?'

'More,' they say, summing me up.

Then I reach a white-washed chapel and beside it, astonishingly, a small wooden bullring. Perhaps these lonely shepherds of the sierras sometimes treat themselves to a *corrida*. A man hoeing his vegetables doesn't look up as I walk past. In time – half an hour or an hour, measureless and unending though suddenly it ends – I am back on *el general* again. The giant black bull on the skyline, advertising Osborne brandy, has never looked so good.

Almuradiel has a three-star hotel with an American bar, sauna and swimming-pool, and lesser places for the lorry drivers and me. My thirst is infinite. I drink four bottles of orange juice before having a shower, swallowing half the water trickling down my face, then two beers before supper and a bowl of garlic soup, the wettest thing on the menu, with a bottle of wine. The meal isn't spoilt by the flies, or the electioneering on TV, or the bad-tempered waiter who keeps a cigarette burning in an ashtray near me, or the pork chop I order, remembering the huge pigs I saw copulating somewhere today, that turns out to be beef. I'm too tired even to groan when the TV announces that the serial of *Don Quixote* is to be repeated – an animated cartoon in thirty-five episodes that cost 340 million pesetas and has been shown in fifty countries, with special success in China.

I have walked only twenty-five kilometres today, but it seems a hundred.

TWENTY-FOUR

Childhood was finished. I had no parents. From now on I would be this – whatever I was – for all my life and to emphasize it, a week after my mother's funeral, I had my first orgasm. It was a joy I hadn't imagined, more thrilling than anything the housemaster had warned me about: the shock among the bigger boys, perhaps, that my mother had predicted. Watching my virility shoot out in happy rhythmic jets, not caring about the waste, I felt the promise it held for the years ahead. This would go on for ever, and nobody could take it from me.

A psychotherapist, a perceptive woman, once suggested that my type-writer was a masturbatory object. We lived in Islington, Deirdre and I with our three children, and I had built a hut at the end of the garden, for writing in. It was an intense pleasure each morning to go down there and join my characters – my friends – where I had left them in typescript last night. They had their own lives too, independent of me, and secrets they kept from me, though I could try to control them while we were together. But nobody else would meet them till the book was finished, or know what was going on in my hut. Sometimes I wished I could share it, but it was too precious and fragile, it might fall to pieces if I let go of it – even if I let Deirdre handle it, though I knew how gentle she could be. It had to be solitary and sometimes, to prove the psychotherapist's point, it became almost physical. To find myself laughing as I write, or crying, or with an erection, has always been one of the joys of it.

Back at school I bicycled out into the country with other boys to enjoy what we had discovered about ourselves, fumbling between guilt and laughter. My fictitious character Paul (we are unrelated, beyond a vague dependence on each other, though he was conceived in that garden hut), meeting an old school friend long afterwards, burrows anxiously into his eyes, 'searching for a distant summer afternoon, for a corner of a school dormitory, for a memory of muddled ecstasy and shame'. I'm not sure what Paul so badly wants to be buried in mutual silence, he doesn't describe it, but at Winchester it was dangerous and each year one or two boys were expelled for being caught. They left 'under a cloud' which, whether no bigger than a boy's hand or an eruptive cock, was a poor euphemism for this bright activity. It was something to revel in, radical and alive, better than illicit cigarettes or pubs, and free. For me the significance matched the fun: I didn't need a father now, I could be one myself, though it was twenty years before I was.

Chamber music was another new delight, also with a promise for the future. In her Sussex home, which was now mine, Aunt Margy arranged Brandenburg concertos, trios, quartets, with a flute part for me: she was the first person to treat me as anything but a child. When I wasn't playing, I listened to the others in string quartets – it would always be a regret that I couldn't play in one myself. (I spent a happy Christmas, the last before I got married, alone in a London flat with records and the score of Beethoven's last quartets: the most abstract art, telling more about the vivifying agony, the impossible but exultant hopes – the quixotic truth of life – than anything I know.)

In my one success at school I won the Spanish prize, a fifteen-shilling war savings certificate, and had my first encounter with Don Quixote. The Spanish teacher, a myopic clergyman who had once been a great cricketer, inspired the class with a faintly lunatic, sideways look at life. Before the war he had taken his boys each summer to Spain where he encouraged them to pursue their adolescent fantasies, and even in war-time he pointed to a fresh angle on the monotonous conventions of school. Each of us was absolute, he suggested, and there was no harm in being at odds with the world. The secret was to live on our own faith, in pursuit of our particular mania; to let nothing outside us destroy or even tarnish the single axis within us, round which events revolved; to know that, in prosperity or adversity, the answer was in oneself. It was a stoic message, straight from Spain. 'There is no other I in the world,' Don Quixote said.

Otherwise the last two years at Winchester brought more freedom but no glory. I forged the headmaster's signature on a pass to London and cheated over sports tests, running and jumping and throwing a cricket ball, which I couldn't do. I might have escaped games altogether because of asthma, but I kept quiet about it, trying to live down the delicate child in me even if it meant running in the appalling annual steeplechase. Another boy in my house suffered far more seriously – less secretly too: he wasn't ashamed of his pigeon chest which was so bad that nobody noticed mine. (He became a stockbroker and died after an asthma attack in the London underground.) On my eighteenth birthday in 1944 I would be liable for call-up into the services or down the coalmines, though if I admitted to being asthmatic I would be exempt. But nothing could be worse than the shame of being unfit. I volunteered for the navy in time to avoid the army or the mines, and lied my way through the medical. It wasn't heroism.

The war went on, becoming less dangerous each month. We were lectured to by famous men who told us what a great defeat Germany and Japan were in for: Mountbatten who had looked better in a film played by Noel Coward on his sinking ship, Montgomery whose son was in the school, Wavell who was an old boy, a fleet air arm pilot who had torpedoed a battleship, an infantry officer who had won the Victoria Cross in a raid behind enemy lines. We cheered them for their immodesty and stamped our feet, but less loudly for the Czech leader Masaryk, who spoke of peace. Most of us were destined for the guards or the commandos and had no time for other people's patriotism. But the drama – crowding round the radio to hear Churchill, scuttling down to the air raid shelter – was passing. At night drunk soldiers rolled past our house and in the morning we found a wallet dropped in the street. We handed the money and army paybook to the housemaster, but kept the condoms for ourselves.

I bicycled into the country with friends, not always for love, sometimes with two ferrets in a sack. We stood for hours at the edge of a wood, waiting for the rumble of animals underground and the sudden bolt of a rabbit into a net; then broke its neck, slit out its guts for the ferrets and slung it on our handlebars by its hamstrung legs to be sold in the town, a shilling a rabbit. Once, lying in a field, bored with sending ferrets down rabbit holes, Tony and I put one up Nigel's trouser leg, expecting it to come down the other side. But it got lost or tangled and bit the juicy thing blocking its way. Nigel screamed and dropped his trousers, the ferret jumped out and we saw the spurt of blood from four small tooth holes puncturing the smooth knob left by circumcision.

Years later I heard that Nigel was working in an airline office off Piccadilly, and went in to call on him. He was behind a desk with timetables and seating plans and a sleek model airliner flying past his telephone. But I was a stranger to him, another customer.

110

'Good morning, sir,' he said. 'Can I help you?'

I might have been inquiring about a ticket to Johannesburg or a holiday in the Bahamas. Didn't he remember me?

'I don't think so, sir, I'm sorry – have you been in here before?'

In a moment it would come back: an afternoon during the war, a ferret up his trousers. Perhaps there were four little tooth scars still. He wore a wedding ring, I saw.

The telephone on his desk rang and he picked it up. 'Excuse me a moment, sir,' he said to me, his hand over the mouthpiece, 'and I'll be with you.'

But I left him talking and went out into Piccadilly.

I thought of Nigel – or of what the ferret had done to him – long afterwards in Vietnam. In Hanoi, the capital of the North, I noticed unfamiliar signs on myself, a circlet of small blemishes on the place where he had been bitten. In that austere Marxist state, to reveal my decadent western morals and ask for help was more than I could face. I tried to remember the films shown to warn me as a young sailor in the navy, to frighten me with the price of frailty, but this fitted none of those vivid symptoms. Nor did it look too serious, and I felt safe as long as the damage didn't spread.

In a few weeks I reached Saigon, capital of the licentious South where my problem might be viewed less harshly, and took it to a French doctor who laughed: 'Ah, it's nothing.' While his nurse, a lovely Vietnamese, held the afflicted part in her fingers he injected a local anaesthetic; then, between them, they delicately removed the marks. 'We call it *crête de coq*,' he said, and left the nurse to bandage me.

Poor Nigel, after the ferret's mouthwork, never received such gentle care from Tony and me.

Tony, who introduced me to mountains as well as to T. S. Eliot, also took me sailing. The school kept an old dinghy on the river Hamble, now a base for torpedo boats and landing craft preparing for the invasion of France. We bicycled hard for an hour, had two hours' sailing through the crowded naval moorings and bicycled back, with time for a few beers in a pub before school supper. It was better than cricket. Then one June afternoon the river was empty: the fleet had crossed the Channel, the invasion had begun.

Later Tony took me rock-climbing in Wales. At first I was terrified, but it lit a love of climbing that shone for twenty years and could never quite be put out. It was ironic, and sad for Winchester, that these things were started by another boy, not a master. Tony became a medical student in London, where I went to see him in a Bloomsbury flat. Books, bottles, stethoscopes, ice axes, a skeleton, a pile of shillings for the gas meter, a bath in the kitchen full of dishes, an outside lavatory – the picture of transient, immoderate Bohemianism touched me as sharply as Eliot and the mountains. At one moment a girl walked through the room in nothing but her bra and pants, more wonderful than anything. I hardly knew whether to cheer or look away, and only blushed.

Our friendship faded and Tony ended up as a consultant pathologist in Sussex with a fox-hunting wife, keener on horses than poetry, and eventually a churchwarden. But he was useful once when I was writing a novel about two twin brothers, Geoffrey and Tom, in a house somewhere on the wild Atlantic coast of Britain – in Cornwall perhaps, where I wrote some of the book, or Pembrokeshire or on the west coast of Ireland.

One night the brothers sail far out to sea in their boat to watch an eclipse of the moon. Next day Tom comes back alone, to tell Geoffrey's wife Cleo that there was an accident in the dark. Geoffrey's body is washed ashore and at the inquest a pathologist gives evidence of his post mortem.

The novel was filmed and the director, checking my pathology, found I had got it right.

I went to watch the filming, flattered that someone had thought enough of my book to take it into another dimension. I was curious too. As well as a writer a novel needs a reader, who also has to do some work, and now I could join him at it. So far from wanting to interfere with the script I was happy to see what a stranger did with it – to watch him indulge his private view.

I thought I was remote from it now, distanced by time and two more novels I had written since. When I have finished a book it really is the end – it stops growing and I move on to the next. I don't feel possessive about it any more. I forget it, I often can't remember my characters' names and have to be reminded. If I look at it again, I'm surprised to find things I didn't know I had written.

But one can't write about people, live with them obsessively for months, without loving them. This was like going back to an old affair. Cleo, Geoffrey's wife, was a woman in my past and I was excited, though disturbed, to see her again. Would she be the Cleo I remembered? Would I still love her? But I was reassured. And I got the feeling that she was happy too – not the actress but the real Cleo behind her.

The director specified the coast of Scotland, though I had left it vague. But my dialogue was almost unchanged and it was gratifying to hear words I had once dragged from myself, in agony or delight, being quoted by actors with such facility. They were still actors, not my characters – whose behaviour and feelings I knew, if not their faces – and the location was utterly unlike my own picture of the coast and house, but I didn't complain. I was entering a reader's mind and found it so weirdly moving that I had to ask the director, if he caught me in tears at the sight of my forgotten child being coaxed into another life, not to draw the film crew's attention.

He wanted to know if the characters were based on real people. It was the wrong question. 'Real people are crowded out by imaginary ones,' Graham Greene has said. 'Real people would wreck the design. The characters in my novels are an amalgam of bits of real people; one takes isolated traits from many; they are fused by the heat of the unconscious. Real people are too limiting.' My characters were real already, before I began writing about them. The true question was – what was it like to be them? I had tried to find out and put it into words. If anything they were based on myself: myself as Tom, as Geoffrey, even as Cleo and her small boy. All of them were me, but transmuted.

I told the director about the Chinese poet who was asked the secret of writing a poem about a waterfall, or a bamboo. First, he said, you must read all you can about bamboos, even if it takes ten years. Then sit down and watch a bamboo closely, for another ten years. Then become a bamboo, for ten more. Then with luck you might write a passable poem about a bamboo – but it would be a beginner's job.

The sense of remoteness returned when I watched the finished film. This was a story, independent of me and waiting out there in some infinite reservoir of stories, which I had taken to make my novel. Kingsley Amis has described the feeling: 'It does encourage the view, even in a reasonably unromantic person like me, that the novel all exists somewhere already, and that you are uncovering the bits.' The film was another man's version of the story and he was welcome to treat it another way – to uncover different bits.

Actually his version was clearer than mine, to suit the camera's precision – or its limitations – instead of the multiple possibilities of words.

In the book Tom says at the inquest that Geoffrey, during the eclipse, got knocked overboard by the boom as the boat gybed and though he did his best to save him, searching the sea till dawn, he saw no sign of his brother. But he is plagued by a persistent dream that comes to him. In it, Geoffrey falls overboard and struggles in the sea, shouting, trying to swim but dragged down by oilskins and seaboots. Tom stands up, pulls the tiller off the rudder and hits his brother's fingers as they grab the boat. Then he hits him on the head, again and again. Geoffrey swallows and sinks and comes up, and Tom hits him once more, a crack that smashes the skull. He puts the tiller back on the rudder and sails home alone, leaving his brother to drown.

The dream is as valid as the truth, no less real for being a dream. Accident or murder – it hardly matters. Geoffrey fell overboard or was pushed, he was knocked unconscious by the boom as he fell or was battered on the head with the tiller, he sank before Tom could do anything or was deliberately abandoned: they are the same in the end. At one level, deep in the darkness of the night – in the middle of the eclipse – the dream supplants the truth. It *is* the truth, for all the difference there is.

'One shouldn't underestimate the element of choice,' the clever psychotherapist told me when I was making excuses for the vagaries of my life. In this case I chose to make no choice. Like Tom I was in doubt myself what happened, but unlike the film director I didn't want to know. It was enough that consciously or not (I couldn't even decide about that) Tom wanted Geoffrey dead because Geoffrey was a terrible man and was destroying his wife, whom Tom loved. It was psychological, if not actual, murder, and I was content to leave it ambiguous, for the reader to settle; and as a reader the director made up his mind. Though he seemed to share my uncertainty by having a single actor play both twin brothers, one with a moustache and one without, he made Tom firmly the murderer of Geoffrey.

The same with the end: the director had clearly had trouble with it. I was glad – so had I. It's obvious from the beginning that Tom is going to end up in bed with Cleo. It's corny, and too neat. I had to re-write it several times, trying to suggest something else to follow – something dark, glowering, a threat in the mood of the last pages. The eclipse of the moon isn't the only one, and when the shadow passed nothing is the same as it was before. It's a happy ending – but not quite.

I couldn't tell the director anything about the book that I hadn't said in it, except that life is like that – open-ended, unresolved. For him, and his cinema audience, that wasn't good enough: he couldn't get away with my untidiness. And though I regretted his shifts of emphasis, minor omissions and insertions – why leave out that and put this in? – I could applaud his clear-mindedness and was relieved to have decisions taken from my hands. Watching the film I was reminded of the book, which was a pleasure. But the writer in me reserved a small protest: I had meant it the way it was, being the man I am.

'I know who I am,' Don Quixote said. Self-knowledge, in that vividly human being, matched the self-delusion.

In me the man I would be, or what I could see of him during my last year at school, wasn't clear. Other boys had parents to guide them into life but I was independent now, which gave me a sense of maturity, treacherously false. There was nobody who would show me what to become, and briefly I fooled myself with dreams. In the holidays, cantering round a field on someone's pony, I was destined for the Canadian mounted police with a red tunic and a gun in my holster, till I began to wheeze with asthma. I read Cronin's novel *The Citadel* and was set to become a doctor, there was nothing else, till I went once to sit in the gallery at the House of Commons and knew I would be a member of parliament.

At times I did consult my dead parents, but they weren't much help. My father, in my mind, was disappointed that I wasn't a scientist like many of the ancestors or heading for an acceptable profession. My mother had sometimes tried to excite me with 'business' or the 'civil service', but had soon given up. Neither of them would tell me what they thought of me and, guessing what they would say, I didn't ask. On leaving school I would go into the navy, which was a temporary answer. I might even stay in it, not for the life of routine and discipline but because of a pull from the sea less vague than from elsewhere. I wasn't in danger of being killed – the war was nearly over – though at least it would save me from the next decision. Death has always been an alternative.

Beyond being what I already was – myself – I could see nothing. And I expected nothing, which would become a lifetime habit: to take little for granted. Friends, for instance: I have been surprised as well as pleased when someone, by seeking me out or writing to me or making an unsolicited gesture, shows that he – or she – is a friend.

Winchester, often blamed for turning out its sons in one mould, failed to form me into anything it could be proud of. There was only a handful of teachers, including the Spanish one, who inspired me enough to make me still grateful. Another was a saintly old missionary who admitted to preferring Zulus to English schoolboys, who introduced me to Browning – 'What's become of Waring, since he gave us all the slip?' – and opened the possibility of escape, wandering and perhaps vanishing enigmatically, only to be glimpsed years later in some oriental seaport. Most of the rest remain as shadows haunting those five years, though a few are too unshadowy. One of them, foxy-tempered with a moustache and clenched teeth, stood behind my desk and swiped at my head with the corners of his gown, whirling them like slings and cracking them on my ears till I gave the history answer he wanted. Another, proud of having been a major in the trenches in the First World War, for whom everything modern was a betrayal of the soldiers killed, turned apoplectic and sent me out of the room when I suggested learning a passage from *The Waste Land* instead of Kipling. (He was known to snatch off a boy's straw hat and stamp on it to vent his rage, which could mean a beating for being hatless.) Nobody showed me the beauty of the place, which I only saw when I went back afterwards.

I learnt to play the flute but it was a lifetime before I was told, by a girl who put mine to her lips, that a one-eyed flute is another word for phallus. I was very ignorant. I didn't even know which way up a man and woman usually copulate, and didn't find out for another year. When I was a midshipman in Singapore a Japanese prisoner, overcome with humiliation, pulled out his silk handkerchief and gave it to me. On it was a vivid picture of the act. I was amazed.

My only school contemporary to become a writer is the novelist Thomas Hinde – not the name he had there, as if to make clear that the boy I remember in a football match or doing stylish things in the gym, watching the world with a sideways smile, wasn't him at all. Winchester may be grateful for his pseudonym. He wrote once that the proper subject for a book is the area of life that seems most taboo, and anything less painful must be rejected: 'Ultimately some part of a writer's character must be both ruthless and absurdly optimistic. Against all the odds, often against normal rules of decent behaviour, he must believe that his book is important and that no pained aunts or injured parents matter as much.' It seems a quixotic opinion, unlikely to be blessed by a school with the pious motto, 'Manners makyth man'. But a writer's job can mean trampling on other people and I have sometimes thought I might be a better one if I cared less about the damage.

The old boys we were expected to revere were cabinet ministers, bishops, judges, generals, men of Whitehall and the Empire – men of power. It was implied that all the ones inscribed on the chapel door, killed in action soon after leaving, would have reached the top of one of the great professions: conservatives without exception, naturally. Socialist old boys like Stafford Cripps and Hugh Gaitskell were treated as aberrations, more unfortunate than significant. Something had gone wrong since they left school – nothing that Winchester could be blamed for. The same with Oswald Mosley: he must have a flaw in him, slightly funny but not really dangerous, which nobody had spotted when he was at school, otherwise it would have been beaten out of him.

Eccentricity – quixotism – was quietly forgotten, even among heroes. Years afterwards I heard of the young Winchester scholar, a poet and communist, who in 1944 – during my last term there – parachuted into German-occupied Bulgaria and joined the resistance fighters. With twelve others he was captured and given a mock trial at which he calmly smoked his pipe, leaning against a pillar. Called to defend himself, he argued in fluent Bulgarian that the war was something much deeper than a struggle of nation against nation. 'I am ready to die for freedom,' he told the court, and after the death sentence he led the condemned men to the castle for execution. It was said to be one of the most moving scenes in Bulgarian history. 'I give you the salute of freedom!' he called out before being shot, raising his fist; raising the spirits of his comrades too and of the spectators, who wept at such bravery as they watched. He was twenty-four. At the old school, if he had belonged to a smart regiment and been blown up in his tank at El Alamein, cheated of his career in the City or as a Tory MP, he might have been more honoured. But he spoilt things by dying for his ideals, rather suspect ones, and for *Bulgarians*.

At the end of my last term the housemaster called me into his study and told me that it was I, more than any other boy leaving, who made him uneasy. After the navy he wondered what the future would be, and couldn't tell. I wasn't good enough at the flute to be a musician. I didn't fit into any of his regular slots. It worried him and he made me feel it should worry me too, but he had nothing to suggest. He could only urge me to be the man my mother would have wished, which left me in the dark.

But I felt flattered that he cared, and that I didn't belong to the obvious old boys' world, and that it left me to myself, whoever that might be – my uncertain, possibly unique, usually feckless, sometimes

117

optimistic self, responsible to nobody's expectations but my own. He hadn't meant to please me, I was sure.

TWENTY-FIVE

May 22, Valdepeñas. In an old house round a covered courtyard, in a tall room with a tiled floor and a balcony over the narrow street, I read *Don Quixote*. Alone, I can think myself into the mad knight's adventures which, shared with someone else, would be difficult. 'Unfortunate is he,' Unamuno wrote in sympathy with his hero, 'who is sound of mind in solitude as well as in public.'

But I must go out into the town, defying my idleness, in search of experience or ideas. There are times when I have to keep telling myself I'm a writer, like a wavering believer who repeats the creed again and again for fear that somehow, unless he says the words, they will stop being true.

In the Plaza de España, surrounded on three sides by blue and white arcaded buildings and on the fourth by the stern and dominating and gravely splendid church of the Assumption, the liveliest bar is the 'Penalty', a haunt of football fans. Among photos of teams it offers frogs' legs and English lessons and three-day trips to the shrine of Fatima for ten thousand pesetas, bus and hotel and meals included. A pretty girl comes to sit next to me, and rehearsing my opening sentence I begin by offering a smile. But she doesn't return it, I'm not worth her scorn.

Next door is a funeral parlour, 'Our Lady of Consolation'. Round the corner in John Lennon Street the Manchegan wind blows the last blast of winter, and on a wall is written, 'We do not want more planes, we prefer the humming of the bees.'

Don Quixote would agree. At supper once he surprised the company with a perfectly sane speech on warfare, swallowing not a mouthful while the others ate. 'Have you considered, gentlemen, how far fewer

119

people profit from war than perish in it?' Even to a knight in armour, ready to fight injustice anywhere, the greatest good that man could wish for in this world was peace. But it grieved him to have chosen a soldier's life in such a terrible age: 'It was a blessed time before the invention of these hellish weapons . . .'

In La Mancha, cracked across the sky too often by the noise of jet fighters, there is still a preference for bees.

TWENTY-SIX

For a fortnight in September 1944, after my eighteenth birthday, I went to the Butlin's holiday camp at Skegness. It had been taken over by the navy, with an officer of the watch on the quarterdeck – a strip of tarmac inside the gate, to be saluted on crossing – and liberty boats down the road into town every evening. I was an ordinary seaman, given a number I can't forget, PJX/717014, and three shillings a day.

Other boys arriving in the same batch were assigned as stokers or cooks, clerks, radar operators, sick berth attendants or officers' stewards. I was thankful to be a real sailor in square-rig uniform with a black sash under my blue jean collar in mourning, they said, for Nelson. Later I began to think I was wrong: I might have learnt a useful trade.

It was a fortnight of kit issues and inoculations, lectures on tooth decay and venereal disease. Thanks to a virtue called OLQ – officer-like quality – I was labelled as a candidate for a commission. 'You've had all the advantages, haven't you?' I was told by an officer who had worked his way up from boy seaman on the lower deck to be first lieutenant of a submarine and resented this appointment to a holiday camp, selecting schoolboys for quick promotion. The remark stuck, like a sharp review.

Over the years the OLQ, with most things that went into my kitbag – oilskins and tropical white ducks, a bosun's whistle, a seaman's knife – got lost. All that is left is my naval 'hussif', housewife, with needles and thread which Deirdre sometimes uses.

Among the Butlin's chalets, between the roller-skating rink and paddling pool, past the ballroom and Ye Olde Pig and Whistle, my squad was drilled by a frightening gunner, Dusty Miller, who prided himself on being the only chief petty officer in the navy to hold a certificate of sanity, having once been mentally deficient. To his terrible screams I marched and doubled and sweated with the threat of seven days' Number Eleven punishment if my cap ribbon was tied wrongly or my lanyard wasn't white enough, wondering if I had joined the army after all. And under his hideous eye I learnt to fold my bell-bottom trousers and lash my hammock with seven half-hitches, so tightly that it would hold me up in the sea if my ship was sunk.

In 1963 I went back to Skegness as a Butlin's camper, to see if it was true – that I had been there before as an ordinary seaman – and found it unlikely. But Dusty Miller turns up again in a novel, the terror of a battleship with the loudest voice and foulest mouth on board, a mad gunner shouting through a gale at a squad of stupid sailors. And now the Dusty Miller of fiction, even nastier than the one at Skegness, is more believable. It is the original who has become unreal. Was there ever a man like that, drilling those trembling boys of eighteen – one of whom, just as improbably, had my name and number? I have a photograph of the squad in their new uniforms, arms all folded the same way, smiles all ordered for the camera by Dusty who is grinning maniacally in the centre. But it proves nothing, not even that the sailor on the left at the end of the front row is me.

From Skegness I went to a naval camp in Staffordshire, as far from the sea as possible, where I watched my friends go off at night to the whores of the Pottery towns; and to another at Torpoint in Cornwall, where I drilled on eight-inch guns from the First World War, and rowed twelve-oar cutters in the river Tamar, and got drunk on rough cider. Though it was the year of the atom bomb we were taught the points of a sail, the parts of a yardarm, the drill for exchanging topmasts with another man-of-war and how to tie a sheepshank. In the gym we were lined up, tallest forward, shortest aft, and paired off by height for a boxing match. Tall but thin and hopelessly unmuscular – an adolescent Don Quixote without his faith or courage – I was put with a heavyweight who laid me on the floor with his first punch. It never struck me that I could escape by pleading asthma. And anyway perhaps, I sometimes thought, it wasn't happening to me at all and soon I would wake from this unlikely dream.

At each stage the sailors without enough OLQ were strained off and sent to barracks somewhere, then to fight the war. I watched them pack their kitbags with embarrassment, almost pity, knowing that I should be envious. They were going to sea as proper seamen, not being kept for more training on the assumption of some phoney superiority. For

122

me, because of my school and accent if not my height and profile, life was to be postponed.

I was sent to an old cruiser at Rosyth. We patrolled the Firth of Forth, sometimes venturing into the North Sea, retreating behind May Island if anything showed up on the anti-submarine detector. On dark winter mornings, barefoot on the rolling ship, hungry for breakfast, we scrubbed the decks. 'Scrub forward! Scrub aft!' the petty officer yelled, throwing down more sand and soft soap for our brushes – for our frozen toes.

We washed the lavatories and steered the ship and weighed and dropped the anchors and kept look-out at the masthead. I had been rock-climbing and enjoyed going up a wire ladder to the crow's nest – too small to hold two of us, so one had to cling outside while the other climbed past. I blew a whistle down a tube, as they might have done at Trafalgar, and shouted, 'Masthead – bridge! Bearing red one-five, a fishing-boat!' In rough weather the crow's nest rolled beyond the ship's side. And away over there, sometimes, was the unknown coast of Scotland.

We peeled potatoes for the galley, we played tombola, the navy's only gambling game, we bought tobacco at half a crown a pound and wished we were old enough for a rum ration. Some of us were very sick, but I escaped. Off watch at night we smoked and wrote letters; and slung our hammocks, climbed into them and swung in unison under the deckhead, rocked by the ship – a unique pleasure. Often I had wet dreams and woke in stickiness, to tumble out into the winter dawn and scrub the decks again.

The ship was used for target practice by fleet air arm squadrons and once a plane failed to pull out of a dive, dropping into the sea close to us. Our crash-boat was launched to bring back the young pilot, the first dead man I had seen: a scarecrow with no frame, his trouser legs hanging limply over the gunwale, all bones broken.

'How did your father die?' the captain asked me in an interview. From his face when I told him (I never told my friends, it was too precious) I knew he would recommend me for a commission: I had the OLQ.

On Sundays we sang hymns on the quarterdeck 'for those in peril on the sea' and were dismissed with Nelson's last prayer. I hardly thought of any other life outside the ship, though in harbour, with a half-day's leave, I took the train across the Forth bridge to Edinburgh, to visit a cellist friend of Aunt Margy's. She borrowed a flute for me and we played sonatas in a Georgian house, tall and grey and icy. It was already dark at teatime – another lump of coal on the fire to toast the scones – and I was glad to get back to the cruiser's stuffy messdeck.

More than forty years later, with Deirdre who was working for a doctorate at Edinburgh university, I drank at a pub on the shore of the Firth of Forth, by the bridge. I could see a young sailor she had never known, at the masthead of an old cruiser, involuntarily ducking his head as they sailed under the bridge; or crossing it by train on his way to play Bach and Handel with a forgotten cellist.

TWENTY-SEVEN

May 23, Alcaraz. Long journeys have shortened as travelling becomes faster, and short journeys have disappeared. Don Quixote could ride all day and be sure of reaching an inn. Now there might be a bar after the same distance, but the hope of a bed or a meal is forlorn.

It was at a country inn, asleep on a rough bed in the loft, that Don Quixote dreamed he was fighting a giant. He stood up in his shirt, on his long thin hairy unwashed legs, and lashed out with his sword, drawing blood at every swipe and making a noise that brought the landlord up in alarm. The enemy was a row of wineskins hanging on the wall and the blood was the landlord's vintage, now flooding out across the floor. A bucket of cold water over him only woke the knight enough to show him what a victory he had won.

Sancho blathered over the lost wine, the other guests laughed, the landlord swore, his wife screamed, but his daughter kept quiet and even smiled: one person in the mob, a pretty girl, could feel compassion for Don Quixote.

Next day, fully awake, the knight's confidence was intact. 'I had the fiercest battle of my life,' he told Sancho. 'With one stroke, wham! I cut the giant's head off and the blood poured out like water.'

'More like red wine,' Sancho said. 'Your dead giant is a punctured wineskin and the blood is fifteen gallons from its guts, and the head you cut off . . .'

'Are you out of your mind, you fool?'

'Get up, and you'll see. And we'll have to pay for it.'

Faced with the evidence Don Quixote began to falter, resorting to silent scorn rather than being contradicted by the facts: 'I'll say no

125

more, in case I'm accused of lying. But time reveals everything and will explain it when we least expect it.'

Sancho persisted: 'I swear to God I'm right – look at the empty skins by your bed and the lake of wine across the room.'

'Sancho, you're an idiot. Enough said.' A shred of doubt was disturbing Don Quixote. Reason lay uneasily close below the surface madness.

I came here by bus a hundred kilometres east from Valdepeñas across the wonderfully coloured plain: bright greenery of vines, rust-red earth, sand-pale barley, dark trees. But this upland part of Spain, far from the coast and the moderating sea, has a breath of austerity, introspection, individualism. It is a land of mystics as well as conquistadors; a place made for the solitary.

A man works far out among the vines ('vineyard' is no more suitable than 'olive grove' for the vast acreages of Spain), hoeing or pruning, his motorbike propped under a tree. A man drives his tractor alone all day. In a deserted village a boy plays marbles against himself. Even an eagle seen from the bus window flies without a mate. But the people on board, like survivors on a raft, make the most of this chance of sociability, hailing new passengers at each village, catching up with news, exchanging family photos. They don't have time for the TV over the driver's head, showing a Hollywood thriller.

Alcaraz is a small decayed hill town at the edge of the plain, once prosperous, with signs of baroque grandeur, arcaded houses and two church towers leaning almost to kiss across the street. There are signs of restoration too, cranes and skips and cement mixers, probably for the sake of tourism. But the inhabitants seem mean and unfriendly, unlike the generous people of Valdepeñas. They have a sullen bitter look as the highway rolls past at the bottom of the hill, avoiding them. In the bars there are no *tapas*, little dishes of olives or fish or *chorizo* sausage with your drink, unless you ask.

Streets fall in steps from the plaza, too steep for cars. Old women of different shapes, some deformed with a hip or shoulder in not the usual place or a badly matched pair of legs, pad up and down in slippers. Two of them are white-washing a house. Their faces are not so much carved from olive wood as growing out of it.

I have seen a notice about the Sanctuary of Our Lady of Cortes, 'a place of spiritual and bodily peace', and decide to walk there in the evening, an hour or two over the foothills. A young man calls from the doorway of the last house and asks where I'm going. He is sorry I'm not French – he was born in France, he doesn't know where, and would like to meet another Frenchman.

I follow a track towards the two white towers of the Sanctuary, like horns above the trees on the far side of a valley. A shepherd with his hungry, diligent flock – bells ringing, sometimes a whistle from him – wishes me luck. In time I reach an ancient farm, a walled-in courtyard with huge wooden ox-yokes hanging in the archway, though no oxen have been seen for years, and a lamb bleating at me from a cart.

In the empty evening, standing in front of the ripening barley, an old man is startled from his deafness when I cough behind him and say, 'Buenas tardes!' Yes, he tells me, the path to the Sanctuary is down there, follow the hedge, cross the stream, climb through the trees. His wife comes from under an olive tree where she was stitching a pair of trousers and asks if I'm English. Once there was an English nun in the Sanctuary who used to walk over the valley to visit them – last year or the year before or perhaps two years ago: the past, like England, is too remote to be placed exactly.

I take the path, the old man shouting when I go wrong, across the valley and up the other side. Mostly, to reach this site of spiritual and bodily peace, I walk through rubbish – beer cans, broken glass, plastic, cardboard, metal. The gate is open and I walk in, but there is no appearance of sanctity. I enter the chapel where, in the darkness facing me, a figure in white is kneeling in silence: some solemn rite is in progress, an uninterruptible daily office of the nuns. I make a gesture of apology – can I come in? – but the figure doesn't flicker and I see it's made of wax, with a box in its hands for donations.

In the cloister there is nobody, of wax or flesh. Cells are ranged round the upper floor, but no sound comes from them, no female chanting or subdued voices in prayer or gossip. Over a wall there is a washing-line between two trees with nothing on it, no private nunnish garments, and beyond it a swimming-pool full of leaves and dirty water. Perhaps later in the summer there will be shrieks and splashing, with the novices ducking the mother superior. Or perhaps the Sanctuary is an illusion: something in oneself, to be invented if it's to be real.

At the end of the cloister I find a bar where two men are drinking gin and Coca Cola, watching football on TV. I have a beer, and walk back at sunset to Alcaraz where I have another beer and a dish of winkles, copying the man next to me, sucking the fish out of the shells, our eyes on the TV.

Madrid is playing Barcelona, and though Alcaraz is far from either there is no hope of a meal, hardly of a drink, till the end of the match. Children scamper up and down, babies are rocked in prams while their parents watch. An old woman, nearly bald and with a huge goitre under her chin like a punitive collar, looks less disapproving than perplexed: this is the life she might have had in a later generation, and perhaps been saved the goitre.

TWENTY-EIGHT

In early spring 1945 I went to a naval base on the seafront at Hove, in Sussex: once a lido with swimming-pool and ballroom, now the last stage in converting sailors into officers.

We drilled on the terrace above the beach and slept in the car park where the sea, in a storm, rolled down the ramp and flooded us. We were tested in morse and semaphore, navigation and seamanship; instructed in ship-handling with motor yachts, playing at being captain; watched by psychologists; checked for ruptures or pigeon toes, the pox or clap; measured by naval tailors for the uniforms that some of us would need. I played the last game of football in my life and one day – awkward in peaked cap and stiff white collar and eight brass buttons, uneasy at this infliction of a rank that I knew was false – I became a midshipman. My OLQ, or my pretence of it, had got me through.

Not much in the training survived though I have sometimes enjoyed, in sailing-boats, splicing a rope or plotting a course across a chart. My semaphore vanished – I couldn't now send even an SOS with flags – but the morse code lasted longer. At a cynical moment while writing a novel I sat in Israel – or anyway a man in the book did – listening on a small radio for a secret call sign from somewhere in the hostile Arab world outside. It wasn't what the navy intended: being taught the role of phoney officer, I learnt to masquerade as phoney spy. In time, against the sham reality of both, the fiction became the only truth.

Soon afterwards the war was over. When Germany surrendered I was at Sheerness, firing an anti-aircraft gun at a flying target over the Thames estuary, playing billiards in the wardroom at Chatham barracks, being saluted and called 'sir' by men twice my age. The navy stayed in harbour now and I chose to go to minesweepers, which still went to sea, clearing up the mess.

We practised on an old steam trawler, on the Firth of Forth again. Tired of putting out a sweep where there were no mines left, we put out the trawl: dragging it all day, winching it in, hoisting it up the mast, untying the net for the fish to spill out on desk, a treasure of flapping silver. The skipper came out of the wheelhouse to help with the gutting, and we ate cod fillets straight from the sea, fried in the galley on deck.

I went trout-fishing too, thanks to a lady who offered her loch to young officers; and walked over the Pentland hills on a summer Sunday, sweating in my doeskin uniform. It was a pleasant unbothered time. Another midshipman had a three-wheel car, with bicycle-thin tyres. The single back wheel would stick in the Edinburgh tramlines and we had to stop to lift it out, or helplessly follow the last tram the way we didn't want to go. Sometimes at a street junction the man with a lever changed the points for us.

Down an almost empty Prince's Street, on his election tour, Winston Churchill came driving in an open car. Was this the man who had beaten Hitler, the dark momentous voice growling to us on the radio at school? Was he even real? Victory had lost importance now and few people came to watch him pass. His face was plastered with make-up, his tired old V-sign was a stale joke, the cigar had gone out. Someone clapped, nobody cheered. 'Up the Labour!' a man shouted, and suddenly I knew that that was how I felt: treacherous to everything in my life so far. Churchill tried to smile, and his Clementine beside him turned away. Within a week he was defeated by the Labour landslide.

Next time he passed me he was in a coffin, coming down Fleet Street on a gun carriage. I held my one-year-old daughter on my shoulders, knowing she would remember nothing. 'Horse! Horse!' she cried – one of her few words.

I asked to be sent to the Far East where there was still a war, but the atom bombs were dropped before I left and Japan surrendered too. I wasn't surprised, I had always known I would escape the fighting, but there were still mines to be swept. I sailed in a cruiser and at sunset a week later, to my wonder, we entered the Grand Harbour at Malta, a fantasy of ringing bells and golden stone and coloured bum-boats lolloping out to sell us lace and fruit. I hadn't seen grapefruit for six years, it seemed a sin to eat them.

In the Suez Canal we passed a troopship bringing home prisoners of war: rows of men at the rail coming back from something unspeakable, jeering at us for having missed it. In the Red Sea an owl came to perch on the bridge and the officer of the watch sent me down to steer the ship in the 'lower conning tower' which took me half an hour to find, an armoured compartment somewhere below sea level, roasting hot; and I remembered the child who was once told that there was usually a death among the stokers. At Bombay, a stew of abject beggary and Buicks where young sailors went off to the street of cages full of whores and came back with disease and raw tattoos, I made myself ill with sunburn by the swimming-pool of the cricket club. Another midshipman – a well-fed tweed merchant, years later, in a Regent Street pub – added my four-hour watch to his own while I nursed my burns.

At Colombo, still blistered and peeling, I waited in the old Fort barracks for an appointment to a minesweeper. The navy was going home, the ceiling fans in the Grand Oriental Hotel revolved with effort, running down over the last gin fizzes of an empire. Some of us, too young to see how silly we were, too late to win the war, had a rickshaw race round the town.

There were arcaded streets with jewellers and American taxis and a smell of drains, sandalwood, dried fish; and a harbour full of ships from Malacca, Batavia, Shanghai (would I ever reach them? did they exist?); and a fleet of fishing canoes on the horizon, mere beetles with a delicate sail-wing to catch the onshore breeze, scuttling home at sunset after the daily monsoon downpour; and nothing to do but stand against the breakers that rolled three thousand miles from Africa or hitch-hike to Kandy to see the Buddha's tooth, while waiting for someone to tell me where to go.

In the end I left by train, through coconut and rubber plantations northwards to the ferry for India. Beggar women at the stations, with withered limbs, blank eyeballs, oozing sores, stretched out their whining septic fingers or held up their flyblown babies to my first-class window, reaching for my humanity. But I slammed the shutters down – I didn't cry or laugh, I only wished the train would move.

In the old quarantine camp at Mandapam on the edge of India I had a bearer to bring me morning tea and take my clothes to the dhobi boy. Pale gekko lizards whistled and snapped at insects on the thatched ceiling of the wardroom, where we drank pints of pressed lime juice to wash down the gin and peanuts, with little else to fill the days. Waiting was a naval habit. I wrote to Aunt Margy, too sententiously, that I longed to sit in a concert hall and listen to an orchestra tuning up. Sometimes we shot at vultures with old services rifles, but missed.

131

The captain was invited by a sporting raja to shoot a peacock, which we had curried for dinner. The commander, shrivelled by gin and the hopelessness of promotion, suddenly became a demon sailor and organized whaler races across the lagoon, shouting at his crew, cheating to win, before going back to the bar. On empty afternoons we sailed out to the reef or landed far down the infinite beach, to swim and throw coconuts at each other. Though this was teeming India, which I knew from *Kim* and *Rikki-tikki*, and I had bought a book on Hinduism to prepare for the multitudes and their mysteries, there was nobody in sight.

Once a big dhow sailed into the lagoon, a swan among our graceless minesweepers, a migrant of the monsoon trade from Africa and Arabia – ivory, rugs, brassware, tiles. Creaking in its huge blocks and tackle, leaking between its fibre-sown planks, it was beached against the palm trees for de-barnacling and tarring. The crew, hardly more than scraps of cotton and dark sinew, natives of nowhere but their wonderful ship, camped on the sand under its hull, coaxed fire out of some flotsam and brewed a blackened stewpot of something unimaginable.

At last I was appointed as Number Two – navigator and junior of three officers – on a BYMS, a wooden minesweeper built in America. We had a gun on the foredeck which nobody knew how to fire and high-speed engines which often broke down, but the temperamental iced water machine was kept going by the coxswain, a Yorkshireman who had spent thirty years in small ships and could fix most things with sailmaker's twine or a marline spike.

He fixed me quickly, without either. It was my duty to watch him draw the daily rum ration and mix it with two parts water, which he thought was an insult to the crew. Sometimes I had to inspect the messdeck where thirty men lived, beset with prickly heat and cockroaches, among broken ventilators and diesel fumes, often flooded in rough weather. Neat rum seemed the least concession. Besides, the coxswain could buy it from any sailor willing to sell his tot and hoard it to get drunk with the petty officer engineer. I didn't want to lose their favour.

The captain was a young butcher rescued by the war from the East End of London and promoted to lieutenant. He swore never to go back to the chopping block, but hoped for a job one day with a cold storage firm. Long afterwards, touring Sainsbury's for a magazine article, shivering in a warehouse of frozen turkeys but remembering him more warmly than anyone in the navy, I had a strong feeling that we were about to meet again. I wish we had.

The Number One was a year older than me, a Glasgow art student who was trying against the odds to grow a beard. He stopped smoking after a cigarette lighter scorched his few hairs and gave up drink in case it washed away the rest. He would become a commercial artist after being demobbed and drew cartoons on the wardroom table, the same figures a hundred times, two hundred, which he claimed would bring facility.

From Mandapam, with an old British coaster for mother ship, the flotilla sailed to Trincomalee, a superb harbour backed by the Sri Lanka forest; then across the Bay of Bengal to Penang, our base for months. Along the coasts of Burma and Malaya, among a million jungle-swamped islands, every little port had been mined – by the Allies to stop the Japanese supplying their army in the interior, by the Japanese to hinder the Allies. We had charts of the minefields, but mines dropped by aircraft or laid like fish's roe by a submarine or slipped overboard at night from a torpedo boat couldn't be fixed accurately, and anyway might drift. Most were magnetic mines, but we were small and built of wood, with degaussing wires round the hull to cancel our magnetism.

We worked in formation, towing long electric cables, often in tropical rain. Every five seconds we pumped a short pulse of current into the cables, strong enough to connect through the sea with the next ship's current and create a magnetic field between them. Any mine in the field was detonated.

We could only sweep by day, starting at dawn, keeping strict station with each other. If we got too close the magnetic field became dangerous, if we drifted apart it lost power. All day I stood on the bridge with the captain, checking the distance and bearing of the next ship, synchronizing our pulses, plotting a track through the minefield on the chart. At the end of each run we turned, dropped a buoy as marker and swept back.

We might sweep for hours in silence, then blow up a clutch of mines that threw lovely geysers into the sun, shaking the ship and bringing the engineers up on deck to watch. If a mine went up close astern I waited for the captain's nod that sent me down to tell the coxswain to write off another jar of rum, cracked in the lazaret where they were stored, to be distributed to the crew with a bottle for the wardroom.

At sunset we pulled the sweeps in. The cables, damaged by blast, were waterlogged and had to be drained and patched; or the winch had broken down, which meant man-hauling. With luck an evening downpour fell on the ship and we stripped on deck to soap and sluice ourselves, then wash our clothes, before anchoring off another unknown shore. We took the dinghy for a sail and explored the beach – some unbelievable place on the fringe of Asia, caught for a night of fireflies and forest noises but abandoned at dawn next day.

We cleared the channels of the Tenasserim archipelago, the tiny harbours and river mouths, the inlets of the Kra isthmus of Thailand. We lowered a steel box with an electric hammer inside to blow up acoustic mines; put out wire sweeps for contact mines, speeding in single file down a narrow passage between two islands; swept into Mergui one evening when the old pagoda gongs were ringing – or it may have been Moulmein or Ye or Tavoy or any of the others – and exploded six mines in front of the astonished town. After dark the people discovered our anchorage and came to barter the fish we had killed in exchange for tins of naval stew.

Back at Penang the crew, half with gonorrhœa from the last visit, went to the doctor for treatment before returning to the brothels. 'Get yourself laid,' the captain told me, going ashore to his Chinese girl, but I was terrified.

Among my charges – charts to be kept up to date, chronometer and sextant to be checked, food and tobacco and rum to be ordered, library books to be changed – was the ship's store of condoms, to be handed out to liberty men. I stuffed a packet into my hip pocket and braved a dance hall, but the first whore coming at me out of the crimson gloom, groping for my virginity, sent me back into the street in panic. I wandered round Penang, wondering where the captain had got his girl and what they were up to now, my white shorts bulging with lust and these awful things. Rather than smuggle them back into my store for some braver sailor's pleasure I threw them into the harbour, and went up to the bridge to mark the latest chart corrections. Anyway the captain's girl, from the photo in his cabin, looked very silly and not even pretty.

I was a sub-lieutenant now, and could take a sun sight and shoot the stars, whose names I liked – Betelgeuse, Rigol, Vega, Arcturus. Voyaging – laying a track across the chart, giving the quartermaster a course to steer, fixing our noon position, making a landfall, entering a new anchorage – was a seductive pleasure. We moved down to Singapore, sweeping into Port Swettenham and Malacca on the way. A line squall spanned the world from horizon to horizon, a huge bridge of cloud for us to sail under, ambushed by winds from all directions. A waterspout twisted into the tropical sky, electricity flickered and rumbled over the Sumatra mountains, my sunburnt skin fried in the Nivea cream Aunt Margy sent me. On the bridge at night I drank cocoa with the signalman as new constellations lifted from the south and the pole star sank astern.

I hated the navy, the hierarchy and bureaucracy, the repetition, the huge machine devoted to such futility and waste. But the sea and these East Indian places weren't the navy. Perhaps there was another way I could have them; and I teased myself with a thought that might be an answer to the future, or at least a postponement of it.

Plying between the ports where we had swept a channel, busy with their cargoes, steaming away to somewhere else, were the little ships of the Straits Shipping Company. They had tall funnels and awnings over the deck, sometimes a few passengers, a Chinese crew but British officers. It looked a romantic, independent life, more enticing than any career I had thought of. My housemaster's doubts had followed me: I fitted none of the usual slots but perhaps I would find my own, in a small coaster trading out of Singapore.

It was a dream, but not impossible. I could take my demob out here. I need never go home to face the aunts and wrestle with my parents' ghosts and start a profession which, if it existed, hadn't shown itself. My watch-keeping certificate and navigation would help towards a second mate's ticket, my OLQ was proved by the gold stripe on my uniform – I was halfway there.

I saw myself, forty years on, as one of the Company's most respected captains, nearing retirement, and would have been astonished to learn that instead I should be writing books in Suffolk. But memory can take an ironic turn; I have a clear picture, not of the twenty-year-old navigator I was in 1946 but of the weathered sea-dog, the Conrad character I would have become, sipping a sundowner on a veranda above some aromatic harbour, telling yarns of those years that didn't happen. The fantasy, which I never shed in the way that I grew out of my naval personality – and out of the OLQ, I hope – is more vivid than the young man who imagined it.

In the Singapore naval base teams of Japanese prisoners slaved at the toughest jobs and prostrated themselves in front of us in disgrace. I hitch-hiked over the Johore causeway and fifty miles up into Malaya, through immaculately ordered rubber trees. At Christmas I staggered to the foredeck and vomited a bottle of South African brandy over the side, the equatorial night revolving helplessly with my doubts and self-disgust.

We sailed for Borneo across the South China Sea and swept the harbours of Sarawak, Brunei, Labuan; then into the Sulu Sea, to the port of Sandakan, thick with jellyfish and the fate of thousands of Australians slaughtered there – we went ashore as if treading among their corpses. Further east on my charts were the exotic shapes of Celebes, the Moluccas, New Guinea, a chain of islands from here to the Pacific. In purple ink I marked the latest admiralty signal to mariners – an altered lighthouse, a missing buoy, a recent wreck – knowing that I should never stand waiting on the bridge for any of them to come up on the horizon.

The navy was disbanding. Unsmiling men of the regular service, wary of their future, were impatient to be rid of us amateurs and demobbing became a rush. A letter came from King's College, Cambridge, keeping a place for me next autumn, asking what I wanted to study. While trying to think of an answer, wondering if there was one, I was sent home in an aircraft carrier, its hangars converted into dormitories. Before going on board I bought a crimson silk dressing-gown with dragons on it.

Driving through a winter gale into the English Channel the huge ship, like an elephant, tossed aside the seas breaking over the flight deck and a young seaman saluted me: 'Enjoy yourself, sir – did you? Like me?' We had joined the navy together at Butlin's, but he had failed on OLQ. 'Was it worth it, sir – Nick?' he asked, somehow confident that he had had a better time on the lower deck. Instead of a dressing-gown, he was taking home a mongoose.

TWENTY-NINE

May 24, Alcaraz. There is no bus today, Sunday, so I must stay another night.

I get into a tangle over politics with a man who lets me share his plate of young broad beans, uncooked, at the bar. He works in a *huerta*, a vegetable garden, and asks about the British general election and the *Dama de Hierro*, the Iron Lady. He has read about a London demonstration where the crowds shouted '*Margarita fuera*, Maggie out!' and wants to know why she isn't admired at home as much as in Spain. I try to tell him what I think of her and catch myself fumbling for quixotic ideals – humility, perhaps, or liberalism – or anyway quotations.

In return he explains the spectrum of Spanish parties from ultra-blue to infra-red. But it's difficult to converse with someone whose Spanish isn't much more orthodox than mine and who makes no allowance for me. As soon as he hears my opening sentence he believes I'm fluent. We aren't helped by a battle raging between four men close to us, shouting in each other's faces with great force: the Spanish love to shout. They are fighting about the ownership of a house, I think.

Though the only hotel in Alcaraz is cheap enough, it provides the best dish of beans tossed in olive oil with bacon and the tastiest pork fillet I have had. But the peach I order for *postre*, as I should have known, comes in two halves out of a tin.

For the winy evenings, apart from *Don Quixote*, I have only Lorca who is wrong for La Mancha: too lyrical, not stark or austere enough for this blank landscape. But his own duality, the gaiety and darkness of his character, match the temperament of Spain, the *sol y sombra*, sun and shade, of the bullring. 'Oh Spain!' another writer, Galdós, sang: 'One half of thy face fiesta, the other misery.'

Another duality, equally Spanish but more universal, is Don Quixote's and Sancho Panza's. I see features of them both in myself, feeding the old dilemma. True and false are so mixed in experience, it's hard to be sure of reason. There seems to be a need for ambiguity and no escape from uncertainty, though a little comedy helps. I have dreamed of Dulcinea, knowing she exists only in my optimistic thoughts – the elusive woman, shadow of a shade – but I have also doubted if Sancho's wife and family are my own. The fantasy is real, and reality another illusion.

THIRTY

Cambridge in 1947 was full of majors and squadron-leaders back from the war, undergraduates for two years on a government grant. They had moustaches and wounds and medals, and often wives and babies. At twenty-one in my demob suit – too wide in the jacket, too short in the trousers – I was among the youngest and far from confident that I should be there at all. Everyone else had a purpose, a degree to be got and a career beyond it. Sometimes in that winter of austerity and rations, shivering in front of a gas fire with an essay to write or gorging on doughnuts to make up for college food, I caught sight of the second mate I never was, trading in a small cargo ship from one steamy port to the next.

This was the town of my childhood but there was another family, a Nobel physicist's, in our West Road house. Boldly I rang the bell, thinking of myself in those pre-war pre-pubic days, and gave my name. The great scientist and his wife weren't interested and told their children to show me round. Down in the cellar where I had once smashed a bottle of my father's whisky they pointed to the insults written by my sisters and me in candle-black on the ceiling, for them to find. Everything was half the size it had been, and my mother wasn't there.

Walking back through King's College fellows' garden I suddenly saw the Greek play she had taken me to as a child: the summer-house turned into a cave where the one-eyed Cyclops was blinded, and half-naked undergraduates acting sailors or goats on the lawn; and I remembered my perplexity, not just at the story but at feeling for the first time the intensity of sexual excitement. I wondered if my mother knew what was going on, either in the drama or inside my shorts.

At King's the porter touched his bowler hat and shook my hand, proud to meet my father's son. I was proud of nothing, except of being a victim of that summer afternoon seventeen years ago. A don helpfully told me that there were still bullet holes in the wall of my father's room, but I didn't go to look. I thought I might ask to see his ashes in the chapel crypt, and put it off, and never did.

In a black gown I bicycled to a weekly tutorial and a few lectures, and in a white surplice I went to chapel services. I practised my flute and played in college concerts, even once or twice as substitute in the university orchestra – it was something I could do quite well. With disreputable friends I drank a lot and in the summer we played croquet on the college lawn or punted up the river. After two years of this I should be a Cambridge BA, qualified for life. It was an unbelievable prospect. What life would it be, anyway?

At the end of my fourth term a friend, Dick, a rock-climber and the troubled lover of two women, decided to emigrate to South Africa. He bought an old army lorry and asked me to drive overland with him. On the way we would climb the Hoggar mountains in the Sahara.

It was an easy way out. Uncle George's family business, a leather company, had expanded to East Africa and he agreed to employ me there. One of his sons, my cousin and future boss, asked if it was wise to chuck away a degree into the desert, but I did it gladly. In Nairobi I could leave Dick to continue south, and present myself at the company's local office – they would pay me five hundred pounds a year.

We loaded up in Hampstead and drove through France, our heavy tyres singing on the tarmac. At the Spanish frontier, nearing midnight, the customs officers' eyes sparkled at our foolishness. Open that box. Unroll that tent. Why these big fuel tanks? And ice axes? And *armas de guerra*! I had bought an old rifle, Dick had a shotgun and pistol. They must be impounded.

Iron-shod boots rang through the chilly building, the winter came howling down from the Pyrenees, Franco watched sternly from the wall. Often in the bleak courtyard at the back, beyond barred windows, men must have been executed. A bottle of wine was produced and we pleaded for our weapons. Our road lay through mountains and jungles and swamps, with wild animals and wilder natives: if not for defence we would need to shoot for food. Another bottle came out. Well then, for the drive through Spain the guns must be sealed. The customs chief, who doubled as mayor, was also the village carpenter and in the small hours he knocked up a box, nailed it down, wired it and stamped it and sent us away.

140

We drove for a week down the Mediterranean coast, camping on limitless beaches, moonlit and empty, washed by phosphorescence. Tourism hadn't broken out yet, the roads were full of shell-holes from the Civil War. Oranges lay in a luscious carpet under the trees and our petrol poured across the road when a mule shied at us, upsetting a cart of fruit and puncturing the tank. Villagers collected to give advice, lighting cigarettes among the fumes.

We were hoisted aboard a ship for Tangier, then headed across the mountains, among eucalyptus and mimosa and wild lavender, and along the coast to Algiers. Egrets pecked among the goats, farmers in brown sackcloth ploughed between the stones with a mule and camel yoked together. 'You should visit the Sphinx,' someone said in a back-street bar, and for our pleasure two women with a giant dildo and some juicy noises performed their unenviable, exhaustive comedy. The Cambridge term was just beginning.

We turned south, making for Kano fifteen hundred miles away. Colonial farms and vineyards rolled over the hills, little grey monkeys scampered on the cliffs of a gorge, the tarmac ran out and we were in the desert. For a fortnight we drove over small sharp stones, or followed tyre tracks in the sand, or watched them vanish under a new sand-hill and had to drive a long way round to pick them up on the far side, or got bogged down in drifts. Water stretched in phantom lakes ahead, evaporating as we approached. In the oases mongrels scavenged round the bare baked houses and baggy-trousered French officers sipped their *pastis*.

We climbed one of the Hoggar mountains, a tower of rock in the dazzle of the desert with a view from the top of our little tent far below and the impossible Sahara beyond. 'Six hundred miles over there is Timbuktu,' Dick said, and an eagle flew out from the cliffs to sail round us.

The desert gave way to bush, where gazelles skipped and quail scurried and at sunset flocks of crested cranes, honking overhead, settled in the marshland behind the thorn trees. I tried to shoot a gazelle with my rifle but it sprang away unharmed, thank heaven. Then, pointing Dick's shotgun at a flight of geese, I killed one and at once regretted it: bringing down this lovely bird, now a mass of bloody feathers to be plucked, butchered, stewed and somehow swallowed.

From Kano we turned east, thankful to escape playing cricket at the club, but came back next day with both front springs broken. Then on again, in and out of empires – French Equatorial Africa, Belgian Congo, back into our own Uganda. At rivers the lorry, balanced on a raft of dugouts, was ferried across by Africans paddling to a drum, singing of these white men who should be tipped overboard for the crocodiles. Grass-skirted girls ran from their huts to cheer us as we passed, and we slept to the piercing ring of jungle insects, the wail of a distant animal, the too-close crack of a twig.

At Bangassou we found we had left our passports at Fort Archambault, six hundred miles back. There was no petrol, we were out of money, we settled down to wait in the government rest-house, made unwelcome by the Greek caretaker and his staff of convicts. An American Baptist missionary rescued us and lent us an empty house – a man tormented by traders who sold alcohol to the Africans, by witch doctors who kept a grip on their souls, by the Catholic fathers who offered salvation through a beautiful white Virgin instead of immersion in the river, by the difficulty of getting proper canned corn and steak from South Dakota for his family who wouldn't eat the local stuff, and now by us, English overlanders, for accepting his hospitality but not his invitation to sell our lorry and its contents for the benefit of his mission and sup, as he put it, with the Lord. We held out, as we had against cricket in Kano, and in three weeks our passports caught us up.

Dick wanted to climb in the Ruwenzori, the mountains of the moon, before the rains broke. When we got there the tracks were streams of mud, the lower valleys were hung with cloud and nothing was visible higher up – we were too late. But secretly I wasn't sorry. There were footsteps up there that I didn't want to follow. More than forty years ago my father had explored in those mountains and was the first to climb any of them. His name was on the map, pinned to the summit he had reached, and he might himself be somewhere up in those tropical mists. I couldn't face a meeting, I preferred to leave him there.

Camped beside the lorry, brewing tea and contemplating the invisible snows, we were puzzled by strange rumblings from behind the bushes. I went to look. It was a herd of elephants feasting on the prickly shoots, having trouble with their digestion.

Over the next three years, though I could never plunge my hand into a pile of warm dung and tell from the temperature how long ago the elephants had passed by, I saw plenty of them. Elephants and antelope and zebras by the thousand and toy giraffes from a giant child's Noah's ark, and the landscape they inhabited, the tawny plains with amazing trees and escarpments falling into the infinite Rift Valley and drifting hills that might be clouds and often an old volcano – it was a benumbing country, a sop for a reluctant businessman. Uncle George's company had branches throughout East Africa and in time I visited them all.

Uncle George, aged seventy when the Nairobi office opened, never went there but left the business to his sons and nephews. Our job was to buy hides and skins, mostly from the descendants of Arab slave traders, and ship them to tanneries in England and America. One of my cousins claimed to know more about goatskins than anyone in the world. He loved them and would stand for hours in a stifling warehouse – 'godown' was the quaint imperial word – holding them to the light, checking for scabs and scratches, seeing in each greasy, filthy, smelly skin a lady's shoe or her glacé kid handbag; stroking them as he would her thigh. Once, for a rich man who thought that a goat's scrotum would make a perfect lady's purse, he had tanned fifty of them – beautiful soft leather pouches in different colours.

I knew I could never catch his enthusiasm, and wondered if I might be happier handling coffee or cotton or diamonds. I heard of an Englishman living in a hut on the coast who caught turtles, strung them on his bicycle and pedalled down the beach to Mombasa, to ship them to Fortnum and Mason's for soup – it seemed a more African thing to be doing. Somewhere there was another life, as there always has been: the rumour, anyway, of something better not far away.

A man in the company had a pilot's licence, an excuse to hire a two-seater Auster and do business, as we called it, in Mombasa or Dar Es Salaam. My job was to crank the propeller by hand for take-off and read the map. Elephants could be teased, for diversion, by flying at treetop height and buzzing them into a stampede. Once we crossed to Zanzibar, climbing above the sea as high as the plane would go and breathing more freely at the point when, if the engine stopped, we could glide down to beach it on the other side. Following the railway up from the coast to Nairobi, panting for a drink, we dropped on the grass near Mack's Inn, then commandeered a gang of plate-layers to push us on their surveyor's truck to the pub – black men running coolie-fashion along the lines and two white men sitting under a big umbrella. The tiny nerve of guilt, though it improved the ride, was soon drowned in beer.

At Easter we flew to Lamu and landed on a strip of sand by the creek, taxiing through someone's cows to a jetty. Between banks of emerald mangroves, in a boat with a car engine needing constant mugs of seawater for the radiator, we were ferried to the island town. There, among white-gowned Arabs and Swahili urchins on the quay, an elderly Englishman with a stick and a black eye-patch shouted, 'How long have you come for?'

He was Petley, peppery owner of the hotel, anxious that we shouldn't overstay. The black patch was in memory of a wounded bull elephant that had once tossed him, trampled on him and knelt on his head – luckily the ground was soft. His arm was scarred and distorted by a hand-to-claw fight with a leopard that had nearly scalped him before he stuffed his fist down its throat and throttled it.

A fleet of dhows waited in the harbour for the monsoon to blow it back to Arabia. Traders from Oman with thin black beards and daggers in their robes stalked the narrow streets. Carved doorways glowed under the casuarinas. Two cannons pointed impotently from the district commissioner's lawn while above the fort, protected by almond trees and flamboyants, the sultan flew his scarlet flag. A blackboard outside the prison gave the score: fifty-one convicts, one debtor.

In his bar, part of an Arab house decorated with native pottery, carpets, jewellery hammered out of silver rupees and the skin of the leopard he had gagged, Petley pressed a spike into the glass ball in the neck of old soda bottles ('early Victorian, like me') for our whisky and tried to sell us an antique door ('make a lovely fireplace'), a model of a dhow, a dancing girl's belt hung with silver bells and tassles ('you'd rather have the dancing girl? – you're all the same these days'). He hadn't been back to England for thirty years ('they say it's changed') but he didn't want to hear about it. He was disgusted with us for buying nothing.

We walked along the beach, swam in the ocean, knocked down coconuts and drank the milk; had lunch of curry and fat Alfonso mangoes at Petley's hotel and met his old friend Coconut Charlie, who had been on Lamu even longer. 'D'you want to buy a plot of land?' Charlie asked.

But Petley dismissed it. He was impatient for us to go ('you couldn't sell a box of oranges to this lot') and lifted the black patch to stare at us with a sightless eye that had last focused on a wounded elephant.

We should have bought the land.

I sailed round Lake Victoria in a wood-fired steamboat. It had been shipped in pieces long ago from England, brought up from the coast by rail and assembled on the lake. As a white man I got a cabin and travelled in Edwardian style – a *bwana* looking down from the rail at the natives on deck. The lakeside ports were very pretty and I was being paid to enjoy them. 'Boy!' I called for a barefoot servant in fez and commerbund to bring a beer and peanuts. But I never forgave myself for this imperialist act. My father, in a more authentic period, would have done it better.

Living for a time in Mwanza, once a German colonial town and not yet spoiled by the British, I sent bales of skins by boat to Kisumu at the other end of the lake; and sometimes for a moment, in an airless sun-baked building, I can catch the peculiar sour flavour of sweat mixed with the stink of dried skins as the 'boys' in the godown, chanting while they worked, turned the handle of the baling press. I drove my Chevrolet pick-up, with a few Africans in the back to change a puncture or push me out of the mud, on collecting trips to northern Uganda, across Lake Albert to the western Nile province, close to the Sudan; and through the White Highlands where Englishmen lived more or less as they would in the Home Counties ('pure Haslemere,' a visitor from the London office muttered when I took him to a half-timbered hotel hung about with teapots and wrought iron and bits of taxidermy for local colour); and up into the northern frontier district of Kenya, a dusty scrubby country on the brink of Ethiopia and starvation, far from the settlers' lush properties.

I ended up, my last year in Africa, as manager of the company's tannery at Thika, thirty miles from Nairobi. For being Uncle George's nephew – perhaps for the last traces of OLQ, soon to wear off – I was put in charge of five white men, all older than myself, a Goan clerk, two French-speaking foremen from the Comoro Islands and two hundred Africans. The smell of leather-making, which once involved soaking skins in dog shit though now we used a synthetic, was sharpened by the climate; also by our glue plant, a stew of horns and hooves and pieces too putrefied for leather.

I stayed mostly in the office, walking through the factory once a day, feeling myself followed by resentful, mocking eyes. Sometimes there was a letter from London to answer, a sales report to sign, a telephone call from a Nairobi shoemaker complaining about the quality of our product. I couldn't be enthusiastic about profit and loss accounts, trial balances, the world skin market: a penny down on goats, twopence up on crocodiles. This wasn't my life but someone else's, passed to me for temporary keeping. I wrote articles and sent them to *Blackwood's*

Magazine and the *Field*, the proper places for stories from the Empire, among adverts for pipe tobacco and winter cruises: an escape from the falsity and boredom. Writing, though I didn't see it yet, was becoming the one reality.

A dog slept under my desk, a mixture of boxer, bulldog and bull terrier bought for ten shillings from a coffee farmer in the Thika club. It was normal, almost compulsory, to keep a dog but this one showed me I would never be a doggy man. The coffee farmer, a pillar of amateur dramatics whose wife doubled as leading lady and local abortionist, threw in a sack of dahlia bulbs as part of the deal. I gave them to my garden boy who planted them upside down.

I had a garden of bougainvillaea, plumbago, alamander, jasmine, with a mulberry tree, a mango orchard and a view down a path of canna lilies to a fountain crowned by Mount Kenya in the distance. The house had been built for a previous manager by Italian prisoners of war, a fine cedar-tiled stone bungalow that I shared with a colony of bats in the roof. My four Kikuyu servants – houseboy, garden boy, cook and kitchen toto – made the most of my domestic laxity. They dreaded a memsahib coming to live with me.

They were safe enough. Sometimes there was a woman in my bed, though sadly never a black one. Kenya Colony had a reputation for free love, an early version of permissiveness, with a mythology of scandals that brightened the suburbanism. That suited me. No longer the nervous midshipman of Penang I was only anxious that marriage should be put off. Though I was too late for the Happy Valley days, when men played cards in the club for each other's women who waited for their fate in old Ford box-bodies outside, and affairs were likely to end in murder, there were actresses in the Nairobi repertory theatre who, for the price of sitting to the end of one more *Importance of Being Earnest* or *French Without Tears* and supper in the only night club, would come home for breakfast. And the thriving game of adultery, more fun than bridge or golf or poker dice, was easy to learn.

The immorality of it all didn't, thank God, escape me. Not just the promiscuity, or my being boss over men who knew the job better than me, or my company house and car with four Africans to attend me, but my connivance as one of the white minority, arrogant and unimaginative, who ruled the Kenya people and used their country as a playground. I was participating in something I didn't believe in.

I did nothing about it, beyond learning a little Swahili to make life easier. I hardly protested one night after the club bar closed when the engineer from the tannery asked me to come with him to check that the watchman was on duty. We left the car, the engineer taking a *panga* from the boot and letting out his Dobermann dog – 'quiet, boy, quiet' – and walked softly up to the gate. There was a light in the watchman's hut, but the door was shut and we threw it open.

The watchman, a huge ex-corporal of the King's African Rifles in nothing but his underpants, got up from the floor. A woman, pulling a blanket round her in terror, crept into a corner. The Dobermann charged in, biting everything in reach. The engineer let loose a stream of mixed English and Swahili and with the point of his *panga* flicked the enormous watchman out into the night, the dog's teeth locked on his ankle. Then he pulled the woman to her feet and with a terrible crack on her head with the flat of his blade beat her down again. She whimpered into silence on the blanket – she was knocked out, if she was still alive.

'They've got very thick skulls,' the engineer said, back in the car. Perhaps he had seen me wince or perhaps, just possibly, he was trying to excuse himself. 'Not like us at all – their bones are different. It's something in the chemistry.'

Hypocrisy was beginning to tell on me. Who did I think I was? – helping this deplorable white man condemn a black man's behaviour when mine was no better. Conrad wrote that the white man's incursion into Africa isn't a pretty picture when you look into it too closely. And Graham Greene wrote, 'No one can adequately write of his own life without humility.'

A few nights later, astonishing myself, I went to an Old Boys' dinner. I had never worn the Winchester tie, I didn't even have one, not because it was made up of three such ugly colours but because I didn't want to be hailed by other Old Boys as one of them. The same with dinners. Since I left school a notice came annually, naming the guest speaker and asking me when I sent my cheque, wine extra, to say who I would like to sit next to. It was a painful thought, bringing back the dread of football or a beating.

But here in Kenya I was an Old Boy anyway. We white men were eternal prefects, keeping the blacks in their place. I couldn't guess how the local branch of the Winchester Society had found me out, but the invitation came like a summons and there was no escape. In my dinner jacket, thankful it wasn't pyjamas, I turned up at the Muthaiga Club,

Nairobi's most exclusive for the palest of the white, which I had never been inside. There were eighteen of us, none of whom I knew, in a private room. I was the youngest. All we had in common was a five-year chunk of our early lives spent within the same medieval walls.

Before the soup, as junior boy at the bottom of the table, I had to recite a long Latin grace. Luckily it was printed on the menu but I felt the others watching me, hoping I would make a slip so that they could howl for blood. The head boy at the top was Grogan, a famous pioneer who had once walked from Cape Town to Cairo and had bought land when Nairobi was only a railway station, and who was already commemorated in a suburb, Groganville. As a member of the Legislative Council, in a debate on African trouble-makers, he cried, 'Shoot 'em! Shoot the lot of 'em!' – as he must have cried fifty years earlier, faced with unruly younger boys, 'Beat 'em! Beat the lot of 'em!'

We sat down and began: When were you there? Which house were you in? Was it you who got the steeplechase record? Remember the Bobber? The Jacker? The Woofer? The Dicker? The Tout? The Bin? Been back recently?

The ancient Winchester language, more fluent for most of us than Swahili, came back effortlessly with the nicknames and legends and jokes. We were at school again, talking about this morning's class results or next Saturday's house match. Looking up the table, feeling the old alarm I got from senior boys – colonial and army officers, import-export agents, accountants, farmers, all becoming adolescent as the drink went down – I might have been only fifteen, wondering if I could get away with one and a half pages for my history essay or a plea of hay fever to avoid cricket; wondering too what I would have thought on being told that ten years later I would be manager of a tannery in Kenya.

When brandy and cigars were brought in, when Grogan had toasted William of Wykeham, our founder, and I had recited another Latin grace, when it was a struggle to forget what we had been once and remember what we were now, we stood up on our chairs and sang *Dulce Domum*, bluffing through six Latin verses from memory. It isn't a school song to glorify the place but a lament from a homesick boy and we sang with passion, nostalgic now for our boyhood, caring nothing for the club servants who stood round the room and watched. The drink was finished off, the chairs were piled to the side, we divided into teams and played Winchester's own version of football with a cushion round the table. Damage to club property was added to the bill: the effect on the servants was uncountable.

I felt I had been caught out, both as a schoolboy in some nightmare of the past and as myself, whoever I was behind this dinner jacket, this costume of managership and Old Boyism. I was glad to stagger out of the Muthaiga Club and look for my car.

I had driven back to Thika so often in the middle of the night, tired and drunk, that I thought I could always do it – the car would get me home. But within a mile I had gone off the road and down a bank, and overturned near a swamp. I lay upside down, blood coming from my forehead, sobering up while the chorus of *Dulce Domum* throbbed round my head; also the ringing of bullfrogs – I was in Africa after all.

It was a white man, thank God, but not an Old Boy, who pulled me out. He introduced himself: 'My name's Mungo Park.'

'Oh yes?' I laughed, half sobered up, half in shock. 'That makes me Stanley, I presume.'

He repeated it: 'Mungo Park.'

'That's ridiculous – he was an explorer,' I said, ungratefully. 'In West Africa. Murdered by the natives a hundred years ago, two hundred . . .' Perhaps the nightmare was still going on.

'I'm sorry, but it's true.' He took me to the European hospital to be bandaged. 'Funny way to end a dinner party, wasn't it? But count yourself lucky you weren't at Eton. They had theirs at the Muthaiga too and picked the night the long rains broke – three inches in an hour. They treated it like the Thames, standing up on the club sofas and punting with umbrellas down the road.' He began singing: 'So we'll swing, swing together . . . But I'd better tell the police before they find your car.'

A police officer came and took the details: 'A reunion, was it? I know the sort of thing – we have them in the freemasons. We like to think we do it with less noise, but I often wonder.' He told a sergeant to take me home to Thika in a police van: 'Got to help our own, haven't we? One of these days we'll be up against the wall. Hang together, before the crunch comes. Or we'll hang separately.'

My own crunch was almost on me, a private version of the bigger one. Anyway, if it came to hanging – the fate that Potts had escaped – I would rather do it my own way, alone.

I was told, but didn't much care, that Kenya was simmering. In the

Kikuyu country all round Thika a man who called himself Jomo Kenyatta was stirring things up. He had lived in London, visited Moscow, picked up dangerous ideas. He even had a white wife – poor woman. It could turn nasty if we didn't watch out. Like woodsmoke coming out of the villages or the sound of tribal drums the whisper of *Uhuru*, freedom, reached us if we bothered to listen.

'They won't be ready for it in a hundred years,' we told each other in the Thika club, for comfort. But the government was dithering, they seemed to be on the side of the Africans: 'They bring them down from the trees and cut their tails off – next thing they'll be handing over the country to them.'

Africans were getting uppish. The worst were the detribalized ones who had forgotten their origins. We admired the Masai for wearing no clothes and carrying spears and being too proud to copy white men. Some of the others tried to behave like black Englishmen. One drove up to the tannery in a big new Vauxhall with zebra skins on the seats, in a suit and tie, smoking a Dunhill pipe, and offering a bigger load of cow hides than any Arab had ever brought us. He gave his price and wouldn't be beaten down. Probably he was richer than us six white men together – we told each other that he was absurd. But secretly, knowing that my own *Uhuru* was getting close, I wished him luck.

They were the last days of the Empire, the end of the pantomime. It wasn't very impressive – a provincial show put on by a touring company of second-rate actors glad of a job. For reassurance Princess Elizabeth and Prince Philip drove past on their way to Treetops Hotel to watch for wild animals, and we gave the tannery workers the afternoon off, to line the road and cheer. 'With monkeys like this lot,' the factory engineer joked, 'who wants Treetops?' Two days later, cutting short her holiday and returning in a hurry, Elizabeth was Queen.

'What's the betting? – Jomo for King!' the club secretary's wife said. She was a rarity in Thika, almost an anti-imperialist.

'Over my dead body,' her husband told her.

'Very likely,' she said.

Misbehaviour was catching up on me: too much smoking, drinking, adultery. I was harbouring a tapeworm as well as a bad conscience. Sometimes I pretended to myself that I was waiting for something to happen, someone to come, but I knew I was only waiting for myself. In the end it was asthma, my friendly old enemy, that freed me. A Nairobi doctor filled my lungs to take X-rays, muttered something about my expectation of life and said I should go to a chest hospital in London.

I decided I wouldn't come back. I was getting old, I would soon be twenty-five, a good age to retire. I would write to Uncle George and take back my contributions to the Scottish Widows, an insurance scheme to give me a pension in forty years' time. I had never liked the Scottish Widows – I saw them in the far distance, a clutch of auntish women in tweeds, grown fat and rich on what had been deducted from my salary, waiting grudgingly to repay it if ever I reached them. Well, I never would.

I gave a party in my Thika house, borrowing the band from the Nairobi night club. A woman, pregnant by the wrong man and doctored by the coffee farmer's wife, aborted in my bathroom but her husband wouldn't take her home yet, he was enjoying himself. Besides, she had brought it on herself.

Next morning my houseboy, a one-eyed Kikuyu, was drunk. He had finished up the bottles and was trying to stack the glasses, missing them in his half-blindness, knocking them to the floor, sweeping the pieces into a heap with his bare feet. I had never sacked anyone in my life and didn't want to start on him but, like me, he knew he had to go. Giggling helplessly he zigzagged down the road and never came back. He had stolen a pair of my father's cufflinks. Though I wouldn't have given them away I was relieved to be rid of them, especially to a one-eyed African.

I thought of him thirty years later in Monrovia, capital of Liberia. One night I had supper in a restaurant run by an ex-dancer, Julia, the survivor from a Paris troupe that had been stranded there when France fell in World War Two. I came out into a tropical storm and began the dash to my flea-bitten Lebanese hotel. Rain hammered like gravel on the tin roofs and guttered into the dark streets. Torrents spewed from the drains, rivers swept between the shops. Cars lurched among the potholes, people shouted and ran, and I dodged from one shelter to the next, avoiding the worst floods. An enormous friendly African came splashing out of the night to greet me: 'Hi, mister! How ya doing?' – pumping my hand up and down in the excitement of the storm. 'Nice to meet ya, mister, nice to meet ya!' He laughed and did a little dance with me among the puddles, and let go and vanished. My watch strap was hanging loose on my wrist – the watch had gone, leaving a drop of blood on the skin. It was beautifully done, and quite painless. I didn't mind the loss, I was too full of admiration – I only wanted him to come back and show me how he had done it.

Before leaving Kenya in 1952, in a Nairobi shop, I met a senior colonial officer, a man I hardly knew but liked. We exchanged news. I was giving up my business career and he was starting as secretary to the new governor. It gave him an idea: would I be his assistant? 'Nothing very strenuous – just another flunkey at Government House. A different face for His Excellency to look at. Have dinner with him sometimes, when I want to escape, and let him talk to you.'

I was grateful to him – later he became governor of his own island in the West Indies – but declined. I was on my way out.

I didn't know where I would go or what I would do. Writing was no more than a hint to the future, not yet a compulsion. To give me time rather than for more education I wrote to King's College, Cambridge, asking if I could go back for a year to finish my degree. They agreed – for my father's sake, I was sure.

Soon after I left Kenya the Mau Mau rebellion broke out among the Kikuyu and both my neighbours at Thika were murdered – one in his car, ambushed on the Nairobi road, the other on his coffee farm. Near the club a strangled dog was found hanging from the arch of a twisted sapling. I hoped it wasn't mine, which I had given to the secretary's wife. It was a useless watchdog and would have run up to the killers wagging its tail, to lick the hand that throttled it.

THIRTY-ONE

May 25, Valdepeñas. This journey becomes more madly unsystematic and quixotic, with the desultory character of life, as I criss-cross and back-track over La Mancha.

Don Quixote let his horse Rocinante choose the road, following it haphazardly, though it puzzled Sancho Panza: 'What's the profit in this desert? What are you looking for at these crossroads? Even your victories are wasted – there's nobody to see you win. We ought to join the army and fight a war, so someone can write about your heroism and it'll be remembered.'

'There's something in what you say, Sancho,' Don Quixote agreed. But first he had to wander through the world, as if to prove himself and find fame alone.

Suddenly, walking from the bus stop into Almagro, I'm in an oasis in the Manchegan plain: high wooden galleries, painted green and white, facing each other across the plaza and a perfect little theatre, brown and white, where they do the plays of Don Quixote's time. I should like to be watching *La Vida es Sueño*, 'Life is a Dream', and as if they heard me a bunch of leggy schoolgirls come bursting in for an impromptu performance, play-acting on the stage, striking bright-eyed poses, singing pop songs, giggling in the galleries. Life may be a dream, but there is no need to fall asleep for it, or even to wake up.

Their performance finished, the girls go back into the plaza and play a game of hopping over an elastic ribbon stretched between two of them, higher each time, hip to hip, waist to waist, neck to neck. Tall girls can do a high kick and twitch the ribbon down, to hop over. Then a small girl does a lovely cartwheel, her hands on the pavement, her toes catching the ribbon, and beats them all.

Boys kick a football round the statue of a man on a horse, *hijo de la ciudad*, son of the town, who became captain-general in the kingdom of Chile and died there before Cervantes was born. Two white-haired old men kiss each other on both cheeks under the arcade. At ten o'clock at night a barber is still shaving a customer, holding the tip of his nose in two fingers and sculpting his moustache with a razor.

I have a room in the kind of place where Don Quixote might have stayed, with a gallery over a courtyard and a tractor and plough parked among the potted flowers. For lavatory there are china footprints astride a hole, primitive but better than a dirty seat. Down the street are houses with grand doorways and elaborate stone shields, relics of Almagro's past, but a convent has become a Parador to show the presumptuous modern style.

Wondering what I am here for, reaching back to recover last night's half-drunk lucidity or the illusion of it, I have nightmares in the dawn before deciding whether to stay another day or move on. Travelling to the next place with such an elusive purpose, I ask myself where I'm going.

Perhaps the answer will be at the end of one of these inflexible Manchegan roads. They impose a ruthless discipline, they must lead somewhere, unless they are frauds or tyrants. I reach the top of a rise, expecting at least a bend, but it goes straight on to the next rise. If there is no conclusion I shall not be surprised – or disappointed, I hope: answers are too neat and final, leaving nothing to prolong the journey for.

Unexpectedly I find myself caught in vivid shafts of memory, flashes of recognition from another time. For a moment I'm a child, one Poppy Day morning in Cambridge, being buttoned into an overcoat to go into the town and see the parade – the undergraduates' annual riot to collect money for the war they missed, half-aware of the one that is coming. The gun goes off and we freeze for two minutes' silence in the agitation of gloves and scarves, buttonhooks and shoehorns, trying to think of slaughter in the trenches, impatient to reach the fun.

Excerpts from the past, prompted apparently by nothing, come with the inexplicability of dreams, though these are real. In an instant, against all reason, I'm a naval officer on leave, shooting rooks in a wood in Warwickshire with some lawyers and estate agents. Adult birds fly high above the trees, out of range of a .22 rifle, but young ones flap around their nests and make easy targets, falling to the ground like parcels of black feathers. I find I'm good at it.

Visions strike at random, shaken out of their proper order, shuffled backwards or forwards in time. Suddenly I'm a freelance journalist in the Cock and Monkey pub in Rotherhithe with a doctor (soon to be driven by alcohol to give up medicine and work in his father's garage). I need injections urgently before going abroad and he has lined them up on the bar, typhoid and cholera and yellow fever, with double brandies – it's luck which are swallowed and which injected.

Next, puzzlingly, I'm marching for nuclear disarmament from Aldermaston to London. On the fourth day, Easter Monday, as the column of ninety thousand people turns out of the Haymarket into Trafalgar Square, the singing and skiffling stop and a great weary but passionate silence drops on us, broken by the soft tramp of rubber soles and the squeak of a push-chair; also a reverence and humility, something like religion, immeasurably strong, before the speeches begin. I have never again felt that infectious sense, while close to some hopeless ideal, of sharing a vast generality yet remaining infinitely insignificant.

Then I'm a lover: in a tent above the Cornish cliffs; on a beach in Portugal, in front of the Atlantic breakers; in a cheap hotel on the Ile St Louis. Or I'm a husband in the car with Deirdre, jammed in the traffic outside Selfridge's, shouting at each other. 'God, you're a beastly man to live with,' she says. I admire her honesty and audacity – I could never say that. I only lose my temper and blurt stupid, boorish things. Who isn't beastly to live with? Living with anyone is a beastly thing. At home an hour later I can't remember what I said – it was another man who said it – though the shame, humiliation, barbarity will last for days. But for Deirdre it has cleared the air and she already feels better.

And now, one quiet African dawn, I'm a young businessman having coffee with the crew and other passengers in the airways hut at Entebbe, bound for London. A mist lies over Lake Victoria which in a few minutes will be sucked up by the rising sun, when a motorboat will take us out to the flying-boat. The pilot says that on the outward flight he saw some spectacular herds of game up in northern Uganda, and suggests we take a closer look.

Half an hour later, a heavy double-decker trying to be a bird, we swoop on antelope, scatter elephant, laugh at hippos below the Murchison Falls where once, in a chartered launch full of roast goose and champagne, I spent Christmas. For lunch we drop on Khartoum, skimming to a mooring on the Nile. Back in the air, cruising through the Egyptian afternoon, the engineer comes to join us in the bar: 'Rather warm, isn't it?' and he opens the door into the sky, hooking it back.

It's tempting to walk out – I have always been enticed by the quick drop, somehow confident that I will survive. Nine thousand feet down there, one step over the sill, our shadow creeps northwards over the desert.

We stay the first night at Alexandria, the second at Port Augusta in Sicily; climb the snows of Mount Etna after breakfast to look into the crater and land at teatime off Cowes, to taxi through thick fog up to Southampton where a bus for London is waiting.

THIRTY-TWO

In 1952 I returned to Cambridge for a year and worked just hard enough to get a degree. I spent more time and care on letters to a woman I thought I was in love with. Later, with mixed horror and thankfulness, I watched them being torn up and burnt in front of me. I also wrote articles and stories which were mostly rejected too.

I played the flute again, and in a university concert for the Coronation I was one of eight percussionists at the back, banging and blowing bits of wood and metal in a piece by Villa-Lobos. But the professor of music, trying to conduct, was too drunk to control us. Counting bars, waiting for my cue, missing it in the general noise – it was a metaphor for my life, playing a triangle in someone else's symphony. I had no idea, when we reached the end, what I would be playing next.

Mysteriously in the summer term I was called for an interview by an admiral in London. He enclosed a return ticket and told me to discuss it with nobody. But a Cambridge postgraduate I knew, an unconvincing theology student with a beard and a black eye-patch who slept on a mattress on the floor and often went to Tangier – to see his mother, he said – had spoken of his 'friends', raising a single eyebrow. He thought they might be interested in my future, something that concerned me too, and I guessed that he had given them my name. Next time we met he didn't mention it and his one eye, darting and hovering and probing like a hummingbird, got nothing from me. I was halfway to being a secret agent, another Conrad character like the mate of a cargo ship I might have been.

In an office overlooking the royal stables behind Buckingham Palace the admiral questioned me about my plans. There was little I could tell him, beyond a wish to travel and write.

'So why did you leave Africa?' he asked.

Because, I said, keeping quiet about the Nairobi doctor, I wanted to return to Cambridge for a degree.

'Do you speak a foreign language?'

A little French, a little less Spanish. And I knew the Arabic alphabet.

The admiral reached for the telephone: 'Perhaps you'd like to talk French to a colleague of mine?' He only had to dial a number.

Quickly I protested – I was rusty, I needed practice.

'But why exactly,' he persisted, 'did you give up the job in your uncle's firm?'

Because I didn't like the business world. Because I wasn't in love with tanning. Because I wanted to work for myself, be my own boss, do something that satisfied me, something less ordinary. Because I was a traitor to the white man, because I was on the side of the Mau Mau, because I was an equivocator by nature, weak on loyalty, strong on duplicity . . . I waffled on, reaching for answers that dissolved before I uttered them, not knowing why I was being questioned in that office, with Buckingham Palace through the window.

'I think I should warn you,' he said, 'that we don't go in for excitement in this outfit.'

What outfit was it? I was in the dark.

'Forget the cloak and dagger stuff.'

And the beard and eye-patch, and the mother in Tangier?

'You might find yourself as an embassy secretary in Argentina, say, sitting there for years. Keeping your ears and eyes open. Collecting data for a treaty on frozen beef. Does that appeal to you?'

Well, I said, warming to the promise of night clubs in Buenos Aires and trips across the pampas, perhaps down to Patagonia, if it gave me a chance to travel. . . .

'There'd be no medals at the end of the day, you realize? You'd be lucky to get an OBE.' The admiral had a knighthood. 'Do you mind?'

Well, the British Empire could get along without me and if it meant I could write. . . .

'Now there's something we must get straight. Have you ever been ill?'

Never.

'Never suffered from any disease?'

None.

'Are you sure about that?'

Of course.

'So what about this?' He picked up a paper. 'Didn't you give up your job in Africa because of your health?'

Well, in a way, yes. But it was perfectly good now. I had recovered totally.

'Asthma, wasn't it?'

I did have it once, but not badly – it had never stopped me from doing anything, I climbed and sailed, I was as fit as anyone. . . . How had he found out? I had lied my way into the navy but this time I was caught out, getting deeper into untruth. I was a midshipman again, facing a senior officer. I wouldn't take a job in the admiral's outfit even if he offered me one, but I wanted to refuse it for my own reasons.

He smiled: 'Perhaps you'd like to think about it and let me know.' The interview was over.

I went down to the street in confusion, ashamed of being trapped in fiction. But soon I began to feel grateful for being exposed. I would become a writer, aloof and solitary – a different kind of spy. And eventually I saw that fiction was the best place for me. Asthma was on my side.

THIRTY-THREE

May 26, Almagro. Waiting in the street for a bus to Ciudad Real I'm joined by a priest in a white cassock with a cigarette in one corner of his mouth, a toothpick in the other. *'Buenos días,'* he says, between the two. I hope he will sit next to me in the bus – Don Quixote met a priest on the road, a canon of Toledo whom he impressed with his talk about books, mixing intelligence with nonsense, fact with fiction – but instead I get a girl who cracks seeds in her front teeth like a parrot, spitting out the shells round us. I feel myself beginning to hate her, and I see she knows it.

In another bus to Puerto Lápice there is a woman who suddenly can't control herself any longer. She cries to the driver who pulls quickly into the side, and dashes out, hitching up her skirt to squat behind the first olive tree; and comes back on board, beaming with relief and gratitude.

The same urgency once gripped Don Quixote. He had been tied up and put in a cage and was being carried back to his village on an ox cart, to be cured of his madness at home. Sane men, perhaps from envy, couldn't tolerate his eccentric vision of the world and had to reduce him to their own level of normality, ruled by the tyranny of common sense. But to Don Quixote it was a spell cast on him by the enemy, another ordeal for him to survive through virtue, faith, courage. Under armed escort the cart rolled along the hot straight road while Don Quixote sat in the cage, leaning against the bars, as silent and patient as if he wasn't a man of flesh at all – which in a way was so.

Sancho Panza wasn't convinced, being a realist, and when they stopped for a siesta he saw his chance for a word in private. There was a question he wanted to clear up: 'With all respect, while you've been locked up in this cage under a spell, as you call it, have you by chance been taken with any desire, any inclination, any . . . ?' His dithering made Don Quixote restless and he came to the point: 'Have you had no mind to do what nobody else can do for you?'

'Indeed Sancho, very often – in fact I want to do it now. Get me out of here, or I'll be in a mess.'

'Ah!' Sancho cried. 'I've caught you now. Anyone who wants to do that can't be under a spell.'

'Sancho, I've told you before – there are many kinds of spell.' Don Quixote was no more prisoner of his body than of the cage, and though for his squire nothing existed that couldn't be seen or touched or smelt, for himself the truth was above such deceptions of the senses. After warning his escort that the offence to their nostrils might otherwise be awful and promising not to run away, he was let out of the cage. Glad to be free and stretch his limbs, he disappeared to a remote spot from which in time he returned, much relieved and with his integrity intact: 'I know I'm under a spell – I feel it, and that's enough.'

At Puerto Lápice a friendly woman in a bar tells me that the bus to Madridejos has just passed and I have two hours before the next, so I drink some of her wine which she gives me with *tapas* – a fried prawn, a piece of cold *tortilla* – and then eat a dish of squid. Old bullfight posters decorate the walls, the way London pubs have old theatre playbills.

In the late afternoon, after three buses in one day, I try faint-heartedly to hitch-hike from Madridejos to Consuegra and stand by the road, beyond the last house. Three cars pass, eyes down on the tarmac ahead as they speed away – guiltily, I hope. I soon give up. What the hell! – I'm too old for this, but young enough to walk.

It's warm, with only seven or eight kilometres to go, and I'm led into the orange-green sunset by a line of windmills on the skyline. There are vines all the way; incredible that so much care and wealth and land are devoted to alcohol. But my scorn is kept for the motorists on the road, though I know it would melt if one of them stopped to pick me up.

A man on a mule cart passes in the other direction. A man in a straw hat on an old motorbike overtakes me, going only a little faster than me – I might jump up behind him. Outside Consuegra a putt-putting engine is linked to a wheel of tin cans, once driven by an ox or donkey, to hoist water from a well for someone's vegetables. At the entrance to the town I pass an advert for a hotel in 1200 metres, but I walk twice as far and out the other side without finding it.

'Is there no hotel in Consuegra?' I ask.

Nobody can tell me. They might be strangers here too. 'Try the lower part of the town – there's nothing up here,' two women say, glad to get rid of me. In the end I try the Guardia Civil in the main plaza and am told that the only hotel is a new one, two kilometres away on the bypass. Hotels are for travellers, and travellers go by car.

I walk there – to a concrete building smelling of new cement and already shabby though unfinished. The waiter won't let me eat in the bar, I must go into the expensive dining-room, so I don't eat at all; and he tries to cheat me, charging for four beers when I have drunk only three.

THIRTY-FOUR

Naval men kept cropping up. This time, in 1953 at a party in Pimlico, it was the Commander. With a quixotic vision of life on his chosen Pacific island he had bought a sailing ketch, eighty feet long and solid oak, that had once carried cod from the Newfoundland banks to Europe and had later traded in the Baltic. Now he was collecting a crew for the voyage to the Solomon Islands.

'You mustn't mind my bagpipes,' he warned.

'What about my flute?' I asked.

He frowned, and signed me on as bosun. I would leave Cambridge for the second time, not in a lorry to Africa but in a ketch to the Solomons – it offered something better than the admiral's outfit. But before sailing away I was confronted by another inadequacy, one I regretted more till I wrote a story about it, giving it a new reality.

It concerned a pretty girl from South Kensington, a virgin drenched in Arpège perfume whose first lover failed to staunch or mop up her grief. She had a classy voice and strong enthusiastic legs and a tiny two-seater Fiat in which, stopped one night in the Knightsbridge traffic, she turned from the wheel to tangle with her passenger. 'Drivers have been prosecuted for less than that,' a policeman said, stepping off the pavement and opening the door. She drove to her flat where she grabbed her chosen ravisher and hauled him eagerly in; and later wept for losing, not her chastity but that callous, callow young man who was embarking on a voyage halfway round the world.

She sent me a Simenon novel, *Banana Tourist*, in case I felt sentimental about the South Sea islands. And years afterwards she wrote to say that another man had picked up the pieces – she had a flair for the right cliché – and married her. I felt those desperate thighs scissoring me again, and caught a whiff of Arpège.

Soon we were bowling down the Atlantic, laughing and sunlit, all sails set, the waves spraying shrapnel over the bows, lifting and sucking round the poop. Storm petrels skimmed the sea and at night drops of phosphorescence beetled in the water. Off watch I sat on deck sewing a topsail for the trade winds; or perched on the bowsprit, shouting to the dolphins; or took a book up the mast to escape the Commander's bagpipes. He marched up and down playing *Westering Home* at sunset for the next five months.

Beyond Madeira a whale came to play with us all day: dropping astern, racing ahead, diving deep, pushing out his snout to squirt at us or roll over, belly up. Sapphire-bright flying fish skated the surface in a game of ducks and drakes – if they flew aboard we fried them. After four weeks, when the Atlantic blue changed to the Orinoco green, we reached Trinidad; and after another ten days the Panama Canal. A bosun bird with black eyebrows and a long white tail, his marline spike, sometimes came to look. All night we carried a blue-faced booby at the top of the mizzen mast, a welcome passenger till we saw the mess of shit it left. Frigate birds chased gulls till they vomited their catch, then swooped on it as it fell. The phosphorescence turned to riches, a brilliant carpet unrolling from the bows. Jewels swam across the deck when a wave spilled on board and the logline became a silver thread.

In the canal, through the locks and out into Gatun Lake, we took short cuts between the flooded trees. During the construction Paul Gauguin, also on his way to Polynesia and running out of money, briefly swung a pick – an unlikely navvy – and was eaten by mosquitoes. These wooded hills, the watershed between two oceans, were our last land for four thousand miles.

Sunset, after the bagpipes, was the best time – the sequence of blue to green to orange to purple to black. The first stars pierced the sky and the Commander with his sextant called to someone with a watch, 'Stand by for Betelgeuse!' Lightning burst over us or glinted on the horizon like a distant battle. Or shooting stars broke loose, tumbling down the sky. Or a rainbow was cast by the moon.

Christmas came somewhere beyond the Galapagos Islands. We drank a gallon of rum and listened to carols from King's chapel: shepherds and herald angels defying the creak of rope and spar, the slap of waves on our hull, even the Commander's pipes.

Drifting in a calm, swinging round the compass while the sun slanted into the depths where a piece of bacon hung, we caught a shark. It glided into the trap, a black and white pilot fish riding above its nose; sniffed and unhooked the bait, and swam away. Presently it came back for more. We tried slices of spam and then a big lump, half the tin. It bit, and was hooked. But there was no fight or death plunge to the bottom, only a feebly lashing tail. We pulled it over the side, hammered it on the nose and cut off steaks.

Five weeks from Panama I climbed the mast and saw ahead, close to the setting sun, a small cloud. Or was it? There were no others like it – a smudge above the sea. The more I stared the fluffier it looked. But it was Polynesia.

Next day we sailed through the Marquesas Islands: one a desolate volcanic pile streaked with furrows, steeped in a haze of pale colours; another a pointed craggy outline; a third, our island, the long heap of Nukuhiva. That evening we slipped through the rock gates of Taio Hae bay and anchored opposite a jetty.

'The first love, the first sunrise, the first South Sea island,' Robert Louis Stevenson wrote, 'are memories apart and touched a virginity of sense.'

Nukuhiva was his first landfall too. In a schooner the size of our ketch, sailing from San Fancisco in 1888, he slipped into the bay on a dying wind and dropped anchor: 'It was a small sound, a great event. My soul went down with these moorings whence no windlass may extract nor any diver fish it up.' He was enslaved to the Pacific and never left it. Perhaps he saw in its huge dimensions the scope for comedy and tragedy that La Mancha held for Cervantes. 'That's what I am,' he said, 'just another Don Quixote.'

The swell rolled into the bay and spent itself on the beach – a hiss and froth of surf. The scent of copra drifted from a schooner anchored near us, loading for Tahiti. The skipper was a halfcast, the supercargo a Russian. The kanaka crew were tying green bananas to the rail, herding goats into the bows, throwing water over pigs. Ashore, a crescent of houses curled under a vault of scarlet flamboyants. Horses grazed in the tepid light of coconut groves, chickens pecked at fallen mangoes, kanakas fished from the jetty. Some of Gauguin's girls, with the green-gold ripeness he painted in their skin, played guitars and sang outside their huts. A frangipani in their hair, an old Englishman told us, was a signal – over the right ear for 'I've got a man', over the left for 'I want one'.

The Englishman, among five Frenchmen on the island, was a Liverpool sailor who had jumped ship in Tahiti, built a boat and sailed to the Marquesas where he had lived with his kanaka wife for forty years. When his sister threatened to come and join him as a missionary he wrote back quickly to say there were more souls to save in Liverpool. He still took the *Evening Standard*, which arrived months late in bundles and put him off ever going home.

We walked up the valley through breadfruit trees and banana palms towards the mountains. Beyond was the valley of *Typee* where Herman Melville fell among cannibals. He escaped, but the cannibals were less lucky. Banned by white men from eating their enemies, with nothing left worth living for, they settled down to fade away, helped by the white man's opium and diseases. In the forest the sun, splashing through the branches, covered the ground with pools of light. Beyond the trees it fell in a sheer cascade of heat.

Two young men stopped us on the path to ask the time: 'We must be back in prison by four o'clock.'

'Prison?'

'We're let out at eleven each morning for five hours.'

'How long are you in for?'

'A year for me, four months for him.'

'What crime?'

'Women!' they said proudly, and showed us with their hands. They were only sixteen, hungry in another way for flesh. Out of nine in prison five were there for rape.

We climbed to the highest ridge and basked all afternoon. Below lay the ketch at anchor, ringed by the bay, the yellow beaches and rocky headlands; and far into the haze another island. In the dusk we broke coconuts against a rock for a drink, and splashed through the surf for a moonlight swim; but splashed back quickly, stung by medusas, jelly-worms drifting in transparent millions.

For another fortnight we sailed between empty horizons. In the evening shoals of bonito joined the dolphins to dance for the bagpipes. I kept the middle watch, the heart of the night from twelve to four, and woke the Commander to catch the stars at dawn. In a line of crosses our noon position crept across the chart.

One morning, checking the time, the Commander announced that Suvorov would be visible from the deck in fifteen minutes. I climbed the mast and there it was, a bristle on the edge of the world, growing taller each minute, stretching to left and right till an arc of the horizon was sown with palm trees standing on the sea: a lagoon ringed by a thread of surf and reef, the atoll of atolls. The bottom rose to meet us, blurred by heat and light, and dropped into the lagoon on the other side. We slipped through the gap, turned to port to miss a rock, swept round to starboard and anchored near a half-mile strip of palms, coral, sand.

Suvorov was meant to be uninhabited – too tiny for a native village or a white man's plantation, too dangerous for a harbour. But at the splash of our anchor a figure in shorts and straw hat ran along the beach, pushed a boat into the water, rowed out to us and stood barefoot and sunburnt on deck: a man of fifty, sinewy and probably hungry, slightly agitated. There was a moment of silence. We were cheated – this wasn't the desert island it was said to be. He must have been shipwrecked or marooned, a hermit, a castaway from Homer, a madman if not a myth: another quixotic character in search of himself.

He too seemed disappointed: 'I wasn't expecting you. Nobody was due for quite some time. I'd have shaved if. . . .'

It was our fault, we said, for having dropped in unannounced. We hoped we weren't disturbing him.

'That's all right.' His annoyance unfroze at the pleasure of having visitors. But his conversation was out of practice, he was unused to passers-by. 'Make yourselves at home.' He waved a hand round his little kingdom: 'It isn't much.'

He was a New Zealander, put ashore by a schooner sixteen months ago to test himself alone and discover his capacity for solitude. Some mother of pearl fishers had come once, and a Dutchman in a yacht, but for six months he had seen nobody. He wasn't writing or painting or studying anything – the struggle left him no time. Now that his chickens had stopped laying eggs he had to spend all day fishing on the reef. We caught him eyeing our lump of bacon on a shark hook.

'How long are you staying?' he asked guardedly, perhaps unsure how much he wanted company: it would spoil the test.

The Commander said we must be out of the lagoon before sunset, and settled down to a lunch of gin and pickles. The rest of us went ashore. The New Zealander broke open young coconuts for us, slicing them in a few chops; then went to his hut to write letters for us to take away. From the beach, a pile of coral bones washed from the living reef, we waded towards the breakers – they piled up and balanced in a wall of black and blue to topple, curl over, roll up from one end to the other, spill with a crash and hiss. Small black sharks' fins waved through the surface and brilliant shoals of fish, more like flowers, hung in the coral pools.

The New Zealander came on board to see us off and stayed till the anchor was aweigh. We offered to take him with us and he seemed to hesitate, half willing. But the test wasn't finished yet. So how much longer would he live on Suvorov?

'At the end of the year – if a ship comes I'll probably go. There'll be no point in staying.'

We filled his boat with corned beef and he shook hands before climbing quickly over the side and rowing back. By sunset Suvorov was a bristle of palm tops again and next morning it had sunk with its lonely islander. We were a six-hour oasis in his ocean desert.

Next landfall was Samoa. Squalls driven in from the sea swept the grey coast of Upolu. Something white flashed between curtains of rain – the church at Apia. We altered course and headed in, steering for a gap between the breakers in the reef. Three days later we sailed away and Samoa was washed out by the rain, leaving only scraps of landmark.

A row of stores along the waterfront. Verandas and a smell of copra, a whiff of Somerset Maugham. A rickety bus ride through clustered villages, insistent laughing children, cotton *lava-lavas* wrapped round tattooed hips and stomachs. Roofs of pandanus leaf, walls of rolled-up matting, giant brass beds. Churches and mission schools with, instead of bells, a hollowed drum-log. Little sanitary sentry boxes along the shore, reached by catwalks, and fishing canoes inside the reef, and the Pacific crashing beyond.

A meal of bananas and hot *taro*, tasting of chestnuts. A boy who swarmed up a tree to knock down coconuts; peeled off the husks on a stake, cut a perfect hole with three strokes of a knife for the milk; opened the nut, sliced a spoon from the husk to scoop out the meat. And an old engineer from Bristol among the fishermen on the wharf – another man lured to Polynesia, never to return – who had lived thirty-five years in Samoa and spoke wistfully, not of England but of a crater lake full of goldfish up in the hills; and persuaded us to go there.

A taxi through rubber and coconut plantations, twenty miles up a worsening track to be stopped by a forest tree, a cathedral of pillars and buttresses. A boy in a hut who knew the way to the crater, and his brother and sister and the taxi-driver, a caravan wading through streams, over savannas, into the forest. Rain rattling on the leaves, cooling the body. Two hours of slithery mud and then, pushing through the undergrowth, the lake. Splashing in and swimming to the far side for a picnic of bananas while the boys trapped goldfish in their *lava-lavas*.

Another hot climb to the hilltop tomb of Robert Louis Stevenson. 'Under the wide and starry sky' – on a grass terrace with Vailima, the house he built, framed among the trees below. Idealism, a romantic dream that presaged disappointment, guided Stevenson as it did the Knight of the Sad Countenance. He called *Don Quixote* the saddest story he had ever read, which is what Byron said too – 'and more sad because it makes us smile'.

A barefoot wide-eyed girl, black hair to her shoulders, came out of the forest to read the epitaph in Samoan for us, harsh and glottalized. Twenty years later, with a red flower in her hair, with a flock of parrots cackling over the trees and another storm building up, she came into a novel.

In time (time? – it plays with the years like a trickster) we reached the Solomons. Mirage trees floated above the horizon ahead, settled firmly on the water as we passed, hitched themselves up again and melted in the sky astern. Rainstorms sprayed the forests on the high volcanic islands, but between squalls the sea was broken only by the flop of a shark's fin or a bobbing coconut.

For our last anchorage we pushed into a creek wrapped round by a huge coconut plantation, the source of infinite margarine and soap. And margarine or soap could have formed the yellow moon that rose over a clearing in the trees where the copra cutters danced for us and sang about the pretty white ship with two masts that had sailed round the world to visit them, and about the Commander with his funny musical instrument, 'squeeze 'im belly, make 'im squeak', and about my beard, 'grass belong face'. We slept to the chatter of insects and rustle of trees, the incessant forest noise.

For his dream the Commander chose Rendova Island, twenty miles long with an old volcano in the middle. The chart called it densely wooded, with no exaggeration. Between the lagoon and the forest we hacked a clearing and pitched a tent. It was a beautiful but lonely place, far from the nearest village, with no other white man on any of the islands in sight. Once it was famous for its cannibals – it was what the Commander wanted.

He would restore an old coconut plantation, derelict since the Japanese invasion, and plant cocoa in the hills. Later he might try citrus fruit or vanilla or a herd of cattle – the scope was fit for such a man. From the Marquesas he had brought some seed pods of flamboyant trees, to splash the greenery with scarlet. He saw something in the future there, precious and very private, which he couldn't share. He would climb the old volcano to survey his paradise and play a pibroch to the cockatoos.

First thing was to get a cook, then collect some workers. Canoes were already coming into the lagoon with people curious to see him. He was impatient for us to be gone, he wanted to be alone. We unloaded some food, books, a case of gin, the bagpipes, and sailed away.

As the island vanished in the dusk astern, though glad to be spared *Westering Home*, I could only admire a man's wish to be marooned. And over the years I couldn't help wondering how he was getting on.

Twenty-six years later I went back to Rendova to find out. I was doubtful about the truth, I wanted to make sure. Half my life ago, according to the facts, I had sailed across two oceans with a man who was still living alone on the island where I left him.

But the facts were dubious, as Don Quixote knew: they weren't enough. The Commander wasn't in my travel books where he could be verified. Perhaps he belonged in fiction, though so far he hadn't appeared. In a sense all the characters in my novels – whatever their age, sex, virtues or lack of them – are aspects of myself. Yet they are more than me. Their lives are beyond my own, beyond time and place. Their truth is beyond doubt. They surpass the facts.

The Commander, an insistent man, demanded a novel. Only then, stripped of his actual self and engendered more vividly in words, would he be real.

This time, instead of a five-month voyage in a ketch it was a four-day journey that began in a jumbo jet and ended in a dugout canoe with an outboard motor. The Commander's arrangements too were rather different, but luckily I guessed they might be. As well as a present of whisky and cigars I brought him a large Stilton and some biscuits from Fortnum and Mason. It hit the right note.

The man in the novel I wrote later, living on a Pacific island, ruling his people like a king, guarding his motives, preserving a corner of the past for himself and defying a future he has no place in, isn't the Commander. He is closer to an image of myself, a conceit I tried to define in words. It's immaterial that the Commander may still be living in more or less that way on another island, in a fantasy of his own – if he ever did.

THIRTY-FIVE

May 27, Consuegra. All morning I lie on the hill above the town, with a castle and a dozen old windmills at my back, the roofs and church towers beyond my feet and the plain going on for ever all round. My slog from Madridejos yesterday looks a mere step across the floor, among strips and squares of cultivation. Thin roads are ruled from here to the horizon, dwindling towards misty hills. One way is Ciudad Real and Almagro where I came from, the other is Toledo where I shall be tonight. But east and west are no different till the sun comes through the cloud and puts shadows on the windmills. Their sails should be flailing the sky, spinning in the dry Manchegan wind.

Noises from the town come up – a school playground, a dog, the chatter of birds, the traffic. Over the roofs I can see trees in the plaza where I had breakfast in a bar while English lessons were being given on TV, and a flag above the Guardia Civil, and away on the bypass the awful cheating hotel. A goatherd comes slowly over the hill, eating a loaf of bread and an apple, with two somnolent dogs and his fastidious goats.

Storks have built their nest, a mop of sticks, on a pinnacle of the church at my feet. The young are now hatched, tottering to the ungainly edge, their parents watching. Sparrows have nested in the overhanging twigs. In a transept of that church this morning I saw carts with life-size statues of the Virgin and other holy figures, parked under dust sheets, waiting to be pulled through the town at a fiesta.

Don Quixote met a party of men with strange objects under white sheets, some upright, some lying down, and asked what they were. When the covers were taken off he saw images of the saints, carved and painted. 'What luck!' he cried. 'They were knights like me. They fought with holy weapons, being saints, but I'm a sinner and fight with human ones.' A saintly life was the highest, though Don Quixote wasn't so mad as to believe he could achieve it. Writers have sometimes felt the same. Graham Greene has confessed to a half-wish that he could have had the dedication of a priest or even have been a saint-turned-sinner.

In the town centre a great sombre building presides, roofed with a million tiles, embracing courts and cloisters: a seat of past power, spiritual or military, now withdrawn into near-abandonment. I have seen them elsewhere – empty monasteries and barracks, locked up, used as billboards for election posters. Power has settled on the fringe, in the shiny grain silos and tanks of petrol or olive oil, the wineries and meat factories.

Also at the edge are reminders of another power. On my left the bullring; and on my right, pushed out of town down an avenue of dark trees ('here if you die, you die,' V. S. Pritchett wrote), the walled and whitewashed cemetery. In Spain, where life plays strangely to the dance of death, they are the two inevitable meeting-places of both. *La vida es sueño*, life is a dream, and the symbols of its end are the sword and the tomb.

In the early afternoon I go down from the hill into the town for lunch. I'm hungry, I had no supper last night. Through a window a fat man with a beard is cooking behind a bar. He offers veal cutlets, pork chops, prawns, squid – I can't choose. Which is best? He laughs: 'Nothing is less good than anything else. What do you want?'

The bus to Toledo stops at Los Yébenes and Orgaz. Everywhere banks are a constant, emphatic feature – Banco Crédito, Banco Rural, Banco Popular, Caja de Ahorros – as familiar as the photographers' windows where, town after town, I see the same children dressed up for communion, girls in white ribbons, boys in sailor suits or bow ties, posed like angels with hands in prayer and holy revelation, or a child's pretence of it, in their eyes. In one place, on a great church of pink brick and stone, a tablet commemorates a local boy who, in the time of Don Quixote, became a bishop in the Philippines.

Old country families inhabit new town flats in the big honeycomb blocks, swelling the surplus urban throng. As more land is cultivated – the stones cleared, the soil fertilized and irrigated ever more profitably – fewer men are wanted for the work, riding out by day from the towns in Renaults or on mobylettes. Farmhouses are abandoned, barns roofless, walled stockyards padlocked for ever or left open for shepherds to move in and out.

THIRTY-SIX

'The lure of the Pacific islands is not a myth' is the start of my first book.

I might have fallen for it like the others: the Liverpool sailor on Nukuhiva who had jumped ship forty years ago; the New Zealand hermit on Suvorov, living off coconuts and fish; the Bristol engineer in Samoa who had been there thirty-five years. And now on Rendova we had marooned the Commander with his gin and bagpipes, and his vision of happiness ahead.

If I had stayed, that first sentence would have been my last – another lie. I was twenty-eight, and had been briefly a sailor and dubiously a businessman. Wandering, without the writing, would have been easy. Here was a chance to drift through the islands as a banana tourist, the scatterbrain who dreams of rattling palms and silver sands and big brown nipples, drunk with the simple life, escaping to emptiness. But I got away in time, in a small cargo boat to Sydney, sharing a cabin with the retiring Bishop of Melanesia, thankful for my own renunciation. I would be a writer.

'Ah yes! – so you prefer to travel alone,' an elderly Muslim in Swat, the tiny Himalayan kingdom, remarked later that year. 'Very wise. And such good practice for the future. The last journey of all, you know, is made alone.' He overtook me on a bicycle one evening of Ramadan, the month of fasting, as I was walking down a mountain road.

'Peace to you,' I called as he passed.

'And to you, peace.' He put his feet to the ground and slithered to a halt – he had no brakes.

For a while we talked in mixed Urdu-Pashtu-English, becoming old friends in a few minutes. There were several miles to the village capital of Swat and a storm was coming over the mountains. Seeing the chance of a ride I suggested sitting on the Swati's rear mudguard. He had a better idea: the back tyre was flat, down to the rim, and as I was heavier I should sit on the saddle and pedal the bike while he rode behind.

Brakeless, downhill all the way, I rang the bell non-stop to warn people off the road – they stood back and cheered. Soon the storm caught up and hailstones like sugar lumps were jumping round us, twanging in the spokes. The man gripped my belt and said something, probably a prayer. He had eaten nothing all day, he wanted to get home for supper safely. At the beginning of the village the road flattened out and I could stop.

'Peace to you,' the man called over his shoulder as he pedalled on alone.

'And to you, peace.'

The storm passed. A scent of wet blossom enriched the air. Above the mountains the fading apricot clouds turned grey. The sunset gun, booming up the valley for the ending of the fast, left a puff of smoke over the village. A muezzin, recorded long ago and amplified by electronics, called from his minaret as the hungry dusk was breaking.

Yes, I prefer to travel alone.

For one thing, being unprotected by anybody else, I'm more sensitive to what I find in the world. For another, I feel more acceptable to strangers. I can slip into a brief, tenuous intimacy with someone, like the Swati on a bike, and slip out of it when I choose, to put it in my notebook. But two people make up a small society of their own, self-sufficient and less welcome. They can look after themselves, or so it seems to others, and don't need to be approached, helped, entertained. They even discourage interference – the Swati would never have stopped for them. And, more dangerously for a vagabond, their dual journey becomes a trail of half-and-half ideas, an alternative route belonging to neither of them, without a single style.

With no companion, between leaving the Solomons and reaching London fifteen months later, I was alert to my own thoughts, free to indulge any fancy when it struck; free from any need to be unselfish. And as well as practice for the future, as the Swati told me, it was part of finding out how to write. Writers, Truman Capote said, tend to learn more than other people how to be alone. They have to, I discovered. So the lonely road became a book.

I walked over a pass to Lahul, a wild unvisited corner of the Himalayas. Patches of barley and millet in the empty valleys, villages set about with willows, meadows of summer flowers, shepherds fluting to their sheep and shaggy goats, monasteries of sleepy lamas, feudal lords happy to feast a stranger, the relief after too much rice beer of camping in high mountain country that nobody had been in – it was a time of discovery and contrast. With an army captain I climbed four mountains that hadn't been climbed before, the highest a gothic peak of ice and snow and rock with a goddess on top but not the view I wanted – only windows in the cloud and through one of them the line of steps I had cut up a steep ridge from the glacier, with last night's little tent far below.

I found myself in Mashobra in the Simla hills, an English transplant of gabled villas, tennis courts, rose gardens among the pines, where a girl in a cotton sari roasted chestnuts for me in a log fire, rolling them from the embers to peel them and laugh quietly at our pleasure. She was a painter, happily unresolved between her restlessness and peace, with jasmine in her hair and the sudden astonishment of love in her large eyes. But she wasn't Shashi who comes into a novel; who wears a crimson spot between her eyebrows and dozens of tinkling glass bangles that touch a young Englishman's heart and ripple through his veins; who tells him he is too English, asking her so many questions; who plays her sitar for him, wrenching a twist of beauty from India's hopelessness; whose fingers he watches scattering over the strings, so that he longs to be taken by them and gently tortured; who meets him at dusk in the old English cemetery where they make love in a tomb while she cracks her bangles one by one like tiny sobs of glass, instead of keeping them to be broken over her husband's body at his funeral.

The girl at Mashobra, last time I heard, was living in another Indian hill station, now a grandmother. Unlike Shashi in the novel who exists as vividly as ever (I only have to open the book), her reality is uncertain, a shadowy figure still roasting chestnuts in the embers. But in 1954 she moved me to search for more revelation in her country, and one day to put it into fiction.

'Put it' suggests putting it down like an old dog, or putting it on a pedestal, equally dead. But really it's putting life into it – the enhanced vitality of truth.

I travelled by bus and tonga and bicycle rickshaw, stayed in dak bungalows and unforgettable cheap hotels, talked to princes, shrank from beggars. I worshipped Buddha under the tree where he received enlightenment, and Surya the sun god in his glorious chariot at Konarak, and St Francis Xavier in his basilica at Goa. I applied for an alcoholic's licence when I was caught by Christmas in Bombay, a city ruled by teetotallers. I smoked hemp, ate curried oysters, chewed pan and drank champagne one morning with a maharaja who saw himself as a lotus floating in a dirty pond. 'I don't believe in royal families,' he said, 'only in royal sentiments. But being a practical man I also believe in money – and now I have none. All my life I have searched for truth and what have I found? Grey hairs. How did I find them? In the mirror. And there also I found the truth.'

I took the night train across the Deccan, crammed into the third class, the heat and lurching rhythm inducing, like my sailor's hammock, erotic dreams – fired also by the chilli-filled samosas handed through the window at country stations. I watched the moon rise over the Taj Mahal and over the prime minister, Nehru, speaking in a football stadium. I was fed with holy coconuts, strung with marigolds, smeared with the mark of Shiva. I climbed the sacred mountains of the Jains, and among Christian evangelists at the edge of the great hot plain I walked over the fields with a bag of chickpeas round my neck, sowing as I went.

I was given roast sucking-pig by an Englishman who had stolen the wife of the Indian commander-in-chief; and invited to sleep on his veranda by a strict Brahmin who said it would have to be purified with liquid cowdung after I had gone; and promised release from the wheel of life by a Tibetan priest; and offered fellatio by a buck-toothed police detective who crept under my mosquito net.

At Sanchi I met another girl, a *yakshi* reaching up into a mango tree, as provoking in her way as the painter at Mashobra and as alive as Shashi in the novel. I stared at her all afternoon – at the quiet sensuous-ness, supple twisting, almost visible breathing of her sculptured stone, twenty centuries old; and went back next day to stare again.

I turned west into Pakistan, and on into Iran and Turkey. On a borrowed horse I rode with a troop of Pathan tribesmen up into the mountains of the Afghan frontier for a huge feast spread on carpets under a walnut tree. In a public bath I was douched, scraped, soaped, rinsed, pummelled, slapped, boiled, twisted, racked and skinned by attendants who had never seen freckles before and thought they could be scrubbed off.

At midnight in a teashop on a bus journey across the desert I smoked opium with the driver, who said it would help him stay awake at the wheel and see in the dark. But it sent him to sleep till dawn and did nothing for me but make me cough and nearly vomit. I hitched a ride in a lorry with a white handkerchief on the gear lever to save the immaculate driver's hands, while his greasy mate squatted on the front bumper, half under the bonnet, keeping the engine running. (Deirdre has sometimes said I ought be a lorry-driver – there would be fewer worries, perhaps, and better pay.)

At a small town in Kurdistan I was arrested for straying into a military zone without a permit. A corporal took me to his lieutenant, who drank vodka with me and put me in a house with sentries at the door and fetched a major, who gave me tea and passed me to a colonel, who smiled sadly and went back to his game of swatting frogs with a stick, leaving me to a general who quoted the Koran: 'Verily, God is with the patient.' Asleep I dreamed of friends and places, happiness and freedom, and was drowned in music, but woke to hear the sentries shuffling outside my dirty little room; and I cried. They kept me under guard for a fortnight before letting me go.

Two years after leaving London I was back, and wrote a book. In his blurb Jonathan Cape called me a traveller without a purpose. He said he didn't usually give advances, but could spare fifty pounds if I was desperate.

THIRTY-SEVEN

May 28, Toledo. I'm getting to know the faces of these Spanish election candidates, fixed in huge fading photographs in every plaza or mouthing their promises in every bar, as glib as TV commercials.

The United Left is a row of workers, open-necked and practical, lusty for power. The multiple men of the Centre, liberal-democratic-christian-socialist or whatever, are in virile middle age, managers, executives with degrees in law or accountancy or business studies, salesmen for their policies with good hair styles, well-knotted ties, plausible smiles. The Green young man is an amateur, long-haired and casual, diffident and hopeless. The Right wing candidate from the National Front is a true old Francoist, his slit eyes gazing at some future resurrection of the past. I'm not surprised to see him wearing a Winchester tie and I search for features I might recognize in that handsome empty face. Could we have been at school together? Nothing is impossible. I imagine him going back for an Old Boys' cricket match, deploring how the place has slipped since his time: 'They don't beat them any more, they'll be taking girls next. Girls – I ask you!'

I'm in danger of being caught up and voting in Spain on election day, instead of in Britain the day after. Not that it would make any difference: some of these men look like David Owen or Neil Kinnock, or actors imitating them. Who shall I vote for – the gang of the United Left? But they are somehow false – male models posing as revolutionaries. The Centre men? They confuse me with their contradictory but overlapping programmes, their alliances and splinters, their identical suits and steadfast looks. There must be selfishness, greed, cynicism behind those faces – the things I came here to escape. Probably I will settle for the Old

Boy on the Right, in the school tie. His kind of corruption is at least straightforward – he would give me a drink if we ever met.

Vans covered in hoardings and loudspeakers edge through the crowded streets and park in the Plaza de Zocodover. Perhaps on second thoughts I will vote for the Green party. They have no money, they make less noise. And Dulcinea's eyes were green – it's a man's favourite colour in the dry brown land of La Mancha.

The Plaza de Zocodover is where the poet Laurie Lee, busking in the cafés with his violin before the Civil War, met the poet Roy Campbell who was making a living horse-coping and trick-riding. Campbell claimed that humanity could be divided roughly into the Don Quixotes and the Sancho Panzas: 'I belong emphatically to the former,' he wrote. 'I live three-quarters of the time in my imagination.' He invited Lee back to supper in his house where he read his poems aloud late into the night. 'I was young, full of wine and in love with poetry,' Lee wrote long afterwards, 'and was hearing it now from the poet's mouth. What had I read till then? – cartloads of Augustan whimsy. This, I felt, was the stuff for me.'

For Roy Campbell, who was baptized, confirmed and remarried in the Catholic church, Toledo was the heart of Spain, the city of God that embodied the crusade for Christianity against Communism in the Civil War. During the siege, living on cucumbers picked at night in his garden, he gave shelter to Carmelite friars who brought the archives of St John of the Cross to his house for safety. But though he was a friend of the Governor, a tavern-keeper under whose rule a thousand unarmed citizens were killed, his quixotry, a private brand of fascism, couldn't save the friars from being shot and he found their seventeen bodies under a tarpaulin. He was lucky to escape himself; and lived to translate the mystic poetry of St John of the Cross, songs of the soul that yearn for God: '*Oh mi Dios*! When will it be, that I can truly say – I live at last because I shall not die?'

In the Plaza de Zocodover now there is a pavement artist, for ever touching up his enormous crayon version of St Peter in tears, more El Greco than El Greco. He has a baby in a pram beside him and drops his crayons to give it a bottle. Behind him old men sit along the wall – the faces of Spain. Some are Don Quixotes, long and solemn, gravely courteous; others are Sanchos, round and wrinkled, good-humouredly patient; a few could have heard Laurie Lee fiddling for pesetas. They like to compare walking-sticks – there is great interest in a silver band or a carved head or candy striping. A party of teenagers, bored with culture and ice creams, start dancing in the plaza, stamping and clapping to defy the loudspeakers. A little old man, mad or drunk, trips in among them and they dance on, laughing at him.

Up the hill from the Plaza de Zocodover is the massive four-square Alcázar, fortress, palace, barracks, a monument to nationalism and autocracy. In the Civil War the garrison held out against the republicans till they were relieved, though the building was half destroyed. For the third time in its history it was rebuilt: a huge, absurd castle – one day, perhaps, to become a Parador for tourists.

Across the city in the evening, under the cathedral walls, someone has parked a big Peugeot in a narrow cobbled street. Nobody can pass and soon a line of cars forms, tailing back into a small plaza. One driver shouts and sticks his tongue out, another slips into a bar for coffee, the rest blow their horns, then settle down to wait. Patience is part of the Spanish soul: *paciencia y barajar*, patience and shuffle the cards – the maxim that Don Quixote learnt in the cave of Montesinos. A better deal may turn up next time. Optimism is the essence – meanwhile, patience. People look out of their windows, pedestrians stop to watch.

Three policemen arrive with truncheons, pistols, radios. The drivers blow their horns again, the police tell them to stop: 'We'll sort this out, don't worry.' They peer through the Peugeot's windows, talk into their radios; and soon there are four policemen, then five and at last a sixth turns up with a man in a breakdown truck. Slowly he unshackles his chains, bars, hooks, and crawls under the Peugeot, hoists its back wheels, drives away with it. One of the policemen pulls out a ticket – *'vehículo retirado por la grua*, vehicle removed by crane' – and sticks it to the cobbles, pressing it down with his foot. By the time all the cars, kept waiting an hour and blowing their horns for relief, have driven over it there is nothing left.

In a bar the man beside me has a sack of fish the size of cod, their gills gasping for breath, on offer to customers. I ask him what they are.

'*Campo*,' he says.

I'm no wiser: 'From Galicia?'

'From the Mediterranean.'

Trying to imagine a man selling live fish in an English pub I go upstairs to the little dining-room – six tables with one other man enjoying his dinner alone and a woman with a cleft palate, in an apron, cooking behind a curtain: beans with bacon, pork fillet and salad, custard flan and half a litre of wine for six hundred pesetas. The TV is in black and white which makes the electioneering less strident.

Descending to the bar afterwards I catch sight of a half-familiar figure, not one of the politicians but a lean, harrowed man, no longer young, not yet decrepit, his eyes a little agonized by some misty private vision, blind to the facts of life around. He might be a crayon portrait of Don Quixote by that pavement artist in the Plaza de Zocodover, in the style of El Greco.

Of course, he is myself in a mirror.

THIRTY-EIGHT

I knew a man who would introduce his wife: 'This is my wife, who is my third wife, who was also my first wife.'

He was a Greek with a long nose and the laugh of Dionysus, who worked for the shipping tycoon Niarchos. Any time I wanted to go somewhere, he said, there would be an oil tanker going there too. I must find my own way to the refinery at Southampton or Rotterdam, but after that it would be free. I only had to telephone him and be ready to sail.

My journey had more purpose this time. In 1957 I applied for a visa to China and began learning Mandarin. I would write a book – I was a professional now, my passport said so – and pay my way with journalism. To hasten the visa, after waiting six months, I invited the cultural attaché at the Chinese embassy to come to *The Entertainer* with Laurence Olivier. (His name was Hu, which caused misunderstanding on the telephone: 'Hu speaking,' he would say.) He wouldn't come to the theatre alone and brought a colleague, but they didn't enjoy themselves – it was decadent, immoral, frivolous. After three more months I considered joining the Anglo-Chinese friendship society but a friend, a Labour MP, said it would blacken me for ever if I wanted to join the Labour party. I had never wanted to belong to any party, but didn't care to be blackened.

I risked something nastier when a man rang to say he had heard about me from someone – he had forgotten who – and asked me to lunch at his club. I would recognize him by his Winchester tie. We hadn't been at school together, he was ten years older, but in the club hall I could have picked him out anyway. The superiority verging on sarcasm, putting me in my place, and the confidence, knowing the club rules, and the air of conspiracy, reaching out to another old boy, were unmistakable. We had a thing or two in common, didn't we, he suggested with a wink.

'In my office,' he said, at a reserved table in the corner of the dining-room, 'there's a lot of interest in your journey.'

I asked what office it was, remembering the admiral and his outfit.

He dismissed it: 'Research – that sort of thing. Economic stuff, you know. A few hard facts to support the hunches. Putting two and two. . . .'

So why were they interested in me?

'There'd be something wrong if we weren't, don't you agree? Your story's pretty good.'

Story? I hadn't written it yet.

'Look here, old man – I mean to say, perhaps we haven't got the clout we used to have, but there's still a lot going for us around the world. And it's a way we can stay in the game. Keeping our finger on the old pulse.'

We? Britain, did he mean? Or the old school? The house? The club? I didn't belong to the club and my membership of the others was shaky.

He passed the menu: 'Steak for me – rare. And sauté potatoes.'

The same for me, I said – but medium. With a green salad.

'Lettuce?' he queried, giving me a chance to change my mind. 'Never go near it. Only good for rabbits.'

I was a junior boy confronted by a prefect. If I wasn't careful I would be in trouble. I was beginning to sweat, I noticed.

'Now China. . . .' His eyes swam towards the windows and out into London, trying to focus on the Yellow River, the Forbidden City, the wart on Chairman Mao's chin. 'We might be useful to each other.'

I didn't think I was really qualified.

'We wouldn't ask much. Nothing out of character, old man. We don't stick anyone's neck out for him. But imagine you're in some tinpot place at the back of nowhere and there's a cement factory with two chimneys – we'd like to know if they've both got smoke coming out of them. Small things like that – they tell us a lot.'

I told him I hadn't got a visa yet, and needed money.

'We thought of that.' He passed an envelope across the table with a hundred pounds in it. 'Might help you on your way. Pudding? Fruit? Ice cream – any of those things?'

Pocketing the money, guessing his opinion of sweets, I said a coffee would do.

'Good man. Two black coffees.'

Though I hated him and what he stood for, I knew that at some final judgement we were on the same side. I couldn't escape. It wasn't just that he had bought me with lunch and the envelope of money: I could never cut the terrible link between us.

'Someone in Hong Kong will get in touch,' he said, hailing a taxi for himself outside the club.

Wasn't it a mistake to be seen leaving together? Had I sold my soul for a hundred pounds? But I heard nothing more and nobody approached me in Hong Kong. When I told the Labour MP, who had written a book about spies, he said he knew of at least three different intelligence departments, all working against each other. The men in them often didn't seem to know what they were doing but they were harmless enough, merely boring – mostly ex-majors whose army careers were finished.

After a year the Chinese visa came and I rang the Greek. He said there was a tanker at Rotterdam due to sail empty to Kuwait where it would load up for Japan, and from there I could easily reach Hong Kong. His wife said she hoped I would be in Peking for the chrysanthemums. I arranged to write articles for the *Observer* and talks for the BBC, cancelled the milk and left. It wasn't an ordinary hitch-hike, more a luxury cruise with myself the only passenger. Niarchos built a private suite in his tankers next to the bridge, in case he fancied a voyage. If it was good enough for the owner it suited me.

This tanker had once been the world's biggest, but was a tenth the size of later ones. The chief engineer remembered a storm in the Irish Sea when they had been in ballast. Feeling a bump he looked out of his porthole near the stern and saw the bows of another tanker sailing past, rather close. On it he read the name of his own ship: the ballast had been badly distributed and it had broken in half. He waved at the captain on the bridge as it floated away, before going down to stop the engines. Later the two halves were welded together and now there was a steel strap across the deck.

The radio officer, an Englishman, spent his time reading Galsworthy or discussing women with his friends in other Niarchos tankers around the world. The captain, who had been blown up and sunk in a tanker – the deck peeled open like a sardine tin – was careful not to show his nerves on the bridge, but shared them happily with me over whisky in his cabin. One more voyage after this, and he would retire to his flat in Athens.

At Kuwait, tied up at the end of a pipeline coming out of the desert, the ship got orders to sail back to Rotterdam, not to Japan. There was no other Niarchos tanker in sight but the harbourmaster, a Welshman, promised to fix me up with something going my way. Give him a couple of days, he said, and in a coffee shop in the bazaar he told me about his early career in the Persian Gulf.

In a room over the coffee shop I started to write a story about a young Welshman, son of a sheep farmer, working for a shipping agent in an oil port at the edge of the desert. But I was interrupted by a Norwegian tanker coming in to load for Singapore. They had an empty cabin, the captain would like a passenger – a new face, someone who hadn't heard everything he had to say – and the radio officer wanted a chance to exercise her English. She was the wife of the second engineer, and I started a story about her too – discussing men by radio with her friends in other tankers around the world. But before I reached the end we arrived at Singapore.

Glad to have come so far for nothing I bought an air ticket to Hong Kong where I found a cheap hotel that doubled as a brothel. I wrote another story about a bar girl, Daisy Jane, who has a gold tooth and halitosis and gets an Englishman to write a letter to her last lover, a sailor in the US fleet. This time I finished it – Daisy Jane was too entrancing to abandon – before crossing into China.

THIRTY-NINE

May 29, Toledo. '*Olé!*' the children shout as I walk past. And a crippled lottery seller calls, '*Hombre!*'

But generally I'm ignored, which is a mercy, though at times I have to run the gauntlet of the idle old men who stare with something more menacing than curiosity: bunched at street corners, or perched like death's harbingers on benches in a plaza, or sitting in the window of a *casino*, their club, or in a bar with a glass and a cigarette and a scrap of memory in their dim resentful eyes. I see myself among them, not many years from now, shabby in a black beret, remembering those lost days of lust in the summer sunshine. I hurry past, hoping that it will be different for me, knowing that it won't.

Towards midnight a young man walks into the Plaza de Zocodover with a big square basket which he props against a tree. From it he takes a football and runs it up one arm, over his shoulders, behind his neck, down the other arm, spins it on his finger, on his head, throws it up, catches it on his chin, still spinning, tosses it on to his toe, flicks it up again and goes on for five minutes, then puts it back in the basket and fishes out three plastic dumb-bells which he juggles up and down, behind his back, round and round under his legs till a girl joins him, a clever scholarly-looking girl in jeans and glasses who takes out three more dumb-bells and they juggle together while a crowd gathers, enough to encourage them to show off, adding more dumb-bells, laughing when they miss one and let it fall, flipping it back into play with a foot and not even stopping when the man pulls an old black sombrero from the basket which he throws up among the dumb-bells, then leaves it on the ground for anyone to put money in. Nobody does. Nobody believes they aren't juggling for fun, they are enjoying it so much. They will juggle all night. But I can't ignore the hat and drop a hundred pesetas into it as I walk away, wishing I could do it less uncomfortably.

Don Quixote never came to Toledo, but there is a slab of black marble in the huge gothic cathedral with six Latin words that might have been left there by him; and his shadow hovers not far from it.

Set in the floor among the wealth of embellishment and treasure, carving, sculpture, El Grecos, boastful monuments to fame and glory, flickering electric candles and surly ticket-collectors, troops of indifferent schoolchildren and sweating tourists with their bubblegum and zooming cameras, trampled on by a thousand pagan feet an hour, it covers the tomb of a nameless, dateless cardinal-archbishop, primate of all Spain. On it, in big letters, is written simply, 'HIC IACET PULVIS CINIS ET NIHIL – here lie dust, ashes and nothing.'

Perhaps the corpse buried there was an ecclesiastical prince of surpassing arrogance and ambition, confident that his name was unforgettable and would be revered for ever without being spelt out. I prefer to think he was a modest man who, in the face of eternity, saw the futility of worldly things and chose to be remembered for it, anonymously. Like Don Quixote, whose true greatness showed in defeat, he saved his soul when all else was lost.

FORTY

Madame Xoum's was the place to go when everything else in Pnom Penh closed down for the King of Cambodia's three-day birthday. After dark I took a pedicab which dropped me in a lane at the edge of the town, where the rice fields began. The driver took my money, pointed into the night and pedalled away. I went through a gate, under a mango tree, round a hut, up a ladder. At the top a girl, after a word with someone inside, let me enter.

I was in a large room, but for some moments I could see nothing. A single oil lamp hung in a veil of insects. From the darkness pale features began to appear – partition walls of woven matting, the bamboo rafters and dim angles of the roof. Presently I noticed a little old woman in black sitting motionless on a table – Madame Xoum.

'What do you want?' she asked.

'I would like to smoke.'

'Have you been here before?'

'Never.'

'How did you hear about it?'

A friend had told me. Madame Xoum was famous throughout Cambodia. Cabinet ministers and ambassadors were said to be her clients. The élite of Pnom Penh society had attended her daughter's wedding.

She turned and spoke softly over her shoulder. A figure, or the ghost of one, showed itself at the fringe of the lamplight, then vanished. Five minutes passed and my eyes reached further into the dark. Someone gave a laugh, too muffled for me to tell whether it was a man or woman. The wooden floor creaked when another figure, barefoot in a sarong, crossed the room. Madame Xoum got off her table to take a closer look at me, up and down: not to check that I wasn't a police informer, probably, but that I was respectable enough. Then without a word she led the way along a passage to another room where she abandoned me.

I was half in a dream already. Something was happening, but I couldn't be sure if I was in control of it. Which was the illusion – this phantom house where I had come for some unknown enlightenment, or the possibility of retreat, going back down the ladder into the lane and finding another pedicab to take me away?

Among my possessions in a hotel not far away – clothes, camera, typewriter, washing things – was the book I was writing. Or was it? Did it have the substance even of this shadowy room in which I now found myself alone? Did it exist any more than the long journey through China and Indo-China, which it was supposed to describe? Were those travels – one man's unreliable account of himself passing through improbable places – as real, factual, solid as this mystifying arrival on a dark night at a rickety house beyond the town, outside the law?

I had travelled through China from Harbin in the north of Manchuria to Kunming in the south-west; then down into North Vietnam and on into the South. Back in Hong Kong I applied for another visa to China and settled down to wait on the island of Lantao, then in Macao, while writing articles and chapters of the book. But no visa came, so I went by cargo boat to Bangkok; and by train and bus up to northern Thailand where the Mekong river, rising in Tibet, slipping past China and Burma, comes through the mountains into Laos. For five days I lived on the roof of a river boat, plying between the magic hills, diving into gorges, dropping to Luang Prabang, the holy royal capital of Laos, a village of monasteries and silence where fishermen with hooped nets stood bird-like in the river's shallows. Then to Vientiane, another village but of embassies and intrigue, the seat of power not of God, where new Mercedes quickly grew old among the open drains and potholes, and Americans brayed about the free world, stretching out a desperate hand for someone to shake.

I interviewed a communist prince and stayed at a tin mine in the hills, and moved on down river to Thakhek, Savannakhet, Pakse. I spent ten days (or ten weeks? ten years? – nothing would be long enough for a lifetime) among the forest temples of Angkor: the silent nymphs and goddesses, snakes, lions, elephants, giants, devils, the devotion and in-spiration, pride and humility, the scope and size, the cicadas and bats and squirrels, the immense carved faces staring through the trees, some-times with a flicker of secret happiness, often with only a tired but patient hint of understanding, a look of love, a timeless father's look.

I had come far enough and was saturated. Soon I would be back in London, putting it into words. But at the moment I was in a dim room somewhere on the fringe of Pnom Penh; on the threshold too of consciousness, waiting blankly for whatever would happen next.

A woman – I couldn't see her clearly, she might be any age – brought a sarong. I undressed and put it on, and lay down on the rush floor, thankful to have a cushion for my head, not a china pillow. Slowly, as I got used to the dark, I made out the partition walls, lit by lamps in other rooms reflected from the high roof. Shadows passed through doorways, and someone put a plate of biscuits on the floor beside me. Like the light that faintly filled the room there was a soft, diffused noise: the tread of bare feet on rush matting, the creak of floorboards, a girl's whisper, a man's brief words in French, a cough, a stifled cry, the grunt or gasp of some unknown emotion, the chirrup of gekko lizards, the hum of mosquitoes. Or were they hallucinations, no more solid than those haunting the twilight of Don Quixote's mind? Suddenly, acridly, there was the whiff of opium through the rattan wall.

In time an old woman with a dried leather face brought smoking materials on a tray: tiny bottles and bits of wire, a small lamp, a pipe, a wine glass full of red beads. She placed it on the floor, squatted beside it, lit her lamp. The flame inside its glass globe near my face threw the room into deeper shadow, bringing a glow of appetite and conspiracy to the pair of us. The woman dipped a needle into the treacly opium, held it over the flame, let it burn and shrivel in the heat; then pressed it with her wizened fingers and burnt it again. Lying back I watched with qualms, almost with horror, as the obscene blob melted, swelled, sizzled on the needle over the lamp.

The woman pushed it into a little hole in the ivory pipe-bowl and handed it to me. I put the mouthpiece, like a trumpet's, to my lips and breathed in deeply while she held the bowl over the lamp for the opium to burn and bubble as I inhaled: a whole asthmatic lungful, or bodyful – the smoke reached through me to my feet. But I couldn't manage one pipe in a single breath, and the woman clicked her tongue in scorn.

I had four pipes, and after each she counted a red bead out of the glass for Madame Xoum's accounts. But there was no instant rapture, I was assailed by none of the expected dreams. It was simply a deep and unfamiliar pleasure. Instead of going to my head or stomach like alcohol the opium affected my whole body, numbing it with lethargy and euphoria. It was a happy feeling – blurred, gentle, exhausting. After a while I had four more pipes.

The woman was gone, absorbed back into the dark house. Now there was another, even scraggier, standing over me and offering a massage. She rolled me on my front, pummelled up and down on my ribs like someone playing a xylophone, and down my thighs. Then she stood up, planted a bare foot between my shoulder blades, caught hold of an arm and the opposite foot and jerked them sharply up and back towards each other: dropped them to the floor and caught up the other two. She knelt across me and kneaded through my flesh, wrung my ankles, bent my wrists, twisted my neck like a chicken's till it cracked, and cracked the joints of my fingers and toes one by one. She left me limp and breathless with muscles freshened, sinews stretched, bones loosened, all infused with opium, floating on eight pipes of it – eight red beads picked out of a wine glass – drifting helplessly a fraction above the floor, neither awake nor asleep.

The last woman was one of the *apsaras* from Angkor, a half-girl and half-dream carved on a temple wall. I had seen her in stone one morning recently, the sun climbing over the trees to warm her. She was younger than the *yakshi* I once met in India, and smiled at being caught in only her jewellery and a sarong so transparent that it hid nothing. To stop it slipping from her hips she held one hand modestly in front and lifted the other above her head – in boredom or anticipation, I couldn't tell. The curve of fingers, lips, eyelids, nostrils had been lovingly followed, like the wrinkles round her navel, the munificence of her breasts, the exact quality of her nipples. I watched her on and off all day, and photographed her several times. As the sun slowly altered her colour and the shadows melted on one side of her to reappear and lengthen on the other, she shifted and turned a little, an offering for whoever wanted her.

I wanted her. Imagination may have been enough for Don Quixote, but the Sancho Panza in me needed flesh as well as figment. And from her forest temple, out of the darkness of Madame Xoum's, the *apsara* stepped on to the rush matting beside me and pushed those coffee-bean nipples towards my lips. She no longer wore her necklace and ankle rings, and the sarong was soon off – so was mine. In sculpture at Angkor she looked generous, agile, a virtuoso. And here, quite simply, she kept the promise.

When I woke, with cracks of light breaking like dawn into the forest, the room was empty. A mosquito was whining round my head, other-wise the house was silent. I dressed and went out. The ladder seemed more rickety than when I had climbed it in the dark. At the end of the lane I found a pedicab parked under the trees, the driver asleep in it. I nearly pedalled away with him as my passenger, feeling a defiant energy, but the first touch on the handlebars stirred him awake and soon I was racing through the cool morning, to the hotel and breakfast.

I had a journalist's job to do that day, with an American publicity officer on some colossal, immensely important project of US aid – an excuse to escape the shut-down in Pnom Penh for the king's birthday. But I would come back to Madame Xoum's tonight, I promised myself.

Perhaps one should never go back.

Once I lived in Jerusalem and wrote a novel there, which meant tearing something out of me and leaving it behind; or more dishonestly, stealing a piece of Jerusalem and calling it mine. I thought it might be dangerous to return, but seven years later I did. On the night drive from Lod airport up through the Judaean hills I felt sick with nostalgia and apprehension. Had I spoilt the real Jerusalem by putting my imaginary one in a book? But at dawn next morning the old magic, hoisted from the eastern desert across the Jordan valley to touch the hilltop city, worked as potently as ever. I wandered in the old streets, tasted pistachios and Carmel brandy again, remembered things I had never known. The book I had written was about another place.

Perhaps, all the same, it was a mistake to go back to Madame Xoum's for a second night, though the damage might have been done already. In London a month later I saw something suspicious on me. I was being punished, as Sancho Panza would say, in the part where I had sinned. Opium, those innocent red beads counted out of a wine glass, wouldn't leave a mark like this – there must be treachery among the *apsaras* of Angkor. They were better left in stone, on a temple wall in the forest.

Later it appeared in a novel too, on a man who discovered it after his honeymoon: 'It wasn't much. Hardly more than a pimple that itched a little but didn't hurt. For the next week or so he watched it hourly but it didn't grow or erupt or change colour, it stayed just as he had found it on the Isle of Wight. Perhaps he shouldn't be surprised after the work it had been through. Any delicate piece of skin could be rubbed into a blister – a case of wear and tear. Give it a rest and it would recover.'

But I was frightened, knowing that it wasn't only *crête de coq* this time. It was something dangerous and I thought I knew its name. In a hospital clinic it was confirmed – the specialist welcomed me into a club with some very honourable members, his noble army of martyrs – and cured.

It didn't take long. The fright, disgrace, joke wore off like the evidence. And anyway, if it was good enough for Schubert, Goya, Nietzsche and all the others . . . I began to note who else had caught it.

Blaming it on foreigners like everyone else (to the Florentines it's the Naples sickness, to the Japanese it's the Chinese disease, to me it's the Pnom Penh pimple) Sancho Panza called it *el morbo gálico*, the French pox, long before it poisoned the wild oats of Baudelaire, Flaubert, Maupassant, Daudet and Jules de Goncourt, and of Poussin, Gauguin and Toulouse Lautrec. But Germans have been touched too – Heine, Schopenhauer and the tragic Crown Prince Rudolf who committed suicide with his seventeen-year old mistress at Mayerling – and sinners everywhere, some of them perhaps while smoking opium. Writers seem especially liable though often, like the first symptom, it's hardly more than a suggestion, merely hinted at in their lives. Keats and Tolstoy may have had it, and possibly Oscar Wilde, Norman Douglas, Dylan Thomas, Edward Lear, Isak Dinesen and Katherine Mansfield, with Donizetti, Smetana, Paganini, Delius, Lord Rochester, Lord Northcliffe and Lord Randolph Churchill. Even kings aren't safe – Francis I of France and Henry VIII of England were victims. It haunts a family in Ibsen's *Ghosts* and afflicts the old madman King Lear who, with his wise fool, is Don Quixote translated from La Mancha to an English heath (Shakespeare's play was published the same year as Cervantes's novel). In a different world the Chicago gangster Al Capone escaped the electric chair, but not the spirochaete.

The specialist seemed sorry when he discharged me, apologizing because I no longer qualified for his club. To have been briefly eligible was nothing to be proud of and wouldn't make me a better writer, but it was an honour of some sort to have shared such company. And soon I could speak about it without a blink, though I never did – except once, to a girl who asked. (We were on a paddle steamer crossing the Lake of Geneva – or was that also in a novel?) I might never have had it, till I put it into fiction. Imagination gave it authenticity. It was no longer a scar but a word, a string of words, part of a story: something of my invention, not a legacy of Madame Xoum's.

It's also the subject of a misogynistic ode by Nahum Tate, better known for re-writing *King Lear* with a happy ending, sparing the pain.

> *Blame not the stars; 'tis plain it neither fell*
> *From the distemper'd Heav'ns, nor rose from Hell. . . .*

194

I don't blame the stars. Nor do I curse, like Tate,

. . . that baneful source of all our woe,
That charming, wheedling sex that draws us in
To ev'ry punishment and ev'ry sin.

It was my fault, nobody else's, least of all that lovely *apsara*'s, lured from her temple at Angkor to Madame Xoum's opium house, and I regret it far less than other things I have done or failed to do.

FORTY-ONE

May 30, Tembleque. The summer has dropped on the land while I was in Toledo, the spring greenery has turned to the colour of breadcrust. Somewhere on the way here yesterday, along a baked escarpment, there was a castle on a cliff. It formed images of attack and defence, or of total uselessness like a missile base, the surplus effort of military vanity, the wasted imagination of soldiers.

Half a kilometre off *el general,* the north-south highway, I walk into this astonishing plaza where sometimes there are bullfights, now deserted, its two-tiered wooden galleries, archways, white-washed houses self-consciously preserved. The lamps are in authentic style, adverts are forbidden except election posters, the barber's shop has a brass basin like Don Quixote's hanging from the balcony.

It was raining when Don Quixote, on the road between two villages, met a donkey ridden by a barber who had put his brass basin on his head to keep dry. Don Quixote urged Rocinante into a gallop and attacked with his spear. The barber jumped off his donkey and bolted over the plain, dropping the basin. Don Quixote put it on himself, amazed at the enormous head that had worn it, but Sancho Panza couldn't help laughing.

His master silenced him: 'Do you know what I think, Sancho?' He had fought and beaten a knight on horseback, and won a golden helmet; and what Don Quixote thought, even if people like Sancho laughed, was what mattered. It took a madman, who would never laugh at anyone's mistake, to stifle a sane man's joke. He knew about appearances: the world was only what it seemed to each observer, and each made of it what he wished, whether sensible or absurd. 'What looks to you like a barber's basin looks to me like a helmet, and to another man will look like something else.' Basins, and windmills and rough village girls, led Sancho nowhere. But helmets and giants and the incomparable Dulcinea were landmarks of discovery, steps into the imagination of a man in search of himself.

I'm back in La Mancha, picking up Don Quixote where I left him. He might ride into Tembleque at any time and call for a meal and a bed, though he doesn't properly belong in a town, but on the open road or in the mountains, sleeping under the sky or in lonely inns.

Women come out to sweep the streets in the morning. One of them starts making *churros*, doughnuts the shape of sausages, at a stall by the church, a fine plain building of brick-and-tile angles and haphazard shadows – random purity after the extravagance of Toledo. Matins are being sung inside. But the convent down the street has been abandoned and its great windows, barred to defend the nuns, are now boarded too. Storks have balanced their ragged nest above the gate, spiked on a pinnacle with a dizzy view of the ruined cloister. A notice promises that the Ministry of Culture will restore the building, without any mention of the storks. Pecking among each other's feathers and stretching their wings, more faithful to the old convent than the departed nuns, they risk being evicted by the Ministry. A stork's nest on a tidy national monument, a blot on the picture postcards, would never be tolerated.

FORTY-TWO

Deirdre was sitting on the grass at a party in a London garden, smoking a pipe. ('Did you marry your mother?' the psychotherapist asked, not knowing that she too had smoked a pipe.) Vaguely doing a George Sand act, she called it. Wearing black trousers and a shirt of wide improbable stripes with something silver round her neck, possibly Inca – she was born in Peru. The loveliest woman in sight. Only nineteen – the age that Potts, the young murderer, had been. A summer evening in 1959, off the Fulham Road. Every husband must keep a picture of that meeting; must feel it in the blood even if he can't still see it. My pulse does a skip, goes into a dotted rhythm at the memory. There are photos from that time that have the same effect, and letters that nearly half a lifetime later I read with a surprise close to both laughter and tears, disbelieving my luck.

She had come alone to London and was attending Latin classes for an exam. In the autumn she would go to Oxford to read history. Poised at the beginning of something, waiting to see what it would be like. I too was freewheeling, carried by the momentum of writing my second book. Now it was finished and delivered to the publisher. The next journey could begin any time – I was ready.

Two orbits touched. They might glance off and separate; or merge and travel on, side by side, a short way or into the distance. Someone in a novel says, 'The *accident* of life – that's what I find exciting.' But often the orbits must narrowly miss, never to know how close they were.

So we came from different pasts one evening to a London garden. The sky dimmed behind the roofs, a summer chill grew from the darkening grass, the trees crept closer, getting bigger in the dusk. We left the party together and had supper at an Italian place in Gloucester Road. I absorbed the lucid eyes, the comma-crescent nostrils, the unsparing mouth; the quality of gift.

'I hate you, I hate you,' she said after supper, with good reason, years later. 'You're the snake in my life' – though she was the woman in mine. The hate and everything else began in that summer of 1959, the last of the angry nineteen-fifties.

I had a flat at the top of a tall house near Notting Hill Gate: a gaunt studio room with a big north window, a stove, a painting of trees by a friend, my mother's piano which I couldn't play, a pot of bulrushes which I had picked by a Sussex river, some bookshelves, a bed; up a ladder to a platform with another bed and a window on to the roof. Friends often came, and sometimes stayed. The room could look like a camp of refugees – they might be from Africa or India – among the bottles and coffee cups.

I can see a woman with fair hair and wide grey eyes on the sisal carpet, a journalist in nothing but her scarlet tights. With an effort I can put a misty story to her and trace the brief track of our affair, but that one bright vision comes easily. And there was a second virgin, a vicar's daughter driving a red Lambretta scooter, with a unique tip-tilted nose. Like a grasshopper she stalked up my long stairs on springy insect legs, and was springy in bed too. This time there was no Arpège, but the faint scent of smoked bacon – I wondered why. She exchanged the scooter for a bubble car and turned up one awkward evening simultaneously with the journalist. The coward in me said that the best way out was to leave them together, so I went to a pub for an hour or two, trying to guess which one of them would still be there when I got back.

Often I was alone for days, glad to meet another tenant on the stairs or the milkman at the street door. As well as a book I wrote articles and reviews. Occasionally I played my flute. Or I eyed the telephone, wishing to be rung up: even someone with the wrong number would do – a stranger to have a few words with. Once, to make sure it was working, I went out to the nearest callbox, dialled my number and ran back to find it ringing in the empty flat. I picked it up and said 'Hello,' half hoping to hear my voice at the other end. But the silence answered with a laugh.

It may have been my aloofness up there, seeming proud and lonely, or even my asthma, the wheezing writer with weak lungs – or possibly the thin, angular, idealistic, slightly absurd character, the horseless Don

Quixote without a Sancho Panza – that drew Deirdre. Perhaps she could join my fantasies, or perhaps become one.

She lay on the roof one empty day, sipping wine, flicking olive stones into chimneypots; talking of her history teacher at school, Frederick the Second, a Jesuit she had met, St Francis of Assisi. In Italy she had gloried in the renaissance, unlocked by the miracles she saw. In France she had filled her eyes with cathedrals, abbeys, castles: already she was launched on a lifelong drift into the Middle Ages. In Spain she had fallen for the apricot afternoons and lemon-scented nights, the gypsy life that would end at Oxford. With me, on the way there, she found a brief refuge from Latin translations where predictability could be postponed. The heavy summer air, humming-full of London, settled over her and the talking stopped.

Leaning against the warm brick, excited and alarmed, she wondered what we were about to do; feeling a hollowness inside, yet a fullness too. Stretched along the parapet, my eyes closed by the bright sky, I put out a hand and took hers. Deirdre, you are gorgeous. So brown and beautiful. Her fingers, curled in mine, spoke of a desire melting in the sun, of her translucent fears and tenderness. But I was thirteen years older, a friend of her uncle, and she thought it faintly indecent to love a man old enough to be her father's brother's friend. Anyway I didn't love her, she was sure, but just liked holding hands.

We could be spontaneous and impulsive, there was nothing else to do. We went to films and galleries, explored the docks, drank beer in riverside pubs – it wasn't very original. I took her to East End places and showed her churches, tombs, inscriptions, finding new pleasure in them with her. Cranes hung over the water, barges nudged the tide – London was still a port. Deirdre added her own ingredients. In Wapping she went into a warehouse and from the astonished storeman bought some purple hessian bags she liked. At a dockside mill in Rotherhithe, where men were loading sacks of flour, she tried to carry one; strained, staggered, heaved it to its place – this strong and obstinate girl powdered with flour in front of the cheering porters and my humiliated self. She stopped a horse-wagon that came lurching over the cobbles, trotting among railway lines, and pulled me up into the back among a load of tea chests for a ride through the traffic to Tower Bridge. The driver winked at Deirdre, an ally against my awkwardness, then whipped up his horse and drove away.

This enchanting girl – at times a child, a tomboy, a fragile woman, inchoate yet sage. The most unprejudiced person I had known, but infuriating too. Soft, sultry, languid; fierce, untidy, impossible. The big black pupils, showing happiness or horror. The vitality and intelligence. The nerves, alert and tense. The strong back, thin wrists, dirty feet, loose brown hair. One rare day when she was in a cotton skirt, not trousers, it blew up and I saw her thighs – her best part, she said, surprised that I hadn't admired them before.

They were bright, tantalizing days. Algerian wine cost four shillings and ninepence in Old Compton Street, coffee was six-and-six a pound delivered from Soho once a week, our happiness was free. In my little kitchen over little Mediterranean meals we explored each other and ourselves, teasing for the truth. I struggled with a Bach prelude on the piano, Deirdre lit a joss stick. Each of us was stubborn, independent, perplexed. Will you go back to your room tonight, Deirdre? Or stay with me?

Usually she went away, to do some Latin for tomorrow's lesson. Sometimes she stayed the night and slept with me, for extra torture. I would kiss her eyes, ears, breasts, toes, but she kept her jeans on. Before the end of the rumpled sweat-damp night, sick with lust, I would have a bath and make coffee, leaving her asleep in the tormented bed. Crudely, to my shame, I left the Oxford Book of English Verse in the kitchen, open at Marvell; 'Had we but world enough and time . . .' It was the banality she resisted. If I had been one of the bristly garlic-breathing lovers of her dreams she might have let me tear her trousers off.

But she could hate me even then. She couldn't stand my arrogance, still less my patience. If I grew morose or cold she looked frightened: I might drop her, abandon her to her precious innocence. So what was she afraid of? Of being disgusted? Of the pain? Of a baby? She had no real arguments. But I was a fool, she said, to suppose there was any reason in it. It was a tussle between two instincts in her. You'll change, I told her, and pushed her away.

Once or twice she cried. Or else she laughed, which was the best thing, and ran away. Yet she wanted to make love as badly as I, and hardly knew why we didn't. 'Don't sleep with strange men,' her father had said before she came to London. She had made a sort of pact, a variation of a childhood promise. And that was another thing: she had a superstition that she had got into Oxford, not on her history but her virginity. She would keep her part of the bargain at least till she arrived there.

The summer passed. One evening, with friends of mine in a pub, she drank too much – from nervousness, or to make me proud of my tough girl who could put down beer like the others, or because she felt young and lonely among my older friends. I steered her home and somehow up the long stairs, swaying as we climbed. We cooked spaghetti and she swallowed it, trying to show that nothing was wrong. Her voice thickened, she lapsed into uncertain French, then further into Spanish. In the end she bolted for the bathroom and was sick. Behind the locked door I heard sobs of rage and shame, and cold water being splashed. (Long afterwards, exasperated by three small children and an unperceptive husband, she locked herself in the bathroom again and beat herself with a hairbrush till it broke – our house groaned with pain.) I had been like that myself, I remembered how it felt, I would be kind to her when she came out.

Next morning we side-stepped, trying to see if we were in new positions. The gap between us was of experience, not of years. I wasn't her lover but her uncle's friend, I was tempted to treat her as a niece, and subdued by the night she was tempted to respond as one. She must get on with her Latin if she was to pass the exam. I was going away to Wales with a friend, to walk in the autumn hills and wash myself of London.

When I returned I knew at once that she had been in the flat with her friends. ('Shall I tell you a secret?' I had once said on the stairs. 'I love you. Shall I tell you another? This is where I keep the spare key.') Perhaps the clues were deliberate: an empty whisky bottle, cigarette ends in the dustbin, half the coffee gone. I was annoyed, more with myself than with her: with my silly cult of self-sufficiency, my jealous privacy, my foolish hopes. When she came to explain I felt no better – I wasn't her confessor any more than her lover.

She had had a party, a double celebration for her twentieth birthday and for passing her Latin, and with two other girls had finished up in my flat. She told them it belonged to a man she knew. A writer. Nobody they had heard of. Much older than them – thirty-three at least. He was away in the mountains somewhere, he wouldn't be back. They were safe, they could make themselves at home. Use his telephone, drink his drink. Read his books, have a bath. He wouldn't mind, he needn't know. She had often stayed there before. It was a kind of revenge, a way of getting at him: the man who hadn't quite seduced her. Instead she had broken into his flat. So they laughed and danced and spent the night, one on the sofa, one in the spare bed, Deirdre in mine.

In a novel it might be funny. I would come back and find three naked girls in my room. Fucking hell! – what's going on? Or fucking heaven, more likely – which of you will have me first? I might try them all. But Deirdre, as if my bed was still a risk even without me in it, slept in a shirt of mine.

Now she was sorry and I was cautious, remote but not indifferent, though I couldn't tell her why. The gap between us, once so narrow, had opened up again. We both felt sad. We had missed something, we had made a mistake somewhere and now everything was wrong.

I kissed her and suddenly she began to cry, spilling great tears. She had expected me to be angry and instead I had kissed her which made her weep – which wasn't what I expected. Puzzlement, compassion, irritation, helplessness – I was inadequate to cope. I sat with her and got up and went to the window and sat down again and got up. She looked so lovely in full spate and I told her so (she made a mental note, she admitted later, to cry more often), and the tears came flooding on. I kissed them like a dog till my shirt was soaked, till at last they stopped. There was nothing more to come, except the return of sunshine in her eyes, breaking through the storm. In her way – versatile, volatile, a phenomenon of nature – Deirdre was rather like the weather.

It was her last night before going to Oxford. We feasted on gin and avocados, her atonement gift. Soon she would take her trousers off, but not tonight. Though we slept together a new need, more peaceful and understanding, lay with us. I longed fiercely for her body, and at last she shared the longing. But to make love now, after the strain of chastity all summer and with only a few hours left, seemed an affront. It would be ironic, it could wait.

Next day she went to Oxford. Go away, I said, on the brink of unkindness. Don't get me wrong but I can't stand it any longer, no man could. Go to Oxford and come back a woman. I can't manage girls. Take your precious treasure with you. You'll soon get tired of it. Give it to a nice young man. You'll find him waiting for you – he's been there a year or two already, he knows his way around. He'll be looking out for you among the new girls. He's called Julian, probably, like so many of them. Studying medieval history. In Christchurch, I expect.

She laughed: 'Why Christchurch?'

God knows, I said, but send me a postcard if I'm wrong. And don't treat him as you treated me. He won't like it and he might not be so patient. Sometimes it's been hell. That's why I've been so beastly – I'm sorry. So be nice to him, I told her. It wasn't a good speech and Deirdre took no notice of it, but I didn't mean to sound abrupt or sarcastic.

Enjoy yourself there, I added. And when you've had enough, come back and stay with me. For as long as you like. I'll try not to be too bloody, but it's in me. Perhaps you can do something about it. And I kissed her goodbye.

So Deirdre went to Oxford. I have invented her, of course.

FORTY-THREE

May 30, Tembleque. At times I wish I had brought a bicycle to Spain. I wait three hours at a bar beside *el general* for a bus to Madridejos and three more for another to El Toboso. On a bike I could have taken cross-country roads.

At times also I wish I had a companion. Don Quixote had his Sancho Panza and – a real presence, a real woman – his Dulcinea. But there is a need to be self-centred and another person has other needs. To be alone is to be vulnerable, exposed only to oneself and one's own imagination.

Two Moroccan families in big estate cars with Paris number plates, loaded to the ground, have parked for a picnic behind the petrol station. Children are sent off to squat in the ditch while veiled women tear loaves of bread apart and the men escape to the bar for coffee. At a table outside, buffeted by the draught of passing lorries, I'm joined by a threadbare man in a black cap, carrying a plastic bag, who asks for money. He kisses the hundred pesetas I give him before dropping it in the bag; then picks up my *El País* and reads it aloud, slowly, sitting beside me.

The bus from Madridejos to El Toboso takes me finally away from *el general* through vines, barley, wheat, more vines. The fields are becoming poorer, the villages more silent and faceless. Even the bus is nearly empty. After a soldier gets out at a lonely crossroads I'm left with one other passenger, a girl who talks non-stop to the driver in a throaty voice loud enough to reach the sierras (I remember Sancho's story of Dulcinea shouting from the church tower, being heard far away in the fields) and tries to bring me in.

We pass a small lagoon with a café beside it and signs, not very lively, of water sports; and later a string of salt pans. Outside a village there is a row of wooden doorways into the hillside.

'Are they houses?' I ask the girl in the bus.

'Caves,' she tells me.

'Do people live in them?'

She laughs: 'Long ago.'

We discuss Tembleque, Toledo, London, and I ask her about El Toboso. '*Muerto* – dead,' was what Benito, the young bar owner who gave me a lift two weeks ago, called it. This girl uses another word, one I don't understand, but from the sound and shape of her lips it's worse than death.

A small white chapel stands in the fields, more like an Asian pagoda than a Spanish church. Children are kicking a ball against it. Under a tree a dozen men and women are having lunch. The summer has occupied the land, each day is a few degrees hotter.

Don Quixote rode into El Toboso at midnight, hoping for the blessing of his incomparable Dulcinea who lived here. The village was asleep, there was no sound but the barking of dogs, grunting of pigs, mewing of cats, braying of a donkey. 'Sancho, my son,' the knight said, 'lead me to Dulcinea's palace. Perhaps we shall find her awake.'

Sancho was at a loss, knowing only a peasant girl in a cottage. And was this the time for knocking up people? Were they a pair of pimps, going round the whorehouses at all hours? They began to quarrel, the knight admitting he had never been inside Dulcinea's palace in his life, though he adored her, and his squire confessing he had no idea who Dulcinea was. 'Sancho, Sancho!' his master cried. 'There's a time for jokes and a time when they fall flat.' But a young farmer, on his way with two mules to start ploughing before dawn, couldn't help: 'I don't believe there's any such lady in the place.'

Cunningly, though touched by his master's madness and becoming unsure of Dulcinea's reality, Sancho said they shouldn't be found wandering round El Toboso at night. They went back into the countryside and hid in a wood till daybreak, when Don Quixote told Sancho to return alone in search of Dulcinea and beg her to receive her knight. Sancho mustn't be frightened at such beauty, but watch her slightest move, her nervousness, her colour, her voice – anything to betray her secret feelings. 'Trust me,' Sancho said, and rode back towards El Toboso, leaving the knight full of muddled, melancholy thoughts.

Sancho too was troubled, and sat down under a tree to ponder. He was being sent to look for a nobody – for a princess as dazzling as the

sun, living in a palace. The people of El Toboso would beat him up if
they found out. His master ought to be in a strait-jacket, and he himself
was no better – even more of a fool to follow him. But Don Quixote
mistook one thing for another, black for white, windmills for giants, so
he might be persuaded that the first girl he met was Dulcinea. And if
he didn't believe it, Sancho would swear it.

In the afternoon, riding on donkeys, three girls from the village came
along the road. Sancho hurried back to Don Quixote, who was sighing
a thousand sighs of love.

'What luck, Sancho?'

'Your lady Dulcinea is coming out to meet you with two others.
Come on – you'll see them in a blaze of gold, all clusters of pearls,
diamonds, rubies, brocade, their hair to their shoulders like sunbeams
in the wind, on three fine horses . . .'

'Holy God!' Don Quixote cried. 'What are you saying? If you're
cheating me . . .' His squire must be trying to cheer him with false
hopes. 'I can see nothing,' he said when they emerged from the wood.
'Only three village girls on donkeys.'

'Nonsense! Rub your eyes! Pay homage to the lady of your dreams!'
Sancho dropped to his knees and addressed one of the girls: 'Queen,
princess, beautiful duchess! – may your high-and-mightiness be pleased
to receive your captive knight who stands there turned to stone . . .'
Trying to convince his master he almost deceived himself, while Don
Quixote knelt beside him in confusion at this moon-faced, snub-nosed
wench.

'Out of the way!' she shouted. 'We're in a hurry!'

She must be bewitched for him alone, Don Quixote thought. This
ugly peasant, treated by Sancho as a princess, was an insult to his
imagination. Years of hoping for the impossible – more deeply hoped
for, being impossible – couldn't be wiped out by bleak reality. 'Oh
perfection of all desire!' he began. 'Pinnacle of human grace! Sole remedy
for this afflicted heart . . . !'

'Tell that to my grandmother!' she yelled. 'You think I want to listen
to that crap? Out of the way!' Kicking her donkey into a trot she fell
off and Don Quixote ran to pick her up. But she jumped on the donkey's
back, far from ladylike, and sped away with her friends.

'Look what my enemies have done!' the Knight of the Sad Countenace
cried. 'Not just transformed her, but turned her into that hussy. And
even robbed her of the sweet scent that comes from a life among flowers
and perfume – I got a whiff of garlic that stank to my heart.'

The hypocrite in Sancho, or the coward or the liar or the half-quixotized Sancho, joined in: 'The swine! I'd like to see them strung up by the gills like sardines. Wasn't it enough to turn those pearls of eyes into acorns and her golden hair into a bristly cow's tail, without meddling with her smell? Though to tell the truth I never saw any ugliness about her, only beauty, and it was set off by a mole on her lip, with some long red hairs like threads of gold.'

'Then she must have another one to match it on the fat of her thigh,' Don Quixote said. The true Dulcinea, whoever the one in real life might be, was a creation of his mind and he was free to see her as he pleased. 'Nature has put nothing on Dulcinea that isn't perfect. If she had a hundred moles like that, they would shine like stars. But I didn't see it, Sancho – I'm the unluckiest of men!' It was his most tragic moment.

In El Toboso this afternoon the sun bounces from the white houses and dusty streets. After a drink with a few olives in a bar I walk through the little town. A museum, 'Dulcinea's house', is fitted out with massive furniture of the period, walnut chests and tables, wine jars, a big double bed, an ox cart in the backyard and a wine press made from a single tree trunk. The Cervantes centre, where they keep copies of *Don Quixote* in thirty languages, is locked, but I'm too lazy to knock up the caretaker. There are texts from the book written in tiles on the street corners and the usual grotesque statues of the knight and his squire.

I feel a growing resentment at the bony, knobbly, ineffective figure of Don Quixote, a sense of personal insult. That bundle of shreds and patches is too like myself. It brings back the anti-imperialist demonstrations in China thirty years ago where the long-nosed scarecrow being ridiculed by the crowd was uncomfortably familiar. Sometimes I was recognized as a genuine example and laughed at in disbelief.

I find a shady place where I can sit out this soporific afternoon. There is almost nobody about. A priest, a boy, two girls, an old man walk past. A church bell strikes each quarter-hour for an hour, two hours, while I sit under the trees. Someone starts a motorbike and roars away into the distance. The old man walks past again. I think I can hear the jingle of a fruit machine reaching through the heat, but it may be an echo in my empty head. A quarter of an hour later the old man comes back, keeping time with the church clock. In another quarter of an hour he is back again.

'*Buenas tardes,*' I say.

At once he tells me about his cataracts, in both eyes. Then he wants to know where I am from, and I tell him. 'The children learn English,

French, all those things in school now,' he says. 'We were never taught them.'

I ask him where I can stay in El Toboso. There is no fonda or hotel here, the nearest is the Venta of Don Quixote five kilometres away on the main road from Madrid to Valencia. The old man tells me to go to the Martinez brothers' bar where someone will find me a room. 'You have no companion?' he asks. 'You shouldn't travel alone – it's bad for you. You need someone to talk to. Even Don Quixote . . .'

I half think I might sleep out in the open, but later I go to the Martinez bar. A big card game is going on, with spectators watching over the players' shoulders, more popular even than the TV. Some of the older men wear short black smocks. A lunatic in a peaked cap and uniform jacket covered with military badges stamps his boots and salutes me – a pale descendant of Don Quixote. I salute back. He begins to shout. The barman hisses at him. He shouts louder. Everyone hisses and the barman gives him a beer to keep him quiet. I have a beer too and ask about a room. I can have supper here, they say, but not a bed. The man next to me tells me to try the house at the end of the street, the last door on the left.

I go there and knock once, twice, three times, banging and ringing a bell, louder each time. I like El Toboso, I want to stay here. At last an old woman, Antonia, opens the door.

'Yes, yes,' she says, 'I was expecting you – you want a bed for the night, I know.'

How did she know?

'The girl on the bus from Madridejos is my nephew's wife – she told me about you. They all come to Antonia.'

She locks her door and leads me back down the street, past the huge old convent of the Trinitarias to another big building, also monastic with high walls, its lower windows heavily barred; through an archway into a court with a fountain where children are playing and a woman is hosing the plants; up a staircase in the corner to the second floor, into a modern flat.

'It's my brother's,' Antonia says. 'He's working in Madrid.'

I have a room overlooking the court, better than in any fonda or hotel. Next door is a Japanese – I can't escape them: here, in a small Manchegan town, the only other foreigner is a Japanese. He speaks no English and almost no Spanish. Over the roofs the sun drops behind pink-grey clouds towards Toledo, the crickets start chattering in the roadside thistles, and night comes with a sharp chill. On such a night

Don Quixote and Sancho Panza rode into El Toboso in search of Dulcinea.

I go back for supper at the Martinez bar, at a table next to the card players: *sopa de cocido*, a big salad, two pork chops and fried potatoes, bread and as much wine as I can drink, with a coffee, for six hundred and fifty pesetas – value and friendliness and general happiness around – better still when I'm praised for my terrible Spanish. Off the tourist trail the people are very polite, untouched by the rough and ready manners elsewhere. George Orwell wrote that the Spanish have 'a generosity, a species of nobility, that do not really belong to the twentieth century.' The common idiom for the pronoun 'you' is still what Sancho called his master, 'your honour', without any irony at all. And whatever his humiliation, Don Quixote stayed dignified and courteous.

FORTY-FOUR

Deirdre came back on a December day after her first term at Oxford. It had been a confused, unhappy time. At the beginning she decided to shut herself in her room with a gramophone and whisky, live a silent Cistercian life, work hard and get a First. (She got it twenty-six years later at another university.) Then, finding things to enjoy, she thought it would be pleasant to treat her college as a sort of hotel, a base for Oxford life. But she had to work and her tutors made her miserable, the lectures appalled her. She found friends in her college, but the men were mostly pink and footling youths, frightened of women whom they tried to impress, or suppress, by talking clever nonsense. At their parties she vented her scorn on them, and eyed Christchurch tower with amusement. She wrote that she might be expelled from Oxford if she didn't abandon it first, though probably by then she would start to love it: 'Like most things, I don't appreciate them properly till I'm on the point of losing them.'

A romantic fool, she called herself when she came to London, feeling pale and pre-Raphaelite in a jersey the colour of winter leaves, a jacket of green moss. Her hair and face were wet with rain as she climbed the stairs to my flat, wild and happy with a touch of Irish.

We went out again through the rain – we had time to kill, as well as innocence – to the Festival Hall, hoping for the *Messiah*, but there were no tickets left. We walked back over Hungerford Bridge, the rain falling on the black river; dropped a coin in a blind man's battered violin case; bought a bag of roast chestnuts at Charing Cross. Deirdre laughed at the London scene, the platitude of tonight's performance: feeding each other, strolling down the Christmas-lit streets among the evening shoppers, the hissing traffic. We passed a fruit stall bright with lamps and

211

oranges, hung with pineapples, bananas, coconuts. She caught the lemon smell of Spain for the last time through a child's nostrils; and absorbed the picture of us two together and our separate lives, aware of each moment's flavour.

We went to a film, *Huis Clos*, Sartre's view of hell, a glittering luxury hotel where the lights are never switched off, the mirrors reflect nothing, the guests stay for ever, neither growing old nor dying, unable to leave or escape each other. *L'enfer, c'est les autres* – hell is other people.

'What would you go to hell for?' Deirdre asked, back in my flat. ('Marriage is hell,' she wrote in a letter years later – not to me, but she left it lying around.)

For being a coward, I told her: a Sancho Panza tonight, more than a Don Quixote. Not only for undressing and leading her up the ladder, naked, to the platform and to bed, but for being who I am. For being frightened of getting hurt, as well as hurting her. Or for being secretive and intolerant and quickly bored. Or for seeing what hadn't happened yet – a future that, if I looked hard and honestly beyond tonight, might be dangerous for us both. Or just for being a nice man, no good for a writer; or a nasty one, no better.

An autobiography that doesn't tell something bad about the author, Orwell said, can't be good. 'Powerful but flawed' was a publisher's verdict on a novel of mine, rejecting it in a few words, and I didn't complain. The power is vital, the flaw is original: the fatal hairline crack in a bell that makes it uniquely imperfect, the deadly blemish in an otherwise sound book that made it mine. It would do for an epitaph, I would want no more: he was powerful but flawed.

We were unhurried, tasting the beautiful pain, the tearing numbing blissful loss, unbearable and unforgivable. Deirdre darling, Deirdre, I love you. Shall I go to hell for this? A woman in a novel says with sadness, 'Even making love one is alone.' Though practically part of someone else she feels utterly separate and the closeness only emphasizes it. She hoped for something more, a kind of uninvited but expected third party.

That night Deirdre, always observant of herself and now the powerful one while her lover died, remembered Munch's painting of Woman as a vampire sucking the blood of Man, holding his limp neck in her teeth. She would never understand this backwards-forwards pattern, the filling and draining of strength, though she would feel it ten thousand times again. And after this there seemed to be no experience left, except childbirth and death. But next day she was wilder and happier than before, loving her new but self-same self.

For months we watched and learnt. At concerts, over curry suppers, in letters, through touch and words we unwrapped our thoughts. On a cold winter walk along the Essex coast, following the dyke between the shore and marshes, Deirdre stripped off her clothes and sprang into the freezing sea. She was often naked at that time, though she liked to keep a ring or necklace on, a talisman against the future. Under the happiness she already heard a sombre theme, a pedal note of doom. Wearing a burnous she had picked up in a Moroccan market, over coffee and toast and gauloises at breakfast in my flat, moving between the kitchen and bathroom or tidying the bed – perhaps seeing us still on it – she would put a Haydn symphony on the gramophone. But when she bought a record to take back to Oxford it was usually a requiem.

Separately we tried to convince ourselves that we liked being alone, defying the truth. Any unhappiness, Deirdre wrote, came from other people – *l'enfer, c'est les autres* – and the worst unhappiness was when someone so interfered with her life that she could no longer enjoy herself alone. A love affair must end unhappily, she felt, through parting or petering out or turning into marriage, disintegrating into habit. But Oxford in the spring was too beautiful for cynicism. She was only twenty and, with no illusions, wouldn't have the fun of losing them at thirty. Bugger Sartre.

Yet loneliness distressed her: the hopeless gulf between individuals, the impossibility of knowing anyone or even communicating with them. It made it no better to see that I was also confused. She recognized that I was deceiving myself, resisting her if not myself, though my ambivalence was no comfort. I like living alone, Deirdre, it's part of my vanity, but I like living with you too.

We didn't live together – Deirdre felt she was a visitor in my flat. Without her I would still get up in the morning, shave, make coffee, read the paper, open any letters. No letters came for her when she had breakfast with me. She was merely passing through and would soon be gone, back to her college room, her essays and tutorials. She sensed my need for solitude and saw how my patience might break.

She wished we were more open with each other. She knew me better than any other man, but felt she knew nothing. I was close, guarded, terribly independent. I hardly spoke of my parents and childhood, having locked them into the past, whereas hers weren't far away. My silence insulted her, though I didn't mean it. I didn't know how much to disclose, I was less sure than she was. And less generous. There's nothing to tell you, Deirdre – it's all so boring.

Beneath the entwining love we shared a helpless isolation, trying to form something greater than ourselves; to give more than we possessed. And sometimes, even then, we quarrelled. I was rude, Deirdre was hurt, she fled downstairs slamming the door in my face, I pursued her. She said, 'I love you and wish I didn't and would be happier to hate you.' (Twenty years later she said, 'I'll never make love with you again – never, never, never,' but it didn't last a week.) One night we slept in separate beds and she told a friend that then she felt really married to me: 'He's a shit, isn't he?' The friend passed it on.

Why couldn't she be cruel too, to match my infuriating self-containment, my pleasure yet near-impatience in her presence? Was I frightened, having lost my parents as a child, of committing myself to something that might let me down again, and so I hardened myself against further hurt? Could she not soften me, letting me respond without risk of mockery or disappointment? Did I refrain from probing deep into her for fear that she might do the same to me, or even expect me to do it to myself? Was I afraid of being found out, exposed in some painful inadequacy? And why did she smile to hide her sadness and keep her own secrets, despite her nature? If she cried, was it because it was easier than to try and express such a multitude of things to someone who was simultaneously so near and distant?

I too was troubled by my contradictions, though I could accept them more happily – they were mine, after all, as personal as my face and voice. I might put out feelers, physical or intellectual, to touch her, but I didn't want to blend. I liked my purity – or rather impurity – the ragbag of bits and pieces that made up my shamelessly inconsistent self. I was nobody's man, except my own. And though I truly, beyond all experience, found joy in making love with Deirdre and knew how she could feel it, I didn't tell her that while doing so, searching in her eyes, I saw only myself. 'In a love affair,' Graham Greene wrote, 'it is our own features that we see reflected flatteringly back.' But I wasn't often flattered.

Nothing escaped her. She watched my movements, collected details, good and bad, knowing that it irritated me. She noticed that when I took her to Paddington station for the Oxford train I spoke about us together in the past tense, but about us separately in the future. She was afraid that I would throw her out soon and was suspicious when I showed kindness. It seemed artificial, not a lover's kindness but her uncle's friend's, to make up for past cruelty and prepare her for worse. She might be glad when the affair was over. 'Goodbye, dear beast,' she wrote from Oxford.

I invented her, of course: she is a character of fiction and exists no more truly, or less fictitiously, than the women in my novels. But did I love her only in the way I love them, as my creation, something sprung – like love itself – spontaneously and unexpectedly from the void, solely for me, to be typed on to the empty page? I couldn't tell, and still can't. And I too was afraid – of the danger that imagination wasn't enough, but reality might be fatal. 'Human kind,' Thomas Becket says in *Murder in the Cathedral* before being martyred, 'cannot bear very much reality.' To test myself, or delude myself, I invented another woman. I think I'm falling in love with someone else, Deirdre. I went to Greece that summer, and Deirdre went to Africa. She never expected me to love her or want her for long, but it made it no less hard when what she knew would happen did.

On the island of Zakinthos I lay all day on a great dazzling beach. I had it to myself, miles of it, and pranced naked in and out of the sea, and longed for Deirdre. It was she I wanted, nobody else, that brilliant day and I wondered, with a kind of fear, how long it would go on. Back in London, after a party of friends in my flat, alone in the mess and desolation, I cried myself to sleep. Deirdre had never seen me cry and it was years before she did. I cried from love and shame, but mostly love.

In the autumn she wrote coolly about the start of her second year at Oxford. She had found another man, perhaps as shadowy as my other woman – perhaps Julian from Christchurch, reading medieval history. A publisher asked me to write a travel book about either the Congo where Patrice Lumumba had been murdered, or Cuba where Fidel Castro had arrived. I chose Cuba, and the *Sunday Telegraph* gave me an air ticket round the Caribbean and Central America.

Deirdre came to London in December, as she had the year before – this time to lose, probably, her illusions. Or lose me anyway. She would prove that our affair was finished and I belonged in the past, with both happiness and unhappiness. It didn't work.

Nobody had stirred me like this; or reached so far into my being; or made life without her seem impaired, crippled. I was flying to Cuba in the New Year, 1961, and would be away till June. We went for a winter walk on Hampstead Heath. I love you, Deirdre – you know where the key of the flat is, if Oxford gets impossible and you want to come to London while I'm away.

I had never asked anyone to marry me. 'I suppose so,' she replied: not the howl of joy or whoop of horror, half a sob and half a laugh as she flew into my arms, that I expected. To her it was perhaps the end of something and not yet a beginning. To me the future was simple, obvious, miraculously inescapable. I would ask her again in the summer when I got back. And I would be faithful for a thousand years.

FORTY-FIVE

May 31, El Toboso. I have the fresh Sunday morning to myself, walking five kilometres from El Toboso to the Venta of Don Quixote, passed by only three cars along the straight bright road. Each day I am astonished at this lovely country, the sheer beauty of the morning.

Families have come to visit the chapel opposite the Venta, before their lunch. I drink an orange juice on the terrace and find myself being stared at, I don't know why. I blow my nose in case of snot and check my trouser zip, and see nothing wrong. But I'm glad to start off again towards Mota del Cuervo, ten kilometres down the highway. Lorries and long-distance buses and disdainful limousines stream past but I'm not troubled, I can walk along the edge of the vine and barley fields.

Soon it becomes very hot and I make excuses to stop for a rest. The vine leaves shift and turn a little in the windless air. The grass occasionally stirs, but after a moment it stands still again as if the effort was too much. The third time I stop, under a tree, I make excuses not to start walking again.

I watch a tractor on a hillside in the distance, harrowing between the rows of vines, too far away for me to hear it. When it reaches the top of a row and turns back the sun flashes on the windscreen like a signal. I wonder what Don Quixote would make of it: a dragon breathing fire or another knight in shining armour. It comes down and drops out of sight in the hollow at the foot of the hill, then crawls slowly up in the next row, turns and flashes at me and comes down again. I will pick myself up with my rucksack at the third flash from now, and walk on.

The tractor flashes once, and twice, and then it stays down in the hollow. It has moved elsewhere or the driver wants his lunch, and I never get my third flash. I feel relieved, though guilty. I must wait for another signal. I watch for it among the butterflies flitting past, but they are too vague and indecisive. Then a grasshopper lands on my knee. I will move on when it flies away. Stay there, grasshopper! – I like you on my knee. But it jumps too soon, and I hoist myself back into the sun.

Once more, before Mota del Cuervo, I slip into an olive grove and pick the shadiest tree for a last rest. The trees are still in flower, a pale grey-green floss lying over them and tiny petals falling on the red soil.

Mota del Cuervo looks unfriendly and I stop only long enough for an orange juice in a bar. I want to know nothing about it, and from the looks I get it's mutual. I walk a kilometre beyond, to the junction of the Belmonte road where I stand beside my rucksack on the verge, waiting for a lift. It's nearly five o'clock and the signpost says sixteen kilometres. I shall be at Belmonte by six, I have no doubt.

A few cars come along – half a dozen in half an hour. One driver waves and points to his load of children, who wave too. Two Belgian cars cruise past, with empty back seats. Suddenly I hate all Belgians and tell them so, shouting after them down the road. I'm close to the town rubbish tip: plastic bottles and bits of polythene blow round my legs. At six o'clock, when I was sure I would be at Belmonte, I start walking.

I don't believe I shall have to walk far before someone picks me up. I keep to the gravel beside the tarmac and whenever a car comes, every five or ten minutes, I turn and put out my hand. It looks better, I hope, not to have just waited outside Mota del Cuervo, but to have started along the road: showing the right spirit or something. Yet I half want to walk all the way – sixteen kilometres. I should be there by nine o'clock, in time to find a room and supper.

The road curls over a hill and settles down to a dead straight line. There is little shade but the sun is behind me, getting low. I trudge up a long rise, reach the top and see another rise ahead; swing down; trudge up. I'm easily deceived: the next rise looks only five minutes away, but it takes me half an hour to get there.

The traffic becomes scarcer. Nobody even seems likely to stop for me and I begin to hate them all. 'Bastards!' I shout after they have passed, into the dust and fumes they leave for me.

At seven o'clock, from the top of a rise, I see a small town not far ahead, though there is no place on the map between Mota del Cuervo and Belmonte. It's good news: I can have a drink and something to eat. All day I have had nothing but two small cakes for breakfast. Then I see a big castle on the hill above the town. So it must be Belmonte already, nearer than I thought – even better news. The road goes straight to it, gently up and down through vines and olives and barley. But the kilometre stones say I'm not yet halfway and they must be right. Though it looks so close, it will be two more hours before I reach it.

Cars overtake me at long intervals. Between them I rehearse the conversation I will have with the man who picks me up. I tell him about my travels in La Mancha and that I have walked from El Toboso today. He asks why I went there, and is impressed – I know *Don Quixote* better than he does. He recommends somewhere to stay in Belmonte and a wonderful restaurant. Better still, he owns a hotel and I can have a room for nothing if I write about it in my book. I need an innkeeper of my own, to compare with Don Quixote's.

But all I do is shout 'Bastards!' at each retreating car. Once, to a Land Rover with three men and a girl and plenty of room for me too, I fling after it, 'You cartload of cunts!' I begin to hate the Spanish too, they are worse than the Belgians. Surely in England someone would have stopped for a man tramping along under a rucksack, obviously making for the town so visible ahead. I will never hitch-hike again, I swear.

I walk more slowly as my sack grows heavier and stop every kilometre. In a dip of the road I pass a big house among trees, a glimpse of tile and whitewash with 'Buenavista' on the gate and a chain across the drive. A nightingale is singing in the garden and perhaps, in the house, a duke or marquis is stirring from his siesta. I hate him for being rich and living in such a place but not inviting me in or caring whether I get to Belmonte before dark. Across the road a man stands motionless like a stork to watch me walk by, while his flock of sheep and goats nibble behind him. I remember the goatherd who invited Don Quixote to share his milk and cheese and fruit, and my feelings soften enough to wish this man *'Buenas tardes!'* But not a croak comes from his lips and my hatred returns.

Belmonte castle stands above the end of the road ahead, touched by the evening sun as if enchanted but getting hardly bigger. The barley has ripened from green to almost white in the two weeks since I came to La Mancha, and the foliage on the vines is massing thicker to cover the grapes. A field of onions is being irrigated with sprays, a cool mist falling on the rows. I feel like stripping off and sluicing myself.

When the next car passes I hardly bother to put my hand out but trudge on, cursing: 'Bastards!' It speeds past, then brakes hard far ahead and the reversing lights come on. I won't run to catch it – I can't. It crunches to a halt on the gravel beside me, a big Renault, and three men look out. Not bastards at all, but young *hidalgos* off for a night in town. I open the back door and start to speak, but I have forgotten my lines, I have almost forgotten the name Belmonte, my voice is dry and weak with dust. In a moment we are speeding down the road again, covering the last two kilometres, sweeping into a plaza. One of the men points to a fonda up the street and they swagger into a bar.

I ring the fonda bell and bang the door. Nobody answers. I go to a bar and swallow two beers. Three girls on a doorstep whistle to me and call me over: 'You are a foreigner?'

'Not at all – I'm pure Spanish,' I tell them, in a foul temper. I go back to the fonda and ring and bang again. This is absurd: nine o'clock, the time when things get going. And I'm hungry. A *guardia civil* comes down the street, adjusting his patent leather hat, and I ask if he knows where I can eat in Belmonte.

'Yes – come with me.' We walk through the town together. 'Where do you come from?'

'From El Toboso,' I say. 'On foot – thirty kilometres.' I don't tell him about the lift at the end.

'But where do you live?'

'In England. And you – is Belmonte your home?'

'I come from Ceuta, in North Africa.'

'Ah yes, in Morocco.'

'No, not in Morocco.' He turns on me sharply. 'It's Spain.' He takes me to the Fonda Manchega where I have a dish of *pisto manchego*, a sort of hot salad mush with onions, tomatoes, peppers, courgettes and bacon, and stay the night.

FORTY-SIX

Starting in Cuba, following a circle of its Central American and Caribbean neighbours and back to Cuba, I went to ten countries in five months; and talked to communists and plutocrats, ambassadors and peasants, soldiers, doctors, shopkeepers, drunkards, priests, prostitutes, presidents. It was 1961, the year I was to be married.

I listened to a four-hour speech by Castro in front of a huge crowd; and interviewed Luís Somoza, dictator of Nicaragua, in his fortified palace. In a night club called the Gato Tuerto, the One-eyed Cat, I heard an Irishman talking Italian to a Yugoslav who was answering in Spanish. I tried to track down Castro's executioner whose name had been given me in a Holborn pub, but when I got there he too had been put against the wall and shot in the empty moat of La Cabaña fort. I also missed the American invasion of Cuba, the fiasco of the Bay of Pigs, having just left for Guatemala ('You'll never make a newspaperman,' someone said in Fleet Street when I got back). I heard Casals play his cello in Puerto Rico – very old and small, his lower lip thrust out and little grunts of apoplexy coming from the rage inside – and Rostropovich play his in Havana, to the crowds in the cathedral square under the Caribbean stars. I flew in a two-seater plane over the Panama Canal which I had once sailed through in a ketch, and climbed to King Henri Christophe's castle in Haiti where the cannonballs were ready to shoot at Napoleon, and drank in a Havana bar with the Russian poet Yevtushenko who said, 'I love you – I love you Rudyard Kipling, I love you Lucky Jim, I love you people, people are good.'

'I want always to love you as I love you now,' Deirdre wrote to me in Cuba. 'I think I shall.' She was living in my flat. Now it was at Oxford that she felt a visitor. She had left it after less than two years, she no longer belonged there. Marriage seemed more important than a degree: 'We must make ours a happy marriage. Why should it be otherwise? I think it will be wonderful. I have complete faith – that is all that is necessary. Don't change your mind.'

But she was going through a turmoil, almost a breakdown. Having impulsively made the biggest decisions of her life she felt she must try to justify them, which was giving trouble: 'How one lies to oneself!' Doubts tormented her, and the torment reached me in airmail envelopes, care of the British embassy in a string of small republics. 'You are a marvellous man and I love you,' she wrote, but in the next letter she was worried: 'I do not know you at all.' After reading Graham Greene she asked me, 'Are you a burnt-out case?' The following day she sent another letter with a match to burn the last one: 'Did I say I didn't believe in your love for me? But I do, I do. I believe in your love and my love and our marriage. I believe more strongly in that than in anything in the world. I have no doubts – not even small ones.'

Though I felt she knew me better than anyone had known me, which made me happy, I was anxious too – for her or myself, I couldn't tell. In Guatemala I read of the quetzal, the national bird with a long beautiful tail that lived in the forest. When it was captured it went into a decline and died, and perhaps Deirdre was like that. Or perhaps I was. I loved her for her wildness – it was wild enough to want to marry me – and she might pine for the treetops. I hoped she would never be quite tamed, I would rather she flew away to be herself. I didn't want her to be different, I even wanted her to exasperate me sometimes, and she seemed glad. 'How do you put up with me?' she asked. 'I am impossible. Other people who have loved me have always tried to reform me, but you just accept me. That is wonderful.'

I still didn't understand why she should marry me. 'Why do I love you?' she asked in a letter, answering my question. 'I love your qualities and I love your faults, I love absurd details. I like your honesty. I like your pride and I like your modesty – not a contradiction. Proud, in that you are reserved and independent, modest in that you don't boast about, even admit, your qualities, your achievements. (Why do you tell me you are vain? I have never understood it.)' Yet I had done nothing for her – on the contrary, I seemed to have treated her selfishly, even cruelly, and knew she minded more than she said. 'You are so perfectly controlled, so completely inaccessible always' was as far as she would condemn me in those days.

Among my feelings as I travelled was an overwhelming gratefulness.

Why should you do this for me? How can I thank you? Deirdre darling, if it's like this at the beginning, what will it become? I questioned and talked to her constantly, and her generosity reached me in return, making me give too. When everything round me was unpleasant I could smile at the thought of her – she would prick my silly bubble of bad temper – and when I was enjoying myself I wished she was sharing it. To me, I wrote back, one of the best things for a human being was to share an emotion with another human being, and sometimes it felt more moving and exciting when the other was half a stranger, and far away: someone perhaps, I might have added, better defined in the imagination than in reality, still being formed by the creative work of love.

In my letters to her I failed myself. I knew what I wanted to say, but when I read it through it wasn't what I meant. The thought had been too brief to trap – it had vanished before I could find words for it. For once they let me down and the ones I chose said something else. They were false or weak or absurd. Sometimes I didn't even understand them, and was afraid Deirdre would read the wrong things into them, and take them up and twist them and toss them back. She must know the truth without my telling her: that we would be together, even when apart, till the very end and then I would have to go off without her.

In the book about my journey the author bought whisky for a bar-girl called Gloria who pressed her sticky hand in his, and was machine-gunned by counter-revolutionaries in the Havana docks, and sang Sunday hymns with a colony of Anglo-Hondurans on an island off the Mosquito Coast, and ate rice and squid with a Hungarian colonel in Nicaragua, and went to a requiem mass for the assassinated dictator Trujillo in the cathedral of Santo Domingo, and toured workers' flats with Kingsley Martin, ex-editor of the *New Statesman*, and brothels with a Christian Arab whose family had come from Bethlehem. But these incidents have slipped beyond memory into a more reliable exist-ence. I believe them because they are there in words, but they seem to have happened to another man, not me.

'You are what I think you are, and what other people think you are, as well as what you think you are,' Deirdre wrote in her last letter before I came home. She would never again have foolish fears and doubts. 'I think we have enough similarities to be happy and peaceful together, enough differences to stimulate one another. That is ideal. It will be a wonderful marriage.'

223

FORTY-SEVEN

June 1, Belmonte. There is a bus to Cuenca at six in the morning. Somehow I wake up in time and let myself out of the fonda into the dark street, slamming the door behind me. I find the plaza where the buses start – for Madrid, Albacete, Cuenca, all at six o'clock – and have a coffee in a bar with the other passengers. But there are only two buses waiting, for Madrid and Albacete, and when they depart I'm left alone. I ask the barman about the Cuenca bus.

'There isn't one today.'

'Why not?' It runs every weekday, and today is Monday.

'Today is a fiesta in Cuenca – there will be a bus tomorrow.'

I go back to the fonda for more sleep, but I slammed the door when I came out and it's locked. I ring and knock, and nobody answers. For three hours I wander round the town, sitting on benches, watching the place wake up, returning to the fonda to knock again. Dogs are plundering the rubbish bins, tipping them over, biting into plastic sacks, spreading bread, potatoes, tomatoes through the streets. A woman throws water on the ground outside her house to keep the dust down. Vans come in from the country with fruit and vegetables, and unload outside the market, the men drifting into the bars for an *aguardiente*. The first housewives emerge with their shopping baskets. A man begins to whitewash a house while two women scrub away the paint he splashes on the street. Children go off to school. At last, at nearly ten o'clock, someone lets me into the fonda.

I stay in my room, reading and washing clothes which I hang on the roof, and in an hour they are parched and stiff. Mulberries are falling from a tree in the garden. Towards evening I walk up the hill to the castle, pay my hundred pesetas to the old caretaker and have it to myself.

For some aristocratic whim in the last century it was given romantic brickwork, palatial chambers, grand staircases and fireplaces, now more ruinous than the medieval walls and towers.

'Go up to the top,' the caretaker tells me. 'It's the Balcony of La Mancha – you can see two hundred kilometres when there is no haze.' Though he is a natural liar the view across the chequered plain, which I have crossed and re-crossed, needs no exaggeration: the immense simplicity, the lack of obstacles to break such an infinity of vision. I can see the windmills of Mota del Cuervo on the horizon, hull down in the west, and the straight road, but not its rises and dips, which I walked yesterday. I can see myself on it, tramping along the verge, cursing the passing cars.

A plume of dust marks a tractor in a field, or perhaps the flock of sheep I passed. For Don Quixote, two clouds of dust drifting over the plain were two armies marching to do battle – a Christian and a Muslim. From the top of a hill he identified the squadrons, named the warriors and their heroic deeds, and could hear the horses neighing, trumpets blaring, drums beating.

'All I can hear,' Sancho Panza said, 'is a great bleating of rams and ewes.'

'You are frightened, Sancho, and it hides the truth from you. Fear upsets the senses. It makes things appear as they are not. If you are so afraid, stand aside and leave me alone.' Sancho's limited vision, his common sense and practicality, were no use to Don Quixote who spurred on Rocinante and galloped down the hill to fight for the Christians, leaving his squire wishing he had never been born, shouting at such madness. The shepherds shouted too as Don Quixote charged into their flocks; then showered him with stones till he was knocked to the ground with two ribs broken, a shattered hand, several teeth missing and seven sheep dead. But still, in the reality of his invention, there had been battle cries and the clash of steel. The retreating sheep and the corpses only proved that a knight's senses could also be upset, though not by fear.

This is the end of La Mancha. Two old windmill towers near the castle mark the frontier of the great plain. I'm on my way out, moving into the sierras. Now La Manchuela begins, the little one: a country of small stagnant towns where churches stand like empty granaries among the huddled roofs, and storks' nests top the belfry towers; of mule carts, and cobblers hammering in tiny shops, and people in the fields doing things the historic way.

225

Don Quixote and Sancho must have come through here on their journey north, though no places are named. I will choose my own route.

FORTY-EIGHT

Deirdre's home was in the Thames valley north of the Berkshire downs. I think of the sickle-chalk White Horse arched below the skyline, caught for a moment from the Paddington train. The steep turf of Uffington Castle, to be clawed and panted up. The Harwell atomic fortress standing like a sin in the great panoramic haze. The wire fence at Aldermaston where three times I joined the Easter march to Trafalgar Square. Hunchbacked stable boys out with a string of racehorses on the gallops. Picnickers exercising their family cars along the B-roads of a Sunday afternoon. A frozen Christmas morning and breaking the ice on a water trough for a herd of grateful bullocks. A summer hike along the prehistoric Ridge Way arranged to fit in with opening time at the pub down in Letcombe Bassett. Eyes sore with hay fever and ears full of the larks ascending. Deirdre in a cotton dress among the cornflowers and bees; then taking off the dress.

To me in 1961 at the brink of marriage, moving deeper into love and trying to write a book about Cuba, it felt a strange and psychic stretch of England. In the middle of a beech wood at the top of the downs was Wayland's smithy. Long ago you could leave your horse there with a silver coin on the stone anvil, and when you came back the horse was shod and the money gone. Wayland still hung around those beeches. I knew a little girl who had never heard of him, but in the wood she danced excitedly and cried, 'Gee-gee, gee-gee!', hearing the ring of the old blacksmith's hammer. Once I met a man on a horse and we had an odd, inconsequential talk about sheep, butterflies, blackberries and the pity of ploughing up the downs, that belied the tall telecommunications mast above us. He cantered out of sight, leaving me to wonder. Had there been something about his speech – not altogether modern? And those little bands of pilgrims, ardently marching from Avebury to the Wash to capture the feel of ancient British travel – did they ever reach the other end?

I would have settled for a registry office with two witnesses, but Deirdre wanted to be married in Dorchester abbey down by the Thames, with the smell of the river and new-mown grass. She would like it to be empty – filled with music perhaps, but not people – and chose the chapel of St Birinus, a Roman missionary who wandered those parts, preaching and converting.

Late the night before, full of wine and emotions, I drove up through ever-dwindling villages – the Wittenhams, Hagbournes, Hendreds, Let-combes – with a vague compulsion to spend my last unmarried night alone on top of the nearest hills. In the dark a signpost pointed 'To the Downs' and I changed into low gear, steering up through the hawthorn. At the top the track flattened out into the open, where I guessed the Ridge Way ran. There, clumsily in the headlights, I pitched my one-man tent. It was the most uncomfortable night of my life – I slept neither the sleep of the doomed nor of the drunk. I hardly slept at all.

At dawn, conscious that I had an appointment at the altar of St Birinus that morning, I crawled out to see where I had landed. There was the car a few yards away, but nothing else. I was in a thick mist. No view, no sunrise. Nothing but the short wet grass vanishing into a summer fog. I pulled down the tent, fumbling with dewy canvas and muddy pegs.

Then suddenly, striding out of nowhere, a man appeared, tall and purposeful in an old hat with a blanket over his shoulders. 'Lousy morning!' he called as he passed, without stopping.

'Yes,' I called back, in agreement and surprise. And because I didn't want to let him go without sharing my awful secret with someone before it was too late, or because I sensed a sympathy with this lonely traveller, I added, 'I'm getting married today.'

'I see what you mean!' he shouted through the mist, and was gone.

I hadn't meant anything at all.

There was time to drive somewhere for a shave and breakfast before my wedding. Lurching back down the lane, out of the mist, I puzzled over the stranger on the Ridge Way. Perhaps St Birinus had worn a blanket and an old hat. Perhaps Don Quixote still stalked the world, not only in La Mancha, hailing strangers and gladdening their hearts.

Later that week, lying one hot afternoon by the lake at Stourhead in Somerset, Deirdre slipped away from me and somehow out of her clothes. Next moment I saw her naked, out in the lake, swimming through the landscape of trees and temples. Other people, strolling in the park, were delighted too. But only I, improbably, could claim her as a wife.

FORTY-NINE

June 2, Cuenca. The election posters are torn. The candidates' faces, breathing idealism and trust, are peeling off the walls, as faded as their policies. The more they shout the more they become the same – noise is all they offer. A team of canvassers in a car roars into the Plaza Mayor, blasting everyone from their café seats with party music and propaganda. They park under the trees, hand out pamphlets and sweets and go into a bar, leaving the tape machine turned up full in their empty car.

The trees – acacias or planes or whatever they hope to be – struggle from tiny basins of earth choked with cigarette ends, beer cans, tooth-picks. Their trunks bruised by car bumpers or stuck with posters, their leaves choked by exhaust fumes, their branches strung with loudspeakers or coloured lights – they are abused, but badly needed.

On a spur between two rivers the houses of Cuenca rise in cliffs twelve storeys high, tottering façades of plaster and wood and brick, overhanging cubicles, forgotten drains, balconies, birdcages, pigeons' nests, bits and pieces of masonry held together by electric cables and TV aerials and strings of washing, great coloured garlands of shirts, trousers, nightdresses, spanning the habitations. Water drips from the clothes into the street far below, with pigeon droppings. The smell of hot olive oil comes from a frying pan somewhere. An aroma of herbs floats up from the valley. Cuenca is famous for its honey.

An old church, till the Ministry of Culture comes to restore it, has a small tree growing on top – I like it with the tree. Students sit on the cathedral steps drinking litre bottles of beer, while a thin woman in black with a plastic bag quietly collects the empties. In a great hall, part of some monastery perhaps, a brass band starts up, drums thumping, trombones and tubas blasting flecks of whitewash off the walls.

A butcher advertises *carne de corrida*, beef from the bullring – fillet, first class and second class. A young man coming round a corner, meeting a stranger, says, '*Buenas tardes!*' Three boys pissing against a wall don't stop for me, but laugh and splash each other, turning to watch me pass.

In the evening a half moon hangs over the old roofs. For supper I have a dish of *morteruelo*, pig's liver and spices. With enough hunger and wine and bread, however stale, I manage to eat it. With more wine I make a promise that one day I will come back to Cuenca and live for a winter in a cliffhanger house – the sort of promise I never keep. In a dark chapel of the cathedral, with an electric bulb over his glossy head, a priest sits in his confession box like a lottery seller. Across the valley a floodlit Virgin defies the moon.

The castle at the top of the town is being turned into a Parador – it happens everywhere: bishop's palaces, monasteries, pilgrim hostels converted into luxury hotels. But the building that looks like a new motel on the road out of Cuenca, red brick for the guests, white plaster for the staff, is a prison.

FIFTY

Deirdre and I shared my one-room flat for three more years – husband and wife now but still with cheap wine for our meals, and love to make before putting on the coffee, and my typewriter waiting on the table. Then for the last year our daughter occupied a corner of the room and I found it easier to work in the public library.

For a time I worked at Bush House in the Strand. The BBC wanted a writer in their Africa service and I was shortlisted, but the job went to someone else. When the winner changed his mind, they offered it to me – I was second best. But I too began to wonder and agreed to try it for six months, writing four-minute 'topical talks' to be translated and broadcast in African languages. Sometimes I recorded a talk for the English service. In a crowded studio a producer took my arm and asked to have a word outside: 'With all those women in there couldn't you do them up?' he said, with a sneer at my unzipped trousers. But there were some eccentrics in that huge building and a good cheap lunch, though nothing to the two-shilling curry in the basement canteen of the Indian High Commission next door.

After six months the department head tried to talk me into joining permanently, at thirteen hundred pounds a year. With twenty-five thousand employees there was room for anyone in the BBC, he said, even for people who wanted to write books: 'I'm trying my best – I think you'd like it.' But I resisted, and he left soon afterwards to become a property dealer in Corfu.

The *Sunday Times* asked for articles on English towns which turned into a book, a journey through the temples and jungles of my own country for a change. It was the time of the Beatles, the Profumo affair, the scandal of half a million unemployed. I visited a silk mill, a butter factory, a steel works; joined Yorkshire grouse shooters, Surrey commuters, Franciscan friars, Butlin's holiday campers; went down a coal-mine and out in a herring drifter the night John Kennedy was shot. At a Newmarket racing stud I watched a stallion covering a mare – a beautiful, moving sight that was too vivid to banish when Deirdre and I next made love. I wrote the book in a cottage we rented in the hills above the coast of Portugal, among olives and figs. It was my last travel book: I was veering away from the factual world to something more imaginative.

But I continued to travel, commissioned by friendly editors. For the *Sunday Times* I sat by a creek of the Demerara river in Guyana with the shabby, battered Indian owner of a fruit plantation, where gaudy butterflies flipped past and a yellow-breasted kiskadee (*'Qu'est-ce qu'il dit?'* he seems to be saying) chattered from a flamboyant tree. I drank my way through four days of carnival in Trinidad, deafened by steel bands, fortified by pepperpot stew. I went to Dublin, Paris, Calais, the Isle of Man.

In 1964 we moved to a house in Islington where our two sons joined us. I watched their births; held them in a blanket for their first five minutes and tried incredulously through tears to see us as close as this ever again, man to man. And what sort of father would I be? More real or less real than my own? More loving, anyway, I hoped. 'Children,' Don Quixote said, though he was never a father, 'are scraps from the very bowels of their parents, and so they must be loved, whether they are good or bad, as we love the souls that give us life.' Through the old knight's madness sudden shafts of wisdom often shone.

Homes and Gardens asked for two thousand words on my favourite English town and I chose Liverpool, though I had spent only a week there. And for a week I sat in Crockford's gambling club, night after night till dawn, watching chemin-de-fer for an article in *Queen* with generous help from Dostoevsky. 'It's all so senseless, so stupid, so vulgar, yet I can't tear myself away from this obsession,' he wrote to his young wife, as if it were a helpless case of adultery and he wanted her to share it with him. 'Can you forgive me, Anya? If we can only suffer this together, perhaps later it will be better.'

I went to Clare Island off the Irish coast for the *Sunday Telegraph* and Bikini atoll in the Pacific for the *Sunday Times;* to Scarborough and Suffolk and Cornwall (John Betjeman sent a note of praise, over-looking the plunder I had taken from his 'Shell Guide' to Cornwall). I crossed the Channel from Cherbourg to Southampton in the old *Queen*

Elizabeth, the world's biggest liner, while the band played 'Lilac Time' among the teacups. I made a film about King's Lynn for the BBC, walking self-consciously but, I hoped, casually through the town with the camera crew trailing me. ('You'll never make it on TV,' the producer said, and though it hurt I knew I would rejoice in the end.) And between keeping up the marital, paternal, domestic appearances I interviewed a couple of dukes, a countess, a handful of socialist millionaires and a Berkshire farm worker who, as I watched, pushed copper rings through the snouts of a load of squealing pigs.

The *Observer* asked for an article on Sainsbury's, the grocery chain. I interviewed a Mr Sainsbury who laid on a tour of their shops and factories: girls knotting sausages, boiled eggs being dropped into pork pies, chickens being plucked and gutted. I turned in an oblique impressionistic essay, a sideways squint at Sainsbury's that didn't suit the *Observer*. They wanted hard journalism with facts and figures, an assessment of rival High Street supermarkets, and got their business editor to do it again. But my effort was too good to waste. I would wrap it up in fiction and, aged nearly forty, I wrote my first novel.

I heard later that Mr Sainsbury had read it and said it was unkind. He must have seen himself in the pink young factory manager with piggish features and a silver pork pie on his desk. It's a common mistake: 'Readers are very stupid about this,' Graham Greene has said.

Though sympathetic, Deirdre didn't like it either. The novel concerns a troubled, unstable man who turns from his beautiful wife and the responsibilities of marriage to the dubious joys of another woman. 'I know the characters are not you and me and people we know,' she wrote in the kindest review it received, 'but sometimes they speak with our words and behave in the way we behave, and though they may remind one of past selves more than present selves, they are sufficiently familiar . . . I kept wishing I was the unknown, wanted woman instead of the other one, bearing babies and reluctantly encouraging Paul to be free. "I do love you, but–" Is there still a but, I wonder? I don't think you are half such a shit as Paul – you've left out the nicest bits and blown up the rest. But he isn't really a shit, is he? Just weak and muddly and a bit hopeless . . . Poor Paul. I can't help loving you and loving the things you make.'

Years later she was still torn between the fictitious people and the author: 'Sometimes you behave like one of the characters in your novels, but I don't believe you are really . . .' Living with me, a witness to the writer's conflict – to be alone and free, responsible to nobody, and to have a family and be a husband and father – wasn't easy.

I was myself torn between unprofitable fiction and the need to make a living. A journalist, David Holden, suggested I might find an arrangement like his own: six months as roving correspondent for a paper, six months writing books for himself. I applied to several editors and got as far as an interview at the *Observer*. But someone more important turned up at the same time and the editor bustled me out. I was sorry at first – I half envied people with colleagues, salaries, secretaries – but later I became thankful. I was still my own man.

The same ambivalence is felt by a poet in a novel, when he visits a newspaper office for freelance work. Can't he join in, play the game, make money as well as any of them? Beat them on their own ground? Writing doesn't have to be done in an ivory tower with an ivory wife and child. This is real life, he tells himself, being lived by real men in a real world; and wonders if it is; and decides it isn't, later, as he walks home. Up there at the top of the house, with his wife and their baby, with a casserole simmering for supper and the double bed afterwards, the flat is at that moment the one real thing to be sure of.

Last time I saw David Holden, at a bus stop in Islington, he was going back to the Middle East for his paper. Soon afterwards he was found in a Cairo suburb, shot in the back of the head and dumped in a ditch. He was someone else's – the wrong master's – man.

Violent deaths have haunted me, perhaps because of my father's. There are several in the novels but they have occurred elsewhere too, less believably. I knew a hunter living by a Ugandan river who was overturned in his boat by a hippo and finished off by crocodiles – he couldn't swim. And a young Etonian, son of a duke, on a coconut plantation in the Solomon Islands, who swam out one night to a ship anchored in the bay but never reached it – also taken by a crocodile or possibly a giant clam. And a clergyman's wife who tried syphoning petrol from her car into the lawn mower, but choked on the fumes. And two Cambridge students killed climbing in the Alps, and a Swiss journalist drowned like Shelley in Italy. I have often tried to share, or fought against sharing, those last moments.

In suicides the moments stretch back into days, months, a life of mounting despair. A boy I was at school with, soon after leaving it, climbed an electricity pylon to touch the high tension wires: typical of

Winchester, they said – short and sweet and no mess for other people, just a flash and a few ashes drifting down. A bishop's son drove half across England, stopping inexplicably to buy a gramophone record on the way, into a lonely wood where he shot himself. A publisher and two journalists also used guns. A great aunt hanged herself over the bath. A cousin dragged firewood to the top of a hill where she lay on it and burnt herself to death. A librarian, like my Uncle Fritz, swallowed pills and so did a TV man, with a lot of alcohol. A priest, after taking off his dog collar, jumped from the church roof. A biochemist took poison in his laboratory. A violinist gassed herself with the exhaust fumes of her car. A woman painter swam out to sea at Brighton, for ever. An architect drowned himself in a river. A novelist cut his wrists. A poet's wife took her small daughter with her. And someone in a novel of mine drove his Mini at speed, head-on into a lorry.

And Potts, after killing my father and the policeman, put the pistol to his own head. He too had a father who gave evidence at the inquest, swaying slightly at the events that brought him to the witness box, stunned by the crime that had smitten him. The son had taken two other lives, but also his own; and the father, refusing to show shame, was proud as well as cruelly bereft. He didn't know where he had gone wrong, he had done his best for the boy, even today, and had been dragged through fire. He could only hint at his bewilderment and desolation, and his family's pain at the behaviour of the press. There was nothing he could tell the court about the company his son kept or the loneliness at the end of that short life – six blank weeks of silence, without news or letters, till the police came and asked him to identify the body. He stepped down from the box, tired by the agony and feeling very old. He would go home and soon retire.

William James wrote that we who cling to life count the man who flings it away like a flower, caring nothing for it, as in the deepest way our born superior: 'The fact consecrates him for ever.' Philip Toynbee agreed: 'Few of us can have failed to feel this, or something very like it, when we have contemplated the suicide of a friend. Death is a serious business, easy enough to talk about but not so easy to practice.' And after someone's suicide Camus wrote that he was 'overwhelmed because I was very fond of him, of course, but also because I suddenly realized that I wanted to follow his example.'

I have felt shock at the sudden news, and horror at those terrible last hours confronted by utter futurelessness, and anger at the consequences – the infliction of guilt, perhaps, on whoever is left. I have also felt a

236

kind of wonder, close to envy: this was someone with far more courage than I have, who faced the fact that each of us is finally alone and who chose an alternative to life. I have admired the defiance, the scorn, the pre-emptive act – getting there first, beating the rest of us to it – and have found it inspiring and ennobling. Such destruction is ultimately creative.

I have wondered how I might do it myself. I think I'm a jumper. At the top of tall buildings, cliffs, waterfalls, even from aeroplanes, I have a feeling of invulnerability – a touch of Don Quixote perhaps. I shall be saved by some private charm, stepping off and floating or flying – into oblivion maybe, though with no appalling plunge or broken corpse at the bottom. Living in Suffolk now I'm tempted by the beautiful bridge over the river Orwell below Ipswich; but in case the charm fails I would choose low tide for a longer drop. It might be better than the likely alternative – years of increasing asthma and diminishing royalties, gasping through heart attacks to the last – and there have been times when death, no worse than any other fate, has seemed like quite a good idea.

I can't imagine the corpse I shall be. Every part of my body is alive, it's hard to think of it without senses. Surgery is the nearest to an objective view of physiology. In a hospital once, after two days of slops and castor oil, I was examined for an operation. The nurse had a hosepipe connected to the water supply – it might have been the fire hydrant – and pushed the nozzle into my rectum, then turned on the tap. With her hands on my stomach she felt the pressure rising – squeezing my waist for complete inflation. In a novel I wrote of an old Hindu giving himself a ritual enema, but it wasn't like this: the ignominy, the confusion of nakedness and hydraulics. I sat on the lavatory and let go. The nurse did it again, and I was empty.

I was put on a steel table, flat on my stomach, where a man in white poured barium into me down a pipe. I felt it running through my bowels, up into my stomach, following the map of tubes while we watched on a TV screen. I was topped up with air like a tyre at the garage, for the X-rays to begin. Breathe in, breathe out, hold your breath, click, breathe again. I rolled over, left and right, front and back, for different angles. Breathe in, breathe out. The table slid quietly along rails under the camera.

I was the corpse in a crematorium. The bronze doors opened, the organ swelled, there would be more men in white to receive me into the kindly flames, and perhaps another TV for me to watch as well as feel. My father was cremated, and most of the aunts and uncles – so this was what it was like. Breathe in, breathe out. The table tilted, dropped, swivelled, rose through ninety degrees till I was upright on my feet. Hold your breath, click, breathe again. Hold your bowels a little longer. I was led away, alive, and given a cup of tea.

The operation wasn't necessary, there was nothing wrong, but I had seen my body without me in it.

Of all violent deaths an execution holds me irresistibly, though I loathe the torture and degradation. Every account of one is precisely remembered.

In an open air cinema in San Salvador, the night before an earthquake, I watched an old film of the Nuremberg hangings: men being hustled up a steep ladder to the scaffold, wives compelled to witness their own widowing from a window, the men's eyes caught by the telephoto lens and flapping wildly just before the drop – seeing what? It was fifteen years after the event but the shame, my shame, is my chief memory of that city, lasting better than the earthquake – being woken by the walls and windows rattling, the furniture jumping like dice in a box. I knew at once that it wasn't a dream, though I hadn't been in one before. It lasted ten seconds, as long as the execution in the film, and I felt the same anger, terror, fascination, without the shame.

In Delhi I saw a newsreel of an execution in Cuba: an officer of the pre-Castro dictatorship standing in front of a ditch, being gunned down, doubling up like a nutcracker, toppling backwards out of sight. Outside the cinema in the Indian monsoon, among bicycles and fruit-sellers and beggars and holy cows, that collapsing figure was the most vivid image in the street.

In Liberia, on the beach at Monrovia, I was shown the thirteen stakes where the last of the True Whig Party, after a hundred and ten years in power, had been shot at dawn: a haunted patch of sand between the Atlantic rollers and the town, the scene of a piece of public theatre so shocking that I could see it still, three years later. And the famous photo of a Vietnamese officer holding his pistol to a prisoner's head a moment before the trigger – like the one of a blindfolded Australian soldier in World War Two, kneeling for a Japanese to behead him with a sword – has at last begun to fade and I have started to hope that I am safe from seeing it again when it turns up somewhere else.

I have a dream, very clear and real, of six men lined up in a trench.

Probably they dug it themselves, probably they were once colonels or ministers or ambassadors. Quite calm and tall, middle-aged, grey-haired or bald – now they are simply men. I'm behind the execution squad, who aim their guns and fire. The men slowly fold up, dropping at each other's feet like children in a game, except one at the end of the line who survives a little longer: breathing hard for a second, two seconds, his shoulders rising and falling – an asthmatic, perhaps – as his lungs work, pumping to fill him with life while there is any left. Another shot is fired and he crumples too. But there is still one more victim. There wasn't room for him with the others, he has to go through it alone. I can't take it, I turn and leave. But he is braver, he stays behind, he can face what I can't. He steps down into the trench among his dead friends and waits for the squad to aim.

One spring morning after a tormented night I lay in bed with Deirdre asleep beside me, waiting for eight o'clock. Somewhere else in London, for a murder he swore he didn't commit, Hanratty was to be hanged. As our clock ticked towards the hour my anguish grew and I buried my head under the blanket, hoping to be unaware of time. I thought I waited long enough, screwed up and locked against the minutes, close to Deirdre's body though she could be no comfort, before pulling back the clothes to face the guilty morning, not daring to look at the clock. At that moment someone's radio gave the time signal: it was being done.

Deirdre didn't know about it, I hadn't shared it with her – it was a death, something to do alone. Stirred by the pips of eight o'clock she put out a hand, turning to ask for love. But Deirdre, how can we? I shrank from her, I was in a prison cell. Warders flinging the door open, grabbing me like a chicken. The end is very quick, they say. The swift, brutal pinioning. The trapping of a man's arms, the snatching of his last free moment. Being frog-marched down the passage. Pushed into the little room I had only imagined and now had no time to look at, no eyes to see with. The governor, priest, the hangman – an expert like Deirdre, knowing what to do, having done it often. Showing me how. His warm fingers on my neck, not hers in my crutch. The prickle of rope at my throat, the pillowing knot under my ear. For God's sake, Deirdre, not now! And the smell of soap. They rub it on the rope to make it slip, they think of everything. Or was it on Deirdre? – she had a bath last night. Not a moment wasted, not a hitch. The mumbled prayers and the blind, screaming, strangling drop to nothing. Not now, Deirdre! Don't you understand? Can't we wait till later? Any time but this.

It's what happens, I have read. There is something in *Ulysses* about it. A hanged man, purple face, bulging eyes, broken neck, dangling and twisting in the pit – and his cock stands up once more. One last erection, a spurt of life in death's eye. It would be the same for Hanratty too just then. Neither of us could help it, neither of us could care any more. And it would have happened to Potts if he hadn't turned the stolen pistol on himself.

For self-defence or for catharsis, like another barium enema to inspect my own purged guts, I wrote a novel round the Cato Street conspiracy of 1820, a plot to blow up the British cabinet at dinner – not a bad idea at the time. The climax was the public hanging of five men outside Newgate prison. I wanted to state my disgust at the killing, my marvel at the bravery, my pity, sickness, enchantment, horror at the scene. The writing – the attempt to imagine the suffering and put it into words – became a sort of absolution. Now I could face it with better understanding and humility.

FIFTY-ONE

June 3, Priego. La Mancha is finally behind me, I'm in the Serrania on my way to the Alcarría and the north. Hills are rockier, fields are smaller and less fertile, rivers are deep gorges full of poplars. Castles are wrecks of history stranded on the hilltops, like the carcasses of whales washed ashore.

Osiers grow on the flat valley bottom, a bright green floor of willow leaves. After being cut they are stood for weeks in pans of running water, then stacked in crimson pyramids to dry. In a yard behind the village bullring men are feeding them into a peeling machine – they come out skinned white, to be cut and bundled by women and loaded on a lorry. I ask where they are going.

'Barcelona – to be shipped.'

'And then?'

'To Germany, Yugoslavia. . . .'

'For baskets?'

'And chairs, tables, even beds – it's better than plastic.'

I walk out of the village in the dwindling afternoon, up a valley cut through the sierra by the river down there, green in the pools, white among the rocks – a valley of cherries, almonds, walnuts, figs, and of vegetable gardens watered by canals. I enjoy the diligence of irrigation, the stopping and unstopping of water among the beans and artichokes. A man in a novel, a prisoner-of-war of the Japanese, found a deep happiness by the river outside the camp where he was allowed to plant a garden. It was freedom from torture and captivity, something good and joyful to nourish the frail roots of his life.

The road is bordered with flowers, a feast for a botanist. And round the next corner I meet one, his nose into the bank, a flower book on the ground beside him, a camera pointed at something blooming in the grass.

'*Holá!*' he says forcefully, too busy with focusing his lens to be disturbed.

I mutter something about rare plants and the enchanted evening, but I see I'm not wanted and walk on. Probably he is English too.

The valley narrows, there is no room for gardens between the enclosing cliffs. But in this stark ascetic place, round another bend, I find a monastery high up on the valley side under the orange-grey ramparts, still golden in the failing light as if with an inner glow. What a paradise for monks! There seems to be no road up to it: perhaps they cut themselves off long ago, choosing to perch up there, untroubled by the material world.

Then I see an eagle, solitary and immense, drifting far overhead, idling in the pale sky. I can't decide at this moment whether I would rather be a monk or an eagle. (Deirdre in the early days would have said there was something of both in me.)

I sit on a rock and draw a sketch of an eagle in my notebook, the first since I drew windmills on Fujiyama for a Japanese girl: the silhouette of two broad wings with spread feathers fingering the sky, a short head and square tail. Then another bird sails out from a ledge on the cliff to join it, and a third, till there are six of them, and I see they aren't eagles but black vultures, perhaps griffons, fabulous creatures, noble and ancient and aloof, patrolling up and down above the valley from their enormous height.

There are other birds too: jackdaws suddenly plummeting like sky-divers, and swifts racing each other across the cliff face, and a nightingale in the poplars down by the river. My father would identify many more (today is the day he died, fifty-seven years ago), but the griffons are enough for me. They are rulers of the lovely valley, kings of the cosmos.

'It's a beautiful place to live in,' I tell the innkeeper's daughter in Priego, a fat girl of twenty-three.

It was the maid, not the innkeeper's daughter, who came barefoot to Don Quixote's room one night. She considered herself a good girl, though down on her luck, and only slipped into guests' beds for their own pleasure, not for hers. Having promised to visit a muleteer upstairs, groping in the dark, she fell into Don Quixote's arms. For him she was the beautiful daughter of this castle, won by his gallantry and coming for a night of love while her parents were asleep. In his hands her sackcloth shift was silk, her glass beads were pearls, her mane of horsehair was golden thread and her breath, though it stank of old cabbage, was perfumed with rare aromas.

'Loveliest of ladies!' he whispered, gripping her tight. 'If only I could repay your favours!' But he lay so battered and bruised after a fight with twenty traders on the road that he could never have made love – anyway he had sworn chastity to Dulcinea. In a sweat of panic the maid tried to break loose and the muleteer, kept awake by lust and jealousy, arrived to claim his woman and deal Don Quixote a crack on the jaw that filled his mouth with blood, jumping on him and kicking his ribs for good measure.

'Ah!' the innkeeper's daughter sighs, less keen about Priego than I am. 'There's nothing here but osiers – nothing, nothing. All the young people leave. My sister is a nurse in Guadalajara, but I'm wanted to help my father in the bar and my mother in the kitchen. I would like to go anywhere – learn English and then go anywhere in the world.' She scowls at the bullfighting from Madrid on TV, and brings me a plate of green vegetables like spinach: '*Acelpas,*' she writes it in my notebook. 'We had a woman here from England – she told me you cook in butter there, but we use only olive oil.'

She trips away to fetch her alarm clock, to make sure I don't miss the five-thirty bus to Guadalajara tomorrow. She longs to catch it too and get away.

243

FIFTY-TWO

I wanted to go back to India and suggested it to the *Sunday Times*. Looking through the news files they discovered a famine in Bihar, a subject for a suitable cry of horror, and sent me there with a photographer famous for pictures of war and butcher's shops. We dragged a dying woman from her hut to get her in better light for colour film and asked a young man, launching his father's corpse into the holy Ganges, to do it again for a shot from another angle: it would make a wonderful double-page spread among the adverts for bathroom suites, leather-covered sofas, electric food mixers.

For a week or two in that tortured land I was grateful to be given a chapatti with lentils or a curried onion, but the photographer sent a taxi-driver forty miles to buy tinned beans. Eventually we fled to Calcutta, not just for a decent meal but for a chance to get into the Kali temple where, with one swipe of a sword, half-naked priests were making sacrifices to the bloodthirsty goddess, patron of *thugs*. They wouldn't let the photographer take pictures but he didn't mind – the victims were only goats.

I took a train to Hyderabad and became a temporary member of the Secunderabad club, a haunt of imperial archaism, a last nostalgic corner of tea dances and bingo nights where young Indians coming in from the cricket field laughed heartily in the bar and slapped their thighs and called each other 'old chap'; where veteran drinkers wore woollen mittens to save being chilled by their iced whiskies; and where I wrote most of a novel.

I took another train down to Kerala to interview the communist chief minister, but he refused to see me. With more success I crossed the Rajasthan desert to catch some maharajas in their fairyland palaces, where they were charming and courteous and pleased to utter princely things for me to quote. One of them was only nineteen, recently returned from Eton. He sat on a wooden horse in front of his palace while an old courtier rolled polo balls at him, which he cracked across the terrace towards a goal. Servants brought back the balls, and peacocks screamed from the palace roof.

I stayed with a Scotsman, once my brother-in-law, on a sliver of land shaved off the coast of Maharashtra. Four times a minute the pale grey Indian Ocean heaved itself up, curling stereophonically from end to end, and flopped on the beach. The fishing fleet hung on the horizon like moths trapped in a cobweb of mist. Before sunset they sailed home, hardening but diminishing as they approached. Thin-hipped boys waited for them among racks of drying fish, an infinity of Bombay duck. In the dusk the Scotsman walked his dog along the shore and at night put Brahms symphonies on his gramophone. Between movements, rolling on the sand, the ocean breakers quietly approved.

At home in Islington, worrying over my career as writer, I wondered if I was any more convincing as husband, father, neighbour. The children went to school every morning and, till I built a hut in the garden, I pedalled off on my bike to a rented room where I kept a typewriter and a wastepaper basket: first in the Canonbury Tower where Gold-smith had once worked and where the Bacon Society pursued their recondite activities; later in Covent Garden flower market where, through the wall, I heard a flower merchant shouting down the tele-phone for more daffodils from the Scilly Isles or gladioli from Jersey, and where I kept a camp bed for the pleasure of an ardent sub-editress who had afternoons to fill. I went there, as I might fly off on another journalistic job with notebook and feelings primed, to preserve the sense of freedom, or the illusion of it; to be myself, the man I most approved of.

Dishonestly – or too honestly, and the dishonesty was only in the secrecy – I collected quotations from other writers to support my duplicity. So Bacon wrote, 'He that hath wife and children hath given hostages to fortune.' And Conrad: 'He who forms a tie is lost. The germ of corruption has entered his soul.' And Jean Genet: 'I can only be truthful when I'm completely alone.' And Pirandello, who said that he had no life outside his writing: 'There is someone living my life, and I know nothing about him.' And an Iris Murdoch character to her ex-husband, a writer: 'You ought to have been a wanderer, a real Don Quixote – that would have given you subjects. Birds can't sing in cages.'

I carried the secrecy too far. I seldom spoke about my writing to Deirdre, but kept it jealously to myself. If I overheard someone ask her what I was working on and she said she had no idea, I was surprised, because I would so much have liked to share it with her that I almost felt I did. In fact I didn't dare. The pages were too tender, too precious to be entrusted even to her. Also I had so little belief in my child – mine alone, this one – and wanted to watch it grow stronger before I could risk exposure.

'Are you married – at all?' someone asked me at a party, making me wonder (that hesitant 'at all' raised doubts), and before I could answer Deirdre said, 'Slightly.'

The distance between us showed, even after ten years. We didn't call each other 'darling' or look like lovers. In company, a friend told me, I could act almost like a stranger towards Deirdre. Sometimes, he said, it must be a great strain for her to live with me, having to bottle up her natural communicativeness: worse than the obvious, unavoidable difficulties of living with a writer. How could she talk freely about my work, giving scope for her vitality and intelligence, if I was so reserved? From what he had seen, perhaps because Deirdre was so young when we married and still felt a need to prove herself, also because of my aloofness, we didn't seem to have the essential equality for a marriage. He recognized that my work was solitary, and didn't suggest I should change into a different sort of person: only understand what a woman of her open but unconfident nature might be going through with a man like me – 'who may have loved her but hasn't always felt like showing it.'

It didn't make me feel any more guilty or solve the old dilemma – the desire for companionship and the desire for privacy; the need to communicate and the more urgent need not to be found; the hope of love but fear of the trap it lays.

I remembered what it was like before we were married, existing for myself alone, and saw how much richer and more solid life with Deirdre was. But marriage often seemed like writing a novel – the hackneyed things were the hardest to articulate and got no easier with practice. I wanted to say something without seeing how to do it, or what it was, and silence was no alternative. Words reached the page with lessening facility, and though I told myself they were more precious for their rarity I knew how I fooled myself. I was certain only that I had to go on trying, even if there were times when I felt I loved someone who wasn't quite Deirdre – or quite anyone else.

FIFTY-THREE

June 4, Priego. From the bus to Guadalajara the country looks kindlier and more intimate, the olives and vines in less huge geometric patterns. Villages are encrustations on the metallic hills. Each has its cemetery set apart, a lonely quadrangle with a few cypresses and the tips of angels' wings over the wall – 'well away from the houses, like a full stop', Jan Morris wrote. A distant lake is visible, and another ruined monastery and beehives grouped beside an orchard. Spirals of dust twist into the air. A red patch in a field where there are more poppies than barley turns into a valley of blood between the hills. On a remote crag, guarding its memories of Christianity or Islam, a castle stands against the sky.

I don't know why a shepherd with his flock is such a stirring sight. And I don't remember having seen hair on a girl's arms as thick as that on a passenger in the bus. Wondering how much of her it covers, staring sideways across the aisle, I lust with sudden curiosity.

From Guadalajara I take a train to Siguenza and sit with *Don Quixote* under the trees by the fortress cathedral. The town has been re-anti-quated with old-fashioned lamps, wrought iron balconies, cobbled patterns in the streets; but the cathedral towers are still pocked with shell holes from the Civil War. In the quiescence that falls between two o'clock and five only the bars, cool and sombre behind bead curtains, show a sort of life. Alcoholism in Spain, my *El País* says, is one of the highest in the world and the third most common cause of death. Those village cemeteries must be a pathologist's dream, a stockpile of pickled livers.

The train to Soria is forty minutes late and the man in the ticket office won't sell me a ticket before it comes in; then in the rush he gives me short change and gets angry when I complain.

'You don't come from Soria,' a nun on the train says to me dismissively. Her only interest in me is as someone to carry her suitcase when she gets off.

Oceans of wheat and barley, still green up here, rise and fall on an endless swell, rippled by the wind, patched with cloud shadows or trees. At a country station a girl in a scarlet cap, the stationmaster, clangs a bell and waves a flag. Modern times – society no less than agriculture and industry – have changed this land but somewhere to the east, lost in the sierras, there are people who live in caves.

Soria seems a mess: houses in ruins with lopsided windows and tumbling roofs, and areas cleared and rebuilt with crude new blocks. I make dutiful, dallying visits to two churches, then walk up the hill to the castle where a Parador Machado has been built, a suburban redbrick eyesore. Poor Antonio Machado. In the bar I sit alone with immense portraits – the same blown-up photo repeated on each wall among signatures and quotations – of the poet who wrote of silver hills, dark groves of ilex trees, wild rocky places, white roads, golden poplars by the river, mystical and warlike (warlike?) afternoons.

'I think of poetry,' Don Quixote said, riding along the road with a stranger who complained that his son at university was wasting time on poetry, 'as a tender young virgin of extreme beauty. She is not to be fooled around with, or dragged through the streets, or shown off in the market place or the palace. She is made from an alchemy of such virtue that whoever knows it can turn her into pure gold, beyond price. She must be kept from crooks and from the ignorant mob, who can't appreciate her treasures. And by mob I don't mean only common people. Anyone who knows nothing, even a lord or a prince, can be counted among the mob.' As the mad knight travelled on, his moments of lucidity became more frequent.

At the Parador Machado a beer costs a hundred and thirty pesetas, a record. A few tourist cars are parked outside and quiet foreign voices – English, German, French – discuss today's plans or interrogate the receptionist. I escape down the hill and find the Plaza San Clemente in the old town, a bright nucleus of drinkers, where for the same money I have a bigger beer with fried potatoes and a dish of olives; and where a trio of musicians in black and white costumes with red bandannas, two oboes and a drum, play to the crowd. I'm the only tourist in sight.

FIFTY-FOUR

Truth is beyond description. Recently, when Deirdre and I each wrote to our daughter who was working in China to tell her about the family Christmas at home without her, she wrote back to say that our accounts were so different she couldn't believe we had spent Christmas together. Though Christmas was a true event, to make it real for her we had resorted to something less than the truth – or perhaps more truthful.

I have a perception of a definitive truth, distorted like everyone's by memory or imagination or wishful thinking, but I don't claim that my version is the right one. It's hidden in the blank sheet of paper I put into the typewriter, waiting for me to release it; to give it reality and pass it on. But the only way is in words, and there is a whole dictionary of them to choose from. All I can do is pick those that suit me, knowing that my selection wouldn't be the same as someone else's, even if we were trying to describe the same thing. I'm an editor of the truth, resigned to accepting at best a travesty but more likely a string of lies. Simone de Beauvoir wrote that words are never anything but 'one way of putting it', which is why writers hate to be taken literally. And the novelist Brian Moore said of a point in his early career, 'Either I became a writer or I found a new lie.' All of us are liars, more or less.

For the *Sunday Times* in 1968, a year after the Six Day War when Israel pushed its frontiers to the Suez Canal and the River Jordan and over the Golan Heights, trebling its land area at the expense of its Arab neighbours, I went to St Catherine's monastery in Sinai, a tiny medieval town inside fortress walls.

At four-thirty in the morning, to the whiff of old incense and the

249

glint of candles among their icons and mosaics, a few Greek monks chanted the first of the daily offices, *Kyrie eleison;* and through the windows the cold desert dawn began to break. I slipped out of the church, out through the monastery gate where camels were waiting with their bedouin drivers. The moon went down as the sun came up, throwing the shadow of our little caravan across the mountains. We had to leave the camels and climb the last thousand feet of the pilgrim track on foot. This was where Moses spent forty days and forty nights and received the Law of God; and it didn't matter, on a brilliant morning such as ours, that thirty Japanese tourists had beaten us to the top. The blinding view reached to Africa and Arabia – not the thunder and lightning that greeted Moses, with the voice of God coming out of a cloud, but a trumpeting of another kind across the world.

The next summer I went back to Israel, writing for myself this time. For some months I lived in Jerusalem, in a room at the top of a French convent in the old city. I looked across the roofs to the Dome of the Rock, the El Aqsa mosque, the Judaean hills. I drank a lot of Carmel brandy and nibbled pistachios, flicking the shells into the Via Dolorosa below. And I ravelled and unravelled the tentative, fragile but totally believable surprises of a novel.

Other things were less believable. I was also working for an Egyptian who called himself Sayid but admitted it wasn't his true name. And though Sayid was unaware of it I was working for an Israeli who introduced himself as Moshe, and agreed when I suggested it was false. And though neither Sayid nor Moshe knew it, I was working for an Englishman who asked me to call him Reid, apologizing for the pseudonym. Everybody was disguised as someone else, in Israel and in London. Nothing was real except the novel I was writing. 'To a novelist,' Graham Greene wrote, 'his novel is the only reality and his only responsibility.'

Under the doleful, baleful eyes of Sayid and Moshe and Reid, whoever they were, I returned to Jerusalem in the autumn of 1969, this time with Deirdre and our three small children; and for almost a year we lived in an old house in the Abyssinian quarter.

My private masquerade was no less absurd than that of the men whose agent, double agent, triple agent, they believed I was. As a spy I swung from occasions of almost gratifying efficiency to moments of helpless frivolity. As a father, catching my breath at the thought that when my own father died his three children were at about the present age of mine and perhaps I wasn't as vital to their future as I hoped, I sweated up the rock fortress of Masada and swam in the sticky stinging water of the Dead Sea and picnicked in stark Crusader castles with names to match – Nimrud, Belvoir, Montfort – and ate St Peter's fish on the shores of Galilee. As a husband, conscious that for Deirdre there were mysteries in marriage that I couldn't reach, I walked with her to Bethlehem on Christmas night, trying to ignore the tourist coaches; and continued the life of alternate happiness and despair that was becoming a pattern, trying to believe it could be something better. Only as a writer, dropping all pretence, could I find a sort of sense among the ironies.

Deirdre bought a donkey to take the children to the Anglican mission school in the Street of the Prophets, where they were filled with Bible stories and simple precepts. One evening my five-year old son, in a pious mood, fixing me with a caring troubled look, asked, 'Father, why don't you open up your heart and let the sun shine in?' Though I knew the answer I couldn't tell him at the time. It was too ludicrous even for a child's belief. And for an instant, in one of those flashes of recognition, I felt myself caught between my own father and my son, sandwiched in the middle. Through me they were briefly joined, they became the same, though they never knew each other. In my son I saw my father. What did my son see in me?

The novel concerns an English writer, Alec, living alone in Jerusalem. It's about deception, deviousness, infidelity; the writer's hunger for material; the novelist as scavenger, feeding on other people. I lived Alec's life so intensely while I wrote the book that now I can't tell how far Alec lived mine.

I had met Reid (or Reed or Reade – I never saw it written, I only had a telephone number which he asked me to memorize) in a block of service flats near Sloane Square. He wouldn't say how he knew of me, but he had heard I wanted to write a book in Israel and had a suggestion that might interest me. He rang to invite me to the little flat.

It was obvious that nobody lived there: a bleak bed-sitter with minimal furniture, not even a telephone (so what was the number Reid gave me?) and only a tin of Nescafé and some teabags in the tiny kitchen. We would always meet there, he said, and I must approach the block by the same street and use the same entrance every time – he came by another route. While we talked, to stop being overheard through the thin walls, he turned up the radio.

I remembered my interview with an admiral behind Buckingham Palace once and my lunch with an old Winchester boy in his club. Beside them Reid was instantly unmemorable – the self-effacing occupant of a flat he didn't live in, with a telephone somewhere else. Faintly scholarly? Faintly sporting? Faintly several things, but all of them suppressed. He was almost non-existent, and the more convincing for it. His most substantial move was to put me in touch with Sayid. But 'touch' suggests a contact between the two men, one a faceless professional, the other a conspicuous playboy, which they didn't have. Reid told me he had once seen Sayid in the distance, but I don't suppose Sayid had the slightest knowledge of Reid.

I met Sayid in a flat off Kensington High Street, a short bus ride from Reid's but large and ornately furnished, with a feeling of the occasional encampment of some rich Arab family, perhaps Sayid's own. There was a programme for a sex show propped against the gold digital clock, a stack of records and magazines, the vague odour of cooking spices or after-shave, and a radio which Sayid kept on – it seemed to be standard routine. We would always meet there, he said, echoing Reid. He was like a fat baby growing middle-aged but probably not as foolish as he looked, though not as clever as he claimed. Whether he was a high-ranking officer or a freelance operator, he suggested that his career was in doubt – my own was also far from clear – and I had come along at the right moment for him. (Reid's career, if he had one, must have been filed away in a nameless office, decipherable only by a few colleagues who knew the key.) Sayid's ability to plant an Englishman in Israel as his agent seemed more important than the value of any intelligence the agent might send out.

In London I went to his flat once a week for training. It was schoolboy stuff. He instructed me in elementary surveillance and showed me silhouettes of aircraft, tanks, torpedo boats. He gave me a pad of soft pink paper which, torn into strips and soaked in water, would make invisible ink – or I could use urine if I preferred; and a small Sony shortwave receiver – we did hours of Morse together, using a simple alphabetical code; and a new lens for my camera and a developing tank. He taught me to make a micro-negative of a typed message – new ribbon, capital letters, single spacing – then insert it in the corner of an ordinary postcard after unpicking the fibres with a needle, glue it up and stick on a stamp without damaging it or leaving fingerprints. I was a good pupil, partly fascinated and partly aghast, weaving a cynical but discreet course between the appalling implications and the utter comedy.

I met Moshe in the Hilton Hotel at Tel Aviv a few hours after a call from a major I knew in the Israeli army: 'He'll be in the Steimatzky bookshop – a small man in a white shirt and grey trousers, with sunglasses.' Moshe sidled up and led me to a corner of the lounge where I began to tell my story. (*My* story? Or the one in the novel?) Struck by the possibilities, or alarmed, or even touched with admiration, he asked me to meet him next day at a flat in a suburb of Tel Aviv. It was neither as austere as Reid's nor as comfortable as Sayid's, but recognizably the home of someone, though probably not of Moshe. We would always meet there, he said, like the others, and he too switched on the radio.

The background noise of those radios linked the three men – perhaps literally, I sometimes thought, as if they had read the same textbooks or even attended the same espionage school and didn't want to lose touch. Though they had different tastes I wouldn't have been surprised to hear Moshe's endless Middle East commentaries break into Sayid's Kensington flat, or Sayid's non-stop pop music interrupt Reid's interminable symphonies. For all I knew their radios contained microphones or cameras, but it was unlikely: pink paper and postcards were their style.

When violent atmospherics came out of Moshe's radio he asked, half humorously, 'Is that your device or mine?' – and took off his shoe in a pretence of examining something hidden in the heel. Sayid would have laughed and banged the machine. Reid would never have allowed himself even half a joke. And when Moshe produced an old photo of Sayid as a young man it confirmed my suspicion that they were not only rivals in the game but, like tennis stars playing the international circuit, somehow friends as well. Reid, perched between them with the book of rules, was umpire.

In Jerusalem once a week, late at night with a single earplug that cut out the Sony's loudspeaker and wouldn't disturb Deirdre or wake the children, I tuned in to my private wavelength and waited for my call sign. It was a moment of nervous excitement till the coded message came through, from Cairo perhaps, tapped out by Sayid or one of his men exclusively for me. I assumed that Moshe was also listening but for him, as for Sayid, it was real. Even for Reid in London, remotely, it may have been real in an almost metaphysical way – the merest detail in some intangible scheme of filing and cross-filing, a trivial memorandum lost in the welter of irrelevances, improbabilities, impersonalities.

For me it was fiction. Any information I could collect was worthless to Sayid, useful only for my novel. I typed my coded reply, photographed it and posted the tiny scrap of negative to one of the names Sayid gave me, the alias of an alias, at an accommodation address that he often changed, concealed in a postcard with an innocent tourist's message written on top – a fiction within a fiction.

At Sayid's request, with Moshe's approval, I spent a night in a fortified bunker on the Suez Canal and went on a dawn patrol along the Jordan and observed at close range the bombing of Syrian positions behind the cease-fire line. Or if I didn't do them – if I didn't watch these astonishing things myself, and put them in my secret reports, and gasp at the balance between deadly seriousness and sheer lunacy, and wonder how I had got mixed up in it – Alec in the novel does. But they weren't experiences to be turned into fiction later, they were the events that followed fiction: not the germ of the book I was working on, but the book itself. It was all round me, I only had to put it into words. This time, while the frontiers of Israel became confused with the frontiers of reality, the novel dictated life – it wasn't the usual way. 'You are doing what Somerset Maugham did,' Sayid once said in Kensington, and in Tel Aviv a month later Moshe said, 'You are following Somerset Maugham.'

Like mine, Alec's duplicity goes further, reaching his publisher, who is also his brother-in-law, and his wife – a multiple disloyalty to everything except his writing. Graham Greene has emphasized the virtue, the secret freedom of disloyalty which is the writer's privilege: 'Disloyalty encourages us to roam experimentally through any human mind, it gives to the novelist the extra dimension of sympathy.' To write freely he must be free to be disloyal with impunity, and Alec is faithful to such treachery.

After an appointment in Geneva for debriefing, which was reflected in my own meeting there with Sayid, which in turn was passed on to Moshe, Alec spends a few days by the lake with a Jewish woman half his age. She too is tangled in the plot, he isn't sure how deeply, and though she may be another agent they can be carefree alone together, responsible only to their love. Her name is Drora, the Hebrew for a lark and also for freedom, and for her alone Alec keeps a sort of fidelity. I love her too, naturally. And I was glad when another woman I knew and loved, twenty years younger than me, who read the novel and recognized quotations from herself, said that she felt not betrayed, thank God, but violated – a less dishonourable offence.

Dishonourable? What had honour to do with it? – unless I retained a vague recollection of some distant quality, not OLQ but perhaps a consciousness of Don Quixote. But unlike him I was doing nothing brave and knew I should survive. Though Alec in the novel is blown up by a hand grenade, I was in no danger. All my life I have been confident of my safety, never to be gunned down like my father – men like me are spared.

Sayid and Moshe have counterparts in the book, more real than the characters who sometimes, with decreasing credibility, can be made to stir my memory – though those too have left tokens that survive to suggest that they existed once. I have a small gold medal in an olive-wood box which Moshe gave me for my trouble. And in my kitchen every morning on Sayid's little Sony receiver, which has more than the shortwave band, I listen to the news.

Reid, of course, vanished with his telephone number, leaving nothing.

Writers, the novelist D. M. Thomas said, are secret agents. John Updike wrote of the useful sensation of being a spy behind the lines, Jack Kerouac called himself a spy in someone else's body, and the film-writer Hanif Kureishi confessed to espionage, 'poking into failures and weaknesses for good stories'. As a spy, literary if not literal, I travelled through the occupied territories of the West Bank, drove to Gaza, talked to Arab mayors and Israeli commanders, politicians, journalists, lawyers, citizens of both sides.

In the same disguise, within a few years, I walked over the island of Hoy in the Orkneys where white hares bounded over the snow, kicking their black tails behind them; and went lobster-fishing in the Hebrides where under the cliffs one morning, full of whisky, we got sixty lobsters from a hundred and forty pots; and pedalled an old postman's bike across the island of Barra to a small loch where, in the rain, I caught three trout for breakfast; and stood on the furthest tip of the Shetlands where I could wave to the lighthouse keepers on Muckle Flugga, the most northerly men in Britain.

More improbably, closer to home, I inspected a girls' finishing school in Belgravia where debutantes learnt to curtsey and make lemon soufflés. And in Islington I kept up the roles of reluctant neighbour, impatient father, unreliable husband.

255

The confrontation of reality and fantasy, wondering which was which, became a theme. 'It's your perpetual ambivalence that I find impossible to live with,' Deirdre wrote, after years of trying. As a family man, helping to keep the rickety but irresistible show on the road, I was an adequate Sancho Panza, but as a writer I had to follow Don Quixote out into the big lonely desert. Though I dreaded going there, back into the unknown in search of the unimagined, it was where I belonged.

Writing could seem a penance, compulsory and inescapable but also beautiful in an oddly moving way. Sometimes, for isolation, I borrowed someone's cottage in Essex, Suffolk, Cornwall, Scotland, to find the solipsism I thought I needed – running away, with typing paper and more whisky, to get a clearer view of the things I felt deeply about; and one of those things was me. A writer needs to love himself a little, but at home there was too much else to love.

FIFTY-FIVE

June 5, Soria. The train to Tudela, like yesterday's from Siguenza, is late. Nobody knows when it will arrive. 'Let my death come from Spain,' an old Italian proverb asks, 'for then it will be a long time coming.'

Passengers at the station begin arguing with the railway staff and among themselves. The bar does good trade, one man is drunk, there is shouting and slapping. Two national policemen driving big Honda motorbikes come slowly along the platform. They park by the ladies' toilet, remove their helmets, light cigarettes and swagger towards the bar on rubber-soled jackboots: in dark green uniform with black scarves at their throats, carrying pistols, truncheons, handcuffs clipped to the back of their belts. One has a red beard. They must have been summoned, unless this is part of their regular patrol, and they stay till the train comes, two and a half hours late.

It stops often at stations that are no longer manned: empty buildings, windows cemented up, tiles off. Platforms have been demolished, sidings ripped out. Sometimes the town is out of sight, lost in a crack between the impossible hills, and a postman has come on a mobylette to meet the train. He should bring a radio to fill the hours of waiting. At one station, deep in grass, an old man gets out with a roll of chicken wire he bought in Soria. He still has a long walk to his village, which also looks abandoned: a few forgotten inhabitants and dogs, perhaps, are living among those ruined houses. He opens his trousers to piss on the derelict platform before shouldering the chicken wire and starting up the road.

All afternoon the country changes, opening into a spacious plain, closing again into the rocky sierra, flattening out towards evening on to the rich Ebro valley where the train's shadow ripples across fields of asparagus, banked in rows like potatoes.

FIFTY-SIX

I'm drawn to the man who lives, as it were, at one remove from himself, perhaps uncertain which identity to believe in. The man, for instance, who announced his own death in order to read the obituaries and find out who he was. The man so ashamed of poverty and his mousy economizing that he would rather be convicted of murder than produce an alibi to show that he had gone to a sixpenny, not a shilling, wash-room. The man who walked out, leaving wife, children, dog, garden, to become in turn a bus driver and a sailor and a gigolo, and returned secretly to observe his home without him – to spy on his past and imagine his alternative present. The man with a pink manilla folder containing a false *curriculum vitae*, a complete set of references covering his life, spotless but faked. 'Cast your eye over those,' he told a friend, 'and tell me if you've ever met a better character.' It wasn't him, and yet it was.

I like the sense of being apart from myself, another I, not the one who did this or that or wrote those books – or is even writing this one. On a plane between San Salvador and Tegucigalpa a whisky salesman, travelling for 'Cutty Sark', asked me, 'Who are you representing?' I wondered what the answer was. Myself? If so, which brand of me? Double lives, like mixed feelings, seem part of the human comedy.

I knew a Canadian who had four children living with their mother in London and four more with theirs in Düsseldorf, the two families ignorant of each other for years. I didn't envy him, but I did admire the member of parliament – once the hero and general wit of a Japanese prisoner-of-war camp, who sustained many inmates' will to live and was tortured for refusing to betray details of an escape route – who later withdrew his acceptance of a life peerage from the Queen on being

259

given four years' imprisonment for indecency with boys and, after his release, pursued his love of poetry and young Arabs in Tangier till he died.

In most lives there must be times when a man takes himself by surprise, or is overtaken by another self. Talking to a foreigner I find I'm speaking with an accent somewhere between his and mine, and think I'm shortening the distance between us, coming out to meet him halfway in a gesture of sympathy, but probably I'm just escaping from my usual self – or anyway from the self who was talking to the person before, and half turned into that one too. I'm so many selves, each available to suit the moment, all reflecting the corruption and chaos that make up my varied, divergent being. A painter friend once claimed, 'All the cruelty, mendacity, phoniness and even emptiness in one are essential if one is to attain their opposites.'

My father had his *doppelgänger*, the look-alike who led him out of the New Guinea forest. Mine, lurking at my elbow, is himself a split personality. Partly he is the man I could easily have been if I hadn't avoided him, who embodies all I have rejected but whom I need, when struck by doubt or worry, standing there to remind me of what I must never forget. Partly he is an observer who watches me, generally with neither approval nor horror though sometimes with an eyebrow raised: the spectator of my life who in his way, like my father's, will save it.

There were times when being a writer seemed more than ever a mug's game and I looked around for something else – or watched myself looking around, aware that in the end I would go back to the typewriter and rejoice. In 1971 a publisher said he could employ me as a reader at £4 a book. I could read a typescript and write a report by lunchtime, leaving the rest of the day for my own work. I thanked him, and went home to draft an advert: 'Seven books but no best-seller. Writer, 45, BA etc., wants job.' The BA didn't bear much scrutiny, the etc. even less. I sent it to *The Times* which put it in the 'For Sale and Wanted' column, the *Daily Telegraph*, the *Guardian* and the *New Statesman*.

The first response was from a nice man, older than me and more down-at-heel, who rang my doorbell and said that since books were my business he could always help me find any I might want. He came in and talked about his life: a country vicar's son, a love of Tudor music, a roomful of books for which he hoped to have his own shop one day. No mention of a job for me. But as he left he asked whether I ever needed someone to do research.

Then the letters began. A man in Croydon set the pattern: 'It seems a pity if you have to involve yourself in a routine job which would give you little time to write. It has occurred to me that you may wish to consider a proposition which, for a very small investment, would make you a distributor of high quality non-polluting cleaning products.' It might not sound very exciting, he admitted, 'but there is a lot of money in it.'

A man in Bournemouth was more forthright: 'Do you want to be a millionaire? I intend to become one and to achieve this goal I am searching for a team of dynamic men to work with me.' He didn't say what they would be doing.

A man in Watford wrote an elaborate letter on paper printed with reference numbers, telegraphic and cable addresses and a picture of a liner steaming into New York – his ship coming home, perhaps. 'Subject to further exchange of mutually satisfactory information I might be able to provide what you are seeking in one or other of the enterprises with which I am connected.' After rambling on about an artist he had known as a child he asked for further particulars, 'by letter please, as I am no longer much good at the telephone.'

A man in Pimlico whom I rang after he had offered me 'a very substantial spare time income' said that he himself had recently made £6000 with a firm called Computax, and when I demurred he suggested I might prefer selling life insurance. A man in Ilford ('If you care to telephone me it may be to your advantage') also had jobs for insurance salesmen. He was saying 'But we have people from all walks of life' for the third time when I rang off.

A man in Sussex said he was looking for men with leadership and enthusiasm to fill the executive posts in his company – shades of OLQ – and promised £1000 a month. Another in Woodford Green had opportunities for anyone with drive and intelligence, but didn't explain how he would employ a writer. An Irish actor in Twickenham for whom my advert brought memories of 'the old days with Brendan Behan' said I could sell schoolbooks for him. An Australian in a Hampshire cottage suggested I might persuade British manufacturers to provide cargoes for ships trading at cut rates in the Pacific – tools, tractors, whisky, food, anything. He already had the ships, he only needed someone educated who could talk with confidence to senior executives. A good man could make several thousand pounds in a month or two: 'This is quite true and no catch, provided you can talk to people.'

As a relief after the promises of quick fortunes an elderly man in Essex who had read one of my books in the public library wrote to say he was now going to buy it and offered to pay for a lunch, anywhere I liked. Another in Suffolk said he was 'most sad' to see my advert, but there was nothing he could do except pass it on to a friend in films. More hopefully the editor of a magazine in Lancashire, also 'saddened', wrote to say he might give me freelance work and his fee was better than my publisher's, but I would have to live in Lancashire.

Half the replies came from Golden Chemicals Ltd. I was surprised that a chemical company should have work for a writer and get so many of its staff to approach me. They invited me to one of their business meetings ('your ticket to a sound financial future,' the card said) and one evening I went along to the London Hilton in Park Lane. I had never been in it before, but a man in a novel had stayed there and I was curious to see inside.

I wasn't alone. Two hundred men and women of every age and colour sat in a room and were introduced to Golden Chemicals: hair shampoo, car shampoo, lavatory disinfectant, bubble bath solution, shoe spray, carpet cleaner – all new inventions, all biodegradable. For an hour and a half two men explained the Golden system, never stopping for our questions but implying that we were privileged to be there. We could be enrolled for only £13, but if we wrote a cheque for £1100 they would send us £1800 of Golden goods and we should be on the way to £400, £500, even £1000 a month. Golden would fly us to a training conference in Miami or Honolulu or Surfers' Paradise, and we were shown a film to prove it – a glimpse of the joys that would tumble from the Golden skies. We could be that man in the sports car at the traffic lights, we could have a skiing holiday or buy a new house, we could retire to our island in the sun.

Golden had just reached Britain and there were a hundred more countries to conquer, so now was the time to join. 'The day Golden gives you a country to run, you're a millionaire.' The two evangelists wished they could make it sound more difficult, to make it more believable. Tonight could be for us what a night like this not long ago had been for them – a Golden opportunity.

The depressing thing, as I slipped away at the end, was the number of people who were already signing on. On my way home I tried to remember what job I had imagined. Some brave and visionary employer must have something for me. I even thought of the publisher's offer with gratitude. At £4 a time I would only have to read fourteen books to pay for my adverts.

Luckily a friend in Amnesty International saw one of them and offered temporary work in their archives. For two months I wrote political reports on foreign countries compiled from news clippings and yearbooks – boring and not lucrative but at least I was busy with someone else's ideas, rescued from my own till the compulsion to start a book returned. Perhaps, though, it might have come to me more quickly as a salesman for Golden Chemicals.

The asthma went on – a protean, unpredictable disease. As neurotic as most people, I caught myself blaming it on things that worried me anyway: depression over my work, cold weather, cigarette smoke, a dog, a heavy meal, a row. It was dishonest to point to a single cause, it needed a combination of several.

Occasionally I was unable to lie down. I propped myself up or sat leaning forward with my heart galloping and shoulders hunched, head down, speechless, panting for every ounce of fresh air I could get. I believed I was dying this time, though I had always survived before. I felt insulted, humiliated, impatient with anyone who interfered or tried to help. This was my problem, I must cope with it alone.

There were periods of near-freedom: climbing mountains and sailing boats and playing the flute, which needed a lot of wind. Sometimes it was easy to forget the day when I was defeated by the short stairs up from Piccadilly underground to the street or, in the London Library, couldn't reach the reading room on the first floor.

I had fluid, thick and opaque like cream, poured into my lungs through a tube down my windpipe or my nose, to show up the faults on an X-ray. A physiotherapist with her hands on my ribs taught me to breathe with different lobes separately, then tipped me upside down and pummelled me to let the sputum run out. I tried most of the new drugs as they were invented.

I was given one of the steroids and it worked dramatically – the difficulty was to get off it. Side effects could be serious, but each time I needed a course it took a bigger dose and more time to have effect. Feeling frightened, I went to a naturopath who prescribed a diet, like the man from Mont Dore in my childhood, and did clever things with his fingers on my spine. (On my daughter, who inherited my asthma, he practised acupuncture which she found soothing, though she too went back to drugs.) I took to carrying two small inhalers, a bronchodilator and a steroid, asking for something stronger when I needed it.

Often I was told of 'wonderful' men to go and see. I had tried too many, I preferred to accept my asthma and get on with life.

FIFTY-SEVEN

June 6, Tudela. Towns are as surprising as the landscape. I arrive in a new place by train or bus, tramp past petrol stations and apartment blocks and small factories, a smell of cement and a white dust on the oleander leaves, a melon patch and a vine between padlocked stores, making for the *centro urbino*, hating what I see, wondering why I came; and find myself in a theatrical scene, a plaza of tiered balconies or stone arcades or a helpless tangle of medieval streets.

Here in Tudela the plaza has a bandstand of glass and iron in the middle, strung in all directions with a spider's web of election flags, a roof of coloured cardboard so thick that the architecture, if anyone cared, is invisible. But they aren't the old slogans that have pursued me across Spain. This is Navarre, a Basque province with ambitions for independence. And the advertisements are not for bullfights but for Clint Eastwood's new film and Jeffrey Archer's book. Nothing is familiar except the family of storks roosting over a gateway in the corner.

The restaurant where I have supper is another surprise: a clutter of brassware and wrought iron, antlers and bellows and stuffed fauna, darkened beams, carved furniture and pictures of jolly yokels quaffing flagons of wine. Spain can fake an antique effect as well as anywhere. But the canary in the cage is fading, the rubber plant is already dead.

Out in the street a man is grilling big red pimientos and a gypsy woman calls to me, *'Caballero!'* It means cavalier, man on a horse, knight. I'm in Don Quixote's land again, the genuine gallant Spain. 'Caballero, you want your fortune told?'

I would love it, if I could believe her.

FIFTY-EIGHT

It was time to leave London. The value of the Islington house had trebled since we bought it, we couldn't afford not to sell it. The rates had risen still more, my overdraft was bigger than the mortgage, I had two novels which nobody wanted. In the country we could buy a house for half the price, leaving me free of money worries – free to get more work done. For a writer who didn't depend on the London scene and hadn't been to a literary party for years the country was the natural place. If it was good enough for Tolstoy. . . .

There was another reason, simple at the time though later it grew confused. Probably it was to do with trying something new. Not only was London no longer what it used to be, twenty years ago, but I too was getting snarled up. Deirdre felt the same, and when our mutual efforts made things worse we turned separately to other people for consolation, understanding. Wasn't there a way out of the tangle? Couldn't we undo things, and learn to think afresh? Why must we suffer this state of confrontation, near-hostility, all the time? Why couldn't our intelligence, strength, dexterity, subtlety, be turned in unison on the same enemy – this dreadful, beautiful world? It wasn't a matter of fault or error, or truth or illusion, but there seemed no signposts to anywhere, and nowhere to go. Perhaps, somewhere else, our marriage could find a new beginning.

We had tried psychotherapy, thinking naively that it might offer a cure. While Deirdre found it painful, I enjoyed the sense of rigorous self-unravelling. It was similar to writing – a way of drawing out thoughts and emotions from deep inside and trying to make sense of them, though this time it was real life, not fiction – and it may have helped with the book I was working on. But otherwise it only confirmed our own diagnosis.

Once, at a time of crisis, we had gone to Wales without the children for a few days to sort things out. We would give ourselves a last chance together, three months, six months, and try harder before admitting failure. Or live apart for a while. Or separate for ever – it might be better now than waiting till everything had turned sour and any love was beyond hope of keeping. We walked over the Black Mountains and the Brecon Beacons, and ate trout and steaks in pubs, and drank too much. It was hard to remember that we weren't on our honeymoon but were meant (by whom? Deirdre asked) to be talking about divorce. Afterwards she told a friend that she had never felt more contentedly in love and couldn't understand what we were up to ('What fools we are – I don't expect anyone to understand us, since we mystify our-selves'), but if she got too merry I reminded her not to get carried away – we were supposed to be on the point of tragedy.

At home in Islington we resorted to bickering over silly domestic details or fell into helpless, lonely silence. 'Quarrelling is easier than loving,' a husband in a novel says. Neither of us wanted to live apart, nor as we were living, and though love hadn't stopped we had ceased to notice it. We had lost the sense of miracle, the apocalypse of those sudden moments when we shared a simple happiness; and were looking for something to blame externally, not inside ourselves; wasting all our ingenuity on a duel instead of deploying it on the whole enormous obscene and marvellous job of life.

But there were enough targets without picking on the nearest and best loved. We should be slinging flowers at each other, not mud; celebrating the good times of the past, not dragging up the bad ones. What had happened to the fun? And the magic? And the generosity? 'Why are you so kind to me?' Deirdre had asked in the early days. 'I feel you ought to be fed up with me.' There wasn't much kindness around now, and if I was fed up it was with shame. Such resourcelessness was barbaric, and a sweat of impatience broke out at my sterile imagination.

I couldn't accept the permanence of things. And there was so much missing. I would read something fine and beautiful, or hear a few bars of Mozart, or catch some outrageous thought beyond the dead-end trivialities that stifled us, and be lifted to a better way to live than this. Though it was romantic and absurd to suppose that changing houses would mean leaving behind the wild unforgivable things we had said and done, life elsewhere might be a half-tone brighter, if not transformed. Perhaps all the ironies could be tolerated, even laughed at, in another place.

We had to move out. But it would still be useful to live within reach of London (Tolstoy was always going off to Moscow), which ruled out Devon and Wales and Cumberland. If one wanted exile one would choose France, Greece, Spain.

We looked at houses, or rather Deirdre did. At the sight of an estate agent's brochure I hardly got beyond correcting the prose. At the sight of someone else's dream house, four miles from a post office and wallowing in nettles, my nightmares solidified, then drifted to a town flat or a cottage by the sea or even a suburban villa.

We spent a holiday in Norfolk because someone said it was cheap and not too far – 'out on a limb, on the way to nowhere' – and trailed round house after house, trying to imagine living in any of them; driving for ever through sugar beet fields, shutting our eyes to the battery turkey prisons, the pig farms like extermination camps, forgetting what we had remembered of the English countryside, in search of one more abandoned farmhouse or derelict mill or de-consecrated rectory. Anything we liked was too expensive, anything we could afford wasn't good enough. Possibly we had been spoilt in our big Georgian terrace house, but we must have room for the piano, the books and furniture, the children's expanding needs.

I pulled the first string and wrote to a man in the National Trust, a writer I used to meet at the parties I wasn't invited to any more. He replied that they were looking for a tenant for the Hall, in Suffolk, and sent me particulars: a fine gabled farmhouse of about 1600, oak framed and yellow plastered, midway between Constable's birthplace and Gainsborough's. We went to look at it on a wet day in February.

Not for us, we decided. Too big, with five bedrooms and five attics above. Too dark, with the East Anglian winter creeping through the leaded panes. Too cold, with the east wind penetrating its lath-and-plaster walls. It hadn't been anyone's home for sixty years, inhabited only occasionally except by the lady in brown who had been heard treading heavily across the floor upstairs and was last seen vanishing through a wall, her finger to her lips.

Perhaps it was she, going about her crafty work while we viewed the alternatives from London, who tilted us in favour of the Hall. Slowly it became inescapable, imperative. It was a ridiculously pretty house –

nothing else came anywhere near it. We went to have another look when the orchard was a flood of daffodils, and I applied for the lease.

Other people applied too: a man who wanted to use it for wholesale antiques, a couple who thought it would make a lovely restaurant, and families who just wanted to live there, like us. I pulled more strings, to a duke on the National Trust committee whose brother I had once known but who never wrote back, and to an accountant on the finance committee who had once led me, with one of his sons and one of mine, up a rock climb in Langdale. The strings touched something in the end and I was summoned to tea with the local baronet, whose family had owned the country round the Hall for centuries.

Over the Earl Grey and sponge cake I must have passed the test – was there a trace of OLQ from the navy thirty years ago? – and in time I was offered a lease. One clause forbade me carrying on any business there, but writing didn't count.

We arrived at the Hall in the golden August of 1975 and opened the windows for the best summer of the century to bless it. After the vertical life of a London terrace it was a joy to move horizontally from one room to the next and on to a third, and out into the garden. But the old house was unaccustomed to being lived in, and needed all our patience and hard work. I would start on a new novel when the children started school in the autumn. Then it was Christmas. Then the spring. And the second summer was even better than the first.

Looking out one day, at the sound of gunfire, I saw we were surrounded by armed men. The baronet was leading the troops, his baronette beside him. They were in battle order, about to attack. Men with sticks were creating a diversion beyond the orchard, snipers were in position, Range Rovers were bringing up supplies. There were women too, in khaki tweeds or jungle green, with dogs for picking up the dead and wounded. When I went out to parley with them someone opened fire and feathers came tumbling from the sky. A square-shouldered warrior raised her shooting-stick: 'Come here, sir,' she ordered. I fled indoors, but later I began to think she was talking to her dog.

At first I grew vegetables. I had never planted a bean and watched it grow. To put a potato in the ground and dig up ten was a new magic. And I was seduced by the names on the seed packets – Fenland Green Longpod, Outdoor Girl, Velocity, Dobie's Purity. Like the fruit trees in the orchard – Herring's Pippin, Ecklinville, Darcy Spice – they belonged to a new vocabulary, unknown to my typewriter.

But nobody had told me about the warfare. Daily I fought against animals, birds, insects, and once when I was bending over my cabbages I was sprayed with gunshot by the baronet's men. The second year it happened all over again, without the thrill.

There were market gardens nearby where vegetables came earlier than mine, and cheaper. Leave it to the professionals – it was enough to cut the grass and tend the shrubs and trees. I ought to be planting sentences, not onions; clipping adjectives, pruning clauses. Each nettle pulled up should be a word crossed out, so that another would live. I sweated, not just with toil but with hate for the lost time, guilt for the book not written. The third year I let the grass smother the vegetable patch and planted a walnut tree in the middle, grown from a nut saved from the London garden. I could wake up in the morning with one less worry to haunt the day.

I found I was no more a countryman than a gardener. If escape from the city was an attempt to regain contact with nature, like adultery as a cure for a dying marriage, it didn't work – the attempt was clumsy, the contact false. As a Londoner I had gone for more walks on Hampstead Heath than I did in Suffolk now. I remembered my elder sister, a farmer's wife, saying she couldn't live in the country if the fields in sight were not her own, but I was thankful these weren't mine. I no more wanted to possess the land round the Hall than I had the park near our London house. I loved the landscape, probably more than the man who had to decide whether to sow wheat and potatoes where last year he had had sugar beet and barley, but I was a passer-by amid the alien corn, which was how I liked it.

The alienation was sharp at first. Early impressions were grim: water meadows drained and ploughed, hedges uprooted or slashed by a machine that left wounds and splinters, chemicals drifting over the fields and into the streams, plastic dustbins of food put out in the fields for pheasants, and the true wild animals – weasels, hedgehogs, crows, foxes, jays, stoats – strung up like gibbeted murderers in the trees. But slowly they grew acceptable and in time I even caught myself, as I fetched more logs from the woodshed for the enormous fireplace, being grateful for Dutch elm disease. Cynicism was seldom disturbed – only if a butterfly flitted past as it had in the summer of perpetual childhood, or an owl – not one of the owls that used to hoot in the London night but a visitor from a pre-modern countryside – settled on an open window and looked in.

There was a risk, I saw at once, from something called Suffolkation. It could set in with no warning – I had to be alert. Soon after moving to the Hall I noticed a previous wave of immigrants from London, like refugees from an earlier pogrom, who had settled in the neighbourhood. They carved, they spun, they potted, they wove, they grew macrobiotic food and sold goat's milk yoghurt and brewed elderflower wine, they wore the sad fashions and kept up the earnest attitudes of the sixties. In their eyes was a sort of melancholy vengefulness which made me uneasy. How would I look after being here as long as that?

Not like one of them, I hoped. I felt no nostalgia or resentment. I could see myself as a pale version of Don Quixote, past the prime of life, indigent and alone, with no resources but my optimism and any energy or enthusiasm that might survive. Like him I would show contempt for worldly riches and hope I could do it without hypocrisy, convincing at least myself.

To discomfort me, or just to bore me, people asked if I didn't feel precarious in a rented house, with no bricks and mortar I could call my own. Property, they said, was the only safe investment. It was true: soon after we sold the London house the market launched into flight, heading for space, while the money we got for it melted. Over the years, watching my mishandling of such things – like Don Quixote trying to finance his journey, 'selling one thing, pawning another and losing every time' – I worried about them less and less. Through indifference, negligence, incompetence, I became free of values that I didn't understand. In time I had lived at the Hall longer than anywhere in my life and felt attached as firmly as I could to any house, but I was thankful it wasn't mine. I now had nothing that could be priced by some index quoted in the news. And precariousness was what I chose when I gave up being a tannery manager in Kenya.

I enjoyed the sense of camping, of being nomadic, at liberty to move elsewhere – and wondered if I ever would, and where to. I had no yearning to belong. Though I put down roots they weren't my own but oaks, chestnuts, poplars, willows. I planted a hundred trees and imagined them maturing in the future, for someone else's pleasure – mine was in the imagining. And my capital, at the mercy of nobody but myself, was in the unwritten words waiting to stain the page.

I told myself that it didn't matter where I lived, it was at best stimulating, at worst irrelevant. Convenience was the thing to go for, apart from peace of mind, which wasn't a matter of geography. The blank sheet of paper in the morning looked the same whether the background noise was a tractor or a London bus, a partridge or a starling. But in the country the traps, to someone who only knew about the town ones, were more treacherous for their rural camouflage. The pit could seem bottomless and the weather, the seasons, the beauty of it all, could too easily become excuses for another diversion – or delusion.

All the same, the mirage of London refused to fade and a cheap day rail ticket was something to relish. At Liverpool Street I inhaled the first draught of the foul familiar drug as an old friend and slipped into the underground like returning to a previous life. It was easy to forget the horrors of the Holloway Road or of getting jammed in the Euston underpass. London, so loud and bright and quick, was where the action was. Perhaps I enjoyed it more for not living in it, for no longer being married to it. But divorce was a formality, heedless of feeling. I was glad when foreigners stopped me in the street to ask the way – I didn't tell them that I was a visitor too. I sat in the London Library, half believing that I would be going home on a number nineteen bus; watching the people and wondering about their London evenings ahead, while I would be in the train back to Suffolk; and trying to remember why we moved.

I wasn't exempt from the usual ravages. 'Sometimes,' the narrator in a novel says, playing adultery in Paris, 'I saw a middle-aged man caught in a shop window acting like a young lover with his girl, and felt a little foolish.' In Suffolk at a Sunday midday gin swill, a feature of local folklore, I saw myself as I thought I wouldn't look for ten more years: skinny, scrawny, bald, trying in a polo neck sweater and with a light tenor voice to strike a note of youthful middle age. As I got thinner my jeans – not this year's cut or even last year's – fell off my hips. I grew old, I grew old, I would wear the bottoms of my Levis rolled.

'Should I have heard of you?' I was asked on being introduced as a writer. I could think of no reply. That apologetic 'should' somehow put the obligation on me – it was my duty to be heard of. 'Do you write under your own name?' The famous thriller writer in the next village used several names. 'What sort of novels do you write?' Not famous ones, was the answer.

But I loved my books, as I loved my children – better than other people's. If their creator didn't love them, why should anyone else? It was gratifying when someone, privately or in a review, showed pleasure at having read one, though I tried to tell myself I shouldn't be affected. Secretly, on the fiction shelves of the public library or a bookshop, I would look for one of mine between P. G. Wodehouse and Virginia

Woolf, and pretend it didn't matter if there was nothing there. The therapy for disappointment, as for all afflictions, was to write and go on writing. Every day I tried to squeeze something out, for me to find tomorrow, like the dry little pellets left on the grass each morning. Otherwise I felt polluted by my own waste.

'I hate your books,' Deirdre said one night, kneeling by the big fireplace at the Hall, a glass in her hand, a bottle beside her. She always looked beautiful when she was drunk, on life or love or alcohol. She had been to a London psychiatrist who had told her things that friends as well as I had said before, but from a man in Harley Street they were more convincing. He must have lanced the boil and now the poison was coming out.

So my wife hated my books. Yet for twenty-five years, longer than our marriage, I had been a writer. A writer, and nothing else; or rather the other things – husband, father, householder, taxpayer, gardener – were secondary to the writer. What sort of writer, I had sometimes wondered? – zigzagging between fiction and journalism, dragging my uncertainties through middle age. To have been more single-minded might have brought more profits, but a ruthless writer would surely have been a worse husband, displeasing Deirdre still more. And though the small cold flame burnt fitfully, often eclipsed by doubts and debts that threatened to extinguish it, it never went out. Starting a new book, when it could seem a silly thing to do, I knew it would be a sillier thing not to do it. If I didn't write, nobody else would do it for me. To give up wasn't only a matter of pride or self-credibility: it would be a kind of suicide. 'You start by writing to live,' Carlos Fuentes said. 'You end by writing so as not to die.'

'I hate your books,' she said, pouring herself more wine. 'I hate your friends, I hate your family, I hate your money, I hate your bony face.' I didn't argue or protest. This was a solo performance, erotic almost to the point of orgasm, and to interrupt would be an insult. I could only watch the two of us – a woman spewing out invective on her husband who sat and took it.

And why was I doing nothing about it, I asked myself? Because nothing was the only thing to do? Because anything I tried would be the wrong thing, and there wasn't a right one? Because helplessness might break into impatience, which would be worse? Because I thought I understood her hatred, which was really something else, and I even shared it? Because I wished that I too could rage aloud like this, if only

273

against the pettiness of things, the cheapness of life's nasty little joke? Or because even then – especially then – I loved her?

I watched to see what I would do, with interest and even excitement. Part of me was involved in our behaviour – wife and husband across the room – while another part stood aside, involved in a different conflict, one within me, hoping that out of it something surprising might be created. Tomorrow Deirdre would have got over it, I knew, cancelling the memory and shocking me as much by her recovery as by this tirade. She would be dismissive, laughing at the episode, and I would feel hurt. But probably she was right, and this was just the scum of marriage bubbling to the surface, which we could spoon off, leaving a more wholesome brew underneath.

Yet even this, or some of it, might be rescued from the garbage – saved from death – by the writer's imagination. 'Even in married love,' Richard Hughes wrote, pointing to the superiority of fiction over life, 'we are still each in solitary confinement, only tapping out loving messages on the dividing wall.'

Having reached the age at which my parents died, and outlived them, I seldom thought about them. Could their marriage really have been the bliss that, in childhood, I thought it was? They were married for less than seven years, hardly enough to strain it, but as my own marriage lurched from one spell of happiness to the next, through short bouts of pain and uneasy periods of a quiet desperation saved by the hope of another happy spell, I asked myself – futilely, irrelevantly – if my parents would have done much better.

Sometimes I wondered what they would have been like at sixty, seventy, eighty, and was neither glad nor sorry that they had never grown old. My father, the year we moved to Suffolk, would have been a hundred, but for me he had hardly existed at fifty and to be twice that age was to double the shadow.

Only the facts survived, which could never make up the truth. Though for years I had tried to find somebody behind my father's name – searching for him, inventing him, meeting him at last but rejecting him, then searching again – in time I gave it up. The authentic man escaped me. I might look through his books and see the great explorer, the naturalist, the handsome face with unswerving eyes, but never catch a glimpse of fallibility to make him human, or hear his voice or feel the pressure of a father's hand in mine. Where memory failed, there was nothing but imagination. He couldn't live, or die, unless I put it into words on paper. He became a character of fiction, like someone in a novel I had written but forgotten, though I only had to read a few pages for the reality – the vitality and thrill of his creation – to return.

But even now, though more rarely as his contemporaries died, I was reminded that for other people he had existed less illusorily. At drinks at the vicarage I was approached by a bright old lady who had been a Cambridge student at the time of his murder and remembered the general shock with a twinge of disappointment: a man she loved had invited her to the King's College summer ball, but it was cancelled for my father's funeral. She laughed over her sherry at the memory of her annoyance, and for a moment I was taken back fifty years to the day when the myth began.

My mother's image, though I knew her better, faded more thoroughly than my father's, as if her actual presence in my life couldn't be as permanent as his invented one, which to a writer shouldn't be surprising. Looking at old photos with my children I would find myself sharing their remoteness from her, their disbelief in a grandmother they had never known.

Old photos: but somehow they are less believable than the snapshots the camera didn't catch. It isn't the group pictures with me as a school-boy or sailor, but the sound of a boot on a football or the feeling of panic at some misdemeanour that evokes Winchester, and a mug of strong sweet tea or the smell of diesel oil that brings back the navy.

Likewise I have images of myself, neither in colour nor black and white but printed more vividly than on any paper. There is an early one of me as a child, playing with the triptych mirror of a dressing-table, catching my profile and asking my mother in alarm to promise that my nose wouldn't grow any bigger – no wonder I was teased at school. And one of me as a student, climbing with a friend on a cliff in Wales, or the Lake District or Skye – the place, like the date, isn't recorded – while the sun warms the rock and we sing what we can remember of Bach's B minor Mass. And another of me sitting in the house of an old Dutchman overlooking a lake in Guatemala: a room full of windmill calendars and plastic tulips to defy the hummingbirds outside and the purple volcanoes reflected in the water. And one of me with sun hat and notebook in a lonely teashop beside the Ganges, being enraptured by a Rajput girl straight out of a miniature painting, with a princess's profile and a voice like a temple bell. And a surprising shot of me in Bond Street, being accosted by a scruffy man in a raincoat who walks

275

with me along the pavement, almost arm in arm though I try to throw him off, and leads me into a police trap – three policemen stepping out of a car parked by the kerb. Having checked my identity they explain, to me and to the little crowd collecting round us, that they are looking for a suspect and I answer to his description: my *alter ego*, perhaps – the man I too would like to find.

FIFTY-NINE

June 7, Tudela. I take the train towards Zaragoza down the flat harsh Ebro valley. It stops at a station called Buñuel where there is nothing but a man pushing an empty wheelbarrow, perhaps an actor in some abandoned film. A flock of sheep drifts in a perpetual cloud of dust, a NATO plane tears across the sky.

After fifteen minutes I get out at Gallur. At eleven o'clock it's already hot – the summer is overlying Spain. Beyond the waste land between station and village I find the Imperial Canal of Aragon, a brown waterway flowing down the valley a little slower than my walking pace.

For four hours through the bright heat I follow the canal, raised above the countryside. Sometimes a figure bent among his beans and onions looks up, without stopping work. Two men in blue nylon shorts, running along the other side, wave across the canal. Cut through the bank, padlocked against greedy farmers, sluices release water into the fields: a land of dykes and channels like an overheated Holland. Somewhere the river Ebro lies invisible, and beyond it the Pyrenean foothills falling out of the mist.

When Don Quixote and Sancho Panza reached the Ebro they found a boat tied to a tree, clearly put there for Don Quixote to sail to the rescue of some noble in distress. 'Cross yourself and cut the rope!' he ordered, jumping aboard, and in a moment they were drifting downstream, Sancho shaking with fright, crying for his donkey left with Rocinante on the bank. Don Quixote turned on him: 'What are you afraid of, you coward? Butter-heart! Mouse-brain! You're sitting like an archduke on a lovely smooth river, and soon we shall come out into the sea. . . .'

Soon, he was sure, they would be crossing the equator when all their lice would die on them – it was one of the signs – and he told Sancho to examine his legs for anything still alive. 'Fish around – I believe you're cleaner than a sheet of paper.' Sancho felt inside his trousers, but the test was faulty or they hadn't reached the equator yet. 'What?' Don Quixote asked. 'You've found something?' Sancho had found many somethings and flicked them off his fingers, then washed his hand in the river.

'Look, my friend!' Don Quixote pointed to a great watermill ahead. 'The castle! – where a wronged knight lies in danger. Or a captured princess.' Though Sancho swore it was a watermill, Don Quixote was adamant: 'It may look like one, but it isn't. Things can be changed by magic from their natural shape. Not really changed – they only appear to be, as we saw with Dulcinea.' There was a double truth – Sancho's facts, obvious to anyone with eyes, and Don Quixote's vision, poetic and inspired.

Facts, in the short run, proved unarguable. In midstream the boat was dragged into the mill-race and the millers, covered in flour, came out with poles to stop it: 'You devils, where are you going? Are you crazy? You'll drown!'

'Didn't I tell you?' Don Quixote said, seeing the ugly gang. 'Look what villains I'm up against!' He stood up in the boat: 'Swine! Let your prisoner free, whoever he is! I am Don Quixote of La Mancha, destined for this by heaven.' He struck out with his sword while Sancho fell on his knees to pray, but the boat overturned, throwing them into the river, and the millers had to dive in and pull them out before they were cut to pieces in the wheels. Calmly, as if nothing had happened, Don Quixote commanded them to release the prisoner in their castle.

'Prisoner? Castle? What are you talking about, you idiot?'

Don Quixote knew when he was beaten – he could never persuade these philistines. Raising his voice, gazing at the watermill before turning sadly away, he cried, 'My friend, whoever you are, locked up in there – forgive me! I've done all I can. But God help us, the world is full of trickery.'

Beside the Imperial Canal of Aragon, this bright hot afternoon, the maize fields are turning from jungle green to khaki. Grapes cluster under the vine leaves like purple swarms of bees. Pumpkins lie swelling on the ground, orange balloons of pips and pulp. A patch of bright green feathers – asparagus? fennel? – catches the sun. Waterbirds splash in the reeds, cuckoos call, a nightingale sings and I remember my first walk in Spain, by the lagoons of Ruidera three weeks ago.

Pedrola is a larger village than I expected, with raw new factories on the fringe. Sweating, tired, thirsty, I enter the Amadeus Bar but there is no hope of anything to eat. Everyone's eyes – youths, weathered tractor drivers, businessmen, smart girls – are fixed on a TV space film. No *tapas* at the bar for a hungry traveller. Not even the normal courteous greeting, only a blunt '*Diga* – speak!' The barman grabs a beer out of the cooler and scoops up my money, resenting the interruption.

At Pedrola, in a real castle, Don Quixote and Sancho Panza were entertained by a duke and duchess. The Knight of the Sad Countenance was famous now and his hosts had read the first volume of Cervantes's book, but they were heartless people who would get what fun they could out of their visitor. The first evening, dressing him up in grand clothes, ushering him into the dining-hall, they bowed him to the place of honour. Opposite sat another guest, a snobbish, conceited, dessicated, narrow-minded priest who saw no reason to humour this notorious lunatic. 'Don Fool,' he called him across the table, 'the laughing-stock of everyone.'

Rising to his feet, trembling with scorn for a pedant who knew nothing of the world beyond his own mean view of it, Don Quixote launched into a defence: 'A knight I am and a knight I shall die, God willing. Some men take the easy road of ambition, others that of obsequiousness or hypocrisy, and a few choose the way of true religion. But I follow my star along the narrow path of knighthood. I despise property, but not honour. I have redressed injustice, righted wrongs, conquered giants, chastized the insolent and put down evil. I'm in love, because knights are supposed to be. But I'm not one of those profane lovers – my love is chaste. My intentions are always virtuous, to do good to everyone and harm to nobody. If such a man is a fool, let the duke and duchess decide.'

'My God, well said!' Sancho cried, proud to have a master who, if he was mad, was only mad because he was good. But the priest, furious to find such company in a castle, stalked out without finishing his dinner.

The duchess pressed Don Quixote to describe his Dulcinea. Almost in tears, he could only say that when he went to visit her, to kiss her hand and receive her blessing, he found her changed from a beautiful princess into an ugly peasant, from angelic to diabolical, perfumed to stinking, serene to skittish – from light to darkness.

'For God's sake!' the duke exclaimed. 'Who could have done that?'

'Who?' Don Quixote replied. 'Who but one of the magicians who persecute me out of envy. They wound me where they know it hurts. To rob a knight of his lady is to rob him of the eyes that see for him and the sun that lights him. A knight without a lady is a tree without leaves, a shadow without the body that casts it. . . .'

'But you have never seen her,' the duchess persisted. 'She doesn't exist, she is your invention, so you make her as perfect as you wish.'

'God knows,' Don Quixote confessed in a moment of honesty, close to sanity, 'if she lives on earth or if she is a fantasy. Some things can't be verified.' It was enough for her to live in his mind. The vital thing was to believe.

After dinner, when the duchess took Sancho aside, he told her frankly, 'Don Quixote is raving mad, though sometimes he talks wisdom. He's really and truly crazy. I should have left him long ago. But it's my fate – my bad luck. I can't help it, I must follow him. We come from the same village, I have eaten his bread – I love him.'

At the castle they were treated to charades, teased and tricked with extravagant jokes to amuse the duke and duchess and their hangers-on. Bravely Don Quixote defied anyone to ridicule his vision, while Sancho lied his cowardly way out of trouble. They needed each other and when Sancho, to satisfy an old ambition to be governor of an island, was sent to rule a village on the duke's estate and told it was an island, Don Quixote fretted alone in the castle. He longed to escape from this idle life and blamed himself for being shut up in pointless luxury, with distractions lavished on him to save his melancholy.

Sancho was no happier – his island was a disaster. 'I wasn't born for this,' he lamented. 'I'm no good at governing anything but a herd of cattle. I know more about ploughing and digging and pruning vines than about making laws and defending kingdoms. I'd rather lie out under an oak tree in summer or wrap up in sheepskins in winter, staying free, than sleep between linen sheets or dress in sables and be weighed down by governing. Let me return to my freedom!'

'Freedom, Sancho,' Don Quixote said when they got away at last and were riding through open country again, 'is one of the most precious gifts of heaven.' He was back in his element, his spirits were reviving. 'Freedom is something to risk one's life for, like honour. And captivity is man's worst fate. You saw the wealth and comfort in that castle. Yet despite the rich food and iced drinks, I felt I was in the grip of famine – I didn't enjoy them as I would if they were mine. Having to return a favour imprisons the spirit. He's a happy man who gets a crust of bread from heaven and doesn't need to give thanks for it, except to heaven.'

'All the same,' Sancho replied, 'I came away with a little bag of money for emergencies. We shouldn't be ungrateful, we won't always find a castle to stay in.' The squire was always practical.

From Pedrola I walk for another hour, dead straight across irrigated fields to Alcalá de Ebro, a tiny village beside the great slothful river. The sour smell of manure hangs in the heat, the only bar is shut. People are picnicking on the river bank, bathing where the water is almost free of scum. There is no boat tied to a tree for me but a small island, a strand of shingle and bushes, floats in midstream, as insubstantial as Sancho Panza's.

I park myself on a seat by the river and wait – there seems nothing else to do. A family of storks on top of the church has grown too big for its nest. One bird has to keep flying round in circles, hoping the others will make room for him. Then, showing off to me, he lands on a sharp spike, perhaps the lightning conductor, fixed to the highest cross. It's a good trick, standing up there without a tremor, and I tell him so.

An old man comes to sit beside me and pulls a radio from his pocket for the sports news. I ask him when the bar will open.

'It's open now,' he says.

I go to look, but he is wrong – he just wanted to get rid of me. I walk back to the railway station, halfway between Alcalá de Ebro and Pedrola. It's a ruin with a brick hut for shelter, a sleeping cat for stationmaster. I go down the line to the level crossing where a man in a sentrybox, frying onions in olive oil, controls the gates and ask him when the next train to Zaragoza is due.

'Three minutes to seven,' he says with precision.

I have half an hour to wait and would love some of those onions. The sun is low, the cat wakes up. An elderly couple arrives on the platform – passengers like me. At seven o'clock there is no sign of a train.

At eight o'clock there is still no sign. The man at the level crossing, who has finished his onions, can't tell me how long we shall have to wait. I'm hungry, I have walked all day on only coffee and *churros* for breakfast and a beer this afternoon. The land softens, the heat is drained as the quick night falls. I contemplate spending it in the brick hut, and ask the elderly couple when they think a train will come.

'Today,' they say confidently.

I'm less sure. At nine o'clock there is still no train. The sun has set, it's nearly dark. I ask the couple if this is normal on Spanish railways.

They are indignant: 'Never! Trains always come on time. This is just bad luck – *accidente.*'

'An accident?'

'*Destino. Fortuna.*'

Just before ten o'clock a single headlight shows far away at the end of the line, growing bigger, and at last the train comes in, three hours late, without apology or explanation. We have no tickets and there is no ticket collector. 'At least we get a free journey,' the couple say, pleased to be avenged.

At Zaragoza it's too late for the last train out, except an international express at midnight with a big supplement to pay. After guzzling a plate of green beans and some bits of fish I decide it's also too late to look for a hotel – I will sleep in the station.

In the bar I drink enough Spanish gin and Coca Cola to be sure of sleeping, then settle on a couple of seats. But they have been made for discomfort, to keep me awake. Loudspeakers shout at me whenever I'm on the point of unconsciousness. A young man camped outside the shuttered newspaper stall turns up the volume of his tape-player and starts singing – I hate him. Two policemen patrol the station, stirring anyone who isn't sitting upright: this place is for passengers waiting for their trains, not for dossers.

At dawn I give up and walk into the town to find breakfast. The barman in a café, busy with his coffee machine, says '*Buenos días*' and sets out a cup for me on the counter. A woman smiles, a canary sings, the croissants are fresh, the coffee is wonderful, the sun breaks over the tables and the day, after such a night, is already better than it was ever going to be.

SIXTY

Henry James, speaking of a novelist's chief danger, called it 'the fatal futility of Fact'. Straying into journalism where ideas could be shared with someone else, and expenses were paid and a fee was guaranteed, I tried to keep on my own side of the line, aware of the risk beyond. And later even the facts, treated with suspicion in the first place, began to look less rigid. Fiction could never be deserted, or the record look quite straight.

For the *Observer* I caught a train from New York to California, where I caught another back again. I shook the hand of Chief Harry Jumping Bull of the Sioux tribe, a shy little man in glasses; and kissed the synthetic cheek of Miss Wyoming 1979, dressed in cowgirl hat and pants. With a pack of credit cards I drove slowly from a frozen Maine to a steamy Florida, calling at creeks and boatyards and marinas where I winkled out a score of lone yachtsmen and asked them, as they got their ships ready for a race across the Atlantic, why they did it.

And why, I sometimes asked, was I doing it myself?

I sat one bright afternoon in a waterside bar in Sausalito on the edge of San Francisco Bay, with a man called George. He had been an actor and a journalist, had lived in Putney, had written plays and a novel, had been married two or three times, he had some kids somewhere and a girl friend who was away in Israel. He wanted to be a photographer and at present was driving a taxi.

That morning he had taken me to the old Beat bars of North Beach where we drank a lot of Steamer beer, a local brew, among the sad footfalls of a dead generation, the lingering beatitudes. When George learnt that I hadn't seen the Golden Gate, being content to leave it to old films and preconceptions, he grew insistent and said he would drive me there for nothing, and pushed me into his taxi. Luckily the bridge was deep in mist, quite invisible. So we drove across it and on to Sausalito where the sun shone, and drank a lot more Steamer beers in a harbour bar. Watching his compatriots George said, 'We have to be *Americans* all the time – why can't we just be *people?*' Outside the bar, beyond the crowded sidewalk and cars and yachts lying along the quay, the brilliant water danced all afternoon.

And then Evan walked past the window.

I love coincidences, the improbability of luck: the unexpected but surprisingly predictable crossing of two lives, as if obeying some secret logic. 'Isn't there a mad scheme in it?' a man in a novel wonders, after escaping from a bomb and finding an old friend in the rubble. 'I can't believe it's haphazard. It fits into a plan somewhere. Nothing is random.' For every chance meeting there must be a hundred that are lost because someone chose to walk down the other side of the street or someone else failed to look out of the window. Unmistakably this was Evan. But of course it wasn't.

I swallowed another Steamer quickly. Evan lived in Hampstead with his wife and three daughters. He was a senior civil servant in Whitehall, a quiet man who had no business in Sausalito. But I would know him anywhere. He and I had played flute duets in my home in Suffolk last year. But it was ridiculous to find him here. He had a cottage in Devon, on the Dart, and we had sailed there together. But not in Sausalito, California. Blame it on the Steamers. . . .

I might go out and chase him through the crowd and shout his name and the man would turn, a stranger, and I would be made a fool. Or I could sit at the bar with George and think about Evan and the times we had had, and one day back in England I would tell him about his look-alike in Sausalito, 'a little place you've never heard of on San Francisco Bay', and we would fix a date to play our flutes again. I bought another Steamer for George and one for myself, and soon George bought two more. But it was Evan all right, as surely as it wasn't.

We left the bar. George wanted to look in at a bookshop along the street to collect a poetry magazine he had ordered, for idle moments in his taxi. We went in, and someone spoke my name. It was Evan's wife, with one of their daughters. After the first stunning disbelief we laughed a lot. They said that Evan had just gone along the waterfront, he would be back in a minute, and we waited. Somehow all the Steamer beers enhanced the unlikely likelihood of luck.

Drunk or sober, I never saw Evan walk across my view again. Six months later, on another unreal sunny afternoon, I went to his funeral at the church in Hampstead across the road from where he lived. We hadn't had another chance to play flute duets.

In an amazing yellow trimaran, a forty-foot racer leaping from the Miami jetty out into Biscayne Bay, with the prow ripping forward like a scalpel, one outrigger swooping through the water to hold us upright, the other flying in the sun – with the wheel in my hands and a can of beer beside my foot – I remembered the solider, less sprightly yacht in which I had sailed as cook on the Fastnet race not long before. And a week later, from a tank on the quay at Boston, Massachusetts, I bought lobsters for supper with Deirdre and the children in Suffolk, England, and brought them home alive.

I took the road up to a fortress in the mountains of Oman where a prisoner, his ankles fettered with an iron bar, was hustled out of sight before I could photograph him. I sneaked by helicopter among the outposts of the Yemen frontier where, with a British colonel in a turban who gave me coffee and fishcakes for breakfast in his spectacular HQ, we watched the enemy watching us. By the holy Ganges I listened to a fat *swami*, naked to the waist, give a sermon on a text from *Hamlet*, 'To thine own self be true.'

In one of Bombay's fifty police stations I saw a bearded old man, brought in from the street for entertaining the public without a licence, open a basket on the sub-inspector's desk and release a cobra which uncoiled and slithered over the telephone, round the typewriter, behind a filing cabinet.

In a jeep with the sub-inspector I went on patrol through the shanty slums and watched his constables foraging for crime like dogs picking through the rubbish. Remembering an Arab I had seen counting out ten thousand dollars that morning in my hotel, where a beer cost the price of a labourer's wages for a week, I felt less human than those wretched shanty dwellers.

I felt another humility when we drove our jeep into the bazaar, blasting a passage through the density of fruit, vegetables, goats, children, coconuts, fish; and jumped out at someone's shout and ran down a side alley, round a corner, along a passage, through a low door into a windowless hut, an illicit liquor shop dark with the smell of drink where two men, too slow or too drunk to escape, were arrested: the shopkeeper, a plaintive man praying for mercy, and a Eurasian customer standing stiffly to attention. I dipped a finger into a bucket to taste the stuff, poisonous and fiery but cheap at ten rupees a litre. And while the police did their brutal work with truncheons and handcuffs and the shopkeeper cringed, I caught the contempt of the Eurasian: it was for me, he knew, that the raid had been arranged. And who was I to spoil his day of drinking? I felt no better than an informer. My guilt, I almost hoped, would outlast his imprisonment.

For a week I stayed in one of India's countless villages, trying to catch the infinite rhythm, the essence of a beauty full of contentment yet pierced at times by agony; walking in the fields, sitting in one house after another, sipping tea laced with cardamom or ginger, dipping spiced bits of vegetable into chutney; feeling myself a character in a R. K. Narayan novel or a Satyajit Ray film; observing the details of my performance as carefully as I watched everyone else and hoping that it would add up to a picture in the end.

SIXTY-ONE

June 8, Zaragoza. After leaving the castle with Sancho Panza, thankful to quit the lavish treatment of the duke and duchess, Don Quixote took the road to Zaragoza where he meant to enter the annual jousting match. But to his disgust he heard that a false Don Quixote, a charlatan posing as himself and taking credit for his fame, had got there first. There could be only one Knight of the Sad Countenance, the world was too small for another. He would go to Barcelona instead, and give the lie to his fictitious namesake.

But I can't miss Zaragoza, though I make an excuse for cheating with the dates. On this summer day I find myself transposed to an autumn one a few years ago, the first day of a week's fiesta in honour of Our Lady of the *Pilar* – the pillar. From the Ebro bridge I watch speedboats skittering up and down, spinning circles of froth on the old river: *Motonáuticos*, they are called. *Los más importantes, mejores pilotos internacionales. . . .*

On the huge commercial bandwagon an entire week is inflated with unholy profit. *Felices fiestas!* There are bands streaming down the streets, a tide of brass and drums, and crackers banging, plastic snakes that wriggle out with a squeak, whistles with devil's horns that sprout alternately, midnight dancing in front of great church façades dusted by centuries, rock concerts going on till dawn with groups like The Mentally Sick and Semen Up, and every day a bullfight – forty-two bulls fought to the death for the loss of not one matador.

Outside the immense, astonishing cathedral a pop singer yells his thumping message; and inside, also into a microphone, a priest intones his eternal words. Children are led or carried by choirboys to Our Lady of the *Pilar* – a doll standing on something like a mauve lampshade, dazzled by spotlights – and allowed to kiss her pedestal; then they turn and smile, hands in prayer, for a photograph – a flash, a nod, a ticket – and the next child is brought. Round the back a line of worshippers shuffles past a brass porthole to press their lips on a tiny corner of the *Pilar*'s pillar. Nearby is a vast bank of candles under a metal canopy: the heat is enough to roast any of the bulls they killed this afternoon.

There is non-stop mass all evening, a continuous celebration. The cathedral, full of the same ornamentation, plastered loops, encrusted garlands that fill the confectionery shops, is packed; and the people, who earlier were parading through the streets, eating ices and fantastic cakes, are rejoicing in this palace of God, temple of the *Pilar*.

It's a total occasion, the flummery of worship, a triumph of reverence and wonder, absorbing for anyone susceptible to religious vehemence: the gaudy prelates and surpliced choir, the chanting and preaching, bobbing and crossing, the deaf woman pressing her ear to a loudspeaker to catch the word of God, the silent figures in the chapels and busy confessionals, the men and women of all ages lining up at the altar steps, the vast congregation assembled to praise and pray, a little dog among them and a Velázquez dwarf in a smart suit and red fiesta scarf waiting for the sacrament – all the more moving for my own faithlessness.

After the final mass the party continues across the city, into the night. It's very orderly: nobody jumps into the fountains, hardly anyone is drunk. Young women sigh outside the windows of the bridal shops, *agencias matrimoniales*, before going home. The clack of someone's castanets retreats down the emptying street. In the cafés the children, dropping asleep on their feet, are stirred awake to wipe tables, stack chairs, empty ashtrays, for six more days's fiesta.

'*Mañana será otro día*, tomorrow will be another day' – a useful motto against the buffetings of life. 'Spain is an absurd country,' Angel Ganivet wrote, 'and metaphysically impossible. Absurdity is its nerve and mainstay. Its turn to prudence will mark the end.' But if its head is sometimes in the clouds, like Don Quixote's, its feet are on the ground, like Sancho Panza's.

SIXTY-TWO

I was asleep when a crying, wailing chant came into my head. It took time, two minutes or twenty, to seep through and wake me up. Three o'clock in the morning. Deirdre wasn't in bed with me. Before midnight I had left her drinking by the big fireplace downstairs, after pushing the last of the burning logs to the back, and come up to bed – she would follow soon. A January night, a blizzard outside.

The chanting persisted: not a scream for help or yell of agony, more of a submissive ritual hymn. It was the moan of the wind, or the desolate years, or the helpless pain of life blowing through the old cold Hall. Then the smell reached me like a draught coming up through the floorboards.

I ran down. The sitting-room was thick with brown smoke. Deirdre was on fire. Her hair alight, her clothes burning. Kneeling at the front of the open fireplace under the big stone lintel. Smoke and flames. Gobs of acrylic wool melting and falling off. Little heaps of fire on the hearth round her. Deirdre, Deirdre, what have you done? I caught my own words, choking in the smoke. *What have you done to yourself?* Did I know already?

She had raked the dying fire forward, pulling it round her for warmth. She must have lain down on it. Two empty bottles stood on the floor. She was mouthing something, in a trance of drink and shock and misery: 'The children of Zion – they said they would come for me. They promised, but they never came – the children of Zion . . .' She moaned, cried, blathered on.

I stamped out the patches of fire. Swept up the burning fragments. Began pulling her clothes off, two sweaters, shirt, vest, over her head. The pain was terrible, the children of Zion couldn't help.

I opened the window to clear the smoke and smell of burnt clothes, singed hair. Fetched a tube of antiseptic from the bathroom and squeezed it over her shoulders, neck, back, through the pain and tears, treading in ashes and bits of charred material. I must take you to the hospital, Deirdre, I must.

I found a shawl to wrap over the wounded shoulders. Grabbed a blanket. Went out into the blizzard to start the car. Frogmarched her into it, drove away. The road was white, there were no tracks. Fierce plumes of snow shot from gaps in the hedges. What did you do, Deirdre? Why did you do it?

'I tried, but it didn't work.'

Tried what? And why, for God's sake – why?

'There's no future, nothing ahead, it's all hopeless – the children say so.'

The children of Zion?

'The children say they hate it because we're unhappy together, they can't stand it. There's a letter for them in my jewel box. I tried, but it didn't work.' The wipers crunched to clear the windscreen, the smell of burning filled the car. 'Am I still on fire?' She was nearly sober but in pain.

Eight miles to the hospital through the snow. The casualty department was locked. I rattled the doors and a man came to open up. Deirdre was led away by a nurse while I sat in the waiting-room, cold and bright. A doctor, a man from Asia somewhere, strange on this wild night of an English winter, came to ask what had happened. It was an accident, I said. We have this huge fireplace, we burn logs in it. There's a space all round, and she fell asleep there and got burnt. The doctor looked hard at me, soft brown eyes from Karachi or Colombo or Calcutta, dipping into mine for the truth; then took me to see her, face down on a trolley, her back bare: blotches of puffed white and red tissue, blisters already forming. 'Third degree,' the doctor said.

Creeping home in the car I skidded on the frozen road and slid into a wall, damaging the bumper. I couldn't swear, the words were blanketed like the night, I could only coax the car home. Burns and ice, and no connection unless it was me. But at four in the morning, with windows lit and my children inside, the Hall looked enchanted in the snow – the loveliest house in the world: a muffled life in there and snowflakes falling like clichés on the Brueghel fields.

Next day, after the children had gone to school, I amazed myself with my anger; raved, shouted in the empty rooms, vented my disgust on the absent suffering Deirdre, disgusting myself. You cow, you great cow! What right d'you think you have to mess up people's lives like this? What monstrous egoism drove you to it? Who d'you think you are – Virginia Woolf? Sylvia Plath? D'you want to drag me down to the same depth of desolation? What are you punishing me for?

I shouted, and then I cried; cried at my desk where I should be writing a novel; cried with exhaustion, sorrow, shame. You cow! – look what you've brought me to. Or what I've brought myself to. Let me escape from myself and be myself! I lost control and overflowed, pouring out something ugly though it was close to love. But who was it for, this mixture of fury and compassion – for Deirdre or for me? If hers had been an act of self-immersion, did mine have to be no better?

I drank too much. Loneliness assailed me. I wished I had a regular job to go to, an automatic daily routine I could sink into; colleagues to talk to about other things. I wanted to spend the anxious mind-filling hours doing an unanxious mindless task. I stared at the typewriter, did a crossword puzzle, poured more whisky.

I might ring up my friends – not to grumble or seek sympathy or enrol them as allies but to enjoy myself, to give myself a treat; to treat my wounds the way the hospital was treating Deirdre's; to seize on people who could hold out hope, who laughed or were busy with something different, believing in it, or pointed to somewhere fresh. But I didn't. It would be betrayal, gossiping, telling tales. I must cling only to myself.

Kindness from other people, anyway, was more than I could take. Kindness, sister to forgiveness – pure kindness, unexpected and unasked for – would affect me more deeply, unlock happiness more simply, than anything. But who was I to deserve it now? It demolished me. I broke down, couldn't speak but choked on tears if someone rang to offer help. I deplored my tenderness, but I had to find my own way through the tangle and the only one I knew was blocked. Words wouldn't reach me, imagination was numbed. I tried to write because I called myself a writer, but what would I be doing if I were a greengrocer, a dentist, a chartered surveyor? Unlike them, though they would have the same private anxiety, I had a professional interest in this too, that demanded a sort of cool but passionate judgement. And I couldn't find it. All I could do was stab the blank paper with cries of perplexity, details of feeling, disjoined questions – anything to redeem the failure. You cow, you fucking cow!

She was kept a month in hospital, the prettiest woman there, her scorched hair done up in a handkerchief – like Little Polly Flinders, a nurse said. 'Sorry, sorry – it won't happen again, I promise.' She was recovering more quickly than I was, dismissing it as a mere mishap, a foolish episode: smother the hangover, cover the remorse, let's dance. But it was the pain that I wanted to share, not this sudden chirpiness. Soon she was pushing the tea trolley down the ward, chatting with other patients, and I felt left behind. Could that terrible night be forgotten so easily? Had it happened? Had I really saved her life? In another fifteen minutes she might have been burnt to death, and the house set on fire with me and the children in it.

I must be having a nice quiet time at home, she said, without a wife to disturb me: nothing to stop me getting on with my book. But can't you see, Deirdre, that I don't live in a vacuum? That when you catch fire in the middle of the night, whatever the reason, and lie in hospital for weeks, I can't simply resume work, thanking God for the peace of mind it brings?

She was right, of course, and I was being blind and obtuse. Action was imperative. Nothing good ever merely happened to anyone, but someone had to do it. It wasn't enough to stand and rage. I must write, to turn this into fiction, more real than life. Life was mortal, words were lasting. This wasn't the end of the story, unless it was a very bad one. It mustn't fizzle out now, but go forward, lure the reader on – lure me on, at least. Other considerations were trivial beside this one great singularity. I must write and write and write, nothing else, on into the bright-dark unknown – known to me alone. I should be unstoppable. But I couldn't start.

My younger sister turned up, driving from London after breakfast; walking into the empty house, calling for me. I had sounded so full of gloom on the telephone last night, she had come to lighten the day; to have coffee, then get back in her car and drive away.

When I told Deirdre in hospital her cheerfulness collapsed. She crumpled, wept, sank into the pillows: 'So, I see – your sister comes to rescue you from your awful wife.' Couldn't she see that a man might be loved by his sister or his friends, as well as his wife? Was it jealousy? Had she missed something, lying here in bed? 'I was feeling all right till you told me that. Go away, please – go away and don't come to see me tomorrow.'

I was suspicious of myself: being over-tragic, making too much of the incident. Was I secretly enjoying it, obsessed to the point of fascination? My motives weren't the finest, I knew, but I couldn't pin them down. Was I making excuses for my own behaviour, next year as well as last? Was I making mental notes for future use? When I appealed to the psychiatrist who had been helpful to Deirdre in the past, was it to absolve myself? To let him ring up the hospital and sort out her problem, leaving me free to cope with mine? I told myself that it was the proper thing to do: call in a professional, someone to heal the soul while the surgeons patched up the flesh. But did I know how much it would anger her? Was I being honest to us both? If I wasn't treating her as a mental case I was at least conspiring with someone who did: going behind her back – her wretched blistered back. Was it revenge? I could believe the worst of me, and the best. I was all things, if not to all men, at least to myself.

I wondered what I believed of Deirdre and found no answer that wasn't shadowy, soaked in doubt. Neither pure accident nor deliberate intention, her self-burning was a confusion of both, perhaps a half-conscious test of herself, of me, of fire – even of hellfire. Mutilation was close to mortification, a kind of defiant challenge. In the fireplace, between life and death, she might have been lacerating herself in purgatory, surrendering to some vague necessity if not to a mystic rite.

'*En una noche oscura* – on a dark night,' St John of the Cross wrote of his escape from imprisonment in Toledo, at a time when Cervantes too was a prisoner; but the *casa sosegada*, house asleep, of his poem is not just the monastery he had broken out of, where he had been horribly tortured – it's the prison of his soul. On a dark night 'fired by the yearning of love', sliding down a rope of blankets, climbing over a wall, wandering the hostile streets till dawn, he was guided by the light that burnt inside him. His poetry is lit with flames: '*Oh llama de amor viva* – oh living flame of love, how tenderly you wound my soul!' He sings of the gentle hand, the consoling torment, of fire – a touch so delicate that it savours of eternity and forgives all sins. '*Matando, muerte en vida la has trocado* – killing, you have turned death to life.' Was there also in Deirdre, intense and ardent as she often was, an element of passionate self-destruction, a glorious need to submit? Long ago she had written, 'There is always some ecstasy in suffering, some suffering in ecstasy.'

I watched her in hospital, burnt and haunted, a spectre of herself but beautiful in her ordeal, as if the spoiling of her body had been the initiation to another phase of life. Soothed by daily treatment and the carefree bed-to-bed society, joking with her friends, chasing the ephem-

293

era of ward life, winking at the ironies, chiding me for being so weighed down by doom, she already smouldered with a more promising fire.

I loved her, not for what she was then but for what she had been before and would be, I knew, another time. Our two selves were held under a web of delicate strands: of experiences and emotions shared; of feelings of uniqueness. The web was *us*, our life together, spun over twenty years though often stretched to breaking point. With patching and knotting it had held out against the divisive forces, the rows and infidelities and separate clamours for identity. But at a stroke it could be ripped apart whenever the wish to preserve it failed and the whole fabric of marriage, seeming so permanent, trapping us apparently to suffocation, could be swept away.

At this moment it would be easier than usual. Yet now, more than ever, was the time to stay together, not just because Deirdre was so unleavable but because it was a chance to let understanding and hope return. There was only one word for my multiple responses to her. She could fling her aggression at me, or her resentment or indifference or whatever, and even cut the mutual love that used to join us. But like a raw electric wire, though it was broken, my end was still live. She only had to touch it to find out.

At home I watched myself, no less doubting but almost mesmerized. It was bizarre and, behind the tragedy, there must be comedy if I knew where to look. Despair wasn't an end in itself but a way of touching rock bottom, empty of illusions, where faith could be rediscovered and there was nowhere to go but up. It was a heartening thought. With nobody dead, and the family more or less intact, and not enough tears for all the crying I wanted to do, I laughed instead. And viewed the future with interest, even optimism. And waited to see what I would do next. Think next. Feel next. Would it be what I wanted, or would it surprise me? And was I also allowed burns – to my soul? 'Your conscience is vital,' a poet in a novel says. 'Go through it with a comb. Pick out the nits, watch for grey hairs.' Though I had betrayed nobody but myself and, thank God, felt no guilt – which anyway, like blame, was irrelevant – I had other scars. But behind them, as with Deirdre's, I dimly saw a possibility to be grasped and somehow put to use. It couldn't be made into fiction, it was too suffused with pain. Yet the agony might be repudiated and in time turned to something almost beyond words – another, perhaps stronger marriage.

SIXTY-THREE

June 9, Huesca. In the morning there is a wedding in the cathedral. Grinding on their hinges the big doors open enough to let the bride and groom into the womb of darkness, which suddenly is shattered by photo flashes and video lights. A wedding is the hope and joy of Spanish women. 'There is marriage and eight children in their eyes,' V. S. Pritchett wrote. Afterwards someone brings a broom to sweep up several kilos of rice, with toilet paper and burst balloons, from the cathedral steps.

I take a bus over the hard white plain of Aragon, where the people were once said to be so stubborn they could hammer nails into the wall with their heads. The dry fields of maize and sunflowers are broken by rock ridges, and somewhere among them is the place where George Orwell got a bullet in the throat from one of Franco's snipers. 'This ought to please my wife,' was his first thought. She had wanted him to be wounded, which might save him from being killed, and it worked: he left the battle.

At Lérida an Egyptian student, hearing of a foreigner with an accent like his own, comes to find me and we walk up to the castle above the town. 'Built by Arabs!' he says proudly, in defiance of the truth, and waves to a friend, a rock-climber practising on the massive walls. He should be at the university in Cairo, but his room here costs only two hundred pesetas a day, he will find casual work in the fruit orchards and stay away for the rest of the summer. He feels at home in Spain: 'Seven per cent of the language is Arabic!'

From the old cathedral, which for two and a half centuries was a barracks – the cloister was a kitchen, the aisles were the quarters for men and horses, the nave was a shooting range – we watch the evening settle on the fading plain; then walk down for a student's supper of beans and pork and thick dark wine like purple ink, with the inescapable TV. In the main street, above every other shop, a loudspeaker blasts music at the people.

I have learnt how the Spanish love a good noise. They turn up the radio, they amplify their own voices to shouting point and let their babies scream.

SIXTY-FOUR

In northern Zambia, at the heart of Africa, a missionary took me to the source of the Zambezi: the newborn stream gurgling from the roots of an enormous tree – a sense of genesis, of a life beginning. I dropped sticks and dead leaves into the water and watched them float away, downhill to the Indian Ocean. They would take three weeks to reach it and so did I, at Quilimane in Mozambique, once a centre of slavery, now a Marxist town. In the hotel the neo-colonials pecked at their tripe and onions, the Hungarians watching the Russians, the East Germans eyeing the North Koreans.

In the Barotse plain, a marshland peopled by punting figures and tropical birds, I tied up my canoe at the island of the paramount chief and walked through the village to his palace, a thatched house defended by a spiked stockade. Once there would have been enemy heads on those spikes. Two servants led me slowly across the courtyard. Every few steps they dropped to their knees, bowed and clapped their hands; crept forward, knelt, bowed and clapped again. Solemnly I followed, keeping upright. I wouldn't kneel even for a paramount chief, even at the thought of that spiked stockade.

At the porch I was abandoned, but rescued by a voice from the darkness: 'Come in, please, oh do come in.' He was a tall gentleman in a grey suit, smiling shyly, with an ivory-handled fly whisk. Above, as my eyes got used to the light, I could see the rafters and thatch. For a moment I might have been in a superior version of Madame Xoum's, the opium house in Pnom Penh, till His Highness invited me to take a sofa while he sat on another. It was like visiting a maharaja or a duke: everywhere these ancient chieftains, in these modern days, could only look at the glory of their ancestors and drop a wistful sigh. On the walls were photos of his father and grandfather and one of himself on a throne dressed as an admiral in a cocked hat with plumes. We sat among the coffee tables, wondering what to say.

In a Lusaka casino I watched luscious women in gimlet curls and tight-bottomed pants tossing plastic chips across the green baize. At Kisangani I watched fishermen work on a spider's web of scaffolding above the Congo rapids, balancing and knotting, shouting over the roar of water when they caught a fish. I travelled a thousand miles down the Congo, a week on board a floating market town with perhaps two thousand people and their animals, with shops and laundries, barbers, butchers, kitchens, a beer hall and prison and, if not a brothel, a number of busy market girls. In my article I quoted V. S. Naipaul and Graham Greene and of course, as they did too, Joseph Conrad. We pick each other's brains, we feed like leeches on bigger men who have gone ahead.

My father, whose shadow now fell on my life less often but with a more friendly shape, had passed that way nearly eighty years before. Crossing Africa on foot or by canoe, he developed a taste for hippo fillet and was impressed by the bush telegraph: Congo villages were warned of his arrival in detail long beforehand, by drums beating down the river. He knew few better ways to travel than by canoe with singing paddlers and a moon over the forest, himself in a chair under a little roof of leaves – in the bows to avoid the smell of native sweat. Often he was the first white man to be seen, a prototype with a train of porters carrying his tent and bed, washing-stand, cloth and beads for barter, spare watch glasses and inkpot. He took an umbrella so that he could walk in the shade and stay dry in the rain, though eventually he broke it over an African's head. For company, with Pepys and Robinson Crusoe, he chose Don Quixote.

I stayed in Schweitzer's hospital at Lambaréné, beside a steamy brown river at the edge of the African forest. During the tormented nineteen-thirties and forties, when it was badly needed, a tiny jungle paradise had been lodged in the world's imagination. A suggestion of saintliness came drifting out, to the accompaniment of Bach.

As the myth grew more inflated, cracks were opened up – this man was too good to be true. The news from Lambaréné turned sour, the lens of publicity tracked over the ugly tin-roofed huts and focused on the reality. The tropical hospital, for many people a refuge of ideals, was seen to be a scandal – primitive, squalid, almost worthless medically, a mere frame for Schweitzer's vanity. In his arrogance he rejected modern equipment; in his attitude of uncompromising superiority to the Africans he mocked his own philosophy, Reverence for Life. It wasn't difficult to stick pins into him, but Schweitzer was big enough to take it. Like Don Quixote he knew he wasn't a saint, he only tried to be as human as he could. In old age he spoke out against nuclear weapons but died too soon to hear the crescendo of voices, like parts in a fugue first stated long ago by himself, clamouring for a simple truth in the entangling illusions: for life in a world unconfident of survival.

The shrine, eighteen years after his death, was preserved in his room: a folded nightshirt beside his pillow, the famous sun helmet, a clip-on bow tie, a volume of Bach lying on the battered piano. Less macabre was the new hospital up the hill where the Schweitzer flair, his personal dedication and concern, were alive and well; and where the sounds and smells of an infinite African village, more insidious than the forest, encroached on the white-tiled wards. 'We try to keep the spirit,' the director told me, as if speaking of a man who was both fact and fiction.

'We taught them to wear clothes,' a German economist said in Liberia, tucking into a lobster, 'and now on the beach it's the white girls who go topless and the black girls avert their eyes.'

I drove far down the coast and turned up a track at a sign to the Hopeful Baptist Church. Under a tree a boy was knocking down mangoes and from a corrugated iron chapel, like music from an old gramophone, came the tinny sound of hymns. The boy fetched the minister out – an elderly man with the light of God in his eyes and the courage to say he had nothing to hide, he had told the truth.

After the *coup* he had preached a sermon condemning the executions of the previous rulers and calling for a week of prayer and thought, to consider the revolution. He was beaten up, given five years' hard labour and sent to a dreaded prison in the forest, reached only on foot or by plane – the worst punishment was the isolation. After two years he was released in a Christmas amnesty. 'I can bear anything,' he said, 'so long as God is with me,' and went back into the Hopeful Baptist Church, leaving me to buy the boy's mangoes.

I drove into the interior and at the biggest rubber plantation in the world, in the cool of the twilit groves, I watched tappers cut a sliver of bark from the trees for the latex, a pure white cream, to drip into a cup: to make a rubber tyre, a child's balloon, a lover's condom. At an iron mine I saw monster machines in a pseudo-prehistoric scene wallowing in pools of rusty water, bellowing as they clawed and grabbed at Africa, and shovelled a hundred tons in a mouthful on trucks that tipped it into a pepper mill – peppercorns the size of pianos. One day, the Swedish manager said, the ore would run out and the miners would go away, leaving some useless lumps of machinery and big holes in the world and a lake of ferrous slurry oozing over the hills, swamping the land where men once lived.

I called on a minister, an ambassador, a professor and two archbishops; and listened to Liberia's new ruler promise redemption for the people. Once a master-sergeant, now a five-star general, commander-in-chief, honorary doctor of philosophy (in South Korea), a nice young man with fuzzy hair and glasses – he looked mild enough and his jackboot a light one, more of a plimsoll. But behind the rhetoric and Coca Cola, beyond the end of the tarmac where the microphones couldn't reach, old Africa slumbered in its darkness.

I called on two more prelates in Lebanon, at the biblical port of Tyre, hoping they might be more reliable than politicians or soldiers – more compassionate anyway.

I had come from Beirut by sea, the road being blocked by the occupying Israeli army. For hours, during a mortar battle on the coast, the ship had waited out of range before putting us ashore after dark, too late to pass the Israeli checkpoint. The beach was mined, we scratched a flat patch of sand above it and settled down to sleep. The Mediterranean rolled on the shore, the moon came up, and at midnight a Roman Catholic friar appeared in an empty bus. Up in the hills the children of his school were on holiday and we were welcome to use the dormitories. The friars fed us with great flat rounds of bread and bowls of yoghurt – Christians indeed in that unholy land.

At dawn I was back at the checkpoint, a bridge across a muddy river. One by one we were called forward by an Israeli soldier who stood by a garbage bin and examined us: a boy of eighteen, seeming ashamed of what he had to do – this insult to the bright morning. Behind the wire other soldiers were washing down their tanks. I found a taxi and drove to Sidon for breakfast, then on to Tyre.

Dark lines of cypresses guarded the orchards from the wind, but the fruit trees were neglected, irrigation systems broken, houses flattened. Orchards had been cut back for a better line of fire and roads torn up by tanks for dust to blow into the trees, choking the fruit. What had the oranges done wrong? Nobody could deny the insolence of soldiers – the muzzle in your face, the searchlight in your eyes, the sonic boom of fighters in your ears.

In a refugee camp I drank mint tea with a Palestinian family, among dahlias and roses in the roof garden of their makeshift house. Their concrete shelter was smothered in jasmine – it would be blown up if an Israeli patrol discovered it. The father said, 'We were born in prison, we shall die in prison.' Some went to Europe or America or Australia, and a few never came back. But there was a strange need for the camp – a foothold at the door of Palestine, in case of one day going home. To escape for ever was to accept defeat.

I banged on the Greek Catholic archbishop's door, but he wasn't there. The Maronite archbishop, a sleek patriarch in white soutane and purple skullcap, fingering a hefty cross, gave me coffee and some un-neighbour-loving thoughts about the Palestinians who had disturbed the land. The town had been shelled and bombed, a third of it was rubble. Buildings lay crumpled or ripped, shedding their insides – instant archaeology, it was called.

Frustrated by the present I turned to the past: to the ruins of a city that had extracted a purple dye from shells, the colour of royalty, worn by emperors and kings; and supplied timber and stone and metalwork for Solomon's temple; and sent a princess, Jezebel, to marry Ahab of Israel and bring disaster; and surrendered two thousand young men to Alexander the Great, to be crucified on the beach. Tyre was flavoured with the past, the way its people put rose water in a glass of lemonade or a pinch of cardamom in coffee – it improved it.

Back at Beirut I had dinner with a grand lady on her terrace above the town. Servants brought sumptuous dishes to the table while peacocks perched on the balustrade to defy the smell of drains, and sometimes a bomb exploded in the night. Next day I took a car through the silver hills, past villages whose destruction would be soon forgotten by a world grown callous since Guernica, to the Bekaa valley and the Roman city of Baalbek. My companion had once danced with the Royal Ballet under the pillars of Jupiter, before war fell on Lebanon, and we lingered all the hot afternoon, drinking beer and conjuring lost *fouettés* from the deserted ruins. War at least had destroyed tourism.

But London was suffering from it badly, even in winter. For the *Observer* I came down the Thames from Teddington lock to the Thames Barrier: four days in a small tug, in and out of the creeks, winding through the capital with the skipper's memories of a big port that had vanished. 'They'd straighten it out if they could,' he said scornfully, 'and turn it into a motorway.' With disbelief rather than nostalgia he spoke of the time when barges lay four deep along the wharves, tugs jostled on the tide, ships steamed importantly up and down: the time in the incredible past, before we were married, when Deirdre and I sat in riverside pubs and wondered what we were about to do. Now there was mostly silence except from loudspeakers on the pleasure boats. Dockland without the docks was becoming a dreamland for the new young rich, a Disneyland for the tourists.

At home I tussled with the garden of the Hall, though my fragile aptitude for plants succumbed and I let the flower-beds give way to grass. Besides saving me mindless, resentful hours grubbing in the Suffolk loam it looked better, I thought; and the National Trust horticulturist, the most elegant of gardeners in a gladiolus-coloured sports car, his green fingers gloved in racing mittens, agreed: 'Simplify it,' he said. I also gave up the fight against rabbits and moles – the place was big enough for us all, why shouldn't they enjoy it too? – and watched the nettles advancing out of the bushes. 'Let them be left, O let them be left, wildness and wet,' Gerard Manley Hopkins sang. 'Long live the weeds and the wilderness yet.'

Simplification became an ideal, never quite reached. After toying with a borrowed word processor I saw it was a trap, anchoring me, and went back to the old typewriter – less machinery, fewer complications. I owned too much already. I would sell the dinghy that we had sailed in and out of East Anglian estuaries and taken on family holidays to Pembrokeshire and Devon; and the flute, that had given music for nearly fifty years – enhancing my life unimaginably and once, perhaps, reaching my mother dying in her bedroom next door – but now was never played; and my father's medals that I had kept locked up like holy relics; and the family portraits, those stern faces that still shadowed me; and hundreds of books I no longer needed.

I went through drawers of hoarded paper and gave back the children's letters, but kept Deirdre's. She had destroyed mine long ago, taking them in bundles to Wales when we were thrashing out our marriage and tearing them up one by one in a pub where we had bed-and-breakfast. Sometimes she wished she could shed the past so easily. 'Men are better at it,' she wrote once. 'Women go on brewing old poison, keeping it bubbling on the stove. I despise it but do it all the same, and hate it.'

It was a habitual argument. We carry our past with us, trailing it like refugees who load what possessions they can collect on a cart and drag it along the endless road, in flight to a future somewhere else. But we carry our future too, pushing it in front – the hopes and fears that might be useful wherever we are going.

Already I lived less and less in a house, even such an assertive one as the Hall, and more and more in my mind. And now I thought I saw the chance of something ahead, not emptier but less burdened. 'I would rather sit on a pumpkin and have it all to myself,' Thoreau said, 'than be crowded on a velvet cushion.' In a fit of dispossession, shucking off the clutter like an old Brahmin who withdraws from the world and reduces things to the barest, I would rid myself of belongings, of the diversions and subterfuges, the bits and pieces of too long.

'And emotions also?' a friend wanted to know, with a concern that made me wonder – and remember the love she had shown me, and mine for her. But it was only an ideal, something to dream about. A jettisoning of inessentials. A whittling down to the ultimate – to 'a condition of complete simplicity, costing not less than everything, and all shall be well': lines of Eliot's written on the gravestone of another friend I loved, wife of a painter, in a lonely churchyard on a hill.

SIXTY-FIVE

June 10, Barcelona. Following unfrequented roads Don Quixote and Sancho Panza found signs that they were reaching the end of their journey. At night, passing through a wood, Sancho felt something brush the top of his head. He put up his hand and touched a pair of human feet, in socks and shoes. Under the next tree it was the same – the trees were full of feet and legs. Sancho shook with terror and shouted for Don Quixote, who calmed him: 'There's nothing to be afraid of. These are bandits who have been hanged where they were caught. It means we are approaching Barcelona.'

The dead still give warning to a traveller that he is coming into Barcelona. In an immense cemetery at the edge of the city they are filed away in hillside tombs for safe-keeping.

It was the only town Don Quixote visited on his travels, and he wasn't happy there. Recognized at once, he was greeted with drums and music, and paraded through the streets with a placard on his back, 'This is Don Quixote of La Mancha', for extra mockery. Boys tied bundles of prickles under the tails of Rocinante and Sancho's donkey, which spurred them into bucking their riders off. After being exhibited like a monkey on a balcony while the citizens passed by and stared, the famous hero was entertained at night with a ball, tempted by grand ladies, tormented into dancing till he could only gasp an oath of loyalty to Dulcinea and sit down exhausted on the floor. He didn't fit into this sophisticated urban society, he belonged on the empty Manchegan plain. Only the sea, which he and Sancho had never seen before, could please him here: it was so wide and spacious, far bigger than the lagoons of Ruidera.

Barcelona is a modern place, hardly Spanish at all. The language is a version of Provençal, the flavour is of Marseille or Genoa or Naples, yet with a character of its own – energetic, ambitious, successful. The factories are working, the dockyard cranes are loading and unloading. Tension, action, profit are in the air, with a whiff of violence. Barcelona faces Europe, turning its back on the bleached old heartland of Spain, the land of Don Quixote.

I try to picture the two-day revolution in July 1936 at the beginning of the Civil War, when the city was seized by anarchists and more than five hundred people were killed, some of them army officers shot by their own men. All fifty-eight churches except the cathedral were burned or demolished. Hotels, shops, cafés, banks, factories were taken over or closed. Shoeshine boys were collectivized and middle class habits – giving a tip, wearing a tie, calling a man *señor* instead of *camarada* – were banned at peril of arrest. But the new order didn't last. It was the only occasion in history, Hugh Thomas wrote, when anarchists have controlled a great city and it was remarkable what little use they made of their opportunity.

Dimly I can see George Orwell in militia uniform marching up the Ramblas, the famous leafy boulevard, on his way to the station and the war front. He had trouble with his equipment and had to be shown how to put on his leather cartridge cases by a gentle-eyed Spanish girl, who gave him a bottle of wine and a length of *chorizo* sausage – 'who looked as though her life-work was to rock a cradle, but who as a matter of fact had fought bravely in the street battles.' Back on leave a few months later, he got caught up in the war-within-a-war between rival revolutionary parties, with the Ramblas a battlefield raked by machine-guns on the roofs and at least another four hundred dead. A thousand or so more were killed when Barcelona was raided by Italian bombers.

In a crowded street a girl coming towards me wraps her fingers briefly round my waist as she passes, but doesn't look back. Outside the cathedral the young people playing flutes and jiggling puppets for money aren't Spanish, or even gypsies, but foreigners on the great drop-out trail round the world, the pilgrim route to some misty shrine evoked by dope. The flock of white Roman geese in the cloister, with their private pool, look sleeker and more satisfied.

At midday I sit with a beer at a café in the Plaza Real. Moroccans kick a football among the palms, a pop singer belts out the chorus of Beethoven's ninth symphony. Four times in half an hour I'm offered drugs for sale: *estupefacientes*, stupefiers, is the vivid word. This morning, across the plaza in his hotel room, a man of twenty-three died of heroin. The shock is greater for being in Spain. They have gone from authoritarianism, the dictatorship of Franco and the church, to a novel kind of democracy – from the Falange to AIDS – in double quick time. They are catching up on the sixties and seventies, the decades they never had. I feel sorry rather than envious: to go through all that permissiveness, swinging and rocking and drugging – like going through my early life again.

I move into a restaurant for lunch. A lean grizzled military man, with medal ribbons on his chest and a forage cap clipped under his shoulder strap, sits reading a German newspaper at another table. Could he be a veteran of the Condor Legion sent by Hitler to help Franco in the Civil War? Could he have bombed Guernica? He marches to the bar, brings back a glass of brandy and pours it into his coffee, at which the waiter fetches the brandy bottle and fills his glass again. The TV on the wall is showing a lunchtime medical programme – huge coloured diagrams of human genitals. The German barks at the waiter who switches the channel, and we get close-ups of Ronald Reagan and Margaret Thatcher instead. People staring at the first programme go on staring: penises, vaginas, presidents, prime ministers – they have their passing interest, their moments of curiosity in a crowded Barcelona restaurant.

'The place is dead,' a young women tells me in the travel agent where I book a seat on this evening's express train to Madrid and tomorrow's flight to London.

Dead? – it's what Benito, the bar owner, said about El Toboso three weeks ago. Outside in the street the traffic is as noisy as anywhere in the world.

'Nobody shouts any more,' she complains. 'And today is election day!' In the Franco days she was a university student and remembers their demonstrations, their involvement in a wider game. Now the graffiti stick to local politics, the tiff between Catalan and Catalan over independence for Catalonia. 'Our writers and painters have gone to Madrid. It's too comfortable here – there's no enemy any more.'

Certainly all is peaceful though not quiet in the Ramblas, where Orwell marched to the front. Blue carnations and green parakeets are for sale, and lottery tickets and the London papers. In the evening *paseo*, the daily promenade when everyone comes out to display themselves, to walk and talk with everyone else, the avenue becomes a stream of life. Revolution isn't conspicuous and down near the port the trees, which once gave cover for snipers, are heavily outnumbered by prosti-tutes. They were shamed off the streets by the anarchists of 1936 and during Franco's long dictatorship were said not to exist at all. Few of them are beautiful. Some of the most startling – a dark red-lipped panther lounging on the bonnet of a parked car or an immensely tall, lusciously feminine blonde mincing down the pavement – are men.

Others are more tragic. A pretty girl, no more than a child, totters against a shop window, then lurches blindly round the corner to lean against another shop. She isn't doing much trade. She is someone's daughter, knocked out by drugs.

Barcelona was Don Quixote's furthest point from home. Riding along the beach one morning he was challenged by another knight, a stranger who claimed that his own mistress was incomparably more beautiful than Dulcinea of El Toboso. They charged in mortal combat but Don Quixote was easily unhorsed and the conqueror stood over him, pinning him to the ground with his spear.

'Finish me off,' the shattered old man begged in a voice that seemed to come already from the tomb. Ignominy was piled on dishonour and only the virtue of his faith was left: 'Dulcinea is the loveliest woman in the world and I'm the unhappiest knight.' Whatever else, love was unconquerable: the love, or truth, that he had created and by which he lived.

In fact the stranger was an old friend in disguise who only wanted to force Don Quixote to forsake this crazy life and go home. Sancho Panza agreed and when his master lay in bed, melancholy and brooding, he tried to cheer him up: 'Thank God that though you were knocked to the ground you got off without one broken bone. Stuff the doctor! – there's nothing he can do for you. Let's give up wandering about, looking for adventure in places we don't know.'

Sorrowfully they set off home. 'This is where my deeds were wiped out,' Don Quixote lamented as they left the city, 'and my fortunes fell, never to rise again.' When Sancho blamed it all on luck Don Quixote replied that there was no such thing: 'Every man is architect of his own destiny. I have been so of mine, though not always with the necessary prudence. But I did what I could.'

In his old age, turning back to his own village which he knew he would never leave again, the Knight of the Sad Countenance was beginning to show the faintest recognition of his fallibility.

SIXTY-SIX

One hot summer day not long ago I sat in a studio where the last agony of Captain Scott and his companions, on their fatal return from the South Pole, was being filmed for television. Though their bodies had already been dug out of the snow in northern Canada they hadn't yet died for the cameras and here they were, sweating under the lights, perishing in Wembley. Time after time, to get it right, Captain Oates crawled out of the tent into a howling blizzard of flour and mashed potato ('I'm just going outside and may be some time') – finally into oblivion, followed by lunch with me in the cafeteria; and Scott laboured feebly to pencil the famous words into his diary, mumbling them for the sound track again and again through frost-cracked bloodstained lips.

The drama was enhanced by the casual rubber-soled look of the film crew and the authentic props and wardrobe: the explorers' clothes sprayed with instant age and dirt, the equipment of the period down to the proper brand of biscuits and pipe tobacco, the man behind the tent flicking the canvas to simulate the wind outside, hour after hour. 'Get Scott stubbled up again,' the director ordered after countless takes, and an immaculate girl, tripping over electric cables and sleeping-bags, dabbed at the great man's chin where sweat had spoilt his make-up.

It wasn't hard to believe the illusion – that this was the real Scott, tough as iron, dying in the Antarctic – even when he moaned about the heat. There were two distinct men there, the actor and the character, totally different yet behaving identically. And afterwards, as I walked to the underground station on my way home, it seemed appropriate that they were filming, not at the South Pole but in a London suburb. They were faking it anyway and, like La Mancha for *Don Quixote*, this made a good stage, bleak but fertile for the truth.

Out of another hot summer day, in 1985, was conjured one of those times – not so much the periods of nostalgia, being reminded of past joys, as the moments of vision, catching sight of possibilities in some future we had missed – when I felt almost on the brink of falling in love again. It was a longing for something, not lost but never quite found.

It was at the University of East Anglia. After smoked salmon and champagne under the campus trees I sat sweating like the actor playing Captain Scott – crying too – in the big sports hall to watch Deirdre being given the degree she had never taken at Oxford more than twenty years before. 'One can't live with too much emotion,' she had written long ago. 'If I always loved you as I do now, I would have no energy left to do anything else in life.' Having once abandoned a university to get married she had now gone into reverse, leaving home for another university – a brave, imaginative move – and her energy was absorbed, as she had predicted. 'I can't talk about love, I'm afraid – what does it mean?' she wrote in our twenty-fifth year of marriage, her year of graduating. 'It seems to mean sweat and tears. And rage. And jealousy.'

A so-called mature student, my so-called wife – the girl I once saw sitting on the grass in a London garden, smoking a pipe – lined up with all the others, average age twenty-one to her forty-five but few of them with a degree as good as hers, in costumes of pink and purplish-blue. In turn, while trumpets blew a fanfare from the gallery, they were called to the platform to shake the chancellor's hand and be admitted to bachelorship, to the applause of a thousand parents and one old husband, cheering through his tears.

Had those years really happened – the good times and the others, with the birth and childhood of our daughter and two sons? A friend of mine, dressed like Cardinal Wolsey to be made an honorary doctor of the university, stepped out of the procession when he saw through Deirdre's disguise and gave her a generous, public kiss. 'I feel far more ridiculous,' he said, 'than you could ever look.'

That same friend, a musician, once asked, 'Do you find that the *passing* of time means less and less to you as you get older? Life is much more a continuous present than I ever thought it could be.' I was happy that an occasion in a broiling crowded sports hall, evoking such a span of retrospect and promise, was being witnessed by a man for whom memory and will, past and future, evaporated in the heat of time, leaving only what he called the indulgent and impatient 'now'.

The children grew up and Deirdre went to Edinburgh University to work for a doctorate. In the spring of 1987 at the Hall, after I had mended the water pipes that had frozen and burst during the winter, and unblocked the drains that had overflowed from excessive rain, and changed the oil and sharpened the blades of the grass cutter, and watched the wild daffodils in the orchard bloom and die, I settled down to read *Don Quixote*. And in the second week of May, a month before the general election, I flew to Madrid and took a train to Manzanares in the middle of La Mancha.

I gave myself four weeks.

SIXTY-SEVEN

June 11, Madrid. I have been almost a month in Spain. Election day here was yesterday, and is today in Britain. Before flying home in time to vote I will spend the morning in the Prado.

Down the street from my cheap hotel near the Plaza Mayor, in a doorway as I pass, two painted ladies speak in deep male voices: in search of coffee and *tostada* I have landed among transvestites. But the shops are devoted to missals, crucifixes, rosaries, and the local bookshop has nothing but religion. The nuns who shuffle past look hardly more female than the lipsticked, rouged, wigged men along the pavement.

Don Quixote would have liked Madrid no more than any other city. On the way home from Barcelona, weary and troubled by defeat, he rested in the shade of a tree where pestering thoughts, like bees round honey, settled on him and stung. One of them persisted: he would become a shepherd and retire to a pastoral life. 'I will buy some sheep,' he told Sancho Panza, 'and we will roam the mountains and woods and fields, singing here, weeping there, drinking from crystal springs and limpid streams and great rivers.' His days of dreaming weren't over; he could still win glory, if not by fighting giants and righting wrongs, then by turning into a shepherd and making love to the moon.

'My God!' Sancho cried, catching a glimpse of his master's vision. 'That's the life for me.'

Life: to live, and not to die. 'This is the main thing,' Unamuno wrote, 'the tap-root of quixotic madness – not to die!' The philosophy of not dying, of believing, of creating the truth – a philosophy that can't be taught in schools or explained by logic or analysed by science, because it rises from the heart – is the philosophy of Don Quixote: to live, with one's illusions.

311

Slowly they trudged homeward across La Mancha, sleeping sometimes at an inn, more often under the stars where Don Quixote was kept awake by worry, also by solitude and the beauty of the night. Before dawn, leaning against a tree, he sang a little madrigal of love – 'strange fate, that life should kill and death revive' – a composition of his own, to the accompaniment of sighs (echoing the mystic passion of St John of the Cross, *muero porque no muero*, I die because I do not die'). 'I'm amazed,' he said, rousing Sancho in the morning, 'at your lack of feeling. You must be made of marble or solid bronze, you have no emotions in you. I keep watch while you snore, and lament while you rejoice, and faint from fasting while you get lazy and out of breath from gluttony. Get up, for God's sake!'

After many days on the road, reaching the top of a rise, the two travellers saw their village ahead. Sancho fell to his knees: 'Open your eyes, my beloved country, and see your son Sancho Panza returning! And your son Don Quixote too! Though he has been conquered by another man, he has conquered himself – which he has told me is the victory to be wished for, most of all.'

'Stop this nonsense,' Don Quixote said, 'and let's get home.' So they rode down into their village where Don Quixote was welcomed by his household, Sancho by his family.

If living was the root of Don Quixote's madness, dying was the only remedy. Whether from sorrow at his defeat in combat or despond at never seeing Dulcinea restored to her proper beauty, his end came quickly. A fever struck and for six days he stayed in bed, visited by friends who tried to cheer him, with Sancho always at his side. The doctor diagnosed a fatal melancholy and advised him to save his soul, his body being beyond hope. Everyone wept as if he were already dead, but Don Quixote took the news calmly and asked to be left alone while he slept.

Six hours later he woke up and cried loudly, 'Blessed be Almighty God! I can see reason now. I'm rid of the dark shadows. I realize my folly and the dangers I have run.' He was on the point of death and wanted to meet it in such a way that he wouldn't be remembered in life only as a madman. To his friends this was a fit of the old disorder and they began to humour him, but he silenced them: 'I'm in a hurry! Stop your joking – send for a lawyer to make my will and a priest to confess me.' He knew clearly what he had only caught before in rare shafts of lucidity penetrating his fog-filled mind – that he had been a tragic failure. It was the knowledge that both lit and darkened his whole story.

'Truly he is dying,' the priest said, 'and truly he has come to his senses.'

'Don't die, dear master!' Sancho begged, in tears. 'Take my advice and live for a long time more. The maddest thing for a man to do is let himself die – killed by nobody, just by disappointment. Get up and let's go out into the country dressed as shepherds, as we promised. We might find Dulcinea behind the bushes, no longer a plain village girl but – the sight of her!' While Don Quixote's dementia slipped briefly from him at the end, leaving him cured of everything but death, Sancho was struck by a desperate lunacy. It has been called the sanchification of Don Quixote and quixotization of Sancho, the novel's final irony. At last the dreamer, who had been shadowed by his practical, sceptical, no-nonsense squire, saw that his ideal could never be attained and was dying at the first touch of reality; and the realist, who had suffered so much from his master's deluded fantasy, was on the verge of dreams. *La vida es sueño*, and without the dream there was no life.

'Gently, my friends – not so fast,' Don Quixote said. 'I was mad, but now I'm sane.' He searched for a quotation to leave behind, a suitable farewell. The moment lay in his choice of words, and he found them: *'En los nidos de antaño no hay pájaros hogaño* – in last year's nests there are no birds this year.'

At this hour of disillusion, he may have meant, nothing was left of his imagination. He was empty, sterile, spent – the writer's ultimate dread. Perhaps even Dulcinea faded in his eyes, no longer a mirage to comfort him. He confessed his sins and signed his will and lay half-conscious for three more days till, to the grief of everyone round him, he died. He was a good and brave *hidalgo*, they wrote on his tomb, the world's scarecrow who cared nothing for the world and had the luck to die a wise man though he lived a fool.

In Madrid this morning after breakfast, expecting the worst, I go to see the statues of Don Quixote and Sancho Panza riding through the Plaza de España under advertisements for airlines and banks. I needn't have worried – they are sculpted with more affection, less ridicule, than any I have seen.

Mounted on Rocinante the Knight of the Sad Countenance is standing up in his stirrups, poised forward, arm outstretched, his long fingers like a blessing on this monstrous place. In the Civil War the communists claimed that he was calling them to storm the prison, the nationalists that he was giving the fascist salute – both trying to enlist a visionary who ignored them all. Politics never entered his head, it was full of better things. He was merely pointing – as he still does – like a prophet to something more truly infused with justice than anything in sight: something beyond power or greed or dogma which, with compassion and imagination, or faith and love, or just with a peculiar kind of insanity, anyone can share. I will try to remember him like that, at home this evening, when I go out to vote in my Suffolk village.

Sancho, baffled by the fumes and roar of traffic, follows him on his donkey. A grove of olive trees, thoughtfully, has been planted round them.

WHEN
FRIDAY
COMES

WHEN FRIDAY COMES:

Football, War
&
Revolution
in
the Middle East

by
James Montague

deCoubertin
B O O K S

Published by deCoubertin Books Ltd in 2013.
deCoubertin Books, 145-157 St John Street, London, EC1V 4PY
www.decoubertin.co.uk

First hardback edition.
ISBN: 978-1-9092450-5-1

A CIP catalogue record for this book is available from the British Library.
Cover by Zoran Lucic.
Typeset by Allen Mohr.

Printed and bound by Korotan.

In memory of the 74.

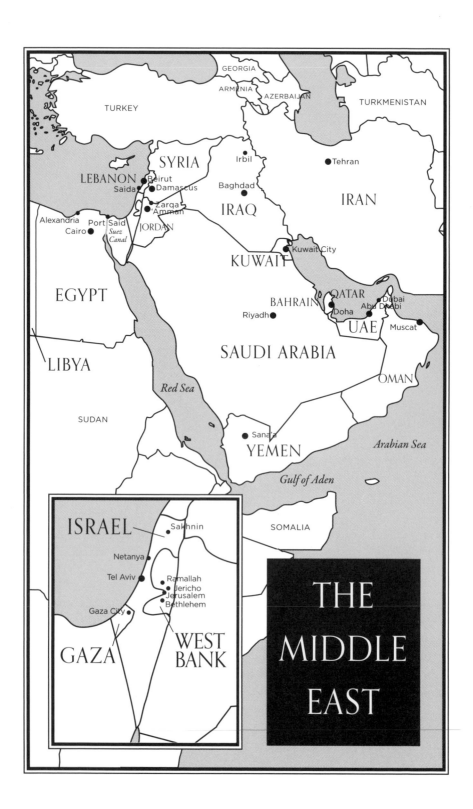

THE

MIDDLE

EAST

CONTENTS

FOREWORD

by Bob Bradley

In football there is the journey. As a manager the journey is about leading, analysing, experimenting, solving, hoping to build a team that can be successful, maybe get somewhere it's never been. My journey has me in Egypt where the hopes and dreams of 85 million people lie not only in Tahrir and some new democracy, but in the national team, *Muntakhab*, and the most important Arabic words I have learned. *Kas Al Aalam*. It means World Cup.

A football adventure from the United States to Egypt. Along the way there are many important names, games, experiences, stories. Zak Abdel, loyal friend, goalkeeper coach, Egyptian American. Confederations' Cup 2009. Port Said. Aboutrika. Ahly. Zamalek. Ultras. And yes James Montague.

To begin with the challenges of managing the Egyptian National Team have a lot to do with a personal navigation system. The type of GPS that reads people, situations, politics and emotions. The skills that have been acquired must constantly be improved with new information. This means listening, observing and reading. I threw myself into the columns of John Duerden and James M. Dorsey, and I read *When Friday Comes*. Better yet, I met James Piotr Montague.

He arrived late for our first talk in a hotel in New Cairo, saving a few Egyptian pounds forgoing the taxi for a microbus, Cairo's cheapest and definitely, most interesting form of transportation. That's James. Substance over style. West Ham supporter. Polish Mum. Witty. All about the journey. Whether in Beirut, Gaza, Doha or Cairo. *When Friday Comes* details personal experiences based on relationships and trusts that develop when you are there in the Ultras' sections of the stadiums or in the smoky, out-of-the-way cafes. Asking honest questions and engaging in true conversations with those that live and breath the game.

James Montague's journey is filled with real life insights that have captivated and helped me along the way. Thanks my friend.

Bob Bradley, Cairo, January 2013

INTRODUCTION

All that I know most surely about morality and obligations, I owe to football.
Albert Camus

The shisha café in the quiet, overlooked suburb of Hor Al Anz in Dubai was the only sign of life on the street. It was late, past midnight, and the sticky humidity that always followed a searing Gulf summer's day coated everyone, and everything, in a thin layer of perspiration. My bed was enticing me home, but I still felt the pull of unfinished business. The lone yellow light along the concrete row of shops and shwarma stands threw itself enticingly onto the pavement in front. A distant clatter of porcelain cups and raised male voices in a foreign tongue wafted over. It was an alien sound, and an alien surrounding, but also immediately recognisable. I instinctively moved towards the light.

Inside, the harsh glow from the strip lighting mixed with the fog-thick fug of sweet apple tobacco and strong, dark cigarettes. It stung the eyes momentarily until a few moments of blinking acclimatised you to the toxic atmosphere. It was standing room only. Every available seat was taken, the space tightly packed together by white-robed Emiratis wearing the traditional *dish dasha*. More stood in any available place they could find. I inched along the back wall and, to my surprise, found a solitary seat overlooked by the crush. A young Pakistani boy worked the cracks in the crowd, emptying ashtrays and refilling tiny thimbles full of thick Turkish coffee as his Egyptian colleague darted around the chairs with his metal ladle of hot coals, replacing the dying embers from atop each customer's billowing water pipe. The crowd was oblivious to their services. Tactics had to be discussed and players rated. All eyes were glued to the television in the corner of the room for the big match.

The appearance of white uniformity from the back of the room was a myth. Two tribes had emerged from Dubai's darkness to watch their respective teams do battle. An invisible line had been drawn in the sand, the room divided. To the right, the supporters of France, to the left, Brazil. The only way to differentiate the two was the hastily hung flags in each corner. It was the 2006 World Cup quarter-final and neither side could contemplate going home saddled with defeat. Arguments started to break out between the sets of fans over who was truly the greatest player in the world: Ronaldinho or Zidane. One Emirati supporting France had to be pulled back by his friends, so incensed was he that the great Zidane had been defamed. And the match hadn't even started yet.

Fights, devotion and obsession over faraway players and footballing nations was something I had quickly got used to when I accidentally stumbled into Dubai nearly two years previously. I hadn't even known for sure where Dubai was on the map when the email arrived advertising a job on the city's *Time Out* magazine. Two weeks later I was stepping out of an air-conditioned arrivals lounge into a brick wall of humidity. It was August and a thick, moist air had emptied my lungs the moment I stepped out of the controlled environment of the airport. Dubai was noisy, brash and hellishly hot. I had seen many new arrivals to Dubai react in different ways upon arriving in such an alien environment. Some flew back home in a matter of days. Some were driven slowly mad by the heat. Relationships crumbled, vices fed. Most stayed, but stuck to their own in expat communities, replicating the life they had enjoyed back home oblivious to their surroundings and refusing to mix with the locals to acclimatise.

I had put my faith in football. In the beginning, to appease my longing for home, I would walk to my local shisha café late at night to watch English Premier League matches. More often than not the Egyptian manager would show only Tottenham games, no matter who else was on, given that the Egyptian international Mido was turning out for them at the time. But soon I started to pick up the little threads of local football stories: a 2006 World Cup qualifier where the United Arab Emirates took on the mysterious North Korean national team; the struggles of the Palestinian national football team as they tried, but ultimately failed, to qualify for the 2006 World Cup; riots in the Lebanese league between supporters representing competing sectarian interests; footballers in Yemen struggling to kick the habit of their national drug qat. I devoured each and every story I could find. They were reported matter-of-factly, as if this kind of thing was perfectly normal in the Middle East. In a way, it was. But each story held something of wider significance. At its root football seemed to embody something about the country's psyche, its national character, its place in the world and where it was heading. I wanted to find out more about the Middle East, its mysteries and its contradictions. Football was the perfect prism.

My catalyst was the news that French World Cup winner Marcel Desailly had signed to play in the Qatari league. Qatar was a barren, inoffensive country whose recent discoveries of gas had given it phenomenal wealth. A lot of this money was being pumped into sport, especially football, in an attempt to raise its international profile. Without thinking or having any particular plan I booked a flight to Doha. It seemed an absurd place with absurd ambitions to rule the world. How little I knew back then.

I then booked another flight to Egypt. And then another to Iran. It was the start of a journey that would take me to terraces and football pitches as far south as Sana'a, to Tehran in the east, to Cairo in the west and to Damascus in the north. In all these places I discovered the same thing: a deep and passionate love for the beautiful game and a window of wider understanding.

Talk of the globalisation of football isn't anything new. Neither is it particularly illuminating that passion is something the Middle East has in abundance, though there is a messianic reverence for the game that matches anything in Europe or South America. Yet, in theory, it shouldn't be like this. The Middle East isn't a place pre-disposed to successful Western interventions. Tragedy has stalked every corner of the region and when I first arrived the West's standing couldn't have been lower. Decades of nefarious interference in Iran, Lebanon, Egypt and Iraq to name a few, had created a toxic mix of corrupt regimes, Islamic fundamentalism, poverty, anger and disillusionment. The duplicity and betrayal reached its nadir after the disastrous second Gulf War and the dismantling of Iraq. As the veteran war correspondent Robert Fisk wrote:

> From the borders of Hindu Kush to the Mediterranean, we – we Westerners that is – are creating… a hell disaster.

The chaos and the confusion had been a boon for Islamic fundamentalists seeking to paint the world in black and white, in us versus them rhetoric. It seemed – at least it did when I first wrote the introduction to *When Friday Comes* in 2008 – that the diverse range of people who called the Middle East their home were rejecting the ideals that had once been heralded as the force of modernity. As a Westerner, an outsider trying to make sense of it all, taking the pulse of a region would be nigh on impossible normally. Yet despite all this, one Western cultural export had achieved something that no amount of military intervention, aggressive foreign policy or attempted sub-jugation could. Football had won hearts and minds in the Middle East. Every country in the region was obsessed with the beautiful game. A weekend of English Premier League or Serie A or La Liga football had the power to momentarily disable the most unforgiving jihadist. On the surface the apocryphal story of how Osama Bin Laden would stand on the Highbury terraces of his beloved Arsenal in the 1990s sounded ridiculous. But it was a testament to the game's power and reach that it was almost believable. Almost.

How had the game conquered the land that one might expect to reject it the most? After all, the document that brought the game to life, one of the only documents that

has universal and unwavering approval across the region and across sectarian lines, was
set down in a smoke-filled room by English public school masters in the nineteenth
century. In his Twelve Books That Changed the World, which included the Rule Book
of Association Football amongst the dozen, Melvyn Bragg wrote that football:

*Has caused at least one war and many battles, often tragic, off the
pitch. It has always triggered outbursts of local and national joy, pride
and unity . . . and it all flowed from the meeting of a few Victorian
Oxbridge graduates in a pub in Lincoln's Inn Fields in London 1863.
Before the afternoon was out they had called themselves 'the football
association' and the Rule Book was on its way.*

It was perhaps the greatest imperialist document ever written, allowing the British
Empire to successfully spread the footballing gospel. When the British forces that
helped colonise the game from land, sea and air retreated, momentum did the rest.
Now, whether I was in Amman or Irbil, the first question I was asked in cafés and on
street corners wasn't about George Bush or Tony Blair, or the war or Israel. I wasn't spat
at in the street or harangued for my country's complicity in very bad things. Rather,
it was: 'Manchester United or Chelsea?' with the more sophisticated barracking me
for supporting such a bunch of underachievers as West Ham United. One Lebanese
international footballer in his late 20s even went as far as conceding that the 3–3 FA
Cup final against Liverpool in 2006 was interesting to watch, but that West Ham were
a shadow of the 1966 team, with Moore and Peters. I watched avowed Hezbollah
members profess their undying love for Steven Gerrard, and spoke to Syrians who were
livid – angrier than me, certainly – with Steve McClaren for not steering England to
the finals of Euro 2008.

Simply put, football is the Middle East's great unifying thread. More so, you
could argue, than Islam, divided as it is, sometimes violently, between Shia and Sunni,
and certainly more than the failed forces of Arab nationalism. Even language fails the
test when you throw the Farsi speaking Iranians and the Hebrew speaking Israelis into
the mix.

True, some had sought to drive a wedge between football and the Middle East's
most dominant and uncompromising religion: Islam. The most famous being the
2003 football fatwa issued by a Saudi cleric Sheikh Abdallah al Najdi, which signified
a strange attempt to Islamify football. In it the Sheikh gave a 15-point plan of how to
rid the game of Western influence. These included only punishing transgressions, not
by red or yellow cards, but by Sharia law; playing only one half; not playing in front

of crowds; and urging followers to use the game only to strengthen the body for jihad. My favourite, though, was point nine:

> 'You should spit in the face of whoever puts the ball between the posts or uprights and then runs in order to get his friends to follow him and hug him like players in America or France do, and you should punish him, for what is the relationship between celebrating, hugging and kissing and the sports that you are practising?'

According to the Middle Eastern Media Research Institute in Washington, Saudi newspaper Al Watan had reported that the fatwas had provoked three players from Al Rashid football club to leave and join the insurgency in Iraq, even though the fatwas were roundly condemned in Saudi Arabia. The Grand Mufti of Saudi Arabia, Sheikh Abdul Ibn Abdallah Aal-Sheikh, who was also an adviser for the Saudi Justice Department, told Al Watan:

> [The authorities needed to] prosecute those involved in the publishing of these fatwas in a Sharia court for the crime they have committed [and to] track down those involved and prosecute them, in view of the dangers and the venom with which they are trying to influence society.

Neither was there anything wrong with the supposedly heathen rules that had been incorporated from the West.

> There is nothing wrong with . . . the soccer rules. All things that come from the West but are not unique to it are permitted. Soccer has become a world sport and does not belong only to the non-believers.

When I first wrote this introduction, it was here that I said that *When Friday Comes* isn't a book with a happy ending, where football provided some kind of silver bullet to solve the region's seemingly intractable problems. Football doesn't change things by itself. A two-state solution won't be kick-started by the Palestinian national team playing Israel. Currently neither team would even dream of playing the other. And that still holds true. Football – thanks to its ubiquity and its closeness to the street, the beating heart of its society – is a mirror that reflects the Zeitgeist; a sponge that soaks up the tensions, the flaws, the frustrations and the hopes of society. For those involved it is one of the few forms of catharsis. Which might give another explanation as to why, every Friday from Aden to Tehran, millions of fans leave the mosque and head straight for their local football club. In the absence of true democracy and a genuine public space, the terraces provide a forum for dissent. In Jordan, the songs for a free Palestine sung by the fans of the football team from Wihdat refugee camp wouldn't be accepted by the police on the street. In Iran the frustrations of the women's rights movement are vented, not outside the Majlis, but outside the Azadi national football stadium before every home international. And in Egypt it was the terraces that provided a space for young football fans to air grievances with Hosni Mubarak's dictatorship.

In the Middle East there was the mosque and the terrace, and little in between.

The power and the thought that the mosque has engendered has been well documented. But the terraces and stands of the football grounds of the region had been neglected for similar treatment, often because of a misguided idea that sport and politics are separate entities. Football is politics in the same way music is politics, or art, or film. It is an expression of the soul with a tribal beat. And it played its role – in some countries a vital role – in the greatest political upheaval to affect the region since the end of colonial rule.

When Mohamed Bouazizi a poor, young Tunisian fruit and vegetable seller – blazing with injustice and frustration after having his meagre fruit cart impounded – set fire to himself in Tunisia in December 2010 it sparked a wave of uprisings and revolutions that are still only in their infancy. Tunisia, Egypt, Libya, Syria, Bahrain, Yemen; all saw their people rise up to depose leaders that slowly constricted the life out of them. In the time before the Arab Spring, in the dark before the dawn, the atmosphere was hopeless and suffocating. Nowhere was this more true than in Egypt where Mubarak the elder had crushed his opposition so completely that in the paralysis of the jaded he almost, almost, succeeded in passing the mantle on to his son to continue his immorality. But in Egypt the people fought back. Not on the streets, but first in the stadiums. Then outside the stadiums. And then on the streets. For three years the ultras groups of Egypt's biggest clubs grew more anti-regime with every beating and every arrest. Yet they couldn't be controlled. When the damn burst on 25 January 2011, the ultras were on the front line.

It was now more than simply using the game to hold a mirror to something that I wanted to understand better. The game itself had become part of the narrative. In Egypt the ultras I had met by accident during a match in 2007 became the 'protectors of the revolution'. In Libya, the fledgling new transitional government realised that the national team's qualification for the African Cup Nations was worth more than a thousand show trials of Gaddafi apparatchiks. In Bahrain, the royal family realised the power of football too, but for the opposite effect. It was those involved in the game

– national heroes – who were punished for their role in asking for greater freedoms. Their fame and their talent had been reversed, turned on them, bastardized to send a message to those that dared to question the status quo. Football didn't cause the Arab Spring. The neglect, humiliation and abuse of the poor and the young did. But in the game many found a voice that would not be heard by any other means, for good and sometimes for bad.

All the while, at its core, the fundamentals of the game and the passion it engenders remains the same: Indivisible, unchanging, sometimes ugly, always beautiful. It is why now, in tandem with the chaos of the Arab Spring, the new oil wealth of the Gulf is being channelled into football, through Manchester City, through PSG and, of course, through the 2022 World Cup which will be held in Qatar. That first trip to Qatar to meet Marcel Desailly and that evening in Dubai, during the World Cup quarter-final, seem like a world away. But they still uphold the central tenant of what makes the game so fundamental to so many people in the Middle East and beyond: its universality. In that cafe in Hor al Anz I watched France famously dispense with Brazil 1–0 thanks to a Thierry Henry goal. The French contingent of Emiratis celebrated as if the United Arab Emirates had themselves put the Brazilians out. They ran into the street and mounted a fleet of expensive, powerful 4x4s before driving them out onto a patch of sandy waste ground, spinning doughnuts and blaring their horns whilst hanging a French flag out of a blacked-out window. The Brazilian fans quickly walked away, heads down, in silence – the defeat tasting every bit as bitter as it did in Rio.

London, March 2013

PROLOGUE

February 2012

Like the blood-red sun that had just drained and disappeared over the Nile a few minutes earlier, the protest was dying; its power darkened and diminished with each passing second. Hundreds of young men and women – most of the women covering their hair with the hijab – stood in front of a steel, stone and razor wire barricade. They chanted at Egypt's hated police, who had formed a line to protect the country's parliament a stone's throw from the cradle of the January 25 revolution: Tahrir Square. Every side road was blocked by newly constructed concrete walls. Every reflective surface smashed; windows, ATM screens, mirrors. Every wall was daubed with revolutionary graffiti.

> *'Fuck the Police'*
> *'Fuck the Military'*
> *'Fuck Mubarak'*

One protester laid down a piece of cardboard and prayed next to a wall under a freshly sprayed anarchist symbol. It had been over a year since the toppling of The Pharaoh. The January 25 revolution that swept Hosni Mubarak and his cabal of criminals, perverts and cronies from power – his sons Alaa and crown prince Gamal included – was the high tide of the Arab Spring. But for the young people who had congregated here a new threat needed to be combated. Egypt had become what they saw as a military dictatorship. The iron grip hadn't loosened since the fall of Mubarak, they argued, but merely changed position from Egypt's neck to its wrist.

Protests continued but not in the same numbers or ferocity. Perhaps it was protest fatigue. Perhaps it was the fact that the directions sent out by the organisers via Twitter were vague. The crowd had slowly drifted away; each revolutionary slogan met with diminishing vigour.

The police line took a step forward, sensing the changing tide.

The darkness was suddenly illuminated by a new blood-red fire. A flare had been cracked open by a young man wearing a distinctive red shirt, held aloft triumphantly. Next to him another unfurled a familiar flag; red, with a soaring eagle embossed on a shield: the flag of Egypt's most popular football club, Al Ahly. The young men were part of the Ahlawy, Al Ahly's own ultras group; thousands of militant, anti-authoritarian football fans.

Suddenly the protest was reborn, as if spirit had been thrown on the embers of a fire. The young men stormed the barricades, urging others to climb with them. Even the man praying by the anarchist symbol had rejoined the fray. They flew their flag and urged the rest to sing.

'*Horriya! Horriya!*'

Freedom.

The police line took one step back.

1
EGYPT

May 2007

After all his planning and high expectations, Assad looked like a man broken by the unforeseen. He sat, along with 40,000 fellow Al Ahly fans, with his face in his hands. The vast stretch of red shirts and flags were motionless in their half of the Cairo International Stadium in Egypt. The silence was stunned and awkward before a brooding malevolence rose, making me feel uncomfortable for the first time.

In the distance, the white half of the stadium was a violent sea of celebration. Furrowed faces darted for explanation between friends and strangers alike. Al Ahly were 2–0 down thanks to a stunning goal worked by Mahmoud 'Shikabala' Abdel Razeq Fadlallah. This was a bad thing for two reasons. Firstly, being 2–0 down to anyone was bad enough. After all, Al Ahly weren't a team that did losing. They had once gone almost three years without losing, a streak that lasted for 71 games and had only finally come to an end a few months previously. But this was worse, for a second reason. Much worse. They were losing to Zamalek, their hated Cairo rivals, their bourgeois city foes.

More people watched this match than any other in Africa, and for the six-figure crowd that turned up to see it in the flesh, the derby meant more than just football. It was about politics, history, identity, colonialism, escapism and pride. And for Assad, leader of Ahly's hardcore supporters group, the Ultras, the battle was equally important on the terraces as it was on the pitch. For weeks he and his band of Ahly fans had been planning for the game by devising the best way to taunt the opposition's fans.

Their group had only been in existence for a few months but they were nothing if not ambitious. They opted for a huge flag, designed to cover most of the north stand, mocking the 6–1 defeat meted out by Ahly in 2002. It was proudly displayed before kick-off. Assad looked behind at it now, an impotent heap of plastic and paint crumpled

1

at the back of the stand. It was time to go back to basics. The explosion was inevitable.

'Listen everybody,' he screamed defiantly to all those that surrounded him, breaking the silence and the gloom. 'I'm going to beat Shikabala, the cunt. I'm going to beat him in the face!'

In Cairo you belong to one of two tribes, one red, one white: Ahly or Zamalek. There are other football teams in Egypt, of course. Ahly and Ismaily have a big rivalry; In Alexandria the biggest team is Ittihad. But nothing gets the blood pumping like Ahly versus Zamalek. Almost every Egyptian has their allegiance. On a taxi journey from Sharjah to Dubai four months previously my Egyptian driver had spilt his colours before he even told me his name. 'I am Ahly, of course,' he said proudly, before regaling me with stories of how 100,000 people would queue from the morning to get in, with another 100,000 stuck outside. Inevitably riots would break out.

'Do not go,' he imparted ominously as I handed over my fare, 'You will be killed.'

His words came back to me as the plane landed at Cairo International Airport in the middle of the night. Arriving at Cairo airport is like turning up on the set of a 1970s British light farce about the last days of the empire. Jack-booted soldiers march around in ridiculously ornate uniforms. Men sit at desks where papers and passports are passed along a large line before disappearing into an unmarked bureaucratic hell. Everything – the walls, the desks, the light – was coloured brown and grey and beige. The humid weight of early summer kept the city's overpowering odour of sewage, as well as the border guards' incessant cigarette smoke, at ground level. Once this was the personification of modernity; a bright vision for visitors arriving in a vibrant and upwardly mobile city. Now it was as if a pane of drably coloured glass had been placed in front of the eyes.

It was Friday, the day that Ahly and Zamalek should have played each other. But the authorities had got wise to the violence and moved it to an early kick-off on Monday, hoping that thousands would be put off by the awkward timing. 'Ahly or Zamalek?' I asked the taxi driver after our conversation in pidgin Arabic, and then pidgin English, had ground to a halt. 'Ahly,' he replied with a shrug, as if there could be only one answer.

The roots of the rivalry can be traced back to when the British army walked the streets of Cairo. Football was almost universally regarded as Britain's only popular cultural import. Al Ahly was started in 1907 as the first Egyptian-run club. The name translates as 'The National' and Ahly, wearing the old red colours of the pre-colonial flag, was seen as a team for the nation, a bulwark against occupation and a chance for the average man on the street to come together for a common nationalistic cause. Zamalek, wearing white, was considered the team of the foreigner (read the British), the unpopular, the outsider. Originally called *Mokhtalat*, the hated King Farouk agreed to have the team named in his honour, before Farouk was changed to Zamalek post abdication. The team traditionally attracted not just the occupiers but also the people who had got rich by what Egyptian nationalists called 'collaboration'. Zamalek was also home to the awkward squad: the authors, poets and intellectuals who were uneasy with Egypt's new-found nationalistic confidence.

As much as the Cairo derby was about nationalism, it was also about class: the truly loyal man on the street versus the effete, shabbily wealthy liberal. But it had always been bloody. As with the majority of the world's great derbies, violence featured prominently in past bouts. Such was the ferocious hatred between the fans that since the 1990s no Ahly versus Zamalek match had been played in their home grounds. Instead, all games were played at Cairo's huge national stadium. The referees were not beyond suspicion either. Foreign officials were bussed in to take charge of proceedings. Scottish referees versed in handling the Old Firm rivalry between Celtic and Rangers were particularly popular. Egypt's notoriously baton-happy riot police took the threat of disorder very seriously and swamped the matches any time the two played. In fact, Egypt's riot police had become even more proficient with their batons in recent months. Hosni Mubarak had recently won what opposition parties called a sham election and had fought off threats to his power, especially from the popular but banned Muslim Brotherhood, a well-organised Islamic movement with links to Hamas. Police prevented voters from reaching the polls, intimidation was rife and opposition candidates were either locked up or denied the chance to stand. Mubarak walked it with 89 per cent of the vote.

Cairo felt hopeless; intractably poor and squeezed between an authoritarian government and Islamic fundamentalism. The hostel where I was staying didn't seem too bothered by goings on in the outside world though. Five young men and a bald pensioner sat in the reception area quickly smoking short joints, giggling hysterically. The pensioner passed it on without saying a word. The keys dropped into my hand as I sucked in the first breath. Welcome to Cairo.

Ayman Younis knew a thing or two about the enmity between the two sides of Cairo. As Zamalek's star striker in the late 1980s, and a regular in Egypt's national team, Ahly fans targeted him in ever more elaborate, vicious and sometimes hilarious ways. These days he was the main anchor for Egyptian and English Premier League football on state television whilst supplying 3-D advertising mats for sports pitches, as well as being on the Egyptian FA's board. If there was anyone who could get me into Ahly and Zamalek's training sessions – which were heavily guarded in fortified complexes – it was Ayman.

I called him from a public telephone in a grocery store near the hostel. He had some bad news. 'There is no training today,' he said. There could have been any number of reasons: the clubs had swapped venue or date to flummox Egypt's vicious sports press; or worried about fan violence, training might have been cancelled. The answer was far more surprising.

'It's the FA Cup final, Chelsea versus Manchester United. All the players and the coaches want to watch it.' Ayman invited me over to watch the match at his place.

His villa was on the outskirts of Cairo, towards 6 October City. This was where the moneyed middle classes chose to live these days, away from the dirt, noise and poverty of Cairo in a newly built and rapidly expanding settlement. It derived its name from the date that President Anwar Sadat – the man who made peace with Israel – was assassinated. It was as if, rather than struggling to integrate into Cairo, the wealthy had instead decided to rip it up and start again somewhere nearby.

Short and with tightly curled black hair, Ayman welcomed me into his huge house as if I were a long-lost family member. His three-storey home told me that, post-football, Ayman had not struggled. Back in the 1980s he was a fast, skilful attacking midfielder who had a reputation for raising his game for the big derby.

'I think I played maybe 11 derbies between 1983 and 1994,' he explained. 'I scored four times. I was lucky, I always played well in these matches.'

It wasn't enough to take his word for it. Handily Ayman had set up his large entertainment room, which doubled up as his trophy cabinet, so that I could experience some of his magic on television. He sat me down, passed me a Pepsi and slid the first videotape in. The screen blinked to life, initially a distorted mess of popping feedback, Arabic and neon-green. It was a compilation of his best goals: a scissor kick against Ahly in 1988; goals in the African Cup of Nations; the final of the African Champions League. He looked on engrossed, oblivious to my presence.

'Mubarak was there!' he shouted, pointing at the screen, lifting himself out of his seat at the same time. 'There, he was there!'

The crackling Arabic on screen gave way to a Brazilian-esque surge from the overexcited commentator: 'AyyyyymanYyooooooooooounis!' And there he was, with his tight retro-shorts, large Afro and barrel chest, wheeling away in celebration after volleying it into the top left-hand corner. The camera focused in on the mass of white celebrating the goal. Men were standing on the terraces holding their babies up in almost sacrificial celebration.

'Ahly fans say this goal was offside,' he said, turning around, breaking his grin and taking on an air of seriousness. 'But it wasn't. That was the goal of the season. But 1990 was my best season, I scored a horrible number of goals.'

Ayman's best form coincided with Egypt's World Cup appearance at Italia '90, their first since a brief, one match appearance at Italy 1934. The stage was set for Ayman's goal-scoring prowess. But he never made it onto the plane.

'I was in Scotland for the last [warm-up] game [before the World Cup] and the fucking number eight,' he spat, still angry at the memory of Egypt's 3–1 victory in Aberdeen 18 years later. 'The number eight[according to the Scottish FA that shirt was worn by Aberdeen midfielder Jim Bett] had a problem with me, he kicked me in the knee and *khalas*, finished, I had to go to Germany for an operation.'

Bett may never realise it but he might indirectly have had a hand in England's greatest World Cup performance since 1966. Egypt had a strong, defensive-minded team that drew its opening two group games with the Netherlands and Ireland. The crunch match came against England, which Egypt lost thanks to a solitary Mark Wright goal. The group was so tight that if Egypt had won 1–0 England would have finished bottom. But Egypt had struggled to score goals without Ayman and, as one of Egypt's most creative forces, he would almost certainly have played in the final game. A 1–1 draw would have created a first in World Cup history: every team finishing on the same points, with the same goals scored and the same goals against. England, Egypt, the Netherlands and Ireland's World Cup future would have been decided on the drawing of lots.

The next season Younis went back to being a thorn in Ahly's side, but he paid a price off the pitch.

'If I go to the stadium I have to go without my car as they break everything,' he said of Ahly's fans who, to this day, still hound him in the street. 'When I was playing I had a lot of problems with Ahly fans. In 1990 I found my BMW car on its side and they signed it 'Ahly fans'. And that was when we lost, 2–0, but they remembered that I scored in the first game earlier in the season.' That, however, wasn't the worst of it. 'Then there was the time they attacked me in my home. I had to phone the police. Five thousand Ahly fans came to my street and shouted against me, my wife and kids, throwing things at us.'

The FA Cup final turned out to be turgid and, with the game instantly forgotten, Ayman offered to drive me back to Cairo. For Ayman his love of Zamalek, along with its fans, transcended nearly every other impulse in his life, even religion.

'Ask a Zamalek fan, can you change religion?' he said as his sleek black BMW pulled away down the empty highway. 'He wouldn't answer. But you ask them: 'Can you change Zamalek?' They'd say 'No!' And if you see a policeman, they won't ask you whether you are Muslim or a Christian, they'll ask you whether you are Ahly or Zamalek. It's true.' But there was a historical demarcation when it came to religion. 'Fifty years ago Ahly became the team of the devout [but] Zamalek was the team of the middle classes,' he said.

The car's average speed dropped as we neared Cairo and the conversation turned to Israel. Ayman sucked air sharply through his teeth. 'If you have been to Israel, trust me, someone is following you.'

'What, even now?' I asked, looking around for any suspicious black cars keeping a steady distance behind us.

'I hate Israel,' Ayman continued. 'Not Israelis, but Israeli politicians and the wars. We've had three of them and lost something like 15,000 people. Everyone has lost someone.'

Ayman's BMW pulled to the kerb when we reached Zamalek Island. He offered me his card and pulled out a fat wedge of Egyptian notes, counting them out in front of me.

'Do you need any money?' he asked. 'I can give you money.'

'I'm OK, Ayman, I have money.'

'Are you sure?' He looked a little offended. 'OK, but if you need anything, ANYTHING, call me. If you need something, tell the person you're a friend of Ayman Younis. Exactly that.'

Ayman was a useful person to know given his status as the Egyptian Alan Hansen. On Monday he would be giving his thoughts in front of the biggest television audience of the year. As much as he was a White Knight to his marrow, he begrudgingly recognised the hold Ahly had on Cairo. They had already wrapped up their fourth consecutive title long before the game.

'Ahly already own the championship,' he conceded through his car window. 'So whatever happens tomorrow, Cairo will already be red.'

He pulled away into the stream of traffic and left me on my own, on the pavement checking over my shoulder for spies.

✦

Zamalek's training ground looked like it was about to collapse. With Ayman as my golden ticket I'd arrived at their huge grey complex on Zamalek Island, by far the most run-down structure in an upmarket and aspirational part of town. Outside, a couple of hundred Zamalek fans had turned up to catch a glimpse of the players as they arrived. They could afford to be more optimistic than Ayman about the derby. Rumours had surfaced in that day's papers that Ahly, who were fighting for honours on four fronts, were to rest the majority of their first team. Even more encouragingly, Manuel José – their crackpot Portuguese manager who had won them their four successive championship and back-to-back African Champions League titles, and regularly boasted he was a better manager than his compatriot Jose Mourinho – was out of the country. He was on holiday, apparently, although most fans believed he had been asked to step down for a few weeks after infuriating Egypt's religious conservatives by stripping off on the touchline during a league game in protest at a poor refereeing decision.

Still, Manuel claimed that his players were 'bored of success' which had in equal parts infuriated Zamalek and given them a glimpse of their first derby victory in over three years. But they didn't want to look overconfident and their recently appointed and notoriously secretive manager, Frenchman Henri Michel, had banned his players from talking to the press.

Michel was one of those managers that stalked the leagues and national teams of Africa, taking one generation to the heights of World Cup qualification before dumping them (or being dumped) and moving on to the next African job. His last job was taking the Ivory Coast to Germany in 2006, where they were knocked out in the first round despite having a team that included Didier Drogba, and the Toure brothers. They were, however, in the same group as Argentina and the Netherlands.

At the training ground the only player who would talk to me was Shikabala, Zamalek's best player who was in his second spell at the club after playing briefly in Greece.

'I came back because I played with Zamalek since I was very young and Zamalek is my home,' he admitted outside the dank, damp changing room. 'The derby is like a championship in itself: if you win it you win the biggest trophy since football started in Egypt. The players will do their best to win tomorrow, Inshallah.'

On the other side of Zamalek Island, things were equally tense at Ahly's purpose-built 25,000-seater training ground. Security wouldn't let me in until I lied and said I was from the BBC. But that was just the first layer. Inside three separate flanks of security guards were on hand to keep the press away from Ahly's players whilst they trained. The closest I got was when the team boarded the bus to leave. Even

Ahly's genial Vice Captain Osama Hosny, famed for his strict adherence to Islam, impeccable manners and beautiful singing voice, looked guiltily at the floor as he appeared, mumbled an apology and climbed onto the coach.

Hosny had recently become one of the most famous voices in Egypt after embarking on a second career as a pop star. Sort of. Osama had combined his love of Islam and his magnificent voice into one package and released a tape singing passages from the Koran, which were selling like hotcakes.

'He always speaks to me [but] the press get so crazy that the players have stopped talking to us before the match,' sighed Usama, a journalist for an Ahly news website who had hung around for the past three hours just to get a few scraps of gossip. With any hope of a quote gone, we walked to a nearby café to talk about tomorrow's game.

'Ahly and Zamalek hate each other,' he told me over a mud-thick Turkish coffee.

'Is there much trouble at the games?' I asked.

Usama grinned. 'Ahly has an ultras group, they're crazy and they hate Zamalek. I can't tell you how much they hate Zamalek! At the Ahly versus Sfaxien African Champions League final in 2006 they had a lot of bombs and flares and entered with them into the stadium. When Ahly scored. . . the Ultras were the only fans who had travelled to the game let off the bombs.' It was the first time I'd heard of the Ahly Ultras but their reputation seemed to be legion. 'The Ultras are everywhere,' continued Usama, partly in disgust, partly in admiration at their commitment. 'Cairo, Alexandria, 200km away, everywhere. There are maybe 200 officially but a lot of fans want to go with them when they travel so it's a lot more. You have to see them.'

Assad readily agreed to meet me. After a few phone calls I'd managed to get through to the Ultras' leader. But it all seemed a little civilised. 'Of course, you can come with us, it will be a pleasure. Do you need a lift? We'll pick you up at Tahrir Square, you know where that is? 5.30pm.'

Years of conditioning in British football made you expect an Ultra to look a certain way: fat, skinhead, tattoos. But the hierarchy of the Ahly Ultras looked like they'd just finished a shift at a Cairo library. Assad, tall, painfully thin and wearing thick-rimmed glasses, jumped out of the car and shook my hand before we squeezed into the car with Mohammed and Ishmail for the short drive to the stadium.

'We are very unique, we are the only club who have several Ahlys named after it in Jeddah, in Yemen, Libya, in the Emirates, Qatar. But Ahly is THE Ahly, it was the first ever in the whole region to be the first 100 per cent Egyptian so it is very nationalistic,' he explained. 'Zamalek have changed their name so many times we sing: 'You used to be half-British, you guys are the rejects'.'

The Ultras were the exact opposite of what you would expect. The hardcore were all university educated, with good jobs and liberal views on women, religion and drugs. Assad started organising the Ultras after spending time studying in England and immersing himself in the football cultures of the English Premier League and Serie A. It was time, he reasoned, that Ahly had its own fan movement that was separate from the sycophantic organisations that tried as hard as possible to 'suck up to the board'. They had a lot of things to rail against, but Zamalek was at the apex.

'In the past Zamalek used to be the bourgeois club, and Ahly the people's club, although that's changed a little these days,' explained Assad. Zamalek, however, still couldn't shake the foreigner tag which had existed for over 100 years. 'Now we mock them and say they are the door tenders club because it has such popularity amongst Sudanese security guards. Seriously. They still think they are high-class.'

As we neared the ground, I asked Assad why Ahly were so popular today. 'The two biggest political parties in Egypt are Ahly and Zamalek', he said. 'It's bigger than politics. It's more about escapism. The average Ahly fan is a guy who lives in a one-bedroom flat with his wife, mother-in-law and five kids. And he is getting paid minimum wage and his life sucks. The only good thing about his life is that for two hours on a Friday he goes in the stadium to watch Ahly. That's why it is such an obligation to win every game. It makes people's lives happy. We are probably the only club in the world where we [the fans] expect to win every single game. Ahly is the only thing that makes people happy.'

And with the frustrations of modern life came the inevitable violence. 'You're asking the right people!' Assad exclaimed. 'Between Ahly and Zamalek the stadium is segregated now so we don't meet and with so many police it's difficult. So we take another route and the violence happens in all sports. There is attacking each other's buses or going to the basketball derby between Ahly and Zamalek.'

Mohammed, who with his large beard, baggy fatigues and baseball cap, looked like an East Coast stoner, agreed. 'Egypt is like a police state, they [the police] are the most powerful institution in Egypt without doubt,' he said as we got out of the car. 'So you can't even reach a Zamalek fan, but you can be as open as you like and say what you like in the stadium.'

It became clear as we pulled into the stadium what he meant. Thousands of black unformed riot officers stood menacingly as a deterrent from the main road up to the stadium entrance. Plain-clothed security officers in dark glasses darted between them, asking suspicious-looking fans for their ID papers and tickets. Twenty thousand fans were already inside Cairo's national stadium chanting songs against their hated rivals: 'You are the white bitches', and the catchy 'Come on, come on, come on, fuck the mother of Zamalek'.

The Ultras took their usual place at the back of the lower stand and discussed the best way of unwrapping their vast flag, the highlight of their achievements thus far. The stadium's huge electronic screen fluttered into life. There was Ayman, his face now the size of a bus, talking the audience and the crowd through great moments from AhlyZamalek derbies of old, many concerning his input as a player.

The Ahly fans jeered and whistled when they saw him appear. 'He was good, but he was always fat,' retorted Mohammed as the rest of the Ultras, now 50-strong and rapidly growing, broke into hysterics. The reverie was broken by the piercing sound of the call to prayer. The more devout rushed to the nearest piece of flat ground next to the popcorn sellers. In the absence of a prayer mat, they used their Ahly flags instead. The Ultras launched their flag. It was vast, far bigger than anything else at the ground, and provoked rapturous applause from the Ahly fans. Assad looked on proudly at his creation, his little piece of Milano that he'd brought to Ahly's terraces. It was the last time I saw him smiling.

From the minute the whistle was blown, it was clear that Ahly was in trouble, playing like a team that had made nine changes and had no coach. Shikabala was everywhere, first to every ball, no doubt spurred on by the abuse hurled down on him. By the time he had helped Zamalek take a two-goal lead, he was on his knees, bowing in front of Ahly's fans, infuriating the Ultras and sparking Assad's outrage.

'Why do Ahly hate him so much?' I managed to ask amid the uproar. 'He is pure Zamalek,' spat Assad. 'I had a run-in with him once, when he was playing for the under-20s. There's always horrible fights there. I was by the tunnel and I heard Shikabala say bad things about Ahly so I spat in his face. He tried to slap me so for three months we chanted: 'I'm going to beat Shikabala, the cunt, I'm going to beat him in the face.' I heard he wants to get me but I'll just beat him up with my car and he'll never play again.'

It seemed to sum up Egyptian football. Hatred, spitting and violence at youth matches. Egyptian rage had spread wherever it could find a weakness. It explained why a ring of riot policemen carrying shields and helmets had circumnavigated the stadium.

The second goal had started to divide a fan base unaccustomed to losing.

'It's only one loss,' a man in a suit offered.

'One loss!' shouted Assad, before admonishing him for his low standards.

A Nubian Egyptian, his head piled high with a sloppily arranged head scarf, shrugged and pointed at the sky: 'I hate Ahly, but what can I do?'

The game ended 2–0. Ahly was vanquished for only the second time in three years. Yet the fans didn't recognise the defeat. As Zamalek paraded in a lap of honour, Ahly's fans refused to leave, screaming out their chants louder than before, over and over again: '1, 2, 3, 4, 5, 6, Ahly!'

Bottles and cans rained down onto the thin black line of police, there to keep the Ultras from the pitch. A bottle fizzed past my nose and cracked on the shield of a policeman cowering under the barrage. An unknown signal ushered the crowd outside and the jeering, seething mass, thousands strong, rolled out of the stadium. Momentarily, I was on my own. Fights broke out between police and fans. Fists flew and blood was spilt, but still the fans marched on, chanting: 'Ahly, Ahly.'

Assad, Mohammed and the Ultras were nowhere to be seen as the mob carried us out of the stadium towards the main road, too big even for the phalanx of near-by riot policemen to contain. I spotted a gap in the crowd where the Ultras were waiting, panting.

'It's going crazy around there, we smashed up Zamalek's team bus and managed to get away,' Assad boasted, although not entirely convincingly.

From the muddy patch to the side of the concourse the human river of red rumbled defiantly, and noisily, on. Ayman Younis was right. Whatever the result, Cairo was always going to be painted red.

We stood in the sand car park until the last of the crowd passed by and the Ultras packed their banner back into the car. They had lost, but claimed an immoral victory by deciding to celebrate by getting some beer and getting stoned.

'Until the 1980s it was virtually legal,' laughed Mohammed. 'Everyone smoked it; Muslims, Christians, but even now the police don't care as long as you don't make trouble. My last dealer? Man, he was a sheikh from a local mosque.'

We drove back through Cairo's thick, polluted air to Assad's flat. Rather than arriving at a modest apartment, the car pulled up in front of a walled compound, complete with guards. We sat in Assad's flat watching famous Egyptian movies from the 1960s.

'You look at any Arab television channel at 7pm,' explained Assad. 'Eighty per cent of the films or programmes are from Egypt. We've been making films for 100 years. All the musicians are Egyptian too.'

The Saudis had an authority bequeathed by Mecca and Medina; the other Gulf states have fabulous oil wealth; the Iranians have the legacy of the Persian empire, of poetry and literature; the catchphrase of the tourist board of Syria was 'The Cradle of Civilisation'; the Iraqis had Baghdad and its history of advances in astrology and medicine.

The Egyptians too had a glorious past. A common refrain, as Ayman had told me, was: 'I'm not African, I'm not Arab, I'm Pharaonic.' Modern Egypt had degenerated under the weight of poverty, nepotism and dictatorship, but at 7pm every night the last proof of the country's cultural greatness was there for everyone to see.

By 3am it was time to leave the Ultras and head home. Outside I stood on the pavement and tried to hail a cab. The bookshop behind me was covered in posters of Osama Hosny. His almost-handsome face and ginger hair was advertising his latest tape singing the passages from the Koran that had made him even more famous. I got into a taxi and left Cairo. I had presumed that it was the last time I would hear of Assad and his Ultras. But no. The young men I had met that day would play their part in one of the most seismic shifts in the modern history of the region, and help reshape a new Egypt.

But I didn't know that yet as the driver smoothly drove his way around Cairo's dead streets. We both sat in silence.

'Ahly or Zamalek?' I finally asked him.

'Ahly,' the driver replied.

Of course he was.

2
QATAR

January 2005

Manfred Hoener was nowhere to be seen. The German football coach had agreed to meet me at Doha International Airport but, after running around the brand new arrivals terminal for an hour asking anyone vaguely blond, over five-foot-ten or with a square jaw whether they were the only person in the country who could save me from a night of vagrancy, I had started to become desperate. By 9.30pm, and with the last stragglers from my inbound Dubai flight leaving the hall in the smug knowledge that they would indeed be lying down under a roof, with air con, I still had no idea what Manfred Hoener looked like. I'd even begun to doubt his existence.

Manfred had assumed something of a mythical status in my world. We had first made contact with each other when I came across an old story in the Scottish newspaper, the *Daily Record*. They had reported that legendary Dutch World Cup midfielder Ronald De Boer was close to signing a shock, big money deal for one last huzzah after falling out of favour at Glasgow Rangers. But rather than choose one of a host of ambitious mid-table Premiership teams like Tottenham or Aston Villa, he had opted to decamp to the footballing powerhouse of Qatar on a whopping tax-free salary, with a nice villa and all-year-round sunshine. And he wasn't the first. Dozens of players, Gabriel Batistuta, Christophe Dugary, Claudio Caniggia, Sonny Anderson and Romario, to name a few, had gone before him to play football in a country where the local population was just under a million, the stadiums were rarely even quarter-full and the nearest neighbours for your forthcoming pre-season friendlies would be insurgent-riddled Saudi Arabia or soon-to-be-nuclear Iran. Still, Ron wasn't upset in the slightest. In fact, he had managed to talk his brother Frank into joining him in the ageing footballer exodus east. Or, more accurately, Manfred Hoener had convinced Ronald De Boer to convince his brother to join him in the ageing footballer exodus east.

Hoener was, according to the *Daily Record*, Qatar's 'Mr Fix it', the man who worked on behalf of the Qatar FA to bring high profile, big name players nearing the end of their careers to the tiny Gulf state to play in the Q League, no expense spared. His success had been legion, tempting players who could expect at least a season or two more in Spain's La Liga or the English Premier League to give up their plush cosmopolitan lifestyles in some of the world's greatest cities to move to Doha, a city of such monumental dullness that the US military based their entire Asian Central Command, CENTCoM, here. After all, if your troops have nowhere to rip apart after a few Budweisers on the town, you're unlikely to upset the locals. The man was quite clearly a genius, or a retired double-glazing salesman – or both – and I had arranged to meet him at the airport in the hope he could put me in touch with some of his success stories. But he clearly had more important things to do. As I sat on the deserted kerb outside Doha International Airport in the oppressive humidity, I cursed his father's good name and wondered whether Ronald De Boer had been in the same position just weeks earlier, gently perspiring into his Armani suit as he stalked the arrivals lounge looking for the illusive Herr Hoener.

Manfred was supposed to escort me to a Q League match that night to see one of his charges in action. Pep Guardiola, the cultured Catalan midfielder who would soon become the world's best regarded coach at Barcelona, was, for now, turning out for Al Ahli Doha. I could, Manfred reasoned, catch up with Pep after the game and interview him then. The interview was the last thing on my mind but in desperation I jumped into a shabby, orange and white Datsun taxi and took the short ride to Al Ahli's stadium.

It was immediately clear something was wrong. The floodlights were on but there was no sound. The stadium was a huge concrete bowl that had probably never seen the tens of thousands of fans that could fill it up. Inside the main foyer was abuzz with obscenely tall Qatari teenagers who had just finished playing basketball. If any football had taken place here, I'd missed it. But then, from behind the boys, came a man, striding towards me with a maniacal grin, arm outstretched. He was a big, perma-tanned, silver-haired fox with a handshake like a malfunctioning robot and not unlike a Teutonic Robert Kilroy-Silk.

'Yes, yes, I'm sorry, but the interview is off,' he spat in a manner that confusingly seemed to be both dismissive and friendly at the same time. 'The team was playing in Morocco and got caught in the worst snowstorms in 20 years.' Snowstorms? In North Africa? I'd clearly underestimated Manfred. 'Never mind, I will drive you to a hotel.'

On the way downtown Manfred regaled me with his life story. In coaching terms he was something of a journeyman, a figure you often came across when at the coal face of international football. He had travelled three continents coaching football since he took his first job teaching Peruvian jungle kids the finer technique of the beautiful game in the 1960s. Today he was arguably the most important person in Qatari football. 'Yes, yes, it's all very good but the head, he doesn't want to talk to the press. But I don't tell him! Ha!'

Hoener's boss was the head of the Qatari National Olympic Committee, Sheikh Tamim bin Hammad, a member of the all powerful Al Thani rulling family. Between them they oversaw an odd transfer system where the committee directed Manfred to sign the players they wanted and then, in turn, doled them out to the clubs that deserved them. Manfred seemed to revel in his dissent, giving out a little whoop as we approached my shabby hotel.

'OK, OK. Call me tomorrow and we'll arrange something with Marcel.'

Tomorrow I was to meet Manfred's greatest triumph thus far, the crowning glory of all his veteran baiting achievements: French World Cup winner Marcel Desailly.

Manfred had told me to go right at the mangled car on a podium. I hadn't a clue what he meant until my taxi dropped me off in front of a gleaming new shopping mall. Outside a large podium overlooked a roundabout. Atop sat a mangled car from a fatal car accident, a shock tactic to encourage young Qataris to stop speeding in their powerful 4x4s. It was one of the unfortunate by-products of the Gulf's explosion of oil and gas wealth, a macabre metaphor reflecting one version of the region's own breakneck political, economic and social development over the past decade: too much, too young.

All I could see for miles around was flat, shimmering desert. Qatar didn't have much variety in terrain. The tiny Gulf state is almost 100 per cent desert and has the heat to match – in summer, the thermometer rarely drops below 40 degrees. Each road seemed to lead into a mirage of nothingness. I chose one at random and walked under the blazing midday sun. Soon a gleaming new stadium loomed into view – the ground of Al Gharafa. For one season at least it was to be Marcel Desailly's home. The ground was magnificent, a steel-and-glass edifice that wouldn't have looked out of place in Manchester, Munich or Marseilles. But there was something of the Marie Celeste about it: a beautiful ship prepared for a sumptuous feast, in the middle of nowhere with no sign of life. The place was deserted but rather stranger was the fact that I could just walk into the ground of the biggest club in the country and poke around the changing rooms and offices totally unmolested. This despite the fact that

Qatar was high up on the Foreign Office's list of places likely to experience a terrorist attack, in one of the most volatile regions of the world. In Europe I'd have been garrotted by a phalanx of burly security guards before I'd even got out of the taxi.

Eventually a curious secretary revealed that the players would be back from training any minute and that I should wait in the canteen. The players streamed in – largely African men in their early 20s sprinkled with a few Arab players – for their buffet lunch of chicken and rice before the star attraction arrived. Quietly and without a word to the other players, Marcel filled his plate, retired to a table on his own and silently went about chewing on the gristly meat. I watched for a while, too nervous to approach him at first. He looked lonely in his training ground tracksuit – stripped of fame – yet aesthetically appearing no different from the Desailly that had picked up the World Cup for France in 1998. It was as if, rather than moving to the Middle East for one last bumper pay day, this was the place where football souls came to die.

'Sit down. I don't mind if you eat with me.' After staring at him for so long that other players were beginning to think I was some kind of infatuated stalker, I plucked up the courage to pick up a plate, slop on some of the goo and invite myself for lunch with Desailly. I tried asking him politely why he had come out here, into the heat and the nothingness. Although, after years of media training in Italy and England, the subtext was clear: why are you wasting what was left of your career by playing in the middle of nowhere in a league where you're head and shoulders above your teammates?

'Well, I would say it's no different from the second tier in a European league,' he replied, smiling. Clearly it was an incredulous query he had fielded a lot. 'I was offered the chance to be coach of the Ghanaian national team but I could follow my passion, being paid what I was earning at Chelsea, and I said: 'Yes, why not?'' New experience, new people, new traditions, another mentality, a sunny place.'

And in Qatari terms, Marcel was thriving. Gharafa was top of the league and with Desailly being the most technically gifted player within a thousand-mile radius, he had begun to loosen the defensive shackles and maraud up field, playing as an attacking midfielder and scoring regularly.

The Qataris loved him. As I was getting ready for our meeting in the hotel, the local television station was replaying Desailly's two headed goals from the weekend over and over and over. But Desailly – a French Catholic who found himself in a staunchly Sunni Muslim emirate – was finding it a little hard to get used to.

'I am surprised when they go to pray,' he said. 'I never knew that Ramadan was so respected. It's the little details you discover. Training is at six o'clock and I am on the field ready to train and there's nobody – why? Because they are praying. Little things like that. But you have to accept it because it's their traditions and culture without judging them. We are not in Europe. I realised that they are not really lazy. I thought I was going to get into a country where, you know, maybe sometimes in Africa you get lazy and relaxed. They are kind of lazy. But here they are still motivated to do things. And also they are really educated. I thought I was going to come to a country where they didn't really care. You are from Europe, you are stupid, they speak badly to you. But no.'

Despite Marcel's protestations something didn't sit right. He just didn't look like the brash, chin-thrusting central defender that had smothered wave after wave of attacks in the red and black of AC Milan and latterly the blue and white of Chelsea. But then it became clear why. Anywhere else but on the football pitch, things weren't going well.

'My family, they're in France,' he said. 'I had moved from England to France to settle down but then I signed for Qatar and thought about moving everybody here, the kids, wife, nanny. I have a great wife and my last-born is six months old. I wanted to enjoy it and be with him because with my career I really didn't have the time to give to my kids. But my wife saw that I needed to play on. She said: 'Go on, we lose one year and we'll gain twenty.' People are working until they are 55-years-old and I can give up after one year and start a new life.'

I wasn't surprised to hear that six months later, Marcel had quit Qatar and gone back home to France. After all, he was here for the same reason that 80 per cent of Qatar's population – mostly labourers from the Indian subcontinent who build the country's stadiums, skyscrapers and hotels – were here: to put hardship away from your family to one side, save your wages and send them back in hope of a better future. Qatar is a transitory place, whether you're a world famous footballer or an Indian taxi driver. I was even more surprised to read that, with Portsmouth struggling to survive in the Premier League, returning manager Harry Redknapp had enquired as to Marcel's availability, in the hope that the Frenchman would plug the gaps in his leaky defence. Marcel even considered it, albeit briefly.

As I left the dinner table and thanked him for his hospitality, I asked about such a scenario: what if a European club came back in for you, as Bolton did when they signed former Real Madrid great Fernando Hierro from the Qatari wilderness. Surely you'd give all this up in a shot?

'No, not at my age,' he replied. 'It's finished for me. I realised that I still wanted to play football and that's why I came here. But I would go back to Europe for what? I know everything from Europe. The crowd, the pressure. I did it for 20 years and it's enough. It's enough.'

One thing Desailly was worried about were the rumblings over the Arabian Gulf in Iran. The Iranians, and pretty much everyone else in the world, call the stretch of water separating Persia from the Arab Middle East, two empires that badly disguise a certain degree of dislike for each other, the Persian Gulf and wranglings over its name had got to the diplomatic level. Iran threatened to pull out of the 2006 Asian Games in Doha due to the fact that the event's promotional material called it the Arabian Gulf. Regardless of the gulf (ahem) in agreement, the distance between Qatar and Iran is short and the election of firebrand ex-Tehran mayor Mahmoud Ahmadinejad – an avowed Shiite who proclaimed that, much like George W. Bush, God had guided him to the presidency – had got pulses racing from Yemen to Iraq, not least as one of his first dictates was to restate Iran's right to nuclear power.

In Qatar, Ahmadinejad's chest beating was felt more keenly than anywhere else in the Gulf. The country had only existed as an independent entity since 1971. When the British pulled out of the Gulf, Qatar had a decision to make: join the Emirates of Dubai and Abu Dhabi, amongst others, that had made up the tiny Trucial coast in a pan-Gulf Arab union, or go it alone. Qatar chose independence. The bulbous outcrop that juts out into the Gulf, dwarfing nearby Bahrain, wasn't the richest of Arab states as it didn't have the oil reserves of neighbours in the newly formed United Arab Emirates or the economic and military might of Saudi Arabia. But whilst the West allowed Saudi Arabia to degenerate – economically and politically – in a corrupt, oil-funded fog that helped sow the seeds of Islamic militancy and gave birth to Osama Bin Laden and Al Qaeda, Qatar took a far more enlightened route to development.

Since independence the country had been ruled by Emir Khalifa bin Hamad al-Thani, a playboy who didn't rock the boat, kept a tight lid on any dissent and spent most of his time holidaying in Switzerland. It was on one of his jaunts to the Swiss Alps in 1995 that his idealistic eldest son, Hamad bin Khalifa al-Thani, decided that he was tired of waiting for his old man to die and seized control of the country in a bloodless palace coup. Internecine warfare and benevolent dictators aren't unusual in this part of the world but what was surprising was the path that the new Emir decided to take. One of Emir Thani's first moves was to abolish the Ministry of Information – effectively ending direct censorship in the country. Not content with that, he decided to bankroll Al Jazeera, a new state-owned television network that wouldn't be hamstrung by the clumsy censoring of its Middle Eastern brethren, infuriating his neighbours – and later its allies in the West – with its uncompromising reporting. The money came from Qatar's newly found gas deposits which overnight thrust them to the top of the world's GDP per capita chart. Even more surprising was his decision to introduce limited democracy to Qatar – becoming the first Gulf state to grant universal suffrage – whilst hosting a US military base on its northern shore. The Qataris had also came across a cunning plan. Rather than pump billions into expensive advertising campaigns, allow sport to promote your country's brand for you. The UAE, and especially Dubai, has been particularly successful in doing this, hosting the world's most expensive horse race – the Dubai World Cup; a PGA tour event where Tiger Woods regularly appeared; and the Dubai Tennis Championship, where Roger Federer turned up every year to pick up his trophy with depressing regularity.

Thanks in no small part to celebrity sporting endorsements, Dubai had put itself on the map and, jealously coveting its success, Qatar decided to follow suit with its own tennis championship (another glorified Federer coronation); golf tournament; and, most importantly of all, its star-packed football league. It even managed to win the bid to host the 2006 Asian Games, the smallest country ever to do so. So proud were they of their Asian Games achievement that they threw billions of gas dollars into developing sport in the country, building the dozen or so brand new, gleaming stadiums that each Doha-based club now played in. The jewel in the crown was to be the Aspire academy, which – if the spin was to be believed – hoped to be the biggest, most comprehensive incubator for sporting talent in the world, all hosted in the state-of-the-art, Wembley-esque, 45,000-seater Khalifa Stadium.

What the Qataris hoped to achieve most out of the investment, and the presence of superstar footballers, was to qualify for the World Cup. Languishing close to three figures on the FIFA rankings and struggling in their qualifying group for Germany 2006, it was a tall order, but Manfred and the Qatari FA reasoned that the influx of talented, experienced foreigners could only improve Qatar's national players in their push towards the finals. And if that failed they could always attempt to buy players to play for the national team. After scoring for fun in the Bundesliga for Werder Bremen, Brazilian striker Ailton was approached by the Qatari FA to take up Qatari citizenship – taking advantage of FIFA's then relaxed rules on nationality – in exchange for a huge pay cheque. After being inexplicably shunned by the Brazilians, Ailton was seriously considering it. At 29, he didn't have many more shots at playing in the World Cup. The national coach at the time, Frenchman Philippe Troussier, was in favour. '[Naturalisation was] probably the only means to one day qualify Qatar for a World Cup,' he told French newspaper *L'Equipe*. 'Naturalisations are nothing new to Qatar, 80 per cent of my squad were not born in Qatar.' FIFA, appalled that a rudimentary transfer system akin to club football was developing, stamped down on the practice – much to the embarrassment of the Qataris.

Given his expertise in this field, you sensed that if a forensic accountant went through the paperwork, Manfred's fingerprints would be all over it. The surreal meeting with Marcel in Gharafa's futuristic stadium had made me wonder about some of the other players who had come out to Qatar. Surely money wasn't the only thing that had persuaded them all to move themselves and their families to within an hour's flight of Baghdad? I decided to phone Manfred and see if he could hook me up with anybody else.

'Yes, yes, I know Gabriel [Batistuta] is in the country, maybe you can call him. But be careful, he hates journalists,' he helpfully offered before handing out Batistuta's mobile number anyway. 'You should speak to Ronald [De Boer] as well. He's very friendly.'

There's a strange slowness to Qatar that doesn't seem to affect the other Gulf states. Whilst the hyperactive capitalism of Dubai and the rest of UAE would appear in a neoliberals' wet dream, and with Bahrain racked with poverty and internal political struggles between the Sunni royal family and its restless Shia majority, life in Qatar is quieter, more spread out and far more relaxed. Certainly that's how Ronald De Boer had found it.

'There are some great golf courses here and I play with Batistuta, Guardiola, Frank LeBoeuf, my brother, every week,' he said. 'It's great fun. You feel safe in the country and there's no pressure. The papers aren't on you every day. And anyway, it's in Arabic, so you can't read what they say!'

Ronald De Boer chortled into his delicate porcelain cup at his last joke, as if his ignorance of the world's fourth biggest language was a pre-conceived foolproof way of avoiding bad press. With Batistuta's phone off, I'd speculatively called him and was surprised when he had agreed to meet me straight away for a cup of tea in the lobby of the Ritz Carlton hotel. Obviously he was at a loose end. But rather than seem glum, resigned and insular like Marcel had earlier, Ronald had adjusted to the role of the rich, Western expat with too much time on his hands rather easily.

'The life here, I love it,' he said. 'Dubai is nearby and that's like New York. For me if I could get another year and move to Dubai for another two I would love to do it.' Ronald was happily playing for Rangers when the first call from Manfred came and, after agreeing to bring his brother Frank with him, they signed lucrative two-year contracts. The football, he explained, wasn't exactly La Liga standard but his team Al Rayyan could give most Scottish teams a run for their money. 'The standard is a little bit higher in Scotland but I don't think any of the lower teams would beat us. I must say, when I look at Rangers now, I think they might struggle against us,' he said. 'I mean, the last game we played to 12,000 people, and then you play some weak teams and only your wife and mother-in-law turn up. But they have some big rivalries like Al Rayyan versus Al Sadd. Sadd is like Ajax and Rayyan more Feyenoord, more with the working-class people, whilst Al Sadd is from the upper-class people. They don't have hooligans, though. They all want to make music.'

Clearly, Ronald and Frank were loving their new surroundings, and the proximity of some of the most dangerous countries in the world didn't faze them. But Qatar offered them both something much more than money, although it clearly helped. It was a chance to play without the intense pressure they had known all their lives, from the media, from the fans and from their managers; pressure that had defined – sometimes for good, sometimes for ill – the most productive years of their careers.

'After all those years of pressure, it makes sense,' Ronald explained, finishing his tea and smoothing down his expensive jeans. 'Of course your level goes down at the end of your career. I've had six operations on my knee and can now only bend it half-way. I couldn't crouch down properly even when I was at Barcelona for the team photograph. Here you get well paid and do what you like, no stress. Of course it's a graveyard of European footballers at the end of their careers. I don't want to make myself crazy with a second ranked team [in Europe]. They expect so much from you because you are their big star and you probably can't do it. But why do that when you can come here and relax?'

Losing one's motivation for the beautiful game through injury, time, or bitterness is an inevitable part of a footballer's evolutionary cycle. But as someone who never had the talent to even hold down a regular berth in my primary school's starting XI something still rankled that these talented individuals had chosen not to nobly play for one final shot at meaningful glory but instead had taken the safe option for anonymity and a large pay cheque. Perhaps it was my latent rancour that Gabriel Batistuta had picked up on when I called him later that night from my hotel room.

'Hello Gabriel, Manfred Hoener has given me your number, I'm a journalist...', I regaled authoritatively, before being cut down. Gabriel couldn't quite hide his anger.

'Manfred Hoener? Gragghh!'

With that strangled scream, somewhere between rage and incredulity, Batistuta hung up and turned his phone off, lest I had the temerity to attempt to speak to him again. Later I discovered that he never played in Qatar again. Perhaps the phone call was the straw that broke the camel's back, although by the sound of it things clearly weren't going well for Gabriel in Qatar – Manfred earlier complained that Batistuta had missed numerous league games on trips back to Argentina for treatment on a spurious 'injury'. Even the prospect of his weekly golf treat with Ronald, Frank and the boys wasn't enough to keep him there. Despite the money, privacy and his well-practised snake oil spiel, Manfred Hoener had at least one very unhappy customer.

November 2005

Television fools the mind's ability to judge distance and size. In Top Gun, for instance, Tom Cruise strides around like a six-foot, jet-flying colossus. It's only when you see him in real life, or up against something like a phone box that gives you a hint of relativity, that you realise that he's little taller than a garden gnome. The one person this does not apply to is Diego Armando Maradona. Maradona was standing on a football pitch in Qatar looking short and sheepish. A ten-year-old Qatari boy lay prone on the floor in front of him clutching his ankle in agony with tears in his eyes. Diego's curly mop of hair barely grazed the referee's nipples as he was given a telling off for his reckless and slightly inappropriate tackle. He was every bit as small as you imagined he was from those images of football tournaments in balmy, faraway lands. But his presence on the pitch was nothing short of a miracle. There are some things as a football fan you have resigned yourself to never seeing. Bobby Moore effortlessly ushering out an overhit through ball, Puskas tormenting a pack of defenders, Beckenbauer marauding across the pitch. But watching Maradona play football again was at the top, especially given that a few months earlier it appeared that the Argentine legend was not long for this earth.

His was the classic man-plays-game; man-conquers-game; man-takes-Herculean-quantities-of-drugs-shoots-journalists-and-balloons-to-the-size-of-an-ox   footballing story. After being slung out of USA 1994 for failing a drugs test, Maradona went into free-fall, unable to deal with his dwindling talent and no longer able to scratch a living from the game he had been obsessed with since fighting his way out of a Buenos Aires barrio 25 years previously. He had tried his hand at management in Argentina, business ventures, even endorsements, but nothing sat right. By the turn of the 21st century, Maradona was morbidly obese, snorting lines of cocaine every morning and was seemingly just a Cuban cigar away from an inevitable coronary. With his heart unable to take the strain of ten extra stone, nor the quantities of cocaine that could kill an elephant, Maradona had two heart attacks. Lying in the hospital and at his lowest ebb, salvation came from an unlikely source: Cuban dictator Fidel Castro. The pair had been friends for years, both sharing a fiery brand of left-wing politics and a mutual loathing for what they saw as American imperialism in South America. Sensing that his old friend was at death's door, Fidel offered to fly Diego to Cuba for a stomach stapling operation. Within weeks the Diego that had resembled a zeppelin had been replaced by a Diego that was svelte, half the size, and once again looking like the tiny wizard that had lit up two World Cups and disgraced a third. It was the start of a long road to recovery that would see him embrace the world of television, fronting his own hit talk show entitled 'The Night Of The Ten', a reference to his famous number ten shirt, which embraced hard-left politics. But the apex of his recovery was here, on a football pitch in Qatar, where he was once again kicking a ball, and young children, in anger.

At first I thought the email was a joke: Maradona and Pele, it read, would both be present in Qatar to open a new sports academy. Usually such an honour would be reserved for government ministers, or even minor royalty. But somehow someone, somewhere, had persuaded two of the world's most famous sportsmen to come to a quiet, inoffensive country in the Middle East to open the Aspire academy, a glorified leisure centre. For the first time in months I thought of Manfred. Surely not even Manfred could have pulled this one off. Could he? The Qataris had pulled out all the stops to get them. Both were rumoured to have been paid half a million dollars just to turn up and the region's press would be flown in to witness the pair share a stage, putting their enmity behind them to discuss the footballing issues of the day. Qatar's policy of pumping huge sums into sport seemed to be continuing as normal. Yet the country had changed since my last visit ten months previously. Six weeks after I'd left Manfred, Desailly and the De Boer brothers, Omar Ahmed Abdullah – a seemingly normal, friendly Egyptian computer programmer – packed his 4x4 with explosives and rammed into the Doha Players Theatre. Qatar's first suicide bombing killed one person and injured scores more. When viewed against the daily three-figure casualty numbers from Iraq, a single death in Qatar seemed tragically insignificant. But it had a far more damaging effect on Qatar's psyche. It shattered the idyllic complacency that had allowed life to go on as normal as the states around it degenerated into an internecine anarchy. It was clear that Qatar had lost something of its innocence.

Every hotel now had metal detectors at its front door and huge concrete barriers had been universally erected to prevent suicide bombers from approaching by car. The government had been particularly worried that the bombing would jeopardise its huge investment in sporting set pieces, not least its hosting of the 2006 Asian Games, and had responded with police state measures to ensure that the bombing wasn't repeated. All this didn't seem to bother Maradona much as he careered around the Aspire training pitch, looking ten years younger than his forty-one, slide tackling boys a quarter of his age and still getting aerated enough to argue with the referee even though it was a kick around with kids.

It was a Damascene recovery. Sure, some of his pace was gone, but that un-mistakable, blurry-legged, barrel-chested gait was still there. He even had time to instinctively punch the ball into the net, much to the whooping delight of the English journalists assembled. I doubt they gave him the same honour when God intervened to score in the same manner against England in Mexico 20 years previously. Just as Fenwick and Butcher did back in 1986, the Qatari children looked on incredulously. Yet Maradona's impish charm beguiled all who encountered him – presidents, states-men, royalty, even English journalists – which was never more evident than when, sweating from the 20-minute-long exertion, he decided to sign some autographs. The circle around him grew as Arab men in flowing white *dish dashas* and the previously restrained press corps literally threw children out of their path to get to their hero, to touch him, to feel his sweat on their hands. Eventually security guards had to intervene and hauled Maradona out of the ruck, beaming with the knowledge that – whatever FIFA thought – he was still number one. This issue had preoccupied him for some time. When FIFA offered the public the chance to vote for their player of the century, Maradona won hands down. But FIFA, fearing Maradona's exalted position would set a bad example to the kids, chose to give the award to Pele as well. Maradona was furious, debate raged from Sao Paulo to Manila and the two men's already strained relationship was all but destroyed. It consumed Maradona, giving him the impetus to turn his life around and to claim the legacy he saw as rightfully his.

'Who is the greatest? My mother says it's me. And you should always believe your mother,' he joked. The crowd of a dozen or so journalists ignited into spontaneous, sycophantic laughter. Maradona, now wearing a casual shirt and jeans, sat in front of us, slumped in a chair the same way a wayward schoolboy would confrontationally sit in the headmaster's office after he'd set fire to a classroom. He smiled at his ability to make a room of educated middle-aged men fawn at his feet and nonchalantly an-swered questions about football, drugs and his former life as a very fat man. Maradona was articulate in a rough, uncomplicated kind of way. After years of being barracked by the press, you would have thought that he would come across as guarded, even reticent. But he was the exact opposite, sitting for an hour talking about everything from Argentina's chances in the World Cup to how, despite all the money in the game, he would still choose to play for Napoli if he was 21 today. His most interesting mo-ments came when he talked politics, openly criticising George W. Bush for the war in Iraq. '[Hugo] Chavez, Fidel [Castro] and Che Guevara they fought for their people, to give them more equality [and] they fought against the United States and anyone who fights against the US is good for me,' he said when asked about the influence of his friend Fidel.

Maradona famously has a tattoo of Che on his shoulder. Most thought it a pretty adornment rather than a deep affinity with left-wing politics. But they were wrong. 'I was at the summit in Argentina two weeks ago and I know Bush commanded the [Iraq] war from Qatar,' he said when asked about his antipathy towards America and the presence of a US military base in Qatar. 'But I support Qatar and an assassin is an assassin anywhere. Every country has the freedom to make its own laws and make a decision and you must respect that. So even if he leaves Qatar, an assassin can kill from everywhere.'

Pele, on the other hand, had a strangely subdued reception. He arrived at the training pitch where Maradona had previously wowed hundreds of onlookers with his newfound fitness in an electrically powered golf cart. He wore a powder blue 1970s safari suit that he'd obviously kept from his New York Cosmos days. We've got so used to seeing the replays of his magnificent career that you can forget that Brazil's greatest player is now a pensioner. He gingerly disembarked and wandered aimlessly around the pitch. He was too frail to kick a ball. Instead small crowds of middle-aged men politely queued for his autograph. Compared to the histrionics of the previous day, you'd have thought that the Qataris had wheeled out a minor character in world football, but Pele had become strangely accustomed to indifference in recent years. Despite leading an exemplary life on and off the pitch as a clean cut, family-loving ambassador for the game – and a flawless example to generations of footballers – even his countrymen hadn't been totally convinced by him. In Brazil he was mocked for not being very bright, lambasted for a disastrous but well-meaning tenure as Brazilian sports minister and derided for signing up to be the face of Viagra in Brazil. He quickly withdrew his support when the press began to question his virility. His press conference was half full, cut short after 15 minutes. Officially, the Emir wanted to see the two of them for lunch. Unofficially, it provided a handy escape route.

Whilst Pele inexplicably struggled to win hearts and minds, Maradona's failings were all but forgotten. Maybe it's because a flawed genius is someone who we can more easily empathise with. Maradona is one of us: flawed and fallible. Or maybe it's because his fallibility still leaves room for speculation. Pele had become everything he could possibly have been. But for Maradona, the same question still lingered, even after his myriad successes in the game. What could he still have become?

The lights dimmed, the crowd already in their seats waiting for the main event. In the main hall of Qatar's Aspire Zone the local dignitaries in their white *dish dashas* chattered in animated Arabic at the front whilst journalists and photographers crowded around the hastily erected stage. Qatar's policy of sporting investment was about to reach its apex. First, Pele modestly sauntered in. Polite applause followed. Then Maradona entered. Perhaps it was the rabid welcoming from the crowd, or the fact that the spotlight sparkled off his white suit jacket adorned with bright silver thread, but Maradona's entrance tasted like a coronation. And then the two shook hands. A thousand flashes followed, capturing the moment when Pele and Diego buried the hatchet. Except this wasn't the moment they really buried the hatchet. Pele had been Maradona's first guest on his talk show debut earlier that year. There wasn't any real warmth in their reconciliation but the Pele and Maradona show had become big business and useful for both men: a vehicle for Maradona's rehabilitation and an opportunity for Pele to counter his detractors. Both were handsomely rewarded for their time.

Maradona admitted as much when the discussion started – a supposedly adversarial 'debate' on sportsmanship. Presumably the Qataris had hoped that Pele would represent the fair-minded professional, with Maradona taking the role of the Machiavellian magician, willing to bend the rules and invoke God to get the right result.

'We just never clicked,' admitted Maradona, glancing over at Pele. 'We always rubbed each other up the wrong way. We would see each other and sparks would fly.' He kicked out against the press that hounded him and the football authorities that doubted his ability. 'I was addicted . . . drugging myself. Then I would play football without sleeping, eating or even drinking water,' he said, getting increasingly irate. 'The media really only emphasised my drug addiction – they wanted a drugs story. All they wanted to do was publicise drugs. They wanted to kill Maradona and I make no apologies for my behaviour to the press.' His behaviour related to the time he tried to shoot a couple of Argentine journalists, who had been stationed outside his house. But then Maradona exceeded himself, comparing himself to the one person less popular than George W. Bush amongst the crowd. 'To defend my family I will become Bin Laden. And if that's what it takes I'll become the fiercest human being on the planet.'

Everyone took an intake of breath, Maradona looked at Pele and they both laughed. The rest of the crowd laughed with them. The debate finished and, sensing that Qatar was unlikely to see the two greatest footballers of the 20th century ever again, the crowd rushed the stage. The crush pressed in on Maradona. On the left of the stage Pele stood on his own. The crowd clambered onto the stage and surrounded Maradona desperate for one last signature. A white-robed Qatari with a walkie-talkie manfully tried to hold back the hordes, screaming for the crowd to get back. The stage was buckling under the collective weight of the scrum. Diego's unkempt hair poked up from the mess, the rest buried in a sea of adoring fans. Pele was being ushered away. Not for the first time in Pele's life, not even for the first time in Qatar, Maradona had stolen the show.

At the time it was not clear what Qatar gained from this set piece. Some journalists wrote stories of the strangeness of it all, others used it to make tenuous comparisons between Diego and Wayne Rooney, whilst one journalist used the event as a Trojan horse to break a much larger story which appeared that weekend and made headlines across the world: that a memo had emerged where George W. Bush had allegedly contemplated bombing Qatar's meddlesome Al Jazeera television network to stop the bad news stories that had emerged out of Iraq. Whatever the benefit, it appeared slight and even the most enthusiastic of backers were now questioning whether Qatar's huge investment was a wise one. On my last day in Qatar, out on the training pitch, I spotted a familiar figure. A tall, silver-haired bear of a man. It was Manfred Hoener. Immediately he strode towards me and shook my hand, almost severing it at the wrist, whilst affectionately beating me on my back at the same time.

'I take it this is all your work then?' I asked, surveying the scene of journalists, PRs and world famous footballers.

'What, this? No, I've given that all up now. It wasn't working out,' he replied.

As if on cue, one of Manfred's last signings ambled past, including the ex-Derby and West Ham striker Paolo Wanchope. As good a player as Paolo was, he was no Desailly. Manfred had suffered from the law of diminishing returns. Each month it had been harder and harder to attract the big names. The old guard of Desailly, the De Boer brothers LeBoeuf and Batistuta were gone and whilst World Cup winners could once be persuaded to come, now only mid-table journeymen like Wanchope and Jay Jay Okocha could be talked into the moneyed pilgrimage east. The Qatari government had even begun to lose patience. The whole point of the exercise was to raise the level of the league and its indigenous players so that Qatar might qualify for the World Cup for the first time in its history. That dream, for Germany 2006, was over long before when the national team succumbed meekly to Iran in Doha. To make matters worse, Qatar had now slid from 61st to 89th on the FIFA rankings between 2004 and 2006. The Asian Games, too, were an unfortunate failure after being washed out by unseasonable torrential rain and a series of bizarre incidents. To start with, the authorities had incorrectly calculated the number of beds needed for visiting athletes and officials by as many as 3,000 – leading to the unedifying sight of three cruise ships having to be towed in to make up the numbers.

The games were also marred by the deaths of seven spectators and a sportsman due to the conditions. A South Korean equestrian rider, Kim Hyung-Chil, was killed after his horse slipped on the mud and fell, crushing him to death. 'The Death Games', as one local paper referred to them, had been a publicity disaster and Qatar's expensive experiment in footballing immigration and sporting PR had failed. I felt sorry for Qatar. Like a teenager who had unexpectedly won the lottery, Qatar had spent big on expensive, flashy accessories but to little reward or seemingly any long term benefit. It was a shame because, as a young country, some of its other, more enlightened investments had paid off – like a fledgling democracy and its free media. As the veteran BBC journalist Tim Sebastian pointed out, when asked why he had moved to Doha to host a regular televised debate: 'Qatar is building institutions. Places like Dubai are building malls.' But that was cold comfort for the Emir when you compared the name recognition of Qatar's glitzy neighbour, which had neither democracy nor a free media. Seeing the writing on the wall, Manfred left the Q League and the FA before he was pushed.

'So what are you still doing here then, Manfred?' I asked, confused.

He pointed over towards two nervous-looking Indian men, one holding a sound boom and wearing headphones, the other with a large camera strapped to his shoulder. It was his film crew.

'I'm in television now, a football talk show. I talk, they listen. Ha!'

When Manfred Hoener decided to jump ship, you really had to start worrying. I had taken it as an indelible sign of Qatar's sporting failure. And in a way, right then, in that moment, it was. But in a few years the seeds of Qatar's master plan – planted initially with mixed success – would begin to flourish.

3
IRAN

March 2006

Outside Tehran's hulking, grey Azadi national football stadium a riot was fermenting. A mob, 70 strong, with whistles, drums and banners, pushed on the crush barriers and screamed slogans in strangulated Farsi. I hadn't expected my first taste of Iran to involve a loud and angry protest. Iran, we are led to believe, isn't a place where dissent is tolerated. Equally, I hadn't expected my first taste of Iran to involve a loud and angry protest exclusively made up of abaya-clad women, faces painted the colour of the Iranian flag and one and all clutching a national football team scarf. They berated the hundred or so riot officers who had constructed a Kevlar wall between themselves and the stadium, as dozens of men – only men – streamed past unmolested towards the stadium's huge gates and that afternoon's main event: a 2006 World Cup warm-up match between Iran and Costa Rica. None of the passing spectators looked surprised and none looked back. But the riot police looked on perplexed, a dilemma etched into their faces. At riot police school they were taught how to deal with enemies of the state. Wade in first and ask questions later. Instead they were frozen, stuck between a conservative culture where women were revered and protected from the wicked mores of the modern world and the demands of the state. Paralysis broke out. They looked impotently on as the women's angry cries broke on their body armour.

Inside the car, our driver interrupted the silence. 'Not the women again,' he rasped as we slalomed past the protest and through the crowd.

'Again?' I asked, surprised. 'Is this normal?'

'They come here before every game to protest in their scarves,' sighed Amir, my guide, of the familiar sight. I wanted to go and speak to them, ask them about their protest, but the doors were locked. Amir didn't think it was a good idea to try and talk to the women with police around. 'It's dangerous,' he said. I pulled the handle.

The doors stayed firmly shut as we glided past. 'It's not a religion thing why they can't come to a football match,' Amir hastily tried to explain. 'They can go to a cinema with a man. But it's the atmosphere in the ground: the swearing, the bad language. It's just not suitable.'

Three hours before every home game the female fans of Team Melli – as the Iranian national football team is affectionately known – trudge to the Azadi Stadium in the western suburbs of Tehran. And every game they are denied entry and trudge back to whence they came, past a huge motivational sign that mockingly adorns the entrance. It reads:

'The Most Powerful Person is That That Can Keep Their Hunger'

It was a hopeless, unrewarding task. But the protests – along with my arrival at Sharjah Airport in the United Arab Emirates for my flight to Tehran – gave me a glimpse that everything in Iran wasn't what it seemed. I had been denied a visa but had been told I might be able to get in anyway. The trip was certainly worth the risk. The 2006 World Cup was but a few months away and Iran had assembled arguably the best team in their history. For only the second time, a team in the region had a good chance of actually making the second round.

But first I had to get in, which is where Amir came in. Amir was an Iranian who worked for the airline, who had promised to get me in one way or the other. We agreed to meet at the check-in desk. Amir claimed to have connections in the upper reaches of pretty much every Iranian institution: the Iranian FA, the police, even, it seemed, Iranian airport immigration.

'Don't worry, get on the flight and we'll sort out your visa at the other end,' he assured me confidently over the phone. 'Don't worry,' he repeated, sensing my fear of an unfamiliar, unfriendly country. Given the Iranian government's hostile attitudes towards my homeland (Great Britain), the place where I lived (UAE) and my profession journalism) it was not a place I wanted to be stranded. 'My father used to be a minister in the government,' he assured me. I wasn't convinced.

We met the next day at the check-in desk. Amir was young, in his mid-20s, and handsome, a useful tool when flirting with the check-in girls when you have a long, suspicious-looking package to put in the hold. A few sweet words in Farsi and it was in.

'Oh, it's a bumper for my BMW,' he said nonchalantly. 'I went a little too fast in the snow and hit a kerb. It's cheaper if I buy it here.' Even in an Islamic theocracy, it seems, the appetite for luxury cars can't be suppressed.

As we flew the short journey from the UAE to Iran, Amir took it upon himself to put the record straight on a few things, particularly when we discussed the Iranian president's recent calls for Israel to be pushed into the sea and his desire for a debate on whether or not the Holocaust actually happened. The West, he thought, had the wrong idea about Iran and it was his responsibility, nay, his duty as a proud Iranian to make sure I had the correct version of events.

'I'm not anti-Jewish, I'm anti-Zionist, which is what he [Ahmadinejad] was trying to say,' he explained cheerily.

I had the feeling that Amir had to account for the president's behaviour to foreign friends on more than one occasion since his accidental election eight months previously. Sure, he won that presidential election but not without a little help from Iran's Guardian Council. The body of unelected, hard-line clerics – which is essentially controlled by Iran's spiritual leader Ayatollah Khamenei – sits atop the Iranian political system. They had the power to veto everything from legislation to presidential candidates, which they did during the 2005 presidential election, barring dozens of reformist candidates from standing. The liberals shunned the poll in protest and Ahmadinejad, the ultra-conservative former mayor of Tehran, was voted in on a low turnout by Iran's recent standards. Only 59 per cent of voters turned out for the second round of voting. The gentle-looking, lounge-suit-wearing President quickly made a name for himself in the West thanks to his anti-Israel pronouncements and his quest for nuclear power. Now Amir and the rest of the population were waiting for Israel to respond.

'If they [Israel] try to bomb us,' he said forebodingly whilst fiddling with the straw in his coke can, 'It will be the spark that lit a room full of gas. It will explode. I truly believe that it would be the end of the world.'

Few in the West knew of Ahmadinejad's existence before his shock election. The Americans initially accused him (falsely) of being the mastermind behind the 1979 American Embassy siege. Several of the American hostages still maintained he was present. What we did know was that his only earthly possession was a 1976 Peugeot, he held revisionist views on the Holocaust and he didn't wear ties, which, like the George Michael songs he banned from the nation's airwaves, as he saw them as a tool of Western cultural imperialism. His one weakness, which seemed to be a blind spot in his distaste for western cultural exports, was football. The Iranian love of football is so pronounced that even the theocrats couldn't control it. Instead, Ahmadinejad sought to use it for his own means. Iran had qualified strongly for the World Cup and were preparing for the biggest tournament in their sporting history. But the preparations weren't going well. I had come to Iran to watch one of their final home warm-up games: a mid-afternoon clash with fellow qualifiers Costa Rica. It was one of the few times a non-Asian team had made the trip to Tehran. It was supposed to be Ukraine but they pulled out, citing the spurious excuse that Iran was too good for a friendly. Amir was livid.

'They said we should go to Ukraine, but why? There really is no problem here,' he spat as the plane began its descent. All around, women stood and fixed on their head scarves, covering the long dark hair that had been tolerated in the UAE but would be tolerated no longer.

Given the political situation Tehran hadn't been a favoured destination for international friendlies and after failing to entice Italy, Germany and England to the world's largest pariah state, they persuaded Costa Rica to play the greatest crop of players the country had ever seen: Ali Karimi – Iran's cultured midfielder – had become the latest Iranian player to sign for a German Bundesliga club after signing a contract with Bayern Munich whilst Ali Daei, their 38-year-old centre-forward, held the world's international goal-scoring record. The team's popularity and imminent appearance on the world's biggest stage hadn't escaped Ahmadinejad. After landing at Imam Khomeini airport I picked up a copy of Tehran's English-language newspaper. On the front page was a picture of Ahmadinejad, meeting the players before training. Initially it looked like your standard statesman-meets-the-team picture. But closer inspection revealed a telling difference. The squad, including the talismanic Daei, was rapt, sitting legs crossed and intently soaking up the president's motivational words. It looked less like a meeting of adults and more like a gaggle of subservient boarding-school children following a particularly taxing nursery rhyme.

'Excuse me, can you step forward?'

A border guard politely ushered me towards passport control. As Amir pontificated with the man holding the stamp, I waited. A colleague watched nearby before leaning forward. Looking down, I feared the worse – handcuffs; a fist; an open palm demanding to be filled with a bribe? Instead, I saw a polystyrene plate full of meat and rice. 'You want?' he offered with a smile on his face. Not wanting to appear rude, I agreed, grabbed a fork and gobbled a mouthful. Lamb and gravy with sultanas – it was surprisingly good. His colleague cheerily stamped my passport whilst a glass of cold water was pushed in front of me before being genially waved off. Confronted by arguably the most hostile border police in the world, I was offered dinner, pleasantries and a drink. No, Iran wasn't supposed to be like this.

Even the most fervently nationalistic Iranian would admit that Tehran is not a beautiful city. As our battered Paykan taxi veered around other battered Paykans towards Tehran city proper, we were hit by monochrome blandness: rows and rows of stumpy, identikit, grey concrete tower blocks. The bleak urban cityscape is only broken by the huge, colourful murals that cover the sides of whole tower blocks, eulogising the martyrs from the Iran-Iraq war – images of young, handsome soldiers standing in wheat fields, handing poppies to carefree, patriotic children. Yet there are nods to the Persian empire's glorious past: a complex network of channels – full of melting snow water from the nearby Alborz Mountains – laces the city, an ancient anti-flood mechanism invented when the tribes of Western Europe were still working out how to stop their mud huts from collapsing in the rain. Iran's attempt at creating a modern transport network, however, had been less successful. Tehran's roads are some of the most dangerous in the world and are constantly jammed by state-made Paykans and Sepands, flagrant copies of hardy European models like the Hillman Hunter and the Renault 5. Traffic accidents were so frequent that Tehran's drivers had given up caring about the dinks and scratches and thought nothing of bumping or scraping you accidentally before driving off without a second thought.

Whilst Tehran lacks the aesthetics of Shiraz, or the cultural riches of Isfahan, the capital is at the centre of every political and social fad, its delayed ripples inevitably reaching its vast borders. It is Iran's beating heart and a microcosm of a huge country that holds 69 million ethnically diverse people, stretching from Afghanistan to Turkey with, it claims, the world's oldest continuously existing borders. The north of the city is dominated by the rich, middle-class intelligentsia who hate Ahmadinejad with a passion. The south is Ahmadinejad territory; deeply devout and poor, this was the electorate that carried their candidate to the presidency.

The physical division between reformists and traditionalists that bisects Tehran has shaped modern Iranian society. But it wasn't until a little-heard-of liberal cleric called Mohammad Khatami snuck past the Guardian Council censors and won a landslide election in 1997 that the reformist movement really had a voice. Preaching moderation, economic liberalisation and greater individual freedom for its people, Khatami rose to office on a tidal wave of optimism from Iran's young population. In fact, it has one of the youngest populations in the world: nearly 70 per cent are under the age of 30. The theocrats in the Guardian Council – never for a moment thinking that such a man was electable – were red-faced. The powers that kept the spirit of the Islamic revolution alive vowed never to allow such a mistake to happen again, and at every turn, Khatami was met with obstruction and hurdles, while his innate caution saw the conservatives take control again. In the end his government was so paralysed by inaction and bureaucracy, and the people so weary of big promises that were never met, that his popularity collapsed, laying the foundations for Ahmadinejad's red-letter day.

It's no surprise then, given this schism and the political sensitivity that his post possessed, that Branko Ivankovic – Iran's national team coach – chose to live neither north nor south but in the centre of Tehran. The Croatian had made Iran his home since being appointed in 2001 after Iran's failure to make the finals in South Korea and Japan. After being an assistant coach for Croatia during their World Cup bow in 1998, and taking them to the semi-finals, Branko had a strong reputation and was quickly snapped up on a five-year contract. He had fulfilled his obligation, qualifying with a game to spare after drawing against Japan in front of 100,000 fans at the Azadi – officially the highest attendance of any World Cup qualifier in that campaign, although most fans suspect as many as 120,000 were crammed inside – and was now one of the most popular men in the country. Dressed in a preppy outfit of jumper, shirt and slacks and sporting expensive glasses, 51-year-old Branko looked more like a university don than a national coach and seemed much younger, remarkable given the pressure and the average career expectancy of a coach in Asia.

'With my job, you don't know what's going to happen the next morning, especially in the Middle East,' he grinned as we sat down in the lobby of his plush hotel apartment. 'In the World Cup in France Brazilian coach Carlos Alberto Parreira was sacked by Saudi Arabia. This is the destiny of our job and we can't make plans for our future. Sometimes one centimetre is all that matters. The ball might go one centimetre left, go out and I'm terrible, but it goes one centimetre right into the goal I am a hero. Just one centimetre defines my destiny.'

Branko's objective, qualification for Germany 2006, had been made easier by the footballing riches bestowed upon him. Iran had produced something of a golden generation in footballing terms and a number of their key players had already been acclimatised to playing in Germany for a number of Bundesliga clubs – Karimi as Michael Ballack's understudy at Bayern Munich; Mehdi Mahdavikia at Hamburg; Vahid Hashemian at Hannover 96; and Ferydoon Zandi at Kaiserslautern.

'We can beat any side in the world,' Branko declared confidently when I asked about his team's chances. But once the final whistle went against Japan, Branko's job became a little harder. With Ahmadinejad making trouble at the UN, foreign FAs stopped taking the Iranian Football Federation's calls. Friendlies were called off and a tour of England's Championship clubs, held in the aftermath of the July 7 bombings, was cancelled by the Iranians half-way through over security fears. One match against Millwall, whose notorious fans have a long history of violence and racism, was cancelled after far right extremists threatened to exact revenge for the terrorist attack on the London transport network a few weeks previously. After losing 3-0 to Queens Park Rangers, the Iranians returned home. As Ahmadinejad's rhetoric grew, so did the sanctions. Western politicians started calling for Iran to be thrown out of the World Cup. German and Israeli lawmakers tabled motions in their respective parliaments, calling for a ban after Ahmadinejad, in one of his fiery speeches, called for Israel to be 'wiped off the map'. There was also the issue of Iran's continuing uranium enrichment programme. Throwing Iran out of the World Cup, reasoned the British Conservative party politician Michael Ancram, '. . . would give a very, very clear signal to Iran that the international community will not accept what they are doing'. Even the friendly against Costa Rica had attracted media attention, taking place as it did on the eve of a crucial International Atomic Energy Agency report on Iran's nuclear programme. If Iran was deemed to have shown sufficient doubt that its programme was anything but peaceful, it would set Iran on the road towards sanctions, further isolation and possibly war. Branko, like Ahmadinejad, wasn't too concerned.

'One of the very important rules of football is that politics is one side and sport is the other side so I'm sure we will go to the World Cup,' he said when asked about coping under the political pressures. Branko may have rejected the link between sport and politics in Iran, but few politicians in Tehran, Washington or London saw the difference, not least Ahmadinejad, whose visit to the squad was loaded with 'us versus them' symbolism. The national team provided an opportunity for Iran to be seen as equals on the international stage and to prove that, despite the privations and isolation of the past 25 years, the country was strong. The 11 men on the pitch represented what Iran really was, not the fiction peddled by the West's media lies. This nationalism held common currency in Iran. Ahmadinejad was not liked by all in the country, but he had tapped into a strong emotion that resonated with all Iranians, one which he saw embodied in the national team – resilience, independence and national, if not political, pride. Branko was just happy to be taking care of footballing matters, even if his meeting with one of the world's most reviled politicians gave him a somewhat dubious honour: he became one of the few westerners to warmly shake the hand of the Iranian President.

'He's a big supporter of the team,' Branko explained, proud of the memory. 'He told us that football is very important to the country, especially at the moment because the image of Iran is not too good. He expects the players to do their best but that this is sport and everything can happen. He's happy with the players and that we won't have any problems going anywhere in the world.'

The inside of the Azadi Stadium is dominated by two, equal-sized portraits hoisted high up on the west stand. One shows Iran's future, the other its past. To the left was Imam Khomeini, the cleric who shattered Western complacency towards Iran when he assumed control after the 1979 revolution and irrevocably changed the way his country would be viewed by the rest of the world. To the right, Ayatollah Khamenei, his replacement at the apex of Iran's spiritual hierarchy and perhaps the only man who could control Ahmadinejad and either steer his country through the current choppy waters or lead it into oblivion. The stadium was a third full with 40,000 spectators, a remarkable number given that the match was being played mid-afternoon on a Wednesday. After driving past the doomed female protests we parked and entered through large metal doors into the east stand.

'Here, you'll need this.' Amir thrust a bib and a pass into my hand, a hastily constructed piece of laminated plastic with a black-and-white photograph cribbed from my passport. It read: 'Photographer.' Amir shrugged apologetically. 'At short notice, it was the best I could do.'

I had never been pitchside for a football match before, unless you count being an unused substitute in a Sunday league match. Making the most of my chance brush with privilege, and using my old-fashioned camera to try and achieve a modicum of professionalism, I walked around the pitch taking pictures. The crowd opposite the murals of the two ayatollahs banged on drums and chanted the name of Imam Hussein, whose contested status as the true heir to the Prophet Mohammed's legacy is at the root of the region's Shia-Sunni schism. Placards were waved in a language I didn't understand. One, on brightly coloured paper, had been written (and only slightly mistranslated) in English and was cheerily waved by two smiling teenagers. It read: 'Don't With the US.' (sic.)

Just before the match started, a television crew approached. 'Can we speak to you, on camera?' the excitable presenter asked. I couldn't work out why the opinion of a fake photographer would mean anything to anyone. 'We don't see many Westerners here,' he said. 'It's on satellite,please?' He turned to the cameraman, nodded, and began filming.

'How are you liking Iran?' he asked.

'It's very nice and the people are very friendly,' I replied.

The next was trickier.

'Why does George Bush want to invade us?'

Ahh. 'Well, erm, I'm not sure...'.

Flummoxed, I couldn't find an answer. Why did George W. Bush want to invade? I wasn't sure that he did, although the press had speculated that the White House had been putting together contingency plans for an attack. Sensing that the dead air time of me lost in thought didn't make good television, the presenter changed tack.

'How do you rate Iran's chances in the World Cup?'

This was slightly easier to answer. The Iranians had pulled a hard group – Portugal, Mexico and Angola – but if they beat Angola and drew against Mexico, I offered, they might finish second. The presenter beamed, thanked me and walked off. It was what he wanted to hear. The interview, though, had only sparked the curiosity of other television crews, who rushed over just to make sure their rival hadn't scooped them. By the time the two teams came on the pitch for the national anthems, I was on my fourth interview, and had become an expert on Iranian football, firing off clichés and platitudes that would have made John Motson weep with pride.

'Of course, it all depends on the form of Ali Karimi.'

'If Branko can keep his team injury free, they have a great chance.'

'You know there are no easy games in international football any more, Mohammed, but . . .'

Iran were sublime. Within ten minutes they were ahead thanks to the best player on the pitch. Ali Karimi scored with a deft shot across the keeper from the outside of his left boot, and set up the next two, including Ali Daei's 109th international goal. The team tore their Central American rivals apart, who were just four places below them in the FIFA rankings, with Ali Karimi pulling the strings. You could see why the former Asian Player of the year, dubbed the Asian Maradona, had been snapped up by Bayern Munich. They had a perfectly good fourth goal disallowed before Costa Rica scored against the run of play. Half-time arrived and the Costa Ricans couldn't get off the pitch quick enough. The Iranian media were ecstatic and jumped towards me, one by one, pointing at the empty pitch as if it were proof of Iran's inevitable World Cup success. Arash, a young French-Iranian journalist who lived in Tehran and wrote for L'Equipe, was a little more circumspect. 'Yes, it was a good half. But they have a small squad. Any injuries and we would really be in trouble,' he said Arash had lived in Tehran for the best part of a year, taking advantage of his dual citizenship to file stories from a country where western journalists weren't particularly liked.

'I still need a permit,' he explained. 'But it helps that I write stories for France. They couldn't be published here.'

The news had been full of pictures in the weeks before showing the Iranian government's opinions on Western standards of freedom of speech. The caricatures of the Prophet Mohammed in the Danish paper *Jyllands-Posten* – an act that is *haram* (prohibited under Islam) – had sparked violent protest in the Iranian capital. The Danish embassy was attacked and burning barricades were erected. Television pictures bounced around the globe entrenching the view that all Iranians were theocratic maniacs. 'The rioters were the Basiji, everyone hates them,' Arash explained. The Basiji, he went on, were a government-funded religious militia who were set up during the Iran-Iraq war. It was a favourite regiment of the Ayatollah, and renowned for being made up of the devout. One apocryphal story tells how volunteers would walk through minefields to clear them. The ayatollah had promised them a quicker route to paradise for their sacrifice. With the Iran-Iraq war a fading memory, and Khatami's reformist revolution in the ascendancy in the late 1990s, the Basiji had impotently tried to reinvent itself as a moral guardian of the theocratic revolution on the street, harassing women for not covering up enough or for holding hands with men in public. Tehran's young population saw them as a joke. But with the rise of Ahmadinejad, their usefulness as a highly visible example of Iranian indignation at Western arrogance was recognised, and their power was on the rise. 'They are the people you see on television,' said Arash as the second half got underway. 'They are not normal Iranians.'

Arash's pessimism proved correct. Ali Karimi had picked up an injury and was taken off at half-time, whilst Daei and the Bundesliga contingent were rested as a precautionary measure. Branko patrolled his dugout studiously throughout, his bald assistant shouting his instructions onto the pitch in Farsi. The crowd chanted his name. The most popular foreigner in Iran smiled and waved back. With a weakened team, Costa Rica fought back strongly, and could have grabbed a draw. In the end it finished 3–2 to Iran.

As Arash and I filed out of the stadium we talked about football's importance in Iranian society. Much like Catholicism in 1970s Communist Poland, football was one area of Iranian life that even the religious establishment couldn't interfere with, although he did try. The league was suspended in the wake of the revolution, but the clubs quickly set up their own city leagues, albeit purged of pro-Western and pro-Shah sympathisers. Iran had just flown the country's flag for the first time in the 1978 World Cup in Argentina, securing a historic draw with Scotland. Yet six months later that team was dead. Many of those players fled to the US, including defender Andranik Eskandarian, who found himself playing in the same New York Cosmos side as Carlos Alberto and Franz Beckenbauer and eventually became an American citizen. Others simply vanished. After surviving the dissolution of the league, the clubs were then faced with another challenge. The Iran-Iraq war saw the availability of healthy young men collapse, meaning the football league couldn't continue. But the clubs soldiered on with an annual cup competition that drew huge attendances until the war ended and the national league could start up again in 1989, eleven years after the Shah's final football season was cut short, never to be finished. Football boomed in the 1990s, mainly because the terraces of clubs like Pas, a team traditionally funded by the police; Persepolis, Iran's most popular team; and Esteghlal FC, formerly known until the revolution as Taj (which means crown in Farsi) but which had to change its name to Esteghlal FC to break its previous connections with the Shah, were the only places where a frustrated population, tired of the revolution's economic failure, could vent their spleen.

The climax came in 1997. Buoyed by the success of the reformist movement, Iran qualified for France 1998 on a wave of euphoria and a million people took to the streets. It was the first time in 18 years that women had been seen in Tehran uncovered. And whilst now the Iranian government looked to football to give it a shred of international legitimacy whilst securing support at home, the authorities had paradoxically always feared its power.

'Football is the only place where people let go and those in power fear the power football has,' explained Arash as we said our goodbyes. 'Football is a threat to their authority. When a million people took to the streets, women were dancing and throwing off their hijabs. The authorities are scared of that, scared of losing control.'

I didn't have to travel far to my hotel. The Olympic was Tehran's finest, the place where visiting football teams would stay, attached as it was to the national stadium like an angular, drab carbuncle. When the ayatollah's forces took over the country, they did more than occupy the institutions of power. The city's hotels – the Sheratons, Hyatts and Hiltons – had also been forcibly nationalised, stripped of their insignia and given more Persian names. Cutting off Western companies also meant isolating Iran from the rest of the financial world – ATMs didn't work, neither did credit cards. The exchange rate from rial to sterling was so high (£1=IRR18,100) that most Iranians simply dropped the last few zeros to combat inflation. Not surprisingly, Iranian luxury hotels were hard to come by and the Olympic was marked the 'upper class'. My wood-panelled room was sparse with little in the way of entertainment. After flicking through the Farsi television channels to see if I'd made it onto the 9 o'clock news (I hadn't) and making a stab of reading the Koran, I was bored senseless. I called Arash, and went to see what Tehran's night-life had to offer. I wasn't expecting much. Being a dry Islamic country, Iran was always going to be one of the world's few countries not to have an Irish bar but I wanted to find out what young Iranians – and there were a lot of them – did at night.

I met Arash at Vanak Square, the Piccadilly Circus of northern Tehran where handsome twentysomethings with duck-fin haircuts and turned up jeans strolled the streets hand-in-hand with girlfriends sporting hijabs so far back they only stayed on by virtue of a stiff pony tail, making them almost redundant. Arash provided me with my answer.

'The youth are so bored, they don't have anywhere to go,' he said as we walked down to a local restaurant he had recommended. 'Especially the middle class. They have money, but nothing to do. So they sit around and take drugs.' It's hard to imagine somewhere like Iran having a drug problem, but all the vices that are open to the youth of the west also seem to be prevalent in Tehran. 'There are no nightclubs but people have parties at home and drink or take drugs. Tehran has a really big crystal meth problem. You have to remember, Iran has some of the best scientists in the world! Last year, the city was full of heroin and everyone would go to 'ex parties'. They would give you ecstasy at the door and let you loose.'

Arash didn't take drugs, and I got the impression he didn't overly approve. But I thought of my lonely room at the Olympic and secretly wished that an opportunity to attend an impromptu 'ex party' would present itself. We arrived at the restaurant, a small, strip-lit affair that sold Iranian staples like lamb with rice and sultanas and iced vermicelli, where Pegah was waiting for us. She was studying art at Tehran University and wore a brown hijab adorned with intricate stitching at the edges. Again, it hung off the back of her head, as if wearing it was little more than fulfilling a technicality. 'Most would probably say they'd rather not,' she admitted when I asked whether Iranian women resented having to cover up all the time. 'It's just the fashion, the way people wear it a little further back every year.' The incremental inching back of the hijab could be a metaphor for the increasing social freedoms that Iran's under-30s have surreptitiously gained. Even under Ahmadinejad and an increasingly conservative political culture, the small gains that make a young person's life tolerable continue unabated. 'They (the police) know that they can't turn things back,' agreed Arash.

One area where this had been put to the test on a nightly basis was in the field of dating. Although Bluetooth technology had helped people to flirt more easily, explained Pegah, there was an automotive version going on up and down Jordan Street every night. Known as the 'Jordan Game', cars full of single men and women would cruise up and down looking for prospective partners whilst the police sat in their patrol cars and did nothing. We climbed into Pegah's small car to take the short drive to Jordan Street.

'I like this a lot,' she smiled, as she pulled out a well-used tape and jammed it into the dusty car radio. Chris Rea replied back. 'Do you like it?' I didn't have the heart to tell the truth. 'I love him.'

With 'Road to Hell' blaring, we hit Jordan Street and the throng of Iranians looking for a date. Dozens of cars inched slowly up the hill full of expectant cargo: groups of men hoping to catch an eye streamed by and shouted bawdy slogans in Farsi. One group, spotting me, shouted something in unison in their mother tongue before the entire car collapsed in laughter.

'What did he say?' I asked Arash.

'He said: 'Nuclear energy is our right'. It is supposed to be a joke.'

Ahmadinejad's much-used slogan of nuclear self-determination and defiance might have struck a chord with his devout fan base, but to the youth of Tehran, the phrase was something to be mocked, an illogical rant that their elders had bought into but which should be viewed with disdain by their children. A second car passed slowly by us, this time containing a pair of heavily made up girls smiling ferociously. I smiled back and waved before they laughed and sped off. Finally, a lone patrol car glided up the strip. The cars disappeared down side roads as quickly as they had arrived, like in a scene from The Truman Show. The Jordan Game was over, for tonight at least. It was time to return to the Olympic. I said my goodbyes, climbed into my taxi and looked out of the back window as it pulled away. Behind me Arash and Pegah flirted openly whilst considering where to go next. Despite being in a country where pre-marital sex can still be punished by the flick of a whip, I got the feeling that out of everyone I'd seen that night, I was one of the few people going to bed alone.

As it turned out, I didn't have to go far to interview Ali Daei. Four doors along to be precise. Daei had stayed in Tehran after the Costa Rica game to meet up with his Saba Battery team-mates, a club owned by the Ministry of Defence. They were due to play a league match in the Azadi in what used to be called the Iranian Premier League. Now they called it the Persian Gulf Cup, to preserve, the Iranians say, the true name of the waterway that has been appropriated by Arab encroachment. The animus stems from the biennial Arabian Gulf Cup, involving every Gulf nation from Iraq to Oman. Iran hadn't been invited to the party. Even Yemen, which is closer to Africa than the Gulf – be it Persian or Arabian – was allowed to play. For Ali Daei, the league match was a long way from his glory days in the late 1990s when he was considered one of the best strikers in Germany. After playing for Arminia Bielefeld and Bayern Munich, he went to Hertha Berlin and spearheaded their Champions League charge in 2000. Daei excelled and scored twice in Germany against Chelsea and once against AC Milan – the first Asian footballer to score in the Champions League. But even as age advanced and Daei went lower and lower to get a game (first Hertha Berlin, then to Dubai, then back to Iran) he continued to be first choice for the national team and had racked up an astonishing 109 goals, including his well-taken strike against Costa Rica. Sure, four of them came in a 7–0 drubbing of Laos, but a world record was still a world record. His exploits on the pitch in flying the Iranian flag abroad had made Daei phenomenally successful in his home country. He was the closest thing Iran had to a Persian David Beckham: he was handsome, owned a sprawling business empire (the Daei Sportswear company) and was good-naturedly mocked for his gentle, lisping voice. Even his wedding was broadcast on public television. Also like Beckham, some fans had begun to wonder whether Daei was now redundant at the national level.

'A lot of fans think he's past his best,' admitted Arash at the Costa Rica game. 'But the coach won't drop him, he's too important to the team.' Branko had admitted as much in our interview. 'There aren't many in the world like Ali Daei but he's more than a footballer,' he said admiringly of his captain. 'He is a leader, a national hero and a symbol of the country.'

Ali Daei was lying one the floor of his hotel room, naked save for a pair of tight briefs that barely contained his modesty, being vigorously oiled up by his balding masseur. Daei welcomed me in and offered me an oily hand before we were interrupted by a string of excitable children, with equally awestruck parents in tow and totally nonplussed by their host's almost-nakedness. He signed autographs, gave words of encouragement and posed for semi-naked pictures with the kids.

Germany 2006 was Ali Daei's last chance of international glory. Having missed the 2002 tournament when he was at the height of his powers, France 1998 was his only World Cup appearance so far, but it brought Iranian football its greatest achievement. Early on the group fixture against the USA – who had reached the second round four years previously – was marked for its symbolism. It was one of the first public meetings between the two nations in 19 years. Bill Clinton recorded a message before the match preaching reconciliation and Iran's European fans tried to smuggle opposition T-shirts against the Islamic regime into the ground. The world waited for the two countries' political antipathy to spill out onto the pitch. Instead the world watched as the Iranian players showered their American opponents with symbolic white flowers followed by warm, smiling embraces. It resembled a first date more than the opening salvos of a proxy political battle. Iran's goalkeeper – Ahmad Reza Abedzadeh – shook hands with his American counterpart Thomas Dooley and handed over a large silver shield bigger than a small child to show conciliation and friendship towards their American foes. Dooley sheepishly handed over a tiny pennant in reply, too embarrassed to make eye contact with his adversary. It was singularly one of the funniest moments in international football, and the Americans were visibly stunned. So much so they conspired to lose 2–1, provoking the biggest gathering on Tehran's streets since Ayatollah Khomeini's funeral in 1989. Whilst the Americans gracefully took the defeat in the spirit of international fraternity, the Ayatollah back in Tehran was eager to make political capital. 'Tonight again,' he sternly extolled in an address to the national team on state television, 'the strong and arrogant opponent felt the bitter taste of defeat at your hands. Be happy that you have made the Iranian nation happy.' In the end, the only enmity that night was in France, as fights broke out between pro and anti regime fans after the game.

Daei smiled at the memory of that June night. 'All we cared about, our only goal [at France 1998] was to win against the USA,' he grinned. 'But we didn't take it seriously for the last match against Germany so that we could qualify for the second round. But this time around it will be different.'

It wasn't just Daei who was convinced of Iran's impending footballing glory. If Team Melli's performance in France 1998 was all about showing the world that Iran could hold their own at the highest level, the team at Germany 2006 wanted to prove what many fans in Iran – and Branko – sincerely believed: that they could beat anybody on their day and that in Ali Karimi they had arguably one of the finest players in world football. As the squad's spiritual leader the burden of expectation – from fans and politicians alike – had fallen on Daei's shoulders. After shaking hands with Branko, there was no question as to whom Ahmadinejad turned to next. 'The people of Iran, they're living with football so any good result has a big effect on the society and the country,' he explained as he started to get dressed.

Ahmadinejad's words of encouragement and earlier meeting with the squad hadn't convinced him that the team was being used as a political pawn in the West or at home. 'No, politics and football are completely different, totally separate,' he retorted when I brought it up. 'We play football and that's what's important for us. We leave the politics to other people.'

But Daei could, like the rest of the country, see that Iran's stock was at its lowest ebb for a quarter of a century. And even if the politicians wanted to hijack football for its own ends, he – as a proud Iranian – would do everything in his power to prove that Iran and Iranians were a world away from the cartoon baddies caricatured in the Western media. 'We'd like to go to Germany and prove that Iranians are completely different from the way the media show us. We have a high culture and our people work hard. The facts are totally different from the way the Western media are trying to show. It's very important for us to show the world exactly who we are.'

The next day's papers proved just how hard that task would be. The IAEA's report was delivered and it wasn't good reading for Ahmadinejad. There was sufficient doubt that Iran was seeking to enrich uranium to make a nuclear bomb, giving the US valuable ammunition in seeking sanctions, and possibly war, in the UN Security Council. Even winning the World Cup couldn't nullify that. Suddenly, Ali Daei and the rest of Team Melli had been handed the hardest PR job in the world.

From a distance it looked like the Iranian Club was under siege. It was three and a half months since I had seen Iran beat Costa Rica in Tehran. All their preparations had led to this day. Dusk was falling on another asphyxiatingly humid July day in Dubai and the upmarket district through which Oud Metha Road ran was stationary. Irate drivers held their horns down in vain to try and clear the road, but it was no use. Streams of disparate people – groups of teenage girls; pensioners hobbling on sticks; young men wearing expensive suits with mobile phones pressed to their ears – were sprinting across the four-lane highway, creating a human river that turned the straight and true highway into a temporary crossroads. All were frantic to reach the heavily guarded compound on the other side. The ornate front gates were inundated with last-minute arrivals. Women argued with the guards whilst expertly fixing on head scarves, never breaking eye contact. The lone guard tried to hold the crowd back, but like King Cnut sitting on the beach and ordering the ocean to retreat, he was fighting a losing battle. The crowd simply pushed past. Others scaled the tall metal fences that surrounded the compound, falling into crumpled heap on the other side before getting up and half limping, half running towards the lights.

The Iranian Club wasn't used to this many visitors. It was meant to be the conservative social club for Dubai's huge Iranian diaspora, but Iran's conservatism didn't travel well abroad. It was a little taste of home, and they enacted Tehran rules. No booze. Women were expected to cover. Socially liberal Iranians preferred to let their hair down (literally) by drinking in the city's bars or dancing at the many Persian nightclubs instead. The only people the Iranian Club expected to see were devout families and ex-military types in retirement. But today was a national occasion and, like the BBC being the British comfort blanket in times of crisis or celebration, Iranians from all walks of life put their politics to one side and flocked to the only place they could be sure to be on the same side. For many, even for those who rejected the regime, it was the only place in town to watch Iran versus Mexico, the country's first game in its controversial appearance at the 2006 World Cup in Germany.

'It has been like this for an hour,' the taxi driver sighed as he parked up. The guard was having another attempt at hauling the gate shut to stop the already bulging club from bursting at the seams. The guards shut the gate closed, leaving hundreds locked out. One covered, middle-aged woman even tried to hitch her leg up on the sturdy fence to try and climb over, but gave up knowing that age would be the ultimate barrier to her entry. Hopes were rightly high inside. After visiting Tehran a few months previously I had witnessed a self-confidence that hadn't been translated by the world media, both in its football team and its youth. This World Cup, Iranians reasoned, was when Iran took a serious step to being one of the world's footballing powers. They had a good case too. The tournament had come with Iran's 'Golden Generation' at its peak: Mahdavikia, Zandi, Teymourian and, of course Ali Karimi. There was also the figure of Ali Daei to contend with. It was surely to be his last World Cup as a player. But as he had told me back in Tehran when he was sitting, semi-naked in his hotel room, this was a vitally important World Cup for Iran for different reasons.

As the tournament drew closer, President Mahmoud Ahmadinejad's behaviour on the world stage had increasingly become more divisive. The country's nuclear programme was almost universally suspected of being for anything but peaceful purposes, the prospect of an American invasion was now being openly mooted by hawkish commentators on domestic US news networks and the calls for the Iranian national team to be banned from the World Cup had become even more vociferous. The world's media had focused on the Iran versus Mexico fixture to see whether the president, as promised, would turn up in Germany to cheer on Team Melli. Protests had been arranged in Nuremberg by Jewish groups livid at Ahmadinejad's potential presence, pointing out that his views on the Holocaust meant that if these pronouncements had been uttered in Germany he would have broken the country's strict Holocaust denial laws. If the protests didn't keep him away, then they would call for him to be arrested when – if – he landed in Germany. Even worse, neo-Nazi groups had planned on holding a counter demonstration to support the Iranian president. It wasn't exactly the kind of endorsement he or Iran needed.

Only one country from the region had made it past the group stage of a World Cup before; the Saudis in USA '94. But this was probably the best chance for Iran to at least match that, having gained a top-15 place in the FIFA rankings that year. History wasn't exactly on the region's side, though. In fact, most World Cup appearances by Middle Eastern countries had been best remembered for catastrophic failure or embarrassing footnotes. Israel had acquitted themselves admirably when they qualified for Mexico in 1970, drawing twice and losing once. Iran, too, didn't do too badly in their first appearance in a World Cup finals, in Argentina in 1978, where the team famously drew against a Scottish team that had foolishly declared it would return home with winners' medals. The appearance of Kuwait at Spain 1982, however, was remembered for all the wrong reasons. With a creditable draw against Czechoslovakia already in the bag, Kuwait took on France. The French were a bridge too far for the Kuwaitis, who went 4–1 down. Or so the French thought. By the time the fourth goal went in the Kuwaitis were standing stock still after hearing a shrill whistle. Assuming the referee had blown, they had stopped playing. The French played on and scored anyway. The Kuwaitis were livid but the referee had made his decision; it was a goal. The ball had even been placed back on the centre spot. But from the stands a man wearing traditional Gulf Arab dress waved towards the disgusted Kuwaiti players, urging them to leave the pitch in protest. Cue one of the strangest moments in World Cup history, as the white-robed figure of Sheikh Fahid Al-Ahmad Al-Sabah – brother of the emir and head of the Kuwaiti FA – strode onto the pitch with his red-and-white checked headscarf and black-and-gold cloak and calmly questioned the referee's wisdom. Amazingly, the referee backed down and called a drop ball. It was the last time he would referee an international match. The sheikh was fined a paltry $10,000.

Mexico '86 saw the Iraqis turn up. They narrowly lost every game but it wasn't until afterwards that it emerged that the players had been subjected to beatings and forced head shavings as motivation to qualify for the tournament. In Italia '90, the UAE and Egypt made it to the finals, the latter making their debut just 19 years after the country was formed. Whilst Egypt narrowly failed to qualify out of a tough group, the UAE's president Sheikh Zayed bin Sultan al Nahyan, perhaps knowing the limitations of his team, promised each player a brand new Rolls Royce, not if they won a game, but merely for scoring a goal. Sure enough, the UAE lost every game, conceding 11 goals. But two players, Khalid Ismail and Ali Thani, scored. They would later claim they never received their cars. USA '94 was perhaps the region's finest triumph, when Saudi Arabia reached the second round. En route they scored what was arguably one of the finest goals in World Cup history, Saeed Al Owairan picking the ball up near his own penalty box and, aping Maradona's wonder goal against England in Mexico '86, slaloming past the entire Belgium team before slotting the ball home. But then Al Owairian experienced an extraordinary fall from grace. He was jailed after being caught partying during Ramadan with non-Muslim women. 'It wasn't like a jail, jail,' he told the *New York Times* before the start of France '98 as he was trying to break back into the Saudi national squad. 'It was a detention centre, and I was held for questioning for several weeks.' He later claimed he was locked up for six months.

France '98 was less successful for the Saudis – they lost their first two games against Denmark and France and conceded an injury time goal to draw with South

Africa - but the tournament did throw up the match between the US and Iran in one of the tournament's most politically charged games, which the Iranians ended up winning 2–1. After that it was downhill. The 2002 World Cup saw Saudi Arabia humiliated 8–0 by Germany in their first game. It could have been worse; the Germans had 26 shots on target. The Saudis went home without scoring a goal. The Iranians, meanwhile, hadn't even qualified. In total, the Middle East's record wasn't something to boast about: played 30, won 3, drew 7, lost 20.

But no one in the Iranian Club in Dubai was was thinking of Team Melli's failure to qualify for the last World Cup any more, or even the disappointment of bowing out early in 1998 after beating the Americans. Inside the packed lobby children cried and parents remonstrated at the doors to the club's huge cinema. They were too late. Inside, close to 700 people had already crammed into the two tiers of seating, with another 400 left outside. Eventually extra televisions were brought outside when the crowd refused to disperse. Dozens more crammed the walkways or sat at the front. The vast projected screen flickered into life, for a moment casting a green glow over the cheering crowd as the equipment corrected itself. The feed was from Iranian state television and as the commentators pored over the team selection – Ali Daei and Ali Karimi were both declared fit and were to start – the club's manager stood in front of the crowd and urged them to be respectful. Clearly he was confident of a good result and didn't want a repeat of the last time Iran won a World Cup match in 1998, when women threw off their hijabs and danced in the streets of Tehran. Two young women walked past draped in Iran's flag with smaller, smudgy versions painted on their cheeks. 'We wore the flag and painted our faces to show everyone that we really love our country,' Shahrzad and Miadeh told a female reporter from a local paper standing nearby. The noise was deafening when the game kicked off; shouts of 'Eee. . . ran, Eee . . . ran,' rang out. Across town, one newspaper reported, several hundred Iranians watching the game in a pub began chanting: 'Nuclear Energy is our Right!' Given the setting, and what I had heard from the young people on Jordan Street in Tehran, it may well have been chanted sarcastically.

On the pitch, at the stadium thousands of miles away in Nuremberg, all eyes were on the crowd. President Ahmadinejad had decided not to turn up, but instead decided to send one of his deputies, Mohammad Aliabadi, instead. Which hadn't gone down well either. 'Aliabadi's presence means we could have a repeat of the 1936 Olympics, when they were hijacked by Hitler for his own political purposes and presentation,' Rene Pollak, chair of the Zionist Federation of Frankfurt, told *The Observer* before the game. 'We should have denied him entry to the country. Western leaders should know by now that appeasing fascist regimes does not work.' Hundreds of people representing Jewish groups and exiled Iranians attended the protest in Nuremberg. A smaller protest by the far-right National Democratic Party was broken up when the police stopped a group of men marching towards Nuremberg's centre wearing Iranian jerseys and waving Iranian flags. Not that anybody in the Iranian Club watching state television knew anything about the protests as the match kicked off in a sunny Germany. The lights dimmed. It was a tough start for Iran. Mexico was a team that had won three of their last four opening games at the World Cup, and they soon went ahead after some atrocious defending. But the crowd were soon back on their feet after the veteran central defender Yahya Golmohammadi fired into an open net. The Iranian Club erupted as high-pitched screams from the children present added to the roar. Iran pushed on and dominated the rest of the first half but missed a slew of chances. Ali Daei was dire, giving the appearance he was wading through treacle rather than air. More worrying was the fitness of Iran's star man. Ali Karimi had been injured in the build up to the finals but the manager, Branko Ivankovic, knew that his team's bid for progress would be over without him. With 20 minutes to go he was shattered, having run the midfield superbly in the sweltering heat.

Within minutes of his removal Iran fell to pieces. Mexico scored a second, before adding a third a few minutes later. The mood had changed at the Iranian Club. Before it was of hope, now it was ugly. Men stood to barrack Ali Daei, the person the crowd blamed for their defeat. People began trickling out even before the final whistle had blown. Mexico had won 3-1. Outside I had hoped to catch victorious Iranian fans running into the streets to celebrate their victory. When the Iranian Club last hosted a victorious World Cup match involving the national team – that famous match in 1998 against the USA – a crowd had rushed outside and ritually slaughtered a goat. Now a trickle mooched out sullenly, unwilling to talk. 'Daei should not be anywhere near the team,' proclaimed one man, who wouldn't give me his name as he walked back out of the gates that had been the scene of such hysteria two hours previously. He wasn't angry, more upset that he had believed the hype. 'Why do Iran let me believe?' he said. There was still hope though. Iran was to play Portugal in Frankfurt. Win and they were back in with a chance, lose and their World Cup dream was over. The goat slaughter would have to wait for another day.

Ask any German and they will tell you that Frankfurt is the most British of German cities. It's the country's financial centre and is thus – so the stereotype goes – full of yuppies and rapacious, money-hungry capitalists. But for a few days the city would be full of Iranian flags and Star of Davids. The World Cup circus that was following Team Melli – the fans, the politicians and the protests – had left the heartbreak of Nuremberg behind and moved on to Frankfurt instead. Branko Ivankovic, Iran's manager who I'd met back in Tehran, was in the lobby of the team's expensive hotel. Suited security guards stood guard around the room, wires trailing from their ears into their pockets.

'We were very unlucky,' he said, when I asked about the defeat to Mexico. 'The heat was a factor but we will come back stronger for the next game against Portugal.' The previous day's papers had also made an issue out of some of Branko's comments regarding how his players would be happy to meet Ahmadinejad if he came to Germany. 'It would be no different from Jacques Chirac meeting the French team,' he had been quoted as saying. Probably wisely, he failed to mention that he and the players had already met the President before the Costa Rica game back in February.

All the political intrigue was getting to him and he wasn't sure whether, come the end of the World Cup, he still wanted to be the Iranian manager after his five-year stint. For a region where a coach's tenure would typically be measured in months, five years was akin to Sir Alex Ferguson's tenure at Manchester United. But if Branko lost against Portugal, he would have no choice. 'We don't talk about politics,' he said, getting up to leave when I asked him about the controversy that had surrounded his team. 'I am only concerned about football.' It was a sentiment echoed by the fans staying at the hotel. A mixed group of a dozen Iranian fans lounged on nearby sofas. They had flown here from Tehran. The women chose to remain covered throughout. I asked one fan whether the controversy over the President's possible appearance had been reported back home. 'I, er, no. I don't want to talk about politics,' she replied shakily. 'I am here just for the football.' Her brother-in-law jumped in instantly. 'There are maybe five, six thousand of us who have flown from Tehran, I think, but we are here for football only.' The players marched through the lobby towards the team bus that was waiting to take them training. The fans had been hanging around to catch a glimpse of them and rushed to take pictures on their mobile phones. For Branko and Team Melli, tomorrow was make or break.

That evening every country was represented at the International Village, a compound where the fans of every nation could mingle, eat each other's food and drink each other's hooch. The Iranians, however, weren't there. Whilst the centre of Frankfurt was full of second-generation Germans of Iranian descent drinking the city's bars dry, the Iranian federation decided against having their stand anywhere near the alcoholic excess of the other nations. They were allowed to have their celebration of all things Iranian on the other side of the river, hidden away from the debauched revelry. It was early evening and the sun was still warm as a troupe of singers and dancers performed traditional songs in Farsi, only stopping when a prominent member of the federation stood and gave a short speech about 'the need for peace in the world'. Several hundred were clustered around the singers in a circle when a commotion began to break out. A phalanx of European bodyguards had formed a circle around a tiny, bearded man wearing a Nehru shirt and brown jacket. The bodyguards looked around shiftily as he waved goodbye to the Iranians watching the show. A man barged past me as he ran to get a closer look.

'I'm sorry,' he apologised breathlessly.

'Who is that?' I asked, expecting to hear that he was maybe a diplomat, or a famous singer. A popular ex-player, even?

'That's the vice president.'

Vice President Mohammad Aliabadi – President Ahmadinejad's man in Germany and the man whose presence had sparked angry protests in Nuremberg – had turned up the night before the game to be around friends and have a little taste of home. It must have been a tough job, travelling from city to city, having abuse thrown at you for something someone else said. A few dozen well wishers had crowded around him as he walked, making his security detail look even jumpier.

'Mr Vice President,' I called out, not being sure what the protocol was for addressing a vice president.

I was sure I had heard something similar on The West Wing. He remained passive; his eyes met mine. He had seen me, but ignored my shouts. Instead he looked in the opposite direction, waving at a group of confused German tourists who had stopped to see what the fuss was about. The question had also alerted his meat head security detail to the presence of a possibly hostile entity.

'Mr Vice President?' I shouted again, holding up a camcorder that I'd brought on the trip. 'Do you share President Ahmadinejad's view on the Holocaussssss . . .'

I felt a blow to my neck as one of his guards dived in the way of the camera, jumping up and down and waving his arms to make himself as big as possible to try and obscure the shot. Suddenly his security went into overdrive, as if they'd just heard the crack of a bullet emanating from a nearby book depository. The guards nervously looked left and right, ushering the vice president up a nearby stone staircase out of the park and onto the main street. Ironically, he found himself standing in front of Frankfurt's Jewish Museum, which was holding a night of Jewish folk music. The security guard was still in front of me, stepping left when I stepped left, moving right when I moved to the right.

✦

The walk from the train station to Frankfurt's futuristic Commerzbank-Arena offered a contrasting view on the Iranian government. Whilst anyone who had to get back onto a plane to Tehran was scared to mention anything about Ahmadinejad, Israel or whether he might turn up in Germany or not, the Iranians that had lived in Germany since fleeing the country after the fall of the Shah in 1979, and their children, followed a different line. In fact, Germany held the third largest Iranian expatriate population in the world, after Canada and the USA. The stream of fans walking the short distance from the station all flew the Iranian green, white and red. But it wasn't the flag of the revolution they carried, it was a flag from the past. It bore the golden lion, the pre-1979 symbol of the Shah. The flag was a protest against the post-revolution regime.

'I'm Iranian, I was born there, I love Iran but the way they treat women there, I can't believe it,' one young Iranian-British woman, holding the Shah's flag, told me outside the stadium. 'One day I'll go back, but not with a headscarf.' She was also in the same predicament as me. Ticket-less.

'Have you got any tickets to sell?' she asked.

'No, I was going to ask you if you had any. How much are they?'

'800 Euros.'

That was that. The next best place was the fan zone next to the Maine River, where a crowd of roughly 50,000 would be watching the game. We walked back past the convoy of Iranian fans with their pre-1979 Iranian flags. Only the periodic flash of Portuguese maroon broke the ubiquity. It would be as close to a home match for Iran as it was possible to get without holding it in Tehran. I rushed back down town, back on the train and then the long walk along the river in searing heat towards the big screen where we should have watched the game. It was due to start any minute but already, half a mile from the screen, there was a pedestrian traffic jam. Tens of thousands of Iranian fans had turned up to see their team. So many, in fact, that the purpose-built stands were full. Not everyone wanted to be inside though. A gaggle of protesters stood under the shade of a line of trees, each one peddling a different dissident political platform: equal rights for Iranian women; an end to racism for non-Persians in Iran. At the end of the line stood Mansoor, a young student, eagerly handing out leaflets to anybody that passed. He was an Iranian Marxist, campaigning for a socialist revolution in Iran. 'In Iran now, you don't know what it's like, it's hopeless. The theocrats have taken away hope.' Just as he said that a distant, worrying silence emerged from behind the trees. Portugal had scored with 20 minutes left. Cristiano Ronaldo ended the contest a few minutes later. All hope that Iran would qualify was lost. For Team Melli the World Cup was effectively over.

Yet their presence was still provocative. Nearby an anti-Ahmadinejad protest was being held, but as I approached, another silence greeted me. The square on which the Opera House resided was empty. A stage sat empty to the side, as security guards quickly cleared away the crash barriers. The floor was a mat of blue and white. Star of Davids fluttered along the floor. Close to a thousand protesters had been standing in the spot I was in a few hours previously, waving placards that said: 'Israel has a Right to Exist' and 'Support Israel Now'. A former Holocaust survivor and renowned academic, Arno Lustiger, the Associated Press reported, took to the stage and, to rapturous applause, told the rally that Ahmadinejad's presence would be a 'provocation to all German Jews'. Now a single, lone protester stood in the middle of the square, an Israeli flag on his back and a cardboard hat with a Star of David on it. Star of Davids seemed to cover every single piece of his body.

'You can't trust the Arabs, you can't trust the Arabs,' he repeated.

'You mean the Persians?'

'You can't trust them,' he continued as if he hadn't heard me.

The scraps of blue-and-white paper swirled around the square, but the protester remained, standing stock still, awaiting the next battle.

Ahmadinejad didn't show his face in Germany. Protests were planned for the final group game in Leipzig against Angola: a 1–1 draw. But it didn't take place under the President's watchful eye. The national team had been there to serve a purpose. Previously football had been a crucible of dissent. Ahmadinejad wanted to co-opt the national team for his own nationalistic ends, to prove Iran's strength in the face of adversity. But the campaign had been a PR disaster. On the pitch the glittering array of Iranian footballing talent had failed to live up to the hype. Off the pitch, Iran's position as the world's number one pariah state had been confirmed by the protests and vitriol that had spilled out in every German city they visited. Iran's reputation had, if anything, been denigrated even further. Even the team couldn't escape that. Ali Daei was the chief scapegoat for many fans, and he quickly retired from the game along with a slew of other Iranian footballers. Branko quit too, his legacy in rebuilding Iran's footballing reputation tarnished by his team's failure to jump properly at the last hurdle. He would later emerge as manager of Dynamo Zagreb, where he would win the double. Back in Iran the head of Iran's football federation was fired, allegedly by Ahmadinejad himself. The move led to FIFA briefly suspending the Iranian Football Federation for political interference.

But Daei would make an unexpected comeback. A few months after Iran's World Cup débâcle, Daei was hired as coach of Iranian side Saipa. It was his first coaching job yet six months later he was appointed coach the Iranian national team, almost exactly a year since I had spoken to him, naked on his hotel room floor. But the doubts that had dogged the end of his career continued into his coaching. Daei was charged with getting Iran to the 2010 World Cup finals, and things began brightly, going unbeaten in the first group stage and finishing top. But a succession of draws in a tough final group that contained their arch rivals Saudi Arabia and eventual finalists North and South Korea saw Iran struggle. When the Saudis fought back from a goal down to beat Iran 2-1 in front of 100,000 fans at the Azadi stadium in Tehran in March 2009, the writing was on the wall. Daei was sacked with three games left, having lost just one game in qualification.

He was replaced by a popular but unusual choice.

Afshin Ghotbi had arrived at Imam Khomeini Airport 18 months previously under a hail of flowers. Thousands had thronged the arrivals hall. Those that couldn't get in lined the road towards the airport instead. His arrival was big news. He had just been hired as coach of one of Iran's biggest teams, Persepolis. It was the first time he had taken a job in Iranian football. In fact, it was the first time he had set foot in the land of his birth for three decades. Ghotbi was an Iranian American. He fled Iran in 1979 after the revolution with his teacher father, leaving his mother behind. He was 13 years old. But soccer remained in the blood. He cut his teeth first playing and then coaching in college whilst studying electrical engineering at UCLA. By the time the France '98 came about, Ghotbi was on the US national team staff, briefing the team on the group's dangerous, unknown opponents: Iran. He then followed Guus Hiddink to the 2002 finals with South Korea, and worked as an assistant to Dick Advocaat, again with South Korea, at the 2006 World Cup.

He had built a solid international coaching reputation. But he was also an Iranian who had vital foreign experience. In Iran he was treated like a returning rock star. At the airport he saw his mother for the first time in 30 years, before being carried out of terminal on the crowd's shoulders. Initially his time in charge of Persepolis was a success. Close to 90,000 people were turning up to the home games and he dramatically won the league title in his first season. But he was still seen as an outsider, a traitor – in some quarters – for fleeing the country. A whispering campaign began about his coaching methods. Former players criticised his choices of tactics as well as the people he hired for coaching jobs. Previously a star player would usually waltz into a well paying coaching position. But Ghotbi had picked up American sports' love of stats and analysis, rather than the illogical hunch of the pro. There was unease at the Western suits he would wear on the touchline. The subtext was obvious. As an American raised, if not an American born, Ghotbi was viewed with suspicion, not by the public, but by the federation and its political allies. When the national team job came up in 2008 Ghotbi was the runaway favourite. On one TV phone poll he racked up 85 per cent of the vote. But he was overlooked, and Daei was hired. But a year later, in the spring of 2009, and with the national team in dire straits, Iranian football turned to him to save the day.

His contract lasted the length of the remaining qualification campaign: three games. His first was a 0-0 draw in Pyongyang before two crucial matches in quick succession: one against the UAE, the second a few days later against South Korea in Seoul. But the timing of the matches couldn't have been any worse. Iran's presidential election was being held, an election whose outcome was far from clear. Ahmadinejad faced a stiff challenge from Mir-Hossein Mousavi, a former Prime Minister, editor and artist who had campaigned on a reformist ticket. Tensions were high. Iran's standing in the world had never been lower. Corruption and squandered oil wealth had enraged the public as the economy crumbled under the weight of mismanagement and international sanctions. The timing of the UAE match in Tehran was such that the regime feared what effect a defeat might have on the election results two days later. An illuminating diplomatic cable sent from the U.S. State Department in Dubai on the eve of the election – and released along with millions of others by Julian Assange's Wikileaks website – highlighted just how worried the regime was that defeat against the UAE might swing the election against Ahmadinejad. Worse, it might start riots that spread throughout the country. Yet equally interesting to Iran football fans was the fact that Ahmadinejad's reverse Midas touch – which had so far ruined the economy and the country's international relations – had now spread to sport.

The leaked cables recorded:

> *President Ahmadinejad has worked hard to associate himself with Iran's beloved national team - 'Team Melli' - a tactic that backfired in March when he was accused of 'jinxing' the team, which suffered a last-minute defeat to Saudi Arabia just after Ahmadinejad entered the stadium.*

That event, coupled with an unexpected loss by the national wrestling team with Ahmadinejad in attendance earlier in the year, set off a firestorm of SMS messages and internet jokes holding the President personally responsible for the teams' defeats, and has led numerous IRPO [Iran Regional Presence Office] contacts to predict - only partially in jest - that a loss to the UAE team in Tehran on June 10 could further weaken Ahmadinejad's standing among soccer-crazed Iranians...

Contacts tell IRPO that the Iranian government worries that public unrest over a Team Melli loss could add fire to the increasingly volatile political demonstrations that have paralysed Tehran in recent nights.

President Ahmadinejad, in particular, has staked a great deal of political capital in Iranian soccer. A fan and former player, Ahmadinejad had made several press appearances practicing with Team Melli. In an effort to capitalize on soccer's popularity with constituents, Ahmadinejad, a political conservative, went so far as to call for the inclusion of women at men's games in 2006, although he was overruled by Supreme Leader Khamenei in a rare, but significant, open disagreement between the two men.

The cable went on to allege that Ahmadinejad was involved in a string of decisions in Iranian football, including personally sacking Ali Daei before approving Afshin Ghotbi for the Iran job. He even lent Ghotbi his presidential jet, according to the cable, for the awkward away trip to North Korea. Just like in 2006, Ahmadinejad understood the political power of football. Except this time there was also a presidential election at stake as well as World Cup qualification.

Through his decidedly public involvement with Team Melli, Ahmadinejad has inextricably linked himself to the outcome of Iran's bid to qualify for the 2010 World Cup ...

Though many serious issues will draw Iranians to the polls on June 12, one cannot overlook the effect that the result of the June 10 Iran-UAE match, especially an embarrassing loss, could have on Ahmadinejad's electoral fortunes.

But football could be used both ways. As more people used the terraces to vent their opposition to Ahmadinejad's regime, the game also became symbolic, reflective even, of Iran's fall from grace.

'To many,' the cable concluded, *'The state of soccer in Iran today reflects the problems that Ahmadinejad's challengers claim the country has suffered under his administration. Whereas Iran achieved international prominence in the 1998 World Cup under Khatami, Ahmadinejad's politicization of the sport has compromised Team Melli's standing on the world stage, and in many Iranians' eyes, further jeopardized the country's national pride.'*

Iran managed to dodge one bullet only to find itself under artillery fire. Ali Karimi, now captain of the national team, scored the only goal of the game as Iran beat the UAE 1-0, setting up a must win-clash against Ghotbi's *alma mater* South Korea.

But as the team left the country Iran descended into chaos. Just a few hours after the polls closed for the June 12 presidential election Ahmadinejad was announced the winner, an impossibility according to the opposition who alleged massive voter fraud. The result sparked huge demonstrations – the so called Green Revolution – that saw millions of Iranians taking to the streets. It was the first serious challenge to the gatekeepers of the Iranian revolution. For a short time, it looked like the sheer weight of protest might bring and end to Iran's 29 year long theocratic experiment.

News of the protests – not to mention the reports of deaths and brutality meted out by the police and the Basiji in the aftermath of the result – had reached Seoul too. Outside the stadium protesters held aloft banners denouncing the Iranian government. 'Go to Hell, Dictator,' read one. As the Iranian team waited in the dressing room, Afshin Ghotbi noticed that something was different about his players. Most of his starting eleven were wearing green bands on their wrists.

'I did ask about the armbands,' Ghotbi told me a few weeks later when he was safely back at his apartment in Dubai. Karimi told Ghotbi that the green bands were in honour of a revered Shia cleric. 'I respected that,' he recalled.

But after the players had walked on to the pitch, their team photo became an iconic symbol of protest. As they crouched seconds before kick off almost all of the players were clearly wearing the same green bands that had become a symbol of protest against the election back home. At the front Ali Karimi wore his tightly around his left wrist. At half time – as news of the protest began to filter out - Ghotbi's insisted that no one was forced to take off their wrist bands, even though several did. The team came within eight minutes of a poetic victory. But, in the 82nd minute, Ji Sung Park equalized for South Korea. The match finished 1-1. Iran had failed, just as the Green Revolution was due to fail too.

There was to be recriminations. Pro government newspapers announced that the players – with Karimi in particular singled out for vitriol – would be banned from the national team for life. Those that had foreign contracts would have their passports seized. There would be consequences for their actions. Ghotbi, though, denied that any punishment was handed down.

'None of these players have been banned,' he said incredulously. Indeed, one spokesperson for the Bundasliga's club VFL Bochum, where Vahid Hashemian played, explained that the player was returning to training in Germany as normal and that the whole story about passport seizures and international bans had been fabricated.

'I will speak to them both [Karimi and Mahdavikia] on a one to one basis,' Ghotbi said. 'The national team door is always, always, open to them.'

The defeat marked the last chance for many of the team to achieve their potential. This was the fading light of Iran's golden generation, finally snuffed out as the Green Revolution was crushed. Many players in that squad did retire. But Karimi, amazingly, would later return. Ghotbi had been good to his word, but it would mark the end of his honeymoon period with the Iranian public. He may have survived the scandal politically by claiming to not know anything about the green wristbands, but his failure to back the Green Revolution and to willingly profess ignorance at his team's actions had fatally damaged his popularity back in Iran. There would be no more jubilant crowds to meet him when he landed in Tehran. There would be no more flowers thrown at his feet. There would be no clamour to carry him out into the streets on the shoulders of men. Instead he would attend President Ahmadinejad's inauguration party two months later, even though dozens of reformist politicians had boycotted it. Ghotbi's Facebook account was defaced, his home in Dubai attacked. But it wasn't all bad news. Ghotbi was rehired as coach of the Iranian national team and tasked with taking Team Melli to the 2011 Asian Cup in Qatar.

4
ISRAEL

August 2006

Oren hadn't seen business like it for years. The middle aged Maccabi Haifa fan, his face tanned and lined, hands rough from his chosen trade, wore the green and white shirt of his team and stood in the long shadow of Maccabi Netanya's crumbling stadium. He held open a large, flat wooden suitcase of football merchandise, around which a crowd had formed. Oren was used to being ignored by all but a rare few but today, the first day of the 2006/07 Israeli football season, was different. The jumble of cheap, polyester scarves and fake gold Star of David necklaces bearing his beloved team's name was being met with an unusually positive reaction. The fans – so indifferent to Oren's usual mercantile overtures – laughed, fingering and pulling his stock as if noticing him for the first time before putting their hands in their pockets and dropping a few shekels in to his palm. The source of this new-found interest wasn't born in the sun and optimism that every football fan feels on the back of their necks as the season starts; the equality of knowing that everyone begins last, that everyone begins first. Nor was it based on sympathy, as such, even though Maccabi Haifa had endured a torrid time of late. The first game of the season was supposed to take place a week earlier in Haifa, a mixed Arab and Jewish city in the north of the country. But it was impossible to play games there now. For the moment at least, Haifa was homeless.

It was less than two weeks since the end of the Lebanon War, a conflict started by the Lebanese shia militia Hezbollah and which claimed the lives of more than 2,000 people on either side of the border. The majority of the dead were Lebanese civilians but the north of Israel had been bombarded by Hezbollah's arsenal of Katyusha rockets. Haifa, Israel's third city, had taken the brunt of Hezbollah's assault on northern Israel. They were due to play Ashdod at their Qiryat Eliezer stadium the week previously, but when a Katyusha narrowly missed the club's ground, the Israeli FA decided to ban games in the north of the country and put back the start of the season by a week, just in case hostilities resumed after kick-off. The start of the football league, the return to normality, even a week later than planned was still a symbolic moment, more so for Haifa than perhaps anyone else. Haifa had dominated Israeli football in recent years, winning four of the previous five championships in the Israeli Premier League, the Ligat Ha'al. As Israel has been a member of UEFA since 1991 – thanks to a boycott by Arab teams in the Asian Football Confederation in the 1970s that effectively left the Israeli FA rootless for two decades - they had qualified for the Champions League.

It was ironic, too, that Haifa had taken such a heavy toll for Israel's incursions into southern Lebanon following the kidnapping of two of its soldiers. The city is one of the few to have a mixed Jewish/Arab make-up, despite Israel's Arabs making up close to 20 per cent of the population, and the football team had long championed the cause of Israel's Arab footballers who had found prejudice, like in wider society, within some of the country's clubs. In fact, the country's football league had long been a battleground that had little to do with football – Jewish versus Arab, left versus right, Likud versus Labour, rich versus poor.

But, today, fraternity – the briefest, rarest of commodities in Israeli football – was the answer to Oren's prayers. He thrust the key to his sale's boom into my hand; a small, green sticker. Drawn on it was a cartoon of a Haifa fan urinating into Hezbollah leader Sheikh Hassan Nasrallah's mouth. Crude, yes, but for only five shekels apiece, it was a bargain. Oren had struck gold.

'It says: 'Nasrallah you are garbage',' he translated as he shifted another to a still-chuckling Haifa fan. 'He's no good, he shoots rockets where there are civilians. They fire deliberately on civilians and when we retaliate they say we are bad. We have a chant for him today: 'Yallah, yallah, Nasrallah, I kill you, I kill you, Inshallah'.'

Shlomi, his fellow merchandise seller, part confidante, part turf rival, eyed Oren's booming trade with jealousy. 'If it was up to me I'd bomb every house in southern Lebanon,' he spat through a mouthful of semi-digested sunflower seeds, as he sought a more valuable seam elsewhere. 'Give my regards to Nasrallah if you see him.'

Israeli football was some of, if not the, best in the region. But the league was also something of a microcosm of the divisions, hopes and fears of Israeli society. When most people think of Israeli society, they think of something monolithic; a homogenous population defined by Judaism and little else. But nothing could be further from the truth. Each football club had its own distinct identity, rooted in a different political cultures.

'Even before the state of Israel was founded, everything was very political and football was no different from that,' explained Uri, the sports editor of *Haaretz*, the country's liberal left-leaning newspaper, when we met at an Indian restaurant in Tel Aviv. 'Every big political group had its own team: Hapoel teams represented the big unions that were running the country – the workers and labourers; the teams of Maccabi represented the middle class; and the teams of Beitar were representing the right-wing nationalist minority.'

Uri was a supporter of Hapoel Tel Aviv, Israel's most famous socialist club. Until the mid-1980s it had been owned by a union. They were the team of the kibbutz settlements – from Eilat on the Red Sea to Haifa on the Mediterranean coast. To their political and footballing opponents, they were simply and disparagingly known as 'The Communists'. Teams like Maccabi Tel Aviv, the *grande dame* of Israeli football, and Maccabi Haifa had always held the centre ground. Beitar Jerusalem, on the other hand, represented the political right and was closely aligned with the Likud party. Many of its past, present and no doubt future Prime Ministers were Beitar fans, the likes of Ariel Sharon, Ehud Olmert and Binyamin Netanyahu. Many Likud Knesset members had cut their administrative teeth on the board at Beitar. The two sides – Hapoel Tel Aviv and Beitar Jerusalem – had long hated each other for more than their competing styles of play.

'We had a cup final against Beitar in 1999 which was three days after the elections. Labour won and we took a huge banner to the game that read: 'We fucked you in the elections, now we'll fuck you on the pitch'.' Uri recalled.

The rivalry existed on another level too. More than a century of Zionism had brought together groups of Jews from across the world, from Yemen to Ethiopia to Poland, united by a common cause. Israel in itself was the glue that held Israel together. But each community brought with it the essence of their homeland. In many areas – food in particular, but also the renowned beauty of its population – this multiculturalism was a boon. In others it caused deep political tensions on and off the football pitch. For years Israeli society was dominated by the Ashkenazim, the white, European settlers that had fled Europe's barbarism and largely coalesced around the leftist Labor party which dominated politics after the creation of Israel in 1948. The support of teams like Maccabi and Hapoel Tel Aviv were drawn from the more affluent Ashkenazim. But that all changed in 1977. The Likud Party broke Labor's hegemony and won its first general election, an earthquake in Israeli politics. They didn't count on white Europeans for their support. They looked to the Mizrahim.

The Mizrahim where Jews 'from the East', those that had fled persecution in the Middle East and North Africa; from Iraq, Yemen or Morocco or anywhere else in the near-East, the majority arriving after being expelled by Arab governments in the wake of Israel's creation. Many spoke Arabic and came from working class neighbourhoods. They also proved more willing to accept a hard-line approach to dealing with Israel's Arab neighbours than their white, socialist countrymen. It was the Mizrahim that swept Likud to power in the 1977 election. It was the Mizrahim – those that had claimed to know the true enemy best – that also made up Beitar Jerusalem's fan base. In 1977 Beitar won its first ever cup, beating the seemingly invincible Maccabi Tel Aviv. The two events are not seen as a coincidence by Beitar fans, nor its political rulers. The clash between the two – the socialist Ashkenazim of Hapoel Tel Aviv, versus the religious, right-wing and nationalistic Mizrahim represented by teams like Beitar Jerusalem and Bnei Yehuda – was not just a clash between competing teams or ideologies but a fundamental struggle between two competing visions for Israel.

But a further dimension had come to define Israeli football in recent years. Clubs like Bnei Sakhnin and Maccabi Ahi Nazareth hailed from the poor Arab towns of the north, and had a resolutely Arab, largely Muslim identity. The status, motivations and treatment of Israel's Arabs, those who stayed behind after the creation of Israel rather than leave into exile had become an increasingly fraught political issue. Sympathetic to their Palestinian kin, but nonetheless Israeli citizens, Israel's Arabs believed they faced discrimination in almost all walks of life. Their towns were poorer then their Jewish neighbours, jobs harder to come by. But for many they also represented an existential threat, a growing non-Jewish minority that threatened Israel's Jewish demographics. Those on the right also viewed them as potential fifth columnists, their allegiances to be found in the West Bank or Gaza rather than Israel. Yet football was one area of life where race was largely irrelevant. Bnei Sakhnin, a mixed team of Arabs and Jews, had been promoted to the top division and had even won the State Cup. The national team had Arab, Muslim players. Almost every team had signed an Arab player. Except one. Beitar Jerusalem had never had an Arab play for them. Their fans, notoriously right wing with a hardcore that held views considered out and out racist, would simply not accept it. The old left-right political dynamic used to define both Israeli society and its football league. Now the issue of racism was increasingly coming to the fore.

Not that much was forthcoming in Netanya, even given the fact that the Second Intifada and the end of the Lebanon War was still fresh in the mind. Netanya is a shabby coastal town known for little more than its high crime rate and moderate beaches. The stadium was in poor shape, semi-affectionately known as 'The Box' thanks to its enclosed atmosphere. It was also rumoured to have been condemned years before. But Maccabi Netanya still played here, and the fans still filled the terraces without the ground collapsing around them. The crumbling walls and lack of an east stand gave the place a neutered, dilapidated air of a 1970s lower league English ground on the brink of liquidation, like Millwall's Old Den, or Middlesbrough's Ayresome Park. There was little intimidating about The Box, despite the profusion of barbed wire. Still, the inscription on the front gates in Hebrew – 'Welcome to Hell' – seemed to be steeped in irony. Although this was the first game for Netanya, Haifa's season had begun long before, in the North of England. Haifa had narrowly lost 2-1 to Liverpool in the first leg of their qualification match for the Champions League. But with the city under siege and rockets getting worryingly close to the pitch, UEFA ordered that their home match against Liverpool be moved to a neutral location. Despite scoring first Haifa drew in a sub-zero Kiev, narrowly ending their hopes of Champions League glory. They could take comfort from the fact that they lost to the eventual finalist.

Outside The Box the ghost of Nasrallah was everywhere. The fans angrily chanted his name and his image was desecrated and corrupted on hundreds of placards, posters, T-shirts and, yes, Oren's stickers. Which isn't to say that Haifa's fans are virulently anti-Arab or anti-Muslim – far from it. Whilst teams like Beitar Jerusalem refused to sign Arab players for fear of upsetting their hardcore right-wing fans, Maccabi Haifa could boast current Israeli international and the country's most famous Arab player, Abbas Suan.

'The fascists, like Lazio, they are Beitar Jerusalem,' explained Kornel, a 20-year-old soldier who fought in Lebanon and who was also a member of the Green Apes – the team's ultras group. 'We are less political like that because we have no problems with Arabs. The war hasn't caused any problems between us. We are from Israel, they are all Israelis too.'

The Green Apes were here *en masse*. Hanging around in the shadow of their crumbling host, drinking cans of Becks and singing 'I'm Forever Blowing Bubbles' West Ham United's famous song in mockney accents. The fact that their most recent export, Yossi Benayoun, had moved to West Ham was a reason to be doubly proud of their famous son. They all seemed a bit too nice to be considered hooligans – one part liberal integrationists; one part ultras; one part youth club – as they crowded around to show off their initiation tattoos: either a large green ape on the shoulder blade or the letters ACAB, an acronym for All Cops Are Bastards, printed prominently on the forearm. They even had a huge ACAB poster – illustrated by a mean, American-looking cop – to hang on the hoardings during the match.

Proudly liberal, the Green Apes differentiated between 'their Arabs' and 'Nasrallah's Arabs' and insisted that war had only brought Haifa's Jewish and Arab fans closer together. Except for Hezbollah, the only other organisation that united Haifa's Jewish and Arab Muslim fans was Liverpool – or 'Chicken Pool' as they were known. Liverpool's refusal to play their Champions League qualifier in Israel had made them public enemy number two.

'Rafa Benitez is a chicken. Sissoko is Nasrallah's cousin. He fights for Hezbollah!' shouted Tamar, a middle-aged woman escorting her son to the match. She scarily tapped at my notebook just to get the point across. 'Haifa is a safe place. Not even in England is it safe. What about your airports? And games were played after the bombs in London and Madrid, weren't they? You should write it in bold: Israel is safe.'

With their Jewish brethren under attack and the opening game being something of a symbolic moment for the city of Haifa – a chance to show the world that it was bruised but unbowed – you would have thought that Israel's footballing family would come together in a show of national unification. But the fraternity that helped Oren the merchandise seller secure a bumper pay day outside The Box didn't last long. Netanya's fans, jealous from Haifa's near domination of Israeli football over the past half-decade, had a different plan: almost every fan wore Liverpool's yellow away kit.

'It's because we play in yellow as well, but it's to annoy Haifa,' explained Hagai, a 25-year-old Netanya fan who lived by the ground. 'We are glad they were kicked out [of the Champions League]. We hate Haifa because they think they're the best team in the world and take all our best players.'

Inside the stadium one stand was packed with thousands of Haifa fans wearing green and letting off luminous red flares. Having started to watch football in England just before the dawn of the Premier League, when crowd violence could rear its head at any moment and the prospect of electrified fences to keep fleet-footed fans off the pitch was an all too real threat, it was still a shock to see armed Israeli police patrol the perimeter fence through the badly observed minute's silence for the war dead. The favourites quickly went one down, then two, then three. Netanya's fans went crazy, scarcely able to believe that they were there to witness one of the great shocks of modern Israeli football. The game finished 3–1, the Green Apes rolled up their cop-baiting banner and left in silence without apportioning blame on players or management. They knew that the only person to blame for their team's poor preparations was a bearded ideologue, hidden in a bunker miles away somewhere near the Syrian border.

The Israeli landscape undergoes a subtle change as you drive north towards the Lebanese border. The industrial suburbs of the big cities gradually morph into plush, green olive groves, expansive valleys and signposts for flat, sand-yellow towns with names familiar from numerous past newsflashes: Afula, Jenin, Hebron. As the road north skirted the walled enclave of the West Bank an abundance of minarets gave away that more than just the terrain had changed. The majority of Israel's Arab – mainly Muslim – community can be found on the fertile planes in the north of the country, although this wealth of natural resources hadn't translated into any economic or social parity. This was also Katyusha country, the southernmost point where Hezbollah's most advanced rockets landed.

After watching Maccabi Haifa's capitulation the previous night, albeit an understandable one given the team's preparations, Ahikam, an Israeli photographer, and I headed for the small Arab town of Sakhnin to interview its most famous son, Maccabi Haifa's recent big-money signing and Israel's most prominent Arab footballer Abbas Suan. His transfer to the country's most successful team was almost inevitable after his Herculean efforts of the past two years. Abbas came to the nation's attention after leading his hometown club Bnei Sakhnin to the Israeli cup in 2004, a success that shone a light on a community viewed suspiciously both by their Jewish country-men (for being pro-Palestinian fifth columnists) and by the wider Arab world (for being Zionist collaborators). His status as a poster boy for Israel's Arabs was cemented when he was called up for the Israeli national team. Suan came on late and scored a last-minute equaliser in a World Cup qualifier against Ireland in 2005. Now he was a national name. Everyone knew who Abbas Suan was, especially in his own backyard. Unable to find his house, Ahikam stopped to ask a child wearing Bnei Sakhnin's red kit whether he knew where Abbas Suan's house was. The child scrunched up his face in confusion before looking back incredulously, pointing up the road, to the left, as if the answer was so obvious it didn't merit a reply. Everybody, it seemed, knew where Abbas Suan lived too.

We pulled up at Abbas' modest stone town house and negotiated the large courtyard bustling with life: brothers, cousins, uncles – the entire Suan clan had decamped within his modest four walls. His father, whose face wore the deep creases of a man who had worked the land for half-a-century, shuttled back and forth to the kitchen, fetching tea, fruit and plates of dates for his guests, before sitting down and regaling us with stories from his childhood memories: his grandfather had bought land for farming from the Turks and moved to Sakhnin as a child before finally having all but a tiny plot seized during the *nakba* – or 'The Catastrophe' as it is known by Palestinians – when the local Arab population were expelled (or fled depending on your reading of history) in 1948 when the state of Israel was created. As Abbas arrived, his father tidied the empty plates and disappeared into the kitchen, offering the smallest glimpses into a past that was still fresh in at least one persons living memory.

'The Haifa fans accepted me very quickly,' yawned Abbas as he sat down, still rubbing his eyes after being awoken from a lie-in on his only day off. 'I know that in the beginning some kids wrote some slogans against me because I was an Arab but the club stamped down on this because they have so many Arab fans and they've had Arab stars playing for Haifa in the past.'

The Haifa fans might have greeted his signing positively, but it had been harder to convince the fans of other teams of the merits of playing an Arab in a largely Jewish team.

'Generally speaking, Israeli fans are wonderful, one of the best in the world. At the same time there are a few that behave shamefully and we're all shamed by them,' he said, referring to one team in particular. 'I'm speaking about the fans of Beitar Jerusalem which behave beneath an accepted conduct.'

Abbas had a somewhat fractured relationship with Beitar Jerusalem. After scoring his historic goal against Ireland, his next game was an away tie at Jerusalem's notorious Teddy Stadium. The home fans welcomed his achievement by unfurling a banner. It read: 'Abbas, You Are Not one of Us.' After one game, a group of fans managed to break into the stadium whilst he was giving a post-match interview and attacked him. Perhaps most surprising of all, Abbas very nearly became Beitar's first ever Arab player. The club's newly installed billionaire owner Arcadi Gaydamak had close links with Bnei Sakhnin and donated millions of shekels to keep the club afloat. Then one day, on a visit to the club, Gaydamak decided he wanted to sign their star player for himself.

'I said I was ready, I could do it,' he said with an unexpected hint of disappointment. 'I believe he was trying to break the image of Beitar and say Arab players can play for them. But he got into trouble in Jerusalem. In the end he apologised and said he couldn't sign me.'

The past three months hadn't gone well for Bnei Sakhnin. The club were relegated from the Israeli top division, lost their captain and almost went bankrupt before Gaydamak came to the rescue. Then the Lebanon War came and the age old suspicions levied against Israel's Arabs were once again raised.

'I don't take the *Hatikvah*,' he explained of his refusal to sing Israel's national anthem. 'But I stand and respect it. It's the anthem of the Jewish people. So what can I do? I am Arab and Muslim.' Yet he was proud to fly the flag of the state, even before the country's media came to him when the war started. 'When the war broke, everybody asked me what I thought. A drop of blood from a Jewish or Arab child is the same, and the missiles don't distinguish between Jews and Arabs. So I was against the war, but I was worried for my family as rockets fell in Sakhnin. It was a big failure but politicians stick to their chairs. I wish politicians would enter Lebanon in a tank. Maybe then they wouldn't be so ready for a war.'

After we had finished talking, he agreed to drive us to his old home, Bnei Sakhnin's Doha Stadium – so called because the Qatari government stumped up some of the cash to have the place renovated, a remarkable gesture given that Qatar doesn't officially recognise Israel's existence. As he stood on the pitch and surveyed his *alma mater,* the parallels between the club's descent and the plight of his people during and after the war wasn't lost on him. If anything, the role that had been foisted on him – of spokesman and role model for a whole community – had never been as important as now.

'When we won the national cup I was proud for the Arabs in Israel and the fact that we were narrowing the gaps between communities through football,' he said nostalgically. 'Now there are many symbols attached to me and many see me as an Arab symbol in Israel. I will always accept it.'

But times, and opinions, were changing. On the eve of Israel's 60th birthday, the *New York Times* reported that a majority of Israeli Jews now favoured the expulsion of some Israeli Arabs as part of a two-state solution. Transfer, as the policy is known, was once the preserve of the hard right. Now it had become mainstream. On the journey back to Tel Aviv we again passed the distant minarets of the West Bank, an area of extreme poverty ringed by what activists refer to as a new Berlin wall, adjacent to an affluent Western democracy. Anywhere else in the world, such a juxtaposition of wealth and extreme privation would be considered vulgar. But for most Israelis, even Ahikam the photographer – a peacenik who agitated throughout his military service and was eventually given a dishonourable discharge – it's the price that the Palestinians have paid for years of terrorism and duplicity.

'I just can't understand these people like the International Solidarity Movement protesting here, what has it got to do with them?' he spat when I asked him about the wall. Even calling it a wall caused offence. 'It's not even a wall in most places, just a fence. You don't see them [the ISM] protesting in China at human rights abuses.'

But several activists had been killed in the West Bank and Gaza, including 23-year-old Rachel Corrie, protesting against the wall. 'Yes, but look at the reality. Since the fence we have had no attacks from suicide bombings. I was against it at first, too, but we feel safer because of it. If the Palestinians want their own state, fine. But it's crazy. How will they live? They could have been part of Israel and had a better quality of life and, if they were smart, they would have outnumbered Jews.' The fence has created a problem for Israeli liberals, who despised what it represented but were forced to admit that their country was safer because of it. That, plus the seeming failure of Israel's unilateral withdrawal from southern Lebanon in 2000 – a move which the Israeli right blamed for allowing Hezbollah to rearm – and Sharon's disengagement plan from the Gaza Strip had forced everyone to reassess their opinions rightwards, even the most trenchantly left-wing Israelis who would have thought those views to be the preserve of right-wing extremists a decade ago.

The problems of war and racism seem a million miles away in Tel Aviv. With the north shaken after being on the front line for the past month, and with Jerusalem long used to tension for straddling both sides of the divide – the Jewish western half with its foot in the former, the Muslim eastern half seized from the Jordanians in 1967 in the latter – Tel Aviv gives a good impression of a city that hasn't read that day's newspapers. Israelis know the city as 'The Bubble', a reference to the fact that Hamas, Hezbollah or Islamic Jihad still haven't been able to devise a rocket that can reach the country's financial capital. As a result Tel Aviv has remained relatively untouched from the rockets that have terrorised the north and the towns clustered around the Gaza Strip. It is famed for its 'life goes on as normal' detachment, its abundance of drugs and for being the party capital of the Middle East. Not to mention its vibrant gay community, a state of affairs that no doubt angers Israel's Orthodox Jewish burghers as much as the militant Islamists coveting their ancestral lands from afar.

I'd arranged to meet Amir, the editor of weekly listings magazine *Time Out Tel Aviv*. He had achieved a little notoriety in recent weeks after being interviewed by various American television networks along with his counterpart at *Time Out Beirut*. Amir was in his late thirties, with salt and pepper hair and an embarrassing musical past (he used to be the guitarist in Prototype, Israel's early-1990s answer to REM). He was a self-confessed liberal and had been troubled by the war, yet was annoyed by the lack of understanding internationally for Israel's position.

'I feel bad for what is happening in Lebanon, I really do,' he said whilst expertly rolling a joint in his modern, minimalist flat. 'But few people seem to be concerned by how we feel here, the fear of attack, the lives lost. Civilians have been killed on both sides.'

In keeping with his liberal beliefs Amir supported one of Israel's left-wing clubs, Hapoel Haifa, designated by its distinctly political prefix. But even socialist clubs were changing these days. In recent years football had begun to become big business in Israel. Television deals were signed, stadiums spruced up and Israeli football experienced a new phenomenon: billionaire Jewish sugar daddies – some home grown but many coming from abroad - willing to pump their fortunes into their hometown clubs. Some were more welcome than others. Arcadi Gaydamak was one to make the headlines after buying Beitar Jerusalem. The Russian-born tycoon was beloved by his club's fans but his rivals were loath to forget his shadier business dealings – an international arrest warrant outstanding in France due to his alleged dealings in Angola, for one. Daniel Jammer was another, a German billionaire who bought Maccabi Netanya and straight away enquired of Real Madrid as to whether David Beckham would consider moving to the club (he wouldn't, unsurprisingly). But not every infusion of cash had been successful. Amir's Hapoel Haifa had a brush with infamy when Rubi Shapira, a lifelong Hapoel fan whose dad used to be the club's kit man and who had made a fortune in African fishing concessions, bought the club and promised to bring the fans their first championship, which he duly delivered in 1999. The problem was that Rubi was so hell-bent on his dream he bankrupted himself in the process. One month later he flew to Africa and shot himself in the head. They've been stuck in the second division ever since.

Nobody seems to go out before 2am in Tel Aviv. The bouncers stepped aside at one of Tel Aviv's best clubs – a grimy courtyard surrounding a split-level shed with a sunken dance floor. Its warehouse chic was more affected than it perhaps realised. But the city's nickname became abundantly clear the moment you entered. Despite being a few days after the end of hostilities, and with a relapse still very much a possibility, hundreds of people packed the bar, danced on the tables and kissed in corners. Perhaps this was what it was like during the Blitz in 1940s London: people throwing caution to the wind, shagging, taking copious amounts of drugs and generally acting as if the world would end tomorrow. Because, invariably, it could. But Amir was too preoccupied with something far more serious thoughts. The war had exposed Israel to a greater threat than Lebanon or even Hezbollah: Iran.

'If they get the nuclear bomb,' he sighed through a bottle of beer, 'where do you think they'll hit? Here.' As if on cue, behind him two beautiful skinhead boys kissed without inhibition. 'This is everything they hate. Tel Aviv has a big red cross on it.'

The Bubble's unshakeable party atmosphere hadn't been rocked by the war against Lebanon, or even a decade's worth of suicide bus-bombings, but ordinary Israelis had been stung by the bellicose pronouncements of its Persian neighbour. Whilst the outside world saw the war as a simple conflict between a state and an armed militia within a state, Israelis viewed it very differently: as an opportunity to prove its military strength to its wider Arab and Persian foes whilst vanquishing Iran's Shia ally on its northern border. It failed on both counts. The press was having a field day against Ehud Olmert's government: the right was apoplectic with rage for not destroying Hassan Nasrallah's guerrilla army, Hezbollah, and failing to force the return of the two captured soldiers and giving succour to its soon to be nuclear enemy. The left was unhappy at the huge civilian toll that Lebanon had endured. The possibility that Iran might one day destroy everything we could see in nuclear fire was enough to lower the mood, and we retired to a popular café for a nightcap.

'That, over there,' pointed Amir animatedly, 'That is Dana International's manager.' He continued, nodding in the direction of well-known Hebrew singers, middle-aged record producers and an overweight transvestite who was wearing a woman's top so small it sat on top of his rotund belly. 'He is a famous soap star,' Amir gave by way of an explanation. As war raged across the region, it was comforting to know that somewhere in the Middle East, life went on as normal. Or as normal as a bar full of Israel's transgender glitterati can be.

Wearing a red T-shirt and admitting I was a journalist was looking like a bad idea. It was 24 hours after Haifa's capitulation and the Israeli football circus had moved to the Bloomfield Stadium in Tel Aviv for one of the biggest matches of the season: former greats Maccabi Tel Aviv versus the moneyed passion of Beitar Jerusalem. You couldn't guess it was a Tel Aviv home game, though. Outside the ground all you could see was the gold and black of Beitar. But some fans had taken exception to my choice of top. Red is the colour of arch rivals Hapoel Tel Aviv, the polar opposite of Beitar's right-wing terrace racism.

'We hate Arabs and Muslims!' screamed 19-year old Eliran as I tried to explain that I was not a Hapoel agitator. 'If an Arab played for Beitar we'd burn their ass and burn the club. They are our enemy.' Eliran was a member of La Familia, Beitar's infamous, violent and highly strung ultras group renowned for being the most uncompromising in the land. 'Ten supporters went to meet Sakhnin and make peace with the Arabs,' he explained. 'But Beitar found out. They were beaten up and banned.'

They also don't have much time for journalists. 'Beitar have the best hooligans, we'd fuck the ICF,' boasted Itzick, a bare-chested fan who seemed a lot more intimidating than his 15 years should allow. 'And we hate journalists.'

Now seemed to be a good time to tell him I supported West Ham, and by extension Yossi Benayoun.

'Yossi Benayoun!' yelped Itzick excitedly when I told him my allegiance.

'He should come and play for us. You seem OK for a journalist. The rest can go fuck themselves.'

And with that he ran into his crew of bare-chested boys, as they sang in perfectly accented English.

I'm West Ham till I die.
I'm West Ham till I die.
I know I am.
I'm sure I am.
I'm West Ham till I die.

Beitar Jerusalem is not unique for sporting a fan base that holds some un-comfortable views. But what is unusual is the phenomenal amount of power the fans wielded both within the club and within the Israeli political system. Outside of its core activities of organising fights and making racist flags, La Familia also liaised with club officials on the issues that affected the fans, like high ticket prices and whether the management were planning to sign any Arab players. It was their virulent protests that eventually persuaded Gaydamak to abandon signing Abbas Suan. In perhaps no other football club in the world are its fans courted and favoured in such a way.

'Olmert used to be here every game. But now he doesn't turn up any more, the police don't allow him to turn up as he's a security problem,' shrugged Nadav, one of Beitar's few self-styled liberal fans, whilst hanging around in a nearby park waiting for the gates to open. It was perhaps wise. Olmert's popularity had fared badly after what was widely seen as disastrous Lebanon War. The only place he could call on much popular support, surprisingly, was at Beitar.

'He's popular because he introduced Gaydamak to the club. In Israel there are a lot of people who want to come to the government and they come to Beitar Jerusalem, they take pictures with the fans because there are lots of right-wing fans here, especially those that support Likud.' Rumours abound that Gaydamak's acquisition of Beitar had more to do with his political ambitions than any great love for the club. By the sound of the fans who were singing 'I believe the Messiah is here, Arkadi, Arkadi' before the game started, he already had a few votes in the bag.

The Bloomfield Stadium was full two hours before kick-off and the 7,000-strong army of gold-and-black Beitar fans were deafening. In the large north terrace the Beitar faithful accepted me red T-shirt and all. I was offered cigarettes and sunflower seeds. This, I thought as another chant grew and filled the stadium, wasn't as bad as I thought it would be. It was only then I was told what they were singing.

'I know this one,' translated the only other Englishman in the ground, Jeremy, a British journalist working for the *Jerusalem Post*. 'They are singing: 'We Hate Nazareth, We Hate Sakhnin, I Swear on The Menorah There Will Be No Arabs Here.'

Others followed, each darker than the last.

'War, War, War.'

'The Empire Will Return'

'Tel Aviv Will Be Sacrificed By Fire.'

Beitar thought they had taken the lead, but the goal was ruled offside. The fans were incandescent with rage and hurled missiles at the referee and linesman. A yellow smoke bomb, red flares and a volley of half-eaten pretzels rained down on the pitch. The decision stood although it made no difference to the final result: Beitar won 2–1 and the players were on their knees in front of their ecstatic fans as if they'd won the championship already. Unable to escape the heaving mass, I was carried along with the throng of Beitar fans that streamed out into Tel Aviv's southern suburbs. What began as a good-natured celebration started to degenerate into a riot. The fans let off red flares and climbed atop parked cars to get a better view. The police waded in to try and control the melee by charging the crowd, firstly with police horses and then by trying to drive a motorbike through the throng at speed. We ran.

As we did, a Beitar supporter running in front of me was knocked to the ground by a fist to the face from an angry policeman. Another took a swing at me with his baton, but missed. The jubilant Beitar fans danced in the street, partially lit by the smoky glow of flares and firecrackers. For a brief moment it seemed that the fans' earlier promises to set Tel Aviv on fire were coming true. Even the police admitted defeat by falling back to defend a main junction whilst the party continued in the shops and car parks around them. Rarely do you get a chance to sit back and watch a bona fide riot. There was something frightening but exhilaratingly anarchic about it. For a fleeting few minutes, there were no rules, no government, only the pack and an internal dynamic being held together by a common passion. The downside of this was, as two skinheads grabbed me and tried to rip my T-shirt off, that if you appear to be off kilter with that internal dynamic, you're in trouble.

'Take off your Hapoel top, you fuck, it's disrespectful,' screamed one, mistaking me for a Hapoel fan. I begged for mercy, telling them my profession and nationality. They looked at each other, smiled and ceased molesting me – convinced that I was a foreign journalist and not the 'local scum', as they called, who were usually out to sully Beitar's good name.

'I wear this every day, to every game,' the smaller man said apologetically. 'It's special, and I give it to you. I'm sorry.'

He patted me on the head and ran in to the smoke. A thick cotton Beitar scarf – embossed with the Star of David and a menorah – now coiled across my shoulders.

The next day the Bloomfield looked like a very different place. The night before Beitar Jerusalem's fans were threatening to burn Tel Aviv to the ground and wishing death to the Arabs. Now the atmosphere was one, if not of conciliation, then certainly of tolerance: Hapoel's fans were singing the name of Walid Badir, an Arab player famous in Israel for playing for the national team and, more importantly, for a brief stint in the Premier League; his single season in the top flight coming with the now defunct Wimbledon FC. It was a Monday night and this was the final game of the season's opening weekend, a tricky tie against Tel Aviv's smallest but most right-wing team, Bnei Yehuda. The crowd was smaller than the previous evening, but given that the game was on television, it was understandable. The north stand was awash with red and-black and socialist imagery: flags of Che Guevara, hammer and sickles, the large red banner of Hapoel's Ultras and placards adorned with a bottle-green marijuana leaf. It was reminiscent of student protest from the early Seventies, almost anachronistic compared to the prescient hatred of Beitar's travelling support. At the front a bald man surveyed the scene with a mixture of pride and apprehension.

'There is less politics than there used to be, the parties are less important,' lamented Ronin, a wealthy architect who moved from Argentina 15 years ago but quickly adopted Hapoel after being attracted to the club's left-wing roots. 'Most fans now come from the south of Tel Aviv, like Jaffa. They are poorer so they are a different type of fan, more right-wing. Usually you say that the left wing are poor people but not in Israel, it's the other way around. Rich people are on the left.'

He introduced me to Faud, the leader of Hapoel's Ultra group, a young skinhead in his early 20s. Faud was one of the new breed, a fan from the southern suburbs of Jaffa who still clung to Hapoel's left-wing imagery despite voting for Likud.

'The union may have been left-wing, but the workers have always been right-wing,' he announced.

Despite the shifting allegiances within the club, he denied there were any tensions between the fans that represented its past and those that represented its future, especially when it came to the issue that has divided Israeli football most in recent years.

'My deputy is Arab. We have two Arab players. Most have one but we have two. If we don't like [Bnei] Sakhnin it's because they beat us, not because they're Arabs. We love Hapoel, he is left, I am right, but we are all Hapoel.'

But even Hapoel, for all their imagery, was not immune to the new commercial realities of Israeli football. As Uri, Haaretz's Hapoel-supporting sports editor, had told me money had changed the nature of the club and its political identity had faded.

'All the teams now have private ownerships, have a very vague connection with the Labor party or the union and what are left are basically the fans,' he had explained.

Money – in the form of billion-shekel takeovers from foreign and domestic donors, like Gaydamak at Beitar, and lucrative pay-per-view television contracts had begun to flood the game in Israel.

'The only thing that stays the same is hatred – the level of hatred,' Uri said. 'You have 20 teams hating the other side and maybe two or three teams supporting their own side. Israeli society is so tense, there are so many conflicts: religious, political, economic, social. It can get really ugly. In Israel it's not a culture of supporting, it's a culture of hating.'

The match ended 1–1 and the fans trudged out into the balmy Tel Aviv night, all except around 40 that hung around waiting for the referee to emerge outside the ground. When he did they hurled abuse at him. They were The Parliament, Bnei Yehuda's own ultras-style fan group that, in the spirit of parliamentary democracy, met, discussed and abused in the most rational of ways. They were also aligned to the right and came from the same community that filled Beitar's fan base.

'We are Arab Jews,' explained Avi, a member of the Parliament. 'We understand the Arab culture, we speak their language, grew up in their countries. But the others, who came from Germany and Europe [the Ashkenazim] don't. We know the mentality which is why we are what we are.' Uncompromising as this 'know your enemy' maxim was, even Bnei Yehuda had taken the plunge and signed an Arab player. 'We didn't have any Arabs play for us until four years ago and he wasn't very good,' Avi said, although it hadn't dissuaded the 'Parliament' from considering another Arab player for playing for Bnei Yehuda. 'As long as he's good we don't care now. Beitar hate the Arabs but we're a little bit more realistic,' he said as the 'Parliament' walked to a nearby falafel stand to continue dissecting the match long into the night. 'After all, if someone comes and fucks me in the ass, it hurts, sure. But the second time he does it, it doesn't hurt so much. We've had an Arab [Muslim] player once, next time won't be too painful. It'll hurt just a little bit less.'

As I walked past the stadium's main gate someone familiar was standing by the lamppost, illuminated by its yellow light. He wore Hapoel's red shirt, selling cheap polyester scarves and fake gold Star of David necklaces from a large, flat wooden suitcase. It was Oren, who only three days previously had been a passionate Maccabi Haifa fan, selling green and-white scarves and his popular Nasrallah stickers. Tonight, everything he sold was red and black. He cracked into a big smile and began laughing hysterically. He had been caught red-handed.

'I sell everything to everyone,' he replied, unable to contain the hilarity of his duplicitous allegiances. 'Wherever the money is, that's where I am.'

For at least one Israeli, religion, politics and tribalism didn't mean a damn thing.

5
YEMEN

February 2007

The young, machine gun-wielding soldier was the only man – well, boy – standing outside Sana'a's national football stadium. The imposing concrete bowl – ringed by faded walls of the red, black and white of Yemen's flag – was supposed to be filled with the voices of 20,000 Yemeni football fans, cheering on the country's biggest team, Al Ahli Sana'a. But the stadium was silent, and the vast car park was empty, save for the young soldier rhythmically chewing on the bulge in his left cheek as he gripped tightly onto his weapon.

'Is there not a football match on?' I asked, whirling around trying to catch sight of someone. Anyone. It had taken two days to get here, on borrowed money, to watch a match in Yemen. It made sense at the time, but with the grinning boy soldier and his AK47 the only witness to my weeks of planning, it suddenly felt like madness. Silently he lifted his barrel and pointed it to his left, gesturing me to follow its line. In the distance, in the corner of the car park, stood the headquarters of the Yemeni Football Association, an orphaned breeze block box adorned with an unnecessarily large sculpture of a football. The soldier grunted and I followed his cue to leave.

The nerve centre of Yemeni football was equally devoid of life, except for a caretaker who had been roused from his afternoon slumber after hearing me bang on the locked doors of the FA's entrance. 'OK,' he told me after I explained my predicament as he sat in his room, on the floor, with two friends and half a dozen half-full bags of what looked like spinach. All the men had the same bulge in their cheeks. He pointed to his mobile: 'Hamid.' Hamid Shaibani was the only man he knew who might know what was going on. He was also the man in charge of Yemeni football, the FA's general secretary. The caretaker pressed the phone to his non-bulbous right cheek, rattled off an apology in Arabic and handed me his phone.

75

'The match was cancelled!' Hamid sang back enthusiastically. 'We had an Olympic qualifier to play in Sharjah, against the UAE, so we cancelled the match.'

This, I later discovered, was not unusual in Yemen, where the fixture list for the First Division was often treated with the same amount of respect as a stray dog. The fans didn't know when, where or against whom a match would kick off until the day before the game.

When people think of Yemen, football isn't at the forefront of their minds. Usually it's just anarchy, terrorism and guns. This, after all, is a country that was only second behind Saudi Arabia in providing the men who waged jihad on foreign battlefields in Iraq and Afghanistan. It was also the ancestral home of Osama Bin Laden and the place where the American military received one of its pre-9/11 bloody noses, when the USS Cole was hit by a suicide bomber whilst moored in the southern Yemeni port of Aden killing 17 sailors. But I had come across a story, a football story, that had encapsulated one of Yemen's most enduring problems. Being ranked as one of the worst teams, not just in the Middle East, but in the world, meant that few people outside of Yemen cared for its football leagues, cups and invariably disappointing qualification campaigns for the big international tournaments. But one story had reached the radar of the international press.

Yemen Withdrew Following Doping Concerns: AFC Yemen pulled out of the Asian Games soccer tournament because of a lack of cash to drug test their squad following reports that players were addicted to a banned substance, the Asian Football Confederation (AFC) said. Yemeni soccer chiefs withdrew the team on Thursday, citing insufficient funds to carry out dope tests ordered by the Yemen Olympic Council (YOC), the AFC said on its Web site. The YOC had advised the YFA to consider pulling out following media reports that a number of players were using the banned drug qat, a leaf which has a stimulant effect when chewed. (Reuters)

A whole squad of players being banned for drug use was interesting enough, but the fact that the drug of choice was qat made it even more intriguing. Qat is the curse of the Horn of Africa, a drug that is only grown at high altitudes from Kenya all the way to Oman and which has, legally, weaved its way into the Yemeni psyche. It's a small, innocuous-looking leaf that, when chewed over time, produces a mild euphoria and a heightened sense of awakening followed by lethargy. Depending on who you talked to it was either a mild stimulant that had the same giggle-inducing properties as weed or an aggressive cocaine-type high. Just ten minutes at the ground had shown me that every adult, and post-pubescent adolescent, exhibited the tell tale signs of qat abuse from the soldier to the caretaker to the youth-team players from local club Shaab Sana'a who had earlier arrived at the stadium and were milling around outside; the distended cheeks, watery eyes and thousand-yard stares.

'We all know what would happen if the coach caught me chewing qat,' replied Ali, a 16-year-old goalkeeper, whilst running his finger across his throat. 'I'd be cut, cut from the team. If he found out he would carry me out of the stadium himself.'

The other four kicked gravel around in a circle and avoided eye contact when I asked whether any of them still took the risk. The Asian Games debacle had been something of an eye opener for Yemen's sportsmen, and the young players were glad the team had been kicked out.

'It was embarrassing, yes,' admitted Naif, a 20-year-old striker. 'Because, if they had played and were on qat, they wouldn't have been very good. They were lucky because it would have been more embarrassing if they had gone on the pitch.'

Keeping the kids off the stuff long enough to play football was a big problem – even the Shaab youth team said there was pressure from family to chew at big events like weddings.

Hamid was the new general secretary of the FA, and had been drafted in to get tough on qat and wean his charges off the green stuff.

'There will be another game, we are not sure what game, but there will be one,' Hamid finally admitted, putting my mind and racing heart at rest. 'I'll pick you up where you are standing now, on Thursday and we'll talk.'

Hamid hung up, and I walked back to the front gate, past the soldier, and waved goodbye. He was too stoned to lift his arm in reply.

I wasn't that surprised to find Abdul, the manager of Sana'a's venerable Taj Talha hotel, worse for wear. I'd been warned a few days previously by a friend from Dubai to try and get to the towering, ancient hostel deep in the Yemeni capital's old city before 1pm, otherwise: 'The man behind the desk won't know what's going on'. Sure enough, by 2pm, Abdul was half-cut. Tall, with a receded hairline, beak-like nose and a thin Nasser-esque moustache, Abdul's glassy, unfocused eyes scoured his small manager's booth looking for my keys. His right cheek was bulging with matter, a thick green paste that could only be seen in cycles, when a periodic chew revealed his dusted and blackened teeth. After falling over twice, bursting into a fit of hysterical laughter and giving me the keys to someone else's room, he finally, and with shaky hands, found the right set.

'Thank you,' he asked with a half grin on his face, unable to look straight. 'What are you doing in Yemen?'

'I'm a journalist,' I replied.

'Ah, qat is very good for journalists,' he shouted, finding a common ground and pointing at his bulbous cheek.

'You chew and then you write. Later we go to the market and chew together.'

I thanked Abdul for his offer, before he stumbled into a backroom and collapsed onto a filthy mattress for his fitful afternoon nap.

My first half-hour in Yemen revealed four odd but essential facts. The first, and most important, is that this was a nation addicted. No one is quite sure when Yemenis started chewing qat. One study discovered that Yemenis had been chewing it before the discovery of coffee. But by all independent verification, qat had been a catastrophe for Yemen and the other states where it was grown, being blamed for the anarchic situation in Somalia, poverty in Sudan and massive unemployment in Kenya. For Yemen, the consequences have meant flatlining productivity, low economic growth and extreme poverty, not to mention poor performances on the football pitch. The truly addicted would fund their habit to the detriment of food for their family, and the whole economy seemed to be moulded around its consumption. From sunrise until 1pm, life continued as normal. Then an estimated 80 per cent of the nation downs tools and heads to the qat market to buy a fresh plastic bag of the stuff. Midday is when the qat comes down from the mountain and most believe that it has to be chewed within a few hours or the active ingredient that gets you high is lost. The rest of the day is spent chewing and lying around. President Ali Abdullah Saleh, the country's first elected leader since the unification of north and south in 1990, had tried to lead by example by stating that he would not chew qat, nor would his armed forces. But he dared not ban it. There would be riots in the streets, as there were in Aden in the mid-1950s when a political party in South Yemen banned it. The issue destroyed the party and qat was back on the streets a year later. Even Islam was powerless to outlaw it. Whilst the devout and the intelligentsia frown on its consumption, and qat is banned in every Middle Eastern country bar Israel (and only then because of its large Yemenite population), it is not considered *haram* as it wasn't mentioned in the Koran.

The second thing you notice is that Yemen is awash with knives and guns. Every man, when he comes of age, is given a *jambiya*, a curved knife that sits in the front of his belt. The knife serves notice of your position in life: the more expensive the *jambiya*, the wealthier the man. But that's not all. Guns are everywhere, a hangover from the days before reunification when tribal loyalties and deep mistrust of central government meant that few threw down their Kalashnikovs. According to the 2007 Small Arms Survey, Yemen, with a population of around 24 million, had nearly 60 million guns in circulation. Add the knives to the party and you have the world's most highly armed population.

The third is Saddam Hussein's ubiquity. On nearly every street corner, wall, car and shop window, a picture of Saddam stared back at you. You can even buy 4x4 spare wheel covers bearing images of him in his pomp. He was always revered for being a symbol of Arab nationalism, for his financial support to the families of Palestinian suicide bombers and for his opposition to 'Zionist imperialism' during the first Gulf War. But Yemenis have another reason. Yemen had backed an Arab solution to the Gulf War, a stance which angered the Saudi royal family so much, fearful that Saddam's Middle Eastern tour would visit Riyadh after Kuwait, that they banished all of the kingdom's Yemeni remittance workers. In 1991 Yemenis made up the largest proportion of foreign labour in Saudi yet 850,000 were forced home, almost strangling the newly united country at birth. His death a few months before my arrival had only deepened his status as a martyr.

The fourth, rather ironically given the third point, is that the second most common fixture after Saddam on Sana'a's walls was the Star of David. The ancient Jewish symbol was carved on every other building in Sana'a's UNESCO-listed old city, a legacy from the days when tens of thousands of Jews lived here. A small community still existed in the north, but most were expelled by Yemen after the creation of Israel in 1948.

Leaving Abdul to his rest, I traipsed up the seven flights to my room which overlooked the old city. Whilst the rest of Sana'a is littered with half-built concrete buildings and debris, as if an occupation force had recently left in a hurry, the walled, old city is a fragile, beautiful reminder of Yemen's wealthy past, when its abundance of natural resources – coffee and incense – made it one of the richest countries in the world. Yemen's ancient architects had been credited with inventing the first form of skyscraper and this small section of Sana'a was packed with crooked, ten-storey, mud-built proto-high rises, all jostling for air and ringed with plaster. The whole district looked like it was carved from gingerbread. You suspected that one strong gust was all it would take to turn the city to dust, yet it had stood defiant since the second century ad and had seen Christianity, Judaism and finally Islam pass through.

The large key opened the door to my sparse room, its plain white walls only enlivened by the coloured light streaming through the stained-glass windows depicting two interlocking Stars of David. On the roof a sand storm blew through the old city's warren-like passageways, coating everything in dust and turning the air sepia, as it had done since the time of Christ. To help me get my bearings I had been trying to arrange an interview with Adel, a sports reporter at the English-language *Yemeni Times*, but our increasingly heated conversations over a crackly international line ended when it became clear that only a bribe would purloin any time with him. Still, his boss was more forthcoming and agreed to meet me at his offices near Hamdan Street, the Oxford Street of Sana'a. Outside their dreary offices every parked car had a picture of Saddam prominently displayed. Adel greeted me like I was a long-lost friend, forgetting our disagreement, and kissed me twice on both cheeks before leading me up to the *Times'* modest office. Banks of old PCs were manned by silent journalists tapping out the next day's edition. Adel ushered me into the office of Raidan Abdulaziz Al Saqqaf, the newspaper's managing editor. Rotund but with the face of an adolescent, Raidan had been working at the *Times*, which his sister edited, since he returned from studying in Nottingham and had spent most of his life outside of Yemen. He wasn't impressed with what he had come back to.

'Yes, he is quite popular,' he sighed when I asked why so many people carried pictures of Saddam around with them. 'You see, we believe in the conspiracy theory here. It is deeply rooted in our culture. We ...' he emphasised sarcastically, exonerating himself from the same view, '... think that what happened to Saddam is part of a conspiracy and he is a hero. He fought against America.'

Back then the perception in the West was that Yemen, and her imposing President, was an ally, a moderate bulwark against the spread of Islamic fundamentalism. The problem, Raidan explained, was that no one was telling the kids that.

'Yemeni children are taught a subject called nationalism. It blames all the poverty and backwardness of Yemen on occupation and colonialism and the influence of foreign powers. So you grow up thinking that Israel has been taken away from the Arabs by America. If you see the news, you will see that they don't mention the most important news. It's a systematic brainwashing of our culture. If they say Israel, they say 'Israeli enemy'. If they say America, they say 'the occupation forces in Iraq'.'

Our conversation was halted when his phone rang. 'One minute,' he apologised, listening to the anonymous caller's tip, before holding his hand over the receiver.

'Four Ethiopian prisoners have died in Sana'a prison,' he said.

'How did they die?' I asked, expecting to hear about a riot or torture.

'Starvation,' he replied coolly, as if this was quite a normal phenomenon. 'The guards didn't even know they were on hunger strike. We only found out when the embassy was called to pick up the bodies.'

After the next day's splash had been secured and a reporter dispatched, we continued talking, this time about qat. Raidan didn't chew, but he recognised how important the drug was for Yemeni society.

'In order to understand this problem, look at the Yemeni people. About 70 per cent are dependent on agriculture. We've had droughts, diseases and no subsidies. Ninety-two per cent of our wheat is imported. If you produce agri-products you can't compete so there's mass migration from rural to urban areas. Sana'a is expanding by 250,000 people per year, that's 3.5 per cent a year, the second highest [rate of urban growth] in the world.'

Which is how qat had gained its foothold. The only way people could survive was by planting a quickly grown, valuable crop. 'Qat is a plus and a minus. It's bad because of the damage to your health and people spend almost all their wages on it. But there is a benefit. Crop prices are down across the board. Except qat, so many people stop growing vegetables and grow qat. It's a cash crop, the same as poppy seeds in Afghanistan. There have been negative effects and anyone of sound mind would ban it as it's addictive. It's cheap, makes people money and it is sociable. That is why it is so popular in Yemen.' The drug was essential to the social fabric of Yemen. Like, Raidan told me, 'meeting friends in a pub in England.' Every house had its own *majlis*, a room designed for long qat chewing bouts. Some had two, one for the men, one for the women. Female chewers, like Asian teenage smokers targeted by Western tobacco firms, were the qat industry's big growth area, the next big market to get hooked and to exploit. Even a rival newspaper had its own *majlis* for editors and journalists to chew and discuss stories.

I left the offices of the *Yemeni Times* and took a taxi back to the Talha. Abdul was waiting for me impatiently outside the hotel. It was early afternoon, just when the sweet leaves had been brought fresh from the mountains to market, and he didn't want to miss out on the good stuff. He took my hand and led me through the warren-like alleyways of Bab Al Yemen, the walled ancient quarter. Shopkeepers sharpened their curved knives, or sold spices in huge, overpowering sacks that spilled out on to the tightly woven cobbled streets. Another polished picture frames in a shop that dealt with only one extremely popular visage: Saddam Hussein. The impersonal bustle of market day gave way to a crush. There was no laid-out permanent stall or signs that directed you towards Bab al Yemen's qat market. Instead, men streamed blindly towards a pre-programmed, long ago understood point, like homing pigeons returning to a coop. Abdul picked up the pace as others joined us, a half-run every six steps belying a hint of desperation. The market was an unmarked arch guarding an alleyway full of qat sellers. They sat calmly, cross legged, with their produce laid out in front of them on blankets, their steely demeanours contrasting with the frenzied bidding that was going on above and around them.

I didn't have a clue what I was looking for. One bushel, which cost 5,000 rials (about £13), looked exactly the same as another that cost 8,000 rials. Buyers barged past as more men packed into the tiny alleyway.

'This is no good,' Abdul finally said after looking at a third, identical bag, with the squinting half-eye of a jeweller examining the veracity of a newly discovered diamond. Finally, Abdul was satisfied we had a good deal, and I handed over 1,000 rials for a bag. For the money, I would be getting some moderately swanky stuff, the kind of qat that the average Yemeni would take to a wedding. For their daily hit a 500-rial bag of qat would do. Even then that represented half of Yemen's average daily wage of $6. The trick, Abdul said, noticeably more relaxed on the walk back to the hotel now that his daily fix had been secured, was to 'look for the red leaves. The more of them, the better it is.'

Back at the hotel Abdul collapsed back on his mattress and began to unravel the thin plastic doggie bag that held that afternoon's hit. I had read romantic descriptions about the rituals of Yemeni qat-chewing: the drinks, the conversation, the friends all gathered to catch up, as intricate and dainty as Victorian afternoon tea. I watched Abdul, on his haunches, greedily stuff leaves into his cheek in the dark corner of his office, the bright spring sunshine blotted out in the Talha's cool, medieval interior. It wasn't exactly what I had in mind. I said my goodbyes, went to my room and packed the qat into my bag for another day.

The taxi thumped through Sana'a's potholed streets back to the national stadium to meet Hamid, the general secretary of the Yemeni Football Association. I was late and again no one was there. Even the qat-chewing boy soldier who had been patrolling the grounds had deserted his post. In the distance, a Honda Civic approached. It was Hamid, who hadn't forgotten about me after all. With dark hair and dressed in chinos and a jacket stretched over a large paunch, he ushered me upstairs into his large office. The walls were adorned with pictures of great Yemeni teams of the past, whilst the trophy cabinet was, understandably, given that Yemen was ranked 137th in the world, rather bare. Hamid eased himself behind his large desk, a Yemeni flag in one corner and a portrait of President Saleh hanging ominously above him. As it turned out, the

Yemeni FA had only really existed in its current form for the past year. FIFA suspended them in 2006 after the sports minister tried to install one of his cronies in the job, breaching FIFA's rule on political interference. Hamid was drafted in to bring a fresh approach to Yemen's seemingly intractable sporting malaise. He was one of the new breed, a liberal technocrat who had lived in New York, China and the Netherlands working for the UN. Now he was charged with modernising football in the country. His first job was dealing with the fall out from the Asian Games debacle and trying to kick qat out of the game. Even if the modernist had to resort to draconian methods to achieve it.

'We only started looking at this [the issue of qat abuse] last October,' he explained. 'We asked every player to sign a contract to say he won't chew qat and if any test result shows he chews qat he will go to jail.' Jail might be a tough option, given what I'd heard at the *Yemen Times*' office, but for Hamid it was a necessary deterrent. 'Footballers earn $1,000 a month, even middle-class people here only earn $200, so they must look after themselves. We spend $50 a day on national team players, so imagine over six months. If we find he chews qat, he must compensate the association.' The problem was that, with the drug so ingrained in Yemen's culture, it was a hard, almost impossible sell. 'They [Yemen's footballers] were all using [qat for] a long time. We tried to educate them as qat destroys their energy. The next day you are dead [but] when you are chewing the qat you feel like a big man.'

It wasn't just the players whom Hamid was trying to forcibly wean off qat. The fans too had been banned from bringing the drug into the grounds, along with their knives and guns. 'We have security in the stadium to stop that, they cannot bring their knives in,' he added, walking to a window and absent-mindedly looking at a woman wearing an all-enveloping black *abaya* as she slowly walked across the car park to the women's gymnasium opposite. 'We have tight security. Some people smuggle it in, but it's not like it was. Did you hear about last week? At a match the fans started throwing stones at the referee. The problem is that everyone in Yemen has weapons, Kalashnikovs mainly. We have to take them off them before they go into the grounds. Then they come out, get their weapons and fight. That happened twice here.'

The last time was in 2006, when the Yemeni national team unexpectedly lost 3–0 to Thailand at the same stadium. The crowd responded to the insipid display by rioting outside, smashing up windows, setting fire to cars and shooting up the stadium as the victorious Thai team cowered inside. 'Unfortunately, it's a tradition,' Hamid sighed, grabbing his keys and ushering me out of the door to meet the national team doctor. 'No one trusts the government. The new generation, though, they don't chew qat or carry weapons. I don't carry weapons, I never have. But they expect to beat teams like

Indonesia and Thailand. We played India recently and it was 1–1. I was really worried. But we scored a second and there was no trouble, even if we didn't play well.'

The team doctor Mosleh Saleh Ali Salman was waiting for us at Hamid's local, a grimy restaurant near downtown Sana'a. Outside, groups of smiling men slung themselves over the back of their Toyota pickups clutching Kalashnikovs. We settled down on a bench laden with what looked like 18 different varieties of lamb, before the doctor made a startling admission: qat wasn't that bad for you after all.

'We haven't done a study on this [but] there is some British study, I hear about it, about qat and they recommended that you should chew qat,' he shrugged, ignoring the well-researched evidence that qat can cause mouth cancer. 'We have prohibited players from chewing it. They can chew far away from the team but chewing qat reduces the training. They can't perform in the stadium to their best so chewing qat will reduce their promise.'

Hamid was making furious phone calls to find out which match was to be played tomorrow. The rumour was that Yarmouk would take on Al Ahli, a Sana'a derby that was given extra spice by the fact that the owners of Yarmouk were deeply Islamic and had incorporated their religious doctrine into the club's constitution. The club would only sign Muslim players and only pick a player for the first team if they had proved their religious credentials by praying five times a day. Missing prayer, or having a Western-style haircut, were two foolproof ways of getting dropped from the team. Al Ahli, on the other hand, were Yemen's most popular team. The name derived from the Egyptian team Al Ahly, the Middle East's first Arab owned club. As it means 'The National', following the club has been seen as a way of supporting a more secular Arab self-determination.

The doctor continued to slowly chew on his meat. 'There are many clubs, like Yarmouk, that are very Islamic. Islamic men, but very political too,' he added. He liked the devout teams, mainly because they made his job easier as qat use in more religious households, much like smoking, had always been frowned on. So far the new regime's net had started to catch the odd intransigent player leading to a number being banned from playing. 'We have had to throw players out. We have found a player chewing qat in front of the team's official. Even if they are famous, it's no excuse, the rule is the same for everyone.' This, I was about to find out, wasn't exactly the case.

Hamid and I left to meet two of his best friends, both ex-Yemeni internationals who were now part of his new generation of officials trying to clean up football in the country. On the car journey north Hamid took the chance to rectify some of the misconceptions about Yemen: about how it actually pumped one million barrels of oil a day, the same as Iraq, but only declared 400,000, such was the corruption. That

Yemen's Islam was actually far more relaxed than people assumed. That everyone had girlfriends and boyfriends. Drugs and booze were readily available and hip-hop was the soundtrack of choice for Yemen's twentysomethings.

The bustle of Sana'a soon left us behind as we climbed higher into the sparsely populated mountains that protected the city. Decrepit oil tankers inched slowly in the opposite direction, one misplaced tyre away from a fiery apocalypse. Parked cars littered the side of the road in front of a magnificent, panoramic view of the city. As it was 2pm, prime qat-chewing time, I'd assumed it was the view that had attracted so many visitors there. But no.

'We have a lot of gays in Yemen,' he said, jutting his head towards the line of silent cars. 'No one cares, not really.'

Just around the corner from Yemen's premier cottaging site, we arrived at our rendezvous. I'd assumed we'd meet at an office, or someone's house. Instead we were met by piles of rubble on the side of the road. Painfully thin stray dogs gingerly picked their way through the detritus, oblivious to our presence.

Khaleed and Fayad were already there, leaning against their 4x4s. Both players were stars from a bygone era, playing in a team that hated itself. Whilst East and West Germany were basking in the glory of the latter's triumph at Italia 1990 and looking forward to a peaceful and prosperous future together under one flag, a more low-key, less successful version was taking place in Yemen. Unification between the warring north and south, the south under the influence of Soviet communism, the north by religious jihadists, had uneasily taken place in 1990. The reunification of the national team was equally fraught.

'There were two teams, I was with the north, then after 1990 we came together and there were big problems,' shrugged Khaleed, a tall, studious-looking man who, despite a protruding bald pate, still managed to exude youth. 'Politics has interfered with football too much here. A lot of political parties are involved. Some of the clubs have good relations with the regime and they support this club and some clubs follow the opposition and there are some problems. They are afraid but they support them through money. Ahli is the government team.'

The only thing that anyone in the newly united Yemen national team could agree on was qat, which was chewed mercilessly in an attempt to qualify for several World Cups.

'I was one who didn't chew qat,' Fayad stressed, 'But everybody did when I played. Some of them chewed one or two hours before the games, others after. They thought it would give them more energy, that it would make them strong.'

Unsurprisingly, Yemen's performances on the national stage were abysmal. Even Khaleed, a baritone-voiced, bald-headed ex-striker once considered Yemen's most feared marksman admitted that he chewed qat before a game. 'Sometimes,' he shrugged, as Hamid glared at him. 'Maybe once a year, in the last years before I retired.'

Khaleed pulled out a large plastic bag and handed me the reason why we had convened on top of a mountain near Sana'a's gay district. A dirty can of Heineken. He cracked it open, shouted '*Yallah, Yallah, Yallah*' (come on, come on, come on) and downed it in one. 'Heineken is the best beer in the world,' he grinned. 'You can't get it in the shops, but you can from the discos, everyone knows where.'

We sat drinking our beer as the bank of cars rocked to the motion of consensual gay sex below. It wasn't long before the subject of qat came up again. Khaleed asked me if I'd chewed, which I hadn't.

'Drink, and then fuck, haaaahahaha. Yes?' he said, banging his arm against the side of his car.

Hamid jumped in to explain. 'Qat is like Viagra, if a woman takes qat, it is potent.' Everyone agreed whilst frowning about the effect it has had on Yemeni society. 'We could achieve much more economically without qat,' explained Hamid. 'It takes so much money and time and we would have a big middle class with the power to buy commodities. It can take half your income. It's a curse.'

The group solemnly nodded in approval before, a few moments later, Hamid dropped a bombshell with unexpectedly brilliant comic timing. 'OK, we will go to a restaurant, get some beer and chew some qat. OK?'

I'd felt oddly subdued on the journey back to the mountain. Hamid and his gang were singing along to their favourite CD – Eminem – as if they were preparing for a big night on the town. With Hamid's zero tolerance policy towards his players' use of qat and his explicit connection between Yemen's various failures and the drug, I was expecting a footballing Eliot Ness; a whiter-than-white enforcer, living by the same rules he implemented whilst shining the torch of justice under every last stone. We stopped at a nearby Chinese restaurant. The owner ran out, shiftily looked both ways, and handed Khaleed a black bin liner full of Chinese beer. Abdullah, a fourth friend who had joined us, wearing a red-and-white headscarf and a long flowing *kandoora*, was dispatched to the market to buy the qat whilst we went to Fayad's house. Like those of most affluent people in Yemen, Fayad's house was a white, expensive-looking homage to Mediterranean design stuck in the middle of an open sewer. Shoulder-high piles of rubbish surrounded us. We entered into his specially designed qat chewing room, his *majlis*. Fayad's was a large, open room, the edges skirted with cushions and the air full of sweet Yemeni incense, which before the commodification of qat was the country's most valued substance. Before the chewing could commence, we ate as much as we could as qat's main side effect is to suppress the appetite. Abdullah arrived from his qat run hot and bothered. He'd had to first go home to ask his wife's permission to come and chew. She was a doctor and, unlike the national team's medic, knew how harmful the drug was. With permission granted, he assumed his cross-legged position at the edge of the room.

The ritual began. First, tissues and a small bucket are laid out in front of each guest whilst the host empties the qat into five equally sized bags. Each large green stem looked like rocket, and the trick was to pick the right leaves. The best and most potent were the small and slightly reddish ones. Each leaf was pulled, cleaned between the fingers and then jammed into the cheek, where it was chewed to a mush before more was added, and then more, and more, until a large ball of mush could be seen protruding from your cheek like a particularly nasty abscess. It tasted bad like unwashed, bitter spinach, but once your mouth adjusted to the sourness it had a smoky, nearly pleasant after taste.

Then you felt it working its magic: the raised heart rate, the loss of inhibitions, the waves of pleasure that shook through you. It seemed to be one part cannabis, one part ecstasy, one part speed. Suddenly everyone in the room was my best friend; I was sitting with the wittiest people in the world. I felt invincible. After spitting some of the thick green juice into my bucket, we got down to the main reason why people chew qat: to talk. The four men in the room were all desperate to improve the image of Yemeni football. They couldn't have found it in a worse state. Yet Yemen was due to host the Gulf Cup in 2011, inviting the rest of the Middle East to view the steps it had made. It would be embarrassing if the rest of the region saw the current qat-addled mess. Although for Hamid, the problems were bigger than qat. We had only just got confirmation that Ahli and Yarmouk were to play at 3.45 tomorrow afternoon, less than 24 hours before the game. None of the teams had its own stadium. There was no such thing as a match ticket in Yemen: fans just rolled up if they heard about a match on the grapevine and watched it for free. Violence, guns, knives and qat were commonplace. The government owned almost all of the teams. And to make matters worse, unless you were at the game, no one would ever see it or have a record of it. Yemen's (one) state-owned television station got angry when the FA asked them to pay for the rights and had refused to show any more matches since.

More qat was stuffed into our cheeks and as the night drew on we made an action plan. Hamid would rebrand the league, like the English Premier League, and privatise the clubs. He would bypass the local television network and sell the rights directly to a pan-Arab satellite network. That would show them! Season tickets would be sold and for those that missed the game, no fear, a highlights show, an Arabic Match of the Day, would be the centrepiece of Yemen's Friday night television schedule. It would be a ratings hit! Fayad and Abdullah shouted ideas as the room felt the frenzied white heat of footballing revolution.

'That's what I've been saying!' they shouted over each other.

'Why don't we bring over big-name foreign players, like in Qatar?' another asked hopefully.

Someone else suggested Sami Al Jaber, the legendary Saudi striker who had appeared in four World Cup finals. Why not? Why the hell wouldn't he want to play in Yemen?!

'How much would we have to pay him?' Hamid shouted excitedly. In the spirit of change, I made my own suggestion. 'How about allowing women into the stadium?!'

The other four looked at each other quizzically.

'No,' Hamid eventually responded. 'This would not work.'

But still, great work had been accomplished. At last, Yemen's footballing problems weren't as intractable as we first thought. In ten years Yemen would have the best league in the Middle East! No, in Asia! Everyone laughed, and slapped thighs, and clinked glasses of beer. With these guys together we could save Yemeni football! The shout went up: *'Yallah, Yallah, Yallah'* All was great in the world.

Then the qat ran out.

Almost as soon as the last sweet leaf had been chewed, the euphoria ebbed away and the depressing inertia that suffocated almost every single good idea in Yemeni society descended over the room. Sami Al Jaber wouldn't come here. What a stupid idea. Which pan-Arab network would want to pay to show Yemeni football anyway? If the government were so riddled with corruption, how the hell would we buy the football clubs off them? Where would the money come from? Everyone sat in silence, the same questions washing around their temples. What comes up, must come down. I felt utterly hopeless and desperate for more leaves to stave off the inevitable. But there was none left. The gang cleared up their stalks and shuffled outside into the cool Yemeni night. We said our goodbyes and retreated to our respective beds, spent. I knew that Hamid, Khaleed, Abdullah and Fayad would be having the same conversation in 12 months' time.

It was Friday and the big match was less than an hour away. As 3pm approached there wasn't a bushel of qat in sight at the small football stadium on the outskirts of the old city. I'd had a fitful night's sleep, one of the drug's other side-effects, but I didn't have to walk far out of the old city to find the squat, condemnable wreck that passed for the testing ground for Yemen's new policy on cleaning up football. Soldiers with machine guns patrolled the front gates, taking guns and qat off anyone trying to smuggle them inside. But the main weapon against fan-on-fan violence was the *jambiya*, and the police had a cunning plan. Rather than impound the knives, they set up a free cloakroom so the spectators could retrieve their knives after the games. The cloakroom was an engine-less Toyota Corona that sat silently as men streamed to the back window. Inside, two policemen poked their hands through a small crack in the window to receive each spectator's knife. In return they received a small plastic ticket. The system seemed to make sense, until I realised that each ticket was exactly the same. Piled all around the policemen, the curved knives looked indistinguishable from one another.

After being shaken down I took my position pitch side as the terraces filled green and red – the green of Yarmouk, the red of Ahli. Minarets protruded from the nearby slums like gleaming white skyscrapers as the basalt mountains watched over in the distance. Suddenly, the call to prayer wafted over the pitch from every direction. Most Gulf countries have employed a system whereby the call to prayer is called at exactly the same time. Some use a single recorded voice for uniformity. Others, like the UAE, make sure that it's not just the times and the voices that are in unison. Friday sermons are vetted by the government too and sent back to each Iman with the official imprimatur. Yemen, as with almost every aspect of its society, was gloriously oblivious to the technological evolutions in Islamic prayer. Each mosque still had its own *muezzin*, prayer caller, and each keeps its own time. Some calls to prayer start as early as 3.30am. The result is a deafening, jumbled cacophony that had not changed for a hundred years. As the two teams warmed up a tall, balding man with glasses, wearing a long white *kandoora* and sporting a huge j*ambiya*, stalked around the Yarmouk players. Abdul Aziz was still allowed to carry his knife because he was the vice president of the club. The Sudanese manager Mohammad Mahdawi circled the seated players in the other direction. Aziz spotted me watching his team talk, straightened his back and walked over.

'We established this club in 1968 with a group of people who had the same idea,' he explained, before spreading his arms and pointing to both sets of fans. 'We are all Muslims, but Yarmouk is more strict. We pray before matches and we are more strict with our values. We don't allow players to chew qat or smoke. Their behaviour is more important than the way they play. So we choose players on that basis.'

It seemed unbelievable that a team could exist that was chosen not on ability, but on a player's degree of religious devoutness. But Yarmouk hadn't been doing too badly. They sat mid-table and had a reputation for playing fluid, attacking football without ever challenging for the championship, a bit like an Islamic Tottenham Hotspur. Abdul still seemed suspicious and was overly eager to point out that his team wasn't filled with extremists or corrupted by fundamentalist ideology.

'Since the beginning it was like this, not as fanatics but to respect the values [of Islam],' he replied when I asked whether a non-Muslim could play for the team. 'We have a Nigerian, but they are Muslim too. [But] we would have a non-Muslim.'

'Don't you mind playing on a Friday?' I asked.

'It is no problem at all,' he laughed, patting me on the back and walking back towards the players. 'Look,' he said, pointing back to the crowd. 'It will be full today.'

He was right. Despite the short notice, the addictive draw of an afternoon's qat chewing and the demands of the mosque, 7,000 fans had packed into the stadium. It all seemed rather cordial as the players kissed each other's cheeks and rubbed each other's noses. Hamid finally arrived and we took our seats with the Yarmouk fans, who sang and shouted at the Ahli players, targeting those that had ponytails.

'You'll see a good game today and a good crowd,' Hamid assured me as the officials sorted out the paperwork. The linesmen sat atop the only three balls in the stadium as if they were rare and valuable eggs. Another official polished the brand new, $500 electronic substitutes board, Hamid's most recent attempt at modernisation. The referee blew and the crowd erupted.

The Yarmouk fans flew the green flags of Islam and mocked any Ahli player who went down too easily. 'You're not hurt!' the 3,000-strong all-male contingent shouted. 'You have spoilt yourself!'

Then, against the run of play, Ahli broke away with their star player Ali al No No. 'No No' translates as 'baby' and Ali was once the great hope of Yemeni football. He had moved to more lucrative and better organised leagues, first in the star-studded Qatari league, then in the less glamorous Syrian first division. He'd failed in both but in Yemen he was the closest thing they had to Ronaldinho, as he exhibited with a curling shot from all of 25 yards into the top corner just before halftime. The red half of the crowd exploded, the green half fell silent.

With half-time approaching the third official struggled with the electronic board. Two more officials came to his aid, none able to get the requisite number of added minutes to be played displayed on its electronic face. Soon, a whole crowd gathered around, pressing buttons randomly and shaking the lifeless board before giving up and resorting to the numbered cards that had done them just fine for the past few decades. Hamid shook his head before bowing into his cupped hands and leaving the ground.

In the second half, Yarmouk fought back and equalised, the goal sparking a riot in the Ahli stand behind the goal. Police with sticks waded in hitting anyone who dared show a lack of immediate respect. With order restored, the game wound down to its inevitable conclusion, just as dark clouds rolled over the stadium and the first spots of a cold, early spring rain started to fall.

Back in the changing room, Yarmouk captain Usman Salihu was happy with the result. Usman was Nigerian but had played in the region for the best part of a decade in Lebanon, Saudi Arabia and Syria for the army club Al Jaish – which literally means 'The Army' – before coming to Yemen and seeing the country's qat addiction first-hand.

'The players are not treated like professionals,' he said as we sat down in a large changing room, our voices echoing around the four peeling walls. 'The qat contributes a lot to the lack of performance in the team. I don't take it but from the people I know who take it, it absorbs their strength. They can't train. This is their main problem here.'

His manager, who had earlier been stomping around his squad like a recently promoted army general, was equally clear on Yemen's problem. Madawi was a former assistant coach to the Sudanese national team but had been in Yemen managing Yarmouk for two years.

'Every year they say it will change but it doesn't,' he said, slumping slightly as he delivered the news. 'Even the [FA] committee get together to chew.' I shook my head and offered a faked look of shock in response. For the outsiders, it was obvious who was chewing and if the FA really wanted to make examples of players they could. 'I don't want to name any names, but I see those who chew. We know who they are. This is not something that is hidden. It is not like cocaine. It is allowed so they chew. And it is available everywhere.'

Both Usman and Madawi hoped that Yarmouk's example would be the best way to exact change. One of the big advantages of only signing players that adhere to a purer form of Islam is that they would be fitter than the rest of the league. 'Every player prays before and after training and everything that religion doesn't allow, Yarmouk doesn't allow,' Usman explained proudly. 'Of course we are fitter because we stick to our religious obligations. We are seventh now but we hope to have a good position this season and maybe win the championship next year.'

This was arguably Yemen's best hope, that non-qat chewers led by example, excel and are rewarded in whatever field it is they find themselves in, be it farming, journalism or football. I bade farewell to Usman and Madawi and their depressing take on Yemen's inability to break its qat thrall. Outside was anarchy. The crowd was still streaming from the stands to the exit, but an almost reverential clamour had come over them. Ninety minutes of qat denial was more than most men could stand. Almost every single pubescent male was filling his cheeks with the drug, secret stores that had somehow eluded detection from the armed guards outside. The pavement was dotted in the green effluence of Yemen's addiction. The crowd swirled around the engine-less Toyota Corona that doubled up as a knife depository like an unstable storm. Fans from both sides thrust their tickets through the window as the harassed policemen matched them to homeless ornate steel. The chaotic scenes sat in contrast to the lone man standing back from the pavement, watching from afar. Murat had been at the game, even though he was a Ahli Ta'izz fan from the south. Yet he didn't seem the slightest bit interested in joining in the melee. Was he not desperate for any qat too? I asked him. 'I gave up months ago, it broke my teeth,' he replied, before breaking into a bellicose laugh, his huge open mouth empty of teeth. Murat had accidentally stumbled across a foolproof way to kick his habit.

My time in Yemen had come to an end. I checked out of the Taj Talha, said goodbye to Abdul, who was already on his first bag of the day, and hailed a cab on the Wadi Road towards the airport. Mujid picked me up in his ancient Toyota Corona, wearing the Yemeni uniform of white *kandoora*, blazer, headscarf and knife.

'Five hundred rials,' he asked solemnly. Seeing as it was a third of what I was being offered elsewhere, I agreed. The car lurched into life and spun off just before the other marauding taxi drivers could cut in and take his fare. Although, as I later discovered, they may have simply been trying to impart a warning.

Mujid's car was, like every other in Yemen, on the brink of extinction. They regularly cut out whilst traveling down highways and every Yemeni man seemed to have such a union with his automobile that he could sense the precise moment it would run out of petrol, ensuring that, as Mujid did, he glided into the petrol station on nothing but the most cursory of fumes. Mujid's luck had run out, though, as the car wouldn't start.

'Push,' he implored, poking me out of the car. I took my position behind, a passer-by on the right, and grunted. The car came back to life just as I trampled through a stinking, overflowing gutter, and jumped into the passenger side, Mujid speeding up as if he hadn't really wanted me to get back into his cab at all. He laughed, before narrowly avoiding a truck and asking me to give him all my money, using warped but impeccable logic.

'You will not need your money now because you are leaving Yemen,' he said.

Stuck in a traffic jam, Mujid attempted to veer onto the pavement but slammed his brakes on, screeching to a halt in front of two Yemenis casually talking. This was clearly a provocation. Although the *jambiya* is a cultural accessory, it can be, and is, still used as a weapon to settle scores in Yemeni disputes under certain circumstances. I was pretty sure road rage wasn't one of them, but Mujid screamed at the two men before pulling out his *jambiya,* waving it inches in front of my face and stabbing it at the human roadblock. The two men responded, drawing their knives and thrusting them through the passenger window before they clumsily jousted in front of me. I wedged myself back into the seat as far as I could and prayed to the God I had long ago forsaken to let me live. Being outnumbered, Mujid sped off, his knife narrowly missing my throat in the recoil, his cab narrowly missing a lorry as he veered away. Behind us the men continued chasing after the car. Somehow, no one had been stabbed and my face had remained unslashed. I had witnessed, a little too close for comfort, my first Yemeni knife fight.

An angry silence fell over us.

'Have you ever stabbed anyone before?' I eventually asked, still rooted as far back in my seat as possible. Mujid looked back blankly.

'Stabbed someone,' I repeated, making a stabbing motion with my arm at the same time.

'Yes,' he replied. 'Many people. Now, give me a cigarette.'

Without hesitation I passed over a cheap Yemeni Kamaran Light and sat back in silence as Mujid swerved and shouted his way towards the airport, drawing his knife once more at another driver in a Land Cruiser that cut him up. The shell of a taxi careered into Sana'a International Airport. I handed over a 1,000-rial note and bolted, dragging my bag out of the back seat. The last thing I heard was Mujid screaming, demanding the rest of my Yemeni money. I didn't look back, and I didn't ask for the change.

6
PALESTINE:
WEST BANK

March 2007

The protest was already in full swing. Walking towards Bethlehem University, the low rumble of faraway raised voices could be felt, if not exactly heard, until the tall sandstone walls broke at the main gate to reveal the crowd inside. Dozens of young men danced in circles to distorted Arabic pop music, spinning their black-and-white keffiyeh scarves in the air. Those that didn't shook yellow flags. The flag depicted two fists, one clenching a bayonet, another a machine gun above a grenade. Behind the men, banks of women, some covered, some not, stood silently unmoved, as a demonstrator with a megaphone began shouting his call to arms.

'*Allahu Akhbar!*' God is great.

The men mirrored his call. 'It was the student elections yesterday,' came a voice to my side, by way of explanation. It was one of the university's Christian Brothers, who administered the campus. This was a victory parade for Fatah, who had vanquished the likes of Islamic Jihad and Hamas to control the university's student body politic. It was a rare moment of success for Fatah – the nationalist party of Yasser Arafat and now the Palestinian President Mahmoud Abbas; the party that had dominated Palestinian politics had squandered the goodwill of their people through corruption and mis-management. Amidst the discontent Hamas, the Islamic fundamentalist party still considered a terrorist movement in the West and by Israel, had moved in and was in the ascendancy after winning the 2006 parliamentary election. Hamas and Fatah had been rubbing each other up the wrong way ever since and had been fighting for hearts and minds in the West Bank and Gaza, sometimes metaphorically, mostly literally, one espousing a secular version of Palestinian statehood alongside Israel, the other promoting a vision of Islamic resistance and Palestinian statehood on top of it. It might have only been a minor student election, but Fatah needed all the victories it could get.

'I voted for Fatah,' said Jasmine, a 20-year-old studying computer science, as she watched the rapturous scene unfold. 'Muslims and Christians vote for them, only Muslims voted for Islamic Jihad and Hamas. In other universities they have won, but not here. It's supported by the Vatican and Hamas would make us cover.'

The screams from the victory parade couldn't be heard down in a basement office on the other side of campus. Samar Mousa was oblivious to the goings on in the main square as she shuffled important paperwork and fielded excuses from her students as to why they didn't have any kit with them for that day's physical education class. Short, with dark hair and piercingly friendly kohl-ringed eyes, Samar welcomed me into her tiny office out of which she ran the university's women's athletics department. But that was merely a day job that helped her to build a subtler, but no less important, form of defiance: organising the Palestinian women's national football team.

Football had long been a man's game in the Middle East. Whilst women's football had exploded in popularity in Asia and the West, women in the Middle East still had to fight just to get a game. Not a single Arab team qualified for the Women's World Cup in 2007. In fact no team from the Middle East or North Africa had ever qualified for the finals, which is no surprise given the reticence of governments and governing bodies towards the women's game. In Iran the authorities insist that women cover completely, only showing their hands and face. What's more, men are banned from watching them play. In Saudi, the authorities have banned national women from playing football completely. In Egypt, one high-ranking FA official didn't even know there was an Egyptian women's team, even though they are arguably the best in the region and were ranked 85th in the world by FIFA. Kuwait's women footballers looked to have made a breakthrough when a member of the royal family, Sheikh Naima Al Sabah, announced that a national football team would be set up. Fans on message boards joked that it was probably the best chance Kuwait had of qualifying for a football World Cup again. The plan was quietly dropped when Waleed Al Tabtabae, a leading Islamist MP in the Kuwaiti parliament who ran a committee that monitored 'phenomena alien to society', forced the team to be banned by arguing that women's football was 'un-Islamic'. But even these barriers pale in comparison to those faced by the Palestinians, who have to fight, not just the restrictions of occupation, but also their own communities to play the game they love.

The seed of the Palestinian national women's team was planted over two decades ago, in Amman, Jordan, out of an injustice. 'I was studying there and they told me that I couldn't play football,' explained Samar cheerily as she ushered me into her windowless broom cupboard. Framed photos of her proudly standing next to the women's team littered the shelves along with dog-eared black and white prints of her family. 'They said I had to do aerobic dance, it made me mad so I made sure that when I was in charge, girls could play football.'

It was difficult to imagine Samar getting mad; such was her soft, matronly demeanour. Yet her experience of being slighted as a young, football-loving student wasn't exorcised until four years ago. It was whilst teaching physical education at the university that Samar's dream came to fruition. And that was only when she met 23-year-old Honey Thaljieh – the team's captain and star striker.

Samar ushered two girls into the room. 'We started with Honey,' she said, smiling at the brown-haired captain as she found her seat. 'Then we had three players, then five from the university, and then we spread the idea to other towns, in Ramallah, Jericho and Gaza. Now we have 20 players in all.'

Honey and Jackline Jazwari, the team's left-winger, had come to the beautiful game from different places: Honey had played (and beaten) the neighbourhood boys in barefoot practice matches on the streets of Bethlehem almost as soon as she could walk. She was blessed with a powerful right foot and natural leadership skills, and Samar decided to build the whole team around her. Jackie, on the other hand, had never kicked a football before she met Samar.

'For me it was a strange thing to play football,' she recalled. 'But when I saw Miss Samar I was in the first year in university and I was playing in the basketball team and she said why don't you join our team? She said you'd love it and pushed me into it. I love her like my mother so I went to training, saw the girls and the spirit in the team and wanted to play.'

Despite having a strong nucleus of dedicated players, the practicalities of living in the West Bank made it almost impossible for them to actually play any football. To start with the only grass pitch was ten miles away in Jericho, which is largely inaccessible thanks to the ring of Israeli checkpoints that surround Bethlehem. Instead they practised on a nearby concrete court with pre-pubescent boys. No women's club teams exist, which meant no league, no cup and no competitive games. It was also impossible for the girls from Gaza to train with their counterparts in the West Bank without leaving the country.

'We went to Egypt to meet the Gaza girls before a tournament last year. It was the first time I had even met them,' Samar explained. 'We didn't know their names. It's strange playing together as a national team as we met the girls for the first time two days before our match. It was also the first time we ever played on a full-sized pitch once in Egypt. The girls didn't know their positions but they played by enthusiasm. We lost, but we didn't lose by that much.'

The biggest obstacle to progress, however, was Palestinian society itself, which hadn't exactly welcomed the women's team with open arms.

'At first it seemed weird, women playing soccer in our society because it has such a male mentality,' admitted Honey through her warm perma-smile, as we all sipped tea in the cramped office. 'Some families had problems sending their daughters to play football, some still face problems.' The resistance came from a mixture of conservative social mores and a creeping religiosity that has spread from Gaza to the West Bank. Although five players were Muslim, most were drawn from the West Bank's small Christian community centred on Bethlehem. Some towns were so conservative they were totally off-limits for recruitment. 'We don't go to Nablus, Jenin and Tulkarem,' Honey lamented. 'We've had some difficulties. One player – her uncles said she shouldn't play. Then they said she had to wear the veil and kept putting barriers up. But they eventually accepted the idea. Step by step they saw what we were doing.' Then there's the issue of marriage. The team has already lost two first-team players to husbands who demanded their wives give up football for duties in the home, a fact that meant that Honey was the oldest of the team. She had vowed not to get married unless her future husband accepted her love of football. 'I'm single, but if I get engaged and get married I will still play. If he loves me he will love what I am doing.'

Quite how football was any barrier for Honey getting married was beyond me. Aside from the fact that she was arguably the most beautiful woman I had ever met, she was strong-willed, intelligent and obsessed with football. Maybe Palestinian machismo was the answer. After all, if your fragile male pride can't handle a woman with her own ideas, it's hardly likely to survive being nutmegged by your betrothed during a kick-around. Marriage wasn't the only barrier either. The team's kit had become somewhat of an issue. Sepp Blatter may have wanted to 'sex up' the women's game with a new kit that mirrors beach volleyball, but in the West Bank long shorts and over-sized shirts were still considered too risqué, especially for some Muslim families who regarded them as indecent.

'In the north of West Bank and Gaza they are a little stricter,' Samar said diplomatically, but with a wry smile. 'The problem is that they do not respect us if we don't dress honestly. We wear shorts near the knee. This is the biggest problem. But our coach is Muslim, a strict Muslim, yet he still coaches us.'

As if on cue Raed Ayyad, the team's 37-year-old coach, introduced himself. Quietly spoken and with a large barrel chest upon which his whistle lay, he smiled and stroked his thick beard when I asked whether his religious beliefs had been conflicted at all by coaching a team of inappropriately dressed footballers. He was new to the job. The vacancy had only arisen after the last coach quit when the Israelis detained him as he tried to leave the West Bank for a match overseas. It wasn't the inconvenience that made him leave, but rather the unfairness that his presence might hamper the team's attendance at tournaments. The new coach wasn't there for the financial benefits either, as the position was unpaid. Worse, he had to combat a whispering campaign as to his intentions in taking the job.

'It was difficult for me because all the people were gossiping that I was training girls,' he admitted, the fourth person in the small room making it feel like a sauna. 'They would say: 'Why is he training girls? Football is rough, it's not good for them,' things like that. I tell them, from a religious point of view, Muslim or Christian, no one has said that it is forbidden, that women can't play soccer. Islam says that sport is good for the body and if [the players] wear long clothes then it would not be forbidden amongst the Muslim community.'

Raed's moderate voice of reason had become more and more isolated in the previous months. Hamas' parliamentary election win had sent a huge signal to the rest of the world as to the changing nature of Palestinian society – it was becoming more religious, more conservative and more radical. Honey, for one, had noticed the difference, both as a footballer and as a Christian.

'Things are becoming more conservative under Hamas but not all women are the same,' she asserted. 'Some women believe that they can do something and won't just wait for their husbands to come along and make children. They believe that they can change something and I'm one of them, the rest of the girls too. It's one of the most difficult things we face. Sometimes we feel like we are fighting alone. We need some encouragement but you can't find it here. So it's about courage. If we have courage we can achieve anything we want.'

Honey's articulate call to arms heralded the end of our interview. Samar had to get on with her athletics training and Coach Raed was preoccupied with training the university's men's team. As the only games Palestine played were international fixtures away from home it was impossible to see them in action, plus training was a few days away. But Honey and Jackline agreed to go for a kick-about in the basketball court outside. The basketball players stopped what they were doing and stared as Jackline teed up the ball and expertly transferred it from foot to foot, occasionally striking the ball higher only to control it back down to earth with her chest. Even within the university the team was considered something of an oddity. The ball passed to Honey who struck it with her ferocious right foot, the ball flying straight into my face. When the two had stopped laughing hysterically I arranged to come back to see training and interview more of the players.

Holding my throbbing nose I climbed back up to the university's now empty main square. The detritus of the victory rally blew across the concrete floor. A yellow Fatah flag lay crumpled and unloved on the floor. I picked it up, put it in my bag and left through the front gate.

It was a short walk down a steep hill to Manger Square. If there's one thing that defines the West Bank it is an inequality of altitude. The West Bank's uniquely coloured, yellow-white hills are the most coveted in the world, with the incremental battle for supremacy between Palestinian and Israel settlements taking place at their zenith. Each hilltop has its own urban snowcap, clinging precariously to its summit lest anyone replaced it when they weren't looking. Bethlehem's ancient foundations meant it could be confident of continuity, but others had not been so lucky. Silver-walled Israeli settlements rise up on nearby hills, all steel and superiority. At its base, the previous occupants scratched a living in huts made from discarded plastic and corrugated iron, waiting for the day they would once again claim the higher ground. Bethlehem will always be fixed in the mind as a place of worship for Christians and, sure enough, Palestine's shrinking Christian minority almost all live here. It was one of the reasons why the women's team could exist in the first place, operating as it does in a slightly, only slightly, more tolerant atmosphere. It was difficult to imagine such an endeavour being tolerated in the universities of Hebron, Nablus or Jenin.

In one small back alley Mike tended to his customer-free trinket shop, St. Johns. 'Things here are bad,' he told me, lighting up a cigarette on the shop's step, revealing the large cross he wore around his neck buried in thick silver chest hair. 'Most Palestinian towns are industrial but we rely on tourism. The war in Lebanon really hurt us.'

In fact, any bad news – suicide bombings, border restrictions, flare-ups in Gaza – was felt more keenly here than anywhere else. Once Bethlehem thrived on thousands of foreign tourists flocking here to see the Church of the Nativity, the site where Christians claim Jesus was born. Few were coming any more. Bethlehem's nadir came in 2002 when a bloody siege between the Israeli military and suspected Palestinian militants took place, flashing images across the world of bloodshed on the doorstep of one of Christianity's holiest sites.

'It hasn't been the same since,' shrugged Mike, handing me a small wooden cross as a present.

Sure enough the square was empty, the small door to the church clear apart from two Palestinian Authority policemen patrolling nearby. The only other life was a gaggle of American preachers dragging a large wooden cross with a wheel on it. Arthur and

Joshua, a father-and-son preaching team from California, had been dragging the cross around the world since the 1970s trying to break the world record for the longest walk – feeling Jesus' pain before the crucifixion whilst spreading the word of God. Almost everyone had been photographed with him; even Arafat and Gaddafi featured in the black-and-white prints Arthur proudly showed me. I was half-expecting a grinning photo of him shaking hands with Saddam. Everything they talked about seemed to point to a bigger, higher question.

'I've never felt alone on my journey because the Lord has always been with me,' replied Arthur when I asked whether he missed a settled life. 'Jesus knows where I have been.'

I could only think of glib questions – 'Shouldn't you take the wheel off to really feel Jesus' pain?' or 'Do you ever get stopped at customs with that?' But they were used to ridicule and wouldn't allow my facetiousness to get in the way of a possible conversion.

'Here,' Joshua offered. 'Try the cross on for size.' He passed me the six-foot-long timber cross, so heavy it pinned me to spot. I was a captive audience as Arthur gathered his disciples around in a circle: 'Let's pray.'

His sermon was interjected by meaty shouts of 'Yeah!' from his followers every time he mentioned Jesus.

'Let Jesus into your heart,' Arthur intoned, holding my hand. 'You will never feel alone, amen.'

Under my shades, my eyes were closed. Involuntarily I replied 'Amen', Arthur took his cross, thanked me for my time and skipped into the Church of the Nativity, continuing on his journey.

I shook my head, laughed and continued on mine.

Palestinians and Israelis share a joke about Jericho. The descriptions might be different, but the punchlines are the same. Three Palestinians are stopped at a checkpoint. The Israeli soldier asks where they are from. 'Jenin,' says the first. 'Get down and spread 'em!,' shouts the soldier. The second says: 'Ramallah.' The soldier shouts at him to get down too. The third says: 'Jericho.' The soldier hands him his gun. 'Hold this whilst I arrest the other two, won't you?'

There has always been the suspicion amongst Palestinians that if Israeli collaborators were to live anywhere, it would be in Jericho. It isn't refuted by the town's aesthetics. The road from Jerusalem is littered with crumbling towns and dirt-poor villages populated by barefooted children and herds of goats. Once you pass the Israeli checkpoint, a different West Bank emerges, one that Jericho seems to be the only representative of. The streets were wide and clean. Grass and palm trees lined the roads. A swanky hotel and casino could be found on the outskirts. Whilst the rest of the West Bank reeked of poverty, Jericho had the air of a thriving oasis town. After visiting the Palestinian women's team I had been told that one of Bethlehem's local men's teams was due to play a cup match in Jericho the next afternoon, a rare occurrence in the West Bank. Since the so-called al-Aqsa intifada flared in 2000, movement restrictions between Palestinian towns had slowly strangled the life out of the Palestinian football league. With fans, teams and referees struggling to make it to matches, it was impossible to fulfil the league's fixtures. The FA eventually gave up, concentrating on smaller cup competitions to keep the clubs afloat until the day arrived when the league could return. The quarter-finals were due to be played between two of the West Bank's best teams; Tulkarem, a devout town in the north, and Wadi al Nes, a small village on the outskirts of Bethlehem.

Whilst the women's game had struggled to have its voice heard, the men's game in Palestine made international headlines after it tried, and tragically failed, to qualify for the 2006 World Cup. The national team had a higher purpose than most as it is in the unusual position of being a national team without a nation. So when FIFA recognised Palestine in 1998, it was a cause for massive celebration in the West Bank and Gaza. FIFA were, after all, one of the only international bodies to recognise Palestine's existence. Reaching the World Cup finals, the Palestinians reasoned, would ensure that the world couldn't ignore their claims for statehood any longer. With the UN refusing to grant it full membership, it was the next best hope. It all started so well too. FIFA had relaxed its rules on citizenship, allowing the Palestinians to call on its huge diaspora to fill its team sheet. Adverts were put into magazines in Germany, Chile and the United States to attract players. A multinational squad was assembled, followed by an 8–0 thumping of Chinese Taipei and a respectable 1–1 draw with Iraq, two teams that had to play their home games in exile, on foreign grounds. Then the wheels fell off. Movement restrictions between Gaza and the West Bank, not to mention the restrictions within them, meant the team could rarely train together. Training camps were set up in Egypt, but the players from Gaza would rarely get through the border. The coaching staff, realising that nine-man training sessions probably weren't the best sort of preparation for an assault on reaching the World Cup finals, started picking more players from the West Bank, breeding resentment amongst the two groups of players and effectively creating two different national teams. Hope died when some of the team were denied permission to leave Palestine to play Uzbekistan. Five Gaza-based players had been held at the border in the aftermath of a suicide bombing in Beersheba. The Palestinians could barely scrape together 11 players. It was a miracle they only lost 3–0. The campaign was over, the Palestinian dream of statehood through the back door shattered.

The national team had never really recovered after that, nor had local football. Back in the West Bank, the restrictions remained and a league was still a distant memory and a forlorn hope. The quarter-final was due to be played at the rather hopefully named Jericho International Stadium. Covered in smashed windows and looking little more than a derelict car park with a rectangle of grass and sand at its centre, it was hard to imagine the stadium having ever seen better days. Faded posters of Yasser Arafat still adorned the low walls that led to the stadium. Fans crushed through the single turnstile to pay their seven shekels for a ticket. Once inside they took their position in the one functioning stand at the side of the pitch, the Wadi al Nes and Tulkarem fans separated by a thick line of Palestinian Authority policemen carrying clubs. A few left their seats to take their positions towards Mecca and pray in the bright, late-afternoon sunshine.

'This competition is a little like, how do you have, the Milk Cup,' Khaldom, a Tulkarem fan, told me whilst sitting in the stands chewing on a bag of sunflower seeds and showing an almost autistic grasp of mid-1980s English football. The stadium looked half-empty but Khaldom wasn't that surprised. 'It's a long journey and there are three checkpoints to get through. Luckily it wasn't too difficult for me and only took an hour.'

The referee, on the other hand, wasn't so lucky. Half an hour after the planned kick-off he still hadn't arrived. A few minutes later the rotund man in black came puffing onto the pitch to a wall of jeers.

'He got held up at a checkpoint,' Khaldom offered. 'But they are more free here in Jericho. In Tulkarem the police cannot work after 10 pm, then the Israelis take over. But here they are everywhere all the time.'

Tulkarem were clear favourites. The team consisted of a number of Palestinian internationals and were coached by the current national team manager Mohammed Sabah. With the stadium not having any changing rooms, both teams received their last-minute instruction behind the steel fence that separated them from the fans. Finally the referee blew his whistle. The years of footballing frustration poured out. Tackles flew in, players rolled around on the floor as if they had been garrotted and yellow cards were brandished like confetti. Seeing that it could be months before the loser got another game, both teams were desperate not to lose. Off the pitch the situation was worse. One journalist sent to cover the match from Tulkarem was escorted from the stadium after he jumped on the pitch in a rage at one of the referee's many dodgy decisions, clawing at the air between him and the man in the middle as he was dragged away by the police. The armed police had to wade in to beat back a crowd of Tulkarem fans after the perimeter fence protecting the players from the terraces was stormed. Their flailing nightsticks carved through the mass until they stopped, confused. At its centre a wheelchair-bound supporter was repeatedly wheeling himself into the perimeter fence and hurling abuse at a Wadi al Nes player taking a throw.

'Of course, some of these players are for Hamas, others are Fatah,' Ahmad, a Palestinian journalist from Al Hayat, whispered to me as the match unfolded. 'But there isn't one team that is for Fatah, the other for Hamas. We are all Palestinians.'

That might have been the case for the West Bank but I had originally wanted to visit Gaza to see how Hamas and Fatah rivalries were being played out in the football league there. One of the few benefits for Gazans in the chaos that had followed Israel's pull out from the tiny strip in 2005 was the absence of movement restrictions, which meant that the football league could go on. The Israelis occasionally still bombed the odd match – the main football stadium in Gaza had been hit by a mortar a few months earlier as a team trained on it – but other than that, the games and the league went on as planned. But Gaza had become totally inaccessible to Westerners thanks to the continued power struggle between the forces of Mahmoud Abbas' Fatah and Hamas. A lawlessness had gripped Gaza as the two forces fought to exert what they saw as their mandate to fulfil the will of the people; the former presidential, the latter parliamentary. Matters were made worse since the BBC journalist Alan Johnston had been seized a month earlier and was still being held captive. I'd hoped that the Palestinian FA could have given me safe passage to the last game of the season, a title decider in the Rafah refugee camp.

'Not even the FA could protect you there,' Ahmad exhaled.

The game itself reached a frenzied conclusion, 1–1, extra time and then penalties. The two teams chose radically different ways to prepare. Tulkarem huddled, discussed the order of the kicks and took some last-minute instruction from the manager. The Wadi al Nes players and staff, even a few of the fans, put their preparations into the hands of God. The motley crew knelt in a line and prayed in the near darkness, hoping for divine intervention. Football fans may talk about how unfair a penalty shoot-out is, but for the neutral penalties are the most exciting part of any match, like squeezing a whole tournament into ten kicks. But if it's your team, it's hell on earth. For one Wadi al Nes player the tension was too much, and he sparked up a cigarette, smoking it surreptitiously in the cup of his hand so his coach didn't see. The goals, the saves and the misses ebbed and flowed. Finally, Wadi al Nes scored the winning penalty to go into the semi-finals. The players bundled into one another on the floodlit pitch as the Tulkarem players sprinted away and jumped into a waiting bus, before speeding off minutes after the end.

'We played better,' explained midfielder Kader Youssef, grinning wildly as his team-mates celebrated around him. 'It is important to own the cup and it's great for our village and great for our people. Inshallah we will play Al Islam [next]. It's a derby.'

Wadi al Nes' prayers had been answered. Perhaps the England team should try it next time they reach the knockout stages of an international tournament.

With the match over and the onset of darkness now complete, I still had no idea how to get back to Jerusalem. The buses had long ago stopped and I only had a handful of shekels left, not enough for a taxi. Salvation arrived in the form of a blacked-out BMW.

'I'm not going to Al Quds [Jerusalem], but I'll take you to near Bethlehem,' the driver intoned, sensing my desperation at being homeless for the night in the West Bank.

Usually I wouldn't have considered climbing into a blacked-out car, with people I didn't know in a part of the world where kidnappings were commonplace. But I was skint, had no choice and had to trust his intentions. We drove through Jericho, the streets alive with activity after evening prayers, back towards the checkpoint we entered through. A huge tailback snaked back through the desert. It wasn't an obstacle. The BMW jolted left onto the bumpy sand and powered round to the Israeli checkpoint. The driver leant out of the window and shouted at the guard: 'Sahafi Britani!' – British journalist. Suddenly my purpose on the trip home made sense. I was a Trojan horse so that he could get home quicker. My usefulness spent, he dropped me off next to the wall and sped away before I could ask where I was. Isolated, with just ten shekels (£1.50) in my pocket and lost, I reasoned that if I followed the wall I would make a checkpoint eventually. But the wall towered above me, covered in the graffiti of resistance, giving no clue as to where it eventually split to reveal Israel on the other side. Suddenly, a small Toyota bus full of young men pulled up behind me.

'Where you going?' the driver shouted above the noise of crackly Arabic pop music. 'The checkpoint,' I replied.

'OK, 100 shekels.'

'I have ten.'

'OK – ten.'

The van leant dangerously around corners as it clung to the tarmac. The men in the back only spoke English just enough to say 'fuck you' and laugh uproariously. I sat in silence, sweating until the familiar shape of Bethlehem's grey checkpoint loomed into view. The driver turfed me out and relieved me of the last of my cash. I didn't care. I had never been so glad to see Israeli soldiers in my life.

✦

It would be a month before I made good on the promise I gave Honey and Jackline to return. Everything had changed. In the short time I had been away Hamas had unilaterally ended its ceasefire with Israel and its feud with Fatah was veering out of control in Gaza. The Palestinian movement was in the throes of a civil war. Gaza was tearing itself apart as forces loyal to Fatah and Hamas fought for control. With Hamas enjoying massive popular support, Fatah were taking a beating. Both areas had killed or expelled members of the opposite political party and their respective armed militias as Fatah officials fled to the West Bank. Extra judicial killings and revenge attacks were reported across both territories, even in Bethlehem. In return, the Israelis had cracked down on movement through the wall. You could gauge just how 'hot' a situation was – as the Israelis refer to it – by the number and thoroughness of Israeli checkpoints. During my last visit our blue-and-white bus had left East Jerusalem and climbed the steep hill to the walls of Bethlehem unmolested. Now the bus stopped on the Israeli side and weaved away to whence it came as everyone else was ushered through security and towards the wall. A sign that can only have been erected as an exercise in irony bore down on the Israeli side, in Arabic, Hebrew and English – 'Peace Be With You.'

I emerged on the Palestinian side, in Bethlehem, just a few hundred metres from the university. It was Thursday, training day. Coach Raed stood alone in the middle of Bethlehem University's concrete tennis court, a brush in his left hand, methodically sweeping broken glass bottles of soft drink into the dustpan in his right whilst muttering to himself.

'The boys,' he intoned despairingly of the teenagers who had smashed their drinks on the floor overnight. 'Sometimes they get a little crazy.'

The girls arrived just as the sun began to dip behind the trees, casting long shadows over the hot gravelly surface. It wasn't an ideal place to give your national team a workout, but when you don't have a stadium, full-sized pitch or even a state to call your own, the small patch of grey was better than nothing. Raed complained that the surface exacerbated his players' injuries, but there was nowhere else to go. It was either here or the sand. All he could do was to arrive early for every training session and clear the court to make sure the players didn't cut themselves.

Dressed in her Palestine 'home' kit – coloured the red, black, green and white of the flag – Honey was the first to arrive, stretching and setting an example to the other girls, some of whom were as young as 12. They filed through the gates, one by

105

one, some fixing their hijabs around their heads before smoothing down long-sleeved T-shirts over thick cotton tracksuit bottoms. It was prohibitively hot, even for late afternoon, but 22-year-old defender Nevin didn't see her veil as a hindrance.

'I played in the neighbourhood with the boys and they accepted me. Nothing is forbidden, the veil is a choice within my family,' she said, pointing out her uncovered 14-year-old sister Nadine, the second-choice goalkeeper, who was diving around on the hard surface as Coach Raed powered balls at her. Nadine flashed back at me, eager to explain. 'It's the opposite to what people think. Wearing the veil gives me power.'

Raed began to work the girls, but only lightly. He had told me earlier that he didn't want to scare any of them off by being a disciplinarian. They didn't have enough players.

'You can't be so rough with the girls, like the men's team, telling them: 'don't stop here, don't walk here',' he said. 'We give them recreational training, not like hard training for the boys.'

Only seven girls could make the training session. It was late spring and exams were in full swing, but there were enough present for a four-a-side game if I played as well.

'Come on,' Honey implored, dragging my arm. 'You can come on my side.'

This was something of a dilemma. I hadn't brought any kit with me and my jeans had a large hole in the crotch. I was one lunging tackle away from exposing myself to a devout Muslim man and half a dozen teenage girls. But the main problem was my complete lack of any discernible footballing talent. The Palestinian team may have been technically the worst women's national team in the world, but I still wouldn't have made the cut, even if I had possessed an extra 'X' chromosome. Within minutes it became clear just how outclassed I was. Nevin nutmegged me and Jackline sprinted past, leaving me for dead. Fida, Palestine's 21 year-old midfield general, feinted. I responded by theatrically falling over. She skipped around my prone, humiliated figure and powered the ball into the top left-hand corner of the small goal. Raed had a smirk on his face as Nevin held out a hand and helped me to my feet. Honey looked on disapprovingly from the half-way line, perhaps wishing I'd stayed on the bench.

Predictably, my team lost, and with the sun fading from view the girls walked back to the bank of waiting parents and their cars. The silhouettes could have been anywhere else in the world, of proud parents picking up their kids from football training in Colorado, Tel Aviv or Madrid. That was until the huge UN-marked 4x4 came into view. It belonged to Sami Mshasha, whose daughter Sarona was the youngest member of the team. Bald and in his late 40s, Sami worked for the UN agency that dealt with Palestinian refugees, the UNHCR. He too had seen Hamas' effect on the sport, but from a different angle.

'The prime minister [Ismail Haniyeh of Hamas] has done more than any other minister [for football],' he said, lighting a cigarette as we pulled away from the other girls. 'He used to play in his youth. He was a nasty defender too. He used to call them after every game, even now.'

Perhaps less strangely given his custodianship of a hard-line religious party, the prime minister's help hadn't stretched to women's football. Sami had taken a keen interest in his daughter's dreams of footballing stardom, mainly by helping Samar to secure funding for the team. Few, he said, within the Palestinian Football Association or the government seemed that bothered.

'It's basically not their priority,' he shrugged as the Israelis waved us through the checkpoint. Travelling in a UN car certainly had its benefits. 'When I meet them [the FA] you can almost hear them snickering. FIFA allocate 20 per cent of their money for the team but they give Sanar no money. You can't have an open ended pro bono coach or rely on NGOs.'

He also sensed the pressures that are on some of the other girls to give up the game. 'Palestine was always religious, but never conservative,' he said as he drove back towards Jerusalem's old city. 'Now the society is becoming more conservative, which is dangerous, but that tends to happen under occupation. You tend to become fatalistic and things can become violent. The interest is so high in football amongst the girls. And the commitment is there amongst the players. But most of them are over 20 so marriage will be knocking on their door whether they like it or not. The family pressure will start now, even amongst the Christian players.'

The future, as he saw it, was in articulate, intelligent and determined players like Honey, to take on the next generation of players. 'Honey's the future leader of the team. She has to be smart and know the situation, knows the politics. Unfortunately, the politics here in sport are as nasty as in national politics.'

I was back on the other side of the wall, back in Jerusalem, the only place in the world that felt like two separate cities superimposed on top of each other. Damascus Gate was buzzing with traders and old, black-clad women sitting on the narrow cobbled streets selling bread, mint, shoes – whatever it was they had got hold of that day. The old city is a claustrophobic place: dark and slippery, full of the smells that define that culture's quarter – be it raw halal meat from the Muslim butchers, or the incense that periodically catches you in the Armenian quarter. The Citadel Hostel just smelt of sewers, but it was the cheapest place in town. It had stood for the best part of a millennia and on its ground floor you could spend £2 a night and have a bed in the cavern dorm – a dark, dank cave with a toilet that always filled the room with the smell of faeces.

The choices were to sit around breathing in the foul odour or to see what a Thursday night in Jerusalem had to offer. I wasn't expecting a lot when I took the road from Jaffa Gate towards Jaffa Street. Jerusalem is seen as the parochial little brother, in hedonistic terms, to Tel Aviv's towering excess thanks to the huge number of Orthodox Jews living there. This, as I was to find out in the Belfast Bar, mattered little. It was a little rock bar at the bottom of Jaffa Street. I'd never been to a Northern Irish themed bar before, although its name was more by accident than design. The owner, seeing how the Irish bars near Zion Square had cleaned up, decided to open his own homage to Guinness and the Emerald Isle. Unfortunately, his limited knowledge of Ireland and Irish politics meant that he strayed a little too far north. It would be the equivalent of opening an Israeli bar in London and calling it 'Hebron'. Belfast was packed with long-haired kids nodding into their bottles of Tuborg as 'Enter Sandman' by Metallica played in the background. I found a seat upstairs, next to a table of Orthodox Jews sporting the kippa, ringlets and tassels and cradling large glasses of beer. Their New York accents rose sharply. They were arguing. The youngest, with blond hair, wearing glasses and sporting the kind of beard that suggested it was his first attempt at growing facial hair, piped up.

'I'm just saying, if I was a Palestinian I would fight back too. We all would.'

'No way man, there's no way that justifies anything. No way,' replied another with dark hair and a manicured beard. They were having a philosophical discussion on the nature of resistance.

'Hey, buddy,' the dark-haired guy said, turning to me. 'What do you think?'

I had travelled enough to realise that getting into an argument about the nature of Palestinian resistance was to be avoided at all costs. It was almost impossible not to upset someone unless you began agreeing with the often heinous views that your host subscribed to. In Arab countries it was the same, with the same old accusations coming out: Jews controlled the media in the West and all the financial institutions. That's why they don't do anything about Palestine. Countering that one usually riled a few people. And in Israel even the most liberal of Israelis met the mere suggestion that the IDF (Israeli Defence Force) was a little heavy-handed with accusations of being a neo-fascist. You ended up upsetting everyone. The seven sets of eyes looked at me for an answer. Best to go for repetition.

'Well, I agree with you, we'd all fight if occupied, right?'

The blond-haired man, Yosef, laughed, shook my hand and invited me to join them. They were all young Americans who had recently emigrated to Israel – made Aliya – and were building new lives for themselves in Jerusalem. They had also brought some of their habits with them from the States. They were all drunk and started discussing what to do next.

'Man, let's go get some pussy,' shouted Abe, the dark-haired guy.

'Yeah, pussy, pussy!' agreed Shlomo, another, who, in another life, could have played the gangly loser in any number of Judd Apatow films. The group careered out of the Belfast and up towards Zion Square, shouting at one another and only stopping to take in a particularly attractive girl as she walked past. The talk was exclusively of girls.

'Are English girls hot?'

'Israeli girls, man, they're tough.'

'Where can we get some pussy tonight?!'

We decided on a local pool bar. The group swaggered in like they were filming Reservoir Dogs but Yosef had clearly had enough.

'Man, I have a beautiful wife at home. I'm going home to get me some sex.'

Everyone hi-fived him before he slipped me a piece of paper and left. Abe was drunk out of his mind and could barely take his shot thanks to a mixture of booze and anger. The group turned towards a noisy group of fedora-wearing Orthodox Jews playing pool on the next table. Words were said, voices were raised and a stand-off ensued. I quietly left the two groups shouting at each other across the pool hall as they made threats in Hebrew and thrust pool cues at each other, squabbling over turf like a Jewish version of West Side Story.

I awoke in my dark, stinking cave gasping for water. Sketches of the previous night flashed in front of my eyes – the pool hall, the pack of drunk and horny Orthodox Jews. Could that have really happened? Searching through my pockets I found irrevocable proof. A thin paper business card.

Sarah and Yosef
Please join us for Shabbas or Yom Tov!
Have an iPod? We can fill it up with Jewish stuff!

I had agreed to meet Honey and her family at their home. The scene from the night before couldn't have been more contrasted on the road back to Bethlehem. I had used the blue-and-white Palestinian buses that spread through the West Bank from East Jerusalem dozens of times, but I had yet to hear anyone talk. A suspicious silence enveloped the bus as we trundled towards the wall, carrying students, workers and mothers between the two different worlds. But these were the lucky ones, the people who held Jerusalem ID and had permission to work outside of the West Bank. With the World Bank estimating that unemployment in the West Bank was running at 47 per cent with 44 per cent living below the poverty line, any job, even in the home of the Zionist enemy, was a job worth having. It is one of the great tragedies of the ongoing impasse between Israelis and Palestinians. The Israeli economy needs cheap Palestinian labour to thrive; Palestinians need remittance cheques from Israel to survive.

Honey wasn't one of the lucky ones. Her home was a short distance from Manger Square, where she met me. We walked the short distance to her modest maisonette where she lived with her brother, sister and parents. Outside the walls were covered in Arabic graffiti. Life had been tough for the Thaljiehs in recent years. Honey's father had been unemployed since the intifada erupted and both Honey and her brother Eissa were the only breadwinners. Being a Christian had also got harder, according to Honey's mother Nahada.

'The [Palestinian] authorities treat us differently,' she told me as we sat in her comfortable, immaculately kept front room. 'Two of our neighbours were caught speeding by the police. They brought them to the prison for one night and shaved their heads and asked them: 'Why are you Christians? It's easy the life for you, being Christian.' And they beat them.' Eissa agreed that there is an unspoken tension between the groups that is forcing many Christians to flee. 'Day by day the Christians are leaving, emigrating. In 50 years you will not see any Christians in Bethlehem.'

Since graduating in Business Administration from the town's university Honey had worked for the sports charity PACE, whilst Eissa had the unenviable task of trying to attract tourists to the West Bank as a travel agent. But Honey's football had given the family hope of a better future.

'We used to play football together in the street,' Eissa recollected in the family's front room. On his arm he sported a large tattoo of a soldier of Christ carrying a cross, apt for a man whose name translates as 'Jesus' in Arabic. 'It wasn't strange for me, but other people thought it was as they were thinking that Arab girls shouldn't play. They got used to it because she was a lot better than everybody else.' Her mother had also got used to her footballing exploits from a young age.

'She started playing at nine but we thought she'd grow out of it,' she said. 'But she didn't. [What Honey] is doing is good for the women of Palestine. It's necessary to have football for the woman, especially outside America and Europe. It's good to have this team here.'

Honey's own aspirations were like those of any young footballer. She wanted to travel to Barcelona to meet her idol, Ronaldinho. Before she could start dreaming of Spain, though, she had a training camp in Germany and a tournament in Jordan to prepare for. But deep down, despite the huge differences between the problems faced by the Palestinian men's and women's teams, their goals were remarkably similar. For Honey the big prize was one day reaching the World Cup and showing the world, and Palestine's fractured society, that football could triumph where politics had failed.

'The World Cup, that's what I'm aiming for. I was the first woman playing football in Palestine. There was no girl that knew how to play football before, even that women could play football.' She put down her mint tea and for the first time since I met her Honey dropped her infectious smile. 'It will be the next generation that will make it but hopefully I will be the coach then. I won't let the team die. Inshallah.'

Outside it was getting dark, my cue to leave. Honey walked me back through the flickering street lights and tightly wound alleyways back to the main road and my lift back to Jerusalem. As we said goodbye I noticed the same wall covered in graffiti that I'd passed when it was still daylight.

'What does it say?' I asked.

Honey stopped to read the message, as if it was the first time she had noticed it.

'A Hamas member was killed by Fatah here,' she explained, her face blank. 'It says: 'We will never forget. We will have our revenge'.'

7
IRAQ
AT THE WEST ASIAN CHAMPIONSHIP

June 2007

It was the hottest day in Amman in 90 years and Jorvan Vieira had taken refuge in the shadow thrown by the main stand of the King Abdullah stadium. Around him his squad of young footballers joked and chattered in accelerated Arabic, stretching in the green and white colours that had always covered the Lions of Mesopotamia. They didn't know Jorvan well; he wasn't too familiar with them either. It was only the second time he had met his new charges, a few weeks after the thin, stubbly-faced, small-framed man with bookish glasses had landed himself the most difficult job in world football: coach of the Iraqi national football team.

'This is the hardest job in the world, definitely,' Jorvan agreed as we stood pitch side – waiting for the Jordanian national team to finish training. The Jordanians were running late after insisting that they prayed in their dressing room, as they did before every training session and match. The Iraqis didn't want to pray. Or rather, they weren't allowed to pray. It had been decided long ago that religion, such a divisive force in their homeland, should be kept out of the team's pre-match preparations.

'These boys,' began Jorvan absent-mindedly as the Jordanians stretched in front of us, 'I have to deal with many, many problems: social, political, internal. Most of these players don't know where they are. Every minute the situation changes.'

Jorvan wasn't new to the vagaries of Middle Eastern football politics. A Brazilian Muslim, he had spent most of his career coaching in Saudi Arabia, Oman, Egypt and Morocco. He was fourth choice for the job and was only given a two-month contract. Jorvan was brought in to guide the team at the Asian Cup being held in Indonesia, Thailand, Malaysia and Vietnam. It was the region's top tournament, Asia's equivalent of the European Championships or the Copa America, and second only to the World Cup in importance. The Iraqi FA didn't have high hopes for the tournament and

Jorvan was soon given a reminder as to the huge obstacles that faced him and his team.

'We lost our physio, two days before we got here,' he explained as his charges trotted onto the field. 'A bomb exploded in Baghdad and he was passing by. He was on his way to the travel agent to buy his ticket to come here.'

The Iraqi national team had eluded me until now. For six months I had been chasing an audience with them through three countries: first in Kurdish northern Iraq, then the UAE, before finally catching up with them in Jordan. Earlier in the year, in the UAE capital of Abu Dhabi, I had watched the Iraqi team take part in the Gulf Cup, a biennial tournament that involved all the Gulf states minus Iran. The veteran coach Akram Salman was in his third spell in charge of the national team. Actually, it was technically his fourth. After being threatened by insurgents five months previously he quit his post and fled to the safety of the Kurdish north, which had remained stable as the rest of the country burned. The FA refused to accept his resignation and he was talked into coming back.

Iraq's team was still highly regarded but managed to lose to Saudi Arabia in its final group game and were eliminated. After a forensic investigation of the Gulf Cup he was fired four months later without taking charge of another game, proving that, even after you put your life on the line for your country, there's no sentimentality in football.

It would have made sense to bypass Iraq and the UAE and head straight for Amman. Since the war as many as one million Iraqis, fleeing the anarchy in their homeland, were now living in Jordan, an island of peace in a sea of instability. To its east, Iraq slowly imploded. To the west, the West Bank crumbled under the weight of internecine warfare between Hamas and Fatah, agitating Jordan's already sizeable Palestinian-descended majority. Israel, Syria, Lebanon and Saudi Arabia – all with their own internal problems – surrounded it. Yet somehow Jordan had gone about its business, made deals, played countries off against each other and generally done anything it could to survive. Much of the credit sat with the wily King Hussein, father of the current monarch, King Abdullah, who could keep all the diplomatic balls in the air at the same time; making peace with Israel, keeping the Americans onside and staying friends with Saddam Hussein. No wonder Jordan has long been thought of as the quiet man of the Middle East. Huge portraits of both men peered down as the Iraqis trained below.

To make the Iraqi diaspora feel even more at home their national football team had decamped there as well, meeting up for training and playing its competitive matches in Amman, waiting for the unlikely event that peace would take hold so they could return to Baghdad, Irbil or Basra and once again enjoy home advantage. This time, though, they weren't here merely for the sunshine and the easier living. They were preparing for a potentially explosive football tournament.

I'd heard about the West Asian Football Federation Championship, a biennial tournament that brought together the Middle East's best teams for a knockout tournament, the previous year. It had been due to take place in Beirut but the war with Israel made that impossible. Instead it was postponed and moved to Jordan. The problem was that the teams competing all had colourful histories off the pitch: Iran, Iraq, Syria, Lebanon, Jordan and Palestine. Almost every single permutation was charged with political significance. Iran and Iraq had fought a bloody, backward war in the 1980s, a war that claimed as many as a million lives. And with Iraq degenerating into an inter-sect civil war, the country's Sunni minority feared the influence of Iran – who they suspected had more influence over Iraq's Shia majority than the government – more than the Americans. Syria had long had a hand in Lebanese politics, occupying the country from 1976 until 2005, and only pulling out after the country's security forces had been fingered for the assassination of ex-Lebanese Prime Minister Rafik Hariri. One of the UN's investigations into his death put the blame on the shoulders of the Syrian secret service, whose influence many in Lebanon believe still looms large. The Syrians, of course, deny any wrongdoing. The Jordanians and the Palestinians also have a turbulent history. The creation of Israel saw hundreds of thousands flee to what was then known as Transjordan on the East Bank of the River Jordan. The many wars and conflicts that had arisen since 1948 had seen a steady trickle of Palestinians enter Jordan, changing its ethnic mix. Now, depending on who you listened to, Palestinians make up anywhere between 50 and 80 per cent of Jordan's population. Fearing being overrun, political power consolidated in the hands of ethnic Hashemite Jordanians whilst Palestinians struggled against discrimination – as in many other Arab states – to get work, housing or any education. Instead, the Palestinians excelled in making their own future and were known for their successful business interests, further antagonising the 'true' Jordanians.

If the potential for a feisty tournament was already there, several developments had made the tournament potentially even more explosive. Two players from one of Lebanon's top clubs, Nejmeh, a Shia-supported but Sunni-owned club, were killed in a car bombing targeting one of Lebanon's Christian opposition MPs. Again, the finger of suspicion pointed at Syrian involvement. In Gaza, open warfare had broken out between Fatah and Hamas, the lonely, overpopulated strip having been cut off from the rest of the world in response. But Jorvan was preparing for his next game, a must-win match against Palestine for a place in the semi-finals, with by far the most difficult set of circumstances to overcome. Almost every single player in the national team had now left Iraq. The league was only operating in the northern town of Irbil, where the Kurdish Regional Government could ensure relative safety. Every player had been touched by tragedy, threatened by insurgents or feared kidnap by criminal gangs.

'How can they come through? Where can they train?' replied Jorvan when I asked how the next generation of players could emerge under such anarchy. 'Iraq will miss one or two generations because of the war. How can they develop sport in Iraq? Did you hear about the boys from taekwondo? It could happen with any player here.'

Hours before Iraq kicked off the tournament against Iran, news reached the squad of the fate of the 'boys from taekwondo' illustrating just how dangerous it was to be a sportsman or woman in Iraq. In 2006, 15 athletes aged between 18 and 26 were kidnapped in Western Iraq on their way to a training camp in Jordan. A year later, their remains were found in a ditch near Ramadi. All had been shot in the head. The team wore black armbands during a diplomatic 0–0 draw.

The dangers were such that most players chose not to return home and those who did soon regretted it. Goalkeeper Noor Sabri had seen his brother-in-law killed a few weeks previously. Midfielder Haitham Kadim watched as gunmen stormed onto the pitch during a match in Baghdad to execute one of his teammates.

'I'd lost two members of my family,' explained Hawar Mullah Mohammad, the team's Kurdish striker. The executions, bombings and insecurity had got so bad he left his home in Baghdad and signed for Al Ain, an oasis club in the middle of the UAE, to ensure his safety. 'It's difficult when you have no safety. Cars explode all the time. I had to pick up my two guns before going to practice, because I'd been threatened,' he said nonchalantly as he was warming up. 'You can buy guns anywhere in Baghdad. You need them. I don't go back any more.'

With the Jordanians finally departed, Jorvan started running the team through its paces. It wasn't lost on him just what a potential powder keg the tournament was.

'All it takes is one match,' he said grinning before rejoining the squad on the pitch. 'And then, BOOM!'

The Iraqi team's coach moved quietly past the Wihdat refugee camp, over the still-intact tracks of the old, largely defunct Hejaz railway – the great, crazy Ottoman project designed to link Istanbul to Mecca – and into the centre of Amman towards their hotel. The players and coaching staff, exhausted by training in the heat, dozed as the bus rocked and bucked through the traffic and badly tarmacked roads. The only man awake was first-team coach Ahmed-Rahim Hamed.

Captain Rahim, as the players referred to him, was a legend of Iraqi football. He had played in the great Iraqi team of the 1980s, considered to be Iraq's finest crop of players after they reached the World Cup finals in 1986. Back then he was a 23-year-old striker and one of the youngest in the squad, playing alongside the current head of the Iraqi FA, Hussein Saeed Mohammed. The team narrowly lost all three games by a single goal against Paraguay, Belgium and hosts Mexico. To the outsider this was a respectable result for a team from Asia, which received just two World Cup spots in Mexico. But the players knew that anything less than silverware would upset the man who had been put in charge of Iraqi football: Uday Hussein.

Saddam's bloodthirsty eldest son had a myriad of interests – torture, extortion and football. After proving that he wasn't quite yet ready to take the mantle as Saddam's chosen successor by beating to death his father's valet in front of horrified guests at a party hosted in honour of the wife of the Egyptian President Hosni Mubarak, Uday was imprisoned before being sent to Switzerland to lie low. When he returned, however, he was handed the keys to Iraq's sporting empire, which he used to feather his own nest as head of Iraq's Olympic Committee. He also used some of his unique motivational skills on Iraqi footballers. On the journey to central Amman Rahim recalled one incident that still upset him, mainly because Uday had put paid to his homage to his favourite player. 'You knew that if you didn't play well, Uday would do something bad,' said Rahim, running his hands through his dark hair. 'I loved Kevin Keegan, he was my best player, and I had a perm like him. After one game [that Iraq lost] Uday shaved everybody's hair. That's when I lost my perm.' Uday may have been killed in a hail of American bullets but Rahim and the rest of Iraq's football community were still being punished for their involvement with the national team. Rahim had to move to Irbil after he received one death threat too many. 'I got a letter that said we will kill your children and ... make something ... with my daughter. They fired at my house twice. So I moved to Irbil. I'm Shia. I don't care, I'm Muslim and Iraqi. But now I sit in a small flat in a dirty area. It's expensive. My rent is more than my brother's rent in Holland.'

Others were less keen to talk about their time under Uday. Hussein Saeed Mohammed, the president of the Iraqi Football Association's, was also Saddam Hussein's favourite player. He held Iraq's international goal-scoring record – scoring 63 times in 131 appearances – and was the team's talismanic captain, leading Iraq from 1975 to 1990 and scored the goals that secured Iraq's only World Cup qualification in 1986. His goal-scoring prowess had alerted the world's best clubs but he never got a sniff at playing for any of them. 'I had many teams that wanted me to play for them. Real Madrid wanted to know about me,' he said. But his dream move was scuppered. 'The government refused and wouldn't let me go and be professional.' The Iraqi regime's pathological hatred of foreign, Western influences was one reason for it. The other was Uday Hussein. Saddam's sadistic son had a habit of asking for a huge cut from any contracts players signed to ply their trade abroad. Former Iraqi captain Habib Jaffar – who told *The Guardian* how he was regularly beaten with cables and forced to jump into vats of raw sewage – had to hand over 40 per cent of his earnings to Uday when he signed a contract with a Qatari club. Hussein would have been expected to do the same. Despite the hardships he had faced, he didn't want to talk about his time under Uday.

'We don't want to speak about the past,' he replied tetchily when I asked about the influence Uday had over the dressing room. 'I am the President for three years and we have had many difficulties now. No players have suffered like Iraqi players have suffered. All our teams qualify for all the tournaments. And we are proud that we have united our people under the umbrella of sport. There is no violence in Iraq when our team is playing. Everyone is watching television.'

It was a foolproof plan: engender Iraqi unity through a sporting example whilst keeping the insurgents off the street with a steady stream of matches and tournaments. Yet sportsmen and women had increasingly paid a high price for their visibility post-Saddam, along with the fans. 'They have kidnapped my driver and my bodyguard. For what reason? What do they need? Last year we had a match in Baghdad, a semi final, 50,000 people were in the stadium and they fired many rockets at them. Why kill people who want to come and watch?' he asked incredulously. 'The cycling coach was killed; the wrestling coach was killed; the captain of the volleyball team was killed; many killings. But we don't stop because sportsmen are part of the people in Iraq. When the people suffer, we suffer with them.'

The list he left out was even bigger: there was, of course, the boys from taekwondo; Iraq's head tennis coach murdered along with two players; the majority of the Olympic committee, plus thirty staff, seized in one raid by kidnappers wearing army uniforms. To literally survive in his post for three years was an achievement in itself for Hussein. His aim was to get back to the glory years, to the team that excelled in the 1980s even with the constant fear of mutilation and imprisonment. 'I am proud of our players and our coach. We put it here on our logo, on our jersey.' He pointed at the breast of his brown sports jacket – 'I am Iraqi. In the future we will be a great team again.'

✦

Thousands of Iraqi fans sat in the afternoon sun on a working day waiting for their team to take on Palestine. Amman's International Stadium looked like it had once been futuristic, perhaps in the early Nineties, with its plastic-looking cladding hiding an ugly concrete and iron frame. But it was suspiciously busy for a mid-afternoon kick-off on a working day with Iraqi fans milling around outside.

'Jordan is good,' said Nasir, an Iraqi Christian, with the kind of intonation that you knew would be followed by a 'but'. 'But the government doesn't let us work. I brought my savings because if the government catch us working they send us back. It's a hard life, but at least it's safe.'

Another spectator with time on his hands had brought his entire family along for a rare taste of Iraqi pride. 'I've been here a year. I had to come here when my brother was kidnapped,' said Essam, a Sunni sewing-machine salesman who was there with his wife and two kids. 'When we see our team we feel like it's home.'

Given the huge Palestinian diaspora, I had expected thousands of fans supporting the old country. But the only Palestine fans I could find was a gaggle of angry-looking youths who couldn't afford to get a ticket.

'We can't watch because they doubled the prices because the Iraqis are here and they are very rich. It's not fair, it's like 6 JDs [$9], we have no oil, the Palestinians don't even have money to buy cigarettes,' spat Salman, a Palestinian student living in Amman, who wanted to show solidarity. 'This team is important because it brings us together, Hamas and Fatah. This team is unity, this team will give us attention.'

It was an important time for unity. The civil war between Fatah and Hamas, between the West Bank and Gaza, had created an almost total, intractable separation between the two groups and two territories. Salman, who spoke in a strong North American accent from his days studying in Canada, knew who was to blame.

'Israel and America,' he proudly stated.

'Not Hamas?' I asked.

'Not Hamas, my friend,' he replied. 'When you have poverty and unemployment anything can happen. They [Israel and America] have deprived the Palestinian people of everything.'

The football team, though, seemed to be functioning OK despite the chaos back home. The team's Gaza contingent, 13 players in all, managed to make it out before the border was shut.

'Why can they share a football team but not a government?' I asked.

'Why?' repeated Salman before answering. 'Because the football team is from the people. Fatah and Hamas are made from the Israelis and the Americans and we know who they are. Trust me. The solution is for the refugees to go home. I'm a refugee. I was born a refugee, my father was born a refugee, my grandfather was born a refugee and I would not give up a single piece of my land. The UN can sort out Jerusalem, but I just want to go back home. I would die for it.'

Salman was 23 and had never set foot in what he called Palestine. He wouldn't tell me which side he supported although he was clearly no fan of the Palestinian President Mahmoud Abbas.

'I wish he was dead,' he replied deadpan. 'He is a faulty sperm. He shook hands with the invaders. The South Africans didn't shake hands with the whites, the Vietnamese didn't shake hands with the Americans. He is a disgrace to us. So was Arafat.'

Palestine's luck didn't get any better on the pitch. The game itself was a scrappy affair. Even though the Iraqi side of the stadium was full, compared to the 12 Palestinian fans who could afford the steep entry price, the Lions of Mesopotamia were devoid of creativity and had no idea how to get through a Palestinian side that put 11 men behind the ball in searing temperatures.

By half-time the fans had had enough and started shouting for their favourite player: Hawar Mullah Mohammad. Hawar had been on the bench resting an injury, Jorvan had told me. But an Iraqi journalist covering the match for an Australian newspaper had revealed that he had thrown a tantrum when he wasn't made captain and was dropped as punishment. With things going badly Jorvan didn't have a choice. Hawar came on and swiftly dispatched an 86th-minute – twice taken – penalty to break Palestine's resistance 1–0. Later, Hawar was mobbed by more than a hundred fans who had waited for him to appear by the team coach, a swirling pack of Iraqi flags, digital cameras and mobile phones preventing him from leaving. Hawar didn't mind. The adulation was probably vindication for being upset about the captaincy. It took the police to eventually drag him out. He reluctantly stepped onto the team bus.

Each nationality clustered in groups in the lobby of the Arena Hotel. Every group of footballers was demarked by what was embossed onto the back of their tracksuits – the Syrians sticking together in one corner, the Palestinians in another, the Iranians in yet another. The gangs didn't mingle, only giving a cursory nod as they swaggered past one another in twos or threes. Sitting down sipping on a thimble of Arabic coffee, with a shining bald pate and a moustache that made him look a little like Mussolini, was Emile Rustom. Emile was the head coach of the Lebanese national team, a Maronite Christian. This usually wouldn't warrant a mention but in Lebanese football, the demarcation between religious and political groups was arguably more pronounced than even in Iraq.

'Anywhere we go to play everybody says: 'are you still playing football in Lebanon?'', he laughed. 'We are living day by day in Lebanon, we don't know what will happen tomorrow. Every day is a dramatic event.' The problem, Emile told me, was that each team had a strong link to each of the country's competing communities. And when Sunni, Shia, Druze and Christian teams met one another, it tended to end in bloodshed on the terraces. So much so that the authorities banned fans from attending games, such was the fear that inter-religious fighting could spark wider instability at a time when Lebanon was still weak internally, both politically and economically, and vulnerable. 'There are teams for Hezbollah like Al Ahed. But it's a good thing if Hezbollah gives money for a club to help football. Mr Hariri [Saad, former Prime Minister Rafik Hariri's son] is giving money to Ansar and Nejmeh. We don't have the basics. We don't have sponsors, no money. If this political party is giving money then that is good.'

But Emile insisted that, within the national team, there were no differences. To prove his point he called over three players: Paul Rustom, his young son who was a striker for the Maronite Catholic team Sagesse; Ali Yaacoub from the Shia-dominated Al Ahed and Bilal Najarin from the Sunni-owned team Nejmeh.

'When we play against each other me and Bilal make trash talk against each other in the game, but we are best of friends afterwards,' explained Paul, the three chatting easily together. 'Our teams are a symbol for the community. Sagesse is a Christian team [but] we [Christians] are eight out of thirty. There are six or seven Sunnis, one or two Druze and the rest are Shia. We all go out with each other.' The problem was that this fraternity hadn't transferred onto the terraces. 'It is because of Nejmeh versus Ansar,' said Bilal. 'Forty-five thousand would attend the game and half of them would be Shia, half of them Sunni. They would fight.'

'The political problems are reflected between the fans,' continued Paul. 'If the Sunni and Shia leaders have a disagreement, there's trouble. This season the fans were forbidden but next season they will hopefully be back.' Ali, whose team was funded by Hezbollah, agreed but played down the role of the political organisation. 'The club is for Hezbollah, yes, but they do not interfere too much. They give money but they let the club spend it on players.'

'Does Hassan Nasrallah go to the games?' I asked.

'No!' shrieked Ali, the others laughing at the thought of Hassan Nasrallah on the terraces. 'The Israelis will get him!'

Things hadn't started well for the Lebanese at the West Asian Championship. The death of two Nejmeh players after training two weeks before in a car bombing – team-mates of Bilal's – had dampened the mood. Worse, with Syrian involvement being blamed for the spate of targeted assassinations against politicians, who all happened to be from the anti-Syria political bloc, the fixture list had thrown up their Eastern neighbour in the first game. They promptly lost 1–0, which didn't go down well back in Beirut.

'The fans were blaming us,' said Paul. 'They said: 'Why did you lose? You could have lost to anyone by 100 goals, but not against Syria'.' But there was, according to Emile, little animosity between the players. 'This is a political problem,' he stressed, finishing up his coffee and gathering his players for their early-afternoon rest. Tomorrow they had to win the game against hosts Jordan. A victory was the only chance they had of making the semis. 'It's true that the Syrian army in Lebanon made many mistakes against the Lebanese people. They were abusing their power to have money, to kill people, to jail people. It happens during the occupation of any country, thirty years of occupation [but] we met the players before and it was a clean game. Many people back home wanted us to win against Syria. Sports people don't think in the same way.'

With that, the four got up, hugged me one by one, and left. 'Call me the moment you get to Beirut,' Emile insisted, giving me his phone number and promising to show me around. 'The season will start in September, hopefully, and the fans will be back too.'

His son was less sure. 'September? With Lebanon you never know,' Paul added mischievously. 'There will probably be another war in Lebanon in September.' Another coach with off-the-field worries was Mohammed Sabah, who I had met in Jericho during a West Bank cup match earlier in the year. His Palestine side had narrowly been beaten by Iraq the day before but his players had other things on their minds.

'The main problem is the situation in Gaza as we have 13 players from there,' he told me. Mohammed was in the lobby reading the paper, trying to devour as much information as possible on what was going on in Gaza. It seemed that finding out about the political turmoil was equally important a job for the coach of the Palestinian national team as keeping tabs on training. 'What has happened in the past week means they are very worried, stressed.' The tensions between Hamas and Fatah that had simmered since the former's parliamentary victory in 2006 had finally exploded and reached some sort of end game. Hamas was, after weeks of bloody fighting that had killed several hundred Palestinians, in total control of the Gaza Strip. The Israelis responded by closing all the borders and isolating Gaza. Effectively, there were now two Palestinian governments. 'It's very difficult at the moment as some of the players and coaches wanted to go back as their minds and their hearts are with their families in Gaza but they can't because the border at Rafah is closed,' Mohammed explained.

The schism had long existed for the Palestinian national football team. Unable to travel between Gaza and the West Bank, there were essentially two national teams, one set of players training in Gaza, the other in the West Bank. They only met together a few days before a match in a third country, usually Egypt. Yet Mohammed was positive that within the camp there was no Fatah-Hamas rivalry.

'I think that a Palestinian team makes a unit for the Palestinian people,' he said when I asked whether any disagreements had broken out. 'The players are close, they are sharing rooms, training. Every player here is an ambassador. When you represent your country you must be good in every way. No players say I am Hamas, I am Fatah. Yes, some are members, but they are friends. If the people were like the Palestinian team there would be no problems.'

He brought out his captain, Saeb Jendeya, who played for Shajaiya in Gaza City, to prove his point. He refused to say whether he was a member of Fatah or Hamas. All he cared about was the safety of the people he had left behind.

'Every second I am thinking about my family,' he said. 'Every time I'm here I'm calling them in Gaza asking about the border, when they are going to open it and whether my family has food or not. In the past two days it has been difficult for them to get food and I have five very young kids. And my salary from the government hasn't been paid for ten months.'

Oddly, as the West Bank and Gaza indulged in civil war, a star-studded Real Madrid side fresh from winning La Liga was making its way to Israel for a peace match against a mixed Israeli Palestinian side, hosted by Israeli President Shimon Peres and his Peres Centre for Peace in Tel Aviv the next day. It was odd because Mohammed didn't seem to know any of the Palestinian players taking part in the match. Stranger still, the official press release with biographies of the Palestinian players taking part stated that they were Palestinian national team players playing in the Palestinian First Division – which had had to be abandoned several years previously due to Israeli movement restrictions. I emailed the Peres Centre and Roni Kresner gave an explanation:

> *None of the players were from Gaza. Due to the present situation in the Gaza Strip, we were unable to include players from Gaza. That is, had they participated, they would have been severely punished for taking part in such a match. [Due to the dominance of Hamas in the Gaza Strip.]*
>
> *As for the players being part of the national team, there is a Palestinian national squad, and the coach selects players from the squad for each*

game. You are correct in stating that there was a match in Amman the same day. Players from the national squad played in that match. Similarly, players from the national squad took part in our match at Ramat Gan stadium. The coach, who is linked to the Palestinian Football Association, is looking for a way to punish these players for participating in a mixed Israeli-Palestinian team (a sad state of affairs!).

For Mohammed, though, the issue was cut and dried. 'No, I'm not sharing [a pitch with] the occupation,' he said when I asked why none of his squad was in Tel Aviv. 'The Israelis must know that when we have our rights we can play. But when we are killed and they make checkpoints so we can't play like in other countries. In my club [Tulkarem], many times they stop us going to the match, turn us away and arrest some players. It's very difficult to play and want peace when they won't give us our rights. I want peace, two states, but until now we cannot move freely, we cannot go from city to city. It's difficult to a share a team over here, when over there they arrest my brother.'

Mohammed's sentiment summed up what I had heard from virtually everyone I had spoken to who was connected to Palestinian football. For them, football was about attaining international recognition and achieving internal unity. Football wouldn't be used to attain peace with Israel. In fact, Iraq, Lebanon and Palestine all had very different problems to deal with, but had one thing in common. All represented a forlorn, distant hope for unity in their homelands. In Lebanon and Iraq's case, the national football team was a rare chance to build some form of nationalistic pride by bringing together disparate, competing sectarian groups under one flag, something that a weak central government had singularly failed to do. For Palestine, the national team had always given the illusion of that elusive prize: statehood. But now, more than ever, it had to also try and engender its own form of common cause, bridging the ever widening gap between the supporters of Fatah and Hamas which had threatened to drive a permanent wedge between the West Bank and Gaza and undermine the great prize of a united Palestinian state recognised by the UN.

That night another group of Palestinian footballers also had to deal with the grim reality of division back home. I'd received an email from Honey, the captain of the Palestinian women's national team. After we had said our goodbyes in Bethlehem a few months previously, Honey and the rest of the squad had been invited to Germany to take part in a three-week long training camp in anticipation of the women's West Asian Championship taking place in September. Now, however, they were stuck in Amman. The players' floor at the Sandy Palace Hotel was buzzing with activity, girls darting in and out of the different rooms as Coach Raed stood in the middle like some kind of pushover physical education teacher at St.Trinians. He nodded his head in recognition and disappeared into his room, unable or unwilling to control his hyperactive players.

Samar Mousa, the matriarchal team manager, and Honey sat in a large, modest suite on their own, chewing on an Arabic fast-food meal served in a polystyrene tray. They both looked worn-out after 20 days of intensive training and media attention. After such a high, Amman must have proved somewhat of an anti-climax. None of the players knew if they would be allowed back into the country. In Bethlehem, Samar told me, armed Fatah militias were roaming the streets rounding up Hamas members in retaliation for the latter's Islamic coup in Gaza. Not only that, two players and one coach from Gaza had been affected in different ways. One player had been refused permission to leave in the first place thanks to an over-protective father who disapproved of her playing football. A second didn't know how to get home as Israel had closed the border. One coach had to leave early after hearing that a rocket had destroyed her home. Now, all the girls crossed their fingers and hoped they even had homes to go back to. Honey soon perked up when we talked about Germany. 'What was the best part of it?' I asked, before leaving them to try and negotiate safe passage home. 'To taste freedom,' she replied quickly. 'To not have to carry my passport wherever you go.' I left her sitting on the floor, deep in thought, staring at a faraway spot on the opposite wall.

The Iraqi team bus pulled through Amman's city limits, rocking to ear-splitting Arabic music. Training had been light this time, and with good reason. The team was recovering from their best performance of the tournament so far, a 3–0 victory over Syria. The game was held on a Friday yet, unlike every other single Middle Eastern football crowd that gathered on Islam's holy day, nobody prayed. The fans had taken on board the same mantra as their football team: keep religion to yourself.

I had sat through the drills, patiently waiting to talk to more of the players. But on the bus, I was expected to dance. It felt like an ambush. As soon as the bus had started, music from the famous Iraqi singer Hussam Al Rassam screeched and crackled through speakers that couldn't handle the volume. Drums rattled like gunfire as the players danced and shouted in delight, occasionally getting thrown into the lap of a team-mate as the coach driver veered around a corner. Younis Mahmoud, the team's star striker and captain, and Nashat Akram, looked at me strangely.

'Come on,' Nashat implored, taking my hand and leading me to the centre of the bus. 'You can dance.' It didn't seem like a bad idea to be part of the whole team-bonding ritual. Little did I know that it was a thinly veiled trap. The whole team circled around as best they could and clapped me in. Defender Jassim Gholam took the lead, hauling his shirt off over his bald head, bowing slightly, circling his fingers and jutting his neck from side to side. Every few beats he would slap an arm across his chest. I tried to mimic his actions. The whole coach descended into mocking laughter as the players started to mimic my rigid movements. Those that weren't dancing were filming the humiliation on their mobile phones. Jassim took things a step forward, pulling at my T-shirt and slapping his chest whilst urging me to join him in his semi-naked revelry. Standing in the middle of the wild-eyed circle, I had no choice. I slowly peeled off my top, revealing painfully white skin, and stumbled along to the beat as we slapped each other's backs. The two minutes seemed to go on for hours. The only thing you could hear over the sound of the music was the sound of laughter. Nashat slapped me on the back and ushered me back to the seat. Behind me a group of players were watching the video back – me, pasty white, red neck from sunburn, dancing like a middle-aged woman.

Jorvan surveyed the scene and gave a wry smile. 'We have to give the Iraqi people a good mirror. Inside the national team there are no differences between Shia and Sunni. I was asked, how can you coach Iraq? I said 'I don't have ammo, no grenades, no M45, no axe.' I'd like victory to bring peace to Iraq. They don't have to pay me if I can help bring peace.'

Mohammed Nasser and Nashat talked business as we trundled through Amman's darkening early evening. Both had negotiated their way out of Iraq: Mohammed to Apollon Limassol in Cyprus, Nashat to Al Shabab in Saudi Arabia. The key, they said, was getting an agent. 'Most Iraqis don't have one but it's crucial because he can drop you in any country,' said Nashat. He had grounds to be more optimistic than most on the team. Nashat had been promised a top-four club in Europe. What he got was a visit from Sunderland, which was stretching the definition of top-four somewhat, but it at least meant that he was on the Premier League's radar. Nashat had even heard rumours that a Sunderland scout was at the first Iraq–Iran match.

'Iraqis can play anywhere in the world, but it would be a dream to play for [then coach] Roy Keane,' he said. 'I sent them my DVD and, Inshallah, I'll hear something.'

Mohammed had also been made some grand promises. He was promised Europe, and he got it, sort of. 'No one can see me play in Cyprus,' he complained. 'So I sacked my agent. I have one at the moment, an Iranian, and he's promised me a top-four club in Greece, England or Spain.' There were other cultural reasons why Mohammed had wanted to leave Cyprus. 'In Iraq you have your wife and maybe five, six, seven, eight girlfriends. You just don't do it in front of her. She might know, but she'll look away. She needs to feel special.'

'What happens if a wife takes a boyfriend?' I asked. Mohammed bristled as if it was the first time he had ever considered such a possibility.

'Then [the husband] cancels her,' he replied. 'It's different in Cyprus, in Europe. There you have one woman, one boss, the captain. I have a girl in Limassol and she always says: 'Why can't I live in your flat?' But if I did she'd be in charge. She doesn't know about the other girl in Nicosia.' Still, life was preferable to back home for Mohammed, a Shi'ite who lived in Basra. As a footballer who earned a handsome wage in Europe, albeit in one of the continent's lower leagues, he was a target for criminal gangs looking to kidnap players and make a handsome profit. The average ransom in 2006, according to the *New York Times*, was $30,000. But for a high profile hostage that figure could rise one hundred fold. 'When I go home,' he said, 'I just stay indoors. It's safer that way.'

After forcing me to dance, captain Younis Mahmoud now sat at the front of the coach on his own. Younis was arguably Iraq's greatest hope for the European stage. He was top scorer in the star-filled Qatari league and scorer of 30 goals in 49 internationals. French clubs had come in for him yet it was unlikely he was going to arrive in Europe soon.

'Of course I want to play in England or France,' he said, 'but my family is my priority and if I sign for a club in Europe, I can't take my family. In Qatar, it's no problem: they say 'Bring everyone!''

The EU's strict work permit rules meant that if Younis signed for an English or French club, his family would stay behind. Worse, with no reason to stay in Qatar, it might mean they had to move back to Iraq. It wouldn't be the last time an Iraqi player had been stung in this way.

For the players left behind in Iraq not lucky enough to get a move or well connected enough to get a decent agent, there was a different set of priorities. Second-choice goalkeeper Ahmed Ali was one of only four players in the Iraqi squad for the Asian Cup who plied their trade in the Iraqi league. He stood between the sticks for Al Zawra'a in Baghdad and his day went something like this: 'I wake up at 9am, I go to practice at 3pm, go home at 6pm, lock the door and don't go out.' I suggest that he must have some security at games. The players around him howl with laughter. 'I earn $100, a bodyguard gets $1000. I'm not David Beckham! My friend was shot dead during a game once, and they also dropped bombs, five of them, mortars I think, onto the field. It's very dangerous.' The bombs, the revenge and the war were a long way away now, though. The victory against Syria meant that the tournament was going to end as it had begun, against arch rivals Iran. This time there had to be a loser. The Lions of Mesopotamia were ready.

The noise from Iraq's fans could be heard nearly two kilometres away. From the outskirts of the sprawling, wooded Sports City complex, where the Amman International Stadium sat at its centre, the distant sound of drums and chanting grew louder and louder as I approached the front of the stadium. It was still two hours before Iraq were due to take on Iran but as many as 8,000 were already in the ground. Outside hundreds of men crushed at the single ticket booth desperate to snap up the last of the tickets. Their wives, daughters and young sons, holding miniature Iraqi flags, stood respectfully back, away from the unedifying scene. It was as if the Iraqi flag had been grafted onto almost every single available surface. The red, white and black, embossed with the three stars that represented Saddam's Ba'ath party and laced with Arabic script – *Allahu Akhbar* – was etched everywhere; on large pieces of cloth; on handheld banners; on hats; dresses; children's faces.

Back home large-scale pride in the national flag was a distant memory, from a time five years previously when hope and idealism of a new post-Saddam Iraq ran rampant. But here, in Amman, for the Lions of Mesopotamia, Iraqis picked up their flags once again in the biggest outpouring of nationalist sentiment since the bombs stopped falling on Baghdad. The terrace inside the stadium was frightening, a deafening noise that hadn't been articulated into any single song or chant. The years of frustration and isolation, of living in their own private hells of repression, humiliation and poverty, poured out, one third of it coming with a female timbre. Twenty Iranian fans, the only ones who had made the trip from Tehran, looked on from beyond the wire fence that separated them in awe. A young boy, wrapped in the Iranian flag, stood at the front with tears in his eyes. In the Iraqi section a group of men hoisted a different flag high up on a pole they had somehow smuggled into the ground. It was red, white and green and blazed with a golden sun at its centre. It was the flag of Kurdistan.

'We fly this because we are Kurds and Iraqis, but we fly it for Hawar [Mullah Mohammad, Iraq's best Kurdish player],' the young man responded when I asked why. The Kurds had experienced few of the problems that had cursed the rest of the country. After the first Gulf War a no-fly zone was forced on Saddam, making it impossible for him to revert to his genocidal ways. During the 1980s he had instigated the Anfal Programme, a policy aimed at wiping out Kurdish identity by destroying thousands of villages, banning the language and gassing its people. The programme saw thousands of Kurdish villages destroyed, killing some 182,000 people. Saddam feared the Kurds' long-standing desire for independence and was scared they might defect to the Iranians during the bloody Iran-Iraq war. It's nadir was the Halabja massacre, where as many as 5,000 men, women and children were gassed to death by Saddam's forces.

In the freedom created by the no-fly zone, Kurdish nationalism had flourished. When the second Gulf War arrived the Kurds were already in charge of much of their own affairs, with their own army. Now they had their own government and long term ambitions for independence. They had their own unrecognised national football team too and had ambitions to one day join FIFA. Their confidence sat at odds with how the rest of Iraq, and the rest of the crowd, felt.

I didn't get a chance to ask the flag bearer's name. The smiling Kurd's face turned as, out of nowhere, a sick-looking middle-aged bald man – his face deeply etched and mean like a caricature of an officer in the Republican Guard – defied his frailty to leap down two rows of seats and lunge at him, knocking me out of the way. With one hand he had the Kurd by the throat, with the other he had ripped down what he saw was an affront to Iraqi unity. The Jordanian riot police quickly waded in and forced the man outside, still bucking and screaming at the indignity. The Kurdish flag wasn't seen again that night.

The teams emerged to a one-sided roar. Hundreds of fans were still outside when the national anthems were sung. Iran's was booed mercilessly, so much so that the music was drowned out by the screams, causing the Iraqi bench to turn around appalled at the spectacle. On the pitch the Iranian players looked at each other as they struggled through the din, shocked by the outpouring of vitriol. They put their indignation to good use. Within two minutes they had sliced open Iraq's defence, one that hadn't conceded a goal all tournament, and taken the lead at the opposite end of the pitch. There were so few Iranian fans, and with the large LCD screen broken – from which a sign hung that pointed out it had been 'Donated by the People's Republic of China' – no one was sure what had happened. By the time the screen fluttered into life, Iran were two up after a mistake by the goalkeeper Noor Sabri. The crowd began to turn on their heroes, raining plastic bottles down on Mohammed Nasser, who wasn't having his best game, when he came near to the fence to pick up the ball. The second half pacified Iraq's travelling fans somewhat and even gave them false hope of a victory with an 86th-minute penalty. But Iran had done enough and when the final whistle blew they ran to Iraq's fans to bow in mock appreciation, sparking a fight between them and some of the Iraqi players who ran to intervene. Nashat consoled his devastated teammates while Younis – topless and bearing a tattoo of Iraq on his left arm – harried the players to thank the fans, who had stayed in the stadium even as the Iranians collected their trophy, soaking up every last minute of national pride.

Mohammed Nasser was distraught, standing on his own by the dugout, his white tracksuit limply hanging off his shoulders. Tears mingled with salty white beads of sweat that streamed down his face.

'Are you ok?' I asked.

Mohammed opened his mouth, but was unable to respond.

Finally he choked out what he wanted to say: 'The Asian Cup. We . . . we still have the Asian Cup.'

And he was right, they did have the Asian Cup a month later. Iraq's 1–1 draw with Thailand in Bangkok on July 7 in the opening game didn't give a hint of the glory and the tragedy that would follow. But Iraq pulled off the shock of the tournament, beating favourites Australia 3–1 in the next game. Vietnam fell in the quarters. They were to meet South Korea in the semi-finals. The game finished 0–0 and went to penalties. No sooner had keeper Noor Sabri saved the deciding penalty than tens of thousands of fans poured out into the stifling Iraqi summer to dance and sing. For a brief, all too fleeting moment, Iraq was united, celebratory bullets being fired high into the late afternoon sky, the tracer fire from Kurd, Shia and Sunni indistinguishable from one another. Which is exactly what the insurgents feared. As the revellers rejoiced, a suicide bomber quietly approached an ice cream stand in the well-heeled Mansour district of Baghdad, destroying himself and 30 football fans with him. That night twenty more fans were killed across town in suicide attacks, as were five more, accidentally, when gravity reasserted its will and the bullets of victory fell back to earth. The Iraqi team, ecstatic in the aftermath of triumph, were shattered by the news that their victory had indirectly led to the deaths of dozens of their compatriots. The team held a meeting to discuss pulling out of the tournament, but the players, spurred on by a bereaved mother who had begged the team to continue in memory of her murdered son, chose to play on.

On 29 July 2007, the Lions of Mesopotamia proudly marched out into the Bukit Jalil National Stadium in Jakarta to face Saudi Arabia. Younis was the hero, heading the game's only goal, sparking joyous scenes. Suddenly the intractable differences that had blighted Iraq didn't seem that intractable any more. Back home, the fear of attack wasn't enough to dampen the mood. The team and their remarkable achievement was suddenly the biggest story in the world, Younis gracing the front page of the *International Herald Tribune*. Television crews from Japan to Brazil wanted their story. Crowds celebrated on the streets from Irbil to Basra. Increased security measures meant just seven people were killed by insurgents, but it would have been many more had police not averted an attempted suicide bombing in Baghdad.

The risk of such activity meant that celebrations on the team's return home were subdued. The Prime Minister's reception had to be held in the heavily fortified Green Zone in the centre of Iraq, away from most civilians. One person who wasn't there was the hero, Younis. 'I wish I could go back to Baghdad to celebrate, but who will secure my life?' asked the captain.

Typically, every silver lining has a cloud. Jorvan quit after the match as he had promised, despite pleas from fans, players and even the prime minister. 'If my contract was for six months and not for two, they would have had to take me to the hospital for crazy people,' he explained. For some of the players it would be the making of them. Some were signed to regional teams in the Gulf on lucrative contracts. European teams courted others, like Younis, after he had been nominated for FIFA's prestigious World Player of the Year award. One player, Nashat Akram, almost went one step further. Sven Goran Eriksson's big-spending Manchester City side had offered him a lucrative contract to become Iraq's first English Premier League player. The significance of the move couldn't have been overstated. At a time when Britain's standing in the Middle East was at its lowest ebb, huge numbers of Iraqis would watch their hero gracing the grounds of some of the world's most popular football clubs week in, week out. Or they would have if the British government hadn't refused Nashat a work permit on the grounds that the Iraq national team wasn't good enough. Despite just picking up the Asian Cup and surviving against all the odds, Iraq sat below 70th place on FIFA's ranking, the minimum required by the British government to award a visa.

But as Younis, Nashat, Jorvan and the rest of Iraq's national football team walked off the pitch at Amman's International Stadium, no one could have predicted what they would achieve in four weeks' time. Outside the ground, the procession of fans who had gathered in Amman in their thousands for every match had pushed into the streets, singing once more. This time, the incoherent noise had morphed into a single song, sung over and over.

'Do you know what they are saying?' shouted Salif, a 16-year-old who had fled Baghdad with his family. 'They are singing against Iran. 'The Sunni and Shia and brothers. We will never sell Iraq'.'

I stood on a concrete bank, high above the crowd and the police below, and watched as Amman's street filled with red, white and black, the drums beating victoriously in defeat long into the night.

8
LEBANON

October 2007

I awoke when the wheels of the plane hit the tarmac. It was 3am and, out of my window, I could feel the presence of dark, foreboding hills, lit up by a patchwork of crisscrossing lights. It felt like I had been here before. Almost a year ago I had sat in my flat in Dubai, watching CNN as Israeli planes unloaded their missiles into the very same tarmac I was currently taxiing on at Rafik Hariri Airport.

Anyone with a keen eye on the Middle East probably didn't watch the unfolding carnage with any measure of disbelief. Lebanon, after all, had for many decades been a geographical joke. Like twentieth century Poland, Lebanon was coveted, fought over and taken by the neighbours that surrounded it. Lebanon was a place other people went to fight their wars. But for me, I had heard only of the boom times, of the economic revival of the 1990s, of tourists from the West flocking to witness its shabby café charm. The Paris of the Middle East, they called it, and it was surely about to return to its former glory. Then the Israelis came again and reset the clock to 1982, the last time their forces had headed that far north. A year on Beirut was still trying to get back on its feet. The flight was empty. Not many people wanted to come to Lebanon any more. Even the weary-looking border guard happily stamped my passport despite the fact I had an overland exit visa from Taba, Egypt and then into Israel.

After watching the final of the West Asian Championship, and the aftermath of Iraq's stunning, against-all-odds victory in the Asian Cup a few weeks later, my thoughts turned to Emile Rustom, the head coach of the Lebanese national football team. We'd met in the hotel in Amman where all the national teams were staying and he explained just how divided Lebanese football was. In many ways it was an exact mirror of the political crises that had afflicted it over the years. Each football team had been co-opted by a sectarian group and politicians had fallen over themselves to fund teams in the hope of increased popularity that might one day translate into votes. The country's biggest club and current champions, Al Ansar, had traditionally been a Sunni club, funded by ex Prime Minister Rafik Hariri. After his assassination in 2005 his son, Saad, continued to give money to them, as well as Nejmeh, a team that was Sunni-owned but supported mainly by the Shia. Saad had also dipped his toe in with the Christians, funding the Orthodox team Racing Beirut.

Hezbollah had got into the game too, funding their team Al Ahed. The Druze community had Al Safa whilst the Maronites backed Sagesse. Every Saturday was derby day in Lebanon, where Sunni met Shia, Shia met Druze, Christian met Muslim. Violence was inevitable. With the dust still settling after Israel's 2006 bombardment of the country, Lebanon was on a knife-edge. The central government and its army had been humiliated by its impotence both in the face of the Israeli onslaught but also by the power and organisation of Hezbollah's guerilla army. The West demanded that Prime Minister Siniora reined in what was effectively a state within a state. The problem was that Hezbollah's stock – both within the Shia and non-Shia communities – had never been higher after their successful act of resistance. They were also a legitimate political party, with elected members of the Lebanese parliament. Siniora's hands were tied. The only thing he could do was tinker around the edges. So he banned all football fans from attending football matches, lest their sectarian rioting produced the spark that blew his country wide open again, this time from the inside.

This year it was supposed to be different. I had flown in for the first weekend of the Lebanese season and this time, I had been told by Emile, the fans would be back. Or so I'd hoped. I was also flying in to the biggest political crisis to rock Lebanon since the war. However, given that the Lebanese are forced to experience exponentially greater crises every year, there was bound to be another one along in one shape or form. But this one was serious. Ever since Rafik Hariri's 2005 assassination blew away Lebanon's post-civil war innocence two political groups had formed and vied for political supremacy. On one side was the anti-Syrian 14 March group – who had blamed much of the country's instability as well as Rafik Hariri's assassination of the Syrians that had occupied the country for years. It was made up mainly of Sunnis like Rafik Hariri's son Saad and his Future Movement political party, the Druze and some Christian groups. On the other stood the pro-Syrian 8 March group, an alliance of convenience between the Maronite Catholics led by former President General Aoun and the Shia militia Hezbollah led by Sheikh Hassan Nasrallah. Lebanon's constitution had been drawn up on sectarian lines, with each community given a slice of the political pie. The Maronites, who had fought against Lebanon's Muslims and, by proxy, Syria in the civil war, had now jumped into bed with the Pro-Syria camp.

Although the Maronites constitutionally hold the post of president, no one could agree on a suitable candidate – fearing it gave Hezbollah and the pro-Syrians the whip hand. An agreement between the political different parties was due in September but it was postponed and a new date set. It had created the last thing that Lebanon needed: a power vacuum.

The football season was due to start on Saturday, but the presidential vote was on the following Tuesday. The timing couldn't have been worse. I got into a taxi and headed for the Christian area of Ashrafiyeh, home to two of Lebanon's most bitter footballing rivals, Racing Beirut and Sagesse, who were to kick off the season against each other. Paul Rustom, Emile's son and Lebanon's international striker, had told me back in Amman it was Lebanon's answer to Scotland's 'Old Firm'. Only this time the Christian rivalry was between Orthodox and Maronite Catholics. Like the Glaswegian version, from an outsider's perspective at least, both teams seemed to have more in common then they cared to admit: both were from the same small hill in northern Beirut, both were on the same side during large swathes of the country's bloody civil war, both were Christian. The crucial difference was that the Maronites were an Eastern sect of Catholicism allied with Rome whilst the Orthodox Church broke links with the Pope in the 11th century. Both now celebrated different Christmas Days and, in Lebanon at least, rabidly supported different football teams. As I sped through Beirut's deserted suburbs, I didn't share Paul's confidence that the fans would be there to see it.

Beirut by daylight is a beautiful thing. The small narrow streets of Ashrafiyeh were filled with stylish old Mercedes Benzs. The buildings – with their little art deco iron balcony railings and wooden shutters – were magisterial; turn of the 20th-century concrete palaces that had only been enhanced by their corruption over time. They wore the scars of civil war well. It wasn't until I walked outside into the unseasonably hot autumnal morning that I realised that the façade of the hostel I was staying in was riddled with bullet holes. The tell tale dimples seemed to be clustered around the window of the dorm I was staying in, as if my room was once the workplace of a hard-to-dislodge sniper, methodically picking off his prey whilst his increasingly desperate enemies in-discriminately sprayed bullets back in return. The main street of Gemmayzeh is quiet in the morning. This wasn't its time. The idle bars and clubs that are packed on either side tell you that life doesn't truly fill its streets until somewhere around midnight. During the civil war it had a very different reputation: a sniper's alley. Walking down it would mean almost certain death. But even for Hassan, who worked in a mobile phone shop on the street, and Nader, a club singer, it was still unusually quiet.

'Watch what you say, everybody is tense,' warned Nader, a Sagesse fan, when I asked for directions. 'Tuesday is an important day for the country, maybe after Tuesday, no one will be safe.'

Eventually I found my rendezvous point on a dual carriageway near the hostel. Emile pulled up in a brand new black 4x4 wearing a Lebanese national team training top, tracksuit bottoms and trainers. There hadn't been training that day but Emile was evidently a man who was always ready to kick a ball, no matter where he was. Emile was a Sagesse man, an ex-player who still coached and helped out at the club, but the financial hardships – no fans, after all, means no revenue for the turnstiles – meant that for the first time in his adult life Emile would be starting a football season with no football club which made his full training ground attire all the stranger.

'It is still not decided [about the fans] as we are waiting to hear from the Ministry of the Interior,' Emile declared as we drove up the hill that Ashrafiyeh lived on. He didn't seem to think it was that bad a thing. 'Because of the bad political situation the fans are fighting [especially] the Shia and the Sunni. So the FA was ordered not to create more problems. I think they will not change this decision. They will make the clubs wait.'

Emile lived in the tallest building in northeast Beirut, a huge tower block that dominated all around it. Out on the balcony, the Mediterranean stretched out before us. 'We didn't leave here [during the 2006 Israeli war],' he said, looking ruefully out towards the horizon. 'We just watched as the planes came and bombed over there.' He pointed towards the port. 'That was the closest they got.' He continued to storyboard Lebanon's bloody recent history across the panorama: in front, where Israeli planes unloaded their missiles into Beirut's dock; over there, to the left, where Rafik Hariri was assassinated; over here, slightly closer now, the huge Mohammad al Amin mosque which Hariri helped build. 'He didn't see it finished but he was buried in it,' Emile said. Over the past 30 years Emile had seen it all, experiencing the country's bloody civil war first hand. 'I played in 14 Sagesse versus Racing derbies – the first in 1966,' he said as we drank cold water on his balcony. Emile had been a centre-back who had turned out for the national team at a time when there was scarcely a nation. 'We lost many players at that time, five were killed. Once during practice a bomb went off injuring several of us. We were targeted because we were Christians.'

Between 1975 and 1990 Lebanon was plunged into a vicious civil war pitting Christian and Muslim communities against each other as outside powers – in particular Syria, Israel, the USA and the Palestinian Liberation organisation (PLO)

– tried to manipulate the situation for its own ends. An estimated 100,000 people were killed by the time a ceasefire was brokered, leaving Syria as its defacto occupier. The war saw the country divided into two, the north controlled by a Christian government, the south by a Muslim parallel administration. Lebanon's football league also split, with Sagesse and Racing competing in exponentially fiercer derbies. Even though they were both Christian teams that should have been united by a common enemy, the rivalry between Maronite and Orthodox remained fierce. 'There was no solidarity between us, even in the war. We hated each other more when there was a war between Muslims and Christians,' said Emile.

Even those involved in the game were puzzled by the hatred. 'I don't understand it,' Emile admitted, shaking his head. 'It's the 21st century and we still make a difference between Maronite and Orthodox. It's a shame to have two Easters. What, Christ died twice? We make the sign of the cross with a hand, they make it with three fingers. That's it.'

Emile had agreed to make some calls and arrange for me to meet some of the players. With Emile and Sagesse parting ways, he arranged that we visit Racing Beirut. Racing didn't have a training ground. Instead they trained on a rented sand pitch at a local school at the edge of Beirut's Christian district. The drive there was illuminating. The closer we got to the sand pitch, the higher the density of bullet holes in the buildings. Just behind the pitch was Damascus Street, which separated us from the Shia area on the other side of the road. This, for a time, was the frontline during the civil war and some derelict wrecks still stood here, missing chunks of concrete thanks to the blast of tank shells. One building closest to the road looked little more than a shell, with front rooms that once housed life hanging through the blown-off façade. The building looked derelict until you realised that up on the third floor, a line of children's clothes hung messily between two concrete pillars.

Racing Beirut's pitch looked like it had taken a few hits itself. With no nets and large holes gouged in its surface it was virtually unusable for football. If Saad Hariri was funding Racing, he wasn't giving them very much. In the penalty area a used hypodermic needle stuck out of the sand. What looked like a sewage truck rumbled onto the pitch in an attempt to make it playable, spraying water to dampen the coarse surface. Baha Salem Hanoun, the team's Iraqi coach, stood by waiting for his team to arrive. He was used to working with this sort of privation.

'We have gifted players but the situation is ruined here by politics,' he said as the truck bounced through the uneven pitch, leaving wet tyre prints in its wake. 'But they keep going. The players and coaches of both sides serve the country better than the politicians.'

The team's captain, Tony Mikerai, was the first player to arrive. Unsurprisingly given the political problems that had surrounded the first weekend of the season, he tried to take the sting out of the weekend's biggest potential flash point.

'We must not look at this game as a rivalry, simply as three points,' he said before the rest of the squad arrived and began stretching on the potholed surface. 'We play football because we love it. You don't get a good salary but I thought, when the war finished, the whole country will be good, and football too. But there was too much fighting so if the fans are there it will make problems for the country.'

The comparison with the champions Al Ansar couldn't have been starker. We drove south, past the Shatila and Sabra Palestinian refugee camps – famous for the 1982 massacre of as many as 3,000 innocent civilians by a Christian militia allied with Israel – and around a broken-backed bridge that was still to be rebuilt one year after it had been destroyed.

'Nothing rebuilt by the government has finished yet,' lamented Emile. Anything that had been finished had been organised by Hezbollah, using money either from prominent local businessmen or outside sources. Sure enough, we passed under a brand new pedestrian bridge bearing the legend: 'Donated by Tehran Municipality.' Emile pulled his 4x4 into a car park surrounded by rubble. Expensive cars sat juxtaposed sharply to the blackened concrete and rocks that surrounded them: BMWs, convertible Mercedes, blacked out 4x4s. In front of us sat a pristine football pitch, with grass, floodlights and a stand full of well-dressed spectators in expensive suits and smoking Western cigarettes. From the podium we watched as the players below were run through training, including Emile's son Paul. When I had last met him at the West Asian Championships the previous June he was playing for Emile's team Sagesse. Now he turned out for the Champions, for Rafik, and now Saad Hariri's favourite team.

'Football is a reflection on society, definitely [and] I can't deny that we are a Sunni club,' explained Mahmoud Natour, a member of Ansar's board who was there to check on his team's progress before the first game of the season.' But we have mixed players, especially here in Ansar. Our board members are Shia, Sunni, one is even Jewish. We care more about football. It doesn't mean [because we are a Sunni club] we are doing anything for politics. We are trying to build a professional club.'

Without the Hariri family's money, most of the football teams would go to the wall. Even Ansar would struggle without the fans being allowed in. But the fans had recently proved that they couldn't be trusted when football matches were being played, even when they were cheering on the same team.

'We did have a problem with the national team when the fans fought in a game [against Kuwait] because of the political tension,' Mahmoud admitted. 'The government aren't happy with that. It's whether football fans [use] the political tensions on the field to start a fire, that's why the government is doing this. You never know who will use it.'

The club that had fascinated me most, however, was Al Ahed, Hassan Nasrallah's team and a club that I had heard was heavily subsidised by Hezbollah. Hezbollah translates as Party of God in Arabic and was set up as a militia to protect Lebanon's Shia – allegedly with Iranian money – after the Israelis invaded Lebanon in 1982. The Shia had good reason to seek protection. For them, the threat was four-fold – the Israelis; the Americans; the Christian north; and the Sunnis. For 1,500 years the two major branches of Islam had bristled against each other. The split revolved around an issue of succession over who really embodied the true spirit of Islam when the Prophet Mohammed died. Without a son to take the mantle as a natural successor, two sides emerged: those who believed that the line should pass through Mohammed's son in law and cousin Ali and those who believed that the lead should be taken by the most suitable person chosen from the Prophet Mohammed's close personal cadre. The former were referred to as Shia (which comes from Shiat Ali which roughly translates as 'followers of Ali'); the latter Sunni (which comes from 'one who follows the Sunnah' or the words and deeds of Mohammed). The two took different paths and had been in conflict almost constantly ever since.

Today, Hezbollah was the best-known and best-organised militant organisation espousing Shia Islam and the West still considered it a terrorist organisation. The Americans had a particular axe to grind after 300 soldiers and civilians were killed by a suicide bombing in Beirut attributed to the organisation in 1983. But as the insecurity and anarchy grew in Lebanon during the 1980s, Hezbollah started to achieve a form of legitimacy by excelling in overground politics, by winning hearts and minds in their own communities by providing essential services the central government couldn't (or wouldn't): water, healthcare, education and other social and sporting projects. Now many within Lebanon and most countries in the Middle East regard it as a legitimate resistance force. And despite still holding on to its arsenal, Hezbollah had an important presence in the Lebanese parliament too. Blue-and-yellow signs that sit on street corners in Beirut's southern suburbs – two yellow hands enveloping a small, blue collection box – summed up Hezbollah's *raison d'être*: 'The hand that fights, the hand that builds.'

Hezbollah's finger prints were also on Al Ahed's training complex. It was a stone's throw from Ansar's, across the main highway south out of Lebanon, just on the edge of the Shia stronghold of Dahiyeh. To the left of the entrance a large banner hung with Nasrallah superimposed onto a Hezbollah flag. Inside, Haj Mohammad Assi, the club's general secretary, sat in his large, white office. It was harshly lit, the strong strip lighting bouncing off the white tiles and abundance of silverware on show. Behind his large, brown wooden desk hung two flags; one the Lebanese standard, the other Hezbollah's distinctive yellow insignia. But Mohammad wouldn't be drawn at first about his club's connection.

'We are a team of all Beirut,' he replied when I asked him to describe Ahed's catchment. 'This is the Shia area. But the fans of Ahed are not just Shia; they are from all the political parties. But here we don't talk about politics. This is a club of football, and a good club.'

Yet all around him more subtle evidence of Hezbollah's connection presented itself. Next to his desk a table was clustered with photographs in wooden frames. From where I was sitting it looked like a picture of a football dinner of some kind, with a visiting foreign dignitary. It was only on closer inspection I realised who it was: Hassan Nasrallah.

The bearded, turbaned nemesis of Israel was a picture of rude health in the shot, kissing a young girl, Mohammad's daughter, in a touching show of affection. 'Yes, the leader of the resistance. This is after the war with Israel,' explained Mohammad. Two large portraits hung on the far wall, one of the leaders of Iran's Islamic revolution, the other of his successor. Like reading a Where's Wally book, Nasrallah's face suddenly jumped out from every corner, on every wall.

'I take it he's a big fan of the club,' I asked. Mohammad ushered me outside his office and pointed proudly at the large team photo that hung at its entrance. It showed Al Ahed's victorious Lebanese FA Cup-winning squad of 2005. In the middle Mohammad pointed to a picture of himself, standing next to the grinning face of Nasrallah who had dropped in to congratulate the team. 'This isn't an office for the football club though, I would not be able to hang all these pictures, see,' Mohammad admitted, looking slightly guilty. He had been slippery about Hezbollah's involvement in the club ever since I had arrived. 'This is the club office.' He pointed to the lobby outside his office. It was pretty unconvincing, although not entirely surprising. Hezbollah had always been cagey about the scale of its social projects and worked hard to present itself as the party of resistance for the whole of Lebanon, not just the country's Shia community. Anything that seemed too sectarian from the party's members – and Mohammad was a sports officer for Hezbollah after all – was decidedly off message. And there were few things in Lebanon more sectarian than football.

'Hezbollah don't give money to us, not like Hariri gives to Ansar and Nejmeh,' Mohammad continued, trying to distance himself and Hezbollah further. 'He gives money and those in the club are now for him. [Walid] Jumblatt [the long-standing leader of Lebanon's Druze faction] and his party is the same, giving money to Safa.

When Nejmeh get money they send a communiqué to all the media that they [the Hariris] are backing this club. In this team we have many forces within the team. The players are free to believe in what they believe. Hezbollah is backing the team.' He paused, perhaps realising the futility of arguing away Hezbollah's involvement in front of a picture of him with his arms around Nasrallah.

'When we need help, Hezbollah is backing us,' he clarified.

'In what way?' I asked

'I am the sports officer for the Hezbollah party. I am taking care of it,' he replied.

'But what kind of help?'

'If we need any help, administrative help, to push people to back the team with money. They know that the team gets help from the party, and they respect the party, so they come and help the club.'

Despite the obvious discomfort about the explicit link between Ahed and Hezbollah, Mohammad and the team were still excited about the prospect of Nasrallah dropping in to see them. The problem was that, with Hezbollah's Secretary General under constant threat of assassination, he couldn't give forewarning.

'Everyone can expect Mr Nasrallah, but we don't know when or where!' Mohammad laughed when I asked whether he'd be there for the first game of the season. 'It is very dangerous. He would love to be here. He is very normal. He supports the team and gives orders to support them.' Still, even if he wasn't watching Ahed's opening-day fixture, he would still no doubt be getting his footballing fix, although it would be from an unlikely source. 'He likes English football too, the Premier League is on Al Mansar [Hezbollah's own television network, itself listed as a terrorist entity by the USA, and which boasts 10 million viewers worldwide] every weekend.'

But like most things with the mysterious Nasrallah, no one was sure where his allegiances lay. 'I think maybe Liverpool,' one of the club's members interjected when I asked who he liked to watch in England. 'I like Steven Gerrard. My father likes Michael Owen but I don't like Wayne Rooney. He is Manchester.' Even in Beirut there was no escape from the animus between Liverpool and Manchester. The smart money, though, was on Nasrallah being a Liverpool fan. But this wasn't that unusual. Most of the big four have their own pariah supporter. Famously, it was alleged that Osama Bin Laden – like Fidel Castro – was a keen follower of the Arsenal. It was even alleged that he watched four games at Highbury in 1994 when he was briefly residing in London. But I wanted Nasrallah as one of my own. 'Do you think he could be a West Ham fan?' Mohammad smiled a knowing, sympathetic smile. 'I will ask him. But it is unlikely to be West Ham. He will need a lot of persuading.' I never did find out who Nasrallah supported. Instead West Ham had to make do with the endorsement of another powerful politician a year later when US President Barak Obama declared his allegiance to the Irons.

The club agreed to allow me to see the rest of Ahed's ground. Outside the front gate I was confronted with a blond-haired man speaking in a thick German accent.

'At last! An English accent!' he boomed as he grabbed my hand with a Teutonic fervour I hadn't felt since Manfred Hoener almost ripped my arm from its socket back in Qatar. It turned out to be the team's manager, Robert Jaspert. Robert was an Australian-born German coach who had worked with the South Korean national team until, out of the blue, someone from Lebanon called. 'I got a call and was asked if I wanted to coach Ahed,' he explained happily as he slowly walked me around Ahed's vast training pitch. The complex was even more impressive than Ansar's, with two pitches, a stand and a fully equipped gym. There was even a heated swimming pool. Ahed had got his number after Lebanon had played South Korea and he had met some representatives from the club. Unbeknown to him when he accepted the offer, they were also representatives of Hezbollah. 'I'm not very political so I was on the plane on the way over here and I was sitting next to a Lebanese guy. He told me about Hezbollah and I thought: 'What am I doing here?''

Almost immediately Robert was immersed into Lebanon's complicated football politics when, back in March and after only a few days in the country, he was caught up in the car bombing that killed two of Nejmeh's players.

'Everyone talks politics, even on the football shows. It was March and my hotel room was wrecked. There was glass everywhere. We all went to the funeral, which is something I will never forget. Now, with the presidency, we do not have spectators. We are artists and need to perform to people.' It wasn't the only difference that Robert noticed. Any ostentatious religious symbols were banned. 'I have to keep this covered,' he told me showing the silver cross he wears around his neck. And Nasrallah was everywhere and nowhere. 'We have a few Sunnis [in the team] but everyone in the club loves him so much. We have a television show that gives awards for the best players. They all dedicated their awards to Nasrallah.' If success followed on the pitch, Robert was even told he might meet the man himself. 'I was told: 'If you get to the cup final again we are sure Nasrallah will meet you and shake your hand.' In Germany they have the wrong journalism about Hezbollah. They think it's like Al Qaeda. It's not, they do a lot of social work, for orphans.'

Robert disappeared to prepare his team for their first match and I was left to roam the grounds. It was inconceivable that the money for Lebanon's most advanced training facilities had come from anywhere other than Hezbollah. Through a metal door that was left ajar, I walked into a high-walled gym, itself bigger than Racing

Egypt A young fan of Al Ahly smokes
a cigarette before his team takes on arch rivals
Zamalek at the Cairo International Stadium
in 2007. It was a rare defeat for Ahly.
It was also the match where I met Assad,
the founding member of what would
become the Ultras Ahlawy.

Egypt Police form a barrier between the fans and the pitch at the Cairo International Stadium before the Cairo derby. The police's heavy handed approach to the fans was one factor in transforming Egypt's supporters into something more political and anti-authoritarian.

Israel Oren, an Israeli street hawker, shows his best selling piece of merchandise outside 'The Box' stadium in Netanya in 2006: a picture of a Maccabi Haifa fan pissing into the mouth of Hezbollah leader Hassan Nasrallah.

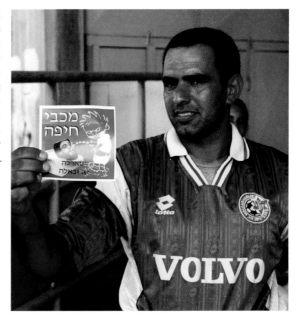

Yemen Fans of Yemeni club Yarmouk cheer on their side during a league match with Al Ahli Sana'a in 2007. Yarmouk is a deeply religious side that only signs devout Muslim players.

Palestine Coaching staff and substitutes for Palestinian club side Tulkarem nervously watch a cup match in Jericho against Wadi al Nis in 2006.

Palestine: West Bank
The Palestinian women's national team celebrate their very first home international in 2009 in Al Ram, near Ramallah.

(Top) One player waves a V for Victory sign at the largely all female crowd.
(Centre) Police officers stand in front of one of the stands. Almost 12,000 people attended the game, higher than attendances for women's football in Europe and the U.S.

(Bottom) The team's star and captain Honey Thaljieh celebrates after the 1-1 draw with Jordan.

144

Iraq *(Right)* The Iraq national team train in the heat during the 2007 West Asia Championships, Jordan. A few months later they would make global headlines by winning the Asia Cup.

(Below) Iraqi fans celebrate a goal. As many as a million Iraqi refuge had fled to Jordan during the war, making it virtually a home tournament for the Lions of Mesopotamia.

Jordan *(Left)* A Jordanian security official guards the doping room during the 2007 West Asian Championship in Amman.

(Below) Fans of Al Wihdat pray before a match against their main rivals Al Faisaly in the city of Zarqa, Jordan. Wihdat has a resolutely Palestinian identity, which cause tensions with the traditionally 'Jordanian' fans of Al Faisaly.

Saudi Arabia Saudi fans can't quite believe it. UAE striker Ismail Matar scores in injury time during the 2007 Gulf Cup semi-final in Abu Dhabi. The UAE went on to beat Oman in the final, their first ever piece of silverware.

Egypt *(Left)* One of the brave few away fans who had travelled to Cairo for the Egypt versus Algeria World Cup qualifier in Cairo in 2009.

(Below) There was an outpouring of anti-Algerian sentiment that stemmed from a similar, vital qualifier that Egypt won to reach the 1990 World Cup finals in Italy.

Egypt *(Left)* An Egypt fan leads the chants during Egypt vs Algeria in Cairo in 2009. Egypt won 2-0, taking both teams to a play-off in Sudan. Algeria won that game and with it a place in South Africa.

Gaza *(Top)* Referees in Gaza take a few moments before officiating the Gaza Cup final, at the Palestine Stadium in Gaza City in 2009.

(Above) Journalists, armed guards and football officials all pray at half time during the Gaza Cup final at the Palestine Stadium, Gaza City.

Egypt *(Top)* A young Palestine fan watches a crush develop as fans try to get into the Faisal al Husseini stadium near Ramallah for the Palestinian national team's first ever competitive home game, a London 2012 Olympic qualifier against Thailand in 2011.

(Middle) PFA chief Jibril Rajoub, AFC head Mohammed bin Hammam and Palestine PM Salam Fayyad stand for the national anthems.

(Bottom) Palestine lost on penalties, leaving the players distraught. But Thailand fielded an ineligible player and they qualified for the next round anyway.

Bahrain Bahrain national team player Salman Isa wonders what might have been after a 0-0 draw with New Zealand in a qualifying play-off for the 2010 World Cup finals. Isa had earlier hit the post.

Bahrain *(Left)* Bahrain fans hang posters supporting the country's King Hamad (and other Gulf royals) before the New Zealand match in 2009. They would go on to lose the return match 1-0 and miss out on the finals.

(Below) Bahraini children play football on a sand pitch in the capital Manama.

Syria *(Top)* Syrian officials pray before training in Jordan, ahead of the Syrian Olympic team's London 2012 qualifier against Malaysia.

(Right) The players trained as war raged in their homeland. No matches could be played in Damascus. They failed to qualify, falling at the final hurdle.

Libya *(Above)* The Libya national team can't believe they have qualified for the African Cup of Nations after drawing 0-0 with Zambia in Chingola in 2011.

(Opposite, top) The team prepared for the match in Tunisia, with a new kit shorn of the Gaddafhi-era flag.

(Opposite, middle) Fighters injured in the civil war waiting outside the stadium in Tunisia to meet their heroes.

(Opposite, bottom) Libya play a warm up match against a local Tunisian league club. Several of the players had fought against Gaddafhi, only to be called from the front line for this match.

Egypt *(Top)* A young Egyptian revolutionary wears a V for Vendetta face mask and an England woollen hat during a protest near Tahrir Square in 2012.

(Above) The Ultras Ahlawy lead a march in the coastal city of Alexandria in honour of those who died in the Port Said tragedy, where 72 Al Ahly fans perished.

156

Beirut's small sand football pitch. On the back wall two more portraits of Iran's Imam and the Ayatollah looked down.

Unsurprisingly given the plethora of Shia imagery Al Ahed's main support came from the nearby suburb of Dahiyeh. I had struggled to find it on the map, until I realised that it actually wasn't there. It was as if it had been wiped off. But every Lebanese knows where it is. It is Hezbollah country and allegedly the place where Western hostages like Terry Waite had been taken and imprisoned during the civil war. Emile wasn't sure it was a good idea I went when I phoned him and asked for directions.

'Be very careful around there, they think everyone foreign is an Israeli spy,' he said.

I took a service bus with Andrew, a young Hungarian student. He was a militant Arsenal fan.

'Who do you support?' he asked me. When I told him 'Fuck off,' was his abrupt response.

He was headed for the same destination as me, a touching exhibition that had been organised by Hezbollah called House of Spider. It was an exhibition that celebrated the 'divine victory' of Hezbollah over Israel, so called because Hassan Nasrallah had said that Israel was 'weaker than a spider's web'. It was touching because it didn't really deal with any heroic acts of bravery. Instead it exhibited pieces of captured Israeli hardware whilst showing pictures of children mutilated by Israeli munitions. Dahiyeh was also famous for bearing the brunt of the civil war and of Israel's 2006 bombardment. In both cases Dahiyeh was impossible to subdue, and as our taxi inched through the lunchtime traffic, it was easy to see why. With its identical, sand-coloured tower blocks and warren-like alleyways, it was almost impossible to navigate on foot, let alone in a tank – Dahiyeh seemed to have been designed with guerilla warfare in mind. Compared to the excess and the revelry in Ashrafiyeh, it felt like a different country: gone were the church steeples, gone were the countless impossibly beautiful women with long, tumbling dark hair, gone were the bars and the clean Parisian streets. In their place stood minarets, hijabs, shisha cafés and poverty. The unmistakable yellow flag of Hezbollah fluttered on every street corner. Down one road, every two metres, hung a huge portraits of Hezbollah fighters martyred in the most recent conflict with Israel. The district, though, isn't as densely populated as it used to be. Every three or four buildings, a sudden gap appeared, the footprint of an Israeli rocket attack that destroyed the tower block that once lived there, a reminder that the vast majority of the 1,000 Lebanese killed perished in Dahiyeh. 'That was where Hassan Nasrallah lived.' The taxi driver pointed to his right. Two large tower blocks stood guard over a patch of twisted steel and sandstone blocks.

The exhibition itself was on a patch of rubble too. From the outside, the House of Spider had been arranged like a battlefield. Green-and-brown military netting rose up on either side of the main path inside. To the right sat the broken propellers of a downed helicopter, to the left a trench full of boxes that once held ammunition. There was activity, but not as we expected. A pack of bearded men had formed a line and were quickly passing broken pieces of military hardware towards the truck. When it had first opened it had made international headlines for its lurid exhibitions and for its gift shop, where you could buy a copy of a computer game, a first-person Call of Duty style shoot 'em up where you played a resistance fighter who hunted down and killed 'Zionist pigs'. Now they were less pleased to see tourists. One of the men spotted us surveying the scene and turned around.

'We are closed, *khalas*, it's finished,' he barked angrily before turning his back to us once again. We stood there for a few moments, hoping he would change his mind. I offered that I was a British journalist. The back remained unmoved. Andrew said he was a tourist. Nothing. Then Andrew had a cunning plan.

'Allahu Akhbar,' he shouted.'Khomeini Rahbar!'

As if we had just said a secret password, the man turned around and ushered us inside.

'What did you say?' I asked Andrew incredulously.

'I learnt it in Iran. It means: 'God is great, Khomeini is the leader.''

Inside, men rushed past us with hastily packed boxes.

'You can't go in there, only here,' the worker intoned, a little softer now that we were deemed friends of a sort.

The centrepiece of the exhibition was a huge crater where a captured Israeli tank sat inside. Around it dismembered mannequins, each with its own Star of David painted on it, were scattered around, as if they had been blown outwards by whatever force had stricken the prone tank. Its own Star of David was burnt and forlorn, the blue only visible on one side. As I inched closer to the crater my right foot clanged on something metal. I knelt down and picked up a spent rocket launcher with instructions on the side written in Hebrew. Within seconds a guard snatched it off me and carried it outside. The room next door was off limits but I managed to creak the door open just enough to poke one eye through. The large white room was empty except for some large colour prints hanging on the walls. Each depicted a different scene of Israeli misery: a crowd of crying Israeli soldiers hunched over the body of a fallen comrade; a party of Israeli women crying in grief thanks to the destructive power of one of Hezbollah's Katyusha rockets. I had seen enough. Andrew and I left them to finish off their packing. It was clear why they were leaving. If I could find my way here on the back of the press House of Spider had got, Mossad would have no problems. We walked through the district safely, past the new offices of Hezbollah's media office, until we found a local souvenir shop. The shop was a homage to Hezbollah – mugs, key rings, Nasrallah prayer mats. On the floor, in a big pile, I saw dozens of Lebanese flags. They weren't selling too well.

'We sell three times as many Hezbollah flags as Lebanon flags,' explained the young shopkeeper, not moving his eyes from the newspaper he was reading. That said everything about where Dahiyeh's heart was. I bought a Lebanese flag and a Nasrallah key ring before leaving.

Finally, on Saturday morning, the first day of the Lebanese football season, a decision was made. Rahif Alameh sat at his desk in the Lebanese FA's smart offices on Verdun Street with a face like thunder. The FA's general secretary had been forced to make a choice he didn't want to make, even if he understood why it had to be made. 'Football is a little dangerous,' he sighed as I sat in front of him to pick up my press pass and find out whether the fans would be let in or not. Football was indeed dangerous in Lebanon and to illustrate the point he stood up, removed a photo that hung on his wall and passed it to me. It was a picture of Beirut Sports City Stadium, the 60,000 capacity national stadium I would be heading for later to watch Nejmeh take on Shebab Al-Sahel, after the Israelis had destroyed it in 1982. There was no pitch, nor any grass. Any that had survived the bombing had been grazed to dust by the herds of cows that lived amongst the blackened concrete pillars. They belonged to the owners of the shabby tents that surrounded it. In the aftermath of the attack it had been used as a makeshift camp housing refugees from Palestine, Lebanon and Syria.

Rahif had only just learned that the fans would indeed be banned from attending matches for the foreseeable future. 'The prime minister [Fouad Siniora] directly interfered in this case. We said: 'Every club should have to decide how many spectators they can accept on his responsibility, to help the government as the situation in Lebanon is not safe.' But everyone is looking for the [presidential] election.'

The decision had far larger ramifications for Rahif. The game itself was under threat in Lebanon. Even in the darkest days of the civil war, matches would be organised and thousands would turn up for a distraction from the horror. Not any more; the lack of fans had strengthened the hands of those seeking to fund football clubs for political gain. With no money coming in from the turnstiles, the clubs were even more dependent on handouts from political figures eager to secure votes.

'It's not healthy. If the assistance is based on politics it's dangerous. Excluding maybe one team I think all of the clubs receive political money,' he said, signing press accreditations for the game.

I told him of my visit to Al Ahed and how they had tried to deny that they received any help. He could barely hide his anger.

'Of course they get help from Hezbollah!' he said. 'Look at their ground: they have two pitches, a swimming pool and are building an indoor gymnasium for the winter. It's against the future of the game what we do now. If no one can come to the stadiums they will forget the football. Once there would be 40,000 to 60,000 at a game. They will choose another way, like drugs or fighting.'

Or basketball. With the prospect of a second season of no football, many fans had started watching Sagesse's basketball team instead. It didn't help that they added a little bit more glamour than their footballing namesakes thanks to their regularly being considered one of the finest teams in Asia. The Lebanese national team had enjoyed some success too, qualifying for the 2006 World Championships, the World Cup of Basketball, and only narrowly avoiding the knockout stages after beating France and Venezuela. There was less trouble in the domestic league, and the authorities hadn't felt compelled to intervene.

'Basketball,' snorted Rahif handing me my pass. 'It's a big joke.'

It only took a few hours for the word to get out that the fans would be barred entry to football matches this season, but some fans already had a well-prepared plan. In a small, dusty building back in Ashrafiyeh, the Sagesse Fan Club was holding their annual pre-season meeting. Like any fan meeting, the ten-strong delegation discussed the basics of fan politics: from the crisis the club found itself in now that Emile had left the coaching side to the less arch but no less important dilemma of who would play the drums in the team's band. The Sagesse fans, you see, weren't going to let anything as trifling as a government ban, heavily armed troops or arrest deter them. But that plan was further down the agenda and things had already started to get heated. An argument had broken out and swiftly been ended when a gun was pulled out and slammed onto the table. Samir, a board member who had produced the weapon, was forced to act.

'We thought we'd agreed 500 fans with [Lebanese Football] federation,' screamed Bashir, a huge bear of a man who looked like he had slept rough the previous night. He possessed a voice so deep you suspected that in his tender moments only oceanographers would be able to pick up the growls. He was responsible for leading the terrace chants during games, which had pretty much made him surplus to requirements in recent months. Another season of inaction was unthinkable.

'It's not the federation, the government didn't allow it,' replied Patrick Aoun, the young, clean-cut president of the fan association.

Joseph, Patrick's grey-haired deputy, tried to calm Bashir down by covering his mouth. The room descended into farce as clipped Arabic effortlessly segued into French and occasionally English. Six conversations rose at the same time, in three languages. It was chaos. The club's vice president, there to give 'The Management's' perspective, gave up and walked out before Samir pulled out his gun and used it on the table as a makeshift gavel. He didn't say a word. Calm was restored.

'In Ashrafiyeh, you're either a Sagesse fan or a Racing fan, there's nothing else and after the games there were too many problems, fights,' explained Patrick as the meeting continued. 'It was really a derby in every way, like Barca and Real. Look at how much this club means to us.' Patrick qualified the point by sweeping his arm in front of the packed table of arguing fans who were now filing out into Beirut's steaming late summer. But Patrick had a plan.

'This is a secret,' he said, lowering his voice, 'As we don't want any Racing fans to find out. At some grounds they have a motorway which is a little bit higher than the stadium so we are using guerilla tactics. It would kill some people to know Sagesse are playing without them so we are going to watch it at the highway and if the army won't let them we will go to the roofs of tower blocks around the ground. We know the owners. Although we won't bring the band as we don't want to make noise and upset the residents.' I took a mobile phone number and was told to call his right-hand man Joseph when I got to the ground. Samir walked by clutching his gun. He wasn't usually have a habit of turning up with a weapon to football functions, apparently. He had just finished his shift working as a bodyguard at a foreign embassy.

'Here, you want to fire it?' he asked, forcing the gun into my hand.

It was heavy and powerful. I felt weak holding it, as if it controlled me, not the other way around.

'Where shall I shoot it?' I asked, looking at the kids standing by the entrance of the building unfazed, as if men swinging pistols was normal.

Samir looked over his shoulder, kicked open a shoddy-looking white door in front of us and pointed at the pathetic-looking cistern.

'Fire!' he shouted.

Nothing. I couldn't do it. It wouldn't have mattered if I had. Samir laughed, taking the gun out of my sweaty grip, holding up an ammunition clip in his right hand.

✦

The silence that followed Ali Nassereddine's goal covered the empty Sports City
Stadium in a dark melancholy. Ali wasn't sure what to do at first. The pure, blind ecstasy
of scoring had led him to perform an act of gymnastic heroism, flipping backwards in
perfect arches. But then the silence caught him too. His celebration was in vain. No one
would ever see his back flips, his team's initial adulation or his goal. Ali trudged back
up the pitch, shoulders hunched, head down, as if he'd just watched the opposition
score. The shouts of the few soldiers allowed into the ground – the same stadium that
had once been a shell housing broken refugees in the mid-1980s, rebuilt into a new,
allseater stadium in time to host the 2000 Asian Cup – were well-meaning but only
provided relativity, a bench-mark with which to measure the stadium's vast echo.

It was Nejmeh's fourth goal against a fellow, predominantly Shia-supported side,
Shebab Al-Sahel, in the first game of the season. Shebab had already had a player sent
off early in the first half for comically diving and handballing the ball on the goal line.
Nejmeh missed the penalty but proceeded to destroy their opponents. It was 4–0 and
there was still half an hour left. The first day of the Lebanese season had started with
footballing fireworks. But it felt like a pyrrhic victory. After meeting with Sagesse's
guerilla fans, I hailed a cab and went south again, this time to the Beirut Sports City
and the first game of the season between Nejmeh and Shebab Al-Sahel. As soon as I
approached the Roman façade of the national stadium, the troops loomed into view.
APCs scuttled at its base, carrying troops brandishing automatic weaponry. For the
first time at any match in the Middle East I saw tanks, six of them, parked to one side.

The teams came out just as I had taken my seat in the only place in the ground
that exhibited any sign of life, the press bench. The Nejmeh players carried on a long,
plastic poster eulogising their fallen comrades who had lost their lives in a car bombing
during pre-season.

'I think it's better now [the fans are banned] because you know it won't be a
massacre,' argued Pauline Sahyoum, a reporter for the An-Nahar daily newspaper, who
was sitting next to me.

'Before, the fans beat the fans. Even the army couldn't stop them, especially when
Nejmeh played Ansar, there were too many of them. So the Ministry [of the Interior]
had to make a decision.'

The sun was setting now, and the minarets began their call by the time Ali had
scored his goal. The game ended in a rout, 5–0. I was used to a crush leaving a football
ground but outside was dead, the troops still clustered around the entrance whilst

the distant beeping of incessant traffic heralded the Lebanese rush hour. At this game football had become everything and nothing. On the one hand, the fingerprints of the game's importance were there: the need for troops, the banner honouring the innocent bystanders of Lebanon's increasing anarchy. Yet on the other, it felt futile. Who was this game for if no one was there to see it?

Football for these two teams had been so removed from the terraces, the weight which tethers any club to reality, that soon you feared these teams would be playing on empty pitches in parks. A new generation had begun to desert the game, not knowing or understanding what it was to collectively love a team that you could actually breathe in and almost touch. The players too had begun to feel the disillusionment that this might be a permanent state of affairs for Lebanese football. As I was walking back to the main highway, a figure wearing Nejmeh's kit walked past, looking for his car in the dark. It was Ali Nassereddine, the player who had celebrated his goal in vain.

'Normally I score and I am so happy because everyone knows we have the most fans in the East,' he said ruefully when I asked about his celebration. 'But without the fans I score and it feels like I have died.'

Ali continued to look fruitlessly for his lift home. Behind him the army stoically remained, as if not fully believing that Nejmeh's faithful weren't planning a final sneaky attack on the stadium's entrance.

Sunday was an appropriate day to hold Beirut's most prominent Christian derby. Like the previous day's match, the army was out in force outside the ground. An hour before kick-off heavily armed soldiers patrolled the Bourj Hammoud stadium, lest any fan dared get near the ground. Inside, the vast ageing concrete structure was alive with activity. Through a half-open door, I watched as the referee and his assistants prayed to Mecca in their office. A solitary Racing player did the same on the pitch. Meanwhile Christian players from both sides sporting large Jesus tattoos got dressed in their respective changing rooms. Sameer Nagim, Sagesse's team manager, stood guard at his team's door, refusing entry to anyone but players. He apologetically explained that the stakes were too high to risk letting outsiders in.

'Every year one of us would get relegated, so we haven't played each other for so long,' he said, clearly relishing the opportunity to continue the tradition. 'The rivalry is still there, Maronite versus Orthodox, and fighting was normal. I used to be young and run from the police. This is football in Lebanon. We have to do it today, especially for the people of Ashrafiyeh.'

The Racing management were less worried about their tactics being leaked to the opposition and let me sit with the players. The atmosphere was thick with Deep Heat, almost blinding, as Rabih Abouchaaya, the team's midfielder, explained Racing's religious mix.

'There are maybe ten Christian players, ten Shia and four Sunni,' he said, although even this basic explanation sparked a political debate between the players. 'I'm with General Aoun [the Maronite presidential candidate supported by Hezbollah],' exclaimed Rabih. 'The majority here is with him because we are Christian and we have a bond with the Shia.'

Joseph Attieh, the team's long-haired left-back who wore a huge cross on his arm, agreed. 'I'm with the General too,' he admitted, just as other players walked in to admonish him.

'We're not all with him! I'm for Hariri,' shouted the midfielder Moursri.

All mention of politics abruptly ended as the coach began the team talk, mapping out the 4–3–3 formation he hoped would bring Racing its first derby victory in close to a decade. There was just one last thing to do before kick-off. The Racing team huddled in the changing room, with the captain instructing the players to 'each pray to their own god'. For a brief few moments, the eleven men were tightly locked in a circle, three different prayers to three different creeds rising from the group. They shouted: 'Oh Mary, Oh Mohammed, Oh Ali, 1,2,3 Racing!' and ran to the tunnel. Sagesse were waiting for them. 'We are all Ashrafiyeh,' an anonymous Sagesse voice implored. 'Let's take it easy, OK?' The two sets of players got the nod and walked out into the empty stadium and to the faint, almost inaudible hum of applause.

High up on the nearby overpass, Joseph and the Sagesse Fan Club were there in force. Despite the government ban and the threat of arrest, hundreds had avoided the army directly outside the stadium and made it to the overpass that skirted the northern end of the stadium. The rooftops were dotted with more fans, all cheering on their team from their precarious vantage points. On the overpass cars flew past and swerved to avoid the growing crowd on the road.

'It's dangerous, there are mad drunk drivers driving past,' shouted Jeffrey, a Sagesse fan clinging onto the crash barrier. 'You can't blame the government. People are afraid of the fights, some people are crazy and mad [but] I've supported this team for 40 years. Can I stop now? How can I stop now?' Joseph, fiddling constantly with rosary beads, looked on proudly, smiling at the large contingent of support he'd brought. The vast majority were Sagesse, with a few Racing fans thrown in.

'Aren't you worried they'll fight?' I asked him.

'No, I don't fight here. I used to fight for real.' With that he lifted the sleeve on his right arm, revealing a tattoo of a skull, with a red beret and two swords. I didn't recognise it, but Gaith, an Iraqi photographer who had accompanied me on the trip, did. 'That's the insignia of the Lebanese Forces.'

The Lebanese Forces were the feared armed militia of the fascist-inspired, avowedly-Christian Phalange political party. They were widely believed to be responsible for the brutal Shatila and Sabra massacres in 1982, one of the civil war's bloodiest atrocities. It gave a new, wholly unexpected meaning to the phrase 'guerilla fan'. Perhaps the presence of a potentially genocidal maniac could explain the rather genial peace that had descended on the crowd although, as Jeffrey explained, just as Racing missed the first chance of a heated opening few minutes, there was a far more mundane reason. 'The truth is that neither of us, Sagesse or Racing fans, have anywhere else to go.'

Sammy, a Racing fan, agreed that the government ban had forced the two groups of supporters to accept each other just so that they can watch their teams. 'I'm happy we are playing in the first division again, but I'm happier just to be watching. I don't care if there are any Sagesse fans here any more.'

The game descended into brutality. Players were stretchered off and yellow cards brandished. Ironically given the pre-match talk, there was far more animosity on the pitch than on the makeshift terraces. Finally the deadlock was broken by Racing's Sierra Leonean striker Donald Massinter running through and coolly beating the keeper. Suddenly the Sagesse fans came to life, screaming at their own team for their inept display.

'You are playing like kids!'

'I'm too angry to swear at you!'

'Your mother's cunt!'

Things got worse when Sagesse went 2–0 down, Massinter again the scorer. It could have been four. The final whistle went and the Racing players celebrated like they'd just avoided relegation. Joseph flung his arms in the air and stormed off without saying another word as the rest of the Sagesse fans negotiated the perilous path back down the overpass, back to Ashrafiyeh. There were no fights and no arguments. It had taken every ounce of effort just to be there, let alone rekindle decades-old antagonisms. But it also constituted a hope of sorts, that football wouldn't be forgotten, even if it took an underground resistance movement to keep the flame alive.

And what of the presidential vote? Tuesday was tense but passed peacefully. The vote was postponed again, further deepening the country's political crisis and leaving Lebanon in a precarious, rudderless position. By the time I had sat down to write this it had been postponed 18 times and street-to-street fighting was being reported between Hezbollah's forces and pro-government militias in Beirut.

'It looks like it's going to be a long, hard winter,' shrugged Jeffrey as he finally let go of the crash barrier that had kept him safe for the previous two hours. He was right, in more ways than one.

April 2009

The final call to prayer of the day washed down from the megaphone fixed to the roof of the nearby white concrete office block, over the mangled metal and broken glass that carpeted the street below. Armed Lebanese soldiers stood brandishing their machine guns on the perimeter of the carnage to keep the crowd – some curious, but most still angry – at bay. Passers-by pointed at the crushed, blacked out BMW that sat at the centre of the crossroads, wondering loudly whether the street had been the target of another car bomb. Beirut, after all, is a city used to random acts of violence. Crushed cars, some concertinaed in half, littered the road towards the city's main highway, as if a monster from a Japanese horror movie had lurched down the road, indiscriminately squashing passing traffic. But no, this wasn't the scene of a bombing, but rather the aftermath of the final day of the 2008/09 Lebanese football season, which had just ended in a riot between the fans of Nejmeh and Al Ahed.

It was 18 months since I had left Lebanon with it on the brink of another violent crisis. The ongoing political stand-off between the anti-Syrian March 14 and pro-Syrian March 8 groups had been simmering under the surface. Many thought that the continued postponement of a parliamentary vote to elect a new president had the potential to plunge the country into another civil war. It was the reason why the country's sectarian football fans were banned from entering the stadiums. Instead the spark came from another source. Hezbollah had long been able to build its own state within a state but a key component of that was a shadow fixed line telecommunications network that the group viewed as an essential weapon in its war of resistance against Israel. But it was completely out of the control of the government. So when it emerged that the network was allegedly being used to spy on pro-government figures flying in and out of Beirut airport, the government moved to shut it down and show Hezbollah who was in charge. Instead, Hezbollah took its guns to the streets and showed the government in no uncertain terms who really held the power in Lebanon: they did. Dozens of people died in the clashes until an agreement was reached in Doha to end the political impasse and allow a new president to be elected after the vote had been postponed an incredible 19 times.

But Lebanon remained as political divided as ever. A new flashpoint arrived on the horizon to replace the old one: parliamentary elections. The football league had again become the proxy battlefield for competing sectarian interests. Religion, politics and mistrust had combined to produce a flammable mix, culminating in the riot between Nejmeh fans and Al Ahed's players which sounded a dark note of caution ahead of the election in a few months time.

The countdown to the violence began a week earlier. Sitting on the Nejmeh team bus, parked outside Beirut's fancy Commodore hotel in downtown Hamra, Emile Rustom exhaled loudly when asked about the denouement of the Lebanese football season. Emile was no longer in charge of the national team, having been poached by Nejmeh. He had done well too, taking the team to within two matches of its first league championship in two seasons. Like Al Ahed, Nejmeh also had a Shia constituency but unlike Al Ahed, Nejmeh was funded by the Sunni politician Saad Hariri. But even though Emile had landed one of Lebanese football's plum jobs he didn't look happy. The season had come to a dramatic conclusion with both Nejmeh and Al Ahed, the team supported by Hezbollah, taking the championship down to the wire. The fans were still banned from the stadiums but the latest round of political bloodletting seemed to have taken its toll on Emile. Nejmeh were hours away from taking on their arch rivals Al Ansar – a Sunni team that was also funded by Hariri – in the penultimate game of the season. Victory was vital to regain the top spot from Al Ahed, the reigning champions after winning their first ever championship the season before. The money I had seen poured in to the club's superior training facilities had clearly worked. But it wasn't matters on the pitch that were causing him concern, or to lower his voice to a whisper as he spoke to me.

'[There is a] man that pulls the strings everywhere and pays money for the games,' Emile hushed like a bad spy as the bus jolted through Hamra's warren of tightly-knit streets. 'When teams play us, the Shia players play like they have knives out. [In one game] Ahed offered to pay the opposition players $1,000 each to beat us. Ahed won the other day. Did you see it?'

'I hadn't,' I replied. Emile continued anyway.

'[The oppositions'] Shia players were on the pitch, but didn't play. It was a very bad comedy.'

When we had met before in Beirut Emile had been a garrulous host, taking me to meet the movers and shakers at Lebanon's top football clubs irrespective of their religious or political affiliation. He had been greeted warmly by Haj Mohammed Assi, Hezbollah's man in charge of Al Ahed, when he took me to the club. Now, things were different. Tensions, always waiting for an anniversary, a constitutional crisis or an election to rear its head, had returned and the football league, its empty terraces, mistrust and hidden violence, were once again merely an extension of Lebanon's fractured political life. And, like in politics, the Sunni footballing establishment could see Hezbollah's hand everywhere whilst also repeating an oft used criticism that was mostly, but not exclusively, aimed at Lebanon's Shia population: That they were fifth columnists with little interest in Lebanon or its flag. Its true devotion was to its Shia faith, to Hezbollah and to Tehran above all else. That Shia players on other teams would tailor their performance according to the religious beliefs of their opponents found depressingly fertile ground.

'Next week Ahed play another Shia team,' Emile sighed as the bus silently jolted towards the coastal town of Saida. This was true. Al Ahed was due to play Shabab al Ghazieh, from the south, whilst Nejmeh took on Safa, a team from Beirut funded by the Druze community. But, politically, the Druze were aligned with Nejmeh and Ansar's owner Saad Hariri. 'So, of course, they will win,' Emile stated matter of factly. 'It is up to us to win fairly.'

Saida's beautiful seaside stadium deserved better than this. It was built at a different time, when the Lebanese had real hope that the sectarian problems of the past were behind them. Sat on a rocky peninsular jutting in to the Mediterranean, the sea could be heard lapping on the shore from inside the stands. When the sun shone the awnings that covered the stands glistened brilliant white. It had been built for Lebanon's greatest moment in football, when it hosted the 2000 Asian Cup. They hadn't made it out of the group stages but the national stadium had been filled with fans and flags. It was ten years since the end of the civil war. The country was booming. But it was all an illusion, destroyed by the powerful car bomb that killed Rafik Hariri in 2005. Now armed police patrolled the concourses to prevent any fans from gaining access to the game. No one even tried to gain entry. Once, the Nejmeh-Ansar derby would have attracted 40,000 people; now only a few of the club's dignitaries, and the press, could attend.

'I think football is dying, yes,' explained Bilal Arakji, a Nejmeh board member, as his team romped to a surprisingly easy 3-0 victory.

Even without the fans, this was still a heated derby. But Ansar were swatted to one side. So easy was their victory that Emile was surrounded by the press demanding to know why the game (played between two teams owned by the same family) was conducted at such a leisurely pace when so much was at stake. Despite the insinuations of the press, for Emile and the rest of Nejmeh the conspiracy lay in Beirut's southern Shia suburbs. They believed Al Ahed and its pro-Hezbollah hierarchy wanted to steal the championship as a publicity stunt ahead of the June election. Bilal was wise to it, even if no one else was.

'Is it a conspiracy? Of course it is! Everyone knows it, it's as obvious as the sun,' Bilal told me as we drove back to Beirut, three points in the bag. 'Ahed and Hezbollah want to take the championship, by force if they have to.'

'Why by force?' I asked.

'What about Hitler and the 1936 Olympics? Why did he want to win that? Ahed won the league last season and presented Hassan Nasrallah [Hezbollah's leader] the cup. They said it was another victory [for Hezbollah].'

Last season's championship was still a sore point for Nejmeh and Ansar. All three teams went in to the last game with a chance to win the title. Whilst Nejmeh and Ansar drew against each other, Ahed scored in the last minute against a team from the south, piping both to the post. Ahed protested their innocence but Bilal wasn't convinced.

'In Arabic we have a proverb,' he laughed as the capital's city lights loomed into view. 'What a big scene to see a prostitute give lessons in etiquette.'

Bassem Marmar, Al Ahed's captain, wandered slowly around the pitch of Beirut's Municipality Stadium, deep in Sunni territory in West Beirut, an hour and a half before kickoff, counting his prayer beads and poking his boot at the shoddy turf under-foot. 'The pitch is very bad,' he lamented. 'But at least we are not playing in Tadamon Sour [a team from southern Lebanon]. There the pitch is like a farm!'

The final round of the Lebanese football season had arrived. Nejmeh's match against Safa was to be played back at the stadium in Saida. But Al Ahed were to take on Shabab al Ghazieh, a Shia team from the south. The equation appeared simple: Nejmeh led Ahed by one point. A win for Nejmeh was all that Emile needed. But all eyes were on the opposition to see whether the conspiracy theories were true. Bassem knew that that he needed other teams to do Ahed a favour. He knew, too, of the accusations made against Al Ahed: that the club, with money from Hezbollah, had been paying Shia players in other teams to motivate them against Nejmeh.

'We will play a fair game, unlike Ansar and Nejmeh last week,' he smiled, referring to the accusation that Ansar had rolled over for Nejmeh as the Hariri family funds both. 'You could see the coach [Emile Rustom] on the pitch telling his players not to score anymore than three. Everything in Lebanon is political. We are supported by Hezbollah, we are with them. Not financially. It is good for them if we win the title. It shows the outside world that they are not just terrorists.'

Hezbollah itself was cagey about the help it gives Ahed. But the club's yellow shirts are sponsored by Al Manar, Hezbollah's TV network. It was still considered a terrorist entity in the US. In fact, a month before the match, a US court sentenced one man, who had his own satellite TV business, to six years in jail for providing material support for terrorists, simply for carrying Al Manar. The players and officials milled around the pitch, including Haj Mohammed Assi whom I had met 18 months previously. He was less happy to see me now, complaining that I had written about the pictures of Nasrallah that had adorned the club's walls. But the big match was upon us and he soon retreated to the stands.

One the other side of the pitch Shabab al Ghazieh, the alleged stooges in Hezbollah's takeover of the league, warmed up. Not that the manager knew anything about it, laughing at suggestions that his team, a Shia team from the south aligned with Hezbollah's political allies Amal, would roll over.

'Here we will play,' Makram Ghaddar announced defiantly. 'We're the same religion, and we are from the south but, for us, we have to prove that we'll play. This match is on TV. We will not give Ahed the game. We will play for the shirt.'

Jihad Habhab, a sports correspondent covering the match for Hezbollah's Al Manar cable network, was more annoyed by the insinuations.

'This is not true,' he said when asked about the alleged $1,000 payments Al Ahed, and by proxy for many Sunni football fans, Hezbollah had been making. 'This [accusation] is designed to hurt Shia players in other teams. This is to humiliate Shia players, to say that they are loyal to their religion rather than their teams. I can assure you that Shia players are loyal to his shirt, and to themselves.'

The game began in front of empty stands and unfolded like typical, vital last days of the season do. A bearded man in a brown sports jacket pressed a transistor radio against his ear to relay reports from the match in Saida as the championship seesawed between the two teams. Safa were making a fist of it but it was Al Ahed who scored first, tipping the balance towards them before Nejmeh themselves scored, reclaiming the higher ground. Rumours circulated that Safa had scored, causing the stand of dignitaries to erupt in cheering and laughter. The man with the radio sat in silence, knowing the truth. 'Disallowed,' he offered with a conspiratorial hint. Then disaster. Shabab al Ghazieh scored. It took the crowd a full 20 seconds to realise their Nigerian striker Donald had just levelled the score. If there was any collusion Ghazieh hadn't been handed the script before kick off. The match reached its frenzied conclusion, both teams determined to win until, in the last minute, Ahed forced themselves a lifeline when they bundled in what turned out to be the winner. 2-1. It wasn't enough. When the final whistle was blown, the Al Ahed players stood in the centre of the pitch, awaiting the inevitable news in their kits, their morose fug only broken by the growing celebratory moped horns blaring outside the ground: proof that Nejmeh were champions. Confirmation came when my phone rang. It was Bilal.

'We won, we are champions!' he shrieked with a touching, child-like abandon. In the background a similar noise of celebration could be heard, of shouting and horns. 'Safa played like they wanted to kill us, but we won. I will let you know where the party is.'

One place the party wouldn't be was Beirut Municipality Stadium. A different gathering had been planned. The noise outside changed from the distant tweeting of innocent celebration to a bad tempered roar. Al Ahed's players and staff rushed from the pitch to see what had happened. A large group of Nejmeh fans, numbering close to a hundred, had arrived with their unmistakable red flag and gold star. But the club's flag was merely a sop for political motivations. Victory in the league wasn't important anymore, not nearly as much as victory over their political and religious foes in June's parliamentary elections. The crowd began to sing anti-Hezbollah songs before attacking Ahed's players. One young man, a boy really, pulled out a screwdriver, before trying to stab one of Ahed's management. Bassem had to be dragged away from the melee.

'I can't believe ... what they are ... singing,' he stuttered, heaving in big breaths, unable to talk because of the anger. 'What they say, about [Hassan] Nasrallah...I cannot repeat it.'

The Ahed staff were trapped, the coach parked beyond the angry mob. A delegation from the club managed to broker a ceasefire, just enough time for the Ahed's players to sprint to safety. The players scrambled on to the bus but safety was relative. The last person through the door, still wearing his full kit and boots, was Bassem. The mob tried to drag him backwards through the closing glass doors. But he escaped just as the crowd attacked again, fists raining down on the door where Bassem had just stood, cracking the glass with the first thump, shattering it with the third. Hundreds streamed out of side streets to take up their positions as they once more peppered the coach with missiles - broken bottles, pieces of car, plant pots, lumps of concrete.

The driver tried to escape the storm. He was trapped as the crowd swarmed in, battering the windows all around. There was only one exit: over the dense traffic in front. The bus jerked forward, smashing through one car, crushing another, crumpling the side of a third. It pinballed down the street like violent drunk, before disappearing on to the highway and back towards the safety of Beirut's southern suburbs. The street was littered with the smouldering, smoking remnants of violence – at least half a dozen destroyed cars and a mat of oil and broken glass. A grey haired taxi driver with a thin, grizzled face silently stood fixed to the spot by his destroyed old Mercedes, hands alternately clasping his face before pointing at his mangled livelihood in impotent disbelief. Oddly for a football match in Lebanon, and even stranger for crucial league decider involving a Shia team taking place in an avowedly Sunni district, the army was nowhere to be seen. When the machine guns did finally arrive, all that was left was to order the young men off the partially-crushed, blacked out BMW they had started smashing to pieces in the mistaken belief an Ahed official owned it.

The next day a very different story would emerge. Some newspapers and television stations reported the fighting, blaming the violence on Hezbollah or Future, depending on their political allegiance. Both sides tried to make political capital out of the incident. The reporters from Al Manar who I had stood next to at the game claimed that guns had been pulled on them and that they had been shot at by a group of Hariri supporters, a claim taken up by SKeyes, a group named in honour of the assassinated journalist Samir Kassir which campaigns against intimidation of the Lebanese press. 'Three journalists who had been with Al Ahed were attacked and the area where the attack took place is pro-Future,' explained Khaled Soubeih, a journalist himself who worked for SKeyes. 'The reporters from Al Manar said they were shot at. With the election close, tensions are very high. As long as tensions rise there will be many more of these incidents.' Soubeih admitted that eye witnesses had yet to confirm that shots had been fired. I hadn't heard any either.

Bassem, though, was convinced he had been shot at. I called him the next day to check if he was alright. After all, the last time I'd seen him he was being kicked and punched on his way back on to the bus.

'We are all ok, the driver was a hero, but the coach was shot at. This happens only in Lebanon,' he said, an anger rising in his voice that I recognised from directly after the game. 'I didn't think we were going to die, but some of the players did, they were afraid of death. The driver was not scared though because we are with Hezbollah and if anything happened to us, well, we are strong, and all of Lebanon will again be with us as it was May 7.' The May 7 he refers to was the takeover of Beirut by Hezbollah the year before.

It was a telling statement. Bassem's fallback, the place where he felt safest, was not under the protection of the police, or the army, but Hezbollah. Future TV, Bassem claimed, further inflamed matters by showing the damage that the bus had made escaping, without mentioning the rioters that had caused it to flee in the first place.

'It's a bad sign,' he said when I asked what this meant for the June parliamentary election. 'If anything else like this happens, there will not be an election, that is for sure. There will be civil war.'

The slim hope that fans would return next season had been all but extinguished and the Lebanese FA cup final, which saw Ahed take on another Shia team Shabab al Sahel, would take place outside Beirut, in Saida, under tight security. The cup was lifted by Ahed. For the third year in a row, the presentation took place in almost complete silence.

Back outside the stadium I was blissfully unaware of the gunshots as the army spread out over the road and as the final call to prayer filled the streets. The crowd of wired men, jumpily looking for somewhere to channel their adrenaline, disappeared in packs, back down the side streets they had appeared from, Nejmeh's seventh league title, just a few minutes old, was already a distant memory.

Four middle-aged men standing on a street corner had watched the whole incident unfold. 'Ahed players had come out swearing,' said one certainly, although not certain enough to tell me his name. 'They [Ahed] are in our area and started saying things against the Sunni.'

The other men nodded silently in agreement. Bassem and the rest of Beirut would hear the same story the next day. History, as ever, had already been rewritten by the victor.

9
JORDAN

March 2008

Tareq Khoury greets his guests like any politician would, with a warm smile and a firm, over friendly handshake. His office in a quiet suburb of Amman, the capital of Jordan, smelt of money. The desk was covered in rich, dark leather, as were the seats and the large bookcases that covered the walls. His shaved head, boyish face, designer suit and penchant for foreign cigarettes gave him the air of a more mature, circumspect West Coast rapper. Tareq, however, had far more in common with a much more controversial figure. As an evidently successful businessman, a recently elected MP to the Jordanian parliament and president of Wihdat Football Club, Tareq, career wise anyway, was more like a Jordanian Silvio Berlusconi. 'There will be 20,000 fans there [at the stadium], to celebrate,' he said excitedly, pulling his seat tightly behind his desk. 'They will all be for Wihdat.'

Tareq was preparing for a coronation. The last game of the Jordanian season had thrown up a potentially explosive fixture between the country's two biggest clubs: the champions Wihdat and Faisaly, the team Wihdat had replaced as the dominant force in Jordanian football. There was no love lost between either of them, a fierce rivalry that went to the heart of an unspoken enmity in Jordanian society. The roots of the schism were found on either side of the River Jordan, between the country's large Palestinian community and Jordan's self-declared 'indigenous' population, the East Bankers.

Both clubs had gone into the final few fixtures with one eye on this final match. It had been feverishly anticipated by the fans all year. Four months previously I had passed through Amman as it froze during an unseasonably cold winter. In a bar at one of the city's hotels, the barman – a Wihdat fan – showed me some of the footage he had captured on his phone of the previous meeting between the two teams that season.

174

The blurry video showed the intense celebrations as Wihdat triumphed 1–0. But this wasn't just a celebration. Faisaly's captain had been sent off. As he walked he swore at the crowd, causing pandemonium of a level considered a national security risk by the authorities. There were near riots in the stands as the police waded in to restore order. The barman nodded his head in appreciation as we watched the shaky video.

That victory had given Wihdat the advantage in the championship but week after week, Faisaly had matched their results, meaning that the title would go to the last game of the season in a winner-takes-all battle. It was going to go right to the wire. Or so I and Tareq Khoury had thought. A few days before meeting him, Wihdat played Al Buqaa in a late-afternoon kick-off. Faisaly had drawn against Shabab al Urdon, a team that was formed when the directors of Faisaly fell out and went their separate ways. It was the penultimate game of the season and it meant that if Wihdat beat Buqaa, they would go into the final game champions and the last tense, explosive match of the season everyone had been readying themselves for probably wouldn't be as tense or explosive any more, as none of the Faisaly fans would turn up. Wihdat won 1-0, and with it the championship.

The victory made things easier for Tareq. Previously he had made contingency plans for violence, the most likely outcome every time Wihdat and Faisaly played. But now, it was to be a celebration. Tareq, a Christian of Palestinian descent, got involved with the club in the late 1980s, giving money to a community scheme that fed and educated Palestinian orphans. As his business interests grew – importing anything from Ralph Lauren shirts, to food, to oil – so did his influence until at the beginning of this season he was elected president of the club.

'Wihdat club was established in Al Wihdat refugee camp, with Palestinian players but to tell you the truth, there are a lot of Faisaly fans who are Palestinian and most of their players are Palestinian,' he explained when I asked about the background of the club. 'But because of the location it has the look of a Palestinian club. All Palestinians support it as there is no good national team. People look at Wihdat as the national team of Palestine. All Palestinians in Jordan, the USA, West Bank, UAE, Saudi Arabia.'

The club was certainly a symbol of Palestinian identity, one of the few in Jordan. Yasser Arafat once even called Wihdat the national team of Palestine, long before it had one its own. But overt symbols of Palestinian identity were in a short supply, a tacit agreement that many Palestinians had with the Jordanian government – citizenship and rights that few of their kin enjoyed elsewhere in the region in return for loyalty to the King. Tareq represented a new generation, one assimilated into Jordan but proud of his Palestinian heritage.

'I am originally Palestinian, my wife is Jordanian, my mother, brother-in law are Jordanian,' he said. 'It's mixed now. Maybe 90 per cent of the Jordanian families are mixed. Now you can't tell that I'm Palestinian or Jordanian [but] I feel for Palestine. We say we are Palestinians so we can save our country so that all people can have Palestine. In Jordan it used to be in the past that there was tension between Palestinian and Jordanians. After the marriage of all families, education, people are more educated. There is no problem. Only with illiterate people and poor people. The poor people don't feel they have anything from this country and think of Palestine as if it could offer them something if they went back because here they have nothing.'

It was a far cry from 30 years ago when Jordan became the battleground for a Palestinian homeland.

'It started in the 1970s and 1980s,' Tareq said, pinpointing the time when tensions between Jordanians and Palestinians intensified, 'when people had influence over Jordan from other countries.'

That period in the early Seventies was one of the darkest chapters in recent Jordanian history. By 1970 the country had taken in two huge waves of Palestinian immigration. The first, in 1948, saw Palestinians flee from what had become Israel. The second, in 1967, comprising Palestinians from the newly occupied West Bank and East Jerusalem, helped create a critical mass. After the second wave, and with it the realisation that the Palestinians couldn't rely on Arab governments to take on Israel, also came the rise of the Palestinian Liberation Organisation (PLO), a resistance movement formed in the early 1960s but radicalised after '67 and determined to fight the Israelis and create a Palestinian state.

Unfortunately for King Hussein, the West-leaning monarch of Jordan, the PLO was acting with impunity in his country, launching cross-border raids into Israel and ignoring the authority of his armed forces. The Palestinians, who now lived in refugee camps in squalid conditions across the country, were no-go areas for his troops. Instead, camps like Wihdat had their own security, levying their own taxes and meting out their own form of local justice. The PLO had effectively created its own state-within-a-state.

King Hussein struggled to reassert the state's authority, as any action might antagonise what had become a huge proportion of his subjects. But on 12 September 1970, King Hussein had to act. The Popular Front for the Liberation of Palestine, a Marxist resistance force, had kidnapped four planes en route to New York. They were flown to Jordan, to the north-eastern city of Zarqa, emptied of hostages and symbolically blown up in front of the world's cameras. The provocation sparked Black September, an assault by the Jordanian army to rid the country of the PLO, which was now firmly under the control of Yasser Arafat, once and for all.

By October King Hussein had been successful in reasserting his will, but not without its human costs. Thousands, perhaps even tens of thousands, of troops and innocent civilians had been killed in running battles in Amman, Zarqa and Irbid. The PLO eventually fled north, to Lebanon, where their presence had an even more destabilising effect in a country already struggling to deal with an explosive political, religious and ethnic mix. Behind them, though, King Hussein had to deal with a deeply divided population – the Hashemite Jordanians angry at the incursion of foreigners on their land, the Palestinians feeling like second-class citizens and burning with the injustice of Black September's heavy-handed assault on Jordan's Palestinian camps.

The enmity was rarely allowed to be discussed in public. But on the terraces two football teams represented the hopes and fears of each side: Wihdat the downtrodden Palestinians, Faisaly the embattled Jordanians. The Palestinians, who now make up anywhere between 50 and 80 per cent of the population, claim they face discrimination and are barred from positions in the army and the police, dominated by the 'true' Hashemite Jordanians. The Jordanians claim that their country is being overrun by people who have no loyalty to it. When Wihdat and Faisaly met, it was explosive, a blood-letting exercise that let the low-level prejudices that blighted everyday life go on simmering without fermenting into civil strife. Football provided much-needed, twice-yearly catharsis.

'For Wihdat, 99 per cent of the fans are Palestinian. You won't find any Jordanian fans of Wihdat,' Tareq admitted. 'They [Jordanian Faisaly fans] feel that the Palestinians came to their country and control all the business and are well educated. Some illiterate people think this way. They should be proud that Palestinians are living here and have all their rights like the Jordanians. It's a plus to the country.'

The rivalry usually led to anti-Palestinian chants and then riots after each game, so much so that Palestinian players felt uncomfortable turning out for Faisaly.

'My brother used to play for Faisaly but after he heard what the club and the fans said about the Palestinians, some cursing in the games, he is now with Wihdat,' he said. 'It's the same with Rangers and Celtic or Barcelona and Madrid. Here it is between two countries, Palestinians and Jordanians. Because it is between two nationalities it is becoming a big problem. Me, as the president and MP, I don't feel it is between people who are educated, or think right about the country.'

The match also represented something far deeper, beyond the confines of Jordan's small borders. From Lebanon to the UAE, Palestine's diaspora had long been treated like second-class citizens. In Lebanon's Palestinian camps, it was illegal for refugees to work in most professions, to leave the country or get further education. In Egypt, employment restrictions were levied; in the UAE and Saudi, Palestinians could never become citizens. Their reticence was couched in the rhetoric of resistance: normalising each country's Palestinian population would destroy the *raison d'être* for future generations to fight Israel for their return. If the next generations felt, say, Lebanese rather than Palestinian, why would they fight for their homeland? Keeping the Palestinians in a perpetual state of flux was a necessary policy decision that kept them hungry for home. There was domestic political expediency at play too. If the largely Sunni Palestinians were given citizenship in Lebanon, it would have huge ramifications on the already politically explosive issue of which sectarian group had the largest population. In the UAE, granting citizenship for the Palestinians would open the royal families up to awkward questions about the other 85 per cent of the country that were foreign-born residents. Yet in Jordan, those inequalities didn't exist, at least not officially, as long as the Palestinians accepted, inviolably, a Jordanian passport.

The fact, Tareq said, that a Palestinian Christian could be elected to parliament in the first place – making him one of 15 Palestinians in the 110-strong legislature – was proof that differences were slowly being married out over generations.

'Palestinians have full rights and we are happy,' he said. 'I care about Jordan exactly like I care about Palestine, I have the same feeling towards both countries.' Of course, being elected as President of the country's most popular team wouldn't exactly have been a hindrance to his elevation as an elected member of parliament. 'There are two million [supporters] just in Jordan,' he claimed, quite a boast for a country that has an official population of six million. 'It is the highest number of fans compared to population. We have millions around the world too, 10 to 15 million. When we played in Saudi against Al Nasr club, we had 10,000 fans there [who lived] in Saudi Arabia. More than the local team. In Egypt the same thing happened.' Tareq insisted that buying political popularity through Wihdat couldn't have been further from his mind, but when a third of the electorate sing your name every weekend it can't be bad for it either. 'I'll tell you the truth. What made me go to Wihdat is that if you accomplish anything in Wihdat club you make millions of people happy,' he said just as a board member from the club knocked on the door and let himself in. Tareq handed him an envelope with a cheque for $25,000 in it. A gift, Tareq said, to the players who had brought him the league in his first season. 'I love that. I love to make people happy. It has cost me a lot out of my own pocket. I love it. When I see people are happy and people call me from Korea, the States, Palestine, they are so happy we won the league. I can make millions happy.' Tareq got up to leave and made his excuses. He had important parliamentary business to attend to. He had to just put me straight on one last thing. 'You know Wihdat isn't a refugee camp any more, it's part of the city.' He urged I should go there before heading for the game.

'You will be there?' I asked.

'Of course!' he replied incredulously.

'What will the score be?'

He laughed as we left though the front gate and shook hands goodbye.

'You know, now, I really don't care.'

I'd grown to love Amman after passing through it so many times. If Lebanon was the place aggrieved parties went to fight, Jordan was the place aggrieved parties went to party. Or relax. Or spy. Anything but open conflict. They were all here. Israelis pretending they were American, Americans pretending they were Israelis, Jordanians pretending they were Palestinian, Iraqis pretending to be Jordanian. It was a place of calm, if not peace; a place of refugees, tourists and those with enough money to buy a little temporary respite from the privations of Jenin or Riyadh or Baghdad – be they recreational or medicinal. It had the feel of a benign Casablanca. The landscape, too, was something addictive. Amman is often unfairly characterised as an ugly city, yet there was something beautiful about the shabby, identikit flat-topped buildings that stuck out of Amman's 19 hills, and the deep valley that cuts through it, like a mouth of badly kept teeth. On street corners and atop hills, evidence of Amman's Roman past presented itself when you least expected it – a Roman amphitheatre wedged between modern buildings in downtown Amman; dissolving columns that once held the roof of a grand Roman palace left orphaned next to a set of traffic lights.

Yet Tareq was right about the encampments that had arrived six decades previously, put down roots and then grown into permanence. On the morning of the match the sun shone as it did on most days in Amman. The taxi cut through the quiet roads, emptied of traffic for obligatory Friday prayers. From the top of the hill Wihdat, or the Amman New Camp as it is known, sprawled in front of us. It was still, like the rest of the Middle East was at midday on a Friday. But today was different. As we drove into the camp the still-deserted streets gave signs of what was to come. Everything was green and red. Green-and-red ribbons hung from shop fronts. Green-and-red balloons were tied to signposts. Shop displays had been artfully arranged with products bearing just two colours. Green and red, Wihdat FC's colours. No sooner had I noticed the colours than the taxi screeched to a halt. This was as far as he would go. In front of us the road was full of thousands of men blowing horns and boys waving posters adorned with their favourite players above their heads. Bunting of red and green crossed the street along with the bare electricity cables. Pickup trucks sat stationary in the sea of people, each draped in Wihdat flags whilst the fans in the back improvised with their own costumes. One had made his own league cup out of foil, another wore a green sweatband with Wihdat written on it in Arabic. It was a scene of unbridled joy but somewhere in the centre of the chaos was the office for Wihdat football club, and I had to find it.

Tareq had told me to be here by 1pm so that I could meet the team and travel up on the team bus. A small boy wearing a Wihdat shirt took my hand and led me through the maze of stalls and shops and celebrating fans. We came to a long street. What looked like the team bus had been swamped by fans all waiting for a glimpse of their heroes before they left for the match against the old enemy.

'Come back here at seven or eight tonight and then you'll see a celebration,' Mohammad, a bald, dark-skinned 45 year old smoking a cigarette told me as we both surveyed the scene. 'This is all they have in Wihdat,' he shrugged. 'They are poor people, poor Palestinians. For them it is always misery, but Wihdat winning can make them happy.'

A gang of small children ran past begging for a photo. 'America! America! America!' they shouted back positively.

'Britani sahafi,' I corrected them.

They stopped.'Britani! Britani! Britani!'

In the past the Wihdat camp was notorious for its backing for Palestinian radicalism. But not today.

This was no refugee camp in the classical sense. This was a town with the population of Middlesbrough. The concrete buildings had lost their new built lustre some time back in the early 1980s but they were stout. The roads were paved, the mosques stood up like medieval castles, white and impenetrable, all-seeing watch-towers impervious to the sun, the wind and the rain. Where Wihdat ended and the rest of Amman began was now impossible to make out. It was progress, sure, but the camp's permanence was also a depressing reminder of just how intractable the Palestinian problem was. I managed to push through the crowd and into the club's front door. Just as I got through the doors a man thrust a wad of coloured paper into my hand: posters of last season's victorious title-winning side.

In the team manager's office, Wihdat's players had taken shelter from the crowds outside, sitting silently on the sofas that had lined the walls. They waited for the signal, so they could start their journey and plough through the maelstrom to the stadium. On the wall hung a long map of Palestine. In this alternative reality of geographical history Palestine stretched from the Red Sea all the way to Syria. There was no room for Israel.

On the windows an incongruous collection of posters were displayed. Ronaldo in a Brazil shirt; Queen Rania and King Abdullah smiling; Ronaldinho holding an award in his Barcelona shirt; a baby wearing the black-and-white keffiyeh of Palestinian resistance; Raul mid-celebration for Real Madrid; the Star of David superimposed on the Stars and Stripes, burning.

The call came from the bus. The players, all wearing their shirts, got up and silently walked through the dark corridor outside into the harsh sunlight and the deafening roar of the crowd. Car horns blared as their drivers finally got a glimpse of the cargo that would be leading their convoy to the stadium. The rickety team bus crawled through Wihdat as children jogged alongside, giving the two-fingered victory salute and shouting 'Filastine!' It was to be a longer journey than normal. The match had been moved from Amman to Zarqa, 35 miles northeast. Zarqa was famous for two things. It was here that the Popular Front for the Liberation of Palestine had blown up its hijacked planes in 1970, sparking Black September. It was also the birthplace of Abu Musab al Zarqawi, arguably the most notorious Jordanian citizen in recent times. The Islamist militant founded Al Qaeda in Iraq and was responsible for numerous beheadings, kidnappings and suicide bombings, including the last time suicide bombers targeted Amman when three of the city's hotels were attacked, killing sixty people. Our bus careered through the valleys of lower Amman as the bus load of players cheered and sang:

'Allah! Wihdat! Al Quds Arabi!'

God! Wihdat! Jerusalem [for the] Arabs!

The driver, an old man with sunken dark cheeks and a concave chest whom one suspected had been driving the bus since the team's inception in 1956, kept his elbow on the horn, emitting a permanent high-pitch screech whilst singing along, adding his own 'Yallah, Wihdat!' every few breaths.

'The championship gives something to the people of Wihdat,' explained Faisal Ibrahim, Wihdat's captain. He sat at the front of the bus with his young daughter on his lap, watching the trees pass by. 'It is very important for the Palestinians. We are one people, the Jordanians and the Palestinians, but we hope one day Palestine will be for the Palestinian people.'

Faisal summed up the difficulty that his generation of Palestinian-descended Jordanians felt. The two identities were being successfully assimilated, which was leading to a more stable Jordan, but was at the same time reducing the number of Palestinians who would seek the right to return to Israel. He felt kinship with the land of his father, his grandfather even. He captained a team heavily identified with the Palestinian diaspora. His shirt was the colour of the Palestinian flag, and his club's badge, worn proudly above his left breast, showed the Dome of the Rock. Yet he had a Jordanian identity too. His children would be even further removed from their Palestinian heritage. He was also part of something that was inescapably Jordanian: he was a first-choice defender for the Jordanian national football team.

'I would like to play for the Palestinian team, the national team,' he added cautiously. 'But I can't because I have a Jordanian passport.'

'You need the Palestinian ID,' the team's doctor, Mamoun Harb, shouted through the puff of his strong cigarette. 'You can't have two passports here.'

The bus slowed down suddenly. The police had pulled us over and wanted to see what the fuss was all about.

'They hate us for being Palestinian,' spat the doctor. 'Maybe they like Faisaly.'

He had a point. As the team of the King, Faisaly were well supported by the police and military. We waited patiently as the team's manager remonstrated with the stony-faced officer. Eventually, he waved us on our way. Somehow, you knew that Faisaly's coach wouldn't meet the same fate. We arrived at the stadium and already 10,000 Wihdat fans were inside. The stadium's tiny doors were inundated by a crush of fans wearing white, green and red, each man pressed up against the next one's back in the harsh, early-afternoon sun. They began singing as soon as they saw their team arrive, going quiet as intimidatingly dressed riot police sauntered down the line. Only one set of fans would be in attendance, but the full force of the police had been drafted in just in case. They wore all black; huge pieces of Kevlar body armour surrounded their chests and backs whilst bulky arm guards and leg protectors made each police-man appear twice the breadth and twice the height of normal men. On their heads they wore black helmets over black balaclavas, to keep their anonymity. Their gloved hands carried black nightsticks. A judicious thwack kept any stragglers in line. By their appearance they had arrived expecting not just a riot, but war. Yet there was no one for the Wihdat fans to fight. The Faisaly team bus arrived without fanfare, a gleaming, modern luxury coach with AC and blacked-out windows. It parked next to Wihdat's tiny Mitsubishi minibus, dwarfing it with its opulence. Only a handful of fans cheered the team's disembarkation. This match wasn't for Faisaly. They knew it was a victory parade for Wihdat and only a few dozen of the die-hard fans bothered to turn up. By the sullen faces of the Faisaly players, they didn't want to be here either.

Inside the stadium, one half was already full with fans jumping up and down and singing, shaking black-and-white headscarves. I asked one of Wihdat's entourage what they were singing.

'They are singing, *'Allahu akhbar! Al dowry ahdar!'*' answered Ahmad, who ran Wihdat's website. 'It means, 'God is great, the league is green.'' Oddly there wasn't a single Palestinian flag in sight. 'That's because the police won't let them bring them inside [the ground],' Ahmad explained.

Wihdat's faithful sang it over and over again: 'Allahu Akhbar! Al dowry ahdar!' The tiny, embattled minority of Faisaly fans looked on sullenly. Usually they would be in fine voice too, pledging allegiance to the king or singing: 'One, two, divorce her [Queen Rania] Abu Hussein [the King].' Queen Rania, whom King Abdullah – the son of King Hussein – married in 1993, is of Palestinian descent. But this time they kept their silence, only showing any anger when Wihdat's players unfurled a banner heralding their title-winning exploits in front of their small section of fans. Two police officers ran onto the pitch, ripped it out of their hands and escorted them back to the dressing-room. The dressing-room was surprisingly tense as the manager went through his last instructions. Most listened raptly whilst the goalkeeper chose instead to pray next to the tactics board. It being Friday, the fans prayed in the stands too. Officials leant on their knees on the side of the pitch, in the shade, pointing towards Mecca. The players emerged to a one-sided roar. There was no guard of honour for Wihdat; Faisaly were just going through the motions. Minutes before kick-off another roar went up. Tareq Khoury arrived to take his seat at the top of the VIP section. The fans chanted his name ecstatically. He gave a regal wave back, acknowledging his popularity.

The game, predictably, was absolutely dire. With neither team having anything left to play for, it degenerated into an attritional dirge. The fans couldn't have cared less. They weren't here to watch football. Not really. They were here to see their players lift the championship trophy. The sky got dark and the minarets sang again as the game limped to its sorry conclusion. Only a missed penalty by Faisaly gave Wihdat anything to cheer on the pitch. Apart from the final whistle. The staff, substitutes and players' families rushed onto the pitch to celebrate. A makeshift stage was constructed and the players invited to accept their medals. Tareq was there in the centre. It was he who lifted the trophy first. The crowd screamed as he sucked in a few more precious votes.

Looking round I realised that the police were hurriedly ushering the Faisaly fans out of the ground. At first it appeared to be a well worn policing strategy. But then it turned more sinister. As Wihdat's die-hard fans sang the name of each player as he bowed in front of the main stand, I decided to sneak out. It was a long way back and I had no idea how I was going home. But, on the steps of the entrance, the riot police had gone berserk. A wave of well-dressed journalists and dignitaries fell back through the glass double doors. The men immediately scrambled past up the stairs to get away from the beatings. Outside, the men in black battered anyone who came near them. It wasn't immediately clear what the trouble was. After squeezing through the doors into the storm, I could see the prone bodies of green and red as the police went about trying to restore calm, screaming indiscriminately and waving their nightsticks at anyone in the crowd who looked at them. Within seconds, the crowd quietened, bruised and tired. A small boy stamped on a green balloon that had no doubt been proudly tied to the windscreen wiper of a Wihdat fan's car. It was all the provocation they needed, and they returned to beating fans indiscriminately as they passed.

'You can't be here,' said one of the policemen, before marching me to a 'safe spot' where I was ordered not to move.

Nearby a Wihdat fan protecting his wife and young son stood next to their car watching the chaos unfold. 'They do this because we are Palestinian,' the man told me, declining to tell me his name. 'All of the police, all of the army, they are with Faisaly.'

I made a break for the front gates, past the unconscious figure of a topless teenage Wihdat fan, his friends splashing water in his face to rouse him whilst a policeman prodded the group with his truncheon, intimating that he'd prefer if they undertook their makeshift first aid elsewhere. Behind me the man and his family were being screamed at by another policeman for taking pictures.

Dusk had quickly given way to night. As 20,000 people streamed away from the violence and the beatings, there seemed little hope of finding a route home. Stuck and desperate I spotted a man wearing a Pixies T-shirt. Assuming that a fan of Boston's finest would speak English, I asked him where I could get a taxi. He glared suspiciously.

'Are you with Wihdat or Faisaly?' he asked, his crew of fellow Wihdat fans crowding around to listen for an answer.

I pulled out the poster I'd been given whilst boarding the bus earlier that afternoon, of Wihdat's title-winning squad from last year, and held it aloft.

'Wihdat,' I replied.

The crowd were satisfied.

'You can come with us!' he shouted, taking me by the arm.

Salah and his crew of Palestinian 'gangsters', as they referred to themselves, wriggled through the crowd, though a broken fence and over waste land before emerging onto the main road grid locked with Wihdat fans. Car horns and police sirens blared in the foreground. Salah's Nissan was parked in a ditch on the side of the road. We squeezed in, four of us on the back seat. The road ahead was full and stationary, but we were safe. Salah settled into the front seat and lit a joint, inhaling deeply and blowing the thick white smoke into the cabin, before passing it on, turning on the radio. Palestinian pop music crackled through the Nissan's speakers. We shunted along the celebratory motorcade, with the distorted tabla rattling through the speakers like a machine gun and the horns of victory blaring around us. Green and red hung from every vehicle, except the car in front which had a poster of King Abdullah in the back window, a sure sign that the driver was a Faisaly fan.

'He's a son of a bitch!' Salah screamed, bouncing forward and chopping his arm towards the king.

'What about Queen Rania, she's Palestinian, right?' I asked.

Salah breathed in a lung's worth of thick smoke, leant his head back and blew it slowly out into the fabric of the roof.

'She,' he started, coughing through blurry, watery eyes, 'she is the biggest son of a bitch of them all.'

No one spoke for a few seconds, the nodding heads in the car giving their seal of approval. Wihdat football club was finished for them for another season. It was back to their jobs and their normal lives. For a few short, hot months football would be a distant memory. But soon enough August would be back and Fridays would envelop them once more.

The hostilities would soon resume. In 2010 *Al Jazeera* reported 250 Wihdat fans were injured when a metal fence collapsed after riot police had tried used the same crowd control methods I'd witnessed after a game with Faisaly. *Al Jazeera* also reported that two fans were beaten to death by the police, although the police denied the allegations.

More illuminating, however, was the release of a U.S. diplomatic cable by Wikileaks. The classified cable entitled 'Jordanian Soccer Game Halted Amidst Anti-Regime Chants, Hooliganism Towards Palestinians', sent on 28 July 2009, details an incident a few weeks previous where a match between Faisaly and Wihdat had been called off because of chants against the king, his wife and the Palestinians in general. According to the cable:

> *The game exposed the growing rift between East Bankers and Palestinians in Jordan. The King's silence on the event is noteworthy, as is a reluctance among our contacts to discuss the issue.*

The cable, which even noted the score twice (0-0, postponed because of the riot) noticed how the match had laid bare an often unpalatable friction at the heart of Jordanian society:

> *Faisali and Wahdat serve as the proxy champions of the East Banker and Palestinian communities, respectively.*

That U.S. Intelligence believed a football match was a worthy subject to help document the political and social undercurrents of a country is interesting enough. But equally as interesting are the names mentioned. Only one person's name appears in the cable who was not a member of the royal family.

> *The club's current president is Tareq Khoury, a successful businessman who allegedly bought his seat on the Wahdat board. He has since leveraged that position into a political career, and was elected to the Lower House of Parliament in 2007.*

But in that moment Tareq, and the legion of Wihdat fans travelling back to Amman, could savour another league title, their third in four seasons.

'Come on,' Salah shouted, breaking the silence. 'Sing!'

There was only one song left to sing. The six of us replied in unison, through the smoke and over the drums, as the car sped down the dark, unlit highway towards Amman.

'Allahu Akhbar! Al dawry ahdar!'

'Allahu Akhbar! Al dawry ahdar!'

God is great.

The league is green.

10
UAE

September 2008

It was apt that the biggest erection in the building belonged to Dr Sulaiman Al Fahim. The Cityscape property exhibition was the largest real estate show in Dubai, which pretty much made it the largest real estate show in the world. Heavily made up, perma-smiling models milled about the sea of identikit pods, towering in their heels over the short, alpha male money men who had come for a slice of a modern day gold rush.

Dubai – one of the seven emirates in the United Arab Emirates – was deep in a decade long property boom fuelled by what appeared to be unlimited funds and ambition. No project was too big to consider. The exhibition was proof enough of that. Already a collection of new islands built in the shape of the continents of the world was well under way. Another, shaped like the fronds of a palm tree, was almost done. The men in suits talked of a global shortage of high rise cranes thanks to the sheer number of developments under way. There were more cranes in Dubai, they said, than anywhere in the world. A sea of flat screen TVs showed the next generation of futuristic tower blocks and malls that would soon join them. And, in the middle, jutting up like an East German observation tower was the stand for Hydra Properties, owned by the new face of twenty-first century English football.

Sulaiman al Fahim had recently, and briefly, become one of the most famous faces in world football. A month before he was the face of a takeover that would change the nature of football in England, and possibly the world. It would change the way that UEFA and FIFA governed the game. It would change Manchester too. City had been in the third tier of English football a few seasons before. Now they were the richest club in the world, owned by Sheikh Mansour of the Abu Dhabi royal family. They could outspend and out gun anyone thanks to fabulous, despotic oil wealth. And it was

Sulaiman al Fahim who brokered the deal. When City's shell shocked fans arrived at Eastlands for their first home game as a newly knighted, genuine footballing super power, many wore tea towels on their head aping the Gulf's traditional male head dress. Some waved wads of freshly minted 20 pound notes, the Queen's face replaced by Al Fahim's, the number 20 replaced by 500 billion. In those crazy, whirlwind few days, Al Fahim was the embodiment of football's new world order; brash, arrogant, unstoppable.

'I always feel like I'm a kind of bulldozer, a fully insured bulldozer,' he said shortly after the deal that saw the club change hands from former Thai Prime Minister Thaksin Shinawatra to Sheikh Mansour. 'If nobody likes it, it starts moving – even if there are cars in its way, it has to crush the cars and move. I can't stop. If I have an idea, I have to do it.' Grand pronouncements were made about future transfers. For a few days it was as if he was the owner. And then, he was gone, pulled away before he could do any more PR damage. After all, the ruling royal family of Abu Dhabi is one of the most opaque and secretive in the world, in charge of one of the least democratic nations on the planet. Bragging should be seen, and not heard.

'I like the British media when they exaggerate and add words,' laughed Al Fahim after arriving on to his stand with his entourage, wearing a blue *kandoorah*, white head-scarf and flashing a unanimous smile. One of his sycophantic underlings announced just how much money Al Fahim had made so far that year. Another handed me the first instalment of his autobiography which, even by the standards of modern football's pornographic obsession with player's autobiographies, seemed a little premature. 'This just covers the years when I set up my company.' One suited woman cradled the tome as if was an album containing the only photos from her childhood. Dr al Fahim is in his early thirties. He sat down to talk about his time at the centre of a global whirlwind.

'I was the one who did the deal, I was the one who closed the deal,' he explained when I asked what his involvement was in the sale. 'I find myself as chairman, as owner, even our official press release said I was the owner. It was nice, I like it. I like it when they put my picture in the news!'

That was certainly true. Al Fahim had a gift for self promotion. By the time he was 30 he was driving around in a Lamborghini, having made his first billion dollars heading up the fastest growing real estate company in the UAE. He counted Hollywood actors amongst his friends. Piers Morgan would later glowingly profile him for a TV programme about Dubai, choosing him as the walking, physical embodiment of its upstart swagger. He also fronted the Middle East's version of the Apprentice.

The Hydra Executives, as the show was called, had to be seen to be believed. Imagine The Apprentice but set in the desert, staffed almost entirely by imbeciles but with the added frisson of geopolitical competition. The first series saw eight Americans take on eight Brits for the chance to win $1m and a share in a business venture. The second series was planned to have a team from Pakistan fight it out against eight contestants from India. Crying, screaming and idiocy followed. His catch line – 'impress me' – was delivered in the style of a camp Bond villain. He didn't even bother sacking anyone: he handed the winning team a 'pink slip' and got them to do it, Lord of the Flies style. Like a proper Bond villain would.

'TV is the best way to market your company so I tried to see if there was anything we could use for reality TV. When you see Trump, you see Piers Morgan, I see everyone is doing something to promote the company and the country,' he said. 'For me this is the best way to promote Hydra and Abu Dhabi. To give a good image to the people. When we started using American and British [contestants], we showed them this was a land of opportunity. Many Americans only know Dubai, this was an opportunity to show people the difference. It's not about Dubai ... it's about the UAE.'

Al Fahim had encapsulated the *raison d'etre* of the Manchester City deal. Promotion. Football – at least European football anyway – was passionately followed here, true, but it was the English Premier League's ability to convey a message into the homes and offices of billions across the world that really appealed to the Abu Dhabi royal family. It was advertising on a previously unimaginable scale.

'It's a very good opportunity for Abu Dhabi to be in the Premier League. Everyone here loves the Premier League.' Al Fahim admitted. 'Man City is one of those clubs that has real big fans in the UK. It's not just about buying the best club, most profitable club, football is passion but you have to buy a club people will really love. And then you need to make a plan to get it into the top five.'

Of course, Al Fahim's ubiquity was also part of the problem. The Abu Dhabi United Group grew annoyed at Al Fahim's increasingly bellicose announcements and, allegedly, pulled him from the deal once it had been done. Now Khaldoon Mubarak, another young Arab businessman who wore bookish glasses, rarely spoke to the press and who could pass as an accountant, steered the Man City ship. It was felt a steadier pair of hands were needed, although Al Fahim denied he was moved on, insisting that he was only ever there 'to bring this opportunity and to bring it in time, in less than three weeks.'

'In UAE I am a supporter of Al Ain club, but in the UK I am Manchester City,' he said proudly. 'Honestly, after the buy-out of the club almost half the UAE nationals watch the match and follow the team. They are all watching as if it is like a UAE team in the Premier League.' He also wanted to see one player in particular come to Eastlands. 'I am a fan of Ronaldo, he is handsome,' Al Fahim said, bursting into infectious, almost childlike laughter. 'But I don't like to interfere. Mubarak, he knows the player. It depends on the management. They are focusing on the 10-year plan. They are looking for good, talented British players. I hope, what's his name, Mark Hughes and Gerry Cook [sic.] and Khaldoon Mubarak pick good players.'

With the interview finished, Al Fahim got up to shake my hand. He had things to do. Piers Morgan was coming to town and wanted to ride horses on his farm. And he was looking after a very special Hollywood power couple, in town to help him with a new real estate venture that would bear their names. 'I have to go and pick up Antonio Bandaras at 2pm,' said Al Fahim, 'In my Lamborghini.'

It was true that Al Fahim embodied one side of the UAE. For three years I'd lived here, amongst its contradictions; its wealth and hypocrisy; its opportunities and its venality; its prostitution and its religiosity. It was true that 180 different nationalities lived here, making up the vast majority of the country's population. Barely ten per cent were UAE nationals. As much as this was a country where those with cut throat ambition could get ahead quickly, it was also a country where most people could never break free of their circumstances. The vast majority of the population were construction workers from Asia; India, Pakistan and Bangladesh, corralled in work camps and treated little better than animals. I had visited one on the outskirts of Dubai, near the iconic Burj al Arab hotel. Men from India sobbed in front of me as they told how they were trapped here, earning 50 dollars a month, working in 50 degree heat. Human sewage ran through the camp. Suicide was a credible option of last resort. Some threw themselves in front of oncoming traffic on the glass skyscraper-lined Sheikh Zayed Road, not because its eight lanes offered the most certain of deaths. But because the UAE's legal system insisted blood money be paid by the driver to the family of the dead. A very obvious cost-benefit analysis had been made. They were worth more to their families back home dead than alive.

But most stayed for decades to pay back the loans they had taken out to get here in the hope of a better life. As Piers Morgan rode horses with Sulaiman al Fahim, indentured servitude was in rude health a few miles away. Open the door to virtually any bar and club in a five star hotel on any night and you would see the faces of young women trafficked from Eastern Europe and Central Asia for prostitution; wearing looks both hopeful and disgusted at the same time.

There was little freedom of speech and there was virtually no democracy. The UAE had only existed since 1971 when seven emirates that had made up the Trucial

States – a protectorate of the British Empire – won independence: Abu Dhabi, the capital, Dubai, Sharjah, Fujairah, Ajman, Umm al Qwain and Ras Al Khaimah. But it was Abu Dhabi and Dubai who shared the power and hogged the limelight. Dubai in particular, under the leadership of Sheikh Mohammed bin Rashid al Maktoum, had seared itself onto the world's consciousness with a string of high-profile sporting events and increasingly ridiculous building projects. While Dubai got all the press, Abu Dhabi was quietly building one of the world's largest sovereign investment funds from the huge oil revenues it enjoyed (ten per cent of the world's oil in 2008 sat under the UAE, almost all of it in Abu Dhabi).

Yet Dubai was so good at marketing itself abroad – Dubai's airline Emirates sponsored Chelsea, PSG, co-sponsored the World Cup and gave Arsenal $200 million for naming rights over their new stadium – that most foreigners assumed it, and not Abu Dhabi, was the UAE's capital. Dubai had even gone a step further by dipping its toe into ownership of a foreign football club. Sheikh Mohammed's sovereign investment fund, DIC, had been aggressively pursuing Liverpool FC and had got close to securing a deal before the board plumped for an offer tabled by American businessmen Tom Hicks and George Gillett. There was even talk of Dubai having an improbable crack at bidding for the 2018 World Cup, even though it would be held in Dubai in the middle of summer, at a time when the outside air temperature regularly nudged 50 degrees Celsius. They were nothing if not ambitious.

Dubai and Abu Dhabi had a history of low-level antagonism, a state of affairs exacerbated by Dubai's current turn in the limelight. But with the UAE's media forbidden from discussing anything controversial about the intrigues of the UAE's royal families one of the few times this enmity was exhibited was when teams from the two emirates played each other in the local league. The first I knew of this was, when watching the local news on television in Dubai, I saw the unedifying sight of two stands full of men wearing the traditional *dish dasha* fighting during a league match.

'It's a changing relationship,' explained Professor Christopher Davidson, a Gulf expert whose book *Dubai: The Vulnerability of Success* was banned in the UAE. The ban was only overturned when the government was embarrassed into a U-turn after it came to light in the international press. 'Look at foreign policy. During the Iran-Iraq war Dubai backed Iran because of trade links, Abu Dhabi backed Iraq. We have the same issue in 2008, Condoleezza Rice putting pressure to severe money links into Iran. But Dubai's trade with Iran is $14billion, compared with $2billion with the US.' Both Dubai and Abu Dhabi, Davidson added, were building their own distinct brands through sport and especially football. Sport had been used in recent years as a marketing tool by many of the Gulf states as a way of sticking their flag in the sand

and announcing that they have arrived on the global stage. But football had another use. 'Football receives massive backing from the state as it's a replacement for tribalism as they want to limit powers of tribes and eliminate cronyism,' Davidson explained. 'Football is one very secular and easy way of engendering tribalism, it replaces one identity with another. The sheikhs are very visible in the stand, it brings the leaders into contact with your population in a benevolent way. It is an outlet for grievances that has nothing to do with the government. You can shout and scream and forget you can't even shout and scream on the street.'

Yet for all the money and all the glitzy, eye-catching projects, the local league was in a relatively poor state with low wages and an antiquated transfer structure that meant it was the clubs, and the powerful ruling families that held the power. No UAE player had ever played in Europe, although there wasn't any shortage of talent. The country's best player was Ismail Matar, a diminutive, pacey striker who burst onto the world stage at the FIFA World Youth Championships, which was held in the UAE in 2003. Matar won the Golden Boot, only the second Asian player to win the award at an official FIFA tournament. Previous winners tended to have a big impact on the world stage – Diego Maradona, Robert Prosinecki and, most recently, Lionel Messi had all had the honour bestowed on them. The interest of big European clubs was pricked. Inter Milan had been mooted as a possible destination. Yet, oddly, Matar chose to stay in the closeted confines of the UAE first division with Abu Dhabi's Al Wahda rather than seek fame and fortune abroad.

Why? The answer may be found in the bizarre case of his international strike partner Faisal Khalil. Faisal had attracted the attentions of second division French club Chateauroux, who he signed for from Dubai's Al Ahli in early 2006. The saga played out in the UAE press.

'I am very happy with this first step towards a professional career with Chateauroux and I hope it will be successful,' Faisal happily told Dubai television once he'd made it to France. 'I know Chateauroux are a second division side. But I hope I can contribute with my team-mates to win promotion to the first division. I will do my best.'

Chateauroux's manager, Didier Olle Nicolle, was equally happy with the signing. 'I had visited the UAE and watched Faisal play against Al Wahda in the league and also with the UAE national team against Brazil,' he told the *Gulf News*, even though the friendly match between the UAE and Brazil had resulted in a humiliating 8–0 thumping. 'He is a talented player and we are sure he will succeed with us.'

Everyone was happy. Everyone, that was, except his old club Al Ahli who were livid they had lost a key player midway through the season. Instead of getting mad, they got even.

The UAE FA mysteriously refused to issue the proper documentation to allow him to play in France. Even though Ahli were playing hard-ball, Faisal was still confident of fulfilling his dream. 'I think two weeks is a good time to get all these formalities out of the way and I should be in a position to play for Chateauroux after I get back to France in the first week of March,' he said. Al Ahli was demanding an apology from the striker and his immediate return. But higher powers had got involved, Dubai's crown prince no less. Twenty-five year-old Sheikh Hamdan bin Mohammed al Maktoum also happened to be Al Ahli's chairman and intervened to solve the crisis. Whatever he said did the trick. Within days of the royal family's intervention Faisal was back to the UAE and ready to turn out for Ahli. Again.

'It's sad that players are so gullible and they have fallen prey to the empty promises,' Jassem al Sayed, who represented Faisal, told *Gulf News* when his player had returned home. 'Faisal Khalil was lucky as his club has stood by him.'

The one area where foreign influence was tolerated was when recruiting the manager. The impressively toned figure of Bruno Metsu, who had memorably taken Senegal to the 2002 World Cup quarter-finals after beating world champions France in the first game, was now prowling the touchline for the UAE. But he hadn't initially been the first choice. With much fanfare Dick Advocaat had been unveiled as the man to take the UAE on to great heights, and maybe even World Cup qualification in 2010. At the time I was working for *Time Out Dubai* and had planned to interview Dick until a better opportunity came about. Gordon Ramsay, who had opened a restaurant in the emirate, was guest editing the magazine for a day. Gordon and Dick had some form: Gordon had claimed to be a youth team player for Glasgow Rangers who made a handful of first team appearances before injury caused him to retire and seek alternative employment in the catering industry (it later emerged that Ramsay had at best played a testimonial as a trialist); Dick had successfully managed Glasgow Rangers, famously winning the treble in his first season. Both still held a deep affection for the club, so they jumped at the chance to meet at Ramsay's smart restaurant and talk Scottish football.

Dick was pretty happy to see us. He had been living out of a hotel since his arrival a month previously and didn't have much to do as the UAE hadn't qualified for the 2006 World Cup. His next competitive tournament was the 2007 Gulf Cup 18 months or so away, a biennial tournament that was to be held in Abu Dhabi and which Saudi Arabia and Iraq had dominated. The UAE had never won it and Advocaat was brought in on big money to change that embarrassing fact. Every time the Old Firm was mentioned, he lit up, reeling off anecdotes about how he once throttled Fernando Ricksen and called him a 'fucking fucker' after getting sent off in an Old Firm game.

It was, Dick maintained, the finest derby in the world. It was also a long way away from the more sedate environs of international management. His whole demeanour dropped when asked about the World Cup.

'We can't qualify for the World Cup,' he said, looking deep into his plate. 'But we're getting ready for the next Gulf Cup.'

It was added so half-heartedly you felt he was about to cry. Dick poked around his salad niçoise as he tried to summon up a modicum of excitement regarding the UAE's next friendly, against Benin. He seemed pretty unhappy to be stuck in the desert. But lunch was good and his spirits seemed lifted as Gordon shook his hand and we said goodbye.

'He won't stick around long,' declared Ramsay as Dick descended the futuristic staircase. I didn't realise just how soon he would be proved right.

A week later the magazine and the interview with Advocaat had gone to print. On the way home from work, I picked up a copy of the *Gulf News*.

'*Advocaat's Sudden Departure shocks UAE*' screamed the headline.

I stood by the news stand, watching my career flash before my eyes.

'The sudden departure of Dutch coach Dick Advocaat from the UAE to sign with the Korean FA has made the UAE football officials, media and supporters furious for many reason,' the article continued, the writer unable to keep their own anger in check.

> '*The first was the way Advocaat left UAE. He secretly went to Dubai Airport. He left the car keys with the reception of the hotel where he was staying after he arrived last month to start his job with the FA. Advocaat did not inform any FA officials about his departure. When the FA board members read about his signing with the KFA in a local newspaper, they tried to call him but his mobile was switched off.*'

Equally galling for the UAE FA, there was no clause to penalise Advocaat if he walked out. Although Yousuf al Serkal, the chairman of the UAE FA, seemed more upset he hadn't had the chance to fire Dick himself.

'*Never in the past did any coach terminate his contract with the UAE FA,*' he was quoted as saying. '*It was always the FA that had sacked coaches.*'

It was too late to retract the interview. The magazine had already gone to print. The next day I sat at my desk wondering whether this was a sacking offence when the phone rang.

'Hello?'

'Hello James, it's Dick.'

'Dick, where are you?'

'I'm, ahh, in Holland.'

The lunch, it turned out, was the turning point. Dick had to get out and get out quick and with the South Korean FA sniffing around, offering the chance to guide the 2002 semi-finalists to Germany, it was a no brainer. A few phone calls later and he had hurriedly packed and fled the country. He'd lasted less than six weeks.

'I'm sorry,' he said as I tried to work out whether to feel angry or guilty. 'It was too good a chance to miss.' At least he had the good manners to call.

The man the UAE FA turned to next had no problems adapting to the job. Bruno Metsu was a footballing chameleon, a consensus seeker who soaked up his players' advice and acted accordingly. He also arrived in the UAE a Muslim after converting during his time in Senegal. When the 2007 Gulf Cup came around nine months later, the country had gone football crazy. Gone were the poorly attended league matches that would see a few dozen men in white dish dashas watch from the sidelines. The games had been packed and Metsu had steered the UAE into the semi-final and a tie against arch rivals Saudi Arabia.

If the nervous looking Saudi men sitting at the bar in the Madinat Jumeirah in Dubai, wearing their team's green football kit and sipping on large glasses of lager, were to be believed, victory for the Green Falcons was a foregone conclusion. 'We will win 2–0, for sure,' boasted one as he ordered a double whisky. '[Yasser Al] Qahtani is the best.' The game was due to start at 8.15pm, but the Saudis were planning on getting there at 1 pm, such was the expected rush for tickets. Clearly tickets would be at a premium.

I took a taxi down to Abu Dhabi's Jaziera Stadium a few hours before kick-off. I should have taken the Saudis' advice. Already, two-and-a-half hours before the match was due to start, every seat was taken. Thousands milled around outside whilst the police, arguably never having seen so many of their countrymen in one place before, struggled to control the mob. Groups of Emirati teenagers in traditional outfits stormed one fence, half a dozen making it over the sharp metal prongs before the police could beat the rest back with their batons. I doubted I would ever make it over in time before getting a beating. I had to find another way. One stand seemed remarkably quieter than the others. With strict segregation between the fans being enforced, the only seats left were with the Saudis. I picked a green Saudi flag off the floor, waved it at the policeman guarding the gate and he let me in.

Inside, the stadium was deafening. Three stands in front of me were blanketed in the white of the UAE's national dress. A single area of black broke the monotony of colour – the women's section, filled with young female fans wearing the traditional abaya.

Despite being outnumbered, the Saudis were louder, banging drums and singing religious songs, the UAE fans' weak replies only audible during the occasional lulls. The match was tense and tetchy, neither team making any clear-cut chances. At half-time some Saudi fans, along with the policemen charged with looking after them, sought divine inspiration in a quiet corner, deep inside the bowels of the stadium, by praying together. The second half wasn't much better and, with the game heading for extra time, the Saudi crowd relaxed slightly, allowing their gaze to be distracted from the tense stalemate.

Their complacency was to be exploited. The referee gave the UAE a ridiculous free-kick in a dangerous position. 'The referee!' exclaimed Mohammad, a young Saudi in traditional dress standing next to me. He rubbed his fingers together in an accusatory manner. 'Money.' With the game deep in injury-time Ismail Matar smashed the ball into the left-hand corner with virtually the last kick of the game. The stadium exploded from its torpor. Robed sheikhs ran onto the pitch towards the mound of bodies that had covered the tiny striker. The UAE bench joined them, as did one man in a wheelchair, determined to reach the pack, wheeling himself heavily over the grass towards his hero as fast as his arms could take him.

Matar emerged from the melee and sank to his knees as the stadium continued its apoplectic celebratory rage. The Saudi section felt like the eye of a tornado: the barometric pressure of quiet violence bearing down around us. There was stillness and silence. Mohammad brushed past me whilst furiously shaking his head. Others simply sat, stunned, robed heads in hands. There were still people on the pitch when the match continued its last few pointless moments. Seconds later, it was over, Metsu and Matar were national heroes. It wasn't the end of the UAE's journey either. They went on to beat Oman in the final, Matar again proving the difference, scoring his fifth goal of the tournament to lift the country's first ever piece of silverware in front of 60,000 fans at the Zayed Sports City Stadium. He never did get the move abroad his talents merited. But for his efforts one prominent local awarded him two prized camels worth $109,000 each. Even Inter Milan couldn't match that.

For close to 18 months, that victory in Abu Dhabi – alongside the national team's qualification for the 1990 World Cup – were the UAE's greatest claim to footballing fame. And then came Sulaiman al Fahim, Sheikh Mansour and the purchase of

Manchester City. Little was known about Manchester City's new owner. Like most members of the Gulf's royal families, Sheikh Mansour didn't have to contend with a prying press nor divulge his accounts for public scrutiny. What was known was fairly typical for the heir to an absolute monarchy. He was a member of the Nahyan dynasty, the world's second richest royal family with access to an oil fortune that could be as much as $1 trillion. He was one of 19 sons sired by Sheikh Zayed, the country's revered first president who founded the nation and persuaded the heads of the six other royal families that would make up the UAE to bury their dislike for each other. He was brother to the next United Arab Emirates President, Sheikh Khalifa bin Zayed al Nahyan, and held the post of Minister for Presidential Affairs in the UAE cabinet. Whilst Sheikh Mansour's money was being spent on the likes of Robinho and the talk was of City breaking into Champions League contention, back in Abu Dhabi a smaller but no less important football revolution was taking place. Manchester City wasn't Sheikh Mansour's first football love. That was Al Jazira, the Abu Dhabi based club. And as the UAE's money was being poured in to the English game, it was decided that more had to be done about the embarrassing lack of fans and professionalism in the local league.

A stream of brand-new 4X4s lined up to get in to the car park that serviced Dubai's Al Maktoum Stadium. The floodlights buzzed through the humid early evening in preparation for that night's entertainment, a Friday cup match between Dubai rivals Al Nasr and Al Ahli. Young boys in long white *dish dahsas* walked past in groups as the call to prayer abrasively cried out. They were not talking to each other, but talking into the hands free mic connected to their expensive mobile phones. The only thing that differentiated the groups was a slash of colour from their club scarves: blue for Nasr, Red for Ahli. This season the royal families of the UAE hadn't just pumped millions into football clubs in foreign lands. For the first time the UAE's league had gone pro to try to flex its muscle a little close to home.

According to the UAE Pro League's new CEO, Romy Gai, what happened here would provide a good indicator of what Man City fans could expect in the future. Gai was previously a commercial director at Juventus for 14 years but received a call out of the blue earlier in the year. It appeared that the local football league was in danger of being slung out of Asian Football Confederation's international tournaments for being too amateur.

'I got the call telling me about what was happening so I joined them as there is little opportunity in the modern age for something like this,' Gai said as the teams warmed up on the pitch in front of us. 'It was difficult at first, with the heat and then with Ramadan. But then the AFC came for an inspection and said we were the benchmarks for Asia.'

Even by the UAE's standards the turnaround was remarkable. In four months they had formed a professional league, refurbished all 12 stadiums and persuaded the television networks to go from paying nothing to 12 million euros a year – even if the Nahyan and Maktoum royal families agreed to split this cost after the Qatari TV network Al Jazeera threatened to win the rights. Some clubs even started flashing their cash in the transfer market. Sheikh Mansour himself sanctioned the purchase of Brazilian Rafael Sobis from Real Betis for Al Jazira. Still, the change may have come too quickly for some. Only 100 fans lined the stands waiting for kick off.

'Football is the country's sport,' Gai insisted. 'The locals love it. If a European club is bought [by a UAE royal family] then international football offers us lots of opportunities. This is a country that has told us that dreams can become reality.'

✦

London, October 2009

Sulaiman al Fahim had successfully blended into the background. But these days – against every fibre in his being – the art of invisibility was a necessity. We had agreed to meet in the lobby of an exclusive five star hotel in London. I had walked past him several times, expecting to see him in his trademark *khandoora*, ordering the most expensive thing on the menu. But, no, Al Fahim looked anything but the bling-encrusted plaything presented to the world's media 12 months before. Now he wore a sports jacket and baggy jeans, mooching slowly along with prayer beads in hand. Without his Gulf attire his hair was thinning, making him look ten years older. He appeared demure, devout, contrite even.

'People say I am playboy, but I am not,' he quickly explained as we sat down. 'That picture with Pamela Anderson was a normal picture. I was in LA and we had coffee with her mother and she came along. It's a wrong perception. The British media made me look like that.'

It was just over a year since I had first met Al Fahim, the face of the Manchester City takeover. In that time he had been busy, deciding that he too would own an English Premier League football club. But with a slightly different outcome. After becoming intoxicated by his proximity to the Mancheter City deal, he decided to buy Portsmouth FC, just as the world economy – including Dubai – was in full meltdown.

His meteoric rise began when he returned to the UAE after studying abroad in 2003 and began buying up property and land that was being sold for £10 a square foot. Just eighteen months later it was selling for £100 a square foot. In a few years he was head of one of the fastest growing real companies in the world. But then the bubble burst. The Dubai property crash arrived on the ripples of the US sub-prime mortgage crisis, almost bankrupting the emirate. Dubai, far from being blessed with natural resources to fund its booming economy had simply paid for it all on its proverbial credit card, running up debts of USD109 billion. When one property company Dubai World announced it might default its debt payment the news sent stocks crashing around the world. In Dubai, people were laid off. As the non-payment of debt is a criminal offence in the UAE thousands would simply drive to the airport, leave the keys in the ignition and flee. Dubai had to ask for an embarrassing bail out from Abu Dhabi, inoculated from economic contagion thanks to its oil wealth. In return Sheikh Mohammed named Dubai's greatest achievement thus far – the tallest building in the world – after the UAE president (and head of the Abu Dhabi royal family) who saved him. The Burj Dubai would hence forth be known as the Burj Khalifa.

But Al Fahim hadn't been affected by the crash. He already cashed out his chips. 'I was lucky because [before the credit crunch came] I pulled the plug,' he admitted. 'I sold most of my shares at the right time in 2006. I bought stock at Dhs1, but sold it for Dhs48. It was sixth sense. No one told me anything, I just felt it.'

Bruised but undeterred from his experiences with the English press, Al Fahim emerged six months later to buy Portsmouth, a move that once again captivated the UK media. *The Guardian* described his 42-day stint as the club's owner as 'not only the shortest but surely the most ill-fated tenure in Premier League history.'

Heralded as a big money saviour for a club crippled by the big spending of its previous owner Alexandre Gaydamak [son of Beitar Jerusalem owner Arkadi Gaydamak], the money never seemed to appear. Portsmouth fans and the press had a field day. Al Fahim was, according to them, another 'Fake Sheikh', a fantasist who over egged his net worth to play the Premier League game after getting a taste for it when fronting the Manchester City deal. Portsmouth began the season with seven straight defeats and were rock bottom of the table. But, much more worryingly, by October the players and staff had stopped being paid. Al Fahim was mercilessly dragged over the coals.

'I believe Peter Storrie [Portsmouth CEO] from day one wanted the [rival] consortium of Ali al Faraj [because] he brought them in,' he explained. It was only a few days since he sold his share in the club and the criticism, the protests, the threats from fans and internet trolls alike, had wounded him. If anything, Al Fahim believed, it was his financial diligence that counted against him. 'With me there would be no overpayment, everything would be at the right time with the right investment. Mine was £5 million as equity. But…they wanted £10 million in two weeks. So I sold the club. But look how much the [Ali al Faraj] consortium has invested. It's only £1.8

million. So where is the money they [Storrie] were asking me for? I was getting 100 emails a day. Why do they not care now that the consortium hasn't paid this?'

As far as Al Fahim was concerned, he was put in an untenable position. 'I don't know why he [Storrie] thought I wasn't the right guy. He was pushing me out, using the media and website of Portsmouth.' Strangely, the controversy and the bad press that had constantly surrounded the Portsmouth deal hadn't been detrimental to Al Fahim. In fact, the opposite was the case. He insisted that the deal was a success for him personally ('Who would have thought that by investing £5 million you would get ten percent of a [Premier League] club?') but his involvement in Manchester City and Portsmouth had meant that other foreign businessmen were now calling him to broker more Premiership takeovers.

'I get phone calls from the States, from Asia, saying 'Mr Sulaiman, help us to buy a club',' he revealed, prayer beads still tightly held in hands. 'Real businessmen don't ever look at my 90 per cent stake as a failure. Anybody, when they see the deal I have done is really happy. People call me to buy and find opportunities in the Premier League. They also call me to open new football clubs in their own countries. My [new] company understands the football business.'

The traditionalists viewed Al Fahim as an example of everything that was going wrong with the English game. The English Premier League's incredible global success had meant that the game had slowly untethered from its local roots.

'[People] should not criticise foreign owners,' he said. 'Whether I am the owner or the owner is Chinese or from Hong Kong or Saudi Arabia, the reality is we are not the owners. It is owned by the supporters and the community. None of the owners are involved in the day-to-day management of the club. It's the foreign owners' job to secure finance, to expand the brand and help with cash flow, but not more than that.'

When we met he was still involved at Portsmouth as club chairman, and held a ten percent stake. He couldn't quite extricate himself from the role of Portsmouth's commander in chief. At one point during our interview Nader Shawky approached him, the Middle Eastern super agent, who was waving a telephone in his direction.

On the other end was Amr Zaki, the Egyptian international who briefly took the English Premier League by storm a year earlier with Wigan Athletic before falling out with his manager Steve Bruce and moving back to Zamalek in Egypt. He wanted to speak to him. 'I believe that Portsmouth needs someone like Zaki,' he sighed, after a brief chat. 'But seeing that I have sold 90 per cent of the shares I don't have much say. I have one vote though!'

The next day Al Fahim took his place at Fratton Park, assuming pride of place in a seat next to the club's new director of football, Avram Grant. It was one of the few areas of UAE life where an Emirati would openly sit next to an Israeli. 'You should come to the game against Wigan tomorrow,' he had offered. I politely declined, partially due to the distance, partially due to the fact that Portsmouth were bottom of the table and another loss could turn the combustible Fratton Park into an ugly bear pit, with Fahim as its sacrificial offering. 24 hours later I turned on the TV to see Al Fahim, a huge smile on his face, applauding next to Grant and the rest of board. 4-0. To Portsmouth. Al Fahim's famous sixth sense, one that had avoided catastrophe during the Dubai property crash, was clearly in rude health. Yet football may not be where Al Fahim's future lies. He had now moved into the brave new world of the silver screen, pumping millions of dollars in to producing a new film called 'The Road to Darfur', a gritty, political road movie directed by leading Arab filmmaker Said Hamed.

'I play Sulaiman himself, a philanthropist. I want people to see the real me, not what people like you have written about me!' he joked. At least I thought it was a joke. 'And not what people saw in Hydra Executives. You know, my only problem was the first season wasn't me. It showed someone with ego, ignorant, selfish. I want this [film] to show my real, honest lifestyle.'

By the end of the 2009/2010 season Portsmouth had been relegated, having also become the first club in Premier League history to enter financial administration. They were bottom every week of the season bar one: the first. And the film? No trace of it can be found on IMDB nor on the 2010 list of Oscar nominees.

11
EGYPT:
BEFORE THE STORM

November 2009

The Cairo International Stadium was already shaking to the sound of 100,000 victory songs six hours before kick off, but by the time The Pharaohs were ready to take to the pitch the deafening screams had created a seemingly impenetrable wall of sound. No one knew for sure how many people were there. The official capacity stated 70,000 but anywhere up to 100,000 had squeezed in, evading the draconian riot police who were beating the ticket-less and the poor outside the gates. It had been two years since I stood with Assad and his Ultras in the same stadium – the same stand in the same stadium – to watch Al Ahly take on Zamalek in the Egyptian league. But this, a World Cup qualifier against Egypt's north African rivals Algeria, was different. Ahly versus Zamalek had become, under Mubarak, an increasingly sanitised exercise in catharsis, a bread and circus diversion designed to allow a little anger out, but not enough to dent even the lowest cog of his machine. This time, it had got out of hand; frenzied, cathartic and ugly.

Such was the noise that every single note of the Algerian national anthem was obscured by a backdraft of hate. The big screens focused on the worried faces of the Algerian players as they tried to sing against the tide. Several of them wore white bandages on their heads and across their faces, signs of recent, violent injury. If I'd been in any doubt about the ferocity of the rivalry between Egypt and Algeria up to that point, the boy standing on the seat next to me, head tilted back, screaming into the night, provided further evidence: the words 'Fuck Algeria' had been written on his and his friends' faces in crayon. A huge Egyptian flag with the words 'Welcome to Hell' written on it faced the pocket of Algerian fans, high up in the main stand. More than 2,000 seats had been left fallow around them, a protective barrier that gave sanctuary to the tiny rectangle of green and white flags.

After months of anticipation, mob violence, lies and political interventions, Egypt was about to take on the Desert Foxes in one of the most politically charged football matches since a World Cup qualifier in 1969 sparked the so-called Soccer War between Honduras and El Salvador. At stake was a place at the 2010 World Cup finals, Africa's first. But like the Honduras-El Salvador conflict, it wasn't what was at stake but what lay beneath. History was repeating itself. The match marked two decades since Egypt and Algeria had played in eerily similar circumstances in 1989 for a place at Italia 90. That match, consequently known as the 'Death Match', became notorious for being one of the most shameful incidents in the history of world football, a game marred by violence between players and fans of such ferocity that it has soured relations between the two countries. Egypt won that game 1-0 but, incensed by defeat, a dodgy offside decision and accusations of bias against the Tunisian referee, the fighting continued after the game, culminating in the Egyptian team doctor losing an eye. Algerian legend, and former African Player of the Year, Lakhdar Belloumi was convicted in his absence and an international warrant was issued for his arrest. Belloumi claimed innocence, pointing the finger at a former team mate in an interview with Algerian daily Echorouck. For two decades the shadow of the game hung over Belloumi until the reverse fixture between the two teams earlier in the year. Then it took the personal intervention of Algeria's president Abdellaziz Bouteflika to have the warrant quashed.

Algeria won that game 3-1, meaning that Egypt had to win in Cairo by three clear goals to qualify for South Africa 2010. Algeria merely needed a point. A 2-0 victory meant that the two teams finished on the same points, goal difference, goals for and against. A play off in Sudan had been scheduled for a few days later, just in case. The players carried not just the pressure of World Cup qualification, but also the joy and heartbreak of '89 on their backs. Every little bit of help was required. AmrZaki, who for a brief few months would lead the line for Wigan Athletic in the English Premier League, stood alone in the centre circle facing the Algerian players, his eyes closed, face in his hands. As two tribes swirled around him, and the referee prepared to blow his whistle to start the game, he was offering a simple, solitary prayer to Allah.

Saleh Zakareya had got up before dawn for a chance to get a ticket for the game, but his efforts turned out to be fruitless. The 23-year-old engineering student had travelled down by train from the northern port city of Alexandria and queued for five hours in the hope of getting one of the official 70,000 tickets, but like the tens of thousands standing outside Zamalek stadium, his efforts were in vain. The police announced that they had come on the wrong day. They should come back tomorrow. The crowd was incensed.

'This is because of the big people in the government who will get all the tickets and then sell them on the black market,' shouted Zakareya, a short, bookish young man wearing glasses, as the angry crowd jostled with the policemen.

The commanding officer, dressed in a black uniform, large Aviator sunglasses and adorned with numerous impotent honours approached me and grabbed my camera.

'You can not film here!' he shouted, before getting distracted by the rapidly worsening situation.

'There is so much corruption here,' Saleh shouted over the noise. 'They are supposed to be on sale for EGP15 [£1.50] but they will sell them for EGP150 [£ 11.50].'

In the two years since my last visit, life had got visibly worse for the Egyptians I spoke to. Poverty, unhappiness with President Mubarak's authoritarian rule and endemic corruption in all walks of life had proliferated. A perfect storm of rocketing wheat prices and inflation had sparked bread riots the year before, calling to mind similar protests over the price of bread in 1977 that led to nearly 80 deaths. The national team, though, had thrived. The Pharaohs were champions of Africa, winning the 2008 championship by beating Cameroon 1-0 in the Ghanaian capital, Accra. Mohamed Aboutrika had scored the winning goal.

Aboutrika was Al Ahly's inspirational midfielder, one of the greatest Africa had ever produced. He was adored by all Egyptians thanks to his pious nature and devout faith. In an earlier round of the 2008 Africa Cup of Nations he had scored and revealed a t-shirt with the words 'Sympathize with Gaza' written on it, a reference to Israel's Cast Lead operation that would cost the lives of over 1,000 people, mostly civilians. 'It was a personal statement form myself,' he explained afterwards. 'I feel great sympathy from the children of Gaza, who are under siege. I wore the shirt for Gaza's children who are suffering, who are starving, who are vulnerable and fear for their safety.' He was booked by the referee and warned by African football's governing body CAF. Aboutrika had only further enhanced his heroic reputation in Africa and the Arab world.

The victory in Ghana meant Egypt had won back to back titles, making them one of the country's few current sources of pride. 'There is no Ahly or Zamalek today,' Saleh explained, in hope that the national team could unite Cairo's deep footballing divisions. As he spoke the police began to clear the crowd with their batons. The crowd replied by chanting what they felt about the Egyptian FA's president: 'Samir Zaher you are an asshole!'

'Unfortunately the media has made this match so huge. Some people will have heart attacks,' Saleh said exasperated, now realising he would be taking the long train back to Alexandria empty handed. 'They have even asked that the female fans, the 'ice cream fans', don't come so that the true fans can come and make the stadium rock. They are making it like a fight between two armies.'

Saleh was right about that. After landing in Cairo it had become clear that the match had taken on a huge political importance. A media war between the Algerian and Egyptian press had slowly escalated since Egypt beat Zambia in an earlier round and the permutations needed for both countries was known. Suspicion was everywhere. There had been no press conferences and training was closed to the media, just in case any tactical secrets were leaked. Before Algeria's home match against Egypt earlier in the year veteran coach Rabah Saadane, who had led his country into their last World Cup campaign at Mexico '86, broke down into tears, such was the pressure from the home press for victory. Every player and official was sworn to silence. The Egyptian league had been suspended for the previous month so that the team could prepare properly for the game, but the move had one unforeseen effect: the Egyptian press filled the vacuum with incessant coverage of the build up which had further stoked tensions between the two countries.

Many countries have been guilty of whipping up xenophobic feeling before an important match. But Egypt's press was tightly controlled. Mubarak was a canny politician, and a huge football fan. He understood the power of a successful national team. He was there at the opening of the 2006 African Cup of Nations, waving to the crowd with his wife Suzanne. When Egypt won it, it was Mubarak who handed coach Hassan Shehata his medal. Before the Algeria game he would grace the team with his presence to offer words of encouragement, but behind closed doors. Aside from state television, the press was not invited.

It had been Mubarak's appropriation of the national team for reflected glory that had angered Assad, the leader of the Al Ahly Ultras I had met at the Cairo derby. His group had boycotted national team games. 'This is Mubarak's team,' Assad had told me over the phone as an explanation as to why he wasn't going to the game.

But there were other reasons too. In the two years since they formed, Assad and his ultras had become virtual enemies of the state. As they grew from a few hundred in to a few thousand, with their choreographed banners and increasingly poetic and political songs, the group had been harassed by the police. Arrests had been made to intimidate them. They were painted as violence addicted hooligans in the state run press. They had re-branded themselves the Ahlawy, and were regularly involved with violent confrontations with the state more than with their opposite numbers at Zamalek. It was best for everyone involved, Assad thought, that the Ahlawy stay away.

The media, both in Algeria and Egypt, had been trading insults, invoking the

'Spirit of '89' and using war-like imagery in their coverage. *Shoot*, Egypt's popular weekly football newspaper, ran with the game on all 20 pages. On the front page was a scene from the film 300, the Egyptian player's faces superimposed on the rippled bodies of the soldiers. At the front, leading the charge with Egyptian flag in hand, was the coach Shehata. The headline read: 'Attack', written in Arabic and smeared in blood. Even Coca Cola handed out t-shirts that read 'I was there in 1989'.

In those circumstances it was surprising to discover that anyone from Algeria would risk travelling to the match, but some were still determined. A short drive from Zamalek's stadium journalists were ducking in and out of the guarded, high walled offices of the Egyptian FA.

'It is a war in the media only,' dismissed Fodil Lyes, a correspondent for the Algerian newspaper *Echorouk,* who was there to pick up his press pass. 'The game in 1989, Egypt deserved to win, even if the goal was offside. I have been here a week and I haven't had any problems. The people have a good relationship.' He looked down at his press pass, with the word 'ALGERIA' splashed over the front and quickly stuffed it into his pocket. 'But Saturday is another day.'

The situation was different for the travelling supporters. Outside the Algerian embassy on Zamalek island, the 2,000 protesters knew they were on neutral, if not exactly safe, ground. The long, white-walled, tree-lined street was coloured green and white. They had gathered to show their displease at the way they and their country had been demonised and to secure arguably one of the most dangerous tickets in world football. And they were not happy that so few tickets had been allocated to them.

'The Egyptians are so scared they will try any means to make sure there are only Egyptians in the stadium,' explained Elias Filali, a well-dressed British-Algerian businessman who had flown from London to get a ticket. 'It has become a dirty game in the press. The image of Egypt is at stake.'

Others had driven from Algeria, through Libya, to get to Cairo. Some had travelled even further. Touiza Mohammed stood with a stiff military back and small moustache, dressed in an immaculate grey suit with a Algerian scarf tied around his head. The 73-year-old had followed the team for decades, back when Algeria was under French rule. On his lapel he wore the flag of the FLN – the National Liberation Front – the guerrilla movement that fought and won Algerian independence in 1962. The FLN had even launched a rogue 'national' team to promote its cause, attracting some of France's best French-Algerian players, several of whom had already represented the French national team. They had to leave the country under the cover of darkness to join the squad, never to return to European football. But Touiza had been much more directly involved.

'I used to be an FLN fighter and I got life in prison, life in arm and leg shackles, in a prison called the 'Corridor of Death',' he bellowed, half to me, half to the crowd that had gathered to listen to what the old man had to say.

What were you in prison for, I asked.

'I killed someone, a French policeman and a *harki* [Algerians who collaborated with the French],' he replied, without a hint of remorse.

'I killed them with grenades, then I shot them. I killed him [the *harki*] because he informed on me. I was tortured in prison, they electrocuted my balls before they let me free after independence three years later. Football makes people popular and united. This match will make us forget the [Algerian] civil war.'

Although the 1989 match had been a pivotal moment for recent relations between the two countries, the enmity ran deeper than that, touching on the colonialism that Tiouza Mohammad fought against. As regional rivals, both have vied for supremacy: Egypt positioning itself as the leading force for Arab nationalism, Algeria assuming the position of tormentor in chief of colonial expansionism in Arab lands. Yet the Egyptians question Algeria's view of themselves, joking that they send language teachers to Algeria so that the Francophone nation can learn to speak Arabic properly. The Algerians, in return, accuse the Egyptians of cowardice, of selling out their Palestinian brothers by signing a peace treaty with Israel. One disgruntled computer literate fan managed to hack President Mubarak's personal website to air exactly those views.

But for most ordinary people, there was still an Arab, Muslim fraternity that trumped all other grievances. As the crowd protested a large group of Egyptian youths holding flags of both nations aloft approached. Rather than attack they applauded the Algerian crowd, who returned the favour.

'We wanted to let them know,' said one teenager who had bothered to paint his face both the colour of the Egyptian and Algerian flag for the occasion, 'That not everyone felt the same.' They were quickly bundled away by the police.

The limited fraternity didn't last long. 'Have you heard, the game is going to be cancelled, they have attacked the Algerians,' an Egyptian friend told me by phone that evening. Sure enough, within an hour the footage of the attack had been edited and uploaded on to the Internet. The first video was dark and shaky, occasionally zooming into a huge hole that had been blown through a coach window. The second showed the aftermath: several Algerian national team players showing their injuries, blood pouring from head wounds. A hundred or so Egyptian fans had gathered to welcome the Algerians as they arrived in Cairo, and had pelted the team bus with paving slabs, injuring three players.

'They let them do it,' defender Antar Yahia told Algerian state radio, accusing

Egyptian security guards of standing back and allowing the attack to happen. 'You can't launch five kilo rocks from 50 metres. They let them do it and watched. It's shameful. In our home game we welcomed them with flowers.'

The Algerian sports minister condemned the attack. The president of the Algerian Football Association asked for the game to be called off, citing safety fears. FIFA demanded the Egyptian FA guarantee security.

'I saw it with my own eyes, I videoed it,' Filali, the Algerian journalist I had met at the Egyptian FA picking up his press pass, told me later that night. 'I was standing in my hotel room, at the window, looking down at the bus. I saw them [the Egyptian fans] attack the bus.'

But not everyone would be sure that he, or the Algerian team, was telling the truth. The next day the streets of Cairo feel silent, the calm only punctuated by the rising, distorted cacophony of a thousand *muezzins* singing a thousand calls to prayer. Friday morning is usually a time for quiet reflection but the Egyptian press had gone on the attack. The initial reaction from the Egyptian authorities was to deny that the attack ever took place, feeding into a popular belief that the Algerians were using the incident to call off the game out of cowardice. The government-run daily newspaper *Al Ahram* then accused the Algerians of fabrication. 'The bus carrying the team from the airport to the hotel was at the centre of a strange incident in which some of the players started to smash the vehicle's windows claiming that they were the target of stone throwing,' it stated.

Every Egyptian I spoke to was utterly convinced the attack had been staged by Algeria to try and get the game annulled, so scared were they of playing in Cairo. For Zakareya, the engineering student I met outside Zamalek's ground who, as feared, had to resort the black market for his tickets, the truth was obvious. 'They destroyed their own bus, of course. Why? So after, when they lose, they can blame it on the Egyptian fans.'

Even Ayman Younis – the former Egyptian international who I'd met in Cairo before the Ahly Zamalek match – was suspicious. Ayman had actually played in the Death Match in 1989 and vividly remembered its viciousness.

'It was an incredible atmosphere, the Algeria team was full of stars,' he recalled, pointing out that it was Algeria that were the favourites back then, having qualified for the 1982 World Cup and beating West Germany in their opening match. 'On the pitch it was very crazy; 11 fights between every player. Everybody forgot what the coaches had to say and just fought instead. It was a battle, not a football match. It was like our war against Israel in 1973.' Ayman had driven to meet me outside Al Ahly's training ground and had managed to procure me a rare ticket.

Ayman claimed he had incontrovertible proof of Algeria's duplicity. Security sources had told him that there was glass on the *outside* of the coach. Clearly, this proved they had broken the window themselves. The bus driver, who he said had no axe to grind, had been assaulted by the players and had seen what was going on.

'What they did was make a movie,' Ayman said of the bloody video evidence that emerged afterwards. 'A very, very bad movie. The Algerian team are very bad people.'

He warned me to be careful at the match and to leave early if I wanted to get in for the evening kick off.

'Don't worry I'll get there a few hours before,' I assured him.

'No, no,' he implored, leaning in as if I had quite grasped what he said.

'You have to get there at midday. A ticket doesn't mean you'll get in.'

Kick off was at 7.30pm.

A burning sun greeted Egypt's big day. Despite it being November, the Cairo International Stadium was heated by an unseasonably warm sun. It was midday, seven and a half hours before kick off, but the side streets and concourses were packed full of supporters and an almost equal number of security officers. The seas parted when a coach, led by a police escort, arrived full of Algeria fans. The Egyptian crowd closed around it as soon as it stopped, hurling vitriol at the scared passengers inside. One of the windows was missing. The Algerian fans filed out under a line of riot shields to protect them.

'They threw stones at us and gave us the finger,' explained Attef Al Akhas, an Algeria fan based in Cairo who had travelled with the convoy and had now been taken behind the relative safety of a police checkpoint. His friends eagerly showed videos on their mobile phones of their vehicle being attacked minutes earlier. Others displayed cuts and bruises from flying glass.

'Not all Egyptian fans are like this,' he added. 'It's the kids really.'

For the home fans the police set up three check points on each route, harassing and beating those that didn't have a ticket at the first opportunity. I was carried through in the crush. The line thinned out as more and more fans were snatched away. Even having a ticket wasn't a guarantee. At the last gate I had begun to take pictures of a man in civilian clothes beating supporters who had tickets but weren't allowed in. They waved them impotently as they limped away. Immediately I was grabbed.

'Delete!' the balding man in the camel jacket demanded as he held tightly on to my wrist. 'Or you will never see the game.'

I flicked on the camera. The screen beamed back an image of the same man, launching himself into a crowd of teenagers, his hand and stick a blur of rage.

'Delete. Next.'

The next was a close up of his face, contorted and puce as he swung wildly.

'Delete. Next!'

The next one was a picture of my pet dog, back home in England, licking the patch where his balls used to be.

'DELETE IT!' the bald man screamed, nonetheless.

Hours passed as the stadium filled and the sun set. Hosni Mubarak was nowhere to be seen. Instead it was an opportunity for his sons Alaa and, more importantly Gamal, to step into the spotlight. Gamal had been an unpopular figure in Egypt, yet was second in command of his father's political party and was being being groomed as his successor. The match offered him the platform for statesmanship.

The hysteria rose until the teams walked onto the pitch, Amr Zaki prayed and the referee blew his whistle. Zaki's prayers were answered almost instantly. Two minutes after the kick off, and with Algeria unable to get a touch of the ball, Egypt surged forward. Mohamed Aboutrika hit a post and Zaki was there to poke in at close range. The outpouring was almost viscous, a soundwave able to knock a grown man off their feet. Everything: 1989, the World Cup, the accusations, attacks, fabrications, they had all led to that moment.

Oddly, the goal had an almost anaesthetic effect on the crowd. It was as if the histrionics and bullishness of the past month were the bravado of a condemned man. The goal had suddenly brought hope, but with it the reality of expectation. After the initial burst of euphoria the anti-Algerian chants died down, the crowd subdued. Whereas before obscenities were screamed at the small patch of green and white high up in the stands, now the Egyptian fans stared blankly at the pitch, transferring their nervousness to the players. Egypt's initial fearlessness meant they had overawed Algeria in the first few moments. Afterwards, they could barely string two passes together.

Chances came, half time went but it was Algeria, their team punctuated by the white head bandages that marked those injured in the team bus attack, who edged towards the finals. After hours of queuing and singing, days of tit-for-tat media exchanges and a month of frenzied anticipation, and with 90 minutes on the clock, it looked like Egypt had fallen short of the World Cup finals by a solitary goal. Objects started to be thrown on the pitch. Grown men began to sob. The riot police lined up, fixing their stares on the crowd and raising their shields. Unless a miracle happened the tension would inevitably explode on to Cairo's streets. But just as all hope was lost, in the sixth minute of injury time, substitute Emad Moteab rose and nodded in a looping header. The Algerians were silent, halted just 30 seconds from the finishing line. The Egyptian bench stormed the pitch, the crowd erupting in disbelief. Egypt and Algeria had finished the group on level points, unbelievably with the same goal difference and the same goals scored. They would have to do it all again four days later in Sudan.

Hundreds of thousands poured into the streets, firing plumes of fire from make-shift flame throwers fashioned from hairspray canisters into the air.

'That we scored at the beginning and the end shows that we played until the last minute with the same soul,' shouted Essam Bilal, a celebrating Egypt fan, over the din of car horns from the gridlocked streets outside the stadium. 'Algeria are so disappointed now. It was bullshit that they were attacked because I know the bus driver and he said they invented everything so they deserved to lose,' he continued. 'Now we will beat them in Sudan, *Inshallah*.'

On the other side of the stadium, just as Essam and virtually every other Egyptian fan still insisted that the attack on Algeria's team bus had been a hoax, rocks once again rained down on the Desert Foxes as their crushed fans left the stadium, another twist of an already deeply plunged knife. 32 people were injured in the clashes around the stadium that night, 20 of them Algerian. But the reverberations from Emad Moteab's late, late goal were felt around the world. In France, hundreds of youths, mostly of Algerian descent, rioted in Marseilles, smashing shop windows and setting fire to cars and boats. In the Saudi city of Mecca 50 Egyptians were arrested after celebrating too exuberantly on the Kingdom's conservative streets. The next day, in Algiers, fans who had gathered to try and buy tickets for the match in Sudan rioted, smashing up Egyptian businesses and ransacking the offices of Egypt Air. Somehow the two nations had to get themselves ready to do it all over again, a few days later, in Omdurman, Sudan.

Sudan was a step too far from me. Without a visa, which was impossible to get in Cairo, there was no chance of making it. It seemed a strange place to have a neutral match. On the one had, Sudan neighbours Egypt, and a huge number of Sudanese live and work there. On the other hand they usually fill the most menial, lowest paid jobs and have to deal with endemic racism. It would not be the fraternal home match many in Egypt were expecting. Waiting at the airport, my phone rang. It was Ayman Younis. He could get me a seat on a plane for Sudan if I still wanted for just a few hundred dollars. But without a visa it would pointless. Instead I would watch the match in the next best place I could find.

✦

*The green and white scarves had arrived early t*o find sanctuary in the Babylon Café in West London. A faded Truman Brewery sign hung on the wall, testament to its previous life as a pub. Now it was dry, taken over by an Algerian who had turned it into a *halal* café. Gone were the cigarette and booze soaked carpets of the English working class, replaced instead by oriental lamps, grilled lamb and beautiful women in green *hijabs* shouting: 'One, two, three, viva Algerie!'

Directly opposite, through the former pub's dirty windows, I watched the Rose Café fill with Egyptian fans. Nasim Mechouri, a young university student stood and watched with me.

'At the end of the last game, you had the Algerians on one side of the road, the Egyptians on the other and the police lined up in the middle to make sure there was no trouble,' he said, not moving his gaze from the nervous men opposite. 'I didn't realise the Arabs hated each other so much. You could see it in the Egyptians' eyes, the Algerians' too.'

As kick off approached cities across the world prepared for war. London's Edgware Road, famous for its Arab cafes like Babylon and Rose, had divided itself for the night. Almost every café within a half mile radius was full of Egyptian fans. The Babylon was Algeria's only ally. They didn't need many more than that. When Antar Yahia's first half thunderbolt gave Algeria the lead, and eventually a place in the World Cup finals, the café emptied into the street where the Thin Blue Line of the British police stood, separating the grimfaced Egyptians from the hundreds of celebrating, horn blowing Algerians.

Down Edgware Road they ran, the Egyptians on one side, the Algerians on the other hurling insults at each other. I ran with them, towards Marble Arch and Oxford Street. The noisy mob snaked loudly through British Christmas shoppers, confused by the rattling drums and the Islamic prayers.

'This is a big victory for the Algerian people,' shouted Qassi Ait Touati, a young chef who spoke with a deep French accent. 'After what happened, Egypt deserved to lose.'

In Egypt, the accusations, rumours and conspiracy theories came thick and fast: Sudan had allowed its fans to be attacked; the Algerian government had sent thousands of violent criminals from its jails to teach the Egyptians a lesson; scores of people had died; Mubarak was about to send special forces into the country to protect his citizens. All weren't true. In fact, the Sudanese government summoned the Egyptian ambassador to explain the media coverage back in Egypt. Only five fans were lightly injured, they told the ambassador. Thanks were in order, not accusations. Such was the schism the Arab League even approached Colonel Gaddafi to see whether he would mediate between the countries.

The whole sorry, ugly incident had left its mark and humiliated Egypt further.

The biggest loser, though, seemed to be the Mubarak clan. The ailing dictator had placed the stewardship of events in the hands of his two sons, but it had gone badly wrong. Dictators can never resist the nationalistic catnip of international football for reflected glory, but the danger is in reflected defeat. Both sons were prominent at both matches with Alaa phoning an Egyptian TV show from Sudan to hysterically attack Algeria's 'terrorism' and vowing to avenge the attacks on Egyptian fans in Sudan next time the two teams played.

'These are not fans, these are terrorists,' Alaa Mubarak had whined. 'Thank God we've lost the game. Otherwise, it would have been a massacre.'

The two matches had broken something in Egypt. Something had been stirred. It was the first time I had seen a whole propaganda machine lie so shamefacedly in the face of irrefutable facts. Egypt would later be punished for the attack on the Algerian bus. For all the conspiracy theories, a TV crew from French network Canal Plus had filmed the whole thing. A representative from FIFA was on board too and had watched the incident in horror. Egypt had been humiliated completely. If the Mubaraks had hoped that football could boost their support, defeat diminished their standing further. The brothers didn't look statesmanlike. The looked petty and jingoistic. The match would prove to be the dark before the dawn.

The Pharaohs did exact some revenge. Before the World Cup, Egypt beat Algeria 4-0 in a heated Africa Cup of Nations semi-final. It would lead to their third title in a row, a record in Africa. But when the World Cup came about, it was Algeria in the spotlight, even if they didn't make it past the group stage.

But, back in London in the afterglow of the Sudan play off, retribution and revolution was far from the Algerians' thoughts. One group of fans surrounded a thin, besuited middle aged black man, out shopping on his own. The men joyously started chanted 'Sudan! Sudan! Sudan!' before hoisting him up on their shoulders with a huge smile on his face. They ran down Oxford Street, with him teetering on their shoulders, towards Trafalgar Square where every Algerian had agreed to meet in case of victory.

His name was Dave.

He was from Brixton.

12
PALESTINE:
GAZA

October 2009

The metal walls of the Erez Crossing sizzled under the mid-day sun. Around its heavily guarded entrance stood a group of angry, desperate people, mainly women. Each covered their heads in a shawl. They shouted and swore at the Israeli guards standing between them and the only entrance to the terminal, pointing to imaginary wrist watches. The guards shrugged indifferently back before they turned and slowly marched away, machine guns in hand.

Israel's only crossing into the Gaza Strip was about to close. Once this had been an important entry point between the two, but the stream of visitors and businessmen had been constricted to a tiny trickle in recent years. Since the 2006 kidnapping of Gilad Shalit, a young Israeli soldier seized by the armed wing of Hamas, the Israelis had blockaded the entire Strip. The restrictions had continued, through the civil war that saw Hamas rout Fatah in Gaza and through Operation Cast Lead, the Israeli as-sault on Gaza in 2008 – designed, they said, to stop cross border rocket attacks aimed into Israel – that led to anywhere between 300 and 1000 civilian deaths.

That was ten months ago. Now nothing went in or out of the Strip, except the barest of essentials, NGOs, journalists, the sick and the dead. There was the Rafah crossing bordering Egypt in the south. But Hosni Mubarak's border police seemed gleefully efficient in maintaining a blockade there too. The only way of getting many goods in to Gaza – from generators to luxury cars – was through Rafah's network of illegal tunnels, piece by piece.

But, today, for some reason, the Erez crossing had yet to be opened. Something had happened. I was headed for Gaza City where, the next day, the biggest football match of the year was taking place, the Gaza Cup Final between Al Shate, a team from its largest refugee camp, the Beach Camp, and the Al Salah Islamic Organisation.

The internecine warfare between Hamas and Fatah had ended. Hamas had won and some stability had returned. Yet football was now in chaos with no league and just a short cup competition for sustenance. This was, I would later discover, as much to do with the Palestinian civil war as the Israeli blockade. With the Jewish holy day fast approaching, the border would be closed for two days. Once in, you would be stuck in Gaza until the border opened again.

Just as the impatient had begun to drift impotently away, the guards ushered the crowd forward. Whatever had gone wrong had been resolved. We walked into the gleaming metal edifice. Entering the Erez crossing was like walking in to a hellish, disembodied theme park ride. It stank of efficiency. The crossing is a series of chambers, each with automatic metal sliding doors that hissed opened and closed behind you. In one room a metal table was all that greeted you. A voice from above delivered instructions to empty your bag for inspection by an unseen eye. More chambers followed. More disembodied voices. More metal. Until the final door lifted.

The floor was covered with dozens of spent bullet casings, spread like shattered teeth. There was no voice. No instruction. No explanation. Just a silent, metal room, the smell of cordite and the evidence that something very bad had just happened. I crouched down, picked up a single bullet and walked out into the sun light.

On the other side two dead bodies lay on gurnys, with ambulances parked nearby. Judging by the shapes of the body bags they looked like adults, but I couldn't be sure. 'They are going home, to Gaza,' said a dark skinned porter in a baseball cap as he tried and failed to usher my bags on to his trolley. As if there wasn't enough death in Gaza, it had to be imported too. It was a 1 kilometre walk through no-mans' land before you reached the Gaza checkpoint. Men with beards and black uniforms stood outside a portacabin to check everyone's credentials, as if they believed they were truly the masters of their land. Behind them hung a sign. Alcohol would not be tolerated. Instead it gleefully informed visitors that any bottles would be opened and 'Poured down in the drain in front of the owner'.

Gaza was now firmly in the control of Hamas. The civil war between the secular nationalist Fatah of Yasser Arafat and the Islamic fundamentalist Hamas in 2007 had created a violent vacuum of kidnappings and tit-for-tat killings. The conflict had broken out when I was with the Palestinian national team at a tournament in Jordan. As the team travelled to Amman to take place in the West Asian Championships, Hamas forces had seized control of the Gaza Strip, trapping the entire squad in Jordan as the Israelis denied entrance to the team back into the West Bank. It was worrying enough for the players based in the West Bank. But for the 13 players that lived and worked in Gaza, it was a disaster.

I had come to Gaza for the cup final but also to see the spiritual home of Palestinian football. Every fan and official conceded that Palestine's best players came from Gaza. But for the past few years, football had slowly been dying there. The blockade and the internal fights had brought Gazan society to the brink of collapse. Gaza City was a hopeless place. Bullet holes, piles of rubble – once former housing blocks – and broken buildings sat untouched from the bombing that destroyed them months previously. The import of cement was banned by the Israelis in case it was used for military purposes. The black uniforms of Hamas now kept order on the streets, pacing in front of large, colourful murals of Palestinian martyrs. Huge piles of rubbish burned permanently, throwing up acrid plumes of thick black smoke. Manic children danced around them, throwing glass bottles at passers by. One whistled inches past my head.

Gaza's football league had managed to survive even the darkest of days of the conflict, but it couldn't survive Hamas. When they took over Gaza they cancelled it. It wasn't just the political and economic apparatus they seized: they had also forcibly taken over Gaza's top football clubs, angering the Fatah-dominated Palestinian Football Association [PFA] based in the West Bank, leaving the fans, players and senior politicians angry. Now all that was left was a hastily arranged cup, branded as a so-called 'Dialogue and Tolerance' cup, organised by the clubs themselves, and resentment at the politicians that had tried to control the sport for their own ends.

Ibraheem Abu Saleem, vice president of the PFA and the man in charge of football in Gaza, made some last minute phone calls from the PFA's office on the morning of the cup final. These days they shared space with the Palestinian Olympic Committee, not out of choice, but because the head quarters of both organisations were levelled when Israel bombarded Gaza the previous winter. Now, though, the biggest threat to the game didn't come from Israel. 'We as sports people want to remove sport from politics but politicians on both sides – Hamas and Fatah – play on this, they try to make politics come into sport,' explained Abu Saleem. 'The main problem lies with Hamas. When Hamas hands back the clubs to their legal board of directors, sport will be running again in Gaza as in the West Bank.'

More precisely, it was the military wing of Hamas that had refused to hand back the clubs to their rightful owners. 'The political wing wants this to return the clubs to their legal owners,' Abu Saleem explained. 'But they [Hamas' military wing] want to be within the Fatah clubs, to have control and channel the minds, the thinking, of the youth.'

The chaos reminded me of my visit to the West Bank a few years earlier. Back then movement restrictions, checkpoints and a lack of political goodwill meant that no league could take place. But that had all changed when a new Palestinian Football Association president was elected. Jibril Rajoub was not a man to be messed with. He was a former National Security Advisor to Yasser Arafat – once known as the the hard man of the West Bank – who had spent 18 years in and out of Israeli jails for throwing a grenade at an army checkpoint before being exiled to Lebanon. He spoke fluent Hebrew and English and had also just been elected to the Fatah Central Committee, making him one of the most respected political figures in the West Bank. He was known for his fearsome ability to bash heads together to reach agreement and had achieved some stunning results. He had managed to persuade the Israelis to allow the building of new national stadium in Al Ram on the outskirts of Ramallah right next to the Israeli separation barrier. The easing of Israeli checkpoints had allowed a new professional league to be started.

A women's league was started too, giving Honey, the captain of the women's national team I had met in Bethlehem, the chance to finally play on a full sized pitch against other international players. Football was thriving in the West Bank. So much so that Palestine played its first ever home match, a friendly against Jordan, almost exactly a year previously, just before the Palestinian civil war had broken out. As many as 15,000 fans turned up to watch their team draw 1-1 with Jordan in a hugely symbolic match. Hopes were high that it would usher in, if not a new era of Palestinian football, then at least a normalisation of a game scarred by political infighting, Israeli movement restrictions and poor results.

But in Gaza the civil conflict between Hamas and Fatah, and the subsequent Israeli war, had shattered all that.

'The women footballers,' said Abu Saleem as he signed a pile of documents, 'They now can only play football in their bedrooms.'

The crisis had hit the players hardest. Sitting in Abu Saleem's office was Hamada Shbair, Al Shate's captain. Tanned with his hair cropped close to his skull, Shbair had played in the 2007 West Asian Championship, which marked the beginning of the end – at least for now – of a united national team. For months now no players based in the strip have been allowed to leave. A lucky few, around 50, had been poached by the West Bank league. But Hamada had remained, angry that his career had been put on hold due to internal and external conflict. 'As a national team player I've had big difficulties in playing because of the siege,' he explained. The last time he was allowed to leave was for a tournament more than a year ago. 'I can't play outside, to be the member of another team. I was offered chances in Jordan and Egypt, but I'm still here.'

Some were even unluckier. When Mahmoud Sarsak packed his bags and travelled to the Erez Crossing, he believed that he was leaving to fulfil his potential and play for one of the West Bank Pro League's newly minted teams. Instead he was arrested by the Israelis, who believed he had taken part in a recent bombing. He was never charged with a crime, but was put into administrative detention – essentially being held without charge for an indefinite period. For three years he maintained his innocence whilst the PFA suggested that his arrest might come from the fact that Sarsak's brother had allegedly been a member of Islamic Jihad. He wasn't freed until 2012 when he decided to go on hunger strike. His act of self destruction brought his cause to global attention. FIFA president Sepp Blatter – the man behind granting Palestine FIFA membership – personally called for his release. The pressure worked. Sarsak returned home to Gaza having lost half his body weight. He would never play professional football again.

But the Palestinians were just as adept at fighting amongst themselves. Now the money from Ramallah had stopped. 'There's a lack of funding for the PFA to launch competitions and so we can support ourselves,' Shbair said, articulating the player's concerns that funding has been cut because of fears that any cash would end up in Hamas's hands. 'Jibril Rajoub is the President, we appeal to him to support soccer in Gaza like he does in the West Bank. Political conflicts are the reason for this. I blame both sides [Fatah and Hamas]. They both have demands that harm the players.'

Ribhi Sammour scrawled his instructions in exaggerated flourishes on the faded green chalkboard that hung from the wall of the Palestine Stadium's decrepit dressing room. The coach of Al Shate Sporting Club had gathered his players, all sitting in nervous silence, for one last briefing before the biggest match of the season would decide who would be Gaza's undisputed champion. They had good reason to be nervous and for Sammour to be especially exacting about his tactics for the big match. For one, their opponents, Al Salah Islamic Organisation, a new team aligned with Hamas, were an almost unknown quantity and the match was to be watched, if rumours were to be believed, by Hamas Prime Minister, and one of Israel's most hated men, Ismail Haniyeh. Equally as important was the weight of expectation. Al Shate, a mixed team of Fatah and Hamas members that hailed from the 80,000 strong Al Shate refugee camp, known as the 'beach camp', and Gaza's oldest and most popular team. They had not won any silverware in almost a quarter of a century. But the most recent impediment to breaking their poor run wasn't the lack of talent or even motivation. There simply hadn't been any other teams to play against.

'We have no championship and we haven't won any trophies since 1983,' Sammour explained after he had directed his players on to the pitch. 'Hamas and the Fatah government in Ramallah do not give us the chance to play, so the 16 teams got together and we were given some money by the UNDP [United Nations Development Programme] instead.' Sammour strode out into the warm autumn afternoon to a deafening crescendo of cheers and drums. With little to do and even less to get excited about in Gaza, 5,000 hyperactive fans had made the journey to the stadium in Gaza City, the blue and yellow of Al Shate dominating the terraces. In front of them stood camouflaged members of Hamas' security forces armed with machine guns, ready for any crowd disturbance. In the spaces under the concrete stands, dozens of fans laid out their football jerseys and prayed as the referee blew his whistle.

The final was anything but an exhibition in dialogue and tolerance. As Hamas' forces prowled the touchline, fierce challenges flew as both sides desperately sought a breakthrough. The only time any unity was displayed was during half time, when the press, Hamas security forces, players and officials lined up, fifty strong, to pray together on the pitch. They prayed in front of whatever they had in their hands at the time: a camera, a pair of boots, goalkeeper gloves, a club, a machine gun. By the time Al Shate scored in the 90th minute, the entire bench was on the pitch celebrating their unassailable lead. The referee had a brief stab at enforcing injury time before giving up, awarding a 2-0 victory to Al Shate and trudging back to his changing room, his authority neutered.

Now all eyes were on the small selection of dignitaries in the stand. The increasingly fraught armed guards gave a hint that someone important had arrived. Ismail Haniyeh took to the pitch in a camel coloured jacket, flashing a wide smile before he climbed the hastily constructed podium that had, moments earlier, been dragged onto the pitch. Haniyeh himself had been a tough tackling defender for Al Shate, where he grew up a few metres from the football club. He had been surrounded by machine gun-wielding special forces in black flack jackets, eyeing the crowd with suspicion. Hamada Shbair took the trophy offered by Haniyeh. The two spoke, Shbair animated, as if pressing home an important point.

Haniyeh's appearance was fleeting. Al Shate's fans, still in the stadium to witness their rare piece of silverware, had begun to let off fireworks. The Prime Minister's stern faced personal security men, sensed danger. After all, the Hamas politician had been targeted for assassination by Israel and, he claimed, Fatah in the past. Taking no risks, his security detail closed around him, forming a human battering ram that charged through the crowd. Haniyeh was bundled, still waving, into the back of a waiting parked limousine, past the lines of celebrating fans, seconds after he had handed out the last medal. The car screeched off into the distance.

It was the last time Hamada saw the cup he had just won. It would later emerge, outside the ground, in the hands of a yellow and blue mob, who proudly chanted as the cup was held at the apex of a tenuous human pyramid. Thousands of fans rolled down the dusty path towards the Mediterranean in the glow of the setting sun, before they, and their cup, disappeared, into Al Shate camp. Hamada didn't mind too much.

'There is not a lot to be happy about here,' he shrugged. 'The Beach Camp is very crowded, maybe 80,000 refugees. The Al Shate team wanted to make the people happy after the war and the martyrs and the siege, and we managed that.'

Later that night Shbair would sit in his home in the Beach Camp receiving wellwishers before a party was held in Martyrs' Square. But there was one thing that puzzled me. What did he say to Ismail Haniyeh as he was handed the cup?

'I told him: 'You used to be a player, please solve this problem of the players quickly,' Hamada retold with a wry smile.

And what did he say? I asked.

'He replied: 'I hope so, I hope so, *Inshallah*'.'

March 2011

The Palestinian national team trained in the cold, freezing light as a gaggle of young boys were being admonished on the touchline. 'Everyone is watching you, your mother, your father, everyone,' shouted a rotund, Singaporean match official, to a dozen or so teenagers dressed like West Coast skateboarders.

'Don't play with the ball!' he shouted in English.

'Don't slouch!'

'Don't look unhappy!'

An interpreter rattled the rules back in Arabic to the ball boys, unhappy and slouching, their hoods pulled tight against the chill.

The Palestinians were preparing for their first ever competitive match on home soil, an opening qualification match for the 2012 London Olympic games against Thailand. The basics needed to be prepared. For one the ball boys were being instructed how best to discharge their duties. It was unsportsmanlike, the Singaporean official explained, to not throw the ball back to opposition players during the match. Next to them another official taught a group of school children how to unfold and carry the flags of Palestine, Thailand and the Asian Football Confederation the right way up.

It had been just over a year since I left Gaza. The situation there was still dire, but in the West Bank Jibril Rajoub's football revolution continued. The President of the PFA's private office was a large villa in a quiet suburb of Ramallah, the colour of Jerusalem's famous sandstone. He sat behind his desk stymied by an ugly cold, occasionally coughing roughly into a well used handkerchief.

'Getting the league started here was not easy but we have 15 to 20,000 coming now to games from the north, the south, from areas that are difficult to travel from,' he explained proudly.

Rajoub looked fearsome, a huge bear of a man with a bald head and the gruff gait of a prize fighter. The blame for the failure of Gazan football to progress, Rajoub insisted, lay with Hamas.

'In the West Bank we have two members of Hamas on the board. We have teams for Hamas, the PFLP [Popular Front for the Liberation of Palestine],' he explained. 'There is a wall here between politics and factionalism in sport [in the West Bank]. I think the same should happen in Gaza.'

The comparison between Ramallah and Gaza City was stark. The former had an abundance of three things: bullet holes, burning rubbish and claustrophobic, manic children scarred by the horrors of war. Everything that lined a Gazan shopkeeper's sparse shelves, along with the cars and motorbikes that bumped along its unpaved and pockmarked streets, had to be smuggled in through the Hamas-controlled tunnels that stretched into Egypt. By comparison, Ramallah looked like Las Vegas. Brand new, alien-looking shopping malls announced their arrival like visitors from the future. Basic foodstuffs in Gaza were scarce; in Ramallah a sign stretched across one road proclaiming that the new Nintendo Wii was back in stock after selling out, yours for just 1,690 shekels.

But this was Palestinian football's biggest game so far, a chance to show the world that it could organise itself to an international standard. Yet some problems endured. Four Gazan players were granted permission to play in the Thailand game, but eight were refused, half of the starting line up according to Palestine's Tunisian coach Mokhtar Tilili who was himself denied entry to the West Bank until the night before the match. Even AFC President Mohamed bin Hammam was held at the Jordanian border.

Rajoub's success had brought him popularity. He was an enigma, a member of Fatah's inner circle and seen by some as a future Palestinian president. And yet his brother was one of the top ministers in Hamas, dealing with religious affairs no less. He was Yasser Arafat's National Security Advisor in the West Bank, known as an enforcer and loathed by Hamas and Islamic Jihad for targeting its members. But he was also known as a moderate, backing a two-state solution. At the age of 17 he went to jail for throwing a grenade at an Israeli soldier. He wasn't released until he was 34, but by the time he came out, he was a very different man. He learned Hebrew, translating some of the works of key Israeli Zionist thinkers into Arabic so that the Palestinians would 'know their enemy' better, as one PFA official put it. During the second intifada he was injured when his home was attacked by the Israeli Defence Force. Yet he now espoused the virtues of non-violent action.

'I think this is a rational decision by the Palestinian political leadership to focus on football,' he said.

'We need to expose the Palestinian cause through football and the values and ethics of the game. I do believe this is the right way to make business and pave the way for statehood for the people. The non-violent struggle is more productive and fruitful to the Palestinian cause. In the current situation in the 21st century, this is the best means... to achieve our national aspirations.'

Football was the medium Jibril now fought through. In fact, such had been his success in furthering the Palestinian cause through sport – he was also the head of the Palestinian Olympic Committee – that, as one unnamed PFA insider put it, 'he is popular and, more importantly, he is not corrupt. He will be the next President [of Palestine]'. Whilst Rajoub himself claimed to have no political ambitions, he left the door open, as any good politician would.

'My ambition is that sport has a national Palestinian identity. I have no personal ambition,' he replied when asked about any future political role. 'For me the [political] position is an option, rather than an obsession. I was popular, I am popular, and I will remain popular as long as I contribute to my people's cause.'

'I was part of the freedom fighters, I spent 17 years in Israeli jails, I suffered a lot...I contributed to my people's cause, I want my cause to achieve something. This is the ambition of a person like me.'

Many within the Palestinian government believed that football not only provided a symbol of nascent nationalism, but was also part of Prime Minister Salam Fayyad's attempts to normalise the economic and civil institutions of the state so that, if the need arose, Palestine could announce unilateral independence.

'People know Palestine throughout the world because of the national football team,' said Palestinian defender Nadim Barghouti who, like the PFA, hailed from Ramallah.

'It is a perfect way to prove to the rest of the world that we are human beings. We are not terrorists. In the past, all the world thought that Palestinians threw stones. I consider the players to be soldiers without weapons. We are playing for freedom in Palestine. '

✦

The big day had arrived. The bus from Ramallah hugged the silver, graffiti-scarred separation barrier as it approached the Faisal al Husseini stadium. The wall was a mere 100 metres from the pitch, the stadium barely 4km from Jerusalem's old city. Thousands crushed inside three hours before kick off, the sky dark and ominous from the earlier rains, coating the fans, the seats and the stands in a thick but lightly coloured mud. The police wore modern riot gear pedantically removing poles from the supporter's Palestinian flags, confiscating fizzy drinks and checking for weapons, to prove that the Palestinians could organise a match to the newly required standard expected of competitive international football. But the numbers were too great; hundreds surged through the single metal door and into the stands, causing a crush. Fans scrambled up the sheer concrete walls, pulled up by other fans, to escape the dangerous ebb and flow of bodies until the police regained control.

Around the stadium, posters illustrated the importance that the Palestinian Authorities placed on football; huge portraits of Yasser Arafat, the Dome of the Rock, President Mahmoud Abbas, Jibril Rajoub and FIFA President Sepp Blatter all sat side by side. A hastily erected poster of AFC chief Mohamed Bin Hammam, also here to witness history, hung from a nearby building.

'When this team plays, the people of Palestine are free, and these people [in the stands] are too,' shouted Motaz Abutayoon, a 21-year-old engineering student from the Askar refugee camp near Nablus. Around him fans chanted: 'Jerusalem, for the Arabs!'

'The Israelis are not here. I am very, very happy,' he added.

The ball boys successfully carried their flags on to the field, the national anthems passed without incident, and the politicians basked in the glow of international media attention. But it took 45 minutes for the stadium to come to life when Abdul Hamid Abu Habib, a player from Gaza, volleyed in Palestine's first goal. The stands erupted in song, chants, tabla drums and whistles. The captain took off his armband, kissed it and pointed towards the Prime Minister Salam Fayyad, sitting in the crowd.

'The national team is very important. It is an important symbol. The national football team is a symbol of this country. It has that kind of significance, for sure. That [a player from Gaza scored] makes it all the more sweet,' Fayyad said whilst sheltering from the driving rain at half-time. But he urged a word of warning. 'We have the second half now. If the score stays as it is, we have an extra half hour of football.'

It proved prophetic. Chances came and went until the final whistle blew at

1-0.; 1-1 on aggregate over two legs. Salam Fayyad, with his white and black keffiyeh wrapped around his neck, paced through the stand, watching every minute of extra time unfold.

'I hate penalties,' he offered, rocking back on his heals with hands in pockets for protection against the freezing cold early evening. 'I won't watch penalties. I'll look this way!'

He pointed to the sky.

The collective weight of expectation rested on the lonely shoulders of a man called Zidan. A storm had now enveloped the stadium as freezing sheets of hail hammered down on to the pitch, and into the face, of the white-shirted midfielder. A whole people, if not yet a whole nation, held its breath.

Amjad Zidan stood twelve yards from goal facing the crucial penalty that would either continue Palestine's Olympic dream, or likely condemn them to familiar disappointment. As Salam Fayyad had feared the match had gone to penalties. Everyone had scored. It was 5-5. Now it was sudden death.

The crowd of young men behind the goal, the players in the centre circle, even Salam Fayyad froze as they prepared for the ball to bulge in the back of the net. Zidan stood nervously in front of the Thai goalkeeper, awaiting his cue, the hail seemingly falling harder as the referee blew his whistle.

But Salam Fayyad did watch; as we all did. For Zidan – not to mention the crowd and the world's press – there would be no fairytale ending. The whistle blew, and the spot kick was saved. Half the crowd was gone before Thailand's Seeket Madputeh sealed Palestine's fate. The players, shattered from bombarding the Thailand goal, missing chance after chance even after the away team was reduced to ten men, left the field with heads bowed. It was too much for Nadim Barghouthi, the 'soldier without a weapon', who ran down the tunnel with tears streaming down his face, inconsolable.

It was a common narrative for the Palestinians; small, rare victories tempered by the reality of failure. Of one step forward, two steps back. Certainly Palestine's Tunisian coach Mokhtar Tilili didn't find comfort in the moral victory.

'This leaves a bitter taste in the mouth,' he said in the tunnel as the press and fans melted away, back to the buses ferrying people to Nablus, Jericho and Jenin.

'We played well. But my heart aches tonight...It was a political victory, but I wanted it to be a sporting victory as well.'

13
BAHRAIN

October 2009

Milan Macala was a man with a very obvious dislike of the press. The 66-year-old coach of the Bahrain national team had – like any coach who had weighed the cash benefit of working in the region against the insane pressure that followed – good reason to be suspicious of the circus that had just enveloped him and his team. The Czech had spent the past 15 years hopping from one managerial job to the next in the Gulf, hounded by the Middle East's sclerotic, demanding football scribes whilst both being adored and pilloried by the all powerful royal families that controlled every aspect of the game in the region. He had largely succeeded wherever he went, winning two Gulf Cups with Kuwait, for example. But sometimes he was not, brutally fired by the Saudis after his first match, a 4-1 defeat to eventual winners Japan, at the 2000 Asia Cup in Lebanon, a common demise for most coaches of the Green Falcons. After all, since his sacking 13 years ago 13 more have followed. Now he was on the verge of arguably one of the greatest achievements in international football. But the veil of secrecy and suspicion remained.

'I will speak to you for five minutes, but that's it,' he barked down the phone. Macala was busy preparing for the biggest game in Bahrain's history: a first leg intercontinental play-off against New Zealand in the Bahraini capital of Manama for a place at the 2010 World Cup finals. 'The training session will be closed,' he added, 'so you won't be allowed in or to speak to the players, ok?' Somewhere in Bahrain he slammed down the phone.

This was a problem. I had travelled to Bahrain in the hope of seeing one of the unlikeliest qualifications in World Cup history. By all measures Bahrain shouldn't have been anywhere near South Africa. The tiny Gulf kingdom was one of the smallest countries on earth, a tiny island next to Qatar and Saudi Arabia that nonetheless had such geopolitical significance that the US military had stationed its Fifth Fleet there. It had a population under a million where the local football league was semi-professional at best. Unlike its Gulf neighbours, Bahrain was poor but more democratic. The kingdom was still ruled by a powerful monarch, Hamid bin Isa al Khalifah, who picked the prime minister, but there was a parliament that gave voice to Bahrain's unusual sectarian mix. Unlike the rest of the Arabian side of the Gulf, the majority of Bahrain's population was Shia – Iran even declared it part of its territory in the 1950s – but its royal family followed Sunni Islam. During the 1990s there was an uprising in Bahrain by the Shia majority against the Sunni elite. There were allegations of torture by the security forces, then led by a former British police officer called Ian Henderson, dubbed the 'Butcher of Bahrain' by one 2002 British documentary. When the current king came to the throne it was seen as clear step towards reform and reconciliation between the two communities. Bahrain, a place where one Lebanese journalist had told me had endured unreported bombings almost every night in the restless Shia villages outside the capital, was now quieter and more peaceful.

The small numbers of citizens and the deep sectarian divisions had not impacted on the national team, which had become one of the strongest in the region. In 2004 they reached only their second Asian Cup finals and shocked the continent when they reached the semi-finals. Two brothers in that team accounted for over half of Bahrain's goals: Mohamed and A'ala Hubail. A'ala had finished joint scorer in the tournament alongside Iranian midfielder Ali Karimi. He scored twice in Bahrain's quarter final victory over Uzbekistan, as well as the winning kick in their victorious penalty shoot out.

That was just the start. Both the Hubail brothers starred as Bahrain tried to reach the 2006 World Cup finals. A'ala scored six times, the second highest in Asian qualification, setting up a play-off match, again against Uzbekistan. After a bizarre scandal the first match between the two in September 2005, which the Uzbeks won 1-0, was annulled after FIFA judged that the Japanese referee had made a technical error. He had awarded Uzbekistan a penalty but, after spotting an Uzbek player encroaching in the box, blew for an indirect free kick to Bahrain. FIFA said he should have ordered the penalty be retaken. The Uzbeks were incensed, especially as they won the game and should have had a retaken penalty anyway. Bahrain went on to draw the replay 1-1 in Tashkent before holding the Uzbeks 0-0 in Manama, going through to the final intercontinental play off against Trinidad and Tobago on away goals. If Bahrain had won that tie against Trinidad and Tobago, they would have been the smallest country every to qualify for the finals. They almost made it too. After grabbing an away goal in the first leg in the Caribbean, hopes were high for the return leg in Manama. Both the Hubail brothers had started that match. They held out until the 49th minute when Dennis Lawrence scored for Trinidad. It was they, and not Bahrain, that became the smallest ever nation to qualify for the finals.

Their journey towards the 2010 World Cup finals was equally as dramatic. A'ala was again joint top scorer in qualification for the Bahrainis as a new star emerged. Sayed Mohamed Adnan was a leggy but cultured central midfielder who could also play at centre back. His performances had caught the eye of European clubs as well as the Asian Football Confederation, who nominated him for their 2009 Player of the Year award. They, along with evergreen winger Salman Isa, helped set up a play-off against their much disliked Saudi neighbours. A historic, sectarian dislike existed between the two, deepened by the regular pilgrimage made by young Saudi men driving over the King Fahd causeway that connects the two every Thursday night to get drunk and start fights. The first leg in September 2009, almost exactly four years after that Japanese refereeing debacle in Tashkent, ended 0-0. As the second leg, played just four days later, entered the 90th minute, the score was 1-1 and Bahrain was going through to the final round on away goals. The board went up showing three minutes as the 50,000 crowd started to get restless. The Saudi's pumped the ball forward. Yasser al Qahtani somehow volleyed a cross over from the right hand by-line. Asian Player of the Year Hamad al Montashari rose to clatter the ball into the top left hand corner. The game was over. The crowd exhaled into a state of what turned out to be premature ecstasy. With ten seconds left of injury time Salman Isa burst forward and won a corner. Isa swung the ball in, a last, desperate, futile attempt. Time seemed to stop as Sayed Mohamed Adnan and Ismail Abdulatif both rose for the ball. It glanced off Abdulatif's head. The ball looped goalwards, as if in slow motion, and nestled into the bottom right hand corner. 2-2. It was one of the most incredible four minutes of World Cup football you could ever hope to see. The whistle blew a few seconds later. Macala, his white hair and rotund frame giving him the air of young Boris Yeltsin, seemed shocked, conflicted even, hugging his players before they collapsed in tears around him. It is on such small margins that heroes are made and broken.

'At 1-1, 90 minutes, the game was over,' Macala said as we met after nightfall outside the offices of the Bahraini Football Association. It was October but a late summer heat wave made the air feel like warm soup. Nearby his team was warming up for training as a dozen frenzied local journalists buzzed around, taking advantage to speak to the players as Macala was looking the other way. 'I nearly had a heart attack,' he said. 'It was 30 seconds in to injury time. But then we scored again. What can I say? It was luck!' Luck only gets a team so far. Unlike the UAE and Qatar – two Gulf countries now leveraging their wealth to change the shape of global sport – football in Bahrain was a street game. Rusty goalposts jutted out of almost every spare patch of sand in the capital, where young children play until dusk. 'I don't know how to explain it, you compare the leagues to Bahrain to Kuwait and Qatar, they have much more money and better quality pitches,' explained Macala, now much more amenable than he was on the phone. 'But spirit and desire is much more important. We have had many, many positive moments to help us dream the dream. They have talent and they have speed and flexibility. They [Bahrainis] are playing football every day, everywhere. It's a small place but they play football, it is in their nature. But now they need organisation to prepare, and to have a strong league.'

Much of the team had now moved to the better paid professional leagues in places like nearby Qatar. There was also Jaycee John, a naturalized Nigerian who played in Belgium. But the key dynamic was one of faith. Macala believed that a mixed team of Sunni and Shia players sent an important message to the rest of the country that was still coming to terms with life after its uprising.

'It [qualification] is very important to them because this is a great moment for the country, because of football,' he said 'Everybody on the street is talking about the Bahrain national team. The team is a representative of the country as a whole. This island is small, only 700,000 people [nationals], and everybody loves football.'

The match was also viewed by many in Bahrain as a last chance. The heartbreak against Trinidad and Tobago four years previously had left a mark. 'After what happened four years ago we are desperate,' said Sheikh Ali bin Khalifa al Khalifa. Sheikh Khalifa was the excessively genial vice president of the Bahraini FA and a member of the royal family. He incessantly asked whether I'd like a cup of tea as we talked. 'Every Bahraini is desperate to go to the World Cup for the first time. It's a dream for every Bahraini…we have been through hell.'

Macala had seen enough of football in the region to know that chances like these rarely come along once for a country the size of Bahrain, let alone twice. 'This is the moment for our players,' he said before heading back to the pitch and ushering the local press off the pitch as if swatting away a swarm of flies. '50 per cent of this team played in the game with Trinidad and Tobago. Everyone was crying… we need luck.'

The large doors, covered in green tarpaulin were shut and the press pack thrown outside.

By 3pm on the day of the match, the flags that adorned the walls and fences of Bahrain's National Stadium, in Riffa outside Manama, had already been meticulously hung. Usually the groundsmen on flag duty busied themselves in silence in front of empty stands but not this time. With three and a half hours before kick-off thousands had already arrived in their seats in anticipation of Bahrain's first leg World Cup play off against New Zealand, creating an incessant, deafening din that didn't stop until the final whistle. The red and white of the Bahrain flag didn't flutter alone. Portraits of King Hamid had been tied to the hoardings. Flags from Sudan, Palestine, Kuwait and Saudi Arabia, among others, flew in solidarity. The message of Arab fraternity was clear. If Bahrain were to be the region's sole representative at the 2010 World Cup finals, than the Middle East would rally behind it.

'They play good football and Bahrain is like a second country to us,' said 24-year-old Abdulatif Hamed, a Kuwaiti who had flown to the game with a gang of friends. 'The whole of the Arab world will be behind Bahrain, inshallah.'

By kick off the stadium had far exceeded its 25,000 limit as hundreds of fans filled each spare walkway in the main stand. The conditions were so humid you could almost see the air. But the atmosphere was perfect for Bahrain. A few hours previously the New Zealand team appeared so hot they struggled to get off the team bus and walk the few meters to the stadium. But the All Whites were made of sterner stuff. Sayed Mohammed Adnan controlled the game but Bahrain just couldn't score. The pivotal moment came when Salman Isa was put through on goal and, after rounding the keeper, contrived to smash the ball against the post with the goal at his mercy. It finished 0-0. At the full time whistle the Bahraini players left the pitch grime faced, knowing a wonderful opportunity had been lost. Isa lay shattered and motionless by the bench, his blank, thousand yard stare a depressing moment of calm amongst Kiwi celebration. For the All Whites it tasted like victory. The players ran to their jubilant section in the corner of the stadium, just 1,000 supporters strong, to link arms and acknowledge what must count as the longest away trip in the history of international football.

'Any team that has beaten Saudi Arabia back to back will be tough. Australia found it hard too,' said Kiwi coach Ricki Herbert, a veteran of the All Whites team that had qualified for their only other appearance at the World Cup in 1982, as his staff celebrated pitch side. 'We wanted to take the tie back home to have a chance and we did that.' He was less circumspect when he thought he was out of earshot. 'We've done it!' he shouted whilst bear hugging members of the New Zealand delegation. 'We're going all the way now. We've fucking done it!'

Outside the ground the crowd trickled home, muted but unbowed, dragging their multinational flags behind them in the sand. '0-0 is not a bad score and it's not a good score but there is a saying in Bahrain that we play better outside of Bahrain than in it,' shrugged Mohammed Alwadhi, a 17-year-old student making the long trek back to Manama. 'We just couldn't find the goal. Even if we put a goal above the goal we wouldn't have found it.'

Ricki Herbert's confidence wasn't misplaced. Back in Wellington New Zealand took a first half lead before conceding a second half penalty. It was Sayed Mohamed Adnan, the beating heart of Bahrain's qualification campaign, that stepped forward to take it. He hit it low to the goalkeeper's right, but it was too weak and too close to Mark Paston who saved it. Adnan still had his hands on his head in disbelief a few minutes later. New Zealand won 1-0 and would go on to draw all three of their group games in South Africa. They were the only team in the tournament to go unbeaten. It is on such small margins that heroes are made and broken.

The Bahrainis knew they wouldn't have another chance like this, especially A'ala Hubail, the team's top scorer for the past six years. He wasn't in Wellington. The striker had snapped a cruciate ligament in his knee playing for Al Ahli in the Bahraini league a few days before the tie. He would be out for six months. But he sent a message to his team mates before they embarked on their long and ultimately fruitless flight down under. 'We don't know what will happen in the next four or five years, and it is difficult to know who will still be playing with the national team at that time,' Hubail had told the *Gulf Daily News* of his fear that, after coming within one match, and one goal, on two occasions, he would never play in a World Cup finals. 'I think this will be the last chance for at least four of our national team players, and I hope they can grab this opportunity for all of us ... the national team is more than just one player. If I am out, there will be someone there who can play for me.'

His words were both prophetic and cruel.

February 2011

The Arab Spring came to Bahrain on Valentines Day. Protests had spread across the the Arab world, breaking out from barren landscapes where no dissent had existed before. Bahrain was different. Antagonism had simmered for decades, between the Shia majority who believed that the Sunni minority used royal patronage to subjugate them politically and economically. The reform process had stalled. The King still reserved the right to pick Bahrain's prime minister, a key demand of the opposition. Although King Hamid had never needed to pick a new prime minister, Bahrain had only ever had one. Khalifa bin Salman al Khalifa had been in place since the country's independence in 1971. He was the longest serving prime minister in the world.

Memories were also still fresh of the last uprising that had ended just 15 years previously. But the discontent had burst forth in a much different world. The Sunni's had always believed that Bahrain's Shia political leadership were mere puppets controlled by Tehran. It was a familiar refrain for the Shia everywhere in the Middle East, be they in Lebanon, Iraq, Saudi Arabia or Bahrain; that their allegiance was to their spiritual leader in Iran and not the country they called home. For those on the street on Valentine's Day at the Pearl Roundabout, the issue of Iran was a smoke screen. They wanted greater democracy, not an Iranian style theocracy. They wanted more accountability, not an infallible ayatollah. They wanted jobs and a future that was based on meritocracy, not patronage.

The crowds that gathered were from all areas of Bahrain too, Shia and Sunni. And amongst the crowd were dozens of sporting heroes, wrestlers, hand ball players, and most significantly of all, several national football team players. It had been just over a year since Sayed Mohamed Adnan, A'ala and Mohamed Hubail had watched their World Cup dream die in Wellington. A'ala and Mohamed now played on the same team, Al Ahli Manama, whilst Adnan had stayed in Qatar playing for Al Khor. But when the protests came they decided it was their duty to take to the streets too. According to an interview A'ala gave to the Associated Press he'd only agreed to go on the march after hearing that the royal family had sanctioned, even encouraged, peaceful protest. It was the biggest mistake of his and his teammates lives.

The Pearl Roundabout protest was crushed. Activists claim four people were killed when the military rolled their tanks in to clear the makeshift camp that had been erected. Eventually they destroyed the monument at its centre too, in case it became a symbol, a rallying point, for protest. A Pakistani migrant worker in his forties was killed when one of the arches collapsed on to the cab of his crane as he demolished it. The King Fahd causeway, once the conduit for a thousand young Saudi men to travel to Manama every weekend to raise a little hell, now rumbled with a new convoy: a GCC force from Saudi, Qatar, the UAE and beyond to help the Bahrainis mop up what ever opposition was left.

The players survived. But they were marked men. The three, as well as Bahrain's goalkeeper, had been spotted at the protests. Those that played in Bahrain – like the Hubail brothers - were fired from their clubs and effectively banned from the national team. Then they were all arrested, along with two other national team players. Shortly before his imprisonment A'ala was shamed on national TV, the host of one talk show labelling the protesters 'stray hyenas' and subjecting him to a 15 minute grilling about his 'treachery' on state TV. The next day they came for him and his brother.

'We saw some masked men get out of the car. They said: 'Captain A'ala get you brother' and we went with them,' A'ala later explained in an ESPN documentary. 'They put me in the room for the beatings. One of the people who hit me said I'm going to break your legs. They knew who we were... We were forced to endure it. I had to endure it. If I didn't something worse would have happened to me.'

Yet no one spoke up for the footballers initially; not FIFA, not the AFC and not the US or British government that had supported other such uprisings in Libya or Syria but who considered the Bahrain Royal Family a vital ally against the rise of Iran. It was British and American made tear gas and rubber bullets that silenced the uprising.

'The violence and abuse is so huge. We have too much work. We can't cope here. A lot of doctors, a lot of people have been targeted, soccer players, basketball players, teachers, unionists,' explained Nabeel Rajab, head of the Bahraini Center for Human Rights. He had agreed to speak to me over Skype. He wouldn't speak on mobile phone nor write by email. He was worried that, as the most visible opponent in the foreign media, his communications was being tapped. Rajab was himself arrested in the middle of the night on charges he had fabricated a picture showing a dead protester, allegedly killed by the army. He claimed he was tortured, threatened with rape and then released. 'The people who are in charge, they don't care about international image,' he said. 'They are military people. All of the sport associations are headed by the royal family. We have 100 associations headed by the royal family.' But Rajab reserved his harshest criticism for FIFA, 'The silence of FIFA and of the AFC raises a question. Either they [the Bahraini FA] have a green signal or they [FIFA and the AFC] accept such violence against football players. Footballers have rights like any other human to be a citizen. It's time for FIFA to raise their voice. The people of Bahrain are looking at them and asking: 'Where are you?''

The three players were imprisoned for up to three months. After media pressure made ignorance impossible, FIFA belatedly enquired whether their detention broke their rules own rules on political involvement in the game.

'The players have obviously been in custody after their involvement in the demonstrations and acts of violence against governmental officials was proven,' said Sheikh Ali bin Khalifa al Khalifa, the genial vice president of the BFA who had been achingly friendly when I met him in 2009, in a statement when I contacted him. 'The players have been arrested, investigated and detained for having opposed the general laws and by-laws of the country. The fact that they happen to be footballers and national team players is highly irrelevant...If tolerance was shown to those who happen to be athletes, it will result in the disintegrating of the equality under the law spirit, a matter that goes beyond everything our revered government stands for.'

When the players were released their national careers were over. Mohamed Hubail was sentenced to two years in jail, later thrown out on appeal. A'ala fled to Oman where he played in the local league, his family still in Bahrain. Sayed Mohamed Adnan left for Australia and starred for the Brisbane Roar as he powered them on to win the A-League championship. But what had once united a nation had been broken for a generation. The national football team had been shorn of its best players, its legends tainted and abused. Former Leicester coach Peter Taylor, who famously took charge of England for one game and gave David Beckham the captaincy, took charge of Bahrain's attempts to qualify for the 2014 World Cup finals. He had never heard of A'ala Hubail, he said. Nor was he on a list of players handed to him for selection. Now the national team, and its under-23 team trying to qualify for London 2012 was more interested in showing unity for the King. After Bahrain defeated Palestine in one Olympic qualifier the players gathered around to kiss a portrait of King Hamid. Taylor's World Cup campaign was not a success. Bahrain was eliminated in the first group stage. They lost 6-0 to Iran and won just two games, both against the lowest ranked team in the group, Indonesia. The second was an incredible 10-0 victory in the final game of the group. But as Bahrain needed to beat Indonesia 9-0 and hope Qatar lost to Iran, FIFA launched a 'routine' investigation.

The golden era of Bahraini football, an era that saw one of the smallest nations on the planet humble Asia's giants, an era that saw a team which, in Milan Macala's words 'represented the whole country', an era that produced two of the finest Asian players of the last ten years, was over. A'ala Hubail's words in 2009, after a serious injury ruled him out of that second leg inter continental World Cup play off against New Zealand, also returned to haunt him.

'We don't know what will happen in the next four or five years, and it is difficult to know who will still be playing with the national team,' he said. Instead he was left to reflect on his evisceration. As he told ESPN whilst living in exile in Oman : 'I didn't do anything wrong to deserve this humiliation.'

It is on such small margins that heroes are made and broken.

14
SYRIA

March 2008

Colonel Hassan Swaidan wasn't best pleased and wanted to see me straight away. Outside the training complex of the Syrian football team Al Jaish, six armed soldiers had surrounded me, shifting awkwardly from foot to foot. They knew what the rules said, and the rules were the rules. This was the army after all.

'Did you take a picture?' the taller of the six asked, as another went into the guard post to phone his superior.

There was no use lying: I'd been caught red-handed. After being dropped off at the training ground I had walked past the heavily armed entrance to the club, the first time I'd ever seen a football club protected by such a show of brute force. But then Al Jaish wasn't any normal football club; they were one of Syria's most decorated teams. They were also the team of Syria's huge and all-powerful army. Al Jaish literally means 'The Army', and the club had long dominated Syrian football, as the army had dominated Syrian society, winning ten league titles and at the beginning of the twentieth century winning the AFC Cup, a kind of second tier Asian Champions League, making them one of the best teams in Asia at the time.

They weren't run like other clubs either. Al Jaish was run by the Ministry of Defence, with a strict chain of command. A general sat at the top whilst The Colonel took the role of technical director and oversaw the day-to-day running of the team. Every aspect of the team was run like a military operation, even player recruitment. It was a beautiful arrangement. As Syria still enforced national service, every 18-year-old had to complete two years in the military. So as soon as a good player hit 18, Al Jaish would force rival clubs to hand over their star man. It was no wonder they had enjoyed such dominance on the field.

The soldier repeated his question: 'Did you take a picture?'

A few scenarios ran through my mind. I could run and jump into a taxi. But I'd probably be shot dead before I got off the kerb. Or I could lie. I had been desperate to get to Syria ever since one of Yarmouk's players in Yemen had told me about his previous club, Al Jaish, and how it had used its position to recruit conscripts to its cause and sweep all before them in the Syrian league. It seemed to encapsulate something about a heavily militarised country that possessed an army numbering close to half a million, trained for its inevitable next conflict with Israel, a country with which it has already fought various bloody wars in the past 60 years. That fact is drilled into every Syrian's psyche, not by propaganda but by geography. The surprisingly short road from Jordan to Damascus is dominated by the eerie, snow-capped mountains of the Golan Heights, policed by the peak of Jebel Al Sheikh. Israel won the Golan Heights in the 1967 Six Day War and, for Syrians at least, it's a line in the sand for any potential peace deal. You understand why it is so important when you reach the outskirts of Damascus. The city spills out before you whilst the heights mockingly smile down at all those who pass.

It was when I reached the Al Jaish training ground that the real problems started. If they arrested me at the front gate and found out I was a journalist then my trip was over, at least. I could have offered a bribe. But I only had three dollars and a few Syrian pounds in my pocket, about £2 worth. I would have been laughed at all the way to solitary confinement. I came clean.

'Yes, I took a photo.' They had me bang to rights. The soldiers had watched as I approached the entrance to the training ground, stopped to see whether I'd been seen, and taken a photo of a sign that said: 'Military Zone, No Entry, No Cameras.'

'You can't do this!' the young soldier shouted, more out of exasperation and fear than anger. 'The Colonel, if he found out he would . . .'

His voice trailed off as he crossed his wrists in an unambiguous sign that transcended any language barrier. Jail.

'Give me the film,' the shortest soldier, carrying a chipped machine gun, demanded. I considered handing them a roll of unprocessed film, hoping they wouldn't know the difference. Instead, I pathetically blurted out the first thing that had come into my head.

'Please, I was just taking a picture of a kitten.'

'Give me the film,' the soldier repeated, more menacingly than the first time.

Just as I was about to hand over my camera, a breathless young recruit with a sketchy teenage moustache ran into the crowd with new orders. The tallest soldier seemed relieved.

'The Colonel will see you now.'

The gateway cleared and the young recruit led me into the complex, past the stone frieze dedicated to the president, Bashar al Assad; past the huge, Lenin-style bronze bust of his father, the late President Hafez al Assad; through a trophy-room fit for a champion. He marched me up the stairs, along a dark corridor that stank of fresh detergent, the smell you imagine a windowless room deep in the bowels of a football stadium in Pinochet's Chile smelt like minutes after it had been cleansed of a recent and horrific torture. His shoes squeaked as they met the linoleum-covered floors. The walls were plastered with the Syrian flag. We walked past banks of troops as they sat at desks, craning their necks to see who the new arrival was.

This was it. The end.

Deportation at least. If not more. The look of fear in the soldier's eyes at the gate told me The Colonel was not a man to be messed with. The soldier stopped abruptly, pivoted 90 degrees, knocked on a door and walked in. The Colonel was sitting behind a large desk, in a grey lounge suit. The soldier immediately stiffened his back and offered a salute. The Colonel rose and turned towards me. He was short, with white hair and a round cheery face. Out of uniform, he didn't look so intimidating.

'What are you doing here?' he asked in perfect English.

I was an English journalist, writing a book about football in the Middle East, I explained.

'English . . .' he replied, letting the nationality hang in the air for a few seconds. 'Where else have you been?'

'Oh, Lebanon, Egypt, I . . . Iraq,' I had almost said Israel.

'How did you go to Iraq!' he laughed, guessing correctly that I obviously wasn't a man of military bent. 'The Americans and the English have made such a mess with their stupid war!'

He nodded at the soldier to leave, who saluted and spun out of the room.

'Sit,' he ordered. The Colonel squeezed behind his desk.

'You shouldn't have just come here without a letter, without permission. And you cannot take pictures here. This is the army, there is discipline here.' He said the last sentence as if he wanted to smash his fist on the table to emphasise the point, but couldn't quite bring himself to do it.

Behind him a large portrait of President Assad loomed over us. His piercing blue eyes were deliberately hung forward so that it bore down on the viewer. The Colonel smirked and reached under his desk. He pulled out a small wooden box and placed it in front of him. About the same size as a revolver, I thought, as he lifted the lid and stared at its contents before looking up: 'Sweet?'

With the tension broken I brought out my notebook, thinking I had crossed some kind of Rubicon with the man. 'Stop!' he shouted, picking up the phone. 'I have to verify who you are.' It seemed like a good idea to turn on the Dictaphone I still had in my pocket, seeing that I wasn't allowed a written account of proceedings.

The Colonel made a call, and was quickly assured. Content that I wasn't a spy, he called the soldier back into the room. 'I will ask whether you can talk to the players, but there is a procedure, rules to follow' – he was a stickler for the rules. He left the room, leaving me alone with my babysitter.

The Colonel's room was adorned with dozens of pictures of the president. A large squad photo of Bashar with the famous Al Jaish side that won the AFC Cup in 2004 hung behind me. He assumed pride of place in the middle, where the manager should have been sitting.

'President Assad,' I said, pointing to his portrait in a futile attempt to make conversation with the soldier. He placed his right hand over his heart. 'I love him,' he instinctively responded in Arabic. The Colonel returned with a decision. 'The General will see you now.' The General? I was to be shown into the office of a Syrian army general, with a voice recorder still whirling in my pocket. There was no way I could turn it off without The Colonel and the soldier realising my error. Taking photos of a military zone was bad enough, but recording the voice of a bona fide Syrian Army general was bound to be some kind of criminal offence. The General's office was at the end of the corridor. Dressed in a green military uniform, his left breast sagging under the weight of military honours, he sat behind a large, expensive-looking desk as soldiers buzzed around, handing him pieces of paper for his perusal. Each was read and promptly dispatched into the shredder that sat next to him. Even sporting secrets were state secrets. Behind him hung more photos of the president, several of The General shaking hands with the great man himself. He stopped midway through signing a letter when he realised I was in the room. Words weren't necessary. His well-fed jowl, grey side parting and red, important-looking epaulettes smacked of a man who had grown accustomed to privilege. He didn't like surprises any more than The Colonel. He merely went about his business as I sat there, with more soldiers buzzing in with more pieces of paper. They too met with the shredder. Eventually he stood up and walked around to the front of the desk.

'I'm not a big fan of football,' he declared. 'I am more of a track-and-field man. I used to run the marathon.'

And that was it, my cue to leave. A decision had somehow been made. I wouldn't be allowed to visit the training ground or see the players. The day after tomorrow, maybe. If I got the right letter. In Arabic. Then we would see. No promises. Maybe. He shook my hand and I was bundled out. The Colonel walked me back to the offices, arranged for my escort to the front gate and made his own excuses to leave.

'How many generals are there in the Syrian army?' I asked.

'Ahh,' The Colonel winked. 'That is a state secret.'

The soldier saluted, turned on his heel and walked me quickly back down the corridor, back down the stairs and through Al Jaish's trophy room. I stopped briefly to see what they were for. One seemed to be an unmarked plaque adorned with the Olympic rings with a bayonet and a rifle pushed through them. The soldier ushered me forward, out into the spring sunshine and through the front gate. He saluted me before turning and disappearing back into the building. I didn't take out my voice recorder until I was safely in a taxi and well out of shooting range.

Damascus is a city that walks to a military beat. It is often said that the Syrian capital is the world's oldest continuously inhabited city, although pretty much every regional metropolis with a walled old city seems to lay the same claim. What can't be denied is its turbulent and bloody history; of wars, massacres and a merry go round of owners from the Persians to Alexander the Great to the Ottomans, who ruled for 400 years. The forces of Arab nationalism, and the secrecy and authoritarianism that followed its failure, have moulded modern Damascus. Down every Damascene street you'll find soldiers on patrol. Whole districts of the city make their living from clothing the country's new conscripts. An inordinate number of amputees go about their daily business, selling newspapers or cigarettes or pushing a cart full of fruit with their one good arm – testament to Syria's past, unsuccessful, conflicts. You can imagine, however, that Damascus' ancient streets have always been filled with soldiers, its tailors drawing a wage from its warriors, whether sewing camouflage trousers or Roman tunics.

With the army so ubiquitous, it's no surprise that little dissent was tolerated in Syria, either of its political institutions or its armed forces. But then, five years ago, opposition came from an unlikely source: the Syrian Football Association. Al Jaish's player plundering had reached critical level. The league was still amateur, which meant there was no compensation. As it was the military doing the taking, there was no argument. By sucking up the league's talent they won honours and attracted huge crowds, whilst the other clubs had to keep a lid on their simmering discontent. The FA decided that enough was enough. Syrian football was turning professional and if Al Jaish wanted to take any club's players, then they'd have to bloody well pay for them.

'Before, they took all the players,' admitted Taj Addin Fares, vice president of the Syrian Football Association, when I visited its headquarters a short walk down the road from Al Jaish's training ground. 'Any good players, they would just take them and if they played for Al Jaish they played for the national team too.' The military had successfully turned what should have been a partisan league club into a de facto national team, flying the flag for Syria at home and abroad. Not supporting them was akin to treason.

'More than 80 per cent of Damascus used to support the army club,' said Toufik Sarhan, the FA's general secretary who, with his salt-and-pepper hair and thick-rimmed black glasses, looked like a Syrian Michael Caine. 'But now many of the clubs are as good as Al Jaish, if not better, because we made the league professional. Rich men started to support their clubs. Football is much better now.'

Just how much Al Jaish's stranglehold had been broken became clear the next day, Friday, match day. My taxi arrived at Damascus' biggest stadium, the Abbasiyyin. Most Middle Eastern stadiums smell the same, of roasted sunflower seeds, decay and urine. The Abbasiyyin Stadium was no different. Hundreds of troops had been drafted in to police the match even though a paltry 1,000 Al Jaish fans had turned up for the Damascene derby against title chasing Al Majd. Ten years ago all 45,000 seats would have been taken. The Colonel was out on the pitch early, dressed in his neat grey suit whilst keeping half an eye on his team warming up. Anonymous, well-dressed men wearing sunglasses approached to kiss him on both cheeks. The coach was nowhere to be seen. With The Colonel otherwise disposed I had the freedom to roam. In Al Majd's dressing-room the players were raucously preparing to go out on the pitch.

'It always was a big rivalry,' explained Ali Rifai, a Syrian international, as he put his shin pads on. 'I was in the army for two years but the people don't like the army, so they see us or Al Wahda instead.'

In the Al Jaish dressing room, the atmosphere could not have been more different. The room was empty, except for the forlorn figure of Ahmad Rifat, Al Jaish's experienced Egyptian coach who previously had been in charge of the Syrian national team – before a vicious media campaign was launched to have him removed – and Egypt's Zamalek. Rifat had been conspicuously absent from his team's warm-up. After his sacking, for Syria not reaching the final stages of Asian World Cup qualification, he was enticed back into Syrian football with the prospect of building a team that was capable of breaking the new monopoly of Al Karamah, the Syrian champions. They were a team that hailed from the troublesome city of Homs, a Sunni dominated city that had an uneasy relationship with the minority Alawite regime of President Assad. Al Karamah had been the biggest beneficiary of Syrian football's privatisation, winning the past two championships and making it to the final of the 2006 Asian Champions League final.

But now Rifat sat in the changing room as The Colonel strode around outside on the pitch sucking up the plaudits. Yet according to Rifat, it was he who had implemented the changes that the army had previously refused to admit needed to be made.

'When I got here last year Al Jaish's results were not good,' he said. 'I made a young team – only two players are above thirty, the rest under twenty-three. I'm here for two years and *Inshallah* I hope that next year we will have a good team.'

He insisted that he still picked the team and that The Colonel was the team manager off the pitch but he still found it something of a culture shock managing an army team after spending his managerial life looking after civilian outfits.

'It is very different. With the army team you have any facility you like. The only problem is the new rules for professional players,' he lamented. 'Before, Al Jaish would take all the competition. Now this is a different football. The other teams take good players and pay money for them. But the army doesn't buy because they have good facilities but a low budget. It's difficult for us because I see a player, I want this player, but I can't take this player any more.'

The team had also lost something of its military identity. Only two players now split their time between military and football duty – although Ahmad claimed another five wanted to wear the uniform since playing at the club.

'Now the club is down,' he said as kick-off approached. '*Inshallah*, we will be big again.'

Ahmad's prophecy wasn't immediately borne out on the pitch. After the crowd, the players and the soldiers present had stood for the national anthem, in front of a huge Syrian flag, things went downhill for Al Jaish. They were dire and quickly went 2–0 behind. But then something unusual happened. Every decision, it seemed, went in Al Jaish's favour. The small band of Al Majd fans were livid as the full force of the apparatus of the state willed an Al Jaish comeback. When Al Jaish scored, the soldiers celebrated. And then they scored again, and again. The players knelt on the pitch and kissed the grass after each goal as Al Majd tried to work out what had hit them. It was only when the fourth goal had gone in, courtesy of Zambian striker Zacharia Simukonda, that they finally gave in. It finished 4–3 to Al Jaish, and as the players walked off the pitch, the soldiers there to keep order shook their heroes' hands without any pretence of neutrality. Back in the dressing room Zacharia didn't find this odd in the slightest.

'I didn't know I was coming to the army team,' he explained, sitting in the dressing room in his jock strap. 'There is no difference though between playing for a civilian team and an army team. They don't treat you like army, they are professional.' Outside the dressing room The Colonel was busy taking congratulations from a large, jubilant crowd that had gathered. 'It was a good game, no?' he shouted as I walked past.

The conversation was curtailed as yet another man grabbed him and kissed his face, first on the left cheek, and then three times on the right; a sign of true affection. Ahmad Rifat anonymously climbed onto the team bus, in silence, away from the melee and without fanfare. His work was done, even if no one had appreciated it.

In comparison to the next day's game, Al Jaish's unpopularity was only too evident. Al Wahda, Damascus' most popular team, were taking on bottom-of-the-table Al Horriya at the smaller Al Fayhaa stadium. Fans draped in the orange of Al Wahda's shirt hurriedly skipped towards the ticket booths cradling their 100 Syrian pounds for a ticket. The anticipation was no different from a match in London or Turin; children excitedly dragging parents towards the stands, nervous teenagers singing Arabic songs outside the ground. Hope and expectation hung in the air. When watching Al Jaish all you felt was the heavy hand of the law, of conformity, of order. No one skipped to go and watch Al Jaish play, not any more. The complete collapse of their crowd to one forty-fifth of its past glory proved that, for all the cups and the league titles, Damascus' love was essentially bought by a tacit understanding that opposing the government and its powerful institutions was unpatriotic. Al Jaish may have stolen the league, but it could do nothing to steal its supporters hearts and minds.

Walid, a young Syrian working security at one of the stands, explained it to me. 'Al Jaish is hated,' he said as the match kicked off. Twenty thousand had made the trip to watch the game, even though it had virtually no significance to the home team.

'They are hated because when you are 20 they bzzzzzz, shave your head. If they play for Al Jaish they don't shave your head, you don't have to serve. And then there's *wasta* . . .'

Wasta is what oils the wheels of Middle Eastern society. It means influence, connections, money. Those with *wasta* can expect to negotiate the Middle East's labyrinthine bureaucracies with ease, or secure a table at a fancy restaurant, or get off a parking ticket. Everybody else had to wade through a sea of forms and treacle-thick obduracy. No one can expect to get anywhere significant in the Middle East without huge quantities of *wasta*.

'They have more money,' Walid continued, 'and the referees always give them decisions.'

Almost every single football league in the world has its own successful team that its rivals suspect have curried favour with the authorities, but when you hear Arsene Wenger or Jose Mourinho or Sir Alex Ferguson complaining it sounds laughable. In Syria it seemed plausible.

After the impeccably observed national anthem, the Al Wahda band – of three trumpets and a tabla – struck up and the fans sang, until Al Horriya took the lead. And they sang some more.

'Fuck your mother!' they screamed as the Al Horriya team, without any fans there of their own, bowed in front of the nearest Al Wahda stand.

In Saudi I had been told that a popular football chant was: 'I shit in your father's beard'. Having found it virtually impossible to enter Saudi Arabia to see a game I had never heard it myself. Nor could I realistically find any trace of it. Largely because (a) how do you bring it up with a Saudi in polite conversation? And (b) putting the words 'father', 'shit' and 'beard' into Google returned some truly horrific results. Still, Walid and his groups of friends revelled in teaching me the phrases you wouldn't find in your standard Arabic phrase book. Omar, Luqmar, Imad and Aram all worked at the stadium and were Al Wahda fans who detested Al Jaish and the army. 'I will not go to the army,' declared Omar. 'I'll pretend I am crazy.'

We talked about life in Syria as the match ebbed and flowed in front of us, about how, in their opinion, the West had a bad impression of Syria and Islam because of distortions in our media.

'You can see in Syria, we are not all terrorists,' said Assam, a wiry boyish-looking 23-year-old studying English. On the pitch players and coaches from Al Wahda were praying during half-time.

'What do you think of Islam?' Aram asked, before answering his own question. 'We are all Muslims,' he said, turning around and pointing his finger to lasso his group. 'We pray every day. But this is the true Islam, between me and Allah. It's personal. Anything else is not praying to Allah. It's for other people to see that you're praying for Allah.'

He was right; Syria appeared to be the least outwardly Islamic country I had been to in the Middle East, other than Israel. It seemed less hung up on public displays of faith, much at odds with Saudi or Kuwait or the West Bank, where Friday prayer time meant dropping everything at a moment's notice. Most women walking around the centre of Damascus had long ago dispensed with covering their heads and alcohol was easily available in the city.

Syria, like Iran, seemed to have at its core a more liberal, *laissez faire* social attitude than its regional contemporaries, and appeared, outwardly, to be most infused by values of tolerance. Yet a mixture of unbending Islamic fundamentalism and political strongmen with a knack of making bad tactical choices – both Assad and Ahmadinejad fall into the latter category – had soured their relationships with the rest of the world to the extent that war against both countries was talked of as a possibility at the highest level in Washington and London.

But whilst the Iranians were growing tired of Ahmadinejad's increasingly erratic behaviour, President Assad still enjoyed some level of popular support if the terraces were to be believed.

'Yes, people love him,' Omar enthusiastically replied when I asked whether their dislike for the army stretched to the president. The rest of the group nodded in agreement. 'He stands up for Syria. Everyone wants us to get on our knees in front of Israel and America and England. But we won't.' The only thing they were prepared to kneel in front of the West for was the Premier League and the musical talents of former British X-Factor winner Shayne Ward. 'Listen, listen!' Omar demanded, pressing headphones into my ear from his mobile. A saccharine sweet pop dirge blared into my skull. 'Shayne Ward, 'No Promises.' He is very popular here. But Backstreet Boys are best.' Everyone in the group nodded: Backstreet Boys five, Shayne Ward nil.

The match had taken a turn for the worse for Al Wahda as they went two down before another remarkable comeback unfolded. Al Wahda hit back with three goals, one offside, one a foul on the keeper, the other a scuffed shot. Scuffles started breaking out between the Al Wahda faithful as the third goal went in and the clock hit 90 minutes. Al Horriya's players slumped to the floor knowing that another chance at clawing their way out of the relegation mire had gone begging. Al Wahda's fans didn't miss the opportunity to gloat. 'Horriya, go fuck your sister!' they sang.

As the victorious Al Wahda fans piled out of the stadium into Damascus' early evening, only briefly stopping by the exit to harass players as they came out, it became clear from the two games just how successful and vital the Syrian FA's challenge to the army had been. I'd originally planned on heading to Homs to watch Al Karamah play, but had decided to stick to Damascus and been rewarded with 12 goals and some of the best attacking football I had seen in the Middle East. Football had become meritocratic. Players were reaping the rewards of their talent and had been cut free from Al Jaish's monopoly to gain freedom over whom they played for. The rewards were being reaped on the pitch too. The FA's overhaul had also heralded a policy of promoting youth. By beefing up its scouting and training structure, and encouraging league teams to play more young Syrian players, the FA has been able to identify and develop more talent. At the 2007 Under-17 World Cup, Syria surprised even themselves. After drawing with Argentina, beating Honduras and then losing by a stoppage-time goal to Spain, their tournament ended with a 3–1 defeat to England.

At the 2005 Under-20s World Cup in Holland, Syria beat Italy before narrowly losing 1–0 to Brazil in the last 16. Many of these players had been groomed for the senior team and were now spearheading Syria's attempt to qualify for its first ever World Cup finals. An excellent draw with Iran in Tehran, followed by another against the UAE, had put them in a good position to make the final Asian qualifying round for the World Cup finals in South Africa in 2010. In the end, they missed out on goal difference. In the last game of qualifying they had to beat the UAE 3–0 in Al Ain. They fell just short, winning 3–1. But time was still on Syria's side, or so I thought back then. Theirs was a success story, I thought, other emerging leagues would have been advised to follow.

I still hadn't given up hope on gaining entry to Al Jaish's suspiciously fortified training complex. After the senior team had won its match The Colonel intimated that it might be possible for me to return with the blessings of The General, so long as I didn't bring my camera. I agreed and arrived back where I started, at the guard booth at the front gate. The soldiers recognised me but, fearing that The Colonel might throw them in jail if they let in an undesirable, who had been ejected a few days previously, they barred my path. Remonstrating with the commanding officer didn't work either, until 50 metres away The Colonel's white head poked out of a brand new VW hatchback. I was sure his head cocked slightly in irritation as he spotted me waving furiously from the gate before beckoning me with a cursory handshake. He shiftily looked around, avoiding eye contact as he shook, as if he was about to engaged in a highly illegal transaction of some sort.

'Please, please,' he begged, finally meeting my eyes. 'Don't take any photos. Off the field, OK. But anything else. No.'

I walked the short distance to the scrubby green field, where the players were waiting. The Colonel had been chauffeur-driven the short distance, before emerging onto the pitch with a large smile and a skip in his step. Ahmad Rifat was there too, but sank into the background as The Colonel took centre-stage and started giving the team talk. With his motivational words done, the players started warming up whilst The Colonel sauntered over to the rotting wooden stand I was sitting on and shuffled next to me.

'Who exactly is in charge?' I asked.

'I am the manager. The coach is involved with everything on the pitch.'

'So, who picks the team?'

A pause.

'He does.'

'Do you have any influence on it [matters on the pitch]?'

'Well ...'

Another pause before the truth willed out.

'I might say before a big game that a player in the side is weak and that he should be replaced with someone who is a strong player, a player who won't be weak. Then after the season we talk and see which players we will take and which we leave out.'

It seemed that The Colonel was the true power behind the throne at Al Jaish, with Rifat merely a civilian figurehead: A Medvedev to The Colonel's Putin. Which is not to say he wasn't qualified for the role of *de facto* coach. He himself had been a promising player in Syria's lower leagues as well as an international referee. That was in between the 21 years he spent as a lieutenant in the army, which included a stint fighting with the infantry on the Golan front in 1967 and 1973. We sat watching the players circle the pitch as he ticked off his military career and many battles with the Israelis.

'Do you think Syria would play Israel if they ever both reached the World Cup finals?' I asked him.

The Colonel smiled a wry smile. This was a bit of a mean question. Iran, Syria and Saudi Arabia would be powerless in the face of the world's biggest, most prestigious footballing tournament. Qualifying was hard enough and if a Middle Eastern state forfeited its tie with Israel, not only would it push the country into the footballing wilderness, it would also spark riots in Damascus, Tehran and Riyadh. Pretending Israel didn't exist mattered to many in the Middle East, but playing in the World Cup finals mattered more.

'We'll make a decision when we get there. Israel has some of our land, the Golan. If they give it back we can have peace and we can play but every day they are killing women, children, babies, girls, men. How can they live like this? They need peace too. It's like France coming over and taking a piece of England. Would you play them after that?'

The Colonel knew he had gone further than a militarily trained mind should usually allow and quickly changed the subject, charging off to fetch one of the players. Abdul Razak al Hussein was the team's star midfielder and one of the few players who still chose to join the army as well as playing for Al Jaish. The Colonel walked him to the rickety wooden stand to meet me.

'You only ask him about football. Not politics,' he instructed. In the end he decided to translate for me.

'How have you benefited from Al Jaish's new youth policy?' The Colonel sprang into action, collecting the response and offering a reply. 'Al Jaish has good facilities, two fields for practice, swimming pool, sauna, professional coach. I have a good chance to show off my technique and fitness. We have here discipline and it is serious. This is why he has come to Al Jaish. Al Jaish is the best in Syria, it is not just my opinion but of everyone, all the journalists.'

It was clear that The Colonel had started to inject his own opinions into the replies.

'Syria will improve with football only if it follows the example of Al Jaish, with discipline, being serious, good training, good money.'

Then The Colonel dispensed with the pretence of answering the questions altogether.

'Yes I think we have a good chance of qualifying for the World Cup if we win the four games, because two teams qualify,' he replied instantly to the question, without even offering it to the confused-looking player.

'What does Abdul Razak think?' I asked again.

'Oh,' he said, relaying the message and garnering a long reply.

'Maybe,' The Colonel answered.

Despite the club's autocratic tendencies, The Colonel, Rifat, The General – whoever was truly responsible for what went on on the pitch – had started to turn Al Jaish's fortunes around. They had started their own youth programme, training talented kids as young as 13. If they didn't make the cut, it was but a short walk to the recruitment office. They won either way. Al Jaish had been forced to change and was starting to show signs that it was finding its feet in the bright new world of professional football.

The Colonel offered to drive me back to my hotel. On the journey back he was convinced that Al Jaish would rise again, stronger than before and better adapted for the modern world of cash-rich football.

'We are number one in Syria. Number one in terms of facilities and number one in discipline,' he reiterated as we passed the old city before pulling up in front of the hotel. 'Other clubs will be following our lead.'

The Colonel was right. Al Jaish won the Syrian league in 2010. The Army did rise again but not in the way he had intended.

March 2012

It took just one question – the first question – for the press conference to degenerate into a farce. In a half empty room that still smelled of fresh of paint at the offices of the Jordanian Football Association in Amman, Haitham Jattal and Ahmad al Salih, coach and captain of Syria's under-23 team, sat in silence in front of a handful of Asian football journalists as an argument raged around them. It was the day before an important match. Syria was due to play its final group qualifier for the London 2012 Olympics against Malaysia. It was supposed to be a home game but football was now impossible in Syria. An uprising against the rule of Bashar al Assad had plunged the country into civil war, an explosion that began in the belligerent city of Homs before its shockwaves had covered the entire country. As many as 10,000 people had been slaughtered in the violence as Assad tried with diminishing success to reimpose his will on Syria's restive provinces. With the uprising intensifying, FIFA decided that international football was too dangerous to be held in Damascus. Amman was deemed a safer bet. Yet exile had not led to defeat. The Syria team had come within one game of qualifying for the first major football tournament in their history, beating Japan – Asian champions no less – 2-1 in the process. Syria needed to beat Malaysia heavily and hope that Bahrain beat Japan on the other side of the world in Tokyo. It was an incredible achievement in the teeth of such chaos, but the regime was not giving up its control easily.

'We can't answer about this,' a voice shot angrily across the room. A large, middle aged man in a suit who had been watching the press from behind the door had entered the room at the first sign of trouble.

'No comment about that,' he said wagging his finger. 'I am in charge of the media for the team and I say you can not ask that!'

'No questions about politics!' shouted another from the other side of the room who claimed to be an interpreter.

The question asked was a seemingly innocuous one: How had the Syrian team coped playing its games outside the country given the situation back home? The room bickered about the nature of the question with the two men who claimed to be interpreters for the team, although few were convinced by their alibis. The Syrian coach and captain watched on stony faced as the circus continued around them.

'We play in the name of Syria,' coach Jattal was eventually allowed to answer.

'It is well known everyone back home will be watching the match and they will be hoping for us to win. Of course, playing in your homeland in front of our own people would be much better than playing outside. But we have overcome this difficulty and turned it into an incentive to reach the Olympics.'

It was a universe away from what I had seen four years previously at Al Jaish. Back then there was stability, if not peace and happiness. Football had successfully challenged the army's monopoly and won. The league had gone professional. Young players were finally given the chance to reach their potential as Syria's various national youth sides had begun to qualify for international tournaments. There had been hope that Syria might even make it to the 2014 World Cup finals, but the team was kicked out early in qualification after it was discovered that they had fielded a player – George Mourad – who had previously played for Sweden. Still, there was always the Olympics.

But then the people of Homs rose up against Assad and everything changed. Except the suspicion.

Another question about how the coach had managed to forge unity in a squad that included players from across Syria's sectarian and geographical divides, including several from Homs, was met with the same howls of protest.

'It is easy and simple. Everybody came a few days before the match [for a meeting] in the capital Damascus,' insisted the interpreter eventually when pressed on the issue. 'We have no problems with the players.'

When asked whether the coach would like to answer the question, the interpreter stopped, as if taken back by the question.

'He says the same as I said.'

Except this was a lie. The Syrians did have a problem with one troublesome player in particular, the team's goalkeeper, Abdelbasset Saroot. He was nowhere to be seen. But that was to be expected since no one knew where he was. The only way to find him was on YouTube, where he had become a hero of the revolution.

The footage was grainy. A young man stood proudly, defiantly even, if a little nervously, in front of a Syrian national flag. The date on the screen stated that the video was shot in July 2011 in the city of Homs. He was wearing a dark T-shirt, his arms folded across his chest.

'In the name of Allah, the most merciful and compassionate,' the young man began.

'I am Abdelbasset Saroot, a Syrian citizen.'

The video style was achingly familiar from a thousand suicide bombers in Iraq and Afghanistan: the austere surroundings, the ramshackle production values, the confessional of a man looking past this world and into the next. But Abdelbasset Saroot was not prepared for martyrdom. At least not yet. Not in the way a casual observer of the video, nor the Syrian government, might have intended. He was far more dangerous than that.

'I am the national goalkeeper of the Syrian national youth team and of [local Syrian team] Karamah club,' he continued.

'I am now wanted by the security agencies, which are trying to arrest me. I declare with sound mind and of my own volition, that we, the free people of Syria, will not back down until our one and only demand is met: the toppling of the regime.'

The video ended abruptly, but not before Abdelbasset Saroot delivered his coup de grace.

'I hold the Syrian regime responsible for anything that happens to me,' he said, calmer now.

'Long live free Syria, long live our proud people that rejects humiliation.'

The 20-year-old goalkeeper had not turned up for training with the squad the previous summer. Instead, he was so sickened by the army's atrocities in his home city of Homs – the centre of the rebellion – that he left football and joined the rebels. At first it seemed like any other defector. But he soon became more than that, as another YouTube video a few months later proved.

Shot by Al Jazeera it showed Abdelbasset Saroot sat low in the front seat as his car careered from stop to stop. He now had to take special precautions. The regime had already tried to assassinate him on several occasions, claiming the lives of his best friend and his brother. Now he travelled from safe house to safe house. It was too dangerous to stay in one place for too long.

Eventually he arrived at his destination. Abdelbasset Saroot was to sing revolutionary songs for a large crowd of a few thousand that had gathered especially for him, to see the now legendary 'singing goalkeeper' give thanks to those who had died so far in the uprising. His beautiful singing voice had been put to good use since he had gone AWOL from Syria's Olympic football squad. The crowds had got bigger and bigger to see the new hero of Homs. Every time the regime tried to silence him, the crowds grew. In the previous YouTube video, filmed shortly after the first assassination attempt, Saroot had appeared – seriously injured and clearly shaken – to prove that he was still alive. Now he was talking to Al Jazeera, explaining his life of perpetual movement that had become a symbol of hope for the anti-Assad rebels.

'I am free. I have travelled all over the world to play football. But freedom isn't just about me or about travelling,' he told the reporter.

'What about everyone else? Freedom is a big word. Freedom is about freedom of speech and freedom of opinion...the Syrian regime has made it so scary that a son is too afraid to even talk to his own mother.'

Abdelbasset Saroot's defection had been an embarrassment. Now the players were looked on every bit as suspiciously as the foreign journalists sitting in the room.

'You didn't think that guy was an interpreter did you?' a Jordanian official asked incredulously shortly after the press conference had finished. 'If the coach or any of the players talked about politics they would hang them.'

The Syrian squad trained in silence at the King Abdullah stadium on the outskirts of Amman. The team had been chosen from all of Syria's football clubs - including the country's biggest team Al Karamah and Al Wathba, both based in Homs. It was hoped that the team could become a symbol of normality and unity. But Abdelbasset Saroot's absence loomed large in the squad, even if some would have liked that not to be the case.

'Everyone is looking for him, he's hiding in houses in Homs,' one Syrian media officer said dismissively and anonymously pitch side, shortly before the delegation decided to close the training session to the media.

'Every time they look for him they find women in all black [wearing religious clothing]. He's friends with number nine [striker Nassouh Nakkdahli] but they haven't spoken to him for seven months.'

His ghost – a free spirit cut loose from the shackles of the regime be they in Homs or here, in Amman – still haunted those all around. It had been a while since he had posted on YouTube. Some thought he had been killed. But his former team-mates still held out hope that he was alive and might even one day play with them again.

In the stands watching the team train, two injured players sat separately from the rest of Syria's delegation. 'We hope that he will return. He is a good goalkeeper and he was also our friend before,' said Thaer Krouma, a midfielder also from Homs who played for Al Wathba.

For Syrian players like Krouma qualification for the Olympics would be a gift to the people, separate from the politics and bloodshed that had dominated the previous twelve months.

'The players have a strong bond and love for each other and are committed. [Olympic qualification is] a big dream to accomplish but we represent Syria, the people of Syria and anyone who loves the Syrian country. We represent the 23 million people and their hopes,' he said. Krouma was worried about the worsening situation back home. He had spoken to his family in Homs, who were safe despite the army pounding several rebellious districts into dust.

Saroot didn't believe that the Olympics would be a gift for the people, nor that you could separate victory for the Syrian national team from victory for the regime. The Olympics would give Assad more legitimacy than it deserved.

By the time kick off arrived, the King Abdullah stadium was virtually empty. A few hundred Malaysian fans – almost all of them university students – filled one small section despite the fact they had nothing to play for. In the 'home' end just 20 Syrians nosily sang pro-regime chants.

'It's a conspiracy,' argued 18-year-old Jneid, a leather market trader originally from Aleppo, of what he viewed as the anti-Assad media coverage of the conflict in Syria.

'The Gulf countries, like Qatar who own Al Jazeera, and his friends, they make a conspiracy on Syria. [In Homs] After the last prayers they [the Gulf countries] take the money and go to the young people with no job, offer them money and tell them to go and shoot, go and bomb the hospitals.'

They watched as Syria easily overcame their inferior opponents, beating them 3-0. It wasn't enough for automatic qualification as Japan dispatched Bahrain. Instead Syria would have to travel to Vietnam two weeks later to play Oman and Uzbekistan in a round robin tournament. The winner would go into a final play off against Senegal in the English city of Coventry for the last place at London 2012. A downbeat coach Jattal tried to see the positives in the victory and the three potential extra matches, played thousands of miles apart in less than a month, that came with it.

'[We feel] happiness but not that much happiness as we would prefer to go to England without the play off,' he said.

The players barely celebrated as they left the pitch, the pro-Assad chants from the handful of Syrian fans almost, but not quite, drowned out by the drums of Malaysian students.

'God, Syria. Bashar [Al Assad] is all we need,' they shouted.

Syria never made it to London. They mysteriously arrived in Vietnam with a different coach. A draw against Oman meant that Syria had to beat Uzbekistan. They took an early lead too but the intense schedule of matches and travel took their toll. Uzbekistan scored two late goals and Syria's hopes of making it to the Olympics was over. By then others had opened its eyes to the horrors in Homs. Syria's army would crush the rebellion and regain control of the city. The world watched as the district of Baba Amr, the centre of the rebellion in Homs, was flattened and innocent lives lost. The thought that Syria might be represented at London 2012 suddenly appeared abhorrent. The British government even moved to ban any figures aligned to the regime from attending the Olympics.

'If the British government has decided to ban anyone connected to the regime and to President Bashar al Assad, I am telling you in advance they should ban all Syrian citizens, because we all support President Assad and support Syria,' an angry General Mowaffak Joma, chair of the Syrian Olympic Committee told the BBC. But the football team was no longer part of that game, who returned to Syria empty handed.

A few weeks later the British government confirmed the news: The General, the same general I had met in Damascus four years earlier shredding documents in front of a picture of him embracing the president, had been refused a visa to attend the games.

✦

The General may not have travelled to London 2012, but the national football team had enjoyed something of a renaissance. The exile and war had, much like with the Iraqi national team and their 2007 victory in the Asian Cup, focused minds. Many of the same players that had gone so close to making it to the London Olympics had starred in the AFC U-19 Championship in the UAE a few months later. They were knocked out in the quarter-finals but not before they had smashed Saudi Arabia – a country that the Assad regime and his supporters had accused of funding and supporting Syria's rebels – 5-1. A few months later Syria won the 2012 West Asian Championship, beating Iraq in the final. In some respects it had been Syrian football's greatest year. But their success wasn't like the Iraq team in 2007. Back then Iraq didn't have a regime to follow or resist, just the morality of their own unity. The fingerprints of the Syrian state, on the other hand, remain on the country's recent football success.

It had been a while since the world heard from Abdelbasset Saroot too. His last dispatch came on 4 April, 2012, from the Syrian village of Bayada. A huge crowd has gathered in the city's main square. It was dangerous to gather in such numbers here given that the Syrian army was in the middle of razing the district of Baba Amr in nearby Homs to the ground. Thousands had died in the shelling and from the snipers. Countless more had been picked up and disappeared, presumed liquidated in one of Assad's many medieval torture cells. But thousands of people, maybe as many as ten thousand people, had taken the risk to see Abdelbasset Saroot sing. He stood at the front, high above his audience, and addressed the crowd.

'*Allahu Akhbar!*' he shouted to the crowd.

'God is great!' they repeated in unison.

Saroot's voice was strong, his singing clear as he whipped the crowd into a frenzy.

'We won't back down from this revolution!' he sang.

'*Allahu Akhbar!*' replied the crowd.

'We won't be quiet on the wound inflicted on Baba Amr. Either we are victorious or we die. Allah is witness to what we say. If we walk on this path we shall, *Inshallah*, die as martyrs.'

The thousands of people hanging off Abdelbasset Saroot's every word agreed.

15
LIBYA

Oh my country! Oh my country!
With my struggle and my patience, drive off our enemies and survive!
Survive, Survive, survive
All through, we are your ransom.
Libya
Libya
Libya

Libya's rebel national anthem

October 2011

Under an immaculate blue Mediterranean sky, Marcos Cesar Dias de Castro
'Paqueta' stood alone on the sidelines in ankle deep grass at the Stade Adelaziz Chtioui,
Tunis, watching his goalkeeper Guma Mousawrithe on the floor in agony. The coach
of the Libyan national team rubbed his temples with his right hand, exasperated. Many
things should have gone wrong over the past year for the Brazilian, but Paqueta and his
team had somehow stumbled their way around fate. Until now.

In a few days his team was due to play a final, vital 2012 Africa Cup of Nations
qualifier against Zambia. The sporting facts were daunting enough as it was. Unlike
their north African kin – Egypt, Tunisia and Morocco – Libya had never had its own
golden era. They had never qualified for a World Cup finals, instead being forced
into long periods of petty self exile and failure thanks largely to the unpredictable
manoeuvrings of the country's dictator Colonel Muammar Gaddafi. They had
qualified for the Africa Cup of Nations in the past, once as hosts, but this was
different. Paqueta had begun his campaign with Gaddafi's iron grip still in place. He

was about to end it with the country mired in a vicious civil war.

The team had met for a training camp in the birth place of the Arab Spring for a series of friendlies against local Tunisian club sides. So far Libya had lost once, eked out a 0-0 draw against another and were now, in their final game against Avenir Sportif La Marsa, losing 2-0. One of Paqueta's best players had been injured thanks to the insane over exuberance of La Marsa's players. He lay on the stretcher weeping, his knee held together in a leg brace. The coach turned and shrugged sarcastically at the concerned bench as Guma Mousa hopped off the pitch, arm around his physio. That Mousa should have succumbed here, of all places, would have been comedic were it not couched in such tragedy. For the past few months, like fellow national team players Walid el Kahatroushi and Ahmed Alsagir, Mousa had been fighting for the Libyan rebels who had risen up against Colonel Gaddafi's brutal rule and sparked the on-going civil war. He had survived Libya's haphazard front line. He had survived the privations and exposures of a modern insurgency. But he could not survive 90 minutes and the swing of a Tunisian boot.

'Why are they playing like this?!' Paqueta asked to no one in particular, tapping his fore finger against his temple. Mousa lay behind him, grimacing as an ice pack was laid on his injured knee. 'It's crazy,' he added.

Paqueta was right: it was crazy. Everything had changed since he had taken the job in June 2010. Back then Gaddafi and his regime looked impregnable. Gaddafi's football-crazy sons had offered a fine package for the coach. The team was to be a symbol of Libya's growing might. Its oil wealth would build state of the art facilities, some of the best in Africa. In return he was to deliver qualification for the 2012 Africa Cup of Nations and the 2014 World Cup in Brazil. Libya was also due to host the next Africa Cup of Nations. Victory in that was expected. No expense was to be spared.

And then a street seller in Tunisia set fire to himself.

When the first protests against Gaddafi began in the eastern city of Benghazi at the start of Paqueta's Africa Cup of Nations campaign, his key players spoke out in favour of Gaddafi and denounced the rebels. The national team was for the nation, they would tell the press. It was united behind Gaddafi against the terrorists. But the illusion of unity melted away as quickly as spring snow. Players started disappearing from the national team's training camps to go and fight *with* the rebels, unable to stomach the pro-Gaddafi sentiment as they nervously waited on news from family and friends, pinned down in districts being shelled by the army. As the facts on the ground changed, the pro-Gaddafi players disappeared too, more out of self-preservation than their own skewed morality. Now the team took a different role. It was to be a symbol of the new Libya. Before they took to the pitch against Avenir Sportif La Marsa, the team's new kit arrived, expunged of all traces of the old regime. The rebel flag was now stitched on each player's breast. It sat atop black and white stripes, an almost exact copy of the shirt worn by Juventus.

The new kit had so far brought nothing but defeat and injury. It had been an inauspicious start for the new Libya. But the second half brought better news. Paqueta threw on his wild card. Ahmed Zuay was a young battering ram of a striker from the rebel stronghold of Benghazi. Zuay was built like an ox, his powerful demeanour belied his childlike face. Three goals were scored, two from Zuay, securing Libya's only victory during their brief tour of Tunisia. In the tunnel Arab fraternity returned as the players from both teams embraced to exchange best wishes before the Zambia game. The players made sure not to exchange their new shirts. There was only enough for one each. Paqueta did not hang around. He walked straight to the coach.

As they left the stadium, the jubilant players were stopped in their tracks. A group of young men wearing rebel flags waited to meet their heroes on crutches, wrapped in bandages or sitting in wheelchairs. Their faces were fresh, clear and unlined under thick, dark beards. The rebel fighters who weren't so lucky had carried their permanent scars to Tunisia for treatment. The players fell quiet as they solemnly passed the young amputees, shaking their hands – or wrists if need be– whispering thanks for their sacrifice into each of their ears.

The team was due to take a ten hour chartered flight from Tunis via Cameroon to Chingola, a small town next to the Zambia-Congo border that had grown rich on copper. The problem was getting myself on the flight too. Libya's team manager had viewed my letters of invitation with suspicion. Ali wore a red team tracksuit and a bushy moustache that was rarely seen without a cigarette poking through it. He had been with the team for years, essentially a fixer getting the team from A to B whilst trying to navigate, and sometimes negate, the suspicious, bureaucratic demands of a dictatorship. Even though a civil war was now being openly fought, and Gaddafi's days looked like being numbered, old habits died hard for Ali.

Ali, like most Libyans who had essentially worked under the regime, was hedging his bets. His innate suspicion of outsiders was clear. He took a long drag on his cigarette before passing the letters back to me. 'Without a stamp I can do nothing.' He attempted to look sorry that my trip was to end here. But a last minute fax from Libya's National Transitional Council arrived a few minutes before the team bus was due to leave for the airport. Under Gaddafi there would be no chance that a foreign journalist would be allowed to travel like this with the team. Ali looked at the new fax, realising that even with years of experience in obstruction there was nothing he could do. He smiled and put out his cigarette as the team threw their bags into the coach. 'I guess you are coming after all.'

It was moral quandary that almost everyone connected with the national team had to address. How could they explain the years of working *for* the regime now that the team was essentially against it? As the coach crept through the gridlocked streets of Tunis towards the airport Marcos Paqueta cautiously explained how it was he got here in the first place.

'When I was there [in Libya] the first time I contacted only the federation people, but then one time I have one meeting with Dr Muhammad,' he recalled of his life under Gaddafi. Back then Colonel Gaddafi's regime enjoyed the détente of Western governments eager to tap into its vast oil reserves. His son Dr. Muhammad Gaddafi, in charge of the Libyan Football Federation, shook hands with Paqueta and agreed to hire him with one eye on the 2012 Africa Cup of the Nations, the other on the World Cup in Brazil two years later. 'We talked about my project. He was happy because I had made a project for the national team and Libyan football.'

Paqueta was a good choice by Dr. Gaddafi. The Brazilian had taken Saudi Arabia to the 2006 World Cup finals in Germany and held the distinction of winning two World Cups in one year: both the Under 17 and Under 20 titles for Brazil in 2003. He proudly opened his laptop to show me his team photos. He knew where each of his former players were now.

'Do you recognise him?!' he laughed, pointing at one. It was Barcelona's full back Daniel Alves, largely unrecognisable thanks to an ill-judged afro-perm. But he also had experience operating in closed societies, and Libya was one of the most repressive regimes on earth. Like almost everyone that worked in Libya before the fall of Gaddafi, Paqueta was reticent to talk about life under the previous regime. He had a good life, a beach side house and large salary.

'I focused only on sports,' he said. 'At that time you don't know about the country.'

Under Paqueta Libya's Africa Cup of Nations campaign got off to a slow start. But a 0-0 draw was followed by a shock 1-0 victory against favourites Zambia in Tripoli putting them top of the group. It was to be the final game that Libya would play at home as the civil war erupted and the Gaddafi regime crumbled.

The Gaddafis had developed a love/hate relationship with football. The Colonel's son Saadi had grandiose delusions of international stardom. After turning out for Al Ahly Tripoli and installing himself as captain of the national football team he moved to Italian club Perugia, where he played a handful of games before failing a drugs test.

He is still to this day referred to as the worst player in Serie A history. But it was the Gaddafi's tenure as head of the Libyan Football Federation – first under Saadi and then later under the more circumspect rule of his brother Muhammad – that saw his father's brutal streak emerge. Under Saadi's control the LFF was used as a tool of political persecution, punishing fans and teams for daring to show any dissent on the football terraces, which remained, along with the mosque, the only available forum for mass opposition. In 2000, for example, Saadi's Al Ahly Tripoli travelled to Al Ahly Benghazi for a league match. Benghazi had long been associated with Libya's opposition movement and fans would complain that referees and players were bribed to ensure that Al Ahly Tripoli, the regime's team, would always win. But this time the Benghazi fans had a surprise for Saadi: they paraded a donkey wearing his numbered shirt.

'It is a bad story, not a funny story,' 29-year-old defensive midfielder Moataz Ben Amer, the current captain of Al Ahly Benghazi, would later recall. 'The first half, Ahly Tripoli are winning. But the referee is no good. So Ahly Benghazi leave the ground and goes to the airport [in protest]. Saadi Gaddafi turned up with his dogs and the police and said: 'If you don't play the second half, we will kick you.' Al Ahly Benghazi was afraid. We ended up losing 3-0.'

The incident revealed the Gaddafis' dark psychology. When his father heard of the intemperance, he ordered Al Ahly Benghazi's head quarters be razed to the ground. The club was banned from playing any football for six years.

'It wasn't Saadi,' Ben Amer added. 'Muammar Gaddafi said Al Ahly [Benghazi] is finished, and closed it. People in Benghazi who were with Gaddafi came and destroyed their building.'

Unlike other dictators that saw the political and nationalistic benefits of a strong, successful football team, the Colonel himself had a far harder time coming to terms with the passion and the popularity of the game that his sons adored. Ali Laswadi was remarkably stoic about the end of his playing days at the age of 29. The 60-year-old was the current manager of Libya's youth and senior national teams and was a legend in his day, playing for the national team and scoring over 150 goals for Al Ahly Tripoli. Whilst the likes of Saddam Hussein and even Mahmoud Ahmadinejad held their national football teams close in the hope of basking in reflected glory, Gaddafi was deeply jealous of the game, a jealousy that effectively ended Laswadi's career.

'I played until 1979 and do you know why I stopped?' Laswadi asked as the coach approached the airport. Outside hundreds of Libyan supporters has gathered to send the team off with flowers and kisses. 'Gaddafi stopped the clubs and the leagues. He only wanted us to play in the streets and for the national team abroad.'

I asked him why Gaddafi Senior disliked football so much.

'Gaddafi would pass people playing football and see names written on the wall,' Laswadi answered. 'He'd ask: 'Who are these people's names?' He was told they were footballers so he went out to stop it. Yes, he was jealous.'

The jealousy was such that Gaddafi banned all names and numbers from shirts of all Libyan football teams, to prevent anyone from challenging his cult of personality. The only player allowed to carry a name and number on his shirt was his son Saadi.

'We used to call him 'Big Lips' before the revolution,' whispered Esam, the team's masseur, as if careless talk could still, one day, come back to haunt him.

Did you ever say that in front of Saadi?

'No!' he laughed, folding his fingers in to the shape of a gun and pressing it to his forehead.

The most telling example, though, came from Libya's most successful AFCoN campaign. They reached the final as hosts in 1982. Laswadi shook his head whilst grinning sarcastically at the memory of it.

'At the opening ceremony, he gave a speech. You know what he said? 'All you stupid spectators, have your stupid game'.'

Gaddafi stormed off the stage in a rage.

The plane landed at night on the tarmac of Ndola airport. Nearby the lights of Lubumbashi, one of Congo's most important, mineral rich cities, twinkled benignly. Ndola's small airport serviced the workers who came from across Africa to work in the region's copper mines. But it also had a dark footnote in history. It was here that the former UN secretary general Dag Hammarskjold was killed in a plane crash. The official report claimed the crash was due to pilot error. He was due to mediate talks over violence in nearby Katanga province in Congo but there have long been suspicions that the plane was shot down.

The match was due to be played in Chingola as Zambia's national stadium in Lusaka was being renovated, but the benefits inherent in the awkwardness of the journey would not have been lost on the Zambian FA. The flight itself had taken a bizarre turn. Half the Libyan players danced and sang in the aisles to Arabic pop songs whilst the other half lay in their seats reading copies of the Koran. At the back the physio and team doctor puffed away on cigarettes as Marcos Paqueta shot them disapproving glances over his shoulder. The plane had to refuel in Cameroon, but an election was about to take place and Cameroon air space was to be shut. There was only a window of a few hours before the plane was grounded. Libya's crucial game would be over before it had started. Knowing this only too well, the ground staff raised the price of fuel. A stand off followed for the next three hours and the pilots refused to give in to their extortion. But it was they would blinked first. A member of the air crew was dispatched down to hand over several large bricks of hundred dollar bills so that the flight could carry on to Ndola.

Even at night you could see the shifting political and economic landscape of Zambia. The north of the country had seen a huge influx of Chinese money in recent years, part of a wider policy of African investment by China to secure the natural resources needed to feed its rapidly growing economy. And the Chinese had left their imprint. As the coach bumped along the single, unlit road towards Chingola we passed a huge new stadium built by the Chinese government. The 44,000 capacity Levy Mwanawasa Stadium was a state of the art construction with a running track around it. It wasn't ready in time for this match, but would soon be one of the finest stadiums in Africa. The front gate was adorned with two Chinese dragons atop a sign. 'The Ndola National Stadium,' it said. 'In Zambia Aided by China.'

Walid el Kahatroushi sat quietly in his hotel room with his baseball cap pulled down tightly over his eyes, head bowed, as if carrying the weight of the world on his shoulders. The team had arrived in the early hours of the morning the day before the match. There hadn't been enough beds for the team and some had to sleep on the floor. It wasn't the late night or the pressure of expectation that now weighed heavily on the 27-year-old midfielder. It was the guilt that wouldn't leave him.

'If it was about me I would never come back, you would never find me here playing football,' he said firmly. It was an usual statement from an international footballer on the eve of such a vital match. Walid composed himself, as if dragging himself up, getting himself ready for duty against the doubts in his mind. 'But my friends on the front line, they told me: 'This is your future, you must go there [to Zambia]. This is also like a war for you. This is your duty. You must go there and play and then you can come back.' And that's why I'm here.'

The Libyan civil war had broken out eight months previously, midway through Libya's qualification campaign, forcing the players to choose sides. Some, like the 34-year-old captain Tariq Taib, were virulently pro-Gaddafi. When Libya beat the Comoros 3-0 in a qualifier in neutral Mali a few weeks after the civil war started, it was Taib who had declared that the team was 100 per cent behind the regime, even declaring the rebels 'dogs' and 'rats'.

'The whole team is for Gaddafi,' he declared to AP after the game. 'We dedicate this victory to the Libyan people who are suffering.'

But under the surface nothing could have been further from the truth. Kahatroushi had scored the first goal of that game, but when the return leg was due to take place he couldn't bear to pull on the jersey that bore the Gaddafi-era flag.

'I was in the camp for the second match against Comoros [in June 2011]. Some people came to me and told me one of my dear friends was in the hospital and lost his arm,' he said.

Straight away he decided to leave and return to fight for the rebels. The coaching staff only realised what he was planning when they saw him in his civilian clothes waving from beyond the gate. 'I went there [to Tripoli] to see him in the hospital. I saw him and saw many Libyans injured in a very hard situation.' Kahatroushi decided to join the rebellion at Jebel Nafusa, then a small pocket of resistance against Gaddafi's forces near the Tunisian border.

'The first time I went there they didn't let me pick up a gun and try to fight,' he said. 'They gave me some missions, gave me some money to go bring them some food and some help. Living there was so hard. As a football player they wouldn't let me on the front line. They were always trying to give me other missions to keep me alive. At the time even one of my friends said: 'just go behind me, I'll go in front of you so if there's a bullet I can have it'.'

The fighting got so fierce that his status as a footballer in need of protection melted away. 'In the end it was so hard and there's no way [I couldn't fight] so I just took the gun and I went out fighting. It was so hard, you can imagine, you could lose your life at any time. It was so hard.'

Kahatroushi survived, as did the goalkeeper Guma Mousa, but not all were so lucky. Ahmed Alsagir was shot in the shoulder and spent a month in hospital. The squad went and visited him before Alsagir decided to rejoin the rebels rather than play against Zambia. By the end of August Gaddafi had been toppled. A week later the team had to play their penultimate qualifier against Mozambique behind closed doors in Egypt. Aside from the trouble of getting the players out of the country, there were some more practical concerns to deal with. Nobody wanted to wear the old Gaddafi era kit and it would be months before a new official kit would arrive. So the team stitched rebel badges on to their shirts instead. The Libyans fought out a 0-0 draw and celebrated wildly, dedicating their victory to freedom and to the Libyans who had lost their lives.

'In football we don't have to represent politics. We played with the first government, yes, but we represented the people of Libya and the country of the Libya,' explained

26-year-old midfielder Abdalah al Sherif, now sitting on the bed next to Kahatroushi. 'We are one of the people and we are still representing and playing for Libya and the Libyan people.'

Sherif lost family during the NATO bombing of Tripoli. 'The whole family is from Tripoli. I lived a lot of moments during the troubles in Tripoli. We were sitting at home it was so hard to get out. You'd only get out for necessities. To get some food or something like this. To go back home quickly. I had a cousin that died because of a NATO bombing. This situation, this very bad situation we have been through, in the soul of Libya, was caused by the regime because it started the hard way, the way of killing people.'

The issue of what to do with those who had supported the regime was swiftly dealt with by coach Paqueta. Tariq Taib was nowhere to be seen in Zambia, replaced as captain by 39-year-old veteran goalkeeper Samir Abod. 'The first time after the war I made a meeting with the players before we started training,' Paqueta had explained back in Tunis. 'I said: 'Forget the war, forget Gaddafi and focus on the people. Because Libya is Libya. It is not Gaddafi, it's not the revolution. It's Libyan.'

Like in Lebanon or Poland or Spain – countries that had lived under divisive brutal regimes who required compromises just to survive – Libya's footballers were moving on and thinking of the brighter future to face them. In the month since Gaddafi fell, over 20 players had signed for foreign clubs, something that had been banned thanks to the paranoia of the previous regime.

'As a Libyan player you didn't have the right to decide for yourself. You just had to come back to the president's son who was controlling everything,' said Kahatroushi. He recalled the Mozambique match and how that result, even a goalless draw, was met with jubilation back in Libya. The match against Zambia, and qualification for the Africa Cup of Nations, would have a greater effect.

'Things are changing, the future will be more beautiful,' he said. Now Kahatroushi didn't look like he had the world on his shoulders. His baseball cap was tipped to the sky, his chin – covered in a large, well kept beard – thrust forward. Now victory was a matter of duty. 'We will do everything to qualify, *Inshallah*, because this will help our country too much. At least to bring them some happiness after all the sadness they have been through.'

The vuvuzelas and the horns began blowing early in Chingola. It was the day of the match and Zambia's fans had descended on the usually-quiet mining town dressed in green, creating a low menacing drone. The Chipolopolo Boys only needed a draw, even if the majority of the fans expected Zambia to hammer Libya. The Libyans needed to win. A draw would see them at the mercy of other results in Ghana and Nigeria.

The skies above the Nchanga Stadium were a fresh, light blue, disturbed by a few white clouds that meandered by. The stadium was full well before the Libyan team arrived at the stadium. When they did show up they sat nervously in the changing room as Paqueta gave them their last minute instructions before praying together. They all wore the new kit with the new badge and carried the new flag. The new national anthem was a little more problematic. With the political and military situation still fluid on the ground, the Zambian government had yet to recognise the new Libyan administration. Officially they had to play the Gaddafi-era anthem. The Libyan officials ran between changing room and the main stand, trying desperately to avoid a diplomatic incident. The players lined up next to a chain link fence. Walid el Kahatroushi and his team mates bounced from foot to foot before they walked out on to the pitch. Thankfully, a diplomatic incident was avoided. Libya's new anthem was played, but at such low volume that no one could hear it. None of the players realised it had even begun.

The game was atrocious. The few Libyan journalists that had followed the team knelt by the side of the pitch and prayed as the match played out in front of them. The veteran goalkeeper Samir Abod, the new captain, made three stunning saves. Zambia hit the post twice. The referee waved away two certain Zambian penalties. Somehow the game ended 0-0. The Zambian fans were livid at their team's inept performance. So angry, in fact, that shortly afterwards the Zambian FA sacked the team's Italian coach Dario Bonetti, despite the fact they had topped their qualification group. Libya's players collapsed on to the pitch. Some cried, others prayed. But they still did not know whether they had done enough to make it. Abod wept openly on the shoulders of his team mates as they returned to the sanctuary of the dressing room.

There we waited for news.

The players sat in their kit, sweating in silence. No one talked, no one speculated. The room grew heavier with humidity and fear. We could have waited an hour. It could have been 30 seconds. The thick fog of confusion was broken when the kit man sprinted into the room. Ghana had beaten Sudan, he shouted, and Nigeria conceded a late...

He didn't finish his sentence. A 90th minute Ibrahima Traore goal for Guinea in the Nigerian capital Abuja had changed the qualification calculus in Libya's favour. They had made it. The room ignited. The players and coaches held each other as they screamed the national anthem until, exhausted, they sat back on the wooden benches.

Somehow, Libya had made it through, ending their campaign with three victories and three draws. They were undefeated.

Libya arrived at the Africa Cup of Nations in Equatorial Guinea as underdogs but were handed the honour of playing in the tournament's opening game against the hosts. They lost 1-0, but drew against Zambia 2-2 before beating Senegal. It wasn't enough to qualify for the next round, but the Libyan team had already shown the world that war wasn't going to hold them back. Zambia went on to appoint Frenchman Herve Renard after sacking Bonetti, and promptly won the tournament for the first time in their history.

Yet a more significant moment happened three days after that match in Chingola. A convoy of cars near Gaddafi's home town of Sirte was attacked by NATO forces. Colonel Gaddafi and a handful of loyalists managed to escape and hide in a nearby tunnel. But they were caught by rebel fighters. Gaddafi, his face bloated and bloodied from the attack, was dragged through the sand and beaten as his captors shouted *Allahu Akhbar*. God is great. He was executed within the hour. Video footage suggested that, in his last, frenzied, brutal moments, Gaddafi was sodomised with a knife by one of his captors. The civil war was over.

But, in Chingola in the aftermath of Libya's qualification, the civil war and the memories of those who had sacrificed their lives to overthrow a dictator were still spoken of in the present tense. The coach returned to the hotel, the first leg of its long journey home. Ahmed Zuay and Walid el Kahatroushi led the team in song as they entered the hotel lobby. Confused white South Africans looked on before joining in with the celebrations. They clapped, not understanding what the Libyans were singing. It was a song they vowed not to sing, not until they were sure that they could honour the promise that it made.

> *The blood of the dead,*
> *It will not be spilt in vain.*

16

RETURN TO
QATAR

Zurich, December 2010

The hangdog expression on the face of the future British king betrayed the truth long before Sepp Blatter had opened the envelopes in front of him. In the main hall of a cavernous conference centre on the edge of the Swiss city of Zurich, the world waited as its organisation's president fumbled with the contents of one of the most expensive envelopes in the history of sport. Within it was held the secret that the football world had been waiting for with frenzied anticipation for the best part of two years: the hosts of the 2018 and 2022 World Cup finals. England's technically brilliant but politically naïve bid had, it was obvious from the outset, fallen well short of Russia's lucrative pitch.

It had made sense long before today. Russia had a rich football history, a deep and philosophical love and appreciation of the game and, now, post communism, money to burn. It was a new market too, the first time the World Cup had ever been hosted in Eastern Europe. Blatter's desire to terraform had become a compulsion. Africa, Asia, America; Eastern Europe was virgin territory ripe for willing colonisation. All the English FA could offer was the popularity of the Premier League and the limp triumvirate of Prince William, David Beckham and British Prime Minister David Cameron.

It looked like a winning team on paper: a young, popular would-be monarch, the most famous footballer in the world and a newly elected Prime Minister in his honeymoon period. As the FIFA delegates took their seats in the hall, and the sheer scale of England's humiliation had dawned on them, they looked anything but a dream team. Instead they resembled a three piece tenor band thrown together from the rejects of a Simon Cowell produced talent show, a housewife's threesome fantasy that should never have left the warped confines of the FA's subconscious. But the winning Russian envelope gave a taste of what was to come. Russia's victory came as no surprise to anyone apart from England's jingoistic press. But the race for the 2022 finals was harder to call. There was Japan, Australia, South Korea and, of course, the US, all adept at staging large successful events. And then there was Qatar.

It had been five years since I had left Qatar for the last time. It was a place big on gas, cash and ambition, that was clear. I had watched as they poured money into their local league to attract the biggest stars they could; the likes of Ronald and Frank De Boer, Marcel Desailly and Gabriel Batistuta. I had seen how they had tried to pay Brazilian footballers huge sums of money in an attempt to naturalize them for the Qatari national team, only for FIFA to change the rules to prevent their efforts. I had marvelled as Diego Maradona and Pele, sworn enemies, walked on to a stage together and embraced to mark the opening of the Aspire sports academy (and earn a phenomenal appearance fee in the process). All their efforts had been focused on raising the profile of Qatar and the standard of football so that the tiny nation with a population of citizens that could be counted in the hundreds of thousands could qualify for a World Cup finals. Back then it seemed like a distant, almost naïve plan. It failed, of course, but there was a charm to the failure. It seemed so hopeless, so destined to failure. How could anyone buy their way to the World Cup finals? But no one could have predicted what happened next.

There had always been ambition in the Gulf to host the world's greatest sporting prize. Dubai had bragged that it would bid for the 2018 World Cup. Abu Dhabi followed with its own project bankrolling an English Premier League team. Qatar had tried and failed with its own Quixotic bid to host an Olympic Games (it was rejected as they wanted to move the date to a time in October when the temperature wasn't above 45 degrees). But this time was different. Qatar had become a serious contender to win the bid for 2022. In the hall they had the very full and very obvious backing of the royal family. The Emir was sitting with the delegation, a huge bear of a man in a Western suit who had began to emerge as one of the most influential statesman in world politics. There was his tall, glamorous but demure wife. His son Sheikh Mohammed bin Hamad bin Khalifa Al Thani, had been the young, handsome, multi-lingual face of the bid. He had charisma to burn and had clocked up the miles, visiting every corner of the global to press for Qatar's case. They had invested heavily in the endeavour: sponsoring obscure conferences in Africa, paying for development projects in Asia and central America, inviting the world to marquee friendlies involving Brazil or Argentina or Egypt to their magnificent stadium in Doha, named after the Emir, of course.

And then there was the change in narrative. Yes, Qatar was a small country. But this will be a World Cup for the Middle East, a World Cup that could unite a fractured land. Yes, no infrastructure existed yet. But we had unlimited pockets to build a new city, a new country. Yes it could hit 50 degrees in the summer. But we would build air-conditioned stadiums that would cheat nature. The technology would be solar, carbon neutral, and like the stadiums, packed up and sent to the developing world. It wouldn't just change Qatar, it wouldn't just change the Middle East. It would change the world. They had stayed within the rules, just. Both bid contests had been plagued with corruption allegations. FIFA Ex Co members, the body who would ultimately decide the winner, had been caught taking cash and suspended. The was also the figure of Mohamed bin Hammam, the president of the Asian Football Confederation, one of football's most powerful men. He was also Qatari and rumoured to be in the frame to replace FIFA president Sepp Blatter. There were accusations that Qatar had unfairly used its immense wealth to get this far. But there was no smoking gun, at least not yet. They had played the game and, for now, they had a shot. Sepp Blatter spent a few more moments struggling with the envelope until finally he pulled the card from its sheath. Even he seemed surprised.

In the end it was a stroll. Qatar had won every round of voting handsomely. The royal family erupted and embraced. The Emir took to the stage and Sepp Blatter handed him the World Cup. He lifted it with two hands over his shoulder, a gap-toothed grin shining under an unfashionably bushy moustache. Sheikh Mohammed looked close to breaking down as he approached the podium and thanked everyone for a decision that genuinely shocked the world far outside football. After a decade of failure, they had done it. 'We will not let you down,' Sheikh Mohammed promised, swallowing his tears.

Mohamed couldn't make it to the mountain. Instead, the mountain had come to Mohamed.

Doha, January 2011

In Doha the posters of that iconic moment, of the Emir holding the World Cup triumphantly aloft, had begun to warp, whiten and peel from the walls and shop windows they had been fixed to in celebration. It was a month since that historic decision in Zurich, and Qatar had the first opportunity to show the world what a football tournament in the Emirate would look like: the 2011 Asian Cup finals. It was January, and for all the talk of excessive heat and air conditioned stadia, Doha felt a very different place. The sun shone brightly between the *shamal*, the strong desert winds that blew from the planes of Mesopotamia down through the Persian Gulf. The rain fell too, fraying the edges of the posters extolling arguably the greatest moment in Qatar's short history quicker than you would usually expect. But that grin and that moustache and the gold World Cup remained untouched in the centre. No one dared take them down, as if removing them would loosen the Emir's grip from the statue itself.

The sporting world was still coming to terms with FIFA's decision. How could this have happened? The press, especially in England, was having a field day. The legendary football writer Brian Glanville, giving his own viciously poetic spin on the issue, called Qatar a 'wretched little anonymity of a football country' and 'Bin Hammam's dismal desert state'. Almost immediately the calls had begun to re-examine the process. At the very least move the event to the winter, which would in turn cause havoc with the schedules of the powerful European leagues. Qatar must have bought it, the media alleged, without giving any concrete evidence. At one point a smoking gun appeared to have been found when Phaedra al Majid, a female media manager on the bid, went rogue, alleging to the *Sunday Times* that Qatar had paid two ExCo members USD1.5 million. The revelations were aired during a parliamentary select committee hearing on England's failed 2018 bid thanks to parliamentary privilege. Later Al Majid would mysteriously retract her allegations.

Indeed, FIFA's general secretary Jerome Valcke had claimed in a leaked email that Qatar had 'bought' it. He later claimed he meant they had used their immense wealth to inundate the process. All within the rules, of course. The suspicions remained. But less well reported was perhaps the true reason for the bid's success. Not bribes or illegal inducements, but the glorified sports centre I had seen Pele and Maradona inaugurate in 2005: Aspire.

When Aspire had first opened its doors in 2004 it was wrapped in the platitudes of the do-gooder. They would spot and nurture talent from across the world in the hope of finding the next Messi or Ronaldo. They had world class training facilities for all sports at its sprawling Aspire complex, with Qatar's Wembley-esque national stadium as its centre point. But Aspire had also become a Forward Operating Base for the 2022 campaign. The Qataris had opened numerous academies around the global looking to identify and recruit talent in previously overlooked or underdeveloped foot-balling nations. It had set up a programme called Football Dreams designed to mine for talent in Africa, opening a facility in Senegal. Whilst the rest of the world's media had looked for subterfuge in the bidding process, Brent Latham, an American sports writer for ESPN, had found a much more believable and accurate reason for Qatar's 2022 success. 'Football Dreams stands out not just because it throws money around to pluck prospects from the developing world,' he wrote. 'Six of the 15 programs are in countries represented on FIFA's all-power 24-man executive committee.'

Guatamala, Thailand and Paraguay had all seen Aspire arrive on their shores. Each had a member on the FIFA Exco, world football's 24 man governing body. Players would be identified and whittled down to a handful who would then be awarded scholarships to Doha or Dakhar. It was a fast track to success and a better life, in a much more controlled and ethical way than the agent's free for all that usually followed a talented player. Whilst the US and England were bragging to the world about their stadia and their technically sound bids, Qatar was working under the radar funding what they viewed as a humanitarian project in the back yards of the men who would actually vote on the World Cup bids. But, along with currying favour with FIFA's Ex Co, the project may not be as altruistic as claimed for another reason. There was one main fringe benefit for Qatar. The hope of finding players for its own national team.

Inside Aspire small groups of children train in front of five a side goals. The young boys were a mix of ethnicities and nationalities: Arab and African; Qatari and Senegalese. On the touchline Aspire's sporting director Wayde Clews watched as the kids were run through their paces by European coaches. '2010 was a watershed year for Aspire because some of the boys that came through the academy are now starting to find their way into the Qatar Olympic squad,' he said. In fact eight Aspire students had just made it to the Qatar squad for the 2010 Asian Games in China. 'We are also now seeing three or four fours making their way in to the [full] national squad,' he added. He denied that Aspire was an exercise in looting talent from the developing world to build a new Qatari team. 'I think there's no evidence to support those sport of notions. What we have done is brought boys from Third World nations. There is absolutely no obstacle of those boys playing for their home countries. It can be seen as an altruistic move by Qatar.'

This was true too. Various Ghanaian and Nigerian national youth squads had benefited from returning Aspire graduates. But Qatar had form in this area, naturalizing athletes from Africa and Asia so that they could compete in the Olympics. The national football team had also seen several Brazilians and Uruguayans play for it, naturalized before the Qataris got greedy and tried to 'sign' the then Werder Bremen striker Ailton, forcing FIFA to change its rules on eligibility. One Uruguayan, Sebastian Soria, remained Qatar's first choice striker to this day.

Clews was adamant that naturalization wasn't a goal, but it didn't mean a young African player couldn't chose to be Qatari if they so wished. As Aspire's director general Andreas Bleicher explained: 'When making agreements, we are not requiring them to play for Qatar. We leave it up to them. A player might be here for five years, and if he wants to play for Qatar, it is upon the player concerned.' That raised a much more fundamental question. A young kid in Senegal or Kenya or Benin could chose the life of poverty and insecurity at home ruled by governments that had invariably failed to offer much in the way of opportunity or a future. At best they could take a long shot in Europe's talent trafficking network where they could find themselves signing for Manchester United, or playing in the Ukrainian second division or begging on the streets of Marseilles. Or they and their families could be taken to Qatar, educated and fed. If they failed, they at least now had options, an education. The question wasn't why would an African kid chose to represent Qatar? The question was why *wouldn't* an African kid chose to represent Qatar? That was what terrified African and European football. One African football journalist captured those fears when he told me, Aspire was 'stealing' the continent's talent. The next generation of Weahs and Drogbas would be lost. This, at least in theory, was partially true. But for European football they had met an entity that threatened its pre-eminence in identifying and exploiting talent. If Aspire was engaged in theft, as some in Africa saw it, they were simply better at the game than the Europeans, who had engaged in talent plunder in a manner that had no rules and few concerns on what would come of those who didn't make it. At least Aspire offered more than an agent's meal ticket. The young boys walking off the state of the art pitch and into the changing rooms were all between 12 and 14-years-old. By the time the 2022 World Cup came along they would be in the mid twenties, in their prime, and possibly wearing the maroon shirt of Qatar.

The Asian Cup wasn't all about Qatar's suitability as a host. On the pitch, things hadn't started well. In front of a packed 40,000 near all-Qatari crowd, after a lavish opening ceremony, the team had conspired to lose 2-0 to Uzbekistan. The holders, Iraq, also had great expectations to fulfil. The Iraq team trained next to the Gharafa Stadium, the stadium where I had met Marcel Desailly what felt like a lifetime ago. Iraq's previous coach Jorvan Vieira, the Brazilian Muslim that had masterminded Iraq's stunning against-all-odds Asian Cup triumph in 2007, was long gone. Now Wolfgang Sidka was in charge, a German who eyed me with suspicion. He was preparing his team for a group match against their perennial rivals Iran. Younis Mahmoud, the captain that had dragged his team to victory through sheer force of will in 2007, scoring the only goal in the final and being nominated for the FIFA Player of the Year in the process, greeted me warmly on the touchline. He had remembered how his team-mates had humiliated me on the Iraqi team bus in Jordan four years ago by filming me dancing topless.

'It's considered a derby game, just as Saudi Arabia is considered a derby,' Mahmoud explained of the up and coming match against Iran. This was an understatement. I had watched him play in the final of the West Asian Championships against Iran, and seen the outpouring of vitriol from the Iraqi crowd towards the Iranian team. 'There were also problems between us and Iran and years of war. So I think it is considered a derby and also a challenge.'

The team had experienced mixed fortunes since that day in July 2007. It was hard living up to an achievement like that. Mahmoud still remembered those last few matches as if they were yesterday. He remembered being in the dressing room after the semi-final with South Korea. Iraq won on penalties but, moments later, a suicide bomber detonated his explosive vest in a crowd of celebrating fans in Baghdad. Some of the team had wanted to pull out of the final, partly out of grief, partly out of guilt. But something stopped them.

'All our players wanted to take this cup because we saw on television one woman whose baby was dead,' he recalled of that moment in the dressing room when they heard the news. They switched on a TV to see the carnage, and saw the woman who had lost her child, overcome with grief. '[She said] 'I need the players to take this cup ... because my son is dead'.' It made the difference between going home and fighting for the title. 'I was fired for this game, I killed myself in that stadium to take this cup,' he said. 'Before we started the game we had won. Because our heart was in this game. We killed ourselves to win this game.'

After the adulation, the comedown followed. Mahmoud had been close to securing a dream move to France, but the issue of whether his extended family could come with him prevented him from going. He stayed in Qatar. Then the team failed to qualify for the 2010 World Cup, losing a final must-win game against, ironically, Qatar. Later it would emerge that one of Qatar's naturalized Brazilian players was ineligible to play in that game. It was an open and shut case. Iraq should have been awarded the tie and a place in the final round of qualification. But FIFA rejected it on the grounds that they received Iraq's appeal past the deadline.

And then there was the battle within the Iraqi Football Association itself. Hussein Saeed Mohammed, Iraq's all time top scorer and, some alleged, Saddam Hussein's favourite player, had kept his job as president of Iraqi football by the skin of his teeth. The Iraqi sports ministry was now run by a Shia politician, who tried to oust Hussein for his silence during the Saddam years. FIFA suspended the federation, threatening their defence of the Asian Cup. He was reinstated but was on borrowed time. Unity and a common purpose was harder to come by in the new Iraq. Results had suffered and the sectarian bickering – within the IFA, if not the team – had begun to rise.

Yet back then, in 2007, with the country tearing itself apart the squad had found that unity in the face of adversity. Something approaching normality had since begun to return to Iraq. In fact, July 2007 marked a watershed for Iraq. According to US military statistics it was the worst month for civilian deaths since the start of the war. But after July the deaths started falling, and they kept dropping. The surge had been a factor on the ground, but the Asian Cup final had had a marked psychological effect.

'The situation in 2007 was very bad. There was fighting on the streets. We won the Asian Cup and now that situation is gone,' explained Nashat Akram, the midfielder who was a key player in that team and who came close to joining Manchester City only for the British government to refuse him a work visa. 'We don't have kidnap in our country any more,' he shrugged. 'We have a very safe country.'

On the next pitch the Iranian-American coach Afshin Ghotbi was training the Iran team. When we had spoken in 2009 he was trying to deflect accusation of treason away from his players. Several had worn green armbands during a 2010 World Cup qualifier against South Korea. The armbands, it was alleged, were worn in sympathy with the Green Revolution that was taking place back home. It was crushed and the players had to face the music. Ghotbi kept his job, and even recalled some of those players despite claims they would be banned and imprisoned, including the country's best player Ali Karimi. But Ghotbi had been given a hard time by the press, especially those that couldn't see past his American upbringing. Dozens of Iranian sports journalists crowded around him as he left the pitch, shouting vociferously at him.

'You always have big rivalries like this with neighbours, take USA-Mexico, or Holland-Germany, Korea-Japan,' he said as the team filed onto the team bus painted the colours of the Iranian flag.

'There are a lot of beautiful rivalries in football that excite the fans. It is a rivalry. There's a long history of sports and politics. So my feeling is that it will be an exciting game. And I hope that energy from outside the game will be transferred to the pitch. It will be a spectacle.' He wouldn't talk about the Green Revolution protests any more, not now anyway. This was his last tournament for Iran. He would soon leave to take charge of a team in the Japanese J League. But he hinted of more. 'I will tell you the truth when I leave here,' he would later whisper to me conspiratorially. 'Perhaps I will write a book about it.'

✦

As dusk fell on the Al Rayyan stadium, migrant workers sold Iraqi and Iranian flags side by side. The atmosphere was good natured, conciliatory even, a far cry from the hatred that had marred the final of the West Asian Championships a few years previously. Of course, it was Younis Mahmoud who scored first for Iraq but Iran stormed back, winning 2-1. After the game the Iranians, almost all wealthy expats living in Doha, danced and sang in the streets outside. Both teams, in the end, qualified for the quarter finals but that was as far as Iraq and Iran would reach, losing to a single extra time goal against Australia and South Korea respectively. Qatar, too, had reached the quarter finals. I had sat in the Khalifa International Stadium along with 30,000 white-robed Qataris as they prayed for a miracle. They beat China 2-0 but succumbed to Japan in the next round 3-2, despite being 2-1 up with 19 minutes to go and putting in their best performance of the tournament. The two goal scorers were Sebastian Soria and Fabio Cesar, the former born in Uruguay, the latter Brazil.

The tournament didn't go without its problems either. Empty seats were an issue, usually dealt with by bussing in hundreds of Indian migrant workers from their day jobs building Qatar's gleaming future, as if they were little more than human seat warmers. It only went to highlight the plight of the migrant workers in the Gulf, usually on sponsored contracts with no freedom of movement and extremely low wages. Their plight has been taken up by the international trade union movement who launched a 'No World Cup in Qatar without labor rights' campaign. 'It is not too late to change the venue of the World Cup. This is not an industrial skirmish about wages; this is a serious breach in regard to human and labor rights,' Sharan Burrow, general secretary of the International Trade Union Confederation told Turkish newspaper *Hurriyet*. 'The country is incredibly wealthy and is portraying itself as a model country. That is simply not true. Our members are football fans and they don't want to see the game played in a country that practices slavery.' But there was still context to be found here too. During India's match against Australia, a few thousand workers had been given the day off – and free tickets – to watch their countrymen play. None of them liked football, but willingly attended for a glimpse of home. They were mostly from the south, where cricket was supreme. But it was still India, and the tickets were free. Almost every worker was cautious about Qatar. There were still problems but, as one engineer told me: 'Thank God I'm not in Saudi Arabia or Abu Dhabi.' The difference between their list of gripes – some still very serious - and their countrymen's utter despair when I had visited a sewage-filled labour camp in Dubai was telling.

The final between Japan and Australia was chaos too. Thousands of fans with tickets (although the organisers claim only 700) had been locked out, supporters who had travelled from Tokyo and Sydney to be there. The gates had been closed half an hour before kick off, the organisers explained, as part of the Emir's security detail, the kind of move that would have caused a riot at a World Cup finals. Yet, despite the controversy and the accusations, Qatar remain the hosts of the 2022 World Cup finals. Perhaps a smoking gun will be found between now and 2022. *France Football*, amongst a host of other global media, have all tried (and failed) to find it amongst the fog of unaccountability that invariably surrounds the opaque dealings of an all powerful Gulf monarchy. That in itself could be another book entirely. In all Gulf monarchies money flows from the king downwards. Patronage, based on familial and tribal ties, dictates who gets what. Money is seldom self made. Everything is intimately connected. Look at how Manchester City is enjoying a huge boost in sponsorship income thanks to Etihad Airways – also owned by the royal family of Abu Dhabi. Before it Emirates, owned by the royal family of Dubai, had used its money to paint the emirate in a good light. Making a profit was incidental to both.

The same principle could be seen in Qatar. According to one investigation into Russia and Qatar's winning bids in *The Blizzard* by journalist James Corbett, Qatar's state-owned airline, Qatar Airways, unveiled massively subsidised routes to Argentina and Brazil. In August, the Emir of Qatar visited Paraguay on an official state visit to finalise one of the biggest trade deals in the country's history. ExCo members from all three countries – Argentina, Brazil and Paraguay – apparently voted for Qatar. Of course, it all could be coincidence.

Most intriguing of all was the mess that the French found themselves in. It was alleged that UEFA president Michel Platini was asked to vote for Qatar by then President Nicolas Sarkozy. Several commercial and military airline deals with Qatar hung in the balance at the time. The allegations, made in a 15 page *France Football* investigation under the headline 'Qatargate', laid out how the President had hosted a secret lunch for the crown prince of Qatar, Sheikh Tamin bin Haman al Thani, Michel Platini and representatives of the Qatar Investment Authority, the sovereign wealth fund that had recently bought PSG, Sarkozy's team. Platini responded forcefully. 'To say that my choice... was part of a deal between the French state and Qatar is pure speculation... and lies,' he said. 'I do not rule out legal action against anyone who casts doubt on the honesty of my vote.' The smoking gun, if there even is one, remains illusive.

The money and the influence and the power of the Gulf remains in the ascendancy. But as Japan lifted the Asian Cup, another powerful force destined to shape the region, and the world, over the next decade was breaking cover. The capitals of the Middle East were burning with the fires of the Arab Spring. And in Cairo on that same day, on the front lines of the battles for control of Tahrir square, stood a force – nurtured on the terraces of its football stadiums – that threatened to bring down a dictator.

17
JERUSALEM

Jerusalem Syndrome *(n) A group of mental phenomena involving the presence of either religiously themed obsessive ideas, delusions or other psychosis-like experiences that are triggered by a visit to the city of Jerusalem. It is not endemic to one single religion or denomination but has affected Jews, Christians and Muslims of many different backgrounds.*

Florida, United States, June 2012

The T.T. Zion was found marooned but otherwise seaworthy on a sand bank near East Las Olas Boulevard, Fort Lauderdale. The boulevard along Florida's Gold Coast is an upmarket stretch of prime real estate. Dan Quayle once lived here, as did Sonny and Cher, and the T.T Zion wouldn't normally look out of place in such salubrious surroundings. But on this warm and wet summer night, the T.T Zion wasn't where it should be. Its twin engines were running, the lights were on. But the T.T. Zion was empty, abandoned, lost.

Las Olas means 'The Waves' in Spanish, a nod to Florida's deceptively dangerous shoreline. Shark attacks are more common here than anywhere else in the world. Last year the University of Florida's International Shark Attack File programme recorded 80 unprovoked attacks worldwide, 53 of those in the US. Just under half of those, 26, were in Florida, the joint highest since records began. High winds and hurricanes regularly batter a coastline renowned for its strong rip tides, killing dozens every year. The Gulf Stream charges north at 5 knots just a few miles from the coast, its warm waters powering the violent storms that rip along the Eastern seaboard.

It was dark, the winds high. Four foot waves had been recorded that night. It was the start of Florida's most destructive hurricane season in living memory – a total of 12 would be formed over the coming months, including Hurricane Sandy which would go on to batter New York. Over 200 lives would be lost and $78 billion worth of damage caused.

Hurricane season was still in its infancy. Guma Aguiar said goodbye to his wife and young family and boarded the T.T. Zion, christened after the ancient name for Jerusalem. It was an apt name for Aguiar's 31-foot, $2.1 million luxury pride and joy. The 35-year-old Jewish multi millionaire had made Jerusalem the capital of his world. Ever since his natural gas exploration company Leor Energy discovered and then sold a huge natural gas field in the US, Aguiar had pumped millions of dollars into the city.

He wasn't always Jewish. At least, he didn't always identify himself as Jewish. Born in Brazil to a Jewish mother, Aguiar was raised a Catholic but was brought back to Judaism by Rabbi Tovia Singer, founder and director of Outreach Judaism. Outreach Judaism was a self declared 'counter-missionary' organisation 'dedicated to countering the efforts of fundamentalist Christian groups and cults who specifically target Jews for conversion.' The controversial Rabbi had discovered Aguiar's roots and aggressively attempted to reconnect him to his heritage. Aguiar was 26 at the time.

Three years later his stewardship of Leor had netted him an estimated fortune of $200 million. Reborn in his faith, Aguiar became enchanted with Jerusalem. He spent big to attract the attentions of the great and good in Israel, donating tens of millions of dollars to a host of Jewish organisations. But his biggest outlay came in June 2009, when he decided he was going to buy Beitar Jerusalem, Israel's most popular and most controversial football club. He sunk $4 million into the team and was welcomed to the club like a new Messiah. He had found acceptance. He had found home.

But, within seven months, Aguiar wasn't to be seen on the club's terraces any more. He was being held in a psychiatric institution after a series of episodes in Israel. He was flown home, half his fortune gone, deeply embroiled in an on-going legal case against his uncle and business partner Thomas Kaplan, an Oxford University trained historian with a love of conservation who had, nonetheless, made his money in mining and natural gas. Aguiar's wife, Jamie, had asked him for a divorce.

According to the US Coastguard's report on the boat's GPS signal, the T.T. Zion left its mooring on June 19, 2012 at 7.29pm and travelled at 31 miles per hour north east – such a speed that the T.T. Zion jumped the waves, according to one eye witness – until abruptly coming to a halt, turning, and drifting back to East Las Olas Boulevard. Aguiar was gone, his phone and wallet were found on board. At first it seemed like a clear case of suicide, a troubled young man about to lose everything taking his final stand. But a mere few days after his disappearance, a vicious series of court battles erupted over Aguiar's assets. Accusations of opulence, avarice, indulgence, greed and manipulation were made as Aguiar's final resting place remained unknown. The T.T. Zion stopped just short of the Gulf Stream. One coastguardman suggested that the abrupt change of speed and the broken tow bar indicated that Aguiar might have been thrown over board. In the Gulf Stream, his body would be taken north and never seen again. In fact, few involved in the case truly expected a body to be found, but not because of the speed of the Gulf Stream. A very different explanation was gaining traction. His body might not be found because there might not be a body to be found.

Guma Aguiar might not be dead after all.

The Teddy Stadium in Jerusalem is named after the city's greatest mayor, himself named after Theodore Herzl, the founder of modern Zionism. Theodore Kollek, or Teddy as he was affectionately named, came to power in 1965 after running for office at the insistence of then Prime Minister David Ben-Gurion. He ruled over a poor, under developed Western half of the city but made his name when Israel captured the Eastern, Arab half of Jerusalem during the 1967 War, and oversaw the city's modernisation. He was re-elected five times. Teddy was both a Zionist and a pragmatist, indelibly wedded to the idea of a united Jerusalem under Israeli rule but also sympathetic towards the plight of the city's newly disenfranchised Arab population. When he died in 2007 at the age of 95 the *New York Times'* obituary described how Israel's assassinated Prime Minister Yitzhak Rabin called him 'the greatest builder of Jerusalem since Herod the Great.'

Today the vast, modern steel and brick edifice that bears Kollek's name – the colour of Jerusalem's famous, ubiquitous pale limestone – is home to Israel's best supported and most controversial club Beitar Jerusalem. In recent years the stadium has seen little of the pragmatism nor tolerance that saw Teddy demand that the Israeli military's first job after capturing East Jerusalem was to distribute free milk to Arab children. Beitar has long been the team of the religious, nationalistic right, representing Israel's working class Mizrahim population, Jews who have their roots in the Arab world and north Africa. After Israel's creation in 1948, the government was dominated by the white, European Jews who had travelled mostly from Germany, Poland and Romania and who helped to prolong the Labor party's leftist hegemony, the Ashkenazim. But the club's fans backed the Likud party in huge numbers. When Likud finally broke the Labor party's dominance in the 1977 election, it was seen as a watershed moment in Israeli society but also for the Mizrahim and the religious right. Beitar played its part too, winning its first ever cup final in the same year against the country's biggest team Maccabi Tel Aviv, a team steeped in the modern history of the Ashkenazim. Beitar was supported by prime ministers,politicians and businessmen.

I had first met the club's renowned hardcore of fans, La Familia as they called themselves, in 2006. Back then, in a match against Maccabi Tel Aviv, I had heard the chants that had built their notoriety: 'Death To The Arabs' and 'We swear on the Menorah, there will be no Arabs here' were just two. I had watched them riot outside the ground, almost getting beaten up in the process after being mistaken for a fan of Hapoel Tel Aviv – Israel's popular, left wing club – thanks to the red t-shirt I was wearing. It was also a Beitar fan who came to my rescue. I had friends who were both moderate and conservative who supported Beitar and yet deplored La Familia's behaviour. But something had changed over the course of the past seven years. La Familia had once been ignored as an extremist irritant, kids playing at being adults over the Green Line. Now they had Israel's and the world's attention. Not because they had exploded in numbers, but because what they said, what they believed in, didn't appear to be that ugly any more. The club has been sanctioned many times for La Familia's racism: points deductions and heavy fines amongst them. The supporters had been regularly banned from the Teddy too, the team forced to play behind closed doors. Nothing seemed to chastise the hardcore. Nothing seemed able to change the culture at the club.

Yet Beitar exerted a strong pull on the rich and the powerful. With so many politically influential supporters, rich men lined up to help the club. It was often said that Beitar commanded one million supporters. Arkadi Gaydamak was one such man beguiled by the club, a controversial Russian billionaire. He had sunk tens of millions of dollars in to the club, bankrolling it to the championship. But his efforts to try and make Beitar a club for everyone in Jerusalem came to nothing. The fans instead rioted and looted the Israeli FA's offices. At the next game they whistled during a minute silence in the memory of Yitzhak Rabin. They sang 'Mohamed is a Homo'.

'The idiot bastards can leave,' Gaydamak said of the hardcore troublemakers at his club after a particularly nasty pitch invasion. 'The fans that went wild yesterday are bastards, and I have no respect for them. While their numbers are in the thousands, they are not the majority.'

Gaydamak, of course, had his eyes on a bigger prize. He held political ambition and had become a thorn in the then Prime Minister Ehud Olmert's side, staging a series of deft publicity stunts. The finest was setting up a luxury tent village in a park in Tel Aviv for the residents of an Israeli town under siege by rockets from Gaza in 2007. Olmert, who at the time had polled a zero percent popularity rating in one national newspaper poll, had insisted that the residents of the towns near Gaza stay put, otherwise Hamas might view it as a surrender. But hundreds of terrified residents took up Gaydamak's offer. Each child was given a black and gold Beitar scarf, the menorah stitched at both ends, on arrival. Still, Gaydamak's popularism didn't translate in to votes. After setting up his own political party he announced in 2008 he would – like Teddy Kollek before him – run for mayor of Jerusalem. He was routed at the ballot box, coming a distant third. The humiliation, coupled with the financial crash which hit his business interests hard, saw Gaydamak withdraw from Beitar as he actively looked for a new buyer for the club.

Guma Aguiar may have grown up in Brazil but he wasn't much of a football fan. He was a basketball man through and through. But he had quickly gained a reputa- tion for his acts of philanthropy in Israel since selling Leor Energy and his donations brought him to the attention of Israel's politicians – he could count the President Shimon Peres as a friend – and, eventually, Beitar. Without Gaydamak's backing, the club was on the verge of going under. Aguiar was persuaded to sink $4million dollars in to the club, as well as a further $1.5 million in to the city's basketball team Hapoel Jerusalem. That was in June 2009 and Aguiar agreed to a telephone interview where I asked him about how his decision to invest in Beitar and Hapoel came about.

'I love Jerusalem, it's special. You're not in Kansas any more, that's for sure,' Aguiar explained, sounding confident and erudite, as he did in the slew of TV interviews he had conducted to woo the Israeli media. 'I was approached,' he said of how Beitar's predicament was brought to his attention. 'There are a lot of people here who feel strongly about their teams. It reminds me a lot of Brazil, going to the Maracana. A lot people here don't care about anything other than football. I can relate to that.'

Beitar was desperate for a new saviour and Aguiar seemed to be the perfect fit. He was young, rich and eager to please. Unlike Gaydamak, he also didn't have any ambitions for elected office. 'I don't want to use the football as a political tool because that's not fair, as an outsider, to come in and have a [political] agenda,' he said. In fact Aguiar, who despite being married with four young children, had a reputation as something of a flamboyant playboy who liked to burn the candle at both ends. 'Like Madonna said the other night, this is the centre of the universe,' he told a lo- cal TV channel whilst trying to play tennis badly. He wore sunglasses, his head was bowed, voice hoarse. 'The only party I'm interested in forming is just a party.' But he understood Beitar's reputation in the world, and how it was beginning to harm, even define, the city's standing. 'The one thing I would like to see is more tolerance from the fans. In order for us to be competitive and to attract talent we want to play abroad and not be viewed as total hooligans. I certainly wouldn't want to go to Barcelona and hear them singing 'Death to the Jews'.'

Like Gaydamak, he wanted to improve Jerusalem's image. 'I want to see the flagship name of Jerusalem, bring some outsiders to Israel to visit [and] create awareness about this place,' he finished. 'Raising the profile of Jerusalem would be the most positive outcome. It's torn apart by a lot of conflict. But there are Christians, Jews and Muslims here that love the land they live in. I want Christian and Muslim fans here too.'

Aguiar sounded sincere and knowledgeable. He agreed we should meet in Israel later in the year, after he had seen exactly what he had bought into.

On August 28 Guma Aguiar walked on to the pitch at the Teddy Stadium to rapturous applause. It was Beitar's first match of the Israeli football season, against arch rivals Hapoel Tel Aviv, a team with its roots in Israel's left wing union movement. Arabs had long played for the team. The Israeli TV station Channel 1 aired an interview before the kick off with Aguiar. It began with him blowing a *shofar*, a traditional ram's horn blown on some Jewish religious ceremonies.

'It's my first time in the Teddy Stadium,' he said to the camera. His shirt collar was open. Upon his chest lay a silver Star of David on a necklace. 'They say: 'Are you some kind of Messiah'. I say no, I don't want to be associated with a word like that. I have no idea [about the outcome of the Hapoel game]. Only God knows. Maybe he's feeling extra sympathetic to Jerusalem tonight,' he said. 'And if not, perhaps he'll feel extra sympathetic later in the year.'

On the pitch a light and smoke show was under way. Israeli dance music thumped out as beautiful Israeli girls danced in the centre circle. On the sidelines, Aguiar was jumping up and down to the beat, dancing with the team's mascot: a man dressed in a dog suite. Aguiar moved into the centre circle and wiggled his hips in time with the music next to the singer. He closed his eyes, arms in the air, and stumbled through the choreography. The dancers didn't miss a beat.

'This is Aguiar's night,' intoned Danny Neuman, a Beitar legend commentating on the match for the evening. 'He has saved Beitar.'

The game finished 0-0.

It should have been a quiet midweek night in the Irish bar in the centre of Jerusalem but Guma Aguiar was gearing up for a party. Outside, on the quaint cobbled street, a hoard of expensive, blacked out 4X4s sat clustered around the door, paying little heed to the city's parking law. Inside the lights were low and the bar was empty. Dance music thumped around the vacuum. But, in one corner, up on a raised platform, stood the tall figure of Guma Aguiar. A ring of steel surrounded him; pumped, shaven headed bodyguards wearing black jeans and black T-shirts. They stood firm as we approached. Aguiar was standing next to an identically dressed bodyguard, who was rolling him a cigarette. Around him several Beitar players, one an Israeli international, buzzed around, eager for his attention. 'Guma, can you get me a ticket to an NBA game,' one pleaded. Aguiar ignored him and lit his fat cigarette. The strong smell of marijuana filled the room.

It had been a few months since Aguiar and I had spoken on the phone. He had agreed to meet me in his favourite bar along with Jeremy, the Israeli journalist I had met at a Beitar match three-and-a-half years previously and who was now the sports editor of the *Jerusalem Post*. Aguiar trusted Jeremy and was eager to curry favour with a paper that was widely read in North America. Aguiar spotted him, raised his arm, and the black sea parted.

It was clear that not all was well. Aguiar seemed agitated. He couldn't focus on anyone for more than a few seconds before losing his trail of thought. Sometimes he would start the same conversation two, three, occasionally four times. The sycophants laughed. His personal bodyguard rolled him another, and then another. He had no recollection of our conversation a few months previously, nor of what he had said a few moments before. But his generosity remained intact. He bought round after round of drinks, buying a round for the rest of the bar on one occasion. Aguiar couldn't make eye contact when we talked. He hung his head, as if listening. He pressed the half smoked cigarette between my fingers. I inhaled. Stars, a tunnel, silence and then white noise, before the gradual return of the world around me. Time stopped.

Beitar's season had begun in mixed fashion. They drew the first two league matches of the season, against arguably their two biggest rivals Hapoel Tel Aviv and the Arab club Bnei Sakhnin 0-0. A handful of narrow victories against low ranked opponents followed. But as the end of the year approached it was clear that Beitar would not be challenging for the league title, despite the early season optimism. Aguiar's life was taking an equally as rocky path. As his profile rose, so did interest in his private life. A little-written about court case between Aguiar and his uncle Thomas Kaplan – the man whom he had gone in to business with a few years previously, making his fortune when they sold Leor – had suddenly become prescient, a taste of the familial litigation to come. In January 2009 Kaplan launched a legal action in to remove Aguiar as a director of the Lillian Jean Kaplan Foundation, named in honour of Kaplan's mother. According to the South Florida Sun Sentinel Thomas Kaplan had given $40 million to the foundation, money used, among other things, to build drinking water wells in Africa. But Kaplan had accused his nephew of miss-spending as much as $7 million in efforts to 'claim that he is the Messiah and to promote his messianic mission.'

The lawsuit was the latest battle in a legal war with his uncle over the sale of Leor. Aguiar believed he was due $18 million more. Kaplan believed that Aguiar had misappropriated company funds – making inappropriate payments to himself and his family – and wanted Aguiar's share of the sale returned. The Sentinel dubbed it 'The Messiah lawsuit'. 'They are trying to distract and intimidate me from going on with my life,' Aguiar told them.

There was also the issue of his arrest in Florida on drugs charges. He was arrested in June of that year on counts of driving under the influence, possession of marijuana and 'drug paraphernalia', thought to be a bong. Aguiar had countered that he had been abused in custody and refused to pay the $536 court charges. 'When I got to the prison (a police officer) took my kippah off and then tried to convert me to Christianity,' he told the Israeli daily newspaper *Haaretz* in October 2009. 'I told him to leave me the fuck alone. He then took me - after blowing triple zeros on my breath test - to the Broward County Sheriff's Office where they arrested me and beat the shit out of me.' According to the paper Aguiar said he was wearing a skullcap and a shirt with the word Israel on it at the time of the arrest. The Broward County Sheriff's office denied the accusations, saying that Aguiar was 'combative and verbally abusive' and that he had been 'controlled and restrained.'

But now, in an Irish bar in Jerusalem, he looked anything but combative. He looked lost as he swayed from side to side roughly in time with the music. I passed him back his cigarette as the world reformed around me.

'If you smoke that every day,' I advised through foggy eyes, 'you will go crazy.'

He didn't hear me. It was the last time I would ever hear from Guma Aguiar.

On the morning of January 14, 2010, an ambulance and two police cars escorted Guma Aguiar to the Abarbanel Mental Health Center in Bat Yam on the outskirts of Jerusalem. Under orders from his wife, he had been sectioned. Aguiar suffered with bi-polar disorder and had suddenly taken a turn for the worse. A few days earlier he had given an interview with a local newspaper where he had claimed that he was in mobile phone contact with Gilad Shalit, the Israeli soldier kidnapped by a Palestinian terrorist group and held incommunicado in the Gaza Strip since 2006. No one knew of his whereabouts, not even Israeli secret service. But Aguiar had claimed he had snuck into the Gaza Strip and freed Shalit, who was now holed up in one of his properties.

'I wanted to prove that I could enter Gaza and come out alive and that Shalit could come out alive as well,' he told the *Kol Ha'ir* newspaper. 'He [Shalit] said that he wants me to tell his family how much he loves them and Israel, and that he hopes this ends soon.'

Within a few weeks it was announced that Aguiar would cease funding Beitar Jerusalem. As he was only sponsoring the club, and hadn't taken full ownership, Arcadi Gaydamak was now in full charge of the football team again. His money had prevented Beitar from going out of business, but his philanthropic journey in Israel was over. Or so it seemed.

'He's an enigma,' explained Shlomi Barzel, the new sports editor of *Haaretz*. Barzel had met Aguiar shortly before he was sectioned. 'He was smoking [marijuana]. I'd met him at a game Saturday. The day before we had met and had an hour and a half meeting. He could not remember me at all. After a meeting he was coming out of the toilet with white powder all over his nose.' Barzel felt some sympathy for Aguiar. 'Was it Jerusalem Syndrome or was it too much powder in the nose?' he asked rhetorically. 'The man was a lunatic. I thought it was a question of conscience, how Gaydamak took the money. It was clear to me that Guma wasn't capable of taking one rational decision. You have to know that, after Gaydamak, there was a period when people [Beitar supporters] were not looking for the new king, they were looking for a rich man coming from nowhere.'

Things didn't go much better back home. According to a Florida court judgement that found against Aguiar in 2010:

> Aguiar's psychosis manifested itself in both grandiose and paranoid delusions. In the spring of 2008, Aguiar expressed the grandiose belief that he is or could be the Messiah. With respect to his paranoid delusions, Aguiar has stated on multiple occasions that [his uncle Thomas] Kaplan was trying to kill him. Aguiar believes that he has been poisoned, that he was shot in the back from a helicopter, that snipers have been following him and that the medical staff at an Israeli hospital were injecting him with poison in order to kill him. Aguiar's bipolar disorder first manifested itself in 1997 when he was Baker Acted [involuntarily detained as per Florida state law] at a Florida psychiatric hospital for approximately 12 days. At the time, Aguiar was 19 years old.

Most interestingly, the documents claimed:

> Aguiar experienced the onset of another manic episode in mid-June

2009 and is still recovering from this episode. From approximately June 2009 through January 2010, Aguiar was also psychotic. Aguiar is presently in treatment for his mental illness.

June 2009 to January 2010 was the exact time Aguiar had been Beitar's benefactor. It was also claimed that Aguiar was abusing:

alcohol, marijuana, Xanax (an anti-anxiety medication), Ambien (a sleeping pill), anabolic steroids (testosterone) and OxyContin (an opiate).

The judgement is disturbing reading. It lays bare a series of misdeeds and failures: email hacking, paranoia, drug abuse, threats, counter threats and spousal abuse. Aguiar was appealing the decision and had even re-entered the arena of Israeli sports. In 2011 it was announced that he had bought a majority stake in the Hapoel Jerusalem basketball team, the team he had donated $1.5million two years previously. But as his legal battle with his uncle intensified and his marriage deteriorated (divorce was threatened and counter threatened; Jamie made accusations of violence against her and her father) Aguiar boarded the T.T. Zion last June and disappeared without trace.

What had begun as one of the biggest natural resource windfalls in modern American history had ended in a story of mental illness, betrayal and family breakdown. Within hours of Aguiar's disappearance his mother Ellen, Kaplan's estranged sister, had moved to take control of his assets. Aguiar's largesse, philanthropy, generosity, what ever the rival lawyers wanted to call it, had halved his fortune to an estimated $100 million. The speed of the legal manoeuvre raised questions as to what had truly befallen Guma Aguiar. In the aftermath Guma's wife Jamie and his mother Ellen embarked on a costly legal battle that is on going whilst Thomas Kaplan's legal team made clear that they held out hope Guma was still alive. But how, in the twenty-first century, could someone with such a high profile simply disappear without trace? What proof was there? Where could Aguiar go?

'There's certainly enough evidence that one could deduce that he's still alive,' explained Jamie Aguiar's lawyer Bill Scherer, sitting in his smart conference room in Florida. 'It would be a nice chapter in a mystery novel... He could have been thrown out [of the boat], drowned and his body swept north and never found. Or he could have stayed in, it drifted to shore, he jumped out the boat and was picked up by someone who was waiting for him. It could have been either or.'

If Guma Aguiar was alive, where could he possibly go? One theory was the Netherlands. According to Scherer around the time of his disappearance Aguiar's [unnamed] best friend, who was also a business partner, upped sticks and moved to Amsterdam. Now Aguiar's sister and brother in law had followed suit.

'The sister and the brother in law are in Amsterdam and trying to avoid our process so we can take a deposition and ask them, on oath, whether they know where he is,' said Scherer. 'Amsterdam is a place he used to like to go … We learned Guma loved Amsterdam. For obvious reasons...' There was also, according to Scherer, the case of Guma's missing clothes. 'Socks, shoes, custom fitted clothing all removed [from his house in Israel]. Personal items. Things that he would want to have if he was still alive,' he said. 'They [whoever removed the clothes] got in without any evidence of forced entry but they cut out all the internal video surveillance. And they would only know how to do that if they knew the set up.'

The court battle will be long, bloody and expensive, depleting what is left of Aguiar's assets. Without a body, Guma Aguiar will not be declared dead in Florida for another four years, and another two in Israel. Guma's sister and his uncle and former business partner Thomas Kaplan didn't respond to requests for an interview. Guma's mother had denied having any knowledge of her son's whereabouts and believed that he was dead. It would, after all, be almost impossible to disappear without trace, no matter how much money you have, in today's wired world. Especially somewhere as small and visible as The Netherlands. It would take gargantuan planning; the hiding of assets, a passport from a country with no US extradition treaty (the Netherlands has had one with the US. Since 1983), lots of money and a complete break from the technology that dominates our world today.

'It's nigh-on impossible to have an existence where you aren't tracked or traced by technology,' Oliver Crofton, director of technology security firm Vigilante Bespoke, told *Spears* magazine. 'If the person really wanted to hide they'd need to change their name and chuck every device they had in the river. They couldn't even open any emails, and they certainly couldn't use a credit card — just a suitcase full of dollars.' Or Sheckles, of course. But with no Guma, dead or alive, the mystery deepens. When asked whether he had commissioned private detectives to look for Aguiar in the Netherlands Scherer replied: 'We are ever vigilant to work out whether he is alive. That's all I can tell you.' But he believed that the mystery of Guma Aguiar's life and possible death would have another chapter. 'I can write a script where Guma says: 'Look I've been in a psychotic state until just recently and then all of a sudden the fog clears and I realise what am I doing out here?'' he said, explaining one possible scenario. 'He'd say: 'I'm well now and, gee, I don't have any memory of what happened to me over the last year and a half. I've had a bi-polar episode.' Stranger things have happened.'

With a divided family grieving for his return, it would be a fitting end to the story of a man who arrived in Jerusalem to make his mark on the world, hailed and accused of being the Messiah in equal measure: The resurrection of Guma Aguiar.

18

THE TRAGEDY OF
PORT SAID

April 2011

It was 61 days since the fall of Hosni Mubarak and the 7,000 supporters of Al Ahly crowded in to one end of Cairo's Military Stadium for the re-start of the Egyptian football league were finally able to gloat in front of the people that had made their lives hell for the past four years.

Hundreds of police officers stood looking at the crowd as the fans, led by the Ahlawy, gleefully reminded them and their former paymasters of their position in the new post-revolutionary Egypt. Around the group revolutionary flags had been hung: from Tunisia, Libya and Palestine. In the middle of the crowd Assad led the crowd in song.

'Fuck the mother of Hosni Mubarak!' he shouted, as the thousands followed suit.

'Go fuck your Minister, Habib al Adly!'

This show of dissent would have been ruthlessly cut down a few months previously. But now Mubarak was under arrest in a hospital bed near the Red Sea, and Al Adly – the former Minister of the Interior and the man formally in charge of Egypt's hated police force – languished, along with Mubarak's sons, the ex-Prime Minister and other members of the country's elite, in the same jail he would send the former regime's political prisoners.

'Can you imagine? What must they all must be saying to each other! You could write a film about it!' shouted Assad over the deafening sound of abuse. 'The police would abuse us every day. Now it's our time.' It had been a while since I had last seen Assad but the circumstances couldn't have been any more different. When we first met, at the birth of his Ahlawy ultras group during the Cairo derby four years previously, the group numbered a few hundred. But their numbers exploded thanks to their persecution by the police under Mubarak. It was a move he would live to regret.

The world watched transfixed as the Egyptians deposed its hated president after 30 years of stifling repression. Every day hundreds of thousands would turn up to Tahrir Square and fight pitched battles. But what could explain how a country, where civil society had been so sanitized, and any opposition so ruthlessly crushed, could rise up against one of the world's largest police states? This was the 'Facebook Revolution' but, improbably, was also – at least in part - a football revolution too, where organised fan groups, the ultras of Cairo's two biggest teams – Ahly and Zamalek – buried their traditional enmity, if only for a little while, to play a crucial role in bringing down a government.

Assad picked me up outside the same KFC on Tahrir Square we had first met in 2007. He looked different now: His glasses were gone and his hair was cut short like a soldier.

'Living under Mubarak was like living under communism in Eastern Europe... nobody could talk to each other who might have the potential to organise,' he explained as we drove out of Cairo's clogged centre to the Military Stadium on the outskirts of town. 'The whole concept of any independent organisation didn't exist, not unions, not political parties. Nothing was organised, and then we started to organise football ultras. It was just sport then. But to them it was the youth, in big numbers – very smart people – who could mobilise themselves quickly. They feared us.'

The Ahlawy grew into something more violent and anti-authoritarian. Members were arbitrarily beaten and arrested, fans harassed by being stripped searched or humiliated. Assad himself had been arrested and thrown in jail. Ahly's football matches provided a microcosm of the heavy handedness that the rest of the country felt on a daily basis in Mubarak's Egypt. But unlike the activists and the other opposition groups that had been quickly neutered, the ultras fought back.

'The more they tried to put pressure on us, the more we grew in cult status. The Ministry and the media, they would call us a gang, as violent,' said Assad as we neared the ground. The police were now in small numbers, lurking on the periphery in the shadows of the stadium.

'It wasn't just supporting a team, you were fighting a system and the country as a whole. We were fighting the police, fighting the government, fighting for our rights... The police did what they wanted. The government did what they want. And the ultras taught us to speak our mind. This was something new, a little bit of a seed that was planted four years later.'

Now the Ahlawy were in charge As much as the match against Al Shorta – ironically the police's own football club - was a celebration for the Ahlawy, it was also the first large-scale public outing for the police force. After viciously trying to put down the revolution with tear gas, rubber bullets and then, finally, live ammunition, the police fled their positions and melted into the population. Now they had returned, chastened; politely asking for tickets and meekly asking the supporters to go through the turntables. Before, Assad explained, a swing of the club would have sufficed.

The skills that Assad and the Ahlawy had honed during four years of fighting the police came in handy when the January 25 revolution, and the 'Day of Rage' that took place three days later, saw the confrontation between the authorities – who had decades of experience quashing dissent – and a wholly unprepared public turn increasingly violent. 'I don't want to say we were solely responsible for bringing down Mubarak!' Assad laughed. 'But our role was ... letting them know if a cop hits you, you can hit them back, not just run away. This was a police state. Our role started earlier than the revolution. During the revolution, there was the Muslim Brotherhood, the activists and the ultras. That's it.' Fittingly, the final score was Al Ahly 2, the Police 1.

Later we met in the Horriya bar, an old, yellowing relic of Egypt's 1950s heyday, on a road near Tahrir Square. The leaders of the Ahlawy sat around, discussing the day the revolution began.

'After three or four days, you can't really feel the tear gas as much,' said Mohammed, one of Ahlawy's lieutenants. 'But we had been in contact with other ultra groups from Tunisia who had been involved in the protest there. They told us to dab Pepsi under our eyes. It worked!'

And what of their hated rivals, Zamalek and their group the Ultras White Knights, who the Ahlawy would fight when they weren't fighting the police? Did you join forces on the front line?

'For a few hours,' spat Assad, as if he had made a pack with the devil. 'But I couldn't do it for long.'

Tahrir Square felt anarchic. Compared to the suffocating security of the past, there were no police or Army on the street. A camp of activists still occupied the centre. People argued about politics on the street. Sometimes they would end in a fist fight. On one occasion a man wearing a women's abaya was lynched by a crowd when he was denounced as an Israeli spy. On another an angry crowd surrounded a different man after he was denounced as police informer. Both had to be rescued by the army. It was flawed and chaotic. But it was free. There was hope. The police had been bested. Tomorrow would be a better day.

Things had been tougher for the supporters of Zamalek. The Ultras White Knights [UWK] had been in hiding, but agreed to meet me in Nasr City, a district of Cairo, in secret. They had good reason to be careful. The day before four of its 15 leaders had been arrested, along with 18 of its members. Two days had passed since

Ahly had beaten the Police team but the UWK had bigger problems to deal with than the fact that Ahly had cut Zamalek's lead at the top of the table to three points. Earlier in the month Zamalek fans had stormed the pitch during an African Champions League match against a Tunisian club, destroying the goals and attacking the players. The interim military government considered cancelling the league, until the clubs pointed out that most would end up going bankrupt. The UWK had been blamed for the violence, and now the authorities were purging its ranks.

The three men sitting in Costa Coffee couldn't have looked less like violent football revolutionaries. Amir, a gentle-natured, heavy set man in his early 20s, was a production manager. Mohammed was a lawyer; Massoud a student. But they, along with the rest of the UWK leadership were being hunted down by the authorities.

'We have suspended our activities,' explained Amir, who suggested, like many White Knights, that the pitch invasion was led, not by them, but by those seeking to discredit them. 'It is only temporary, we will return....They [the police] want to be in control again. It is some kind of propaganda for them. They want to control us.'

Zamalek had also played their first league match in post-revolutionary Egypt, against Haras el Hodood and also at the Cairo Military Stadium, which Zamalek won 2-1. But the Ahlawy's show of unity and force against the Police team, the UWK were nowhere to be seen. The arrests had forced them underground, and without them, the fans had begun fighting amongst themselves. One group had crossed their wrists in unison as the teams entered the pitch, in solidarity with the arrested. Another group stood in silence, angry that some Zamalek players were complaining about non-payment of wages. A third sung revolutionary songs, ignoring the other two. The crowd was watched by close to 2,000 armed police, some with machine guns, others with dogs.

It was a far cry from the unity that had seen the UWK come to prominence on the front line of the protests. Even the *New York Times* noted that the ultras had been part of the group that stormed, and then torched, the headquarters of Mubarak's despised National Democratic Party. At the so called 'Battle of the Camels' – when Mubarak supporters mounted on camels and, armed with machetes, stormed Tahrir Square – the UWK had used their experience of dealing with the police to stop and then detain the riders. 'There is a war between us and the police,' said Amir. 'We are fighting them in every match. We know them. We know when they run, when we should make them run. We were teaching them [the protesters] how to throw bricks... hit and run tactics... At the beginning of the Battle of the Camels people were afraid but we got up and attacked the riders.'

'On the Day of Rage [January 28th] we made a plan,' Mohammed continued.

'Every group, 20 each, travelled separately... On our own, it was nothing. But together as a group in the square we were a big power... 10,000, 15,000 people fighting without any fear. The ultras were the leaders of the battle.' The victory didn't come without its cost. Three were killed, according to Amir, 'one in Suez, one in Alexandria, one in Cairo. And a lot of injuries. One was shot in the stomach.' Just then Mohammed's phone rang. It was one of the UWK's leaders. The army had just raided his home. He had narrowly avoided arrest and was now on the run. It was time for the interview to end.

Would your old rivalry with Ahly return, I asked finally.

'During the march we celebrated with each other. We were fighting with the Ahlawy on the front line,' Amir recalled. 'We are trying to make a peace treaty with the Ahlawy, because we are fighting in the same direction... You've just heard. The police are chasing our leaders.'

On 1 February 2012, almost a year later, the Ahlawy was preparing for a long away trip to Port Said for what was usually a bad tempered clash in the Egyptian league against Al Masry. There was no deep historical rivalry between the two clubs, just the petty provincial jealousies provoked by the big city. The Ahlawy was expecting a hostile reception. The last time they travelled to Port Said they had been run out of town by Al Masry's fans. It should have been a routine win. But Al Masry pulled off a shock and won 3-1.

Few, however, cared for the score. As soon as the final whistle was blown, hundreds of Al Masry fans stormed on to the pitch. The security for the match had been lighter than under Mubarak but the Al Masry fans got on to the pitch far too easily. Something didn't fit. The Al Ahly players fled for their lives.

'The fans were coming, sprinting after the match,' recalled Egyptian international defender Ahmed Fathi after the event. He was on the pitch at the time and made for the sanctuary of the dressing room. 'I knew they hated me and all the players. All the players ran. I didn't know what was happening outside. But something was happening outside. After this they killed the boys. Not the men, the boys.'

That 'something' was the deaths of 72 young men. Most were crushed to death in a stampede, others – the ultras claimed - stabbed. Some were thrown to their deaths from the top of the stand, four stories up, on to the concrete below. It was one of the worst football disasters of all time. The true horror had only become apparent in the cold light of the next morning. Dozens of odd shoes, discarded by those that had fled and those that had died, piled up as if left for collection by those that could never return. Pools of blood had collected in the depressions of the plastic seats. A huge metal gate had been carefully moved and left against a wall after it had been sheared from its concrete pillar by the sheer weight of the crush. In the aftermath the authorities blamed the violence on thuggery. But as eye witnesses accounts began to emerge, a very different story formed, one of official complicity in the deaths; of a police force who had stood back and watched on as young men were stabbed, beaten, crushed and thrown to their deaths; of an army that, either through foresight or ineptitude, was responsible.

Assad met me under the hanging needle in the lobby of the Ramses train station in central Cairo. It had only recently been built, but already it looked old and worn, as if the chaos and pollution of the city had quickly reclaimed it like an advancing desert. It had been almost exactly a year since I had said goodbye to Assad and the Ahlawy at the Horriya bar. Then he was blazing with hope. Now he looked smaller and older. He stooped slightly as we met, hair now shaved close to his skull (the product, I later learned, of having to be treated for a gash delivered by a policeman's club). A scrappy reddish beard tried to hide his face.

'The military were clever,' Assad said after we embraced, looking at the floor as he spoke. 'They played their cards well so that it looked like the police.'

It was a few days since the Port Said tragedy. Several dozen of the Ahlawy had gathered to take a train north to the famous northern coastal city of Alexandria, once the brain of the Byzantine empire. Everyone present had lost someone at Port Said but the trip has been organised to commemorate the death of one man in particular: Mahmoud Ghandour, the leader of the Ahlawy group in Alexandria. He was 24 years old. A march was to be held in his memory. Thousands were planning to attend, marching towards the northern headquarters of the Egyptian army to demand justice for the dead. 76 people had been arrested, mostly Al Masry fans who had asserted their innocence. But some high profile figures had been blamed too. The head of security in Port Said was arrested. It was rumoured he would face the death penalty, but it wasn't enough for the Ahlawy.

'We don't want resignations,' Assad said as we bordered the express train north. 'We want arrests. Not the people who were holding the knives but the people who put the knives in their hands.'

The group gathered in a cafe close to the Alexandria seafront. At the beginning of the twentieth century Alexandria was famed for its liberalism, Francophile architecture and its parties, where Muslims, Jews and Europeans would mix freely. Now the city was crumbling into the sea, the incongruous metal and glass of the famous Alexandria

Library on the shore of the Mediterranean the only splash of modernity in the city. The Muslim Brotherhood was strong here. Graffiti honouring the Port Said dead was everywhere. The stencilled face of Ghandour had been sprayed on what seemed to be every wall along the seafront.

Assad sat with his lieutenants, drinking Turkish coffee. The weeks after the tragedy had been spent on the streets in clashes with the police and army and visiting the families of the dead. Assad felt responsible in some small way. After all, this was his gang. What had begun five years ago as an expression of support for a football team – catharsis in the face of oppression, even – had ended in the homes of mothers distraught with grief after losing their only son. It had left its mark. So far he had visited 38 families all the time prepared for a backlash against the Ahlawy from the relatives of the dead. But it never came.

'They weren't angry,' Assad said as the group discussed how to get to the march and where to find Ghandour's grave. 'They told us that they were proud their sons were loved by so many people. They all told us one thing: get justice.'

Football had long melted into the background. After the tragedy the league was suspended and later cancelled altogether. The Egyptian FA board, including the hated president Samir Zaher, resigned and Al Masry provisionally banned from all competitions. Such was the fear that violence would break out even Egypt's home 2014 World Cup qualifiers were to be played behind closed doors. The only football left for Ahly was the African Champions League. 'We will play in the Champions League and we will win it to honour the dead,' Assad predicted forcefully. The delegation left for the graveyard.

The taxi bus pulled to a stop outside a high walled compound in a quiet suburb of Alexandria. Inside the graveyard, old women covered head to toe in black sat crying on the tombs of the deceased, as if clinging to a fading memory. It was unclear whether they had been there for hours or years. Dozens of cats stretched and bathed in the warm sun, blissfully ignorant of the grief around them. The Ahlawy weaved silently through the graves until they reached the final resting place of Mahmoud Ghandour.

They were joined by one of Ahly's greatest players. Shady Mohammed was Ahly's most successful captain and in the decade between his first game in 1999 and his departure a decade later he had won six league titles, nine domestic cups and clinched the African Champions League on four occasions. He also won the African Cup of Nations with the Egyptian national team in 2008. He didn't play for Ahly any longer but that didn't matter.

Shady, Assad and the Ahlawy stood by the grave, heads bowed, each mouthing a prayer in silence. A few minutes passed before Assad moved. The rest followed.

Outside the high walls Heema, one of the group that had travelled north from Cairo, pulled on a cigarette. Heema was one of the founding members of the Ahlawy, a working class hotel worker who had tried his hand at making it in Eastern Europe a couple of times. He'd even married a Polish girl at one point, but that didn't work out. And the cold was excruciating, so he returned home. Like the rest of the delegation he knew Ghandour, but not well. But Heema had been there on that day in Port Said. It was his devastating testimony of what happened in Port Said that turned the tide of public opinion. At first people assumed it was just football thugs settling scores, but Heema's appearance on a talk show on Egyptian TV changed all that. He seemed to sink when he recounted what happened, how Al Masry had beaten Al Ahly on the pitch before the police and army turned a blind eye to thousands of charging home fans:

> 'We saw they were not celebrating, but heading towards us. We could see the cops in front of us but we thought they would stop them from attacking us. But suddenly we saw the cops moving and the gates are opened. And the fans are coming like a storm of people. Hundreds of people.

> 'We were so surprised the gates were locked. 800 people were stuck in this tunnel. 60 square metres. We started to fall down on each other. There were like five levels of people on top of each other. We couldn't see a complete human, only half a human. Just an upper part, a head, the body is buried by the other bodies. Just one hand sticking out trying to say help. The cops were just watching. The army were guarding this gate and just watching.

> I was inside the tunnel. The gate which was locked it collapsed under the weight of all the people. The first person who died, his name was Yousef. He was a great hero. He was outside the gate because he went to the bathroom 15 minutes before the end of the game and when he came back the gates were locked. So he got a stone and tried to break the lock off the gate. He couldn't do it. He was pulling it with his own hands and then it collapsed on him.

> We were just waiting for the moment for to die. I couldn't step because there were a lot of guys falling on each other. I was down and someone was on top of me. I had two choices. If I stand up someone will stab

me or burn me. The other choice is to step on these boys. I could hear
they were killing people. I could hear people screaming for help. When
they took the guy on top of me I heard him screaming so bad so I guess
they stabbed him or something. In this moment I took the hard decision
to move.'

Heema got out and managed to find refuge in the dressing room, where the Al
Ahly players held some of the bodies, distraught. The Egypt national team's American
coach Bob Bradley would later tell me how Mohamed Aboutrika held one of the
protesters in his arms as he died. 'You know the story?' Bradley asked. 'The fan says to
Aboutrika: 'Captain, I always wanted to meet you...'.'

Tens of thousands of crying mothers, fathers, brothers and friends awaited
Heema and the other survivors when he returned to Ramses train station that night,
all desperate for news. The carriages had left packed four to a bench. The survivors
spread out in silence.

Heema was under no illusion who to blame:

> *We blame everyone. We blame the army who were guarding the locked*
> *gate. We blame the police. We think it was a mix. It happened because*
> *of the rivalry between the two teams. And also as punishment for the*
> *ultras standing with the revolution, for protecting the revolution. We*
> *are a big pain for the regime because the people of the revolution believe*
> *that the old regime is still controlling the country. It was because of the*
> *Masry fans, it was because of football and it was because of politics too.*

The march began on Port Said Street, behind Alexandria's famous library. Tens of
thousands of men and women filled the streets as far as the eye could see. Those with
the loudest voices sat on their friend's shoulders to face the crowd and lead them in
revolutionary song.

> *They say violence is in our blood*
> *How dare we fight for our rights*
> *Stupid regime*
> *Hear what we say*
> *Freedom!*

Freedom!
Freedom!

The smiling face of Mahmoud Ghandour stared back from T-shirts and banners. Before the revolution a protest like this would never be allowed. Now what little police were there, perhaps half a dozen, looked the other way as two ultras with spray cans rechristened the street sign 'Ghandour Street'.

It took three hours for the march to snake through the streets. All the while they were cheered by the watching crowds on the balconies. An old lady held up a hand made placard denouncing the army. The march eventually stopped at the gates of the head quarters for Egypt's army in the north of the country. Troops stared back atop armed APCs, a tank and a dozen foot soldiers. All their guns were trained on the crowd.

'*The people demand the trial of Port Said*', they chanted.

The troops didn't move. The gate stayed locked. Instead the ultras knelt down and prayed in front of the troops before peacefully dispersing, their point made. Even old enemies were welcomed on the march. White flags of Ahly's main rival Zamalak could also be seen. And in a gesture of revolutionary fraternity, the fans of Alexandria's own Premier League side Ittihad – the Blue Magic – arrived too. They requested a meeting with the Ahlway. It came with an invite back to one their houses.

'They said to me: 'We've wasted 20 years hating each other, let's make peace," Assad explained as we climbed into a taxi.

The Blue Magic were poor men, too poor to rent an apartment and therefore too poor to marry. Instead the group of middle aged men lived together in a derelict building. Both groups squeezed into the front room, overlooking the city's court house. One pulled out a large hunting knife. He plunged it into an empty bottle of Sprite, carefully sawing it in half. In the centre of the room, under a bare bulb hanging precariously to its wire, one member of the Blue Magic crumbled hash into a big brown pile. The plastic bottles were filled with water and hastily constructed into makeshift water pipes as the room broke out in to song and dance. The leader of the Blue Magic – a fisherman blessed with a beautiful singing voice – led the two groups singing sad old songs of regret and longing, as he glided gently across the room. The rudimentary pipe was passed to each and every person. Laughter rose out of the glass-free windows past the closed court house outside. The future and the past were forgotten. Everyone breathed deeply.

✦

The next evening there was a gathering outside the Cairo International stadium.
The meeting had been arranged on the Ahlawy's Facebook page. Assad never looked
forward to the meetings before, but that had changed.

'We used to take these meetings a little for granted, but not after Port Said,' he
said as he swung his BMW into the car park. On the radio was a CD of chants and
anti-regime songs the Ahlawy had recorded long before Port Said. 'After speaking to
the families and what it meant for them to come here and get the shirt, well...'

The crowd were here to buy a new shirt made by the Ahlawy. They were selling
them to raise money for a childrens' cancer hospital. If they sold enough they could
have a ward dedicated to the victims of Port Said.

'We will call it '*Shahid Ahlawy* Port Said'.' Assad said as he took the orders. *The
Ahlawy martyrs of Port Said.*

They took 600 orders in half an hour. The popularity of the Ahlawy could
not have been higher. Nor could their standing in Egyptian society, as the so called
'protectors of the revolution'. But Port Said changed everything for Assad.

'Because of the political situation in the country, we [the ultras] developed so
quickly that I can't really still believe it. We had no political ambitions at first but
when the regime started oppressing us they turned us in to what they feared,' he said.
'Everybody knows Port Said was a set up, everyone knows that.'

Assad regretted the loss of what made the Ahlawy in the first place: the football
team. But now there were bigger things to fight for.

'We are victims for our values and victims for our ideology and we are victims
of what we stand for. It is destiny that we were made to suffer that. We are one of
the purest entities in the country and they are trying to destroy us. Seventy four [72
who died in Port Said and another two who died during the revolution] people is not
enough. If you want to terminate our ideas then you have to finish us all. It makes you
more focused to get what these people died for. They died for certain values ... I don't
know if we will achieve it but what is certain is that we'll all die for them. We'll die for
it if that is what it takes.'

The Al Ahly flag took pride of place on the barricades. The club's crest, the eagle
on the shield, was now flown with revolutionary pride. But there had been no football. With the league cancelled the only competition left was the African Champions
League, which Assad and the Ahlawy believed Ahly was destined to win. In the second
round they travelled to Mali for a two-legged tie. No sooner had the team landed than
a coup started. The players were stuck in their hotel for a week after their 1-0 loss as
vicious street-to-street fighting played out around them. They quickly went 1-0 down
in the first half of the second leg too, in the empty Military Stadium in Cairo. That

was until Mohamed Aboutrika – the 'captain', the man who held a dying fan in his arms in the dressing room on that night in Port Said – scored a second half hat trick after coming on at half time.

There was a rash of arrests in the aftermath of Port Said. The Supreme Council of the Armed Forces blamed hooligan elements on the violence and strongly denied it was a conspiracy, insisting it was a mixture of thuggery, bad luck and incompetence. When the accused were taken before the judge, in a large cage, they protested their innocence – claiming they were scapegoats for a wider conspiracy – and prayed together in an act of defiance. The trial's continued postponement meant the Ahlawy would keep protesting to prevent the league from restarting until they had secured justice for the Port Said dead.

After the T-shirt orders had been taken Assad and Heema led the group to their cafe, their local, in a district near Tahrir Square. It was already full, spilt out on to the street; rich and poor, Muslim and Christian.

'My mother thinks Egyptian society should follow us,' said Heema, fanning his arm around in a semi circle. 'Look. We have low class and high class. Assad is high class. But we have another guy who works as a baker making a couple of [Egyptian] pounds a day. There is no religion here. Christian, Muslim, it's all the same. Everyone is equal.'

Assad agreed as a joint was passed around the group. 'We have members of the Muslim Brotherhood too,' he said, pointing to the crowd. 'Even before the revolution, this place, the cafe, it was a free place.'

But the ghosts of Port Said still walked here. The talk was of sacrifice and martyrdom. If the authorities had hoped to silence the Ahlawy they had instead, as Assad said, created what they feared. They had thrown spirit on the embers of a fire. 'We now have a big battle against all the officials. Nothing will make us calm until we see them all hanged,' Heema said, betraying his anger for only a few moments. 'Everyone who was responsible for this. The Al Masry fans who did this. The police. The cop leaders in Port Said, the Minister of the Interior. Everyone.' Heema lit a cigarette before he and Assad melted back into the night.

POSTSCRIPT

Cairo, January 2013

Red smoke billowed all around, heaving upwards from canisters sacrificially held aloft. The thickness enveloped everyone that had stood for hours waiting for the news, forcing its way through the crowd like a flood, but rising like a fire. A cloud grew yet dissipated with every passing second, allowing the lungs to finally breath but leaving behind a permanent haze of crimson in its wake. It was a sign that word had arrived. It still wasn't clear what that word was. Or whether a word had even been spoken. Had justice been served? Or had, as the 15,000 strong crowd that gathered outside Al Ahly's walled training complex in Cairo always suspected, justice been denied, compromised, denigrated, postponed.

The thousands of Ahlawy stood in front of a huge black billboard, 100 foot wide and 10 foot tall. This was still a good part of town, on Zamalek island in the Nile, one of the few upmarket districts that the rich of Cairo still bothered to populate. Most had left for the gated communities of the new suburbs that had been growing steadily for the past decade. Cairo proper had become too poor, too chaotic and too polluted for those with choice. Most people in Egypt didn't have a choice. The rest remained, struggling with the realities of a city that had become to big for its clothes. But Ahly remained, an anchor to the old world, to the hope that burned and then crashed between Nasser and the assassination of Sadat.

A few dozen of the Ahlawy had climbed on to the shelf in front of the billboard via a pale, sick-looking, leafless tree nearby, to see the expectant but pessimistic crowd below. Aside from the crazy few who had clambered to higher ground, the crowd faced the profiles of the young men that had been eulogised up high.

It was a few seconds after 10am and the verdict of those accused of their role – or complicity or acquiescence – in the deaths of 72 Al Ahly fans killed during a match against Al Masry in Port Said nearly one year previously was about to be known. The billboard, a collage of 72 portraits shorn from Facebook, passport photos and family gatherings, bore down on the crowd as if they too were expecting justice.

Except there wasn't 72 faces. Only 68 had been honoured with a picture. Three of the dead had no picture to prove their existence. At best their photos had been lost in the sands of life. At worst, they had never had a picture taken. *Never had a picture taken.* They had no record of themselves on Facebook nor on celluloid. One of the dead had never been identified. As the grieving families claimed their departed one by one, he was left orphaned at the morgue. All that was known was depressingly medical: he was male, Egyptian, in his forties. He could have been an Ahly fan, he could have just been passing by that night and caught up in the tragedy. He was buried in an unmarked grave. Everyone on that billboard had a name, if not a picture, but under his generic black space he was known simply as 'The Martyr'.

Information crackled through the crowd like a loose electrical wire. Gun fire boomed, ear shattering blasts that scorched the face. The Ahlawy, at least some of them, had come armed for the verdict. They carried home made, sawn-off shot guns, fashioned into pistols. They fired them in the air, bird shot spraying those near by. One young man fired an automatic pistol in the air repeatedly before it jammed. His friends gathered around to try and make it work again, but they didn't have the technical ability, as if the gun had been stolen out of a father's closet. Fireworks exploded too, adding to the chaos. Gunfire and gunpowder mingled effortlessly.

Many of he Ahlawy I had know for all these years, from the Zamalek derby in 2007, to the hope and anarchy that immediately followed the revolution to the aftermath of Port Said and to now, were here too. Mohamed, one of the founding members, crouched down, the hot morning sun burning his face, as he tried to decipher the code. The gun fire and the fireworks suddenly intensified.

'15 death sentences, a lot, a lot, a lot for the Port Said people I don't know what's for the police,' he relayed, calmly, mobile phone pressed to one ear, his other hand trying to muffle the outside world. Next to us a teenager with a home made shotgun, his head covered by a hood, his face smothered by a red scarf, blasted another couple of rounds in the air.

'It's over.'

The court had delivered an unexpected verdict. As the fog cleared the decision was better than almost any of the Ahlawy had expected. Twenty one of Al Masry's fans had been sentenced to death. The year previously, in the macabre glow of Port Said when I had marched with the Ahlawy in Alexandria and spoken to Assad and Heema, Assad the founding force of the Ahlawy and Heema an original member who was at Port Said and had been forced to step on the bodies of his friends as they died underneath him, the ultras had demanded blood. Executions. *Not the people who are holding the knives but the people who put the knives in their hands.*

Since then they had embarked on a campaign to ensure that justice was served. They had successfully boycotted the league until a verdict had been delivered. In some cases the Ahlawy would picket stadiums where matches were about to take place. The Egyptian FA, so tainted by their close association to, and sycophancy of, the Mubarak regime, crumbled in front of the Ahlawy's opposition. August, September, October passed and still no league could restart without the Ahlawy's say so. The only football, other than a handful of Egyptian national team World Cup and Africa Cup of Nations qualifiers, was the African Champions League. Port Said had scarred Ahly's players. Many said they would never play again. It took months for some of them to emerge for training. It was understandable.

When I had said goodbye to Heema and Assad they had vowed justice and victory. Victory in the Champions League, they said, would honour the martyrs. Somehow, despite not playing any league games, Al Ahly progressed. First there was the tie in Mali when the team was caught up in the coup. And then there was the semi-final against Nigeria's Sunshine Stars. The match in Cairo was again played behind closed doors but the hotel where the away team was staying was inundated by Egyptian protesters. They weren't the usual protesters you would see at Tahrir Square, but a gathering of professional footballers, angry that their livelihood had been taken away from them. They were equally angry that Al Ahly had still been allowed to play, tapping into a resentment that had existed long before the revolution that the club received special treatment. The players hoped that if they barricaded the Nigerian team in the hotel, the match would be cancelled, Ahly would be kicked out of the competition and their cause would finally be understood. But Mohamed, now crouching in the street outside Ahly's training complex trying to relay news of the Port Said verdict to his friends, had other ideas.

'We only found out during rush hour that the players were having a march,' he told me at the time. 'We embarked on a mission to 'free' the Sunshine Stars players. We contacted each other by BBM and SMS and congregated. There were fights with the players. I think one of the players had a gun. They prevented the Sunshine players from going to the game. We had to let the game go on. We cleared the way for the bus.'

The Ahlawy led the players to the bus and arranged an escort to the stadium. Nigerian journalist Colin Udoh, who was embedded with the Sunshine Stars, saw the whole thing. 'When the players were coming down the fans were applauding them,' he said. 'On the drive to the stadium 2,000 fans were lining the road applauding

POSTSCRIPT

us. Inside the bus they didn't understand it. They thought they were angry with them … It is a unique position, to see fans with that much power.' Al Ahly won that game and won the final too. Despite having no league, no fans, and experiencing unimaginable horror they had become champions of Africa, and with it a place with the other confederation champions – Chelsea from Europe, Corinthians from South America, Monterrey from Central and North America – at FIFA's Club World Cup in Japan.

A dozen Ahlawy had made the insane trip to the city of Nagoya, south of Tokyo, for the first match against the Japanese champions Sanfrecce Hiroshima. It was December 2012 and the snow fell thick on the freezing stands. Assad, Miha, a Christian member of the Ahlawy and Hassan stood and watched Ahly play in the snow for the first time in their history. It was also the first time the Ahlawy had attended a match since Port Said. It had been an incredible journey for the team, as much as it had been for the Ahlawy. Assad was optimistic. He wanted to get back to the football. Politics was a dirty business. He despised the government and the police, but now they at least had a mechanism for change. Egypt wasn't a post-revolutionary society any more, ready to be moulded into whichever force emerged strongest. It was now a presidential democracy. Mohamed Morsy and the Muslim Brotherhood had won, just as Mubarak feared.

It was better than what they had before, Assad reasoned, and now they had the prospect of justice too. 'Already a date has been set to announce the verdict which should be January 26 [2013],' he said as Al Ahly took the lead. Around him the Ahlawy sung the familiar revolutionary songs that had not been heard in a football stadium since Port Said. 'We are very optimistic and hopefully the court will bring the justice the victims deserve. It will be unimaginable to think of how emotional and special it will be to return to football after 13 months.'

Next to the Ahlawy, a bigger group of Egyptian men, most students studying in Tokyo, watched Al Ahly too. They wore heavy beards and carried banners proclaiming their support for President Morsy. The Brotherhood had been allies of the Ahlawy and the activists during the revolution. They had even accused the military regime in colluding in the Port Said tragedy. But now they were the establishment, the enemy. And the Brotherhood didn't tolerate dissent. They began to chant pro Morsy slogans. The ultras chanted back, louder, about freedom and control. Scuffles broke out between the two. They only ended when Mohamed Aboutrika intervened. With the match drawn at 1-1 Aboutrika took the ball down on the right and the blasted the ball past the goalkeeper. It was later voted goal of the tournament. The banners were put away and the chants stopped.

As the day of the Port Said verdict neared, the new regime of Mohamed Morsy breathed in, fearing the court verdict would spark an already combustible situation on the ground. The sulphuric burn of tear gas now hung around Tahrir Square. Riots raged in its vicinity. Next to the Nile, outside one of the big five star hotels, young protesters, many wearing Ahly flags and scarves, and the police force traded blows. The police would fire tear gas cannister after tear gas cannister high in to the air, smoke marking its trajectory as it looped and then landed at the feet of the crowd 100 meters away. The protesters would pick up the cannisters and hurl them in the Nile before aiming the only weapons they had, fireworks, in the direction of the police. They would impotently explode a few metres after being fired.

None of the Ahlawy I knew were here, still fighting theses battles. They had become more than a revolutionary force. They were now a revolutionary aesthetic. Street hawkers who would sell religious flags during marches by supporters of the Muslim Brotherhood now sold Ahly flags too. Their biggest seller now was the Ahly branded black balaclavas. Being an ultra was now a synonym for resistance. Every young person with a grievance on the street now wore the badge of the Ahlawy and sung the revolutionary songs that had emerged from the terraces. Being an ultra wasn't first an expression of love for your team, it was an expression of discontent. But the core of what had brought them together in the first placed had skipped a generation. There was no terrace to stand on any more, no team to discuss, no matches to watch, no schedule to keep by. The metronome of a football season that should and always have been was gone.

They lamented the loss of their club and the game they loved. Others had taken the mantle and ran with it. But it had little connection to them nor to the roots of what had made them strong in the first place. Justice for the dead at Port Said had already held them together longer than anyone had expected. Many of them were now approaching 30. They had jobs and lives to live. Assad couldn't be here for the verdict. His job meant that he was out of the country. Real life had intervened.

Outside the ground, as the extent of the court's verdict became known, the mood changed from menace, to celebration to confusion. Twenty one were sentenced to death, yes, but the verdict of the other 52 accused, including several security officials, had been postponed. Some believed the verdict was political, a way of taking the sting out of a potentially explosive situation. 'It's a very good decision by the court,' said Miha, the Christian member of the Ahlawy who had travelled to Japan to see Ahly for the first time in a year. 'We hope it will be a perfect ending for this story. We have been waiting for this for so long. For 21 to get executed is a very good decision. So now we wait for the police decision. For sure it wasn't just them that made this.'

Ahmed, another founding member of the Ahlawy I had met in Alexandria was equally as unequivocal. 'I feel satisfied that some of those who committed what we suffered a year ago are going to face what they deserve,' he said, as the crowd began to move inside the training complex and gather on the pitch. 'It's a strong verdict but they don't deserve less than a strong verdict. Nobody ever wants to see someone dying but when someone kills he deserves a death sentence. He deserves that his life is taken. I don't see a way the police can get away with this.'

It was conflicting, watching thousands celebrate an execution on the pitch inside the training complex. But if the courts had hoped to take the sting out of the situation, it had worked. The crowd melted away, satisfied at least until the next verdict a month later. The Ahlawy I had known for the past six years were always accidental revolutionaries. Now the battles were to be fought by other people carrying their flags, the next generation. The Ahlawy left for Mohamed's flat nearby, to spend the rest of the day getting stoned and watching the protests in Tahrir Square on TV.

But what had averted disaster in Cairo had ignited the city of Port Said. The verdicts were greeted with astonishment, disbelief, and anger by Al Masry's fans and the families of the 73 accused who had gathered outside the prison in Port Said where the suspects were held. Like the Ahlawy supporters in Cairo, they too had come prepared. Two policemen were shot dead as the relatives tried to storm the prison. The police fired back. At least 30 people were killed in clashes. Among them was a former Al Masry player. President Morsy addressed the nation and announced a 30-day curfew, from 9 pm until 6 am in the cities worst effected by the violence. A few hours before the first curfew was due to fall, a storm rolled into Port Said. I had taken the last bus from Cairo and entered the city just before it was to be sealed. The streets were empty, the skies dark and pregnant with rain. The only sound was the faint, periodic burst of gunfire. It emanated from near the Al Arab police station by the sea. I walked through Port Said's deserted streets, using the rising smoke and gunfire as a compass. Ominously, down one deserted street, an orphaned tire barricade burned in its centre. Suddenly, the dead streets came alive, as if the entire energy of the city had been focused on one point. Young men exchanged rocks for gunfire over the burning tyres. The clashes had followed the funeral of more protesters, killed the day after the violence outside the prison. Down side streets members of the Red Crescent peered nervously around street corners to check for the injured, before ducking back when the police fired off a few rounds.

'There are some injuries here,' one paramedic said as he sheltered from the latest volley. Ambulances flew by, their sirens blaring. 'We've seen gun bullets from the government. In four days we have seen more than 450 (injured).'

Yet, despite the gunfire and the curfew a march had been arranged. At 8.30pm a crowd of thousands gathered near the same spot the Red Crescent had been waiting to ferry the injured to hospital. They marched through the smouldering barricades towards where the gunfire had previously come from. Now the army, not the police, was in charge. APCs and armed troops were stationed on street corners and outside important military and civilian buildings. At its core were the fans of Al Masry's ultras group the Green Eagles. But they were by no means alone. The marchers had come from all sections of Port Said. Several hundred women marched together, denouncing Morsy and Cairo. The curfew came and went, the crowd mocking its passing. 'It's 9 o'clock!' they chanted as they passed the stationed troops. There was no animosity towards the army. The police were the enemy. Protesters took it in turns to hug and kiss the young soldiers that had lined their path.

No one wanted to admit to being an Al Masry fan, nor say whether they were there on that fateful night almost a year ago that set in motion the chain of deadly events. What they would say was that they believed a miscarriage of justice had taken place, that Morsy had sacrificed Port Said to prevent chaos in Cairo, that traditional antipathy towards Port Said, a poor and neglected city, was at play.

'People are truly sure that these people (the 21 sentenced to death) didn't kill anyone. We didn't do it and they (the Ahlawy) don't believe we didn't do this,' said Tariq Youssef, a 32-year-old accountant who was on the march with a friend. 'Al Masry will not be back for five years. I'm a big Masry fan. But I can't go anywhere. All the supporters for the big teams in Cairo or anywhere believe that Al Masry supporters did this.' For Tariq, admitting to being an Al Masry supporter outside of Port Said was impossible. 'They say, 'You killed them the Ahly supporters. You are like a terrorist.' Nobody believes us we didn't do anything here.'

As the march moved back towards the place it had started, machine gun fire rang out once again. This time it was all around the march, front and back. The crowd scattered. A protester had been shot dead at the back of the march, next to the Al

Arab police station. 'In three days we have lost 21 people, judged to be executed, and also about 39 murdered and many injured so there is no family which have not lost a friend, a colleague, a neighbour. You can consider this a sort of vendetta between the people and the police,' said Muhammad el Agiery, an English tutor who had stayed until the end. 'People are going to stay out all of the night, every day for a month. They reject and refuse the curfew imposed by Morsy.' But they didn't stay out all night. Their message had been already heard and, with one protester already dead, it was time to leave. As gunfire crackled in the night sky, I moved through Port Said's deserted streets, hiding behind cars every time a new volley broke out until I finally reached safety. At the time of writing, close to 50 people had died in the protests in Port Said since the verdict had passed.

In a region as diverse and divided and vibrant as the Middle East, football had provided a window of understanding, yes. But it was also much more than that. It had afforded a voice to those that had no other. It had provided a space to breath where none other existed. It had provoked both fear and admiration in dictators and presidents alike. It had fuelled at least one revolution and provided heroes and villains in other uprisings. To understand football in the Middle East was to understand, at least partially, the Middle East itself. Many of the people I had met – the fans, the Football Associations and the players – would play their own roles in the future direction of their countries. Some big, some small.

In Palestine, Honey Thaljieh would lead her national team out on to the pitch in front of 12,000 fans, mainly women, for Palestine's first ever full women's international match against Jordan. The new men's professional league would go from strength to strength, even able to financially out muscle the Israeli league in signing Israeli Arab players. Gaza fared less well. The pitch on which I had watched the cup final in 2009, and seen Hamas' main man in the strip Ismail Haniyeh present the cup, was almost totally destroyed by an Israeli rocket in 2012. The Israelis claimed that the pitch had been used to launch an Iranian-made rocket which came close to hitting Tel Aviv, bursting 'The Bubble', a claim the armed wing of Hamas denied.

Guma Aguiar was still missing. The responsibility for funding Israeli football club Beitar Jerusalem had returned to Arkadi Gaydamak who made one last attempt at changing the attitudes on the terraces of the Teddy Stadium by sanctioning the signing of two Chechen, Muslim players, causing consternation amongst the Beitar faithful. When one of the players scored his first goal for the club, La Familia booed.

In Syria the league returned as the country burned. All the games were to be played in Damascus, showing what little control the government had outside the capital. Abdelbassat Saroot remains unaccounted for. Next door in Lebanon, tens of thousands of Syrian refugees poured in. The country's football fans had, finally been allowed back to the stadiums, but only in small numbers.

In the UAE, the royal family of Abu Dhabi bankrolled Manchester City to its first English Premier League title. But their money, or financial doping as it was labelled, forced UEFA to take action, introducing Financial Fair Play regulations so that such spending could never happen again, changing the European game in the process. The country did, however, enjoy some success on the pitch for itself. The national team qualified for the 2012 Olympics with ease, bringing through the best generation of players in their history. One, Omar Abdulrahman, had taken the mantle from Ismail Matar as the country's hottest prospect. Abdulrahman would no doubt have the choice to play in one of the world's top leagues, a choice his predecessors had either been denied or forgone.

In Qatar money continued to flow into Europe. French side PSG and Spanish side Malaga were both bought using Qatari money. PSG signed David Beckham and Zlatan Ibrahimovic. Malaga qualified for the Champions League before their Qatari owner mysteriously pulled the plug on funding them. There was a sticky end to one of the architects of Qatar's successful 2022 World Cup bid too. Mohammed Bin Hammam would be caught offering cash for votes in the Caribbean whilst campaigning against Sepp Blatter for the FIFA presidency. In Bahrain the Hubail brothers have still not returned to the national team. Their coach Peter Taylor was sacked after the team's failure to reach the final round of 2014 World Cup qualification. But not before taking charge of a series of matches in Germany that held unlikely significance. Sayed Mohamed Adnan was called back in to the team. Peter Taylor wasn't too sure of his name, nor what position was best for him, but he had pulled on the national team jersey just over a year after his arrest. The *Gulf Weekly*, a pro-regime English language publication, reported the news in typical magnanimous fashion. 'His appearance in the squad shows the world that soccer in Bahrain is above politics and how sport can be a unifying force for good,' they wrote.

And what of Yemen? Three-and-a-half years after Hamid, the head of the Yemeni Football Association, and I had chewed qat together and dreamt of the glowing future football in the country could have, his time in the sun had arrived. But there were problems. In the run up to the Gulf Cup in 2010, the tournament Hamid had been waiting for, a bomb went off in the southern port city of Aden, at the first division club Al Wahda – one of the clubs due to host the likes of Saudi Arabia, Asian champions

Iraq and hosts Qatar. Hamid was summoned to a meeting in Beirut with the other Gulf FA chiefs.

'Don't worry, they have all confirmed their participation, the teams and the technical committees,' he cheerily told me on the phone when he returned to the capital Sana'a. 'The security is the responsibility of the state but football is making love and peace between people and we are sure that they will unite behind the tournament. Terrorists are in all the Arab countries. They will not affect it.'

After that bombing in Aden two senior British diplomats survived an assassination attempt whilst a French oil worker was murdered in a separate attack on the same day. Then came the attempted bombing of cargo planes destined for the US, using explosives stuffed into printer cartridges that had originated in Yemen. 'Holding the tournament in such circumstances,' one editorial in the Arab News claimed, begins to look courageous bordering on the foolhardy.' President Saleh himself promised that 30,000 troops would patrol the tournament and that US-trained anti-terrorist operatives would be in charge of guarding the teams, with extra security placed at hotels too. Hamid was satisfied, especially with the new stadiums he had secured. 'We have never had this before, this investment,' he said. 'We have two official stadiums to FIFA standard and new training fields. It's the first time in Yemen that the government has done this.'

Perhaps this *was* to be the new dawn for Yemeni football. Hamid was an optimist and believed football could even be a trump card to fight against Al Qaeda. 'They [terrorists] do not want love and peace; they are extremists and they don't represent the people,' he explained. 'We want our people to know they are equal to other gulf countries, and this will help development here in society and football. If they put their energies into football they won't put their energies into extremism.' The tournament went without a hitch, but it was also one of President Saleh's last civil acts. He was later ousted after massive street protests. The Yemen team's performance on the pitch, in front of their home crowd, wasn't what Hamid expected either. They lost every game. Today they are ranked 170th in the world by FIFA, their worst ever position.

1 February, 2013

The streets outside Ahly's training ground were deserted now. On the same spot where 15,000 Ahlawy had gathered to hear the first verdict in the Port Said trial a week before, a crew of eight graffiti artists were busy covering the walls of the training ground with the faces of the dead. It was exactly one year since that night in Port Said and the club had arranged for an evening memorial service for the victims of the tragedy. As the sun set the Ahlawy slowly arrived, chaste and introverted. Mohamed and Miha had met with others I had come to know well. They embraced and led each other up in to the stands where thousands more were waiting for them. On the pitch four of the Ahlawy were arranging a pyrotechnic display to mark the exact minute when tragedy took place: 74 flares were to be lit, each held by a different ultra, standing in the shape of a '7' and a '4'. The organisers ran around flustered trying to move the men into the correct position as if herding cats, phoning friends stationed high up in the stands so that they could guide the design below.

The families of the Martyrs walked on two by two. Mothers who had lost sons, sisters that had lost brothers, wives who had lost husbands. They wept as they saw the crowds that had gathered to honour their sons, the name of each read out on the crackly speaker system and chanted by the crowd. When the moment came, and the sun had almost vanished from the horizon, the flares were lit. The number '74' burned brightly. Tomorrow another chapter in the tragedy was to close. The football league would return. The fans would still be banned from attending but that was the next battle, to fight for their rightful return. When the second verdict was read out a month later, two of the main security officials on trial were jailed for 15 years. But 28 were acquitted. Riots near Ahly's training complex followed as the near by Police Club was burned down. Some of the Ahlawy claimed responsibility. But no one could be sure who it was. The Ahlawy had become so big, so stretched, so removed from the original core of fans who had fought the regime in Egypt's darkest days that the claim was virtually meaningless.

Perhaps it was a supernova, the blinding flash of brilliant white that marked the death of a star. Perhaps it marked a new phase under a new leadership. But, at the one year anniversary memorial, it felt like an end, a chapter that had closed on all of their lives. The flares burned and the victims wept as we stood and paid our respects. Tears streamed down Miha's face as the flares began to fade and the Ahlawy began to sing – a song that had never been sung at an Al Ahly match before – into the cold, darkening Cairo night.

Wearing a red T-shirt
Going to Port Said
Came back in a white coffin
I became a martyr in my own country
In heaven a martyr
Revolution all over again.

ACKNOWLEDGEMENTS

This book is a treatise on luck and the enduring goodness of human nature. Over the past eight years I have been blessed with fortune and the kindness of strangers. The list is endless and largely anonymous: The Syrian border guard who took pity on me when I had no visa, the taxi driver in Israel who drove me to the Egypt border when I had no money; the football fans whom I befriended when stranded outside football stadiums in Jordan, Egypt, Bahrain or Yemen when I had no prospect of home. The young men who shielded me under gun fire in Port Said. The young men who protected me on the streets of Cairo after the revolution. The photographers I've worked with who have saved me from the beatings I no doubt deserved. The families in the West Bank and Gaza and Lebanon that invited me in to their homes and shared the last of what they had. I only have fragments of names and places, sometimes just a photo. But mostly I have nothing. Many of these experiences I have not written about. I have kept those memories to myself. But they are always with me and will stay there for the rest of my life.

This book would also not exist without the enduring energy and patience of James Corbett. We met whilst being lightly interrogated in a holding pen at Tel Aviv airport. The two of us were on our way to report from the West Bank, which had raised suspicions amongst the Israeli border guards. He was reading the first edition of *When Friday Comes* and vowed, when we were both eventually let out, to publish an updated edition and was good to his word despite having to deal with my pathological disorganisation and lateness. For this I am both sorry and grateful.

Much of what is new in this second edition of the book has been adapted from reporting commissioned by various magazines and newspapers who enabled me to meet the people that make up the spirit of this book: Rob Orchard, Marcus Webb and Matthew Lee at *Delayed Gratification*; Jason Stallman at the *New York Times*; Jonathan Heaf at *GQ*; Richard Padula at the BBC World Service; Ben Wyatt at CNN; Jeremy Lawrence and Matt Pomroy at *Esquire ME*; Louis Massarella at *FourFourTwo*; Sean Ingle at *The Guardian*; Jonathan Wilson at *The Blizzard*; Thomas Woods at *The National* and, last but not least, Gavin Hamilton at *World Soccer*. Without your support this second edition simply would not have been possible.

I'd also like to thank my family for living with the chaos; my mum, dad, Laura and soon-to-be-brother Rob; each and every member of the Ahlawy for taking me in as one of their own, and especially to Assad (you know who you are); Sir Bob Bradley for his counsel and incredibly kind forward; Ana, for enduring more than I deserved; my agent Rebecca Winfield for her faith and, finally, Alina, for holding my hand to ensure I didn't fail you. I hope that I haven't.